The Microphone Wars

The Microphone Wars

*A History of Triumph
and Betrayal at the CBC*

Knowlton Nash

Canadian Cataloguing in Publication Data
Nash, Knowlton
The microphone wars: a history of triumph and betrayal at the
CBC

Includes bibliographical references and index.
ISBN 0-7710-6712-7 (bd.) ISBN 0-7710-6715-1 (pbk.)

1. Canadian Broadcasting Corporation – History.
2. Canadian Broadcasting Corporation – Management –
History.
I. Title.

HE8689.9.C3N3 1994   384.54'0971   C94-931543-5

The publishers acknowledge the support of the Canada
Council and the Ontario Arts Council for their publishing
program.

Printed and bound in Canada.
The paper used in this book is acid-free.

McClelland & Stewart Inc.
The Canadian Publishers
481 University Avenue
Toronto, Ontario
M5G 2E9

1 2 3 4 5   99 98 97 96 95

To those who have given their heart and soul to make it work.

Contents

Introduction

In 1994, we celebrate seventy-five years of Canadian broadcasting, which began in the cramped Montreal studio of Marconi's station XWA in September 1919, when "radio wireless receiving sets" were selling for $15 – a lot of money seventy-five years ago. It was time, I and my publishers thought, for a book on the subject.

In deciding to sketch the history of the CBC and Canada's "Microphone Wars," I bit off a good deal more than I realized I would have to chew. So many stories could be written about the ever embattled CBC, an institution which has enriched and infuriated almost every single Canadian at one time or another. The CBC is our national whipping boy, our national frustration, and our national dream.

In the beginning, politicians saw broadcasting as a revolutionary way to reach all citizens directly. Entrepreneurs saw it as a cash cow. Educators saw it as the biggest classroom in the world. Listeners and viewers saw it first as a magic marvel, then as a way to share a moment, an event, with all other Canadians, and eventually as their principal source of entertainment and information. Canadians now spend more than half of all their leisure time in front of their spellbinding boxes of mass culture.

Broadcasting is one of the miracles of the twentieth century, profoundly affecting all humankind. Arguably, it has had as big an impact on society as the invention of the automobile or the airplane. At the start, most of the world, led by the BBC, saw it as a cultural instrument for national enrichment. A few, led by the Americans, saw it as a business. Until halfway through the century, the cultural missionaries dominated in Canada and most other nations, except the United States. Then, most of the world began moving toward the American model as commerce pushed its way into broadcasting's driver's seat. In Canada, as usual, we made a compromise, and broadcasting became a cross between the high-tone BBC and the commercial American networks. We had our cultural cake, but with a topping of commercial icing.

The CBC began in 1936 with 142 employees, spending $708,179 in its first partial fiscal year (five months) on eight owned or leased stations. It reached half the country. Nearly six decades later, it had more than 9,000 employees and was spending about $1.4 billion a year operating four TV networks, four radio networks, an international radio service, two international satellite services, eighty-four wholly owned radio and TV stations, 1,152 rebroadcasters, and working through 37 private affiliates and 271 affiliated or community-owned rebroadcasters. It now reached 99 per cent of the country.

The full history of public broadcasting and the CBC is a vast panorama, far beyond anything that could be contained between the covers of a single book. And, thus, I had to make choices, mournfully leaving out much material, largely ignoring whole areas such as the technical development of broadcasting, and concentrating on a few score rather than the thousands of women and men who have played key roles in the CBC's multidimensional history. My focus has been primarily on the English networks with their interweaving strands of bureaucracy, creativity, and politics: a combustible combination, as history proves.

This book is, therefore, selective, not exhaustive, more impressionistic than definitive, something like viewing flowers from a galloping horse. It is also a very human story of triumph, betrayal, inspiration, frustration, brilliance, and stupidity; a story of rascals and dreamers, drunks and missionaries, egocentric stars and bureaucratic barracudas. In short, it is a story of the clashing wills of talented, driven humans under the pressure of building an electronic national dream.

The book is a product of more than thirty years of personal involvement with the CBC as a correspondent, bureaucrat, and anchor, and, for the past three years, of poring over thousands of archival files, private papers, personal correspondence, annual reports, oral history interviews, and a multitude of newspapers, magazines, and books, as well as conducting lengthy personal interviews with seventy-five key players, some of whom preferred to remain anonymous. Not only has the sheer volume of material been daunting, but so, too, has the challenge of reflecting the magic and excitement Canadians felt about early radio and TV.

No organization has faced more inquisitions than the CBC. It has been repeatedly examined by royal commissions, special committees, task forces, parliamentary committees, and study groups, including commissions led by Aird, Massey, Fowler, Applebaum and Hébert, and Caplan and Sauvageau. But since all Canadians are stockholders in the CBC, it is both inevitable and proper that there is an incessant downpour of evaluation and criticism.

Shining through all the reports and evaluations is one clear message: what matters most is not the plumbing of organizational structure, flow charts, or "repositioning" strategies, but the content of programming. Ultimately, the producer has more power than any president because the president is, essentially, a plumber, while the producer is a creator. Ignoring that reality has bedevilled many a CBC president over the last six decades.

Triumph and betrayal are history's legacy for the CBC. Triumph because, given the intensity and immensity of special-interest opposition to national public broadcasting, it is a cultural and political miracle that the CBC exists at all. For six decades, the CBC has reflected to mass audiences the spirit and reality of this country as nothing else could, and without it, Canada would be a soul-starved nation, hiccupping the cultural values and history of our southern neighbour.

But triumph has come amid more than the occasional political betrayal, the ceaseless onslaught of powerful special-interest buccaneers intoxicated with the elixir of broadcast profits and determined to shrivel public broadcasting, and sporadic internal sabotage. Sometimes loved and sometimes hated, the CBC has surged from crisis to crisis under a leadership that has ranged from idiosyncratic to brilliant but always, in the end, dependent on the creative genius of its programmers.

That the CBC could be much better than it is, that it has at times failed, distressed its friends, and sometimes sacrificed principles for expediency, is certainly true. But, in the sum, there are more triumphs than tragedies.

In researching and writing the book, I was overwhelmed by the enthusiastic help offered by so many people: archivists, librarians, radio and TV personalities, producers, senior and junior bureaucrats, government officials, and politicians. Each living president of the CBC gave hours of his time in interviews, and I am particularly grateful to them – George Davidson, Laurent Picard, Al Johnson, Pierre Juneau, Gérard Veilleux, and Tony Manera. The exhaustive files and oral histories of their predecessors provided an intimate glimpse into the trials and tribulations of their times at the helm. Other current and past senior executives who provided extensive insight included Bill Armstrong, Michael McEwen, Peter Herrndorf, Denis Harvey, Trina McQueen, Ivan Fecan, Harry Boyle, and Robert Pattillo. CBC board members, past and present, gave extensively of their time and so, too, did stars and producers such as Juliette, Frank Shuster, Harry Rasky, Norman Campbell, Lister Sinclair, and Patrick Watson, the latter two being stars of both management and the airwaves. I am also appreciative of those who provided background and perspectives, but who prefer to remain anonymous. Throughout the book, thoughts ascribed to individuals come directly from interviews, oral history tapes, letter, memos, and journals.

I am particularly grateful to Ernie Dick, the CBC chief archivist, and Bruce McKay, the director of planning and production for the English TV network, whose fact-checking advice on the manuscript was extremely beneficial. Among those who especially helped in digging out material, answering obscure questions, and steering me to nuggets of information were the archivists at the Metro Toronto Reference Library; George Brandak of the Special Collections Division at the University of British Columbia Archives; Professor Ross Eaman at Carleton University in Ottawa; Michel Filion and his colleagues at the National Archives in

Ottawa; Sylvia Robitaille, Bruno Fortin, and Carolyn Forcier Holloway of the Visual and Sound Archives in Ottawa; Frances Plaunt Hall of Calgary, daughter of the Father of the CBC, Alan Plaunt; and Leone Earls and Anne Mercer of the CBC Toronto Reference Library.

A special note of thanks must go to my ever-patient and supportive editor at McClelland & Stewart, Dinah Forbes, whose skill in pruning, shaping, and clarifying the manuscript was invaluable. Thanks also to Heather Sangster, my copy editor, for her careful work.

And finally, but pre-eminently, my thanks for this book go to my wife, Lorraine, who has not only danced, talked, and produced her way through a vibrant CBC career, but, more recently, patiently accepted the mountain of reference material that overflowed from den to dining room and even into the living room. She will now get back her home. And, too, for tolerating my distraction and encouraging my determination, I'm grateful to Fred and Francesca Parker and our grandchildren, Jesse and Robert.

Toronto
June 1994

Chronology

1827	Word "microphone" coined by Sir Charles Wheatstone.
1844	Samuel Morse sends first telegraph message.
1876	Invention of telephone by Alexander Graham Bell.
1895	Marconi sends wireless signals more than one mile.
1899	Three British warships exchange wireless messages at sea over seventy-five miles.
1900	Reginald Fessenden transmits first human voice by wireless.
1901	At St. John's, Newfoundland, Marconi receives first transatlantic wireless signal.
1905	Wireless Telegraph Act passed by Canadian Parliament.
1906	Reginald Fessenden makes first radio broadcast to ships at sea.
1909	First radio station programming at San Jose, California, engineering school.
1913	Radio Telegraph Act passed by Canadian Parliament.
1916	KDKA Pittsburgh on the air with experimental broadcasts.
1919	First Canadian station, XWA Montreal, begins broadcasting to hams.
1920	Dutch station begins broadcasting concerts.
1922	First Canadian commercial station, CJCG Winnipeg, on the air.

First French-language station in Canada, CKAC Montreal, on the air.

British Broadcasting Company (BBC) begins.

1923 First publicly owned station, CKY Winnipeg, on the air.

1924 Canadian National Railways (CNR) opens its first radio station in Ottawa.

1926 First demonstration of television in London, England.

British Broadcasting Corporation (BBC) formed.

1927 First nationwide hook-up of Canadian stations to mark Canadian Diamond Jubilee.

1929 Aird Commission recommends national public radio for Canada.

1930 Graham Spry and Alan Plaunt form Canadian Radio League (CRL).

Temporary network of private radio stations carries opening of Parliament for first time.

1932 Canadian Radio Broadcasting Commission (CRBC) established with authority over all broadcasting. Hector Charlesworth named CRBC chairman.

First parliamentary committee on broadcasting established.

1935 Controversial "Mr. Sage" political programs aired by CRBC.

1936 CRBC broadcast of Moose River, Nova Scotia, mine disaster.

Canadian Broadcasting Corporation (CBC) replaces CRBC.

Leonard Brockington appointed CBC chairman.

Gladstone Murray named CBC general manager.

BBC begins world's first television program service.

1937 CBC carries coronation of King George VI.

1938 CBC French network begins farm broadcasting.

1939 CBC English network begins farm broadcasting.

CBC carries declaration of war by Prime Minister King.

CBC war correspondents begin war coverage.

Leonard Brockington resigns as CBC chairman.

1940 Alan Plaunt resigns from CBC board.

CBC school broadcasts begin in Nova Scotia.

1941 CBC News Service established.

1942 Gladstone Murray resigns as CBC general manager.

1944   CBC Dominion Radio network begins.

1945   CBC International Service begins.

Davidson Dunton appointed CBC chairman and CEO.

Golden age of radio begins.

1946   First CBC FM stations in Montreal and Toronto.

1947   CBC broadcast of royal wedding of Princess Elizabeth and Duke of Edinburgh.

1951   Massey Commission reports, urging continued CBC authority over all broadcasting.

1952   CBC-TV begins.

1953   Radio receiver annual licence fee of $2.50 abolished.

First private TV station in Canada, CKSO-TV, opens in Sudbury, Ontario.

1955   First CBC telecast of opening of Parliament.

1957   Fowler Commission Report issued.

1958   7.8 million Canadians watch CBC-TV as Prime Minister John Diefenbaker is re-elected.

CBC opens world's longest TV network linking Victoria to Halifax.

Board of Broadcast Governors (BBG) takes over CBC broadcast regulatory functions.

CBC Northern Radio Service begins.

Alphonse Ouimet replaces Davidson Dunton as CBC chairman and president.

1959   CBC Montreal strike.

"Preview Commentary" cancellation controversy.

Pioneer broadcaster Ernie Bushnell resigns from CBC.

1960   Twelve million Canadians watch CBC-TV for wedding of Princess Margaret and Anthony Armstrong-Jones.

1961   Canadian Television Network (CTV) established.

1962   CBC Dominion Radio network closed.

1966   "Seven Days" crisis erupts.

First regular CBC colour TV programming.

1968   Alphonse Ouimet resigns and George Davidson becomes CBC president.

"Air of Death" controversy.

Canadian Radio-television and Telecommunications Commission (CRTC) replaces BBG as broadcast regulatory agency.

Nine million watch first televised debate of party leaders.

1969   Prime Minister Trudeau attacks separatism in CBC.

1970   CBC coverage of FLQ October Crisis.

1971   CBC "radio revolution" begins.

CBC Radio and -TV admitted to regular sessions of Nova Scotia legislature.

1972   Laurent Picard becomes CBC president.

Global TV system begins.

1974   CBC French FM stereo network begins.

1975   Al Johnson becomes CBC president.

CBC English FM stereo network begins.

1977   Special CRTC committee of inquiry investigates separatism in CBC.

CBC-TV begins regular live coverage of House of Commons.

1982   Pierre Juneau named CBC president.

1989   "Newsworld" on the air.

Gérard Veilleux named CBC president.

Patrick Watson designated as CBC chairman.

1990   Major CBC budget cuts.

1992   Repositioning announced.

"The Valour and the Horror" controversy.

1993   Gérard Veilleux resigns as CBC president.

1994   Tony Manera named CBC president.

Patrick Watson resigns as CBC chairman.

Prologue

The Founding Fathers

One early October night in 1930, at a corner table in the crowded dining room of Café Henry Burger in Hull, Quebec, two men were sipping wine and talking excitedly about the potential of radio to forge a Canadian national identity.

Hovering waiters in this popular restaurant were ignored by the two men – Alan Plaunt, who was twenty-six years old, and Graham Spry, aged thirty. Through their membership in the newly formed Canadian Institute of International Affairs (CIIA), they had met for the first time a few weeks earlier and had been attracted to each other by the friends, views, and aspirations they had in common. Both were Oxford graduates who admired the British Broadcasting Corporation (BBC) and despised American radio. Both knew everybody who was anybody in Canada; Plaunt because he was to the establishment born; Spry because he travelled the country as national secretary of the Association of Canadian Clubs, getting to know what he called "the business gentry." Both were at the forefront in promoting Canadian nationalism, which had taken the country by storm in the 1920s; both were in love with the national symbolism of the Group of Seven artists; and both had joined other talented, activist young Canadian intellectuals in organizations such as the CIIA and the Canadian League.

Plaunt was an organizational wizard; Spry had boundless energy. In their campaign for public broadcasting, Spry was the public Sir Galahad while Plaunt was the backstage Machiavelli. Together, they were the most effective lobbyists in Canada's twentieth century, almost single-handedly convincing prime ministers, Parliament, and the public of the need for public broadcasting. Without these two men there never would have been a national public broadcasting system and radio network programming in Canada would have been almost totally American.

This cool early October evening in Hull, they swirled their wine and plotted strategy, and before they got up from the table, they had a plan. Earlier and separately, they had talked to their friends about the potential of radio and of the dangers of the Americans taking over Canadian airwaves. They had held lunchtime conversations in the Rideau Club across the street from Parliament Hill, conversations at friends' homes, and conversations at meetings of the Canadian Club, the CIIA, and the Canadian Teachers Federation. Four years earlier, in a little dining room behind the Grill Room of Ottawa's Chateau Laurier Hotel, Spry had talked to the executive committee of the Association of Canadian Clubs about using radio to unify the nation. He had proposed that Prime Minister Mackenzie King broadcast a speech to the nation on July 1, 1927, in celebration of Canada's Diamond Jubilee. His advice had been taken, and the broadcast had been a national sensation.

Now, in 1930, Spry and Plaunt were plotting how to strong-arm the government into establishing a public radio system in Canada.

They knew the 1929 report of the Aird Commission, which advocated a national public broadcast system, was languishing on a back shelf, ignored by the newly elected Conservative government of R. B. Bennett. The stock-market crash of 1929 and the resulting Depression had meant that money was now needed for projects of far higher priority than a national radio system. They also knew they faced formidable enemies in the government bureaucracy, among private radio entrepreneurs, advertisers, American broadcasters, and politicians. On the face of it, they couldn't win; it seemed inevitable that Canadian broadcasting would drift into American domination and control.

But they knew, too, that Charles A. Bowman, editor of the *Ottawa Citizen* and a member of the Aird Commission, shared their views and was avid to expand his "Listeners Group," which he had formed a few months earlier among young activist civil servants in Ottawa. Bowman had written a lead editorial in the *Citizen* in 1928 that had expressed Spry's and Plaunt's thoughts. In it he complained of American "radio fumes" inundating Canada and wrote, "There are great possibilities of building the bridge of understanding through the medium of radio broadcasting. . . . There is only one way to meet this American radio competition and that is to raise the standard of service in Canada. It is about time to begin." This was what Spry and Plaunt were now seeking to do.

As Plaunt later remembered, he began the conversation at Café Henry Burger by asking, "Spry, what do you think of the broadcasting situation in Canada?"

"Damn bad!" Spry replied.

"What, I wonder, can be done to bring about an improvement?"

"Let's form a league."

"How do you mean, 'a league'?"

"It's very simple," Spry explained. "You get a number of people interested, you form a league for the advancement of such and such an interest, and that's all there is to do."

"That certainly is worth considering. Let's talk about it."

"The League began as it will no doubt end – in vino," Plaunt scribbled afterwards in his small brown notebook in his almost indecipherable scrawl.

Both men knew Canadians were spending 80 per cent of their listening time glued to American radio programs, and they both felt this was a cancer eating into the Canadian sense of nationhood. Both abhorred the insistent, ceaseless hucksters who sold soap, laxatives, and toothpaste on the radio; the programming that aimed for the lowest common denominator; and, worst of all, the cultural invasion of Canada by American values, American performers, and American stories. But they also knew that the more than 300,000 Canadians who had radios were devoted listeners to "Amos 'n' Andy," Rudy Vallee, and Eddie Cantor. They believed that if Canadian radio could offer an exciting alternative, it would win over the fans of American programs.

The only Canadian programming Spry and Plaunt thought worthwhile was heard on the Canadian National Railways (CNR) radio stations across the country. This, they felt, might provide a model for a future national Canadian public broadcasting system.

"Canadian radio for Canadians" was the motto of these two young revolutionaries, who believed radio was potentially the greatest of all Canadianizing instruments. Each saw it as both an instrument of nationalism and an educational vehicle that would raise standards and tastes through the broadcast of music, drama, and discussion. Radio was so majestic in its potential but so tawdry in its reality. They also saw public radio as a model for experiments in the conduct of public business in Canada. It might, they thought, be the beginning of a much bigger social revolution.

After more talk on how to organize a league to lobby for public broadcasting, they paid their restaurant bill to Madam Burger, went out into the crisp, moonlit night, and agreed to meet again with several friends the following Sunday night, October 5, at Plaunt's three-storey house at 1 Clemow Street in the fashionable Glebe section of Ottawa. (It now houses the High Commission of Ghana.)

It was actually a meeting of the CIIA program committee, and at first the members talked of the crash near Paris that day of the British dirigible R-101 and of Prime Minister Bennett's trip to London for the Imperial Conference. After the meeting ended, Spry, Tom Moore, president of the Trades and Labour Congress of Canada and, as Spry called him, "a huge-belly'ed Englishman," and Margaret Southam, of the Southam newspaper family, stayed behind. "Let's have a drink," Plaunt said, and then they got down to the business of broadcasting and national unity and what Spry called "genial and even convivial plotting."

There was no doubt Spry was running things. After they agreed to form the Canadian Radio League (CRL), "I nominated myself as Chairman and Alan Plaunt as Secretary," Spry later recalled. And with that settled they plunged into the details of organizing the league, including how to raise money, who to recruit, and how and who to lobby. "I was hammering a typewriter indefatigably for hours on end each day and rushing about," Plaunt scribbled in a note to himself remembering those days. Their crusade would have an impact that lasted for the rest of the century.

I

Magic in the Air

Radio and television were hatched from a thousand eggs.

The idea that sound and pictures could actually fly through the air over hills and across lakes, through walls and between cities, must have seemed mystical, magical, and impossible to those who listened to broadcasting's first dreamers. But in the mid-1800s, scientists in Britain, Russia, France, Germany, Italy, Denmark, Sweden, and the United States all began tinkering with experiments in transmitting sound. In the United States in 1844, Samuel Morse sent the first telegraph message from Washington to Baltimore saying, "What hath God wrought." That same year in Germany, C. A. Steinheil conceived the idea of telegraphy without wires. A quarter-century later, the Scottish physicist James Clerk Maxwell found it was theoretically possible to communicate using electromagnetic waves. Alexander Graham Bell invented the telephone in 1876. In 1888 in Germany, Heinrich Hertz made a practical demonstration of using these waves to communicate, and shortly afterwards, English inventor Oliver Lodge transmitted sound by waves as far as sixty yards. In 1892, the most dramatic experiments yet were conducted in Italy where eighteen-year-old Guglielmo Marconi sent sound waves thirty feet across the attic of his parents' home. He then sent sound through the air

23

for about three-quarters of a mile on his father's estate near Bologna, and in another test, he covered two miles. When the Italian Post Office rejected his ideas in 1896, Marconi's British-born mother made arrangements for him to go to England, where the British customs officers initially suspected that the "black box" of scientific instruments he carried contained bombs and "infernal machines." He resumed his experiments in England and, that same year, he sent sound four miles across the Salisbury Plain. Two years later, it was eight miles, and in that year, he moved from experimentation to practical use, scoring a journalistic scoop for the Dublin *Express* by reporting on the Kingston Regatta Yachting Race by radioing back his reports to the newspaper from a tug following the yachts. It was the beginning of the end for Baron Reuter's news-carrying pigeons.

This demonstration of the "wireless" seized not only the public's imagination, but also the interest of King Edward VII. By 1899, British battleships up to seventy-five miles apart were sending each other radio communications, and radio messages were being beamed across the English Channel.

Two years later, Newfoundland received the first transatlantic radio transmission. Marconi, now aged twenty-seven, had set up a sending station in Cornwall, England, and a receiving station in St. John's, Newfoundland. He and his assistants George Kemp and P. W. Paget climbed Signal Hill on the cold, blustery, rainy morning of December 12, 1901, carrying six kites, two balloons, and a length of copper wire. The idea was that the kites, each trailing a 500-foot wire aerial, would catch the sound sent out from Cornwall, 2,232 miles to the east across the stormy Atlantic Ocean. Marconi had instructed his colleagues in Cornwall to send the letter "s" in Morse code continuously for three hours in the afternoon. With the high winds, he and his assistants had trouble keeping the kites in place over St. John's. The previous day one balloon had blown away.

At 12:30 P.M., Marconi was sitting at a small table inside Cabot Tower on the windswept hill above St. John's harbour with an earphone clamped to his ear when he heard a faint letter "s" come through. Marconi let out a whoop of excitement and handed the earphone to Kemp, who later noted in his diary, "Got three dots." They got them again at 1:10 P.M. and at 2:20 P.M., and transatlantic wireless telegraphy was born.

In a page-one story, the *New York Times* said, "Guglielmo Marconi announced tonight the most wonderful scientific development of recent times . . . electric signals across the Atlantic Ocean from . . . England."

Marconi was quoted as saying, "Fog has no effect on the signals, nor has even the most solid substances. The waves can penetrate walls and rocks." To public disbelief, Marconi talked of radio that could "girdle the globe in a flash." It was yet another miracle in an age of miracles which saw horseless carriages and flying machines.

At the same time, there was an even more revolutionary, but less heralded, radio experiment being carried out by a bearded and short-tempered man called Reginald Fessenden, a young Quebec-born inventor who grew up in Fergus, Ontario. Fessenden wasn't just making dots and dashes fly through the air, but human voices, too. Working for the U.S. Weather Bureau, he was developing a new way of transmitting weather forecasts by Morse code at a laboratory on Cobb Island in the Potomac River near Washington, D.C. Now, on December 23, 1900, the thirty-four-year-old Fessenden attached a crude microphone to his new system (the word "microphone" had been coined in 1827 by Sir Charles Wheatstone for a device he had built to magnify sound), and spoke into it with a question for an assistant sitting in another laboratory in Arlington, Virginia, about fifty miles away. "One, two, three, four. Is it snowing where you are Mr. Thiessen? If so, telegraph back and let me know." Thiessen sent back in Morse code a message saying it was indeed snowing. "This afternoon here at Cobb Island," Fessenden excitedly scribbled in his diary, "intelligible speech by electromagnetic waves has for the first time in World History been transmitted."

Fessenden continued his local voice experiments, and in the fall of 1906, he was startled when an assistant reported he had heard a voice from across the Atlantic. Fessenden had set up a radio receiving station in Machrihanish, Scotland, for Morse code experiments between Scotland and his lab at Brant Rock near Plymouth, Massachusetts. His engineer at Machrihanish wrote him, "At about 4 o'clock in the morning I was listening in for telegraph signals from Brant Rock when to my astonishment,

I heard instead of dots and dashes, the voice of Mr. Stein telling the operators at Plymouth how to run the dynamo. At first, I thought I must be losing my senses, but I'm sure it was Stein's voice, for it came in as clearly as if he were in the next room."

About a month later, Fessenden produced the world's first radio "program." Under a contract with the United Fruit Company, he operated the wireless systems aboard some of the company's banana boats, and at 9:00 P.M. on Christmas Eve 1906, puffing one of his favourite, foul-smelling cigars, he sat in his makeshift studio at Brant Rock wishing the banana boats at sea, hundreds of miles away, a Merry Christmas. Fessenden played a recording of Handel's "Largo" – the first recording ever heard on radio – and then, on his own violin he played "O Holy Night" and sang the last verse of "Adore and Be Still." He concluded by reading several Bible passages, wished everyone season's greetings, and announced he would have another "program" on New Year's Eve. At age forty, Fessenden had become the world's first radio producer and performer.

Three years later, the principal of an engineering school in San Jose, California, who was also a radio ham, started what, for the first time, could be called a radio station. Charles David Herrold of the Herrold College of Engineering and Wireless began regular broadcasting once a week on Wednesday nights in January 1909 in order to publicize his school, and later that year, he expanded the airtime to half an hour every day. "This is San Jose calling!" was the signal for hams to tune in to Herrold, his wife, Sybil, and a colleague offering news and music on records provided by a local store. Sybil Herrold became the world's first disc jockey.

In 1915, David Sarnoff, a twenty-four-year-old whiz kid at the Marconi Wireless Co., who started as an office boy at age fifteen and later became a giant of radio, dreamed of a day when radio would be listened to by a far larger audience than hams. "I have in mind," he said, "a plan of development which would make radio a 'household utility' in the same sense as the piano or phonograph. The idea is to bring music into the house by wireless." Marconi, on the other hand, wanted radio to be more than music and entertainment. "Communication between peoples widely separated in space and thought is undoubtedly the greatest weapon against the evils of misunderstanding and jealousy," he said. These differing views on the purpose of broadcasting would echo for the rest of the century in the conflict between private and public broadcasting.

Over the next few years, there were more radio program experiments, including a broadcast of Enrico Caruso singing from the stage of the Metropolitan Opera House in New York in 1910, which was heard by an audience estimated at fifty people, and a special program of musicians and speeches broadcast in 1915 from the United States to Paris. American scientist Dr. Lee De Forest, who called himself the Father of Radio, experimented with broadcasts of the results of Woodrow Wilson's 1916 U.S. presidential election victory, and he also broadcast program experiments involving mezzo soprano Madam Eugenia Farar. He dubbed her the Original Radio Girl after persuading her to sing into a microphone "I Love You Truly" and "Just A'Worryin' for You." Radio was developed further during the First World War, but it wasn't until after the war that experimentation turned into a business.

By 1920, a radio station at The Hague in the Netherlands was broadcasting concerts, and the Marconi Wireless Co. was broadcasting from Chelmsford, England. In the winter of that year, Marconi's Chelmsford station was broadcasting two half-hour programs of music and news daily, and on June 15, 1920, London *Daily Mail* newspaper magnate Lord Northcliffe sponsored a blockbuster radio event. Noted singer Dame Nellie Melba sang "Home Sweet Home," and her voice was heard and hailed by listeners on headphones or clustered around a loudspeaker in London, Paris, and St. John's. Dame Melba called it "the most wonderful experience of my career," and the *British Radio Yearbook* pronounced it "a thrill likely never to be forgotten."

In the United States, station KDKA in Pittsburgh had begun experimental programming in 1916, and its first scheduled broadcast on November 2, 1920, reported on Warren Harding's easy U.S. presidential election victory over James Cox and his vice-presidential running mate, Franklin Delano Roosevelt. KDKA began daily newscasts a year later on September 20, 1921, from the newsroom of the *Pittsburgh Post*.

WWJ in Detroit claims to have begun regular programming even earlier, on August 31, 1920, with the results from Michigan local, state, and congressional primary elections. WHA in Madison, Wisconsin, also lays a claim to being on the air before the Detroit and Pittsburgh stations.

In Canada, sporadic programming began in September 1919 on XWA, a Montreal Marconi station which later became CFCF. The Marconi Wireless Co. of Canada was selling "radio wireless receiving sets" for $15 a set. They were, said a newspaper ad, "Just the Christmas Gift for Your Boy." One of Marconi's salesmen was a young man named Max Smith, who, to stimulate sales, persuaded the company's general manager to let him use XWA's facilities to play records, read news items, and talk about the wonders of radio. Thus, Max Smith became the first announcer, anchor, and recognized radio voice in Canada. Ham listeners also heard Canada's first live performance given by a popular balladeer named Gus Hill and his pianist, Willie Eckstein. They performed in XWA's cramped studio on the top floor of the Marconi plant overlooking a chocolate factory next door.

On May 20, 1920, XWA aired a program that, like Fessenden's Christmas Eve "Amateur Hour" to the United Fruit banana boats, had historic significance. On that sweltering evening, 500 of the nation's powers-that-be crowded into the Chateau Laurier ballroom in Ottawa for a meeting of the Royal Society of Canada. Those present included Prime Minister Sir Robert Borden, Opposition leader and soon-to-be prime minister, Mackenzie King, the governor general, and noted explorer Vilhjalmur Stefansson. Dr. A. S. Eve, a McGill University physicist, addressed the meeting on "Some Great War Inventions." Part of his lecture was a broadcast demonstration in which the audience would hear a program from XWA in Montreal over 100 miles away. Dr. Eve first introduced a recording being played from the Montreal studio, and then at 9:30 P.M., suddenly the voice of a soloist, Dorothy Lutton, came out of a box on the stage.

"WOMAN SINGING IN MONTREAL IS HEARD IN CITY," headlined the *Ottawa Citizen* the next day. "WIRELESS TELEPHONY EXEMPLIFIED." The newspaper reported that "the sound emanating from the strange mechanism" was greeted by rapt attention. "Before their very eyes, a veritable miracle was being evoked," the *Citizen* said, noting that Mrs. Lutton's voice "could be heard quite clearly."

Within a few months, XWA was broadcasting regular programs of recorded music, news, and weather reports, which were heard mainly by ham operators and ships sailing the St. Lawrence River. Later, XWA began broadcasting programs to movie theatres in Montreal which audiences listened to during intermissions.

People everywhere were staggered by this new invention, many simply unable to comprehend that voices could actually fly through the air, through buildings, over forests, farmlands, and oceans. A popular feature of the Canadian National Exhibition (CNE) in Toronto in 1921 was an hour-long Marconi "Radio Concert" at the CNE bandstand that attracted as much attention as the freak shows and rides. A Marconi test station in Toronto began broadcasting experimental radio programs, and another company broadcast concerts twice a week. All across the country, similar broadcast experiments were going on, and Canadians from Vancouver to Halifax became entranced by the wonder of radio.

None were more fascinated and mystified by radio than the 1,100 citizens of Toronto who jammed into the downtown Masonic Temple at Davenport and Yonge streets on March 28, 1922, to hear a radio concert. Some waited in the two-block line-up for hours in a driving rainstorm, huddled against the Masonic Temple's grey stone walls or clustered under a sea of black umbrellas. The doors opened at 7:30 P.M., and hundreds were turned away after the hall was filled. Many of them stood outside in the rain just to be near where the radio miracle was taking place.

The lucky ones inside raced to seats as close to the platform as they could get. They saw in the middle of the stage, flanked by potted palms and sitting on a table, a big square black box and, attached to it, a large horn like an old fashioned gramophone horn. The brightly lit auditorium was a babble of voices as people pointed, whispered, and stared at "the magic box."

This was Toronto's first public demonstration of an actual radio program, and it was sponsored by the *Toronto Star*, whose publisher, J. E. "Holy Joe" Atkinson, saw radio as a promotional opportunity for his newspaper. Atkinson had been introduced to radio by his son, who had been one of Canada's earliest ham radio operators and had made his own crystal wireless set. This "Star Free Radio Concert" would be heard not only by the public at the Masonic Temple, but also by 500 wounded veterans lying on stretchers, sitting in wheelchairs, or standing on crutches in the auditorium of the Christie Street Military Hospital. The broadcast would come from a makeshift studio in northwest Toronto, three miles from the Masonic Temple, where the announcer, singers, and musicians fidgeted nervously and stepped over a maze of wires while they waited for the program to begin.

At 8:30 P.M., one hour after the doors of the Masonic Temple opened, the audience fell silent as John Bone, managing editor of the *Star* (and chairman of the Masonic Temple), strode to centre stage and announced that this was the first such event in Canadian history. "It's quite within the realm of possibility," he said, "... that this occasion is the forerunner of a development which will alter our customs and habits to as great an extent as that occasioned by the invention of the original telephone, of the phonograph or even of the motor car."

With that, a faint noise suddenly crackled out of the big horn at centre stage and a man's voice was heard saying, "First number on the program." Then the strains of a piano were heard tinkling the opening notes of "God Save the King." As Mrs. Evelyn Chelew Kemp played the anthem, all 1,100 people listening in the Masonic Temple leapt to their feet, standing rigidly at attention out of respect for His Majesty and out of wonder that there could be such a thing as music coming from three miles away and out of a horn.

As they settled back into their seats, some muttered that the "talking box" had to be a fake, that it was a phonograph or that the announcer and musicians were really backstage or hidden under the stage. Maybe it was a freak of telegraphy, a hoax, or even "witchcraft," they thought. While many shook their heads in disbelief, others looked at each other and then at the magic horn onstage emitting what one called the "invisible" sound of radio. But believers and non-believers alike were spellbound when the announcer said, "Number two on the program . . ." and the voice of Mrs. R. J. Dilworth, who was standing in the distant studio before a microphone that was nothing more than a telephone on a pole with a horn attached to the mouthpiece, began singing "Down in the Forest" and then "Annie Laurie." The program continued with viola, piano, and cello solos and the Luigi Romanelli Orchestra playing "Oh Me, Oh My," "Wabash Blues," and "Moonlight Serenade."

The audience was transfixed. "Men strained forward in their seats with the hands cupped to their ears. . . . Women were rigid as if carved from stone," reported the *Toronto Star* the next day.

A mighty cheer rose from the listeners as the program ended and, babbling at the wonder of it all, they went back out into the rain to tell those waiting outside, their families, and their friends of the miracle they had witnessed.

"WONDROUS MUSIC WINGED THRO' RAIN-LADEN AIR," headlined the *Star* the next day. "THRILLS, SUSPENSE, AS PEOPLE WAITED, LISTENED."

Three major stories and the banner headline splashed over the front page of the *Star* the next day, and there were two more stories on page two. "Sound waves leap into the air . . ." one story said, and another talked of "a feat of magic . . . an annihilator of distance." "Its possibilities may be described as transcending imagination," the *Star* wrote in its lead editorial.

Equally excited by the wonder of it all was an ambitious, skinny nineteen-year-old cub reporter for the *Toronto Star* who, the night before, had been a technical adviser at the sending station, 9AH, and who was to become the best-known voice in Canada – Foster Hewitt. He had fallen in love with the idea of radio years before, and the previous summer, as an amateur boxer, he had listened in fascination on his crystal set earphones as Jack Dempsey knocked out Georges Charpentier in the fourth round of a boxing match at Boyles Thirty Acres in Jersey City, New Jersey. The Radio Corporation of America (RCA) had broadcast the fight, sending out the signal to 200 theatres and halls up and down the Atlantic coast and to anybody who could pick it up with a receiver.

The potential of radio boggled Hewitt's young mind, and a few months before the Masonic Temple program, he'd gone to Detroit with his father to see an RCA "Radio Show." He was mesmerized by what he heard and bought thirty-five crystal sets and sold them to friends in Toronto. For a short time, he worked in a plant making radio sets and then got a job at the *Toronto Star*, where his father, W. A. Hewitt, was sports editor and where he shared a desk with a flamboyant, newly hired youngster whose name would also ring through the decades of Canadian broadcasting, Gordon Sinclair. In one of their first radio programs together, Sinclair was Hewitt's assistant at a church service broadcast.

Hewitt wasn't the only *Star* man excited by the Masonic Temple "Star Free Radio Concert." So, too, was the newspaper's publisher, Holy Joe Atkinson, who promptly organized another "concert" on April 4 and a third on April 6. And then, still using the facilities of station 9AH, on April 10 at 7:00 P.M., the *Star* began regular programming with news reports, the closing stock markets, sports, and music. That same day, Foster Hewitt was named editor of the *Star*'s radio page and began writing a regular radio column. Within a few months, the *Star* set up its own radio station, CFCA, which remained on the air until 1933. Hewitt was not only writing about radio, he was CFCA's announcer, reading the news and sports, introducing concerts, popular music shows, and church services. He was a tireless promoter of radio for the *Star*. On weekends and holidays he would drive an old Ford pickup truck jammed with radio equipment to county fairs, beaches, and wherever people would gather within the 150-mile listening range of CFCA.

While he loved radio, Hewitt had to be arm-twisted to launch the career that was to be his life and an integral part of the life of almost every Canadian – broadcasting hockey.

On March 22, 1923, at 5:45 P.M., as Hewitt later recalled the conversation, a *Toronto Star* editor, Basil Lake, called to him, "Foster, will you come here a minute? I've got a job for you tonight."

"I've had a hard day. I'm beat," Hewitt replied.

Undeterred, Lake said, "I'd like you to go to Mutual Street Arena tonight and broadcast the hockey game between Parkdale and the Kitchener Seniors."

"A what?" exclaimed Hewitt. "Did I hear you right? Why wouldn't someone in the sports department do that job?"

"They haven't anyone with radio experience," said Lake. "No, you're our man, Foster."

"What if it's a flop?" worried the radio columnist and future broadcast icon.

"Don't worry about that, my boy," said Lake. "You can handle it all right!"

Hewitt later said, "It was one of those 'into the jaws of death' commands." Reluctantly, he headed for the arena, ate two five-cent hot dogs for dinner, and squeezed into a hastily rigged glass box "studio" by rinkside that was four feet high and three feet wide, where he sat hunched on a stool with sawed-off legs.

He was using a telephone line to get the signal from the arena to CFCA, and several times his hockey broadcast was interrupted by a phone company operator breaking in to say, "Number please? What number do you want?"

Hewitt's first hockey broadcast went on for three hours, as the game went into three periods of overtime. Listeners heard for the first time the flat, nasal tones of an excited Foster Hewitt shouting what was to become one of Canada's most memorable phrases, "He shoots! He scores!"

Hewitt, however, was not Canada's first hockey play-by-play radio announcer. That honour goes to a fellow *Toronto Star* reporter, Norm Albert, who did the first hockey broadcast over CFCA on February 18, 1922, when North Toronto beat a Midland, Ontario, team 16–4, with six of the winning goals scored by soon-to-be hockey immortal Lionel Conacher. The second broadcast game was announced by Pete Parker in Regina a month later when the Regina Caps played the Edmonton Eskimos. Hewitt was distressed that the *Toronto Star* didn't pay him extra for doing the hockey games, but he still made broadcasting hockey his life. While he was on his way to becoming a Canadian legend, broadcasting was on its way from being perceived as witchcraft to becoming a part of everyday life.

Radio was simply exploding across Canada. The first commercial licence was granted to station CJCG, owned by the *Manitoba Free Press* in Winnipeg, which reported, "Prominent lectures, great singers will cast their voices through blue space to an audience miles away." By September 1922, licences had been issued by the government for fifty-five stations, including twelve in Toronto, four in Winnipeg, and four in Quebec. In some cases, however, those who got licences didn't put stations on the air or did so and quickly closed them. The owners were companies making or selling radio sets, some religious groups, and newspapers in Vancouver, Halifax, Toronto, Montreal, and Winnipeg with an eye on radio's promotional value. Later, newspapers in Calgary,

Edmonton, Regina, London, Hamilton, and Quebec were also granted licences.

Much listening was still done in large gatherings because, by early 1923, fewer than 10,000 Canadians had paid the one-dollar licence fee required for a radio receiving set, although there were a good many "bootleg listeners" who evaded the unpopular fee. What they heard was mostly music, news, stock-market and weather reports, with occasional unexpected comments from announcers or performers who didn't realize they were "on the air." Radio pioneer Donald Bankart recalled one prominent singer on his first radio performance pausing after his opening song, expecting to hear the applause he usually received onstage. When it didn't come, the radio audience heard him mutter, "Damned ungrateful!" On CKCK in Regina, another singer unused to radio hiccupped in the middle of "Asleep in the Deep," muttered, "Damn it!" and carried on.

On a trip to Canada in 1924, former British prime minister Lloyd George, who called radio "scientific witchcraft," refused to speak into a radio microphone at a Montreal meeting because he was told his voice would be heard by more than 7,000 people. "I won't speak to any more than 1,200 people," he said. "I'm not going to strain my voice." His anxious hosts told him the late U.S. president Warren Harding had spoken to 40,000 people via radio on a recent trip to Vancouver, but Lloyd George replied, "Yes, and Harding died the next day!"

One of Canada's first regular announcers was Jacques Cartier of CKAC in Montreal, who later became a Conservative Party backroom political power in Quebec and played a senior role in the forerunner of the CBC. He was a descendant of explorer Jacques Cartier, who sailed up the St. Lawrence in 1534. A suave, witty, fluently bilingual announcer, Cartier startled his audience when an earthquake shook Montreal by saying in French and English, "The program will be continued later, if we are still alive."

Interruptions and "dead air" were frequent at the best of times as equipment broke down or performers failed to show up, and "There will now be an intermission of ten minutes" became a familiar phrase.

In the early days, some Canadian stations received angry letters from indignant female listeners protesting that announcers were looking at them in their bathrobes or in bed. According to T. J. Allard of the Canadian Association of Broadcasters (CAB), some even claimed the radio was causing pregnancy. It was all due to what was called "radio-itis."

There was worry that radio would make people give up reading and bring about a "passive" society. It was making children "nervous," distracting them from their homework, causing housewives to ignore their housework, and keeping fathers up late, depriving them of sleep, reported *Chatelaine* magazine. The radio is turned on before breakfast and in some homes runs all day long, said writer Harry Hill. "Radio is making our children deaf," he claimed.

Still others talked of "radio maniacs" and "radio widows," some of whom reportedly sought divorces because their husbands ignored them in favour of the radio. There was fear, too, that church attendance would collapse, and ministers would be out of jobs. There were speeches and articles denouncing radio because it would encourage people to stay home and listen instead of going to concerts, movies, and meetings, and editorials denounced the "corruption of the English language" by announcers. Worry about accidental swearing on air led the CNR Radio service to warn its announcers, "It has to be moral if it's oral."

The number of radio listeners rapidly expanded. Canadians tuned in their crystal sets, went to radio concerts, joined radio clubs, and gathered around the "magic boxes" in the homes of friends, much like Canadians would do thirty years later at the dawn of the television age. Farmers hooked up crystal sets to their tractors and listened all day out in the fields, and hospital rooms were equipped with radio sets and earphones. The Mount Hamilton Sanitorium bought 250 headsets and boasted of "a pair hanging on every bedside." As well, a whole new world opened up for the blind. Electric shops couldn't cope with the demand for radio receivers and department stores began setting up radio sections.

In the United States, radio fever was even greater. "The radio popularity is sweeping the country like wildfire. . . . It is one of the greatest marvels of the age," said a Montgomery Ward catalogue in 1922. From nine stations in 1921, more than 550 stations were on the air in the United States by 1924. In one year alone, 1921-22, the number of radio receivers went from 60,000 to 600,000. While Canadians note our first hockey broadcast in 1923, Americans note their first baseball broadcast in 1921.

When commercial radio first burst onto the scene in the United States, there was some sentiment in Washington that there should be a public broadcasting system. Prominent exponents of this idea were the secretary of the Navy, Josephus Daniels, and his assistant secretary, Franklin Delano Roosevelt. They didn't get very far, however, nor did Herbert Hoover, who became the Republican secretary of commerce after the Democrats lost the presidency in 1920 and who sharply disliked radio commercials. They were "outrageous," he said. "Radio communication is not to be considered as merely a business carried on for private gain, for private advertisement or for entertainment of the curious," Hoover told the Congress. "It is a public concern impressed with the public trust and to be considered primarily from the standpoint of public interest." But his modest efforts at urging a public system didn't find congressional favour and the field was left wide open for commercialization. A few years later, Congress passed legislation limiting the government role primarily to the granting of licences and control of frequencies.

The early radio station operators used the new medium to promote the sale of radio sets, their own newspapers, or in some cases, a religion. The first radio commercials were broadcast by the San Jose station in 1909, which exchanged records for on-air mentions of the record store. In October 1919, KDKA in Pittsburgh also began receiving records in exchange for mentions of a local music store in experimental programs on Wednesday and Saturday nights. A few months later, commercials came to Canada through the efforts of Max Smith at XWA in Montreal, who was promoting Marconi receiving sets. But it was, of course, the Americans who perfected the art of huckstering on the air.

At first, the commercials were all spot announcements, but soon advertisers began sponsoring full programs. Credit for that idea goes to the American Telephone and Telegraph Co. (AT&T) which, on August 20, 1922, charged a New York real estate developer $100 for a ten-minute talk on the AT&T Manhattan station WEAF. AT&T argued that a broadcast was "like a telephone conversation [and] should be paid for by the person originating it." In the developer's case, the commercial paid off, for he sold two apartments as a result. The age of advertising on radio had dawned.

It was dawning in Canada, too, where, four years after Max Smith's early efforts in Montreal, stations were carrying "indirect" advertising, which did not promote an individual product or mention a price, and carried "direct" advertising with specific product information only before 6:00 P.M. In allowing advertising the government said, "It has finally been decided to allow stations to undertake advertising as an experiment [on] ... whether advertising can be handled in such a way as to make it popular with broadcast listeners."

But in 1926, the government banned "direct" advertising altogether, except "in special cases" with written permission from the government. As time went on, station managers winked at this directive, and it was enforced with increasing laxity, although specific mention of prices was avoided. Also in 1926, Canada's first radio advertising agency was established in Toronto by Ernie Bushnell, who would become a behind-the-scenes power in the CBC. Bushnell, in fact, may well have been the originator of the singing commercial, a dubious contribution to broadcasting about which, decades later, he mourned, "God forgive us for our sins." Bushnell's vibrant tenor voice had been trained in a Toronto church choir and honed in a travelling quartet called The Adanacs. Bushnell decided to use it to enliven a sponsor's message. To the tune of "Three Blind Mice," he and his business partner sang of the wonders of the Toronto Wet Wash Company.

Most early Canadian stations, however, were less innovative in their commercials, and many survived by selling time to "Bible-thumpers" and pedlars of patent medicines.

British radio had also begun as a commercial enterprise, when the Marconi Wireless Co. and seven other radio-set manufacturers established stations. But the British government wanted to avoid the roaring jungle of the more than 550 stations that produced airwave chaos in the United States. So, in 1922, the British Post Office, which was called the Policeman of the Ether for its supervision of radio, acted as midwife in encouraging these companies to form the British Broadcasting Company (BBC) as a monopoly. It was to be financed by a ten-shilling licence fee, of which the BBC got half, and by the manufacturers of radio sets giving the BBC 10 per cent of the price of each radio they sold. As an inducement to bring the radio-set manufacturers together to form a single broadcast service, the government agreed that no foreign-made sets could be sold in the United Kingdom. Later, the 10 per cent rebate to the network on radio sales was dropped, and the BBC's share of the licence fee was raised.

As in Canada and the United States, in Britain radio captivated the nation, and by 1924, the BBC estimated it had about five million listeners. The 1925 *British Radio Yearbook* echoed the mood: "When we first get the wireless set from the shop, there comes the first thrilling moment when the set is to be operated.... This, like the wedding day and the first ride on a bicycle, gives a thrill such as we seldom feel in this unromantic age."

Within a few years, the British government realized the impact of radio on the public and established a parliamentary committee to chart the future. "Broadcasting," the committee stated in its report, "... is fraught with such far-reaching possibilities that the organization laid down for the British Broadcasting Company no longer corresponds to national requirements or responsibilities." Thus, five years after it was set up, the BBC was changed from a company to a public corporation; in effect, broadcasting was nationalized. "The programs," the new corporation said, "will consist of instrumental and vocal music, lectures, speeches and news."

The man who had run the British Broadcasting Company and who was chosen to run the new BBC was appalled by the North American idea of popular radio programming of dance bands, sports events, news snippets, and amateur talent, with only occasional serious music, serious drama, and serious commentary. "To have exploited so great a scientific invention," the thirty-four-year-old intellectual John Reith said, "for the purpose and pursuit of entertainment alone would have been a prostitution of its powers and an insult to the character and intelligence of the public." While broadcasters in Canada and the United States viewed radio simply as a business, Reith and his colleagues, according to historian Asa Briggs, believed radio "was an instrument of public good, not a means of . . . pandering to their wants." Reith believed in giving the public what he thought it needed, not necessarily what it wanted.

Reith, who came to be known as the First Lord of the Airwaves, was judged by some to be insufferably arrogant in his élitism, but one close colleague said Reith simply had an inferiority complex "so acute as to be indistinguishable from a superiority complex." Nevertheless, he felt he was guided by God to use radio to save the world from immorality, heathendom, and avarice.

The stern, moralistic Reith despised "vulgar showmanship" and, unlike Canadian and American private radio leaders, disliked emphasis on celebrities. He demanded a large share of highbrow programming on British radio. "The desire for notoriety and recognition sterilizes the seeds from which greatness might spring," he said. Reith insisted that, out of respect for the audience, early BBC announcers wear tuxedos when on air. "The wearing of evening dress is an act of courtesy," a BBC official explained. The BBC paid announcers a clothing allowance so they could buy the required formal wear.

On April 24, 1923, the BBC carried the first broadcast by King George V and brought a new dimension to the monarchy with the King's voice reaching people who had never before heard a monarch. Throughout Britain, and Canada too, listeners would leap from their chairs and beds and stand at attention whenever "God Save the King" was played.

Little of the Reithian élitism was evident in these early years on Canadian radio. Its owners saw their mission as hustling profits, not culture. There were some exceptions, such as CFCA, the *Toronto Star* station, which favoured more highbrow programming than most Canadian stations, and there were programs such as the Toronto Symphony Orchestra and the Hart House String Quartet on CFRB in Toronto and "The Nellson Hour" with Geoffrey Waddington and his twenty-seven-piece orchestra on CKNC Toronto. Occasionally a diamond would be found in the rough local talent, as Maj. William Borrett discovered when he was running CHNS in Halifax. "A hungry-looking little fellow . . . came in one day with a guitar and asked for a chance to sing," he later said. "He was pathetic looking . . . [but] I could tell right off this fellow had something. . . . It was Hank Snow." Canada's first regular female broadcaster was Jane Gray who, in 1924, read poetry while an organ played in the background, in a London, Ontario, station. She had a hard time getting on the radio because the station manager felt a woman's place was in the kitchen not in the studio. "Women on the air?" he exclaimed. "There never will be, by the grace of God." He relented, but she wasn't paid for her first broadcasts. Gray went on to become a radio star and a producer.

There had been plays on Canadian radio as early as 1922, but Gray launched Canada's first series of radio mysteries in 1928 on CFCA in Toronto. Her total budget was $12.50 per half-hour program. At the time, her CFCA colleague Foster Hewitt ridiculed the idea of her mystery shows, saying, "You can't kill a man, find the murderer, and hang him in thirty minutes." The mysteries were the exception; for the most part Canadian radio followed the American pattern of broadcasting dance bands, news, weather, and sports, with occasional home-town talent shows and coverage of local events.

CHNS in Halifax was typical, opening at 6:30 P.M. with a stock-market report and producer prices and then a talk, followed by a half hour of recorded music. From 8:00 P.M. to 8:45 P.M., there was "Children's Period," then more recorded orchestra music. At 10:00 P.M., local musicians and singers were featured, and at 11:30 P.M., it was back to recorded dance-band music until the station went off the air at midnight. Commercials on CHNS cost $1 or $2, and sponsoring a half-hour show cost $30. In 1925, when CHNS first went on the air, there were about 7,000 radio sets in Nova Scotia.

Among the early announcers on CHNS were the Willis brothers, who would later become famous as CBC voices and television hosts: Austin Willis, who eventually wound up in Hollywood, and J. Frank Willis, who thrilled tens of millions of Canadians and Americans with his vivid, live radio reporting from the pit head at the Moose River mine disaster in Nova Scotia in 1936, which was carried on a vast network of Canadian and American stations. Much later, he hosted the principal prime-time television documentaries and other major TV programs as the CBC's premier announcer.

Harry Boyle, a mischievous, tousle-haired young boy in the hamlet of St. Augustine, just north of London, Ontario, who later became one of the creative giants of Canadian broadcasting, fell in love with radio when three brothers came into his father's general store lugging a radio set. It was, he says, "a great big horn and batteries. Wires hung out from every-where." They arranged a demonstration for that night, and Boyle's neigh-bours flocked to the store, hearing, after three hours of squeaks and squawks, violin music on KDKA in Pittsburgh. "Everybody cheered and yelled," Boyle recalls.

There were several "educational" stations in Canada in the earliest days of broadcasting, including CKY in Winnipeg, which was run by the Manitoba government and which, today, is run by the CBC as CBW. The provincial government had taken over a few stations in 1923 (includ-ing CJCG, which had been given Canada's first commercial licence a year earlier) when their newspaper owners had decided to close down the sta-tions. Canada's first public broadcaster, CKY, carried commercials along with weekly educational lectures by University of Manitoba professors on everything from architecture to zoology, a program called "Teeth and Health" by the Manitoba Dental Association, and lessons in French and Esperanto. Queen's University at Kingston, Ontario, also began a broad-casting station in 1923, featuring lectures and coverage of sports events. CKUA in Edmonton, the University of Alberta station, began in 1926 and continued into the 1990s. It offered twenty hours a week of symphonies, literary discussions, travel talks, handicraft information, and farming news. The pioneering public broadcasting station was supervised by E. A. "Ned" Corbett, who, a decade later as a leading supporter of national public broadcasting, helped design some of the most successful and significant CBC public affairs programs including "The National Farm Radio Forum" and "Citizens' Forum."

The first Canadian election coverage on radio happened in December 1921 when stations in Toronto, Montreal, Vancouver, and Saint John car-ried the federal election results. Most Canadian stations were reluctant to go further and carry political speeches and meetings because they weren't profitable and besides, they said, audiences wanted music not politics. CKAC in Montreal was an exception, however, covering more political speeches and meetings than any other station. It aired addresses by Prime Minister Mackenzie King on his return to Canada from the 1923 Imperial Conference in London and speeches by other political leaders.

In their search for profits, some stations apparently were even willing to lend a helping hand to bootleggers selling to Prohibition-parched Americans. "Some of the broadcast stations in Canada were actually being used as bootlegging agencies," said Charles A. Bowman, the influential editor of the *Ottawa Citizen*. A station in Vancouver, according to Bowman, would sometimes "tip off the rum runners when the coast was clear for landing liquor [on the U.S. coast]."

There were complaints about there being too little "serious" programming and too much dance music and jazz. "How Can Radio Be Best Utilized to Inculcate National Ideals and Foster National Unity?" was the title of an October 15, 1924, *Maclean's* article by Elton Johnson. "There are," he wrote, "thousands of fans – particularly in the small towns and country districts – who want something more than an orchestra from their loud speaker. They want news stories, often with bright interpretations, they want interesting talks on science, politics, religion, history and literature. They do not want every station in the country at all hours to be broadcasting nothing but . . . music."

One of the problems for Canadian radio in the 1920s was that powerful American stations punched into much of Canada, overwhelming, if not drowning out entirely, Canadian stations. Nowhere was that more evident than in Toronto, where there were an estimated 30,000 radio sets by the mid-1920s. The Toronto *Telegram* surveyed its readers' listening habits in a "Radio Popularity Ballot" in September 1925 and found that the first seventeen best-liked stations were American. The five Toronto stations that broadcast daily at the time were at a distinct disadvantage because, like other Canadian stations, each was on the air only a few hours a day and thus found it difficult to establish an identity. Canadian stations were simply lost in a flood of American radio channels just as, as *Maclean's* complained at the time, "American-made photo-dramas monopolized our moving picture houses."

The most ambitious Canadian radio operation came from the vibrant foresight of Canadian National Railways (CNR) head Sir Henry Thornton who decided, in 1923, to set up a CNR radio network, or "simultaneous broadcasting" as networks were then called. In January of that year, WEAF in New York had established the first American network called the "Red Network" by linking up with stations in Washington and

Providence, Rhode Island. There were also networks set up in the 1920s by private Canadian stations for a single program or event, but there was nothing like Thornton's plans for the CNR. He envisioned a network stretching all across Canada, but first he put radio receiving sets in some parlour cars on CNR trains and in some CNR hotels. The minister of railways and canals explained that the idea was "to advertise Canada and the Canadian National Railways, to furnish entertainment to passengers on long distance trains and guests at the company's hotels and generally to make the service of the railway more attractive. . . . As an advertising medium radio telephony is unsurpassed."

After some experimental broadcasts during the summer and fall, the CNR service began on December 30, 1923, with a musical program and speeches by Sir Henry and other railway officials broadcast from studios in Ottawa and Montreal. They announced plans to build a nationwide network of stations and to equip CNR transcontinental trains and hotels with "the finest of receiving sets." The inaugural program was received by local trains. The first CNR transcontinental train equipped with radio in the lounge car chugged out of Montreal, headed for Vancouver, on January 5, 1924, and by 1930, eighty lounge cars had radios equipped with earphones.

The dashing Edward, Prince of Wales, was one of the early fascinated listeners when he sped across the country in the fall of 1924 on the CNR transcontinental to his ranch near High River, Alberta. He spent several September afternoons listening to CNR Winnipeg's newscasts and music on a loudspeaker in his private parlour car enroute to High River. CNR radio engineer Gordon Olive was dispatched to the royal ranch to install a special radio set for the prince's use during his five-week stay. Olive, who a quarter of a century later became the CBC's director general of engineering, often joined the prince in listening to a Calgary station.

Radio fascinated not only the Prince of Wales, but almost all railway travellers. "I'd hear complaints from dining car stewards that nobody was eating . . . they'd all be out in the observation car listening to radio," said J. T. Carlyle, the first CNR Radio service employee. Hundreds of passengers boarded trains in 1926 just to hear the radio broadcast of boxer Gene Tunney winning a ten-round decision over Jack Dempsey.

The CNR opened its own station in Ottawa on February 27, 1924.

Programming began with the clanging of a big railway bell and then "O Canada" played by the Chateau Laurier Orchestra. Hundreds came to the studio to watch the event, which was heard not only in parlour cars and on home radio sets but also on a downtown Ottawa street corner where "a large horn" was set up. Hundreds of people crowded around the street-corner loudspeaker listening to concert music, singers, and speeches.

In November of that year, the CNR opened another station in Moncton and, in 1925, one in Vancouver. In addition, the CNR operated so-called phantom stations in Montreal, Toronto, Winnipeg, Saskatoon, Regina, Edmonton, and Calgary, and later in London, Ontario; Brandon, Manitoba; Yorkton, Saskatchewan; and Red Deer, Alberta. For these "phantoms," the CNR rented program time on existing stations and, using its own call letters, broadcast its own programs. The rental costs ranged from $25 an hour for stations in Yorkton and Red Deer to $128 an hour on CFRB in Toronto.

Landslides, mudslides, and snowslides which cut off broadcast lines caused many a problem for CNR Radio in the early years. During one storm in 1927, a CNR freight train stalled in deep snow east of Fort Frances, Ontario. Told to seek help, the brakeman climbed a nearby utility pole and connected his emergency phone to the wire he thought was a dispatcher's circuit but was, in fact, carrying a CNR Radio music program. With the temperature at forty below, and hanging on amid the swirling snow high above the snowbound train, he heard the strains of "Honey Love" and nearly fell off the pole in astonishment. "Jeez, I hear music.... Goddamn, Bill ... I can't get the bastard to answer me.... What the hell is going on? Where the hell's the dispatcher?" the brakeman bellowed into the line, inadvertently breaking into the radio program being carried from Montreal's Windsor Hotel and shocking listeners from Winnipeg to Vancouver.

Such incidents didn't deter CNR president Thornton in his dream of a high-quality, coast-to-coast network with minimal advertising. There were some sponsored programs on CNR Radio in addition to references to the wonders of the CNR itself, but Sir Henry disdained the commercial preoccupation of fellow broadcasters. "It is essential," he warned, "that broadcasting be surrounded with such safeguards as will prevent the air becoming what might be described as an atmospheric billboard." Sir Henry, who saw radio as a great unifying force for Canada, said, "We regard the use of radio as a national trust."

The on-air result of this attitude was a schedule of operas, symphonies, instrumental groups, original Canadian dramas, news, school broadcasts, farm broadcasts, and children's programs such as "Bedtime Travel Talks" and "Uncle Dick and Aunt Agnes." Through the CNR, Canadians heard live programs of *The Mikado*, *Faust*, *The Gondoliers*, and *Madame Butterfly*, as well as *The Merchant of Venice*, *Othello*, and other Shakespearean dramas. An astonishingly productive and creative radio drama group was developed in 1925 by the CNR in Vancouver. Called the CNVR Players, it produced hundreds of plays and became the catalyst for early CBC drama a decade later.

Canadians heard weekly programs of the Toronto Symphony Orchestra, the Hart House String Quartet, and the McGill Operatic Society and, in a less highbrow vein, they also heard a blackface quartet, The Continental Porters. Programs in French and English were aired, and comedians, dance music, health talks, economic talks, and political commentaries were featured. One program featuring talks by political leaders, called "Nation's Business," still runs today on the CBC nearly seven decades later. Religious groups were barred from the CNR stations, however, because of the squabbling among the radio preachers.

The first Canadian time signal was heard at 9:00 P.M. on CNR Radio from the Dominion Observatory in Ottawa on March 1924. That same month, CNR broadcast the first radio coverage of the Stanley Cup playoffs, in which the Montreal Canadiens beat the Ottawa Senators in overtime. Altogether, it was an extraordinarily rich diet of programming, rivalling that of the BBC and starkly different from the commercial fare on American and most private Canadian stations.

A handful of soon-to-be movers and shakers of Canada took up Sir Henry's radio ideas, heatedly discussing the potential of radio at meetings of the Association of Canadian Clubs and the Canadian League. They pointed to the contribution radio could make to national unity and cultural enlightenment and extolled the virtues of the British system of public ownership. One of these activists was *Ottawa Citizen* editor Charles Bowman. He'd been intrigued by radio ever since he tucked his young son, Bob, into bed one night and discovered the boy listening to a crystal set. "Dad, listen to this," Bob said excitedly and, taking the earphones, Charles Bowman, who had previously disdained his son's fascination with radio, heard a station in Chicago. Forever after the newspaperman was obsessed by the potential of radio.

In 1926, a chance phone call from Prime Minister Mackenzie King started a chain of events that eventually led to the establishment of the CBC. King asked Bowman to accompany him to London for the 1926 Imperial Conference as his public relations adviser. Bowman agreed, and together they sailed to England and checked into London's Ritz Hotel. Their first visitor was a man called Gladstone Murray, a thirty-three-year-old Canadian from the Fraser Valley of British Columbia who was head of public relations for the BBC and who, a decade later, became the CBC's first general manager and a central player in Canadian broadcasting.

Murray wanted King to give a radio talk on the BBC, the first national broadcast by an Empire prime minister on the network. King's speeches had been broadcast in Canada, but he had never given a radio talk and was reluctant. Murray, a smooth-talking former RAF ace fighter pilot and Rhodes Scholar, persisted, and King finally agreed, provided Bowman wrote the talk. Bowman immediately saw a golden opportunity not just to promote Canada, but also to demonstrate the importance of radio to the prime minister and put some policy-making words into his mouth. He knew that the drafting of speeches was the making of policy.

The date for the talk was set for November 19, 1926. When King and Bowman arrived at the BBC they were met by Murray and BBC general manager John Reith, who envisioned the BBC as a model for the rest of the Empire, if not the world.

Promptly at 9:40 P.M., King entered the radio studio and began talking of "The Problems of Canada." Most of the talk, however, was of the joys of Canada as he spoke of the "sparkling white" Canadian winter snow, of skiing in the Gatineaus near Ottawa, of maple syrup, the red maple leaves of fall, and of the Nova Scotia seashore. Then, with Bowman pridefully listening to his own words, King, for the first time, indicated the kind of radio system he might like to see in Canada.

"It does seem to me," King said, "that the British method of regulating the use of radio for the public entertainment has much to commend it. . . . The radio programmes which are published from day to day do impress me as being maintained on a very high order of excellence. They furnish evidence to me that the British people have not succumbed so completely as they have in some other parts of the world to the craze for jazz and the jangle of some modern dance music. The British radio public is, indeed, to be congratulated upon having the air kept largely free from the clangour of discordant noises."

The radio talk, Bowman said later, "initiated Mackenzie King into the significance of national broadcasting."

Back in Ottawa, meanwhile, Graham Spry, as the new national secretary of the Association of Canadian Clubs, was thinking of ways to promote national unity during the celebration of Canada's Diamond Jubilee in 1927, to be held seven months after King's BBC talk. Spry had been fascinated by radio since he was a ten-year-old experimenting with ham radio. As a teenager he had served in the Signal Corps in the First World War, and later had organized a pioneer radio club at the University of Manitoba. Spry sent a memo to the King government recommending a nationwide radio hook-up from the Parliament Buildings to mark Canada's sixtieth birthday. It would be the first coast-to-coast network program in Canada. After returning from London, and remembering the success of his BBC radio talk, King agreed.

On a hot, sunny morning on July 1, 1927, 40,000 people gathered on the velvet grass of Parliament Hill while hundreds of thousands more across the country tuned in to stations organized into a temporary network by the CNR Radio service with the co-operation of the telegraph and telephone companies. Jacques Cartier, the irrepressible Montreal pioneer announcer, was one of the hosts for the broadcasts. The Peace Tower carillon from Parliament Hill sounded over twenty-three stations, including WWJ in Detroit, at 10:45 A.M. Ottawa time, signalling the start of the first program. "O Canada," "The Maple Leaf Forever," and "God Save the King" were heard. Prime Minister King had just finished his first broadcast speech of the day and taken off his glasses when the iron hands of the Peace Tower clock reached noon and the clock rang for the first time since the 1916 fire on Parliament Hill.

"The most thrilling moment of the whole day was the striking of the new clock in the Peace Tower at 12:00 o'clock noon. . . ." the Toronto *Globe* reported. "The depth and clarity of the tone of that bell thrilled radio hearers in every part of Canada and was an extraordinary living symbol of a united Canada listening to the striking of twelve noon."

The second program began at 2:00 P.M., featuring 10,000 schoolchildren from Ottawa and Hull singing together in French and English, followed by a 1,000-voice choir. The crowd on the Hill was now swollen to 50,000, and a plane circled overhead while women, clutching colourful parasols, and men, dressed in kilts, uniforms, and business suits, perspired under the glaring sun.

The speeches droned on through the afternoon, leading the *Toronto Star* to comment, "Some of the speeches were a little long," and that Mackenzie King "spoke just a trifle too fast" for the radio.

Listeners across the nation were stunned to hear live for the first time the voices of Ottawa officials, and were also amused to hear unscheduled comments. "Sit down, Brown, His Excellency is going to speak!" was one unexpected admonition heard by radio listeners just before the governor general began his address. "One could hear the movements of the crowds and their chatter," said the *Globe*.

The most impressive program was that night's. It went on until 1:30 A.M. and featured music by the Hart House String Quartet and The Bytown Troubadours, a reading by famous Canadian actress Margaret Anglin, and more speeches by the governor general, Prime Minister King, and others who spoke into a microphone that had been gold-plated to honour the six decades of Canadian nationhood.

Across the country Canadians listened on sets in their homes and on loudspeakers in downtown parks, such as in Montreal where 20,000 gathered at Parc Jeanne-Mance to hear the ceremonies.

"NATIONWIDE BROADCAST THRILLS LOYAL THRONG OF EDMONTON CITIZENS," read one headline. "RADIO TRANSMITS CAPITOL [*sic*] PROGRAM TO FIVE MILLIONS," said another. "HEARD PERFECTLY ON BOTH COASTS," was another front-page banner headline. Newspaper editorials lauded the radio broadcast with comments like "unmatched worth," "thrilling," and "that modern genie, the radio." "One of the most significant and useful of all contemporary scientific achievements," said the *Toronto Star*. "Radio," said the Toronto *Globe*, "... is a democratic science, ready to instruct and entertain all manner and conditions of humankind who prepare to receive its blessings."

Graham Spry thought so, too. "This was a turning point in thinking about broadcasting," he later said. "Up to that point, radio was a plaything." He was standing near the platform when King spoke and recalled, "I was looking up at him and he was so thrilled, so enraptured by the thought that 'Here I am standing in Ottawa and every Canadian could be listening.'"

Mackenzie King was simply knocked out by the impact of the broadcast. There was "nothing comparable," he said, noting it was the first time words spoken on Parliament Hill were heard simultaneously across Canada. "It is doubtful if ever before," he said, "... those in authority were brought into such immediate and sympathetic personal touch with those from whom their authority derived. . . . All of Canada . . . became a single assemblage swayed by a common emotion. . . . As a result of this . . . there will be aroused a more general interest in public affairs and an increased devotion of the individual citizen to the common weal."

These Diamond Jubilee broadcasts, together with his BBC talk, profoundly shaped Mackenzie King's attitude toward the potential of radio as a public service and led, in time, to the establishment of the CBC.

2

God in the Air

The roots of the CBC sprouted from the evangelical excesses of the Jehovah's Witnesses.

As the 1920s wore on, the airwaves were increasingly flooded with the word of God. Religious groups excited by radio's potential to spread their faith had been among the first station owners in Canada. "We believe that the radio is one of God's most wonderful gifts to man," said Rev. A. A. McIntyre, editor of the *Canadian Churchman*. "There is no doubt about it," said Rev. W. A. Cameron in Toronto. "Radio can be made a wonderful agency for spreading the gospel." That had been a long-held belief by church leaders and, in fact, the first "broadcast" of any kind in Canada had occurred in 1880 from Montreal's Zion Church. The church service, including choral and organ music and a sermon, was carried by a rudimentary telephone line to an audience of reporters and editors listening in on earphones in the phone company's office half a mile away.

Now, in the mid-1920s, the Presbyterians, the Baptists, the Roman Catholics, and the United Church all had stations and programming in various cities, as did groups like the Christian and Missionary Alliance, the Jehovah's Witnesses, and other evangelical bodies. Evangelist Dr. H. A. Terry exulted in the success of his broadcasts on CKY in Winnipeg, boasting that he had at least three conversions in one weekend alone through his radio sermons. The conversion champion, however, was William "Bible Bill" Aberhart of the Prophetic Bible Institute in Calgary, whose fundamentalist radio preaching – "evangelical bellowing," said Alberta educator Ned Corbett – converted the citizens of Alberta into electing him as premier.

Other proselytizing preachers used radio as a weapon to attack rival churches, as in Toronto where, in March 1926, a vicious Roman-Catholic-versus-Protestant broadcasting battle broke out. The *Toronto Star* station, CFCA, had agreed to carry three broadcasts labelled "Catholic Truth," but after the second broadcast, the station asked the speaker, Father F. J. Kirby, to tone down his attacks on Protestant "bigotry." He refused, and in the middle of his third broadcast, CFCA cut him off in mid-sentence. The *Catholic Register* blasted the station and its owner for "imperiously setting themselves up as a Methodist censor of Catholic Doctrine," and it went on to attack Toronto itself "whose intellect," it said, "is chloroformed by the old Protestant tradition."

This battle paled, however, in comparison with the war that broke out over the radio broadcasts of the Jehovah's Witnesses. This shook the foundation of Canadian radio so profoundly that it was never the same again. In Canada, the strident, zealous Witnesses went under the name of the International Bible Students' Association. They were continually in hot water because of their fiery warnings of Armageddon and their bitter attacks on "the infidel leaders," "Judases and polecats," and "gullible followers" of other religions. They also regarded all governments as the work of Satan.

They were among the first to realize the potential of radio and owned and operated several stations in the United States and had applied for a Toronto radio licence in 1922. They had initially been denied, but within a few years, they had been granted licences and were on the air in Toronto, Saskatoon, Edmonton, and Vancouver, broadcasting attacks on the Roman Catholic Church. In a typical broadcast they lambasted the Church: "That wicked organization, acting under the pretext of being God's representative on earth has crushed every organization that has ever risen against it. . . . The Roman Catholic hierarchy has begun and carries on the assault against God's true people. In every country of earth, the hierarchy carries forward this wicked persecution."

This kind of attack by the Bible Students' Association stations churned up protests across the country. "Un-British," "unwarranted," "unjustified," "unpatriotic and abusive," members of Parliament were told in letters, petitions, and resolutions. Under the Radio Telegraph Act of 1913, the government licensed broadcasting and receiving, and P. J. A. Cardin, the minister of marine and fisheries, and a devout Catholic, was both in charge and in outrage at the broadcasts. "The broadcasting of the Association does not meet with the approval of the listening public," he said. ". . . The tone of the preaching seems to be that all organized churches are corrupt and in alliance with unreligious forces, that the entire system of society is wrong and that all governments are to be condemned."

On March 31, 1928, Cardin revoked the stations' licences and another storm broke over his head. "Censorship!" "Discrimination!" "Muzzle!" screamed not only the Bible Students' Association but also a good many members of Parliament, commentators, and newspapers. "It is unsafe, unsound, unfair; it cannot be justified," said MP W. Irvine of the United Farmers of Alberta.

"When did we appoint a Minister of this government as censor of religious opinions?" the Labour MP for Winnipeg North, J. S. Woodsworth, asked in the House of Commons. Although he personally found much of the Jehovah's Witnesses' preaching "positively grotesque," he said, "Surely it is strange that a Liberal government should seek to deny people freedom of the air."

The general manager of the Bible Students' Association, W. T. Salter, set off on a cross-Canada tour to get a million signatures on a petition of protest about the licence revocation. He collected 458,026 signatures, although few of the signers owned radios, and also claimed that 20,000 letters of appreciation for the Bible Students' programs had been sent to Ottawa. The government, however, said there were only 5,005 such letters, and almost all of them came from the United States.

The assault on the government for "censorship" broadened in the House of Commons to attacks on radio programs in general and newscasts in particular. Even though most MPs at the time did not even own a radio set, they ranted on about what people heard. "Most radio programs are rubbish," one MP said, while another said, "Most of the news that is now on the air should be either severely censored or cut off entirely." "The kind of news they send out over the radio . . . is the cheapest sort of scare headline material and it is unfit for children to hear," said still another MP.

It wasn't just the news that drew parliamentary scorn. "Irving Berlin with his questionable productions is bringing a blight to the minds and hearts of our generation," said Thomas Bird, a Swan River, Manitoba, Progressive Party MP.

J. S. Woodsworth, who became the first leader of the Co-operative Commonwealth Federation (CCF) in 1933, used the crisis to advocate government control and operation of radio. "I know there are dangers associated with the control of radio by government," he said, ". . . but there are even greater dangers in allowing things to drift along as they are at the present time in Canada. . . . I would rather trust our own Canadian government with the control of broadcasting than trust these highly organized private commercial companies in the United States. The government itself should take the responsibility and decide upon a comprehensive national policy leading to public ownership and control of this new industry."

Woodsworth was echoing the words of *Ottawa Citizen* editor Charles Bowman, who had written a few months earlier that Parliament would soon be faced with deciding whether radio should remain private as in the United States or become public as in Britain. "With the experience of the United States where chaotic conditions in radio broadcasting were allowed to develop for lack of public control, it would seem," he wrote, "the height of folly on the part of Canada to allow this great new public service to drift into similar conditions. . . . Canada should act without further delay."

The whole debate on religion and radio, the *Citizen* said in another editorial, "may help to focus public opinion on an impending national problem."

Assailed on all sides, Marine and Fisheries Minister Cardin quickly became fed up with his responsibilities for radio, groaning, "The sooner I can get rid of this and have it taken out of the department, the better it will be for me!"

Like Bowman, Mackenzie King saw both an opportunity and a way out of a public row. After his visit to the BBC two years earlier and listening to Bowman's arguments, King was inclined to the British system of public broadcasting and was privately urged to adopt the BBC approach by his close friend J. H. Cranston, the editor of the *Toronto Star*. The prime minister was also hearing support for government owned and operated radio from his close associate Vincent Massey, a power in the Liberal Party, the Canadian minister to Washington, and, as it happened, a friend of Bowman.

In the spring of 1928, Bowman wrote a series of *Citizen* editorials arguing forcefully for nationalized radio. "Only under a comprehensive national policy of ownership, control and operation in Canada does it seem possible to meet the competition of American broadcasting stations for the ear of the Canadian public," he said. Bowman also complained of the public being forced to listen to "dull advertising parrot talk" by "radio barkers." "Radio broadcasting under private enterprise is permanently handicapped by the necessity of having to raise revenue from advertising," he wrote. It also did not escape his attention, although it wasn't expressed publicly, that newspapers, which were beginning to recognize radio as a serious competitor for advertising revenue, would be better off with commercial-free radio.

Bowman's editorial crusade drew strong support from his Southam publishers, and his articles were reprinted in other Southam papers. Ontario Premier Howard Ferguson also offered his support. But cautious as he always was, King took the traditional Canadian route when faced with a difficult problem by appointing a royal commission.

The prime minister invited Bowman to meet the cabinet to offer his ideas on what to do about radio and also consulted him on who should be appointed to the commission. Bowman made several recommendations, including William D. Herridge who, although originally a Liberal, was now a Conservative Party insider, a personal friend, and adviser of the Conservative Opposition leader, R. B. Bennett. He was also friendly toward public broadcasting. However, Herridge hated King, and the prime minister knew it. So, King demurred but then asked Bowman if he would serve on the commission. Bowman agreed with alacrity.

Bowman's appointment had been urged on King by Vincent Massey, an ardent and influential supporter of Bowman's public broadcasting ideas and the first senior Canadian official to propose a national broad-casting policy. Massey also suggested Sir John Aird, president of the Canadian Bank of Commerce. King accepted Massey's two names and then added Dr. Augustin Frigon, an electrical engineer and director general of technical education in Quebec. The secretary of the commission would be Donald Manson, chief inspector of radio in the Department of Marine, and a man Graham Spry described as "a charming Scot."

In his typical procrastination, it took King six months to set up the Royal Commission on Radio Broadcasting. When it finally was brought into being, the government formally gave the commissioners three options to consider: establish one or more private networks which would get a federal government subsidy; establish a network of government owned and operated stations; or establish stations operated by provincial governments. King privately indicated he wanted the middle route of federally owned and operated stations.

Despite King's preferences and Bowman's convictions, however, the two other commissioners instinctively opposed nationalized radio. Sir John Aird, a seventy-three-year-old banker, was a charming, witty old Tory, and Dr. Augustin Frigon mistrusted national governments and wanted more powers for Quebec. "Neither had any use for public ownership," Bowman later commented.

Only Bowman had spent much time thinking about radio, although Frigon felt the future of broadcasting lay in the answer to a key question which was, he said, "Whether we consider broadcasting as a business or as a medium to be used for the benefit of the country." It was indeed the fundamental question they faced, and the question all Canadian broad-casting continued to face for the rest of the century. Neither Aird nor Frigon, however, had much more than instincts about broadcasting. At their first meeting in Toronto, Aird told Bowman and Frigon, "Of course, I know nothing about radio. I used to have a radio in the house, but I threw the damn thing out."

Aird decided the commissioners should first go to New York to see how the Americans did it. NBC and CBS, however, shocked Aird and Frigon when they learned of the broadcasters' desire to extend their networks across Canada. "We intend to give Canada complete coverage as in the United States," an NBC official told them. Behind the gracious reception the two networks gave the Canadians was the expectation that the Canadian airwaves could be a profitable satellite operation. It was a broadcasting version of the old American cry of "manifest destiny," and it shook Aird, the good Toronto imperialist.

"Canada could become dependent upon the United States for radio broadcasting as we are on films from Hollywood," Bowman warned Aird. Aird decided they should quickly sail to Britain to see the BBC style of public service.

Before they boarded the *Mauretania*, Aird, Frigon, and Bowman also heard indirectly from an American advocate of nationalized radio, Franklin Delano Roosevelt. At the time, FDR had just been elected governor of New York, and at a private lunch with Vincent Massey, Roosevelt recalled how he had tried and failed when he was assistant secretary of the Navy to make American radio a public service rather than a private enterprise. "I don't want to appear to be interfering or intruding," he told Massey, "but I do hope you'll keep the desirability of national broadcasting in mind. It should be nationally owned and controlled and operated." Massey, who fully agreed, made sure the commissioners heard about Roosevelt's views.

The broadcasting education of Aird and Frigon, which began with such a rude awakening in New York, was deepened by their examination of the BBC. Bowman was already sold on a public radio service for Canada *à la* BBC, and Aird found a soul mate in John Reith, a fellow "son of the manse," who was responsible for what was considered the best broadcast service in the world. Aird was impressed with the variety of BBC programs, the absence of commercials, and the funding by a licence fee for each radio set. Frigon was impressed, too, but ever the technical expert, what struck home for him was the quality of British technology, which he judged to be far ahead of the Americans'.

During their visit to London, Aird became the first Canadian to speak on television. He, Frigon, and Bowman visited the small, suburban London workshop of television pioneer scientist John Baird. They saw a demonstration of TV, and then Baird invited Aird into a cluttered, tiny room where the commission chairman sat "looking very uncomfortable in the glare," Bowman later remembered. "It's damn hot in here!" were Aird's historic first words on television.

From London, the commissioners went to Paris where they were told that because private broadcasting was in such disarray, the French were going to nationalize radio. That impressed Frigon, Bowman recalled, "and so we began to get rather closer together in our thinking."

Frigon, always concerned with provincial prerogatives, was also impressed by the German system of a radio public service mix of federal and state program control. His interest would have echoes in a federal-provincial clash he would have with Bowman when the commissioners were preparing their recommendations.

The "three wise men" of Canadian broadcasting visited the Netherlands, Switzerland, Belgium, and Ireland, as well as France, Germany, and the United Kingdom, their inclination for public broadcasting increasing as they travelled. After nearly three months in Europe, in April 1929 they sailed back across the Atlantic to begin a tour of Canada. They travelled coast to coast in the private railway car "Atlantis" provided by CNR president Thornton, whose CNR Radio network told one of the commission hearings that it was "the nation's largest, best established and only national broadcaster." Thornton told Bowman privately that if a national system was not established (and he foresaw a CNR-run radio system), then the Canadian airwaves would be taken over by the Americans. The conflict of interest in travelling in the CNR's luxurious private car while the CNR sought benefits from the commission apparently didn't faze the commissioners.

The president of the rival Canadian Pacific Railway (CPR), Sir Edward Beatty, had his own idea for the future of broadcasting: a private monopoly with minimal federal regulation similar to the American system, which would be run by the CPR.

Characteristic of the private stations' approach to the commission were the comments of Arthur Dupont, radio director of *La Presse* in Montreal, which dominated French broadcasting in Quebec with its powerful station, CKAC. Private radio, he said, means better and more popular programs and an opportunity for Canadian companies to advertise their products. A public radio service, he said, would bring government meddling and propaganda. Ironically, four years later, Dupont went to work for the very kind of public broadcasting system he had denounced. But, in one form or another, Dupont's 1929 arguments were repeated by private station operators through the decades of Canadian broadcasting.

In 1929, those arguments were answered by groups as diverse as the Canadian Legion, the Trades and Labour Congress of Canada, and the United Farmers of Alberta, all of which strongly urged a public broadcasting system for Canada that would be "Canadian for Canadians."

As they travelled to all nine provinces, the commissioners heard many complaints about excessive American propaganda, too many commercials, bad programming, and fears that unregulated private radio would inevitably lead to American domination of radio in Canada as had happened with Canadian movie theatres.

Powerful support for public radio also came from the former prime minister and Conservative Party leader, Arthur Meighen. Speaking to a meeting of Vancouver educators just as the commission began its tour, Meighen said, "If left to private enterprise, like the magazines and moving pictures, it is bound to cater to the patronage that will be reflected in dividends to the stockholders. That is sound commercially, but it will never achieve the best educational ends. . . . The amount of fodder that is the antithesis of intellectual that comes over our radios is appalling while the selection of material for broadcasting remains in commercial hands."

In three months of hearings in twenty-five cities, the commissioners heard 164 oral statements and received 124 written submissions from businessmen, unions, farm organizations, churches, newspapers, veterans, teachers, towns, cities, individuals, and such clubs as the Kiwanis, Elks, and Lions. They also received promises from every provincial government of co-operation in organizing broadcasting. One caveat, however, was raised by the Quebec government, which said it would co-operate in helping to establish control of broadcasting, but that it would not "waive its rights of jurisdiction." That warning translated into a major court action two years later.

In early July, Aird, Frigon, and Bowman retired to make the decisions that would shape Canada's broadcasting system for generations to come. They quickly agreed that a public broadcasting system should be established in Canada; the only questions were in the details. Aird told Frigon and Bowman, "If you two get together, I'll sign whatever you can agree on." Whereupon Aird went back to the business of banking while Bowman and Frigon closeted themselves for two weeks of intense argument on detail.

One of the details they wrestled with was the matter of a name. Bowman suggested the operating body should be called The Royal Canadian Broadcasting Corporation. "Royal," however, was too much for Frigon. Bowman gave up and they agreed on The Canadian Radio Broadcasting Company. Other matters were more weighty, and their biggest fight – regarding an issue that has plagued Canada since the beginning and continues today unabated – was over federal and provincial jurisdiction. Bowman wanted strong federal control; Frigon wanted strong provincial control, especially on program content and appointments to the new company's board of directors. "He was really just thinking of Quebec," Bowman later commented.

Bowman wanted three members of the board to be nominated and appointed by Ottawa and for each of the nine provinces to nominate one member who, in turn, would be appointed by Ottawa. Frigon disagreed. He insisted that the nine board members representing the provinces be nominated and appointed directly by the provinces. Bowman said he would agree, if the provinces would then "be prepared to assume an equivalent share of the financial obligations involved." That wasn't acceptable, and in the end, they weasled out of their differences by agreeing on a compromise: there would be twelve board members, three federally appointed and nine members representing the provinces, "the mode of appointment" to be decided by agreement between Ottawa and the provinces.

With their differences resolved, Bowman and Frigon showed their agreement to Aird, who promptly signed it. On September 11, 1929, in just nine pages, they laid out their recommendations for a national public radio system, saying, "Canadian radio listeners want Canadian broadcasting."

In answer to Frigon's initial question of whether broadcasting was to be "a business or . . . to be used for the benefit of the country," they responded: the country.

"Broadcasting," they wrote, "should be placed on a basis of public service and ... stations providing a service of this kind should be owned and operated by one national company. ... The primary purpose should be to produce programs of high standards from Canadian sources." All private stations (eighty-seven at the time, including "phantom" stations and some granted licences but not yet operating) would be shut down or absorbed by the new national company.

The strong hand of Frigon shone in the statement, "Provincial authorities should [have] full control over the programs of the station or stations in their respective areas." In other words, the director appointed for each province would be the czar of programs heard in the province with advice from a provincial advisory council. The arrangement would have been a nightmare for any national program director. The commission went on to recommend that time be made available for school broadcasts and adult education, and, remembering the fiery broadcasts of the Jehovah's Witnesses, it said religious programs should not carry attacks on the leaders or the philosophies of other religions. The commissioners also said political broadcasts should be made on the basis of "arrangements mutually agreed upon" by the parties.

Aird, Frigon, and Bowman recommended building seven powerful, 50,000-watt stations, one for the Maritimes and one for each of the other provinces. They proposed exchanges of programs among the stations and, occasionally, coast-to-coast broadcasts on events of national interest. To finance this public system, they would raise the radio-set licence fee for the public from one to three dollars a year. They figured that would raise about $900,000, since 300,000 Canadians had paid their annual licence fees that year.

Aird, Frigon, and Bowman all disliked advertising, especially the "direct" kind. At one point during their Canadian travels, Frigon said, "We heard the results of a baseball match the other day on the train, but every now and then the announcers would cut in to advertise. That is poor education. It is a lack of taste." So direct advertising was out, but they would allow generic "indirect" advertising, with no product or price mentions. They estimated that it would earn $700,000 a year for the new company. That figure fell far short of the $2.5 million a year they estimated it would cost to run the public broadcast system, so the commissioners recommended a federal subsidy of $1 million a year for five years. "We believe," they said, "that broadcasting should be considered of such importance in promoting the unity of the nation that a subsidy by the Dominion Government should be regarded as an essential aid to the general advantage of Canada."

Aird sent a copy of the report to John Reith at the BBC, who shot back the query, "Who is going to be in charge?" He couldn't determine whether the chairman, the board, a chief executive, or the provincial director would be in charge. "I do not see one real authority anywhere," he wrote to Aird.

Reith's point seemed to be missed by Canadian commentators, most of whom praised the report. Five Southam papers blessed it, as did *Le Devoir* and other key papers across the country. Even the Toronto *Telegram*, philosophically opposed to any kind of state intervention, surprisingly endorsed the idea of a public radio service. "The air channels are too important and valuable to be allowed to remain in private hands for commercial exploitation," the *Telegram* said. "And in Canada they have been shamefully exploited. . . . The best interests of the Canadian people can be served only if it is placed under national control."

A warning about a public radio system, however, came from *Canadian Magazine*, which said, "[It] would really be the tool of whatever political party was in power." Montreal's *La Presse* joined in the minority opposition, spurred by its ownership of CKAC. The newspaper launched a bitter campaign against the idea of public radio, calling it a "menace" to private enterprise. Warning of "the evil of political control," P. R. Du Tremblay, director-administrator of *La Presse*, said, "The paramount danger is the certainty that state ownership of radio means political control. . . . The Mackenzie King Government is . . . employing a steam roller to dig in a flower pot." He also said nationalized radio as outlined by the Aird Report would eliminate the opportunity for Canadian companies to advertise on the radio because of its ban on direct advertising. Aird disagreed, saying, "People do not like a good program of music to be interrupted by washing machine advertisements." In what in time would prove to be a monumental miscalculation, Aird added, "My impression is that the radio is not an ideal advertising medium and that its value as such is decreasing. The newspaper is the best medium." Sixty-five years later, broadcasting in Canada was earning more than $2.5 billion in net advertising revenue, and the world's figure for broadcasting advertising was $112 billion.

In a series of *Citizen* articles rebutting *La Presse*'s opposition, Bowman agreed with Aird's thoughts on radio advertising and added, "There is no likelihood of private stations in Canada being able to raise sufficient revenue annually from Canadian radio advertisers to maintain an independent Canadian system." He supported the idea of "goodwill advertisers" sponsoring programs, but not direct advertising pitches, and he pointed to the CNR's "indirect" style of advertising as a model.

Bowman reissued his warning of inevitable American domination of Canadian radio if it were left to private companies. "The question to be decided by Canada," he wrote, "is largely whether the Canadian people are to have Canadian independence in radio broadcasting or to become dependent upon sources in the United States." Already CFRB in Toronto had joined the CBS network in April 1929, and CFCF in Montreal had joined NBC in November 1929, about the same time as *La Presse*'s station, CKAC, had joined CBS.

Six weeks after the Aird Report was issued, the "Black Thursday" stock-market crash devoured the economy, panicked business, signalled the start of the Depression, and brought to government, to say the least, a disinclination to spend public money on broadcasting. As financial panic seized the country, political nerves paralysed Mackenzie King. In December, Cardin, the minister responsible for any new radio legislation, said he favoured a national system something like CNR Radio. Finally, in January 1930, Mackenzie King's government announced that a radio bill would be introduced in Parliament based on the Aird Report.

Immediately, private stations exploded in opposition. "Confiscation!" "Civil Service broadcasting," "Unfair," "Programs will get worse!" they shouted. Anti-Aird editorials were broadcast, speeches delivered, and denunciations made.

The *Globe* attacked the very idea of radio nationalization, calling it, "A doubtful and extravagant experiment . . . open to the danger of becoming a semi-political machine in Canada." The *Telegram* returned to its traditional conservative position, rejecting its earlier support of Aird and warning, "Keep radio out of politics." The paper attacked the Aird Report as "a silly idea" which "would soon make your radio a gathering place for dust and cobwebs." One reason for the *Telegram*'s new position was that it had made a deal with the Toronto station CKGW and encouraged the station to join NBC. The paper's managing editor, I. E. Robertson, praised American radio, noting that "the talent of this continent naturally gravitates to New York." One result of the *Telegram*-CKGW-NBC alliance was to bring to Canada, among other programs, "Amos 'n' Andy," the enormously popular "blackface" radio show. This, the *Telegram* glowed, "is but a forerunner to other Canadian stations being added to the Network."

The manager of CKGW, R. W. Ashcroft, took particular aim at Bowman in an address to his station's audience, saying the whole idea of nationalization came from "super Canadians" and "the silly flapdoodle of Bowmanesque origin."

In February 1930, the CPR formally entered the fray, announcing it would sponsor a series of musical programs on stations in Toronto and Montreal, and reports circulated that CPR planned to seek a licence for a network of three high-powered stations. CPR president Beatty said the railway would launch a radio advertising campaign to show Aird and Bowman that there was enough private advertising money available to support private stations.

In face of the onslaught, King paused again and, besides, he had politics on his mind. He asked Bowman to tea at Kingsmere and praised the Aird Report. "I think it's got class," he said, and then, to Bowman's dismay, he added, "But I don't believe we should bring it down this session. And we don't want to make a political football of it. So if you don't mind, we'll postpone it until after the election."

Bowman did mind, but there was nothing he could do. Meanwhile, in April, the report limped into Parliament and was referred to a special parliamentary committee which never met. A draft bill had been prepared but was never presented.

King called the election for July 28, and the future of Canadian radio was put on the shelf. As it turned out, the future of Mackenzie King was also put on the shelf, as Canadian voters threw him out of office and elected the autocratic, quintessential Tory stuffed shirt, R. B. Bennett, as prime minister. The future of Canadian radio was now up to Bennett.

3

The Dream of National Public Radio

As the battle lines were being drawn in the public-versus-private broadcasting war, Canadians were voting with their dials for American programs. They were among the 40 million ardent fans of the shameless, blackface buffoonery of "Amos 'n' Andy," the first national radio phenomenon which started on NBC in 1928, and laughed nightly at the double-dealing Kingfish, the Mystic Knights of the Sea, and at the characters' shuffling but somehow endearing stupidity and their massacre of the English language with phrases such as "I's regusted!" for "I'm disgusted!" and "Yazzah, yazzah" for "Yes sir." Canadians were hooked on American entertainment shows. They listened to Irving Berlin on "Cities Service Concerts," with soprano Jessica Dragonette and the symphonic jazz of Paul Whiteman's Band. CBS and NBC captivated Canadian audiences with crooner Rudy Vallee's "Fleishmann Hour," the music of "The Old Maestro" Ben Bernie, the American marches and Broadway show tunes of "The Voice of Firestone." They also followed the drama series of "The Shadow," "Sherlock Holmes," "Death Valley Days," and Ripley's "Believe It Or Not."

Canadians tuned in to these shows on American stations or on Canadian stations that had American network affiliation. As Graham Spry said, "We were simply swamped with American programs."

Some Canadian stations made a valiant effort to counter the popularity of American shows with programs featuring local oldtime fiddlers, amateur performers, and a few orchestras. CKNC in Toronto was one of the more aggressive private stations. Geoffrey Waddington, its musical director, a few years later took charge of CBC music and conducted the CBC Symphony Orchestra. Ernie Bushnell, its manager, a few years later was running programs for the CBC. Together on CKNC they produced some of the best Canadian popular entertainment programming, including such musical shows as "The Neilson Hour," "The Buckingham Hour," "The Wrigley Hour," and "The Coo-Coo-Noodle Club," a music and comedy show. Imperial Oil sponsored highbrow broadcasts on stations from Sydney, Nova Scotia, to Vancouver, and Rogers Majestic sponsored programs featuring the Toronto Symphony Orchestra and the Hart House String Quartet on twenty-one stations. At CKGW in Toronto and through hosting CPR Radio programs, the handsome, fun-loving Charles Jennings became one of Canada's best-known announcers.

While private radio pioneers were discovering the profits that could be earned by radio, educators were realizing the educational potential of the airwaves. Experimental school broadcasting had been tried in the mid-1920s in Nova Scotia and Manitoba, and regular school broadcasting had started on CHNS in Halifax in October 1928 with French and English lessons, nature talks, dramatized scenes from plays, and a harmonica band. A few years later, classrooms in Cape Breton were listening to Sydney's CJCB "Radio Classes," and they were soon joined by schools in New Brunswick and Prince Edward Island. The CNR Radio station in Vancouver, CNVR, began one-hour Friday night educational broadcasts in 1927. Stations in other provinces soon followed these examples and handed over airtime to local school authorities. In Saskatchewan, private stations broadcast courses for rural children.

The most extensive Canadian programming was mounted by the CNR stations. They carried such events as the Westminster Abbey Thanksgiving service for King George V's recovery from a serious illness and his opening of the 1928 Naval Conference in London, England. One elderly, early rising woman in Saskatchewan was so affected by King George's broadcast, and so unaware of time zones, that she wrote to CNR

Radio program director E. Austin Weir, scolding him for getting "our dear King" up so early in the morning, having heard the program at 4:00 A.M. Saskatchewan time.

By 1929, thirteen CNR stations were on the air in English and four in French, but only the Ottawa, Vancouver, and Moncton stations were actually owned by the CNR. This was the start of the golden age for CNR Radio, even though it was providing only three hours a week of national network programming in addition to local and regional broadcasts. In May 1930, Weir decided the network needed to produce more than music, talks, coverage of big events, and the occasional drama. "Why not dramatize a series based on the epic stories of the early Canadian discoverers, adventurers and explorers?" he wrote in a memo to his bosses. His idea was received with enthusiasm. In announcing the series, Weir's boss, Sir Henry Thornton, said, "We hope to kindle in Canadians generally a deeper interest in the romantic early history of their country." He warned Weir not to get an American producer for the series, saying, "Just one thing. Don't go to New York for him."

Weir went to England instead, where he hired the director of the Festival Theatre in Cambridge, Tyrone Guthrie. Guthrie had been recommended to Weir by the BBC's Gladstone Murray. (A quarter-century later, Guthrie returned to Canada as artistic director for the first year of the Shakespeare Festival in Stratford, Ontario.)

"The Last Voyage of Henry Hudson" was the first of two dozen history plays written for "The Romance of Canada" series, which was the most ambitious and successful presentation of the era. It was produced in a studio which Guthrie later described as "a sty . . . in a cabbage green. . . . No windows, no ventilation. It was a rather sissy version of the salt mines." The opening production, however, was greeted exuberantly by Canadians. "The most wonderful thing of Hudson's last days afloat in Hudson Bay," said Ned Corbett, director of extension at the University of Alberta. "You could hear the groaning of the oars, the creaking, and the talk of the men. It was a tremendous thing."

In one program, Guthrie wanted the sound of marching feet, so for a dollar each, he hired several men to tramp up and down in a separate studio from the one where the drama was being produced. A microphone carried the sound of marching feet to the radio control room and was mixed with the voices of the actors. Since they could not hear the drama the men started marching when a light was flashed in their studio. Guthrie and assistant producer Rupert Caplan, however, forgot to flash the light a second time for the marchers to stop. When the radio play ended, Guthrie and Caplan retired to Caplan's office for a celebratory drink. Suddenly, Caplan remembered the marchers, leapt up, and raced to the studio to find the now perspiring and breathless marchers still tramping.

Other dramas in the series included portraits of the Marquis de Montcalm, Pierre-Esprit Radisson, Laura Secord, the Selkirk Settlers, Prince Edward Island, and Louisbourg. The series, which ran from 1931 to 1932, was much applauded, but there were some complaints, especially from Ku Klux Klan members in Regina, about too many portrayals of French Canadians.

Weir heard complaints of another kind when the government became alarmed at criticism of the United States by the editor of the *Ottawa Journal*, Grattan O'Leary, on a CNR Radio series called "Canada Today." O'Leary, a future Conservative Party power broker, had denounced Washington for insisting that Germany must pay all its First World War reparations. The U.S. Consulate in Montreal complained, and the prime minister admonished Sir Henry. The CNR briefly considered killing the series, but in the end decided to continue it. It was a taste of things to come in government attempts to prevent broadcast commentaries it didn't like.

Meanwhile, the promised CPR Radio programming began airing on stations across the country: "The Canadian Pacific Hour of Music" from 9:00 P.M. to 10:00 P.M. on Friday, "Fred Culley's Dance Band" and "Musical Crusaders" from the Royal York Hotel in Toronto, and "Melody Mike's Music Shop" from 9:00 P.M. to 9:30 P.M. on Monday.

In a decade, radio had gone from being a mysterious and magical box that somehow caught sounds out of the air to being a common instrument. "It has become a necessity in every home," Ottawa mayor Frank Plant said to the hundreds who flocked to "The Ottawa Radio Show," a demonstration of the latest radio receivers held at the Chateau Laurier Hotel in late 1930.

But even so, outside Toronto and Montreal, less than 40 per cent of Canadians could hear a Canadian station. In most parts of Canada, the air was filled with powerful American radio signals. In 1930, 80 per cent of Canadian listeners still preferred to tune in to American programs, prompting Charles Bowman to say, "We would like to see that our Canadian people would get at least a 50-50 share of broadcasting." More than anything, it was this American invasion by airwave and the threat of cultural colonialism that galvanized two stunningly intelligent and passionately nationalistic Canadian young men by the names of Graham Spry and Alan Plaunt.

During the summer of 1930, Spry talked with his friends about a campaign for the improvement of Canadian radio. He asked one Ottawa friend, "Do you know any young man with money who can give us a hand?" The friend introduced him to Plaunt who, Spry noted, "had a car and money" as well as an interest in radio as an agent of national unity. Plaunt's money came from his wealthy father, a lumber baron.

The idea of forming a group to lobby for public radio was conceived in early October of 1930, over a starched tablecloth in the Café Henry Burger in Hull, Quebec, and over many a glass of wine. It was born a few days later in Plaunt's spacious Ottawa living room where he, Spry, and an élite clique of young, intellectual up-and-comers plotted the future of Canadian radio amid a heady combination of Johnny Walker and nationalism. "Britannia rules the waves – Shall Columbia [CBS] rule the wavelengths?" asked Spry. Radio, Spry believed, "should make the home not merely a billboard, but a theatre, a concert hall, a club, a public meeting, a school, a university."

With the war cry "Canadian radio for Canadians" and with the warning that we must "protect Canada from a radio system like that of the United States," Spry and Plaunt leapt into the battle for Canada's radio soul with a combination of the talents of Machiavelli and Sir Galahad, with a bit of Sisyphean determination thrown in. Their bible was the Aird Report, their model was the BBC, their target was the newly elected Conservative government of R. B. Bennett, and their instrument was the Canadian Radio League (CRL).

Writing to Brooke Claxton, a friend and up-and-coming Montreal lawyer, the day after the meeting in Plaunt's home, Spry said, "Our method of operation is, resolutions, delegations to the Cabinet, articles in the press and a highly reputable honorary executive masking the machinations of a small, disreputable executive consisting of yourself, myself, Alan Plaunt, George Smith, R. K. Finlayson, Margaret Southam, etc." Noting Plaunt's key role in soliciting support, Spry added with tongue only slightly in his cheek, "Alan is a gentleman of leisure and will do our dirty work aided by Margaret Southam."

The group cabled Gladstone Murray at the BBC in London for information and guidance and plunged into a tornado of letter-writing, telephoning, buttonholing, and pamphleteering. Their enthusiastic crusade began with their wide and ever-widening circle of influential friends and friends of friends, including future prime ministers Lester B. Pearson and Louis St. Laurent; future ambassadors and high commissioners Norman Robertson and Arnold Heeney; future governor general and Liberal Party insider Vincent Massey; future cabinet ministers Brooke Claxton, Jack Pickersgill, and Ralph Campney; former Conservative prime ministers Sir Robert Borden and Arthur Meighen; and future power brokers A. E. "Dal" Grauer of Vancouver, E. Hume Blake of Toronto, and *Free Press* editor John Dafoe in Winnipeg. Their allies also included William Herridge; Tom Moore, president of the Trades and Labour Congress of Canada; influential McGill law professor Frank Scott; and the leaders of the Canadian Clubs, the Canadian Legion, the Canadian Institute for International Affairs, the Royal Society of Canada, the Canadian Bar Association, and the Hadassah Organization of Canada. Their supporters included prominent business leaders, twelve university presidents, six provincial superintendents of education, and the heads of the Anglican, Catholic, and United Churches. The inner group and its allies bombarded newspaper editors across the country with pleas for support. Fifty newspapers with circulations of more than two million responded positively, as did women's organizations with more than 600,000 members in total and farm organizations representing 327,000 members.

In a note scribbled to himself, Plaunt described his lobbying technique: "I set to work to get every university president, as many bank heads, organization heads, as possible. Graham conceived publicity stunts galore and carried them out. We sent out a news story a day. We lobbied Parliamentarians, we lobbied socially. For example, Diana and Lady K took two hours of a bridge game to convince Sir Robert Borden." In a letter to a friend at Queen's University, Spry said his campaign was "a great education in respectable intrigue. . . . We . . . are now getting our local Duchesses to work . . . we are sparing no weapon, not even afternoon tea!"

The campaign was primarily aimed at English Canada, but Plaunt and Spry took special care to get support from key French Canadians as well, such as St. Laurent; Georges Pelletier, the managing director of the influential *Le Devoir*; Victor Doré, president-general of the Montreal School Board; Edouard Montpetit, secretary-general of the University of Montreal; and Eugène L'Heureux, editor of the Chicoutimi newspaper. What particularly attracted the Quebec supporters was the Aird Commission's recommendation for provincial control of programming.

"Lambs and lions are lying together," Spry said, marvelling at his and Plaunt's success in securing support from almost everybody who was anybody. But while they backed Plaunt and Spry's ideas, few among this élite group were regular radio listeners. Brooke Claxton told Spry, "I have no radio and have never listened to radio if I could possibly avoid it," but that didn't stop him from being a key member of Spry's and Plaunt's ginger group and taking on the non-paying role of legal counsel for the Canadian Radio League.

The objective was to capture the mind and soul of the new prime minister. "The League proposes to bamboozle Mr. Bennett into implementing the principles underlying the Aird Report, i.e. radio as a public service rather than as an advertising medium," Plaunt wrote to Dal Grauer.

Volunteers were appointed as chief organizers in each province to woo big names to the Radio League's cause. Ned Corbett, for example, barnstormed Alberta, soliciting Radio League support and getting resolutions of endorsement from fifty organizations. "Everywhere I went I carried copies of the Aird Report [and] propaganda literature released by . . . the Radio League," he said.

Spry and Plaunt were working fifteen-hour days keeping in touch with supporters secured by Corbett and others like him across the country. "All the time," Plaunt later remembered, "the family were perplexed and mystified. . . . Here I was hammering a typewriter indefatigably for hours on end each day, rushing about with mysterious files, actually taking an interest in life." Unlike Plaunt, Spry wasn't adept with the typewriter, using the old hunt-and-peck system of two-fingered typing to bang out his speeches and pamphlets.

But the "rushing about" exhausted the two men. Spry's weariness was aggravated by worry about the personal money he was spending on league activities. He had no private money as Plaunt had and depended on his job as national secretary of the Canadian Clubs, which he feared might be threatened by critics of the league. Writing to a friend, he said, "Some of those who disagreed in this question have attempted to have me fired. . . . It has cost me several hundred dollars, it has taken days from my holidays. . . . I was working every Saturday and Sunday. It has been great fun, but the only thing it's going to do for me is to get me into trouble. But I can enjoy that, too."

In their whirlwind campaign, Plaunt was the insider, the behind-the-scenes, driven polemicist and tactician. "One of the most charming young men I've ever met," said Ned Corbett. "He was . . . sensitive, intelligent . . . thorough. . . . He was thoughtful, he was kind, he was gentle, but he had the fighting courage of a tiger. Nobody could knock him down. He'd come right back."

Spry was the extrovert – a speech-making evangelist and strategist for public radio. "Here is a majestic instrument of national unity and national culture," he said of radio. "Its potentialities are too great, its influence and significance are too vast, to be left to the petty purpose of selling cakes of soap."

Together, Plaunt and Spry made an irresistible team and built the most effective lobby in Canadian history. "It was really great fun," said Spry. It was, said Plaunt, "a series of coups, of masterstrokes, of strategy and execution."

The "coups and masterstrokes" were aimed at Prime Minister Bennett, but "bamboozling" him was proving to be easier said than done. While Spry and Plaunt were organizing the Radio League in the fall of 1930, Bennett was in London, England, attending the Imperial Conference with, among others, his close adviser and soon-to-be brother-in-law William Herridge, a public broadcast supporter, a friend of

Ottawa Citizen editor Charles Bowman, and an acquaintance of Spry. Spry immediately sought Herridge's help, asking him to urge the prime minister "to create a radio broadcasting system which can draw the different parts of Canada together, which can use the air not only for indirect advertising but more essentially for educational and public purposes." Spry also wrote to other members of the Canadian delegation to pressure Bennett, and he persuaded his friends at the BBC to invite Bennett to visit the BBC studios where, Spry hoped, the prime minister might see the value of public broadcasting. Bennett, however, refused to go to the BBC, and a disappointed Spry told a friend that Bennett had said that "he was not interested in radio, that it was unimportant, that there was little public interest and that he had too many things to attend to at the next session to bother about radio legislation." One ray of hope, however, was that Bennett cabled from London that no new private radio station licences were to be issued.

Back in Ottawa, Spry and Plaunt did get the support of the acting prime minister, two other Bennett cabinet ministers, and Dr. O. D. Skelton, the all-powerful deputy minister who reported that the cabinet was impressed with the groundswell of public support Spry and Plaunt were stimulating. "What at first appeared to be an impossible dream is beginning to offer real hope," exulted Spry.

The dream that began at a small table at Café Henry Burger in Hull two months earlier took on a formal form in the ballroom of Ottawa's Chateau Laurier Hotel on December 8, 1930, when Spry and Plaunt held a general meeting, legally establishing the Canadian Radio League. A few hundred delegates turned up, agreed on a dollar-a-year membership fee, and issued a statement, saying, "Radio broadcasting, while valuable for certain limited commercial purposes is perhaps primarily an instrument for the cultivation of public opinion, of education and entertainment. It should make the home not merely a billboard, but a theatre, a concert hall, a club, a public meeting, a school, a university."

Bowman's *Ottawa Citizen* gave the league the front-page headline the next day: "NAT'L RADIO LEAGUE OF CANADA IS ORGANIZED," the paper bannered. "Urge Public Ownership of Stations and Better Programs for Canada. Outstanding Citizens Throughout Dominion Give Ready Support..."

The league ran its campaign from a cramped, third-storey office in a rickety downtown Ottawa building two doors away from the exclusive Rideau Club to which Spry and Plaunt belonged. Immediately after the formal establishment of the Canadian Radio League, Spry and Plaunt issued a six-page press release and increased the pace of propaganda and lobbying, formally writing to the government outlining the league's objectives and describing its supporters. "The public got the impression of a vast national organization," marvelled Spry at their own handiwork.

When he arrived back in Ottawa, Bennett was impressed with the public support Spry and Plaunt had generated, and Spry was encouraged by a chance meeting with the prime minister, who told him, "Carry on the good work." Spry was not above reminding Bennett that he and Spry's father had been friends in Calgary years earlier and that, as a child, Spry had delivered newspapers to Bennett's home. This was just one of the many ways Spry managed to influence Bennett. "I studied his personal habits," he later said, "and discovered he used to take a massage quite regularly at the Chateau Laurier baths. I would wait till he'd come out and go up in the elevator with him or walk back to the East Block with him and get in my whacks." Spry also had "chance meetings" with "R. B." at the Rideau Club at lunchtime or dinner.

Meanwhile, Spry and Plaunt persuaded the established churches that public radio would bar the kind of evangelical hoopla of the Jehovah's Witnesses; persuaded educators that public radio would give them much more airtime than private radio; persuaded newspapers that public radio would not eat into their advertising revenues as private radio was doing; persuaded influential Quebeckers that Quebec would have more pro-gram influence under their and Aird's proposals; and persuaded nationalists that only public radio could counter the American radio invasion and ensure national unity. Charles Bowman gave Plaunt access to all his Aird Commission files, which Plaunt and Spry studied carefully for policy and strategic planning.

In early January 1931, a league delegation called on Alfred Duranleau, Bennett's minister of marine, who was responsible for radio. Spry's boast of huge support throughout Canada led the deputy minister of marine, who attended the meeting, to say, "A rough calculation of the popular

74

support your League claims to enjoy suggests to me that at least twenty million of the Canadian population of ten million are on your side." Duranleau praised the Radio League, saying "Canada must be protected from alien influences," and adding that the league was the best organized, most effective he had seen.

Spry and Plaunt also got Tom Moore to make a special plea for public broadcasting when the Trades and Labour Congress held its annual meeting with the prime minister.

All this activity was costing money: stationery, postage, telegrams, phone calls, and travel expenses. At the beginning Plaunt paid for much of this, and he and Spry had set an early target of $1,000 to be raised from ten $100-donors. Their campaign was getting more expensive, however, and before it was over in 1932, the total cost of the Radio League's lobbying was about $7,500. Spry and Plaunt provided nearly half, and the rest came from seventy-five large and small contributions, such as $500 from F. N. Southam, $450 from *Toronto Star* publisher Holy Joe Atkinson, $5 from the Victoria Listeners Club, $25 from the United Church, $15 from the Native Sons of Canada, and $2 from H. J. Crerar.

Watching the money, the big name supporters, and the indications of sympathy from the Bennett government come in, Spry and Plaunt were exultant. But a dark legal cloud from Quebec began hovering over them.

As it had warned it might two years earlier, the Quebec government began pressing its claim to jurisdiction over broadcasting, and the issue went to the Supreme Court of Canada in mid-winter 1931. Spry and Plaunt were uneasy about upsetting their Quebec supporters, but nevertheless, Brooke Claxton presented the league's argument that broadcasting was a national not a provincial responsibility. The federal government made the same argument. The Supreme Court agreed, but Quebec appealed to the Privy Council in London, England. At this point, the league had only $80 in its bank account, so Spry cashed in $550 of his Power Corporation bonds, and Plaunt and three others, including *Winnipeg Free Press* editor John Dafoe, an old friend of Spry, provided most of the rest of the $750 it cost to send Claxton to London to join the federal government argument against Quebec at the Privy Council. Claxton waived his legal fees. Ontario had joined Quebec in claiming provincial jurisdiction, and Spry and Plaunt feared the Privy Council might favour the provincial argument because of several recent decisions the Council had made that strengthened jurisdiction of the provinces in some areas.

While the league was arguing in the courts, private radio owners mounted a belated counterattack on the advocates of public radio. The battle had started at the beginning of 1931, when Spry squared off in the pages of *Saturday Night* magazine against R. W. Ashcroft, who ran the most powerful station in Toronto, CKGW, which was in alliance with the *Telegram*. The station was owned by Gooderham and Worts, producer, as Ottawa professor Margaret Prang has noted, of the two essentials for surviving a Canadian winter: liquor and anti-freeze. Under the headline question "SHOULD RADIO BE NATIONALIZED IN CANADA?" Spry said YES! and Ashcroft said NO!

"Radio in Canada is broadcasting of the advertisers for the advertisers by the advertisers," Spry wrote. ". . . The primary consideration of the broadcaster, indeed, is not the listener who hears, but the advertiser who pays." He demanded that all "direct" advertising be eliminated and that the government establish a public radio service. This, he said, "has the support of the leaders of every phase of Canadian life."

Ashcroft complained about the Radio League's "endless streams of propaganda" and called Spry and his supporters "theorists and some, possibly, idealists." "Very few of them," he said, "have any practical knowledge of and experience in broadcasting." He claimed public broadcasting would need a government subsidy of $15 million a year, not $2.5 million as Aird had forecast, and an annual licence fee of $30, not Aird's recommended $3. He said there were not enough Canadian musicians, singers, and actors to provide the amount of Canadian programming Spry advocated. "We would have to import the bulk of our talent from the U.S. and abroad," he predicted. Ashcroft also warned that public radio "would open the way for the broadcast of political propaganda in the interest of the party in power."

Spry snorted about the "pathetically exaggerated statements spread by the private station owners," whose annual conference was held in Ottawa in mid-February 1931 and who launched a two-pronged strategy to defeat Spry, Plaunt, and the Aird Report. In a room at the King Edward

Hotel in Toronto one January morning in 1926, the Canadian Association of Broadcasters (CAB) had been formed by key private stations, radio-set manufacturers, *La Presse* in Montreal (owner of CKAC, the CBS affiliate, which had the most powerful Quebec transmitter), and the CNR. The CNR and several other stations, however, later withdrew when the CAB stepped up its attacks on public broadcasting. Now, at its Ottawa meeting, the CAB sought a mantle of social responsibility. It recommended coast-to-coast network educational programs by private stations. "We intend to pay the various professors for giving the educational addresses," a CAB official said. The private station group also recommended there be no direct advertising on Sundays and that on weekdays after 7:00 P.M. commercials should be limited to a maximum of 5 per cent of program time. The CAB convention combined this approach with an increasingly vigorous assault on the Aird Commission's proposals, saying they were "nothing more or less than a very clever ruse to divert radio advertising expenditures to newspaper columns." Most newspapers did, indeed, support the Aird Commission's proposals and were aware that the less advertising there was on radio, the more there would be available for newspapers. Even so, some papers, such as the *Telegram* and the *Globe* in Toronto, *La Presse* in Montreal, the Halifax *Herald*, and the *Edmonton Journal*, strongly opposed public broadcasting, some because they had their own private stations.

The CAB also decided to issue a pamphlet to counter the increasingly successful lobbying efforts of Spry and Plaunt. "There is no truth in the statement of the Canadian Radio League that Canadian national integrity and business is being threatened by growing American control of Canadian radio . . ." the pamphlet said. "No programmes originating in the United States are broadcast in Canada except when sponsored through Canadian organizations, employing Canadian labour and developing industry in Canada." With an eye to gaining more newspaper support, Spry and Plaunt responded by issuing their own pamphlet headed "Radio Advertising – A Menace to the Newspaper and a Burden to the Public."

With pamphlet in hand, they attended the annual meeting of the Canadian Daily Newspaper Association to lobby for support. Borrowing the Radio League's tactics, the CAB marshalled supporters in its fight against public broadcasting. These included advertising agencies, the Canadian Manufacturers' Association, and major corporations such as the Robert Simpson Co., Swift Canada, Imperial Tobacco, Pepsodent, and Dominion Stores Ltd. Business as a whole, however, tended to be either neutral or supportive of what Spry and Plaunt were seeking. The Canadian Chamber of Commerce took no stand, although most local chambers approved of public radio.

So, while noisy, the level of CAB support was considerably less than that for the Radio League, which had been endorsed by most of Canada's power élites. The CAB was also to prove inept. "They didn't know what they were doing," said Spry. "They were absolute children." Evidence of that came when the CPR general publicity manager, John Murray Gibbon, launched an ill-fated attack on public radio in the pages of the March issue of the *Canadian Forum*, an influential magazine that editorially supported Spry and Plaunt. Gibbon argued that no more than 10 per cent of Canadians would listen to public radio. In fact, he said, public radio would "deprive more than half the population of what they want so as to provide intellectual solace for a few." He said public radio would need huge subsidies for Canadian talent and might "drown out with inferior talent some of the excellent programs originating in the United States which we presently enjoy." Gibbon also launched a bitter assault on the Radio League's "delusions" about BBC programs, which he claimed were far from popular, and he warned, too, of the dangers of political interference in broadcasting

Before Gibbon's article appeared, Spry was given a copy of the manuscript by a member of the *Canadian Forum* editorial board, University of Toronto professor Frank Underhill, a historian, political thinker, Oxford graduate, and, more importantly, a friend of Spry and public radio. "The more damage you do to Mr. Murray Gibbon the better," Underhill wrote to Spry. It was awkward for Spry since Gibbon was one of his bosses in the Canadian Club, but Spry nevertheless crowed, "The Lord has delivered the enemy into our hands." It wasn't the Lord, it was Underhill, and his advance notice gave time to Spry to prepare a detailed counterattack which appeared in the April issue of the *Forum*. "There is no agency of human communication which could so effectively unite Canadian to Canadian and realize the aspiration of Confederation, as radio broadcasting," he wrote. "It is the greatest Canadianizing instrument in our hands."

Spry sent a copy of Gibbon's manuscript to Gladstone Murray at the BBC, suggesting the BBC also respond to Gibbon's attack. Murray quickly answered, thundering that Gibbon's article was "a unique combination of inaccuracy and malevolence," and threatening to refer the issue to the British House of Commons. An embarrassed CPR feebly responded that Gibbon had written the article as a past president of the Canadian Authors Association, and the views expressed were his own, not those of the CPR. "It was lovely fun," Spry later said.

It was a clear victory for Spry, but he still worried about the influence of the CPR and its allies. Writing to a friend at the *Manitoba Free Press*, George Ferguson, he said the opposition was coming from three sources: R. W. Ashcroft and the private stations, American radio officials who were sending "visitors" to Toronto and Montreal "to promote the American system and damn the British," and the CPR. "These three forces are, as you may imagine, quite formidable and perhaps the most immediately dangerous is the CPR," Spry wrote. What especially worried Spry was the fact that Prime Minister Bennett had been legal counsel for the CPR and was a personal friend of CPR president Sir Edward Beatty.

The battle for the mind of the prime minister continued through the year with the CPR and its allies lobbying behind the scenes about the danger of "civil service radio," while Spry and Plaunt were buttonholing allies and warning about the dangers of private radio. "There can be no liberty complete, no democracy supreme, if the commercial interests dominate the vast, majestic resource of broadcasting," Spry told one meeting.

The commercial interests stepped up their efforts and started to spend big money on network Canadian programs as a demonstration that advertising could support quality Canadian radio. Imperial Oil began sponsoring music shows on *ad hoc* networks of stations, and General Motors started sponsoring Foster Hewitt's broadcasts of NHL hockey games. But it was the CPR that led the way in 1931, the only full year of its broadcasting venture. It leased time on two dozen stations, and used a "phantom" station, CPRY in Toronto, as its originating station.

CPR had earlier sought licences for a network of eleven stations across Canada but was told no new licences would be issued at the time.

CPR president Beatty informally offered Spry the job of being general manager of the CPR Radio system once it was established. "When I set this thing up, I'll make you the manager," Sir Edward said in a Chateau Laurier hallway conversation. Spry, who knew the CPR president well from the days when Beatty had been president of the Montreal Canadian Club, declined, saying, "I don't think the CPR could afford me!"

Beatty also sought to win over *Ottawa Citizen* editor Charles Bowman. They met at the Chateau Laurier, where Beatty urged Bowman to support a national, private broadcasting system. Like Spry, Bowman said no.

Not discouraged, Beatty was confident his personal friendship with Bennett and Bennett's aversion to government intervention in business would eventually lead to his choosing private broadcasting. He even made a $25 bet with William Herridge, who was now both Bennett's brother-in-law and the Canadian minister to Washington, that the prime minister in the end would choose a private system over a public one.

As the Dirty Thirties got underway, the Depression bit deeply into the nation, spreading discouragement and disillusionment and reducing radio advertising revenues. CNR revenue fell, and the company drastically reduced its radio operations. In November 1931, the CNR stopped radio broadcasting to its trains. When the year began, there had been a staff of 105 in the CNR Radio service putting out a total of forty-eight hours a week of national and regional programming. But by the end of the year, there were only thirty-three staff members, and they were down to twenty-two a few months later. Some private stations, too, were being hit by the Depression, and they began cutting back on airtime to save money. The average station was now on the air for only six hours a day, and many stations were on for four hours or less. Far from being discouraged, however, Spry argued that the Depression proved the need for public radio, saying, "It has been demonstrated beyond doubt that there is not enough national advertising revenue in the Dominion to finance programs the Canadian people expect."

In spite of the Depression and radio program cutbacks, more than

500,000 Canadians were now paying their annual one-dollar radio licence fee (raised to two dollars in 1932), as many of the 10.3 million Depression-weary Canadians found in radio an inexpensive form of entertainment.

Everybody in the battle for Prime Minister Bennett's mind was waiting for the Privy Council decision in London on whether broadcasting in Canada was a federal or a provincial jurisdiction. Everything hung on that decision. The Radio League executive met at the end of January 1932 to plot its strategy and prepare for another meeting with Marine Minister Duranleau. At that meeting a few days later, the league's delegation was assured the government would act as soon as the Privy Council gave its decision. One member of the delegation, Father Marchand, lectured the minister on the Pope's latest encyclical, which he said "had practically exhorted Canada to set up a nationally owned radio system."

Spry and Plaunt were increasingly hopeful Bennett would choose public radio. They knew he was listening to two close colleagues who were supporters of the Radio League: William Herridge and R. K. "Rod" Finlayson, a Winnipeg lawyer, a Conservative insider, but nevertheless a friend of the liberal *Winnipeg Free Press* editor John Dafoe, and, most importantly, one of the early supporters of the Radio League. Bennett had brought Finlayson to Ottawa as his personal assistant. Spry was close to Herridge and had been friends with Finlayson since they had attended the University of Manitoba together. Through these two men, Spry sought to win Bennett's support for public broadcasting. He later described how, in the spring of 1931, he had won over Herridge, whom he called "our great ally": "To convince such a key person in the Prime Minister's Office," Spry said, ". . . an observation of his habits and routes to and during . . . visits [to Ottawa] led me to take a parlour seat on the CPR train to Montreal in the knowledge that Herridge had gone aboard. I entered the same car and, in due course . . . I began a conversation which lasted most of the trip . . . I had convinced Herridge to accept the broad principle of the Aird Report as advocated by the League!" Charles Bowman provided another Radio League conduit into Bennett's office, through his friendship with Herridge.

They made an odd threesome: the teetotalling, high Tory Bennett, the fun-loving, liberal-minded Finlayson, and the onetime Liberal Herridge, who so hated Mackenzie King he had become a Conservative. But somehow, with them, Bennett, who had a haughty and sometimes brutal personal style, could let his hair down in a way he wasn't able to do with anyone else. "Bennett has the manners of a Chicago policeman and the temperament of a Hollywood film star," British Prime Minister Stanley Baldwin once observed.

Herridge and Finlayson were getting Bennett's attention, however, and later Plaunt would speak of Herridge's "valiant stand on the inside." Later, too, Bowman said of Herridge, "He contributed much toward Prime Minister Bennett's decision to bring down the necessary legislation to establish national broadcasting."

In his efforts to swing over the prime minister to public broadcasting, Finlayson echoed Spry's and Plaunt's warnings about American cultural imperialism. Finlayson said later that he "worked Bennett up to such a pitch of fear about American domination [I thought] the old man would call out the troops." As Bennett later told Spry, "We will show the States that Canada is no appendage."

At last, in London on February 9, 1932, the Privy Council ruled that broadcasting in Canada was a federal jurisdiction, and whoops of joy erupted from Spry, Plaunt, and their supporters. After a year of arguing, jockeying, and lobbying, the stage was now set for the decision that would shape the future of Canadian broadcasting, and all eyes looked to Bennett to see which way he would jump: public or private.

One week later Bennett gave his answer, sort of. Although he was clearly leaning toward a public broadcast system, he hesitated to commit himself just yet. On February 16, he announced the establishment of a special parliamentary committee to "recommend a complete technical scheme of radio broadcasting for Canada." The biggest hint he gave publicly of his private leaning to a public system was to tell the House of Commons that the present system was unsatisfactory and that "properly employed, the radio can be made a most effective instrument in nation building."

The CPR and the private stations fattened their war chests for the battle that would be fought at the parliamentary committee hearings in the spring, while Spry and Plaunt launched their own campaign for donations, raising $987.50, including $400 from Vincent Massey and $250 from *Toronto Star* publisher Holy Joe Atkinson. Most of this money would go towards the cost of bringing over the BBC's Gladstone Murray, who had kept close watch on the broadcast debate largely because of his burning personal ambition to run any new public broadcasting organization set up in Canada. Murray funded some of the costs of his trip himself, and the BBC also helped out.

The four Opposition members of the nine-member parliamentary committee were sympathetic to the idea of public radio, but the five Conservatives had no stated position and were thus the prime target of Spry's and Plaunt's campaign.

"I stayed home and organized Ontario and Quebec and the Maritimes for a 'popular' demonstration," Plaunt recalled. "I lined up all the organizations friendly to us . . . and asked them to appeal to their local bodies for popular demonstrations of support. I even wrote the Trades and Labour Letter to 51 Councils and was authorized to issue it under the signature of Tom Moore [the Labour Congress president]." He also wrote to league supporters such as Brooke Claxton, urging them to stir up support for public radio. The result was a flood of supportive letters, telegrams, telephone calls, resolutions, petitions, and newspaper articles and editorials. He arranged for Gladstone Murray not only to testify before the committee but also to meet privately with the prime minister, Opposition leader Mackenzie King, and other Ottawa powers to enlist their support. Murray's testimony to the committee was persuasive as he described the BBC structure and programming. "Members confessed that he had more influence over their ultimate findings than any other person," said writer Wilfrid Eggleston, who interviewed the committee members.

Spry and Plaunt arranged for American radio inventor Dr. Lee De Forest to testify in writing. In his statement, he said radio was being debased by advertising and added, "We look to you in Canada to lead radio in North America out of the morass in which it has pitiably sunk. May Canada fulfil my early dream."

The two lobbyists persuaded the committee to hear testimony from

Dr. J. E. Morgan, chairman of the U.S. National Committee on Education by Radio, who made a powerful attack on private radio as it had developed in the United States. They also arranged for a message to be sent to the committee from former Conservative prime minister Sir Robert Borden who urged "a government-owned national broadcasting system."

As the hearing got underway, however, Spry and Plaunt were assailed by fears of a new and growing attack mounted by the private radio stations. "Sinister rackets," Plaunt called them. They worried about the effect of private radio editorials, an especially vigorous campaign against public radio by *La Presse*, and the "behind-the-scenes" activity by major radio manufacturers, by CBS and NBC, as well as by the Association of Canadian Advertisers and the Canadian Manufacturers' Association.

Even Bennett, now persuaded that there should be some form of public broadcasting, was worried about this assault. At a cabinet meeting, several Western members questioned the support the Radio League was claiming in the West, and in mid-March 1932, Bennett telephoned Spry at the Rideau Club where Spry was hosting a dinner party for a London friend. The prime minister urged Spry to travel immediately to the West to gather visible evidence of support for public broadcasting. Spry excused himself from the dinner, went home, and made arrangements for a whirlwind trip starting the next day. He met with Manitoba Premier John Bracken, for whom he had once worked on an election campaign, Alberta Premier John Brownlee, whom he also knew well, the attorney general of Saskatchewan, and other provincial and municipal officials and organization leaders.

"The response was simply magnificent," Plaunt said. The Alberta and Manitoba legislatures unanimously passed resolutions for public broadcasting, Saskatchewan's cabinet sent its endorsement, and the mayor of Winnipeg did the same. "The newspapers started a hullaballoo," Plaunt said. With allusion to cricket, Spry exulted, "I had bowled three times and hit the wicket three times and so I cabled the Prime Minister." Fifty telegrams to the parliamentary committee came in from Kitchener, Ontario, alone, along with hundreds of other messages of support and local resolutions, including one from the mayor of Halifax and resolutions from the Canadian Legion (which said public broadcasting would keep "foreign propaganda" out of Canada), farm and labour organizations, women's organizations, and boards of trade.

It was a classic example of effective lobbying, bridging many diverse and sometimes opposing viewpoints, far outdoing anything private radio had mounted. Even before the parliamentary committee finished its hearings, Spry was confident of victory. "We have won," he wrote in his diary. "We have defeated the CPR, the CMA, the NBC, the CBS and ignorance. Today the Prime Minister sent Alan and I, by way of Gladstone Murray, a message of congratulations."

The pressure from outside the committee hearing room had almost as much effect on committee members as what they were hearing from the witnesses. Aird, Frigon, and Bowman testified, as did spokesmen for private stations, advertising agencies, and the Canadian Manufacturers' Association. Almost all witnesses who opposed public broadcasting nevertheless urged a federal government subsidy in one form or another for the private stations.

By far the most dominating witness was Graham Spry, who appeared five times (Plaunt testified twice). In a detailed, lengthy statement, Spry made the case for public broadcasting, lambasting American networks for cultural imperialism and vigorously waving the flag of Canadianism. "The American chains have regarded Canada as part of their field and consider Canada is in a state of radio tutelage," he said. ". . . . The question before the Committee is whether Canada is to establish a chain that is owned and operated and controlled by organizations associated or controlled by American interests. The question is the State or the United States." Spry talked of public radio as a "single, glowing spirit of nationality," which he said was not a business, but a public service. "Here," he said, "is a great and happy opportunity for expressing, for achieving, that which is Canada. It is here and now; it may never come again."

In his testimony, Spry supported the main thrust of the Aird Commission's report, but differed on some aspects, such as, in a tactical bow to private stations, his support for low-powered local stations run by local interests under the umbrella of the national system.

The president of the CPR had very different ideas. Sir Edward Beatty told the committee he wanted to see the establishment of one national broadcast service owned by the railway companies and radio interests, with a government commission to oversee time allowed for advertising and educational programs, to encourage Canadian talent, and to handle other regulatory issues. Network programs would be ten hours a day, he said. There would be regional advisory councils, and the cost would be $2 million a year, half coming from advertising and half from annual licence fees.

The hearings ended in late April after a month and a half, and suddenly everything fell silent as the committee drafted its decision. Despite their normal ability to reach into the political and governmental inner sanctums, Spry and Plaunt could not get anyone to talk. "We had no idea what was going on," Spry said. They heard worrisome rumours that Duranleau had gone to Montreal to meet Beatty. The Montreal *Gazette* ran a front-page story that Beatty's radio plan was going to be accepted by the parliamentary committee. Finally, Spry talked to the prime minister on May 2, and was relieved when he saw an advance copy of the committee's report.

Unanimously, the committee endorsed public broadcasting. It talked of radio as a "medium of education . . . fostering Canadian ideals and culture, entertainment, news service and publicity of this country and its products . . . also as one of the most efficient mediums for developing a greater National and Empire consciousness."

The committee recommended a new public system run by a three-member commission with assistant commissioners in each province who would act as chairmen of the provincial advisory committees. The commission would establish and operate a network of high- and low-powered stations to cover the country with original and purchased programs. It would control the issuing of all licences, prohibit private networks, and "subject to the approval of the Parliament of Canada . . . take over all broadcasting in Canada." The committee would allow low-power private and community stations to operate. The new public system would be financed by revenue from licence fees and commercials, which could take up no more than 5 per cent of program time. There was no ban, however, on direct advertising, as Aird and the Radio League had recommended.

Response to the committee's report came swiftly. "Nationalization of radio would be a colossal blunder," said the Toronto *Telegram*. "Paternalism is to control the air and programs are to be dictated by well-meaning, but mistaken uplift authorities." *The Financial Post* said, "Now the deadening hand of bureaucracy is reaching out to strangle radio broadcasting in Canada." Later the *Post* said public broadcasting was "another step toward communism." The private stations in Toronto and Montreal affiliated with CBS and NBC worried that they might be taken over or at least not be allowed to carry "Amos 'n' Andy" and Eddie Cantor. Some Conservative MPs complained to Bennett that under the new system, French-speaking listeners outside Quebec would soon demand French-language programs, while some opponents inside Quebec complained that the public radio proposals would lead to an English-dominated national network.

But Spry basked in his victory. At a Rideau Club lunch with Spry and William Herridge, Bennett, voicing his worries about the American radio invasion of Canada, told Spry, "It may well be, Graham, that you have saved Canada for the British Commonwealth." Spry later wrote in his diary that he momentarily considered becoming one of the three members of the new commission, "But," he wrote, "when the day came to decide, I was virulently hating my own anomalous position, [and] I wiped out that weakness."

Congratulations poured in to Spry and Plaunt from their many supporters, including Vincent Massey. "All of us who believe in radio as a national service owe you a debt of profound gratitude," Massey said. Spry was exultant. "The public has won a triumph. . . . It is a complete victory for the Canadian Radio League," he said. In private, however, Spry was worried that Bennett might be listening to some of the Conservative Party opponents to public broadcasting, especially "the Toronto Gang" who were "horrified" by the committee's recommendation. Spry and Plaunt cranked up the league's lobbying effort once again, urging newspapers and organizations to demand that the prime minister take immediate action to set up a public system.

Within a week, Bennett, the champion of private enterprise, introduced legislation to establish public broadcasting, and in the process made a policy statement that became a holy mantra repeated to this day by CBC supporters.

"First of all," he said, "this country must be assured of complete Canadian control of broadcasting from Canadian sources, free from foreign interference or influence. Without such control radio broadcasting can never become a great agency for communication of matters of national concern and for the diffusion of national thought and ideals, and without such control it can never be the agency by which national consciousness may be fostered and sustained and national unity still further strengthened. . . . No other scheme than that of public ownership can ensure to the people of this country . . . equal enjoyment of the benefits and pleasures of radio broadcasting . . . I cannot think that any government would be warranted in leaving the air to private exploitation and not reserving it for development for the use of the people."

It was music to the ears of Spry and Plaunt, who said the new public broadcasting system "may well prove one of the [most] important incidents in our national life since Confederation."

Spry and Plaunt sat happily in the House of Commons public gallery as the bill setting up the Canadian Radio Broadcasting Commission (CRBC) was passed with only one dissenting vote from E. J. Young, the Liberal MP from Weyburn, Saskatchewan. The bill essentially followed the recommendation of the parliamentary committee that a commission be established to regulate and control Canadian broadcasting and to operate a national broadcasting system – an "ether highway," as some called it.

In the process of passing the legislation, weaknesses in the bill that would haunt the new commission and lead eventually to its destruction were overlooked. These weaknesses included no mention of a chief executive officer, the commission's limited independence, and its vulnerability to political pressure. It had, for instance, no board of directors to insulate it from government. These problems were, however, ignored by the public broadcast supporters as they shouted hosannas. "We felt we had won a very large part of our battle," Spry said a generation later. "So we endorsed the establishment of the CRBC." It wasn't the BBC model both Spry and Plaunt yearned for, but given the reality that Bennett was torn between his advocacy of free enterprise and his recognition of the need for public broadcasting, it was the best they could get. It was, said Spry, "the art of the possible." Plaunt publicly rhapsodized, "A priceless gift – a veritable fairy child of the Gods – has been dropped into the lap of the present generation. Its name is radio."

Reflecting on the eighteen-month lobbying blitz by Spry and Plaunt, Brooke Claxton called their effort, "One of the most remarkable accomplishments ever to take place in our country. They had to cure ignorance, overcome apathy, arouse support and master interested, organized and unfair opposition." But, in reality, the battle they had joined was far from over.

4

The CRBC's Gang of Three

"What do you think of Hector Charlesworth?" Prime Minister Bennett asked Charles Bowman.

"Oh no!" replied Bowman, who thought Charlesworth was "a nice little fellow but a bit of a joke." The two men were discussing who should be chairman of the new Canadian Radio Broadcasting Commission (CRBC). Bowman urged Bennett to appoint the BBC's Gladstone Murray to the job. Murray, thought Bowman, would ensure that the CRBC would become a BBC-like public service broadcasting system, and he had Spry's and Plaunt's ardent support. Bennett had seriously considered Murray, whose testimony had been so persuasive in the parliamentary radio committee hearings, and he had briefly considered Ned Corbett's recommendation of Vincent Massey, but Massey was too much of a Liberal. The prime minister, however, was also listening to friends and associates who were lobbying vigorously for Hector Charlesworth, editor of the Tory-leaning *Saturday Night*. Looking like King Edward VII, the bearded and charming Charlesworth had originally favoured a continuation of the private system of radio with modest government regulation, but later endorsed nationalization of radio as now planned by Bennett. He also badly wanted the job of running the new system. He wrote to former prime minister Arthur Meighen seeking support for his candidacy and wrote, too, to Bennett himself.

Bennett delayed for four months before finally offering the job to the sixty-year-old editor and music and theatre critic, who, Bennett thought, would be politically saleable as well as malleable. "In offering you this position, Charlesworth," the prime minister said when they met in a room in Toronto's Royal York Hotel on September 30, 1932, "I am giving you a sheet of white paper on which you will be free to work out your own ideas in your own way. If you accept it, you will find the work very interesting. . . . I shall deem it my duty as Prime Minister to take a deep personal interest in your work."

Charlesworth's credentials for the job were slim to non-existent. The lifelong journalist had no administrative experience, no radio experience, no Ottawa experience, and didn't think much of the Aird Report. "A wordy and poorly written report . . . of little value," he said. But Charlesworth eagerly accepted the $10,000-a-year job as czar of Canadian radio. He would, however, never have the freedom Bennett indicated, and while the job would indeed be "very interesting," being chairman of the CRBC would also be unbelievably frustrating and nothing like Charlesworth had ever experienced.

Another of Bennett's promises that would come back to haunt the *Saturday Night* editor was his commitment: "The Radio Commission is not a political body and was never intended to be."

Bennett's choice of vice-chairman belied that promise of a non-political CRBC. He named to the job a Quebec Tory who had run and lost in the 1930 federal election, Thomas Maher. Maher had at least some connection with radio as he was a director of the private station CHRC in Quebec City, but his main experience was in Tory politics and forestry.

The third CRBC member named was Lt.-Col. W. Arthur Steel, a friend of William Herridge and a man recommended by Spry and Plaunt. Lieutenant-Colonel Steel was a technical consultant to the parliamentary radio committee and an autocratic Army communications officer who had been chief radio officer for the Canadian Corps in the First World War. He had written a series of memos to Prime Minister Bennett in late 1931 in which he echoed the arguments of his neighbour in Rockcliffe Park, Ottawa, Charles Bowman. Private broadcasting in Canada, he told Bennett, would mean "broadcasting . . . in the hands of American interests."

The appointments were greeted by distinctly mixed reviews. Spry, Plaunt, and their Radio League supporters hoped for the best. "They weren't villainous people," Spry later said. "Not evil people, but just not good enough. [Charlesworth] was a charming and a very fine person, but absolutely incompetent."

"He [Charlesworth] had great charm," said Ned Corbett, "but [had] no more idea of running anything than your Aunt Susan. Everybody thought that he would be harmless." Spry and Plaunt wrote that "no three men in Canada have before them so difficult and perhaps so thankless a task as the Commissioners. . . . The magnitude of the problem, the difficulty of finance, the circumstances surrounding their own appointment and their own diverse, even contrary temperaments combine to place upon their shoulders unusual and serious burdens." And, Spry and Plaunt noted, "There is no real and effective buffer between the paid Commissioners and the Government."

The well-known Quebec writer Olivar Asselin had a harsher view. He wrote in Montreal's *Le Canada*, "Hector Charlesworth knows nothing; Col Steel knows nothing; and as for that little cock Tom Maher, he knows less than nothing."

They were the classic gang that couldn't shoot straight, doomed from the start by their own naive incompetence and arrogant certainties, by Ottawa bureaucratic and political jealousies, by the fatal imprecision of the Broadcasting Act, and by the failure of the government to back Bennett's rhetoric. "Nationalized radio," Charlesworth later said, "had been brought into being largely by the Prime Minister's personal initiative against a Cabinet partly hostile and partly indifferent, and a caucus somewhat of the same frame of mind."

His own former employer, *Saturday Night*, editorialized on Charlesworth's appointment that it was a relief that radio had not fallen "under the control of some schoolmaster who would set the whole nation doing homework." But executive editor Joseph Clark added ominously, "I doubt very much whether anybody could direct the national radio which will really please anybody."

Flushed with their triumph in getting the Broadcasting Act passed and now watching warily from the sidelines, Spry and Plaunt looked elsewhere for other issues to champion. They quickly found them in the miseries of the Depression, which had put one Canadian worker in three out of a job. Within days of the passage of the new legislation, Spry, who had resigned from the Association of Canadian Clubs, and Plaunt were busy with a new project, the *Farmers Sun* published in Toronto, a run-down, money-losing weekly newspaper with an illustrious past which they renamed *The Weekly Sun*. They turned it into a journalistic agitator for the underdog, especially farmers. "It is, in a word, a sheer gamble," Spry told Plaunt, but he bought the paper and then sold half to Plaunt, and together they plunged into a new campaign for social justice. Within a year, Plaunt founded the New Canada Movement for young farmers seeking a New Deal similar to Franklin Roosevelt's ideas for the United States. It was, said Plaunt, "a movement to discover and support ways of leading Canada out of the Depression . . . a program of thought and action to rebuild Canada and agriculture." *The Weekly Sun* became the spokesman for the movement. Spry joined professors Frank Underhill of the University of Toronto and Frank Scott of McGill University in developing the left-wing League for Social Reconstruction (which Plaunt also joined). Spry became its part-time national secretary at $100 a month, a salary he was seldom paid.

July 1933 found Spry in Regina as a delegate to the first national convention of the CCF, and in public he became increasingly identified as a CCFer. A few years earlier, Spry had described himself as "a semi-detached Liberal" and had been asked by Mackenzie King if he were interested in being the Liberal Party national organizer. He declined, his politics moved left, and that led to a problem with Plaunt and their newspaper. Spry sought to have the *Sun* openly support the CCF, but Plaunt believed the paper should ally itself with ideas, not with a party. As a result of their disagreement, Spry sold his shares to Plaunt for one dollar. In June 1934, after a continuing flow of red ink, Plaunt was ready to close the *Sun* and accepted Spry's offer to buy it back for one dollar. Spry quickly turned the paper into a CCF organ. Even so, Plaunt continued to make loans to the perpetually money-short Spry – loans which he later forgave. With the loss of his paper, Plaunt saw his New Canada Movement fade away. That same year, Spry ran and lost as a CCF candidate in a federal by-election in the Toronto riding of Broadview-Riverdale to Conservative Tommy Church.

All this time, the two activists watched unhappily as their success in establishing a public broadcasting system in Canada turned sour. They began to feel betrayed by Bennett and by the CRBC.

Undeterred by the less than enthusiastic endorsement of his appointment and preening with a self-confidence that bordered on arrogance, Charlesworth had come swinging into Ottawa with his cane, his bald head, and his bow tie, and had immediately stumbled into controversy. "If the politicians will let us alone, we shall be all right," he quipped to a reporter, setting off a night-long House of Commons debate by politicians who had no intention whatever of letting him alone. "Mr. Charlesworth's tongue should be torn from his mouth and wound seven times around his whiskers," Quebec Liberal MP Jean-François Pouliot said.

From the moment his job started Charlesworth had to deal with MPs seeking favours for private stations in their ridings and with petulant government bureaucrats, unhappy at the CRBC taking over some of their former functions, sluggishly dealing with his requests for help, denying him rugs, and providing his commission with what he called "very unsatisfactory accommodations." He complained to the prime minister and was then given "a very fine suite of offices."

Sitting at his glass-topped mahogany desk, Charlesworth complained of "bitter heart burning" among civil servants "pouring poison into the ears of private members and even of Ministers with regard to our Commission." He was baffled by the "star chamber" Treasury Board, which scrutinized his every expenditure and his every appointment from secretaries and office boys up. Charlesworth groaned that when he sent a $10-wreath to the funeral of the president of the Canadian Radio Manufacturers' Association, a government order-in-council was needed to approve the expenditure. He had to apply in duplicate for any request for travel funds to the comptroller of the Treasury, and he felt demeaned by having to explain his own expense accounts to clerks in the office of the comptroller. He pleaded for an extra $15 a day on top of his authorized $10-a-day travel allowance so he could entertain while travelling. "At the present time this is being paid out of our own pockets," he pouted in a letter to Watson Sellar, the comptroller. Sellar referred him to "Form No. 17 . . . Form No. 12 . . . Section 29 (1) to secure encumbrance certificate."

Charlesworth viewed radio as "theatre of the air," but since he knew nothing practical about it, he reached out for the experts. His first major program staff appointment was, to Spry's and Plaunt's joy, the CNR Radio program director E. Austin Weir, who became the CRBC director of programs at a salary of $6,500 a year. "A splendid chap," Charlesworth told reporters, "a real expert on radio, simply invaluable to the Commission." Weir soon found himself in familiar company as most of the early CRBC staffers came from the CNR Radio service. Within a few months, the CRBC bought out the CNR Radio network for the bargain price of $50,000, getting stations in Ottawa, Moncton, and Vancouver, and equipment in several other cities. In addition, it leased time on private stations across the country.

Weir thought he was being hired as the senior executive officer to run the CRBC, an assumption that was soon rudely shattered when the CRBC was racked with personality clashes, rivalries, jealousies, and internal chaos. Weir began his short-lived but pyrotechnical CRBC career by arranging for Canadian stations to carry the first Empire Christmas Day broadcast from London, which meant that for the first time, the voice of the reigning monarch was heard throughout the Empire. The program was a great success, and in February 1933, regular CRBC programming formally got underway. Weir had organized programs that ranged from commentaries on current events to amateur dramas, symphonies from Toronto and Montreal, and musical groups such as George Wade and his Cornhuskers.

At the start, the CRBC had two hours of national broadcasting a week. By May, it was up to one hour an evening. Charlesworth, Maher, and Steel, however, were impatient; while Weir sought quality programs they wanted more quantity. Weir began to sour on the commissioners and they on him. "He took the attitude of a person empowered to sit in judgement on his employers," Charlesworth later said, complaining that while Weir wrote long memos, he seldom answered his own mail, had a "sullen attitude," and was a bad administrator who wouldn't follow instructions. Three months after Charlesworth had heaped praise on him, Weir was demoted, his overall responsibilities were reduced to programs produced west of Montreal, and he grew increasingly contemptuous of Charlesworth, Maher, and Steel. In June, Weir was taken out of program work entirely, put into a relatively minor job in public relations, and his salary reduced by a third to $4,000. A month later, he was fired outright "on account of inefficiency," and given a month's pay. "They never gave him a chance," Spry said. "He stood in the way of Maher's and Steel's ambition to operate the Commission as they damn well please," the *Winnipeg Free Press*'s Ottawa correspondent, Grant Dexter, said in a letter to his editor, John Dafoe.

In a meeting with the prime minister shortly after he was fired, an outraged Weir denounced the CRBC commissioners as hopeless incompetents and appealed for reinstatement. Bennett was sympathetic, telling Weir, "Hold your horses for a few days and we shall see what can be done." But Bennett did nothing. A year later, Weir got his revenge at a House of Commons radio committee hearing when he attacked the CRBC for its "blunders," "chaos," "stupidity," and "inefficiency." He said that Charlesworth, Maher, and Steel had lowered program standards, discouraged creative initiative, and had "become politically suspect." Charlesworth, he told the committee, "knew nothing whatsoever about broadcasting when he was appointed and knew little more now." He said the CRBC programs lacked originality and brilliance, and the announcing was dull and uninspiring.

Graham Spry, Alan Plaunt, and Weir's other allies and many of the supporters of public broadcasting were outraged at the way the CRBC treated Weir. *Winnipeg Free Press* editor John Dafoe called the firing of Weir "a very dirty job." Weir was "demoted, humiliated, and forced to resign," Plaunt told his friends, adding that the CRBC might destroy the whole concept of public broadcasting. "The integrity and ability of Mr. Weir appears to have provoked the jealousy of the Commissioners or some of them," he said.

What particularly galled Weir and Canadian Radio League supporters was the hiring as CRBC program directors two men who were among

Guglielmo Marconi in 1901 in his makeshift laboratory in St. John's, Nfld., where he conducted the first transatlantic radio-telegraph communication.
(*Sandy Stewart Photo Collection, National Archives of Canada, 6016*)

Reginald Fessenden, the Quebec-born, Ontario-raised radio inventor, who was the world's first broadcaster in 1900. (*National Archives of Canada, PA 93160*)

Heavyweight boxing champion Jack Dempsey (front) speaking into a XWA
microphone in Montreal during an interview *circa* 1920.
(*Sandy Stewart Photo Collection, National Archives of Canada, 6019*)

The first studio and control room in Canada at XWA, Montreal, *circa* 1920,
with technicians Jack Argyle (left) and J. O. Cann (right).
(*Sandy Stewart Photo Collection, National Archives of Canada, 12662*)

A late 1920s CNR advertisement extolling the virtues of the radio service available on its trains. (*Sandy Stewart Photo Collection, National Archives of Canada, 6036*)

Foster Hewitt began broadcasting play-by-play of hockey games in 1923. For more than fifty years, he was Canada's best-known voice. (*Sandy Stewart Photo Collection, National Archives of Canada, 12661*)

The Melody Belles were one of the musical groups popular on Canadian radio in the 1920s and early 1930s.
(*Sandy Stewart Photo Collection, National Archives of Canada, 6070*)

From its Winnipeg studios at the Fort Garry Hotel, CNR Radio fed out its programs east and west.
(*Sandy Stewart Photo Collection, National Archives of Canada, 12660*)

On July 1, 1927, the crowds on Parliament Hill celebrated Canada's sixtieth birthday and witnessed Canada's first coast-to-coast radio network program. (*National Archives of Canada, C 18068*)

Members of the Aird Commission. Left to right, Charles Bowman, chairman John Aird, Augustin Frigon, and commission secretary Donald Mason. (*National Archives of Canada, PA 122227*)

The CNR's hugely successful drama, "Henry Hudson," directed by Tyrone Guthrie and performed in the CNR Montreal studio in 1930.
(*National Archives of Canada, PA 92385*)

The Four Porters, a Vancouver blackface quartet heard on CNR Radio.
(*National Archives of Canada, C 66621*)

Playing checkers on the radio in the 1920s. (*National Archives of Canada, 66703*)

Prime Minister R. B. Bennett, the unlikely political sire of public broadcasting in Canada. (*National Archives of Canada, C 7733*)

Graham Spry, the Father of Canadian public broadcasting. (*Courtesy of Robin Spry*)

Alan Plaunt, Spry's behind-the-scenes collaborator in 1930-32 and the force and inspiration behind the establishment of the CBC in 1936. (*Paul Horsdal, courtesy of Frances Plaunt Hall*)

the loudest enemies of public broadcasting. When Weir was demoted and made responsible for programs only west of Montreal, the man appointed to arrange programs from Montreal and the East was Arthur Dupont. He had run *La Presse*'s station CKAC in Montreal, had been a leader in the bitter private radio attack on proposals for public broadcasting, and was a vigorous opponent of the Canadian Radio League.

Even more galling was the appointment of Ernie Bushnell as Weir's replacement when he was fired from the CRBC in July. Bushnell had been a persistent foe of the Aird Report, public broadcasting in general, and the Canadian Radio League in particular, calling the campaign for public radio "the greatest snow job ever" and saying politicians "swallowed holus bolus" the Radio League's ideas. Bushnell had been a leading spokesman for the private radio campaign, giving numerous speeches, writing newspaper columns, and delivering radio commentaries that attacked the idea of public radio.

Bushnell complained that Spry and Plaunt ran the Radio League for their own purposes, that it was a "will-o'-the-wisp" organization whose "big shots on the letterhead didn't know what its aims were." He said public radio would become a pawn of the federal government. A key figure in public broadcasting for a quarter of a century, Bushnell always retained an affinity for the private sector. In 1962, thinking back to the early 1930s, he told an interviewer, "I think had we been left alone, private broadcasters had sufficient honesty and integrity to ensure that Canadian broadcasting wasn't completely swallowed or devoured by the American networks." Despite his lifelong uneasiness with the purposes of public broadcasting as seen by Spry, Plaunt, and the Broadcasting Act, Bushnell, whom Weir called "the old rascal," was likeable, smart, experienced, and, the commissioners thought, more amenable to following orders than Weir.

He was called to Ottawa by Steel, but first he saw Weir. "I presume they are offering you my job," Weir told him. "They fired me yesterday." "To hell with them," Bushnell responded. "I'm not a bit interested." But his role as manager of CKNC in Toronto was about to disappear as its owners were withdrawing from broadcasting. Bushnell reluctantly accepted Weir's old job as program director for Ontario and the West at a salary of $4,500 a year and talked scornfully of the "whole crazy civil service set up" of the commission. It was the unpromising start of a turbulent, high-level career with the CRBC and its successor, the CBC.

The first thing Bushnell did was to hire most of the men who had worked for him at CKNC. "Why the hell not?" he later said. "They were the only ones who knew a damn thing about radio." Bushnell was right, for the newcomers included Charles Jennings, who became the CRBC chief announcer at $46.15 a week and who, on the CRBC and later the CBC, became Canada's first, and some still say best, network news anchor. As his son Peter would be a generation later, Jennings was wooed by the American networks, and he had actually accepted a newscaster role with NBC. He was, for some unexplained reason, turned back at the border by U.S. Immigration, and he stayed with the CRBC and CBC for the rest of his life. A 1934 news story called the twenty-eight-year-old Jennings an "ace high announcer" and said he read "everything from Popeye to Shakespeare."

Bushnell also brought with him to the CRBC Rupert Lucas, who, before working with CKNC, had been with CNR Radio. For half a century he would illuminate the nation's airwaves with his direction of radio dramas for the CRBC and CBC. Another CKNC staffer Bushnell hired was Stanley Maxted, a tenor whose career with the CRBC and CBC later included a senior management position and fame as a war correspondent. Jennings, Lucas, Maxted, and the others brought in by Bushnell were known as the Boys from CKNC.

Still pursuing quantity not quality, Charlesworth directed Bushnell's team to substantially increase the number of programs coming from Ontario and the West. One of his complaints about Weir was that more programs had come from Dupont in Montreal than Weir in Toronto. So Bushnell poured onto the airwaves "Edgar Herring and his Xylophone," "Pianology," "Canadian Capers," "The Serenaders," and "Radio Theatre Guild." These joined other CRBC programs such as "The Young Bloods of Beaver Bend," "Cotter's Saturday Night," which was a lively Scottish music program, "Parade of the Provinces," and "Forgotten Footsteps," an archeological program. The CRBC also covered the World Series, the English Derby, and everything from the United Empire Loyalists annual meeting to Remembrance Day ceremonies in Ottawa.

At the end of 1933, the CRBC began its "Northern Messenger" program, sending news items and personal messages to Canada's Arctic area – a program that continued into the 1970s.

Bushnell had been given an annual budget of $300,000 to produce fourteen hours of programming a week, not much money even in 1933. Through rented time on private stations and its owned outlets in Ottawa, Moncton, and Vancouver, the CRBC had established by mid-1933 a Western network from Winnipeg to Vancouver and an Eastern network from Halifax to Fort William, Ontario, both of which aired about two hours of programming a day, and a national network, which was on the air for another hour and a half a day Monday through Saturday and two hours on Sunday.

At the end of its first year, the CRBC boasted in a report to the House of Commons, "By the daily exchange of radio programs between east and west, the geographical barrier of distance is being surmounted and in this way there tends to be a disappearance of parochialism. . . . Obviously national radio is an effective instrument in nation-building."

But not all parochialism had disappeared. A great deal of programming came out of Montreal, and the CRBC's insistence that programs produced there use both languages set off howls of protest against French "polluting the air." Protest at French being "forced down our throats" came from MPs in the House of Commons, from the Royal Black Knights of Ireland, the Protestant Vigilance Committee, the Orange Benevolent Associations, the Ku Klux Klan in Saskatchewan (which Charlesworth called "this bastard American organization which boasted three members in the House of Commons"), and numerous town councils and boards of trade.

A mass protest overflowed Toronto's Massey Hall, and 10,000 Royal Black Knights of Ireland met in Guelph to protest against French on the air. The Sons of England in Prince Albert claimed French programs were "a plot" to make Canada a bilingual country. "Any government that will permit any other language insults the English-speaking people of this country," said Orange Society leader W. Bro. McComb.

"When the Commission attempts to force the Quebec view on the rest of Canada, these people resent it and instead of building up unity and friendliness, it is building up a wall of hostility between the two races," thundered Regina Conservative MP Franklin Turnbull. "The people of Saskatchewan feel that what is going on is a concerted effort to make Canada a bilingual country and that the Radio Commission is being used to promote this end." Fifty-three residents of Outlook, Saskatchewan, almost the entire village, telegraphed the CRBC, "Humbly requesting to have the broadcasting of programs in the French language discontinued."

"The radio programs are apparently designed to promote the false claim that French is an official language," said C. M. Carrie, past grand master of the Grand Orange Lodge of Ontario West. Moose Jaw Conservative MP W. A. Beynon told the House of Commons radio committee that people in Saskatchewan "don't want to hear French at all."

Austin Weir commented that the CRBC's French programming had stimulated "a queer mixture of prejudice, bigotry and fear." The *Telegram* noted that the CRBC was supposed to help national unity but "under the bilingual auspices of the Radio Commission, it is provoking racial controversies and is becoming an agency of discord." Even Prime Minister Bennett, whose political strength lay outside Quebec (although he had two dozen Conservative MPs from Quebec), became concerned at French on the CRBC. "Government is losing hundreds of votes through the insistence of the French Canadians on bilingualism, particularly at the moment in connection with radio," he noted.

Charlesworth, alarmed at the anti-French campaign, sought to stop all French being heard on CRBC west of the Ontario-Manitoba border. Thomas Maher, however, objected, saying 700,000 French-speaking Canadians lived outside Quebec. He demanded a minimum of one hour a week in French on the full network and that "all programs shall bear a short translation of the principal part of the continuity." His fellow commissioners agreed, and Charlesworth told the parliamentary committee, "French will continue to be used in radio programs. . . . There are French Canadians living in practically all the provinces." Maher noted that even in Quebec only 20 to 25 per cent of programs were in French. "This can hardly be regarded as an undue proportion of French programs," he said.

Nevertheless, as 1933 wore on, the CRBC reduced French programming heard in the West, but it increased French programs heard in Quebec and sought to broadcast to all of the province.

Another assault on Charlesworth came from the Jehovah's Witnesses, who portrayed the beleaguered CRBC chairman as a dictator trying to keep them off the air. Since their station licences had been taken away from them half a dozen years earlier, the Jehovah's Witnesses had been buying time on up to twenty-five private stations to continue airing their beliefs about "wicked" Catholics and "evil" governments. The broadcasts were made by "Judge" Joseph Franklin Rutherford, the Jehovah's Witnesses' leader and an iron-fisted, self-appointed agent of God. His deep voice and machine-gun delivery thundered out threats and warnings against "pagan" Catholics and Protestants and "infidel" authorities.

Rutherford had been jailed in the United States in 1918 for conspiring to obstruct First World War recruiting. His style was similar to the anti-Semitic, anti-establishment rantings of the Fighting Priest, the Ontario-born and -educated Father Coughlin, who broadcast from Detroit through the 1930s.

Charlesworth took umbrage at Rutherford, who used the title judge but never was one, calling him "a heavy-jowled, flannel-mouthed prophet" from Brooklyn who was "abusive and mischievous." It was not their first confrontation; six years earlier Charlesworth had written in *Saturday Night* that "Judge" Rutherford was like the "wandering blatherskates and professional liars . . . Rutherford is a lying demagogue." Rutherford had responded, calling Charlesworth "a liar, thief, Judas and polecat."

Rutherford's broadcasts had been the first item on the agenda of the first formal CRBC meeting of Charlesworth, Maher, and Steel on January 19, 1933. "Evidence of the subversive nature of those broadcasts was provided by Judge Rutherford's own advertising circular," the CRBC minutes reported. Angered by what he called this "scurrilous abuse of all Christian clergymen and lawful institutions," Charlesworth ordered that each of Rutherford's radio broadcasts had to be approved by the commission before being broadcast. "Censorship!" charged the Jehovah's Witnesses. Charlesworth complained that "Rutherford's strong arm salesmen got to work in many parts of Canada with petitions asking the removal of our Commission."

The "Judge," his Jehovah's Witnesses, and the anti-French protesters weren't the only ones assailing the commission in its brief lifetime; the musicians were after the CRBC, too. Protesting a pay cut, the musicians went on strike early in the CRBC's existence, causing widespread program havoc since music dominated the airwaves. After a month, however, Charlesworth settled the dispute over a bottle of whisky in his office with American Federation of Musicians president Joseph Webber.

He was assailed on another musical front, however, with complaints about "syrupy crooners" and "sentimental rot" on the air. "Crooners are positively immoral," preached Rev. John MacFarlane, the United Church minister in Chatham, Ontario. Noted pianist Alfred Laliberté resigned as CRBC musical director, complaining about Charlesworth's taste in music, and saying, "He is just looking for the approval of the mass." A University of Toronto psychologist, Dr. W. D. Blatz, said CRBC programs were aimed at twelve-year-olds. The Canadian Bandmasters' Association said radio music was "trash and jazz and the most degrading type of music." Others, however, called Charlesworth a musical "highbrow. . . . A self-anointed leader of the intelligentsia." In truth, Charlesworth was more low than highbrow in his cultural tastes, loving barn dances, variety shows, and circus clowns.

There were complaints, too, about the absence of comedy on the CRBC. "There isn't a laugh in a whole evening," said popular Canadian entertainer Al Plunkett. "Everything's wrong with radio. In the first place there are men attempting to produce programs who haven't the faintest knowledge of entertainment."

The CRBC's drama programs were criticized by many, including the *Montreal Star*'s drama critic, S. Morgan Powell, who said they were "worse programs than ever before and all of what we did not, do not and never will want." Others complained that the CRBC allowed too many American programs on Canadian stations, while still others complained of too few. Ottawa Liberal MP T. F. Ahearn demanded the CRBC carry all the American programming broadcast by Toronto and Montreal stations affiliated with NBC and CBS. Charlesworth refused, saying to do that "would practically hand over the entire radio business of Canada to the two big networks of the United States. . . . We can't unify Canada if we are to hand over the air to American networks." Charlesworth could have stopped the Toronto and Montreal stations from carrying the American network programs, but he didn't have the nerve to do it, given the popularity of the shows.

Even Prime Minister Bennett had a complaint, objecting to radio being used unscrupulously by mining promoters; Charlesworth promptly took them off the air. He also banned from both the CRBC and private stations medical quacks and such religious groups as the Remedial Movement for the Establishment of Permanent Happiness in the World and the Spiritual Psychic Science Church, Inc. Charlesworth was determined to rid the air of what he called "those gentry [of] financial sharks, medical quacks and the general fellowship of imposter." "The very first program I banned," Charlesworth later said, "was that of a quack who presented a short program of hymns with a discourse to the effect that Our Lord commanded people to use his Indian herb remedies." For all these actions Charlesworth was labelled a dictator and Sole Master of the Air.

Charlesworth and his fellow commissioners were also castigated for wild spending and arrogance. "RADIO COMMISSION SPENDS RIOT-OUSLY," read one *Financial Post* headline. "Broadcast Dictators Plan New Extravagance . . . Autocratic Radio Board Exceeds Powers Given It." H. C. Buchanan of the Moose Jaw Radio Association told a parliamentary committee, "The vast majority of the people of Saskatchewan are now definitely against government or Commission broadcasting."

Complaints poured in about too many commercials being allowed on programs. "I object to being hit with somebody's sausages in the centre of a symphony," said western MP E. J. Garland. "Nor do I want devilled ham in the middle of an opera."

On the other hand, the private stations complained of too few commercials. Among 108 radio regulations it issued in its first few months, the CRBC had ordered that there could be no spot advertising from 7:30 P.M. to 11:00 P.M. and that prices could not be mentioned. It also said total advertising could be no more than 5 per cent of broadcast time, although it softened those rules as time went on to allow up to 15 per cent. Even so, many private stations winked at the regulations without being penalized for going over the limit. Even the CRBC's own outlet in Toronto, CRCT, broke the rules, carrying three times the allowable commercials for Pepsodent during "Amos 'n' Andy." All this violated Charlesworth's own belief that "when you put your broadcasting in the hands of advertisers you no longer depend on the good taste of the artist, but upon the taste of the advertiser."

The Dominion Broadcasters Association (DBA) charged that the CRBC was "illegal" and that its operations were "notoriously unsatisfactory." They were especially upset with the CRBC's realignment of station wavelengths, charging, as did Weir, that it was sloppily done. Public broadcasting's old nemesis, R. W. Ashcroft, president of the DBA, called Charlesworth and his colleagues "chiselers" and "clumsy," and he denounced the whole idea of public radio as "a delusion and a snare, as are many other pious hopes." Charlesworth replied that Ashcroft was an "imposter" and that his group was a "bastard" of the American Association of Broadcasters.

CBS wrote from New York, protesting about the CRBC's "arbitrary limitation" on commercial time and demanding that more commercials be allowed on the American network programs carried on Canadian stations. A more potent and, as time would prove, a more enduring adversary of public broadcasting was Harry Sedgewick, manager of Toronto's CFRB, who forcefully argued that radio was dependent on the United States for advertising and programming. He also began a quarter-century campaign to split the CRBC, and later the CBC, into two separate bodies: one for regulations and one for operations. That way, he said, one public agency would not be simultaneously judge and competitor of private stations.

Charlesworth, fed up with all the complaints, groaned about "the commercial rapacity of many broadcasters" who, he said, insisted "on nauseating overdoses of advertising."

Charlesworth was also angered at the government which he felt, rightly, was shortchanging the CRBC. The CRBC's budget in its first full year was $1 million, less than the revenue the government took in from the two-dollar annual radio licence fees and much less than the subsidy recommended by the Aird Report and the parliamentary committee. Worse still, while Bennett was out of the country, the cabinet tried to limit the CRBC to spending only $500,000 a year. Charlesworth threatened to resign and tell everyone why. The government backed down, and Bennett said he had been unaware of his cabinet's move. The cutback would have been too late anyway as the CRBC had already spent most of its million-dollar budget, not only on buying the CNR stations, but on paying for the programs, which cost $300,000 ($1,000 for a program by the Hart House String Quartet, for example, or $800 for an operetta), on buying time on private stations to air the CRBC programs, which cost about $250,000, and on network lines, which cost about $300,000. There was also the cost of administration and of building and maintaining facilities. All this left hardly any money at all for the kind of public radio system envisioned in the 1932 legislation.

The Bennett government's shortchanging of CRBC funding killed its plans to build five high-powered public broadcasting stations across Canada. When the CRBC began, it reached 40 per cent of the population in prime time. Four years later, it had increased its reach only to 49 per cent. Instead of building its own stations, the CRBC was forced to lease stations and buy time on private stations to broadcast its programs, in addition to using the CNR facilities it had purchased. In keeping with its easy attitude toward private stations, the CRBC did not requisition airtime, let alone stations, as it had the legal right to do and which had been proposed by the Aird Report and envisioned by Parliament in 1932. "From the very start our policy was not to take over all stations," Steel later said. Nor did the CRBC have enough money for a large program staff. The total staff was 132 at the end of its life in 1936.

To compensate for the lack of federal funding, the CRBC reluctantly began seeking more commercial revenue. In a memo to his colleagues, Steel wrote, "If we are to continue to improve the standard of Canadian broadcasting, it can only be done by bringing in commercial advertising." Charlesworth and Maher had been forced to agree, and they began their search for increased advertising. Local CRBC stations carried commercials, but because of an agreement with the line companies, which forbade commercials, there was no network advertising until 1935. In its last year, the CRBC brought in $236,000 from advertising. The lure of commercial revenue in the absence of enough government funding caused problems for public broadcasting for the rest of the century.

It was a particularly sore subject for Charlesworth, confronted as he was by the clash of his anti-advertising principles and the CRBC's financial realities. He was especially hurt when complaints about programs and commercials came from friends, such as J. F. B. Livesay, general manager of the Canadian Press. Livesay had complained about the CRBC in a letter to a colleague at the *Vancouver Sun* that he had copied to Charlesworth. The CRBC, Livesay said, was carrying "a lot of American song and dance junk," and its programs "seem to be deteriorating all over the country, and it's just too bad for those of us who believe firmly in the Commission idea. We are finding it more and more difficult to defend our position. The reason, of course, is the Commission is not getting enough revenue to be able to sustain first rate programs. . . . I think it would be better if they should be starved out of existence than they should be selling their own air time to American programs when the very object of the establishment of the Commission was to combat those by offering in their place worthy Canadian programming. . . . It looks very like selling one's birth right, does it not?"

Charlesworth shot back a letter to Livesay referring to his "deep anger" at Livesay's "unkind and slanderous words." In a second letter written a few days later, Charlesworth added, "Your phraseology upset me a great deal, especially in view of the many trivial annoyances which crowd on me daily." He defended the CRBC's growing reliance on commercials, saying, "If we are to keep programs to our standards, we must seek revenue from advertising sources." Years later, Graham Spry wished aloud that the government had raised radio licence fees enough to allow the public broadcaster to eliminate or sharply lessen dependence on advertising. "If the government had had the guts to face up to the financing of broadcasting by the licence fee," he said, "the whole picture of Canadian broadcasting would be fundamentally different and fundamentally better."

Another problem for the CRBC was that Charlesworth, Maher, and Steel allowed themselves to get bogged down in trivia. Too much time at their meetings was taken up with such things as hiring a tenor in Regina at $45 a week for six months, fussing about musical director Geoffrey

Waddington receiving an extra $140 a program beyond his $3,600 annual salary for conducting an orchestra on the air, or on deciding what to do with "two worn out pianos in Montreal." After some debate they decided to sell one piano and send the other to the Chicoutimi station. They also decided after much debate to pay for the tuning of seven CRBC pianos in Toronto on an annual contract instead of paying $100 a month. At another meeting, and again after much debate, the CRBC commissioners agreed to buy for the Halifax studios "twelve No. 118 Conductors stands . . . at a price of $9.50 each, less 40%."

The biggest surprise for Charlesworth in his CRBC chairmanship was the intensity of the political pressures on him from Conservative MPs and others who wanted favours for their friends. Prominent Conservative and future Opposition leader R. B. Hanson demanded a power increase for CFNB in Fredericton, warning, "From the political standpoint, it is most important that we should have this licence given to those who are absolutely our friends." In another warning he said, "If this matter is not straightened out, I intend to attack Charlesworth on the floor of the House. . . . I want that station in Fredericton for political and other purposes." Within weeks, CFNB got its power increase. One result was that the CRBC closed its own weak and somewhat dilapidated station in Moncton. Similar Tory pressures came from Regina, Toronto, Windsor, and elsewhere. Political interference with the CRBC had reared its head just twenty-three days after the commission was appointed in October 1932, but before it was officially operating, when the Bennett government issued radio licences to the actively Conservative owners of *La Patrie* in Montreal.

The commission was seen to be vulnerable to the governing Tories, acting more like a government department than an independent agency. While there had been virtually unanimous support for the establishment of the CRBC in the House of Commons, within a few months of its birth that support had disintegrated into partisan squabbling. The CRBC was becoming, Liberal leader Mackenzie King said, "a great Conservative political machine." Independent MP A. W. Neill said the CRBC was becoming "a curse to Canada, a curse to the people and a curse to the government." "I am afraid it has developed into simply a Conservative owned and Conservative operated affair," said influential MP J. S. Woodsworth.

Charles Bowman was appalled by the CRBC operation. "An unworkable, clumsy organization that," he said, "has alienated the public, that has been riddled with politics." Vitriolic criticism about Charlesworth came privately from the *Winnipeg Free Press*'s Ottawa correspondent, Grant Dexter, who wrote to his editor, John Dafoe, "Charlesworth is one of the most dangerous, sinister, desperate men I have ever met. . . . A double dyed scoundrel. . . . [His] cowardice is only exceeded by the mendacity with which he puts forward semi-truths."

In 1934, the parliamentary radio committee, heavily stacked with private broadcaster supporters, seriously considered recommending that Charlesworth and his fellow commissioners be dismissed and replaced by a single general manager, possibly Ernie Bushnell.

Bennett, throughout all the troubles of the CRBC, remained a strong vocal supporter, rejecting the accusations of political interference and attacking "private interests," which he said encouraged the "unpopularity for the moment of the Commission." As early as April 1933, he told the House of Commons, "The attacks that have been made are being made for the purpose of destroying this publicly owned service."

The potential for political interference from the government in CRBC activities had always been there. In the parliamentary debate setting up the CRBC, Mackenzie King had said, "Anything that will help remove the possibility of the slightest suspicion of political partisanship will be most helpful. . . . In radio broadcasting, political partisanship . . . might become a very serious affair." Within a few months of the start of the CRBC, Mackenzie King had told the House of Commons that the commissioners were all "well-known members of the Conservative Party."

In its first full year of operation, the CRBC carried speeches by the prime minister and several cabinet ministers, but Charlesworth said he wasn't worried about them because "we have a strict understanding that those talks will not be political. I want to make that very clear. They will not be political in any sense whatsoever." Opposition parties, however, thought they were indeed political and forced Charlesworth to allow other parties on the air for talks. He thought that "too much of it wearies the public," and his vice-chairman, Thomas Maher, said politics should be "banned from Canadian radio."

But Bennett saw radio's great political value, and he used it to shore up his own plunging popularity. On radio, to the horror of traditional Conservatives, the sixty-four-year-old Tory mossback miraculously transformed himself into a hot-eyed Franklin Delano Roosevelt New Dealer. In January 1935, he gave a series of five prime-time radio addresses entitled, "The Premier Speaks to the People," which became known as Bennett's New Deal Broadcasts.

Bennett staggered supporters and opponents alike by saying, "I am for reform. And in my mind reform means government intervention. It means government control and regulation. It means the end of *laissez faire*. There can be no permanent recovery without it." In a nervous, staccato voice and stumbling from time to time, Bennett reversed a lifetime's philosophy and hitched his future to the Rooseveltian bandwagon of popularity, pushed into it by Bill Herridge and Rod Finlayson. Herridge supplied the ideas, Finlayson wrote the words, and Bennett provided the voice and the $10,000 it cost in radio time. The speeches originated in the CRBC Ottawa studio and were carried on thirty-eight stations. The broadcasts earned him the characterization of The Tory Trotsky, and they earned Charlesworth criticism for allowing such blatantly political addresses.

Charlesworth's most dangerous enemy, however, was not a politician, but was Alan Plaunt, who had quickly become disillusioned with the CRBC. When the CRBC was only a year old, Plaunt wrote in the *Canadian Forum* that its "flaws . . . are such as to imperil the principle of a public system." He said that while Bennett endorsed the principle of public broadcasting, his methods were wrong, and now "almost universal support has been turned into almost universal indifference or opposition." Plaunt's formidable temper would soon surge into a vicious and ultimately successful assault on Bennett, Charlesworth, and the CRBC.

Plaunt fumed at what he saw as a Tory stranglehold on his public broadcasting "baby," and he was outraged at the admonition given by Charlesworth to a radio commentator who had warned about the dangers for Canada in a future European war. Professor T. W. L. McDermott, secretary of the Canadian League of Nations Society, broadcast a commentary in which he predicted "either internal revolution or a break up of the Dominion" if Canada entered such a war. The government was outraged, and the CRBC publicly apologized, claiming it had the right to censor all radio speeches and warning McDermott not to say such things ever again on the air. McDermott, who was Brooke Claxton's brother-in-law, later became Canada's high commissioner to Australia and served as a member of the CBC board of directors.

Plaunt bitterly complained of the CRBC's "unbalanced judgement." He was further incensed when Charlesworth told a meeting in Vancouver, "I do not favour total nationalization of radio." Graham Spry was even more outspoken than Plaunt. "The Canadian experiment has failed," he told a Canton, Ohio, conference on U.S.-Canadian affairs. "It provides no satisfactory alternative to the privately operated American networks. . . . Its regulations with respect to comment on public institutions are menacing and vicious. . . . It has failed and some new experiment is called for."

Amid the din of complaints about the CRBC, Charlesworth defiantly boasted, "We have taken the inferiority complex out of Canadians regarding programs." At a Montreal meeting, Charlesworth met his adversaries head on, saying, "There has been no muddle in anything the Canadian Radio Broadcasting Commission has done, the only muddle being the muddle-headed comments in Canadian newspapers. If I went down into my grave tomorrow I would have nothing to be ashamed of."

One of Charlesworth's two vice-chairmen didn't feel quite so confident, however. Depressed and angered by the controversy over French-language broadcasts and attacks by MPs and frustrated by arguments with Charlesworth and Steel, Thomas Maher resigned from the CRBC in August 1934, believing the CRBC to be a failure. He claimed ill health, but it was ill humour that prompted his departure as, in effect, the overall program boss of the CRBC. "There are so many people to please in this job," Maher complained. "One has to be very careful not to offend."

Maher had been a blatant Tory political appointment, and his replacement came from the same ranks, although, unlike Maher, this time the chosen commissioner had a rich broadcast background. He was Jacques Cartier, the pioneer Montreal radio announcer and a strong opponent of public broadcasting. Cartier had been an influential Conservative Party organizer in Quebec in the 1930 election and before that had been president of the Broadcasters Association of Canada, a private radio lobby group. Cartier had begun working with Marconi at the Marconi Wireless Telegraph Co. in 1908 and had also worked with David Sarnoff at RCA. For all his credentials, however, Cartier lasted only a year in the CRBC job. He quit, he said, "to perform a more public spirited service," turning his back on the Conservatives and becoming Quebec organizer for the Reconstruction Party led by renegade Conservative H. H. Stevens. Cartier was replaced by Col. C. A. Chauveau, another Conservative politician and the grandson of the first premier of Quebec.

Within weeks of taking over the CRBC, Charlesworth had faced demands that he stop private stations from "stealing the news." The complaints came from the Canadian Press (CP) which denounced as "theft" the private stations' practice of scalping news stories from local papers for their own newscasts. Under prodding by CP general manager Livesay, Charlesworth agreed to use the CRBC's regulatory power to prevent what Livesay called "news robbery." Some newspaper editors went further; they wanted no news on the air at all. J. H. Woods, editor of the *Calgary Herald*, wrote Charlesworth, "Newspapermen spend years in learning how to handle news with moderation and with accuracy. It is not a job that can be trusted to anyone who speaks into a microphone."

Despite the newspapers' distress at radio news, the Canadian Press thought that newscasts on the CRBC would discourage private radio "news pirates." Charlesworth and Livesay began negotiating a deal. The Canadian Press initially proposed that it supply the CRBC with newscasts for $6,000 a year. Recognizing the help Charlesworth could provide in preventing news "theft," however, CP changed its position and offered to provide the newscasts free of charge. A deal was made, and the CRBC sent a notice to all private stations warning them against using any items from the newspapers in local newscasts, although allowing an exception where the local newspaper was agreeable.

The CRBC newscasts began on July 17, 1933, with two five-minute bulletins a day, one at dinnertime, the other in late evening, and both billed "by courtesy of Canadian Press." Charlesworth and Livesay had agreed there would be no commercials in the newscasts. A year later, the two newscasts were merged into one ten-minute newscast at 10:45 P.M. EST. The newscasts were prepared in CP bureaus, and some of them were delivered to the CRBC stations by teletype, some by boys on bicycles, and often they were late. CRBC Maritime supervisor J. Frank Willis complained, "It is not unusual for the despatches to show up One and Two minutes before the time set for us to go on the air. Last Sunday . . . they did not arrive until Three minutes after the time of broadcasting." Another problem was that the CP newscasts were written on flimsy paper that crackled when announcers turned the pages.

Charlesworth and his colleagues thought radio news was useful, but they didn't think it was truly important. Radio news, they said, was largely of interest only to the more than half of the Canadian population who lived in the country and who got their newspapers "several days or weeks after they are published. . . . Obviously, [it] is not of prime importance to those in urban centres who receive the newspapers within several minutes after the time of publication."

The Canadian Press essentially agreed, feeling radio news could be an appetizer for those interested in news, but certainly not the main course; that was reserved for newspapers. In the Nova Scotia election of the summer of 1933, CP said it would cover the election results for the CRBC but only enough "to whet the public appetite rather than satiate it."

But a few major stories broke during the CRBC years which graphically demonstrated the power of radio news and began the public's historic shift from dependence on newspapers to dependence on broadcasting.

The first big story came in the spring of 1934 with the birth of the Dionne quintuplets at Callandar, Ontario. Shortly after their delivery by Dr. Allan Dafoe, CBS asked the CRBC to arrange a broadcast from the hospital. In a fifteen-minute prime-time program on sixty-four stations in Canada and the United States, a microphone was placed at cribside and an announcer described the scene. "Now we will hear the quintuplets themselves," he said, and listeners heard Yvonne and Marie crying softly, Emilie bawling lustily, Marie squealing and burbling, while Cecile uttered not a sound. "It was a wonderful broadcast," said Charlesworth.

The most dramatic broadcast by the CRBC, however, was aired near the end of its existence in 1936. Its coverage of a mine collapse at Moose River, Nova Scotia, had millions of Canadians, Americans, and Britons glued to their radio sets to hear the fate of three men trapped underground for eleven days by a rock fall. Six hundred and fifty radio stations in the United States, fifty-eight stations in Canada, and the BBC carried reports from the pit head by the CRBC's J. Frank Willis. His rich but increasingly strained voice came on the radio live for two or three minutes every half hour for a total of fifty-six hours, with only one two-hour rest. His last report was at 2:00 A.M. on April 23, 1936, when two of the three men were finally brought out alive.

Willis's broadcasts demonstrated vividly how radio could tie an entire nation – even several nations – together to share the emotions and experience the drama of a single event. It was the beginning in Canada of broadcast news specials. Willis was swamped with offers from American radio stations and agencies wanting him to do broadcasts, make speeches and public appearances, and endorse products. Willis, who had once been a Halifax choirboy, turned them all down, saying, "I felt there was something wrong about capitalizing on a thing like the Moose River disaster." He stayed in Canada to become one of the country's best-known and highly regarded radio and television performers.

In spite of all the criticism and bitterness heaped on Charlesworth and his fellow commissioners and the reality that the government had tied it hand and foot, the CRBC was providing a significant public service through its special broadcasts. As well as the Moose River disaster, the CRBC covered debates between various Canadian universities, Empire Christmas messages, the death and funeral of King George V, and the opening of Parliament. In 1935, it provided the first nationwide radio coverage of a federal election when, between 6:00 P.M. and 1:00 A.M. EST, CP election flashes were aired every fifteen minutes.

There were program successes in addition to the news specials. The zany comedy team of Woodhouse and Hawkins, known as "the two nitwits of the network," became a starring attraction for the CRBC and later the CBC. The show was as popular in the 1930s and early 1940s as Wayne and Shuster were with a future generation. Thanks to the CRBC and CBC, Mart Kenney and his Western Gentlemen became Canada's most famous and most popular big band. Making his radio debut on the CRBC in 1935, Kenney became known as Canada's King of Swing, and his CBC Sunday series "Sweet and Low" lasted twenty years. There was "Atlantic Nocturne" with J. Frank Willis from Halifax, the musical show "Ici Paris," and special presentations of everything from *Les Misérables* and *The Magnificent Obsession* to *Thirty-Nine Steps* and *Top Hat*. The CRBC boasted in 1935 that in the past year it had aired 365 variety and comedy shows, 350 dance music programs, 125 novelty shows, 45 symphony concerts, 29 operettas, and 20 programs of chamber music. The longest program that year was one celebrating the Silver Jubilee of King George V which lasted from 10:00 A.M. to 4:00 P.M. EST.

Ernie Bushnell, who became the CRBC's overall program director in 1935, believed that "broadcasting was the poor man's theatre. The main objective was to tickle the fancy of listeners hungry for entertainment. No one took it too seriously. It was a pleasant diversion." Bushnell's attitude to broadcasting was sharply different from Spry's and Plaunt's and the Radio League supporters who saw radio as a significant social force for enlightenment and nationalism, as well as diversion.

The CRBC also broadcast American programs, including concerts featuring the Metropolitan Opera and the New York Philharmonic, and the CRBC station in Toronto carried some of the immensely popular American programs such as "Amos 'n' Andy" and Kate Smith and Fred Allen. The most popular Canadian show and the CRBC's biggest star was Foster Hewitt, broadcasting the Toronto Maple Leaf's hockey games. At 9:00 P.M. sharp, half an hour after the game began, across the land Canadians heard his tense greeting, "Hello Canada and hockey fans in the United States and Newfoundland." It became a weekly shared experience and a unifying force for its estimated one million listeners. Hewitt once forgot to say "Newfoundland" in his introduction, and protests poured in from the British colony.

The fair-haired thirty-year-old, "never a sore throat" Hewitt rejected three American radio offers. The games were initially sponsored by General Motors, but in 1935, a new company president came in who thought sponsoring hockey was not a good way to sell cars. Imperial Oil took over sponsorship and has been a hockey advertiser ever since. A young Imperial Oil advertising man, Ted Hough, passed notes to Hewitt during the games and in time became the godfather of "Hockey Night in Canada," the unseen hand running the hockey broadcasts for more than four decades.

Despite the CRBC's Canadian programming efforts, American programs remained the most popular in Canada. A Toronto *Telegram* survey showed the number one program in Toronto during this time was "Amos 'n' Andy," and the actors portraying "Amos 'n' Andy" were mobbed on a few visits to Toronto at the time; Lowell Thomas and the news was number two; and Rudy Vallee was number three. Other favourites of Canadians were Bing Crosby, Jack Benny, George Burns and Gracie Allen, Wayne King and his Orchestra, Guy Lombardo and his Royal Canadians playing out of New York, and Major Bowes and his Amateur Hour.

Charlesworth's frustration at Canadian listeners' preference for American programs and anger at his private radio critics was sharpened in the spring of 1935. He saw a "plot" for "a big coup" behind plans by three private stations in Toronto, Montreal, and Windsor which were affiliated to American networks, to persuade the federal government to allow them to increase their power to 50,000 watts. "This meant the complete Americanization of radio in the most populous sections of Canada," Charlesworth said later. "The lobbyists also sought an arrangement whereby commercial programmes, both American and Canadian, should have the right of way on the national network."

In Toronto, the CRBC already suffered from the 10,000-watt power of CFRB, which dominated the city and which had been granted the power increase by the Bennett government shortly before the CRBC came into being. Its powerful signal attracted advertisers, who could reach on this one station about half of the total Canadian radio audience. More high-power private stations would critically undermine the concept of public broadcasting set out by the Aird Commission, the Radio League and Parliament itself, whose 1932 Broadcasting Act envisioned only low-power community stations in the private sector.

Charlesworth said a western Conservative MP – probably Franklin Turnbull from Regina – was "the chief agent of these plans," and he said twenty-seven other Conservatives had joined him in the scheme. The "plotters" were taking advantage of the fact that the prime minister was out of the country. They succeeded in persuading acting prime minister Sir George Perley to introduce legislation extending the life of the CRBC for only two months, after arguing that it should be done away with altogether. As soon as Bennett returned to Canada, Charlesworth appealed to him, and the CRBC chairman said Bennett stopped "this sinister conspiracy" with an "iron heel." A new bill was introduced giving the CRBC a one-year extension to 1936, after the next election.

Again offering strong rhetorical support for public broadcasting, Bennett told the House of Commons, "Always insidiously is the attack made against the publicly owned facility and the effort made to destroy it." Bennett said there had been extremely heavy pressure to hand over broadcasting to private enterprise, but he said he would never yield "this facility to any private enterprise."

Alan Plaunt, however, put the blame for what he now regarded as a "betrayal" of public broadcasting squarely on the shoulders of the prime minister. His and Spry's "baby" was being destroyed, he felt, by that "ignoramus" Charlesworth and that "betrayer" Bennett, and when Plaunt's temper was aroused he was invincible. He decided Bennett had to be thrown out of office, Charlesworth fired, the CRBC killed, and a new, real public broadcasting system established. He surreptitiously began what would be one of the most ruthless, most Machiavellian, and ultimately successful backstage lobbying campaigns of this century. And this time, he would do it alone: Graham Spry "was in very bad odor at the time," as Spry himself later admitted. "They regarded me as not a good thing to have around the [Radio] League. They were quite upset about me joining the CCF." "I am rather afraid that Graham has minimized his usefulness with regard to radio reorganization through his other activities," Plaunt wrote to his BBC friend and ally Gladstone Murray. In any event, Spry's political involvement as CCF organizer in Ontario and his desire to run as a CCF candidate in the October 1935 federal election left him little time for any renewed battle for national public broadcasting.

Plaunt had not only time and money, but also an obsessive mission to recapture the Radio League's broadcasting dreams of five years earlier. This time, however, he would work primarily on his own in the shadows, not with the league in public as he and Spry had done before.

First, he had to get the Liberal leader, Mackenzie King, committed to his broadcasting ideas before the election, and as a lever for that, he provided the Liberals with deadly political ammunition against Bennett. The key to success, Plaunt wrote Gladstone Murray in London, depends "on getting King committed in advance, before the election and the person most likely to accomplish that improbable aim is V. M. [Vincent Massey]."

Early in 1935, Plaunt outlined his ideas to his old colleague, mentor, and public broadcast supporter, Vincent Massey, who was then president of the National Liberal Federation and a close ally of Mackenzie King. He was also the brother of Hollywood actor Raymond Massey, who later performed in many CBC dramas. In a letter to his old friend and *Ottawa Citizen* editor, Charles Bowman, Plaunt said, "I don't see any reason why, should Mr. Massey and his colleagues be interested, they should not be privately supplied with the basic material for a vigorous and devastating condemnation of the radio set up and administration, together with details and specifications for a re-organization based on the proposals of the Aird Commission and the Canadian Radio League. Then, after the election when the proposals are incorporated in legislation, we can, if necessary, rally public support as a counterpoint to the lobby which will undoubtedly be carried on."

In a note to Massey, Plaunt said, "Material should be supplied on which Mr. King could base his attack ... [but] I think it is important that I stay strictly in the background." Plaunt told Gladstone Murray, "For your confidential information, I have been working, one, on supplying V. M. and Co. with material of attack and two, in supplying them with material on which to have a policy more in accordance with your and our original recs." Over the next few months, Bowman met privately with Mackenzie King several times, carrying Plaunt's messages to the Liberal leader.

Plaunt's confidence at winning grew as King and his colleagues showed their appreciation for the ammunition provided by Plaunt and listened to his ideas for a new public broadcasting system. "The people who will handle the re-organization will be King, Euler, Massey, Lapointe, possibly Ilsley, and I think they all have been reasonably sold on the lines to be followed," he wrote to Gladstone Murray.

With help from Austin Weir, Murray, Ned Corbett, and Brooke Claxton, Plaunt prepared a sizzling eight-page memo labelled "Private and Confidential" and titled "Suggested Basis of Attack." In the memo Plaunt attacked Bennett, charging him with having "monomaniacal tendencies," of being "contemptible, evasive and obviously insincere," and of being "guilty of the most flagrant bad faith."

"It can be demonstrated," Plaunt wrote to his Liberal friends, "that he has mismanaged through his stupidity, dictatorial methods, insincerity and bad faith every important reform he has attempted. Radio is the best case in point. . . . Far from honouring the trust delegated to him unanimously by all parties in the House [on passing the 1932 radio law] he has, willfully or from ulterior design or both, violated that trust both in the spirit and the letter."

The revenge-seeking hand of Austin Weir is evident in much of the memo as Plaunt went on to castigate Charlesworth and the CRBC for favouring private stations, moving too slowly on establishing its own stations, having no standards in its programs, failing in its educational broadcasts, and discouraging talent.

Plaunt raged at what he called "blatant evidence of bad faith" and "the total failure to free the new Commission from the stigma of gross partisanship. . . . Of the three original Commissioners, two were palpable partisans. The Commission's staff was similarly tainted with a strong partisan flavour, four of the leading posts going to men who had either been party workers, or active opponents of a public system."

Plaunt's ammunition was helping the Liberals to win and helping to destroy the CRBC, but the *coup de grâce* for Charlesworth was supplied by the CRBC itself during the election campaign in the fall of 1935. Charlesworth would later dismiss the incident as a "piffling affair" and "absurd clamour," but "piffling" it wasn't, although "clamour" it certainly was.

The storm broke over the first creative use of radio as a political tool. The idea, born in the J. J. Gibbons Ltd. advertising agency of Toronto, was for a series of six fifteen-minute dramatized political soap operas ridiculing Mackenzie King and the Liberals, under the title of "Mr. Sage." Conservative Party organizer Earl Lawson arranged for the broadcasts, which were approved by the politically naive Ernie Bushnell and Hector Charlesworth. "We were told," Bushnell later said, "that the fifteen-minute period would be occupied by some narrative and some dialogue of entirely fictitious persons . . . on the role of Parliament, that it would be quite innocuous and, indeed it was hoped that it would be entertaining as well as informative."

Mr. Sage was described as "a shrewd observer who sees through the pretences, knows the facts and understands the true issues of the present political campaign." The character was a village philosopher who sat on his front porch persuading his Liberal friends of the evils of Macken-zie King and the Liberals, describing King as "an old hen always cackling and never laying an egg." The friendly old codger talked of Liberal "slush funds" and "carelessness," and of King leading his party into "the valley of humiliation." "What's worse," Mr. Sage said, "Mr. King's henchmen . . . used to call up the farmers – and their wives – in the early hours of the morning and tell them their sons would be conscripted for war if they voted against King." His Liberal neighbour Bill replied, "Gosh, that's kind of low down stuff. I didn't think King would do a thing like that." At another point, Bill, impressed with Mr. Sage's comments, said, "So King's just talking through his hat, eh?"

The Conservatives were so pleased with "Mr. Sage" that they expanded the broadcasts from the Ontario network they had arranged for the first two programs to the national network for the last four shows.

Ernie Bushnell thought it was all just "good clean fun," but King and the Liberals were outraged. "It stuck in his craw," says Edward Pickering, who was then King's assistant private secretary. King, who didn't hear the broadcasts, branded them as "scurrilous and libelous misrepresenta-tions over government-owned radio. . . . Propaganda of the worst type any party has ever put out. . . . Insidious."

The Liberal fire fell on the weary shoulders of Hector Charlesworth who later lamented that "several grand and lofty liars . . . filled his [King's] ears with tales of my atrocious perfidy toward himself that made him very angry." Charlesworth was, in fact, angry himself that the first of the six "Mr. Sage" broadcasts carried no mention that they were sponsored by the Conservative Party. He demanded the sponsor be identified, but was circumvented when the sponsor was identified as R. L. Wright, head of the research department of the J. J. Gibbons advertising agency. "A rather shabby trick," said the beleaguered Charlesworth.

What made it worse for Charlesworth, and especially infuriated King and the Liberals, was that the first two "Mr. Sage" broadcasts originated in a CRBC Toronto studio. Even more damaging was that the part of "Mr. Sage" in the first two episodes was played by CRBC's drama director, Rupert Lucas, and the production also included CRBC station manager Stanley Maxted and several other CRBC employees. Charlesworth protested to his critics, "I leaned backward to give everybody a square deal," in the election campaign. He said he always stayed by his phone at night and accepted no social engagements during the campaign.

But Charlesworth's gesture obviously wasn't enough, and a livid Mackenzie King resolved that if he won the election, he would ban all dramatized political broadcasts. "I will do all in my power," he said at the end of the campaign, "to see to it that no man in future generations has to put up with that sort of thing through a medium over which a Prime Minister and his government has full control."

Thanks mainly to an electorate that blamed Bennett for the Depression and thanks, too, in part, to the ammunition provided by Plaunt, King did win, and dramatized political broadcasts have been unheard in Canada ever since.

With King and the Liberals triumphant in the election, Charlesworth and the CRBC were now on borrowed time. Having provided anti-Bennett, anti-CRBC election ordnance to the Liberals, Plaunt knew he was in the catbird seat. "This gave me an excellent entrée," he said, "and when the government changed, it was arranged that I should be the first to see Mr. Howe." C. D. Howe was the new minister of marine whose responsibility included broadcasting. Three of Plaunt's supporters were in the new cabinet: W. D. Euler, J. L. Ilsley, and Ernest Lapointe, with King himself giving clear signs of support for Plaunt's radio ideas. Vincent Massey, newly appointed as high commissioner in London, told Howe that Plaunt was preparing a memo for Howe to study on "Canadian Broadcasting Re-Organization." Plaunt took Massey's advice to exclude not only Spry, who had been again defeated as a CCF candidate, from his new campaign, but also Charles Bowman, who had begun to drift away from the Liberals and toward the Social Credit party.

Repeating a conversation he had had with Massey, Gladstone Murray told Plaunt that in the government's eyes "You stand very high." So high, in fact, that King offered Plaunt a job as secretary to the prime minister. "During the course of an eminently amiable interview, I told [King]," Plaunt wrote to Murray, "that while I was extremely flattered by the offer, I felt it was my duty and obligation to see that the public point of view was adequately represented at the forthcoming Parliamentary [Radio] Committee.... If nothing else, it was a marvelous opportunity to get the radio issue before him."

Plaunt admitted privately to Murray that he would like to play a role in the future CBC, but he wouldn't say so to King. "What I did not tell him, of course, was that what I really wanted to do . . . was to join the great venture in an active way.... I should certainly look forward to serving as public relations." Plaunt used this and half a dozen other conversations with King to win the new prime minister to his version of what would become the CBC, but he was careful in what he said because he knew King did not like to feel pressured. He said he "never went to the well too often" as he subtly worked on King, just as he and Spry, four years earlier, had worked on Bennett, wooing the prime minister through his associates as well as in direct conversations. One such associate of King's was Edward Pickering, King's assistant private secretary, who, young, idealistic, and nationalistic like Plaunt, shared his ideas on public broadcasting. In addition, Plaunt solicited and got support from Dr. O. D. Skelton, the potent undersecretary of state for external affairs and key prime ministerial adviser; Clifford Clark, the powerful deputy minister of finance; and Dana Wilgress, deputy minister of trade and commerce. Meanwhile, on another level, Plaunt persuaded Massey to urge the Radio League's ideas on C. D. Howe and other cabinet ministers. In addition, *Winnipeg Free Press* editor John Dafoe, a friend and adviser to Mackenzie King, was enlisted to help win the prime minister's support. Big, shaggy, uncompromising, and modest, Dafoe was the most influential Canadian journalist of the century, and his help in establishing the CBC was invaluable to Plaunt.

In a twenty-four-page memo for Howe, Plaunt detailed the new broadcasting organization he wanted. Using many of the recommendations of the Aird Commission and the Canadian Radio League, he proposed a nine-member board of directors, a general manager, a two-dollar licence fee rising to three dollars after a while, as well as revenue from some sponsored programs and additional federal funds to build new stations. "A national chain of high-power stations covering the whole settled area of Canada would be . . . as important to the continued existence of Canada as a nation as transcontinental railways to its inception." Plaunt banged the same drum of nationalism that he and Spry had used on the Bennett government, saying that in this new broadcasting system, "Canada would have a wonderful instrument of nation-building."

By the end of 1935, after Plaunt had had several detailed meetings with Howe, the new minister seemed to be sold on the broadcasting service Plaunt was advocating. "We will base our reorganization on this material," Howe said, and he asked Plaunt to have Brooke Claxton prepare a draft law. Plaunt was exuberant; he thought he had won the battle for his brand of public broadcasting. But his battle was only the beginning of the war, and Plaunt soon began picking up signals that Howe was also listening to other voices. One of those other voices belonged to Harry Sedgewick of CFRB in Toronto, president of the Canadian Association of Broadcasters. Howe was also forming his own opinions, encouraged by his empire-building instincts. The legislation drafted by Claxton had been sent to Howe and to his director of radio, C. P. Edwards, and as they examined it, they began to back away. "All private stations should be placed under the control of the Minister and not under control of the Corporation," Edwards wrote to Plaunt, noting that the main complaint of private stations "was that they were regulated by, and at the same time competed with the Radio Commission."

CRBC program director Ernie Bushnell supported Edwards' idea as philosophically he sided with the approaches of the private broadcasters. He thought the principal role of the CRBC or its successor should be "good wholesome entertainment" and warned against "idealists and pure theorists" who talked of programs for national unity and intellectual enrichment. Bushnell was clearly marching to a different drummer than Plaunt.

The growing strength of the private station argument worried Plaunt, who met with Howe to discuss this point, but found him won over by the private station ideas. In a letter to Claxton, he said, "He is convinced that the powers of regulation and control should revert to the Department, and I was unable to dissuade him from this view. Clearly, Edwards has convinced him thus." In a note to Gladstone Murray, he added that Edwards "is not altogether to be trusted."

Howe's approach, of course, struck at the heart of the single system proposed by the Aird Commission, envisioned in the 1932 Broadcasting Act and at the centre of the Canadian Radio League's and Plaunt's desires for public broadcasting in Canada. Edwards drafted his own bill for Howe, incorporating the idea of slicing away the regulatory role from the new broadcasting body, a division the private stations had been seeking for four years. "This completely ignores the proposed aim of such a Corporation," Claxton said, "which is not only to broadcast a few programmes over a few stations but immediately to influence and control and ultimately operate and own all broadcasting in Canada. . . . The day of bringing that about is relatively far off but I do not think that we should give up the principle of ultimate public ownership and immediate public control now."

Nevertheless, Howe decided Edwards' bill, not the Plaunt-Claxton bill, would be presented to the special parliamentary committee formed to discuss the proposed legislation. Howe was new to Ottawa, however, and he quickly found himself politically blindsided by wily Plaunt and his friends.

J. S. Woodsworth was a member of the special parliamentary committee, and Plaunt made sure he knew of his clash with Howe. Woodsworth leaked the information to John Dafoe, as Plaunt knew he would. Dafoe, in turn, passed the information to Grant Dexter, the *Free Press* correspondent in Ottawa. Dexter contacted Woodsworth, read the proposed bill, and broke the story that key regulatory powers were going to be taken away from the new broadcasting organization and given to Howe's department.

Major newspapers of both Liberal and Conservative stripes picked up the story and attacked the idea of splitting the regulatory function away from the new broadcasting body. Plaunt himself attacked the idea in a *Saturday Night* article, saying it was "contradictory," "unworkable," and likely would lead to the death of public broadcasting. Privately, Plaunt said, "The publication of the draft was really a godsend." Howe didn't realize what had hit him and, amid the attacks, retreated, withdrawing his draft bill and replacing it with a "synopsis" for presentation to the special parliamentary committee.

Throughout the spring of 1936, the committee held twenty-five meetings and heard thirty-seven witnesses, including Plaunt and Hector Charlesworth, debated the "Mr. Sage" broadcasts, and exoriated the CRBC. Charlesworth was especially angered by Plaunt's submission, calling it "as deceptive a document as I have ever read. . . . A fantastic and erroneous account of our method of doing business. . . . Censorious and malicious." The committee also heard private broadcasters and advertisers who sought to disembowel public broadcasting so that the system owned and operated no stations at all and only offered programs for the commercial stations to carry.

The committee's first draft of its report endorsed the approach of Howe's "synopsis" in transferring regulatory powers to him. But, as usual in Ottawa, the combat and intrigue backstage was much more vivid than what was going on in public hearings. As he and Spry had at the time of the 1932 parliamentary committee hearings, Plaunt stirred up a whirlwind of letter writing, phone calling, and buttonholing to get support for public broadcasting. He arranged editorial support from newspapers, persuaded organizations to make representations to the committee and to the prime minister, provided questions to witnesses for committee members, especially Liberal Paul Martin, and pulled every lever he had to win support. In a letter to Gladstone Murray, he wrote of his wife "remarking bitterly that I had been home six days last month."

On one side of the war were the private broadcasters, the advertisers, and Howe and his department, and on the other side were Plaunt, the Radio League, several cabinet ministers, a large number of national organizations, unions, farm groups, religious leaders, and key editors and publishers such as Dafoe of the *Winnipeg Free Press* and Holy Joe Atkinson of the *Toronto Star*, both friends of the prime minister. But Plaunt's ace in the hole was Mackenzie King. He had to play the King card carefully, however, because of King's dislike of being pressured. But pressure was now needed.

When he found out the committee's first draft bill favoured Howe's position, Plaunt talked with King. Pickering remembers King telling him that the parliamentary committee was "off the rails." He says, "Mackenzie King thought it was going to develop along the lines of the Aird Report. Instead of bringing in the Aird Report, the minister was influencing it towards a commercial, privately owned orientation."

Plaunt gave King a copy of his testimony to the committee and later said it "was undoubtedly the crucial factor. After reading over our stuff, he sent word to the Committee that it was to be implemented which resulted in a first draft of the Committee's report being completely revamped. We want, he said, the Aird Report and this [Plaunt's testimony] is the Aird Report brought up to date."

Describing this battle in the shadows to Gladstone Murray, Plaunt said, "Despite his unequivocal support, there was nevertheless quite a backstage row. . . . The matter of divided control reared its head again, and again a row was on. Mr. King taking our position, Mr. Howe reluctant to give."

Since King did not want to confront Howe personally on the issue, he asked Pickering to get the committee quietly to change its position, reject Howe's, and accept the Aird concept of public broadcasting as championed by Plaunt. It was a typical King backdoor assignment, and Pickering admits, "I proceeded pretty surreptitiously . . . and I was able to influence the thinking of the committee." In this ticklish bit of politicking, Pickering worked closely with the committee chairman who, sensitive to King's desires, moved the committee members day by day, little by little, away from Howe toward Plaunt. Pickering succeeded because the committee heard Pickering's tongue but knew it was King's voice.

"The battle here is proceeding merrily," Plaunt told Murray in one letter, and, "Everything . . . is going beyond our wildest hopes," in another. By June, Plaunt was exultant. He told Murray, "King has come to consider broadcasting policy as a matter of major importance. . . . All in all, the situation, even for a super cautious like me, looks really very hopeful."

Finally, the committee unanimously supported keeping regulatory powers with the new CBC, while giving licensing and allocation of wavelengths to Howe's department. After a private meeting with King, Howe agreed to accept the committee's report, which largely followed Plaunt's proposals. Brooke Claxton called it a "ninety per cent victory." The law that followed formally brought the CBC into being and was supported by all parties in the House of Commons and most key newspapers in the country. A whole new era in public broadcasting was launched.

"It has been," a glowing Plaunt wrote to Murray in London, "an extraordinary experience of intrigue, bamboozling, publicizing – and worse – but it has been successful and very much worth the effort. . . . The whole sordid business . . . is certainly a tale to tell."

Former prime minister R. B. Bennett was oddly pessimistic about the future of the CBC, telling the House of Commons in mid-June, "The private interests . . . have determined that if it is within their power, this facility is not to function as a public enterprise. They have determined . . . to destroy this publicly owned facility." Bennett thought the new CBC would become simply a department of the government and that the head of the CBC would be "the tool of the government to do what he is told to do."

In his moment of glory, Plaunt didn't share that pessimism, but if he thought his troubles were over, he was wrong. Another confrontation with C. D. Howe loomed.

5

A Booze Problem for the CBC

The man Alan Plaunt was determined would run the CBC was Gladstone "Bill" Murray, the forty-three-year-old senior BBC executive who had played a key role in developing Canadian public broadcasting ever since he and Charles Bowman introduced Prime Minister Mackenzie King to a microphone at the BBC in London in 1926.

Murray had everything in Plaunt's view. He was a Canadian, born of a staunch Liberal family in British Columbia, educated at McGill University, and a Rhodes Scholar at Oxford. He was a sports hero, running the mile at four minutes and twenty-one seconds, and was a decorated First World War Royal Flying Corps ace, shot down once over no man's land. He became a major and was selected to drop over a German air base a wreath and a note reporting the shooting down of German air hero Baron von Richthofen. He was a world traveller, had worked for the League of Nations, had been a reporter for the *Montreal Herald* and Lord Beaverbrook's *Daily Express* in London, England, and was a pioneer BBC official, joining in 1924. A burly, handsome, and moustached *bon vivant*, Murray was bilingual, politically astute, a deadly poker player, an extraordinarily hard worker, and a man who desperately wanted to run the CBC.

The heavy smoking Murray was also, however, a heavy drinker, but it was a flaw Plaunt chose to overlook until much later. "More than any broadcasting executive in the English-speaking world," Plaunt said, "Major Murray possesses the combination of qualities and experience which would enable him to make public service broadcasting in Canada a success."

Murray had once had his eyes on replacing John Reith as head of the BBC, but had been entranced with the idea of running public broadcasting in Canada after he first talked to Graham Spry and Alan Plaunt in 1931. Since they had modelled most of their ideas on the BBC, they sought Murray's advice. They saw Murray as being Canada's Reith, a man who could meet the challenge of Canada's unique broadcasting environment with its endless geography and relentless American radio invasion. The BBC was only too happy to export its broadcasting model and allowed Murray to devote considerable time to Canadian broadcasting affairs. When the Canadian Radio League brought him to Canada to testify before the parliamentary radio committee in 1932, Murray not only impressed the MPs, but also Prime Minister Bennett. Murray had met privately with Bennett and other Conservative cabinet ministers, as well as Opposition party officials and many of the key Radio League supporters. Ned Corbett remembered one party at Alan Plaunt's home where Murray was fêted by Plaunt, Spry, Radio League supporters, and such budding Ottawa mandarins as Norman Robertson, a future senior deputy minister and prime ministerial adviser, Jack Pickersgill, a future powerful cabinet minister, and Norman Lambert, a close friend of Plaunt, and secretary of the National Liberal Federation.

Murray wowed Liberals and Conservatives alike with his knowledge of broadcasting, his verve, his charm, and his down-to-earth style. Bennett was so impressed that when he was in London in 1932, he discussed with Murray the new CRBC that had just been set up. Murray told Claxton that he had had "several characteristically fantastic interviews with R. B." who "was obviously in a muddle" about the CRBC. Bennett wanted Murray's advice on the future of the fledgling CRBC and asked him to come to Canada to study and report on how to "put the Commission on its feet." Murray, responding to what he called "stirring appeals to my patriotism and imperialism," agreed, and in the spring of 1933 set off on a three-month, cross-Canada study of the CRBC and Canadian broadcasting.

He wrote three reports, the first, a brief interim one suggesting some changes to the Broadcasting Act, which the government accepted. He sent his second report, which dealt with problems of the CRBC itself, not only to Bennett but also to Mackenzie King and J. S. Woodsworth. His final report was a twenty-seven-page *tour d'horizon* of Canadian radio that laid out a blueprint that bore much resemblance to the public broadcasting system Mackenzie King eventually accepted three years later in setting up the CBC. Murray's central concern was to make certain that the public broadcasting organization was utterly untainted by politics. He worried about the perception that the CRBC was politically partisan, and although he said he saw no evidence of this, he warned, "If this impression is not dispelled the Commission will hardly gain either the support or the independence essential to the success of the work." The commission, however, never did shake the impression of being partisan.

Murray urged the appointment of a general manager for the CRBC, which never happened. He proposed the broadcasting agency be divided into five regions of the Maritimes, Quebec, Ontario, the Prairies, and British Columbia, with regional directors in each one. He also proposed various program areas for the CRBC, including music, religion, and drama, and he urged the appointment of an all-party advisory committee. He spoke of the need to have public broadcasting managed "in efficient, business lines," and he also advocated a partnership between public and private radio in which private radio would play a much larger role than Plaunt envisioned. In this last idea lay the seeds of a future clash with Plaunt.

Bennett thanked Murray and put his report on the shelf, to be joined in the ensuing six decades by innumerable similar reports all largely saying much the same thing. The CRBC commissioners bitterly resented Murray's report and, according to Grant Dexter, "were inclined to think that Weir was Murray's spy or stool pigeon."

From London, Murray had watched the disintegration of the CRBC and, spurred on by his correspondence with Plaunt, his appetite to run Canadian public broadcasting increased. Bob Bowman, Charles

Bowman's son and friend of Murray and Plaunt, was working in London in the early 1930s and had numberless conversations with Murray about Canadian broadcasting. "Night after night we planned what we would do when the opportunity came," he later remembered.

From time to time as the 1930s rolled on, Murray's name came up in Parliament, government offices, and elsewhere as the possible head of Canadian radio. At one point there was a discussion in Parliament of whether he would come back to Canada for a salary of $15,000 to $20,000.

Murray, meanwhile, was climbing the BBC's executive ladder. He was made acting program controller and then put in charge of a number of BBC program areas, including all Empire broadcasting. "My prospects here have brightened a lot recently," he told Plaunt. But in a letter to Vincent Massey he said, "I would gladly sacrifice the definite prospect of the succession to Reith if I could get a chance to put public service broadcasting on its feet in Canada. . . . Without being boastful, I still think I could succeed in Canada where the others have failed."

Even before the 1935 election, Plaunt was confident that, given a Liberal victory and success in his campaign to create the CBC, Murray would get the job of running the new operation. He had already talked to Mackenzie King and concluded that King favoured Murray. "I am now very optimistic of our chances of getting a first rate organization with yourself in command of the executive," Plaunt wrote Murray a few days after the 1935 election. "Mr King, I think, at long last, has grasped the essentials of the problem. Above all, his prejudice with regard to your good self – I may as well be frank – appears to have been dispelled. Bowman had several quite long chats with him this summer and he both agreed on the set up and you as the logical Director-General." The apprehension Plaunt alluded to in his reference to King's "prejudice" referred to Murray's reputation as a heavy drinker. It was a reputation and a reality that endangered his candidacy and plagued his future.

At his first meeting with C. D. Howe after the Liberal win, Howe agreed Murray should run the new organization and suggested a salary of $15,000. Plaunt and Murray began a flood of letters and cables to each other. Plaunt instructed Murray, "Please forward immediately full and unblushing description [of] yourself and achievements." Murray responded enthusiastically with his biography and with ideas on the new broadcasting agency, its functions, and the people who should be on the board. "My dear Alan," he wrote in mid-November, "At the risk of conviction for counting the chickens prematurely, I cannot resist working on plans and schemes for Canadian radio." Increasingly confident of getting the job, Murray worried about the cost of servants in Ottawa. Plaunt reassured him, "The servant problem is not as desperate as you imagine. House maids around 20-30 a month, cooks, female, around 40."

But chickens were being counted too early, and Plaunt's ever-sensitive ear began to hear hints of an anti-Murray campaign by the same people who opposed public broadcasting. First, Plaunt heard that just after the election NBC president Merlin Aylesworth had sent an emissary to Ottawa to meet King, Howe, and others and present what Plaunt called "some fantastic proposal to take over Canadian broadcasting for the NBC." In London, Murray heard the same story from friends at CBS, which wanted to stop NBC for its own competitive reasons. The NBC emissary to Ottawa was Reginald Brophy, head of station relations, former manager of the Canadian Marconi station in Montreal, CFCF, and a man who, a few months later, would be at the centre of a battle with Murray and Plaunt.

Meanwhile, the private stations began lobbying for CFRB head and Canadian Association of Broadcasters president Harry Sedgewick to be the man chosen to run the CBC. They were fighting Plaunt and his friends on two fronts: trying to weaken any new broadcast organization and, at the same time, seeking to have whatever new agency emerged run by a private station man.

Plaunt pinpointed C. P. Edwards, the director of radio in Howe's Marine department and head of the government's radio branch since 1909, as leader of this campaign. "He is trying to spread the idea that Murray is holding out for too high a salary," Plaunt told friends. "I have no doubt that he is playing the double game of his friends the Rogers at CFRB . . . to get their man Sedgewick in as General Manager, if possible."

Ned Corbett also warned Plaunt about the lobby for Sedgewick, but when Plaunt sought counsel from John Dafoe he was told, "Don't worry." Dafoe knew King would never approve Sedgewick. In any event,

Sedgewick turned out to be only a stalking horse for the real danger to Murray, NBC executive Reginald Brophy. The thirty-six-year-old Brophy was dead set against Plaunt's approach to public broadcasting, strongly favouring the populist "good, wholesome entertainment" approach of the CRBC's Ernie Bushnell. Bushnell and Brophy were old drinking pals who had spent time travelling together, sipping rye from paper cups in various CPR lounge cars as they chugged across the country. Like Bushnell, Brophy was an outspoken enemy of everything Spry, Plaunt, and the Radio League advocated. Bushnell had once briefly thought of himself as the new CBC boss, and in a private memo he talked about having "at the helm a man with private radio experience . . . a man who understands the problems of the private station owner and who is willing at all times to lend a sympathetic ear." That description fit Sedgewick, Bushnell, and Brophy, but it was Brophy whom the opposition to Murray and Plaunt settled upon.

The two weapons they used against Murray were that he would try to foist onto Canadian airwaves highbrow, BBC-like programming and that he was a spendthrift and a drunk. With Edwards' support, they sought to torpedo Murray's candidacy in talks with Howe and Finance Minister Charles Dunning. Howe's earlier support for Murray began to weaken. By instinct, Howe favoured a Canadian with New York commercial broadcasting experience over a Canadian with a British public broadcasting background. "I don't think Howe ever really grasped what the concept of public broadcasting was," says Edward Pickering.

By spring 1936, the battle was on. Plaunt wrote Murray, "Brophy is actually putting on quite a lobby, but so are we." As part of his intense backstage lobbying, Plaunt encouraged editorials favourable to Murray. John Dafoe wrote in the *Winnipeg Free Press*, "Murray seems to be an almost ideal man for the position," and he characterized the Brophy campaign as "a sort of last charge" by private broadcasters. The *Ottawa Citizen* said that unless the new CBC general manager had a public service vision, Canadian broadcasting would "certainly pass into the United States orbit."

Even with this influential editorial support for Murray, Brophy was gaining ground, and Plaunt warned Brooke Claxton, "The worst of it is, that lobby is having a considerable measure of success. Howe appears to be 'sold' on Brophy (largely Edwards' influence), and he in turn sold Dunning."

Claxton wrote to his friend Labour Minister Norman Rogers, saying, "Brophy is a Marconi production who has always opposed national radio in Canada, having worked tooth and nail against it. . . . He has the commercial point of view."

"The situation is beginning to look very sinister," Plaunt wrote to Dafoe. Now King himself began to have new worries about Murray's drinking habit. Murray received another and unexpected blow when Howe asked the BBC representative in New York for his advice and, to Murray's astonishment and anger, the representative, Felix Green, urged that Brophy, not Murray, be appointed. Even J. F. B. Livesay, the general manager of the Canadian Press, had to be calmed down by Plaunt. "I have been able to convince Livesay about you," Plaunt wrote Murray. "He was carrying about 'certain prejudices' but I have dispelled them." Plaunt also persuaded Sir John Aird to come out in support of Murray, but another member of the original Aird Commission, Dr. Augustin Frigon, proved more difficult to convert. He initially announced he favoured Brophy, but later was persuaded to switch his support to Murray.

Stories began to circulate that Murray had spent $8,000 drinking his way across Canada when he was doing his broadcasting study in 1933. (He had been paid $7,200, most of it to compensate him for "loss of income" while in Canada.) Ned Corbett later told of Murray being drunk in Vancouver, Winnipeg, and elsewhere. When he was to make a speech at the Hotel Vancouver, Corbett said, "He just walked off. He didn't know where he was. . . . I don't think he ever drew a sober breath. He was drunk all the time." Plaunt admitted to Vincent Massey that "Murray actually was rather indiscreet during his 1933 visit to Ottawa Mr. King fears that he might prove unreliable."

Murray recognized the problem and told Plaunt, "Have noted the importance of dealing with the booze business and shall try to manoeuvre those you suggest." What Plaunt had suggested was that Murray solicit letters of support from British politicians and officials attesting to his sobriety. Meanwhile, Plaunt and Massey began their own campaign to minimize the damage of the accusation that Murray was an unreliable drunk. They persuaded senior British and Canadian political and diplomatic officials to send letters certifying Murray's reliability to the prime minister, Howe, Dunning, other cabinet ministers, and even the governor general. Dafoe telephoned King to tell him that "as a rule, Murray does not drink at all."

Plaunt himself wrote to the prime minister saying, "I have known Major Murray since 1931 and can say absolutely that drinking forms no part of the habit of his life." He attached a cable from Bob Bowman in London swearing that Murray had not touched a drink nor smoked for the past two years. Plaunt also wrote to Howe saying, "I wish to counteract certain false rumors which are being circulated about him. One of these rumors suggests that Murray is an habitual heavy drinker. I personally know absolutely that the suggestion has not a shred of basis." He again quoted Bowman's cable and labelled the accusation "malicious gossip."

It wasn't just malicious gossip to Ned Corbett, however, who later commented, "Having seen Gladstone Murray drunk, Reg Brophy would probably be a more stable type of person." Corbett made known his feelings to C. D. Howe, and Howe asked him to go to New York to see Brophy. Corbett did and was impressed. After another meeting with Howe, Corbett admitted to Plaunt that he admired Brophy. "Did you tell C. D. Howe that?" demanded Plaunt. "Yes, I had to tell him that," Corbett replied. "Oh, you fool!" cried Plaunt. "Don't you know what that guy would do? He'd sell out to the commercial interests right away."

Corbett warned that Howe "was deadly opposed to having Gladstone Murray," and Dafoe now advised Plaunt, "While Mr. King is in favour of Gladstone Murray the majority of his colleagues are not." Plaunt put much of the blame for Howe's attitude on C. P. Edwards. "Edwards continues to be a son of a bitch," Plaunt said. Grant Dexter was gloomy about Murray's chances. "Gladstone Murray seems to me to be fading out quickly," he wrote to Dafoe. "I have never known of such a case – where defamatory stories simply pile up against a man. This place is reeking with stories about how Murray drank himself unconscious while in Canada a few years ago."

At the end of June, Murray told Plaunt, "Whatever happens, I shall never be able to repay you for your efforts and sacrifice on my behalf."

A few weeks later, several cabinet ministers, including Dunning, visited London, and Plaunt arranged through High Commissioner Massey and one of his aides, Lester Pearson, for Murray to meet Dunning. "You should put on a show," Plaunt advised Murray. Later Murray told Plaunt, "I told him [Dunning] that I had never been guilty of such alcoholic excess as would cause public scandal or interfere with my work. . . . I told Dunning I had abandoned all alcohol two years ago and had no intention of resumption. This seemed to please him."

Murray admitted to Dunning that he had experienced "artificial exaltation" during his 1933 trip to Canada, but said it had been "grossly exaggerated." After what Dunning called a "brutally frank" conversation with Murray, Dunning was sufficiently impressed that he made a positive report to the cabinet. At the same time he tried to discourage Murray by telling him the job would pay only $10,000, not the $15,000 that Howe had mentioned the previous November. "I hope to Christ they do make it $15,000," a dispirited Murray wrote to Plaunt.

CPR president Beatty, who was still hoping for a major role in Canadian broadcasting for the CPR, also tried to discourage Murray when he met him in London. "He went out of his way to blacken the picture," Murray reported to Plaunt. "In his opinion, there was really no hope of success. . . . His chief purpose was to frighten me away at all costs." Plaunt asked his supporters to apply still more pressure on King and the cabinet. In a somewhat exasperated response to Plaunt's latest plea for help, Dafoe wrote back, "I am afraid I cannot do much more in the radio matter." Dafoe, in fact, wondered whether it might be better if someone other than Murray and Brophy were suggested for the job of running the CBC.

The most effective weapon that Plaunt had was King's fear of American domination of Canadian airwaves, and Plaunt played hard on that fear just as he, Spry, Herridge, and Finlayson had on R. B. Bennett's similar fear four years earlier. Plaunt said the CPR was plotting with American broadcasters to prevent public broadcasting in Canada and that they were determined to stop Murray's appointment.

In the end, King was worried more about Brophy's American links than he was about Murray's drinking. Plaunt told Murray that King "realizes to the full the sinister character and implications of the Brophy effort." King finally made it clear he wanted Murray but he had one proviso: a majority of the cabinet had to endorse Murray as well.

"Delicate game, this," Plaunt wrote to Murray in early August, and again persuasion and pressure were applied to key cabinet ministers. In the end, Plaunt had more staying power than Brophy. Towards the end of summer, the cabinet finally agreed to appoint Murray, although not unanimously. Once again Howe had lost to Plaunt. He continued to hold Brophy in high esteem and, in 1952, hired Brophy as deputy minister of defence production.

Plaunt wrote to Murray, assessing his victory, "That was perhaps the best job of salesmanship which I ever hope to achieve." King, too, was pleased with himself, writing in his diary, "More satisfied than ever we took the right step in securing Gladstone Murray."

Murray was exultant. On September 8, 1936, he wrote Plaunt, "It is your splendid tenacity and courage that have seen this triumph." Three days later, he cabled, "Many thanks. Stop. Congratulations are yours for tenacity, skill unprecedented. Stop." The next day he sent Plaunt yet another cable. "Krug nineteen nineteen to you in jeroboams with a magnum . . . on the side. Stop. Splendid news. Stop." Plaunt's and Murray's mutual admiration would, however, erupt in a shocking explosion of antagonism within three years.

While the Murray-Brophy fight had been going on, a no less important but much less tempestuous choice was being made for the chairman and the board of directors of the CBC. Plaunt wanted Dafoe as chairman, but Dafoe wasn't interested, just as he had earlier rejected the prime minister's invitation to become the Canadian minister to Washington. The chairman of the CBC would be Leonard W. Brockington, whose glowing imagery and golden throat made him Canada's best-known after-dinner speaker. A prominent lawyer and a cultured, witty, and tough forty-eight-year-old Welshman, Brockington had been recommended for the CBC board by Plaunt and championed by Dafoe. "Dafoe simply got in touch with Mackenzie King and said, "Here's your man! So Brock went," said Ned Corbett.

Brockington had worked in the same Calgary law firm as R. B. Bennett, but was regarded more as a Liberal, although not an overt one. There was, however, a distinct Liberal hue to the full board, which included several members who had been active Liberal politicians while none was known to be associated with any other party. It was, in fact, much more of a political body than Bennett's CRBC. Members included René Morin as vice-chairman, a Montreal banker and onetime Liberal MP; Gen. Victor Odlum, a bond dealer from Vancouver who had been a Liberal member of the British Columbia legislature and was one of the Radio League's original supporters; Nellie McClung of Victoria, pioneer feminist, fiction writer, and a former Liberal member of the Alberta legislature; Col. Wilfrid Bovey of McGill; J. W. Godfrey, a Halifax lawyer; N. L. Nathanson of Toronto, president of Famous Players; Rev. Alexandre Vachon from Laval University; and Alan Plaunt. While the nine-member board was sharply political, it generated little opposition and in its early years was the most prestigious and the best board the CBC ever had.

The board member most knowledgeable about broadcasting clearly was Plaunt. He became the central driving force of the board, working closely with Murray in proposing staff members and with Brockington in renewed battles for CBC expansion against the formidable C. D. Howe.

The board's first job was to choose a general manager who, in truth, had already been chosen by the cabinet. But the ever-cautious Plaunt again revved up his lobbying engine to make certain of Murray's appointment. "I had taken steps to make damn sure there would be no slip up at the last ditch," Plaunt later told Murray, and so the Canadian from the BBC was, at long last, the general manager of the CBC at a salary of $13,000.

The man appointed as Murray's deputy was Dr. Augustin Frigon, a member of the Aird Commission. Donald Manson, who had been secretary of the Aird Commission, was named secretary of the board, Frigon assumed responsibility for all French-language programming, and Ernie Bushnell was put in charge of all English-language programming, his philosophical misfit with public broadcasting being offset by his talent and friendliness. Austin Weir, who had been fired by the CRBC, was brought back as commercial manager. Charles Bowman's son Bob was hired by Murray to be in charge of special broadcasts.

One man Plaunt tried to persuade to take on the job of public relations head for the CBC was Lester Pearson. Reporting to Pearson on a conversation with his CBC colleagues about the ideal candidate to run CBC public relations, Plaunt wrote shortly after the CBC began, "We are agreed that you are such a one if you can be tempted to take the job." At the time, Pearson was a senior officer at the Canadian High Commission in London, and he seriously considered Plaunt's proposal. Although he was tempted, especially with Plaunt's hints of future high office at the CBC, Pearson in the end rejected it, largely because the pay was not high enough. A year later, Gladstone Murray tried to entice Pearson to join the CBC as his deputy in Western Canada, but again Pearson declined. Given his influential friends and his talent, had he accepted the job, Pearson might well have become president of the CBC instead of prime minister of Canada.

With a board of directors and a senior staff largely committed to Alan Plaunt's broadcasting ideas (with the exception of Bushnell), the young activist idealist and nationalist had finally achieved what he and Graham Spry had talked about in a Hull café six years before.

There remained one awkwardness, however, and that was Hector Charlesworth. Throughout all of the frenetic manoeuvring by Plaunt, Murray, Howe, and Brophy, Charlesworth and the CRBC had been lurching through their final days. The CBC came into existence on November 2, 1936, and the last CRBC meeting was held in Ottawa mid-afternoon on October 30, as a dispirited Charlesworth thanked his secretarial staff and concluded his and the CRBC's public life in a twenty-minute meeting.

Aside from the legacy of a hesitant and controversial start for public broadcasting, the CRBC left behind for the future CBC a rich residue of broadcasting talent which included a future president, J. Alphonse Ouimet, who had been hired by the CRBC as a "Class II" radio engineer at $2,000 a year; two future key vice-presidents, news anchor and announcer Charles Jennings and Herbert "Bud" Walker, a handsome young announcer hired at $32.30 a week; a future CBC general manager, Ernie Bushnell; a future chief engineer, Gordon Olive; a future Quebec region commercial manager, J. A. Dupont; and creative stars such as band leader Mart Kenney; hockey sportscaster Foster Hewitt; announcer J. Frank Willis; singer, executive, and future war correspondent, Stanley

Maxted; musical director Geoffrey Waddington; drama director Rupert Lucas; and many other future senior CBC executives.

As for itself, the CRBC had been doomed by Bennett's failure to match rhetorical support with financial and policy support, and by its own political ineptness, its failure to generate a supportive constituency, and its administrative chaos. Its national programming had risen from two hours a week in early 1933 to six hours a day, although only at night and on Sunday afternoons. Programs were heard over its handful of owned stations and about fifty private stations on which it leased time. Even though faltering and tentative, the CRBC at least had begun national public broadcasting.

Charlesworth himself wanted to stay in a senior role at the CBC, and he claimed both King and Howe had promised him as much. In his autobiography, Charlesworth quoted King as saying, "Charlesworth was brought from Toronto to take charge of broadcasting. He has done a good job, and his services should be retained." It's hard to imagine how King could have that attitude after the "Mr. Sage" affair and Plaunt's assault, but Charlesworth nevertheless was confident of working for the CBC in "an important capacity."

He was still on the payroll when CBC chairman Brockington called Charlesworth into his office on November 4, two days after the CBC was formally established, and fired him. "A bolt from the blue," Charlesworth said. He argued that Howe had assured him of a role in the CBC, but Brockington said Howe had no right to make such a promise. Brockington did say, however, that he would ask King to do "something handsome for me," Charlesworth recalled.

"Then I am not to consider myself an outcast," Charlesworth said.

"Charlesworth, you must not speak like that. You are to consider yourself a great public servant on furlough."

"But off the payroll," Charlesworth responded with a feeling of betrayal and humiliation.

Later he talked to Howe who told him, "I don't know what to make of 'Brock.' I never saw such a change come over a man. . . . Wait till I see the prime minister."

Charlesworth asked Howe for two years' salary in compensation for his firing, and he said Howe agreed that this was "not unreasonable." In the end, he got only one year's salary, and he said, "Mr. King, when it was all over, expressed to me his deep personal regret."

Ruminating later about his dismissal, Charlesworth blamed Ontario Liberal Premier Mitch Hepburn and Alan Plaunt. As editor of *Saturday Night*, Charlesworth had called Hepburn "a rather wild-eyed young radical." Hepburn was outraged and threatened revenge. A few years later, Hepburn accused Charlesworth of trying to keep him off the air. "Hector Charlesworth," he said, "is the most contemptible of the Tories I have ever known." Charlesworth said that Hepburn warned he would "have my head on a silver salver" when the Liberals took power in Ottawa. With the 1935 Liberal election victory, the new CBC board caved in to Hepburn's threat that he would undermine the CBC unless Charlesworth were fired, Charlesworth said.

With much justification, Charlesworth also blamed Plaunt and his supporters not only for his dismissal, but for the abolition of the CRBC. "It was this group," he said, "with the collusion of some hostile officials, who foisted on Mr. Howe the new set up and lobbied it through the Commons." The CBC was, he said, "a Frankenstein."

6

Birth Pains

The CBC began on November 2, 1936, with a staff of 132, including 10 producers and 14 announcers, and six hours a day of network programming reaching 49 per cent of the country. A million Canadian homes had radios, but most were tuned in to the sixty-seven private stations or to American stations. Public broadcasting, which had only eight owned and leased stations, clearly was greater in rhetoric than reality. Brockington, Plaunt, and the CBC board's first priority was to get more powerful CBC stations. It would be a major battle.

Two days after the CBC was born and a few hours after he had fired Hector Charlesworth, Brockington took to the airwaves to promise an increase in the hours of broadcasting and an increase in the power and number of CBC stations. Spelling out the purpose of the new CBC, he said, "If the radio is not a healing and reconciling force in our national life, it will have failed of its higher purpose. If Canadian radio makes no lasting contribution to a better understanding between the so-called French Canadian and the so-called English Canadian, between the East and the West . . . then we shall have faltered our stewardship."

Brockington and his board devised a plan for twelve hours of daily network programming and the building of 50,000-watt stations in Ontario and Quebec, with additional powerful stations in the Maritimes and the Prairies. With a new transmitter in Vancouver, this would bring the CBC to about 85 per cent of the population. All this could be done on an annual revenue of $5.6 million and a $500,000 loan to begin the building program, altogether about four times as much money as the CRBC had been getting. The money, the CBC board said, would come from licence fees, government subsidies, and "considerably more commercial broadcasts than at present." Brockington also said all requests for higher power from private stations must be denied. His objective was to keep the private stations strictly local and make the CBC a regional and national network.

When C. D. Howe saw the plan, he hit the roof. Mackenzie King's aide, Edward Pickering, says, "Howe was a hands-on guy. He wanted to run the place." In a four-page letter to Brockington, Howe said the CBC should concentrate solely on making programs, not on improving its broadcasting facilities. Besides, he said, the government didn't have the extra money the CBC wanted. Howe complained bitterly that his earlier advice to the board to develop programs not stations had been "completely disregarded." "I regret to note," he said, "that my discussion with the Board . . . in which I outlined government policy toward broadcasting, left no visible impression on your plans. . . . I sincerely hope your Board will face realities. . . . Efforts are not being directed along practical lines."

Brockington shot back a seven-page letter saying Howe's earlier admonition to the board had not been ignored. "You are mistaken about any such disregard," he said. "I was instructed to write to you not because your remarks were unheeded, but because they were received with attention and astonishment. . . . Any general policy upon such a foundation would constitute a surrender in which we would not wish to participate." Brockington said Howe's views "do not represent the opinion of the government which appointed us. They certainly do not reflect our conception of our duties."

In Brockington's letter was a clear threat of mass resignation by the board, which astounded Howe but which Brockington felt was likely a winning tactic. His belief was reinforced by a report from Alan Plaunt, who had earlier briefed a sympathetic Prime Minister King about the confrontation with Howe. In a note to Brockington, Plaunt reported, "If in the final analysis you and I are prepared to resign . . . we can get what we want if we play our cards carefully."

Howe discussed the clash with King and began backing away. "The correspondence between us has taken a turn that I am sure neither of us really desire," he wrote Brockington in late January 1937. "Your Board evidently has some doubts as to my interest in public ownership. I am as much interested in this as anyone . . . I feel that we can clear the air completely if you and I can sit down quietly and explore the whole position in detail."

In the end, Howe agreed to the building of the two 50,000-watt stations in Ontario and Quebec, but he asked for a delay in the construction of the Maritimes and Prairies stations. By the end of 1937, the powerful Ontario and Quebec stations were on the air, and after further efforts by Howe to delay the building of the other stations, and again after Plaunt and Brockington sought and got backdoor support from King, these two were also on the air by mid-1939. A decade after the Aird Report, Canada had finally achieved its recommendations for a chain of high-powered public broadcasting stations.

There was, however, yet another battle looming with Brockington and Plaunt against Howe. Plaunt's *bête noire*, the director of radio in Howe's department, C. P. Edwards, advised Howe to overrule the CBC's refusal to grant high-power increases to the private stations. Plaunt again sought support from Mackenzie King via his friend in King's office, Edward Pickering. Howe had been attracted to Edwards' idea, but in light of the strong position of the CBC and probably a private word from King, he agreed to increases of only 1,000 watts for the private stations, a fraction of what they had been demanding.

By mid-summer of 1937, much of the battle was over. Howe wrote to Brockington, "I sincerely trust our frank and full discussion at our last meeting will clear the air in the matter of relations between the Board and the Government. It seems undesirable and unnecessary that there should be any friction between the two."

It had been an extraordinary test of wills between Plaunt and Brockington and Howe, and Howe had lost every encounter, an astonishing outcome for such a tough-minded powerhouse. He soon would be known as the Minister of Everything in King's government, but he failed to match the cunning of Brockington and Plaunt. "It was probably the boldest and most severe rebuff Howe ever received in public life without having its donor's head on a platter in return," wrote Howe biographers Robert Bothwell and William Kilbourn.

Paying for more stations and more programs, however, forced the CBC to seek an increase from two to three dollars in the licence fee and to carry more commercials than the CRBC ever had. This planned increase in advertising frightened Canadian newspaper owners. Graham Spry and Alan Plaunt had, from the beginning of their campaign for public broadcasting, wooed and won broad newspaper support. Plaunt now feared this support was in danger. The newspaper urged both the licence fee increase and additional government subsidies in expectation that the CBC's commercial revenue would be kept at a low level – perhaps a maximum of $250,000 a year. The government, however, raised the licence fee only to $2.50 and that meant the CBC needed commercial revenue of about $500,000.

The newspaper publishers were outraged and denounced the CBC both for its advertising and for carrying an increasing number of sponsored American radio programs. After talking with Arthur Partridge, general manager of the Canadian Daily Newspaper Association, a worried Alan Plaunt wrote, "The newspapers supported the establishment of the Corporation and Mr. Murray's appointment on the grounds that they believed public service broadcasting would be increased and advertising decreased. He [Partridge] intimates that a commercial policy will result in the Corporation losing its most important backlog of support."

In a letter to Canadian Press general manager J. F. B. Livesay, Plaunt said the CBC's long-term goal was to reduce commercials. Gladstone Murray sought to reassure publishers that the CBC would not go heavily into commercials, telling a parliamentary committee in 1938, "If we want a million dollars net for advertising revenue, we would so undermine our other functions that we would be indistinguishable from an ordinary profit-making network. . . . My own personal view is that we have got really too much advertising now."

Back in 1932, Graham Spry had estimated advertising revenue for public radio of $950,000 a year in a statement to a parliamentary committee, and the Aird Commission had foreseen "indirect" advertising revenue of $700,000.

Brockington was less agitated by commercials than were Plaunt and Murray, saying later that advertising helped provide many "highly entertaining programs," established good relations with American networks, and helped fund non-commercial programs.

The publishers were not appeased, however, and in early 1938, many of them began a furious editorial assault on the CBC. The Montreal *Gazette* denounced a "flood of American advertising over the air highly injurious and dangerous to those in Canada who are engaged legitimately in the advertising business, a business which the Corporation appears to be determined to destroy." The *Quebec Chronicle-Telegraph* said the CBC, in defending itself, was using the argument "some crook or woman of the street might use equally well to excuse their degradation; their means being insufficient to gratify their vices, selling their honor." *The Financial Post* accused the CBC of endangering Canada by diverting money from newspapers "which are the bulwarks of national unity in this country."

Brockington picked up the national unity theme in a counterargument before the parliamentary radio committee in the spring of 1938. "If radio in Canada had not been nationalized, the great American chains would have dominated Canada," he said. "If tomorrow the CBC ceased to exist every private station in Canada . . . would be delighted to be the member of an American chain . . . [and] there might be a disastrous Americanization of Canada by way of the air."

The anti-CBC editorial campaign eventually petered out, but it marked the end of the powerful newspaper-public broadcasting alliance that Spry and Plaunt had constructed.

As the newspaper assault waned, confrontation came from another direction – private radio revived its attack on the CBC for being a competitor for commercials and audience and at the same time being judge and jury on radio regulations. The stations complained bitterly about the CBC regulations that limited their power and barred mention of prices in radio ads. There was also a demand for a private radio network.

Brockington said no to everything and went on the offensive, criticizing private local stations for not broadcasting more of the CBC's non-commercial programs, urging establishment of more CBC stations, and proposing a limit on the profits of private stations. He accused the private radio critics of attacking "the Canadian Broadcasting Corporation in an effort to increase their profits."

Gladstone Murray, who had sought friendly relations with the private stations, played good cop to Brockington's bad cop. He denied that "the CBC is inspired by a ruthless determination to extinguish these stations.... Private radio stations that are doing good jobs in their communities – and there are lots of them – are an important part of the pattern of Canadian broadcasting."

"An important part" they were, but private stations no longer dominated the airwaves as they had before the CBC. In November 1936, when the CBC began, the private stations' total power was 65,000 watts against the CBC's 14,000 watts, but by mid-1939, the tables were dramatically reversed with the CBC at 213,000 watts, a fifteen-fold increase, against 74,000 watts for the private stations.

In an article about the complaints against the CBC, the American entertainment industry newspaper *Variety* commented, "The CBC has apparently won an easy victory over the private stations. Further strength has been given [to] the position of the CBC in recent weeks through the lessening and almost complete cessation of newspaper attacks due in large measure to the discovery ... that loss of revenue to the CBC network by national advertisers would be inconsequential." *Variety* concluded, "From the viewpoint of radio listeners, the CBC [is] providing more abundant, more diversified and more complete radio entertainment than possible for private interests in this country to furnish."

The greatest improvement in Canadian radio was in Quebec, where French-language programming had previously been limited in most parts of the province and almost non-existent in others. Through the efforts of CRBC commissioner Thomas Maher, outlets had been established in Montreal, Quebec City, and Chicoutimi, although program hours were limited. Even in the early days of the CBC, the Montreal station carried both English and French programs, and network programs out of Montreal were announced in both languages.

In late 1937, the CBC built the new high-power station in Montreal which became the heart of a French-language network reaching almost all Quebeckers. The CBC French network rapidly developed its own music, drama, and comedy stars with variety shows, soap operas, and history programs reflecting life in Quebec. English programming in Montreal continued on the old CBC station, and for the most part the French language on the English network disappeared. From that moment on, CBC broadcasting in Canada speedily developed into its two solitudes.

Before that happened the CBC was assailed for its bilingual programming. "We much prefer U.S. programmes, rotten as many of them are, to the bilingual broadcasts of the CBC" editorialized the *Tribune* of Stouffville, Ontario. "There is more French than ever on programmes in regions where there is no excuse for it."

The CBC was accused, as the CRBC had been, of trying to foist bilingualism onto the country. Gladstone Murray fell into a political hellhole when, in a 1937 Montreal speech, he said, "Broadcasting can help to make the whole of Canada bilingual, to make available to the Canadian citizen of the future the culture, literature and thought of both parent languages. This is not a vague aspiration; it reflects a definite and carefully considered policy."

Murray was attacked in Parliament by the prime minister, who said Murray's speech had not been approved by the government and that he made it on his own. Former prime minister R. B. Bennett said Murray "certainly should be dismissed at once."

Back at the CBC, however, Murray was praised for his leadership. The organizational chaos and helter-skelter programming of the CRBC had given way to the increasingly structured and creative programming by the CBC. Under Murray's exuberant guidance, more producers, program organizers, writers, and performers were hired, and specialized programming began in drama, music, light entertainment features, and talks. Network programming jumped from six hours a day to twelve in the CBC's first year and to about sixteen hours within five years. The staff tripled by 1939, and all the new high-power stations meant that more than 85 per cent of Canadians could hear the CBC. Within the first five years, the total number of programs jumped from 8,000 under the CRBC to 40,000 local, regional, and network programs on the CBC. Altogether it was an astonishing spurt of activity and creativity.

The most popular programs carried on the Canadian airwaves, however, continued to come from the United States. The CBC brought in Bing Crosby's "Kraft Music Hall," "The Jack Benny Show," "Fibber McGee and Molly," "Charlie McCarthy," "Lux Radio Theatre," and others, which not only attracted big audiences but, since they were sponsored, also brought in considerable advertising revenue. Justifying far more commercials and American programs than the CRBC ever dared try, Brockington told an admiring parliamentary committee, "We get first of all a revenue; secondly, we get a high standard of entertainment; and thirdly we get the occupation of broadcast time." The CRBC could never have gotten away with this rationale, but times had changed and, for the moment, the CBC could do no wrong.

The most popular Canadian program continued to be Foster Hewitt's Saturday night hockey games from Toronto, which had rapidly become deeply imbedded in the nation's psyche. Hewitt's nationwide fame was rivalled by the stars of "The Happy Gang." "A small instrumental group ... and they weren't too bad," said CBC program executive George McTaggart when he pushed the Gang onto the network. Their signature sign on of "Knock Knock. Who's there? It's the Happy Gang! Well, come on in" was an instant success and eagerly awaited every weekday afternoon. For half an hour, corny jokes, lively music, and a frenetic, happy talk show lifted the spirits of a nation heading out of the Depression and into a war. Gang members over the years included Bobby Gimby, Bert Niosi, Bob Farnon, Kathleen Stokes, Eddie Allan, Jimmy Namaro, and Herb May. The slaphappy Gang was ruled by pianist Bert Pearl, a frazzled little iron man in his twenties known as the head Gangster, who always chirped "Remember, keep happy!" However, he didn't follow his own advice and was called "the unhappiest man in radio," always fearing he was going to crack up, which he eventually did. Unease permeated the Gang behind the scenes, prompting June Callwood to write in a *Maclean's* article "'The Happy Gang' has one outstanding peculiarity. When it's not on the air, it isn't happy."

There may have been jealousies and backbiting off the air, but "The Happy Gang" delighted Canadians from 1937 to 1959, leaving a legacy of musical joy and laughter across the nation rivalled later only by Wayne and Shuster. Three decades after their heyday, Bert Pearl and the Gang drew 20,000 fans at a special reunion show at Toronto's CNE.

The game show "Treasure Trail" also became a long-running Canadian hit, giving away prizes to listeners and contestants, and for a time it was right behind "Charlie McCarthy" in popularity. CBC stardom also came to a fifteen-year-old future Hollywood comic, Vancouver's Alan Young.

Seventy per cent of the first year's CBC programming was music: symphony orchestras, operas, chamber music, and popular music. The Toronto Proms were broadcast from Varsity Arena, as were summer concerts from the chalet atop Montreal's Mount Royal. Within a few years, music programming was down to 50 per cent, as other programs were developed, and as the years went by, it kept sinking. The drama department was formed in the spring of 1938, and, with Rupert Lucas in charge, 350 plays poured onto the air over the next four years, heavy on Shakespeare but including many Canadian writers, too. Lucas established acting cells in Toronto, Montreal, Vancouver, and Winnipeg to provide actors for radio dramas. Even more drama was aired on the CBC French network, averaging nineteen hours a week in the early years of Radio-Canada, including French classical plays, portraits of Quebec life, and a dramatization of the life of Sir Wilfrid Laurier.

In orchestrating the programming, Gladstone Murray set a dizzying pace, and he complained to Frigon about overworking. CBC board member Nellie McClung said, "He is one of the hardest working men I have ever seen and I am worried about him. He looks so tired and worn." Murray not only had to build a network, but he also had to wade through a flood of program ideas from hundreds of would-be producers and performers.

Among the most insistent were quacks, crystal ball-gazers, tea-leaf readers, mystics, handwriting analysts, and astrologists who pedalled miracle cures and fortune telling. There was the Great King Solomon from Montreal who urged Murray to "Let King Solomon's magnetic and prophetic power relieve you"; Madam Carmen from Winnipeg, "Your Fortune Telling Madam"; and Koram from Calgary, who billed himself as Radio's Voice of Destiny and who offered Murray "hundreds of letters proving that the advice that I gave proved beneficial." The most persistent of all was Astrolite from Toronto, a man named C. Mervin Lewis who sent thirty scripts to Murray and for years bombarded not only the CBC general manager, but also members of the CBC board, cabinet ministers, and members of Parliament trying to get on the air. But Murray rejected them all.

In trying to reach Canadians with Canadian programming, popularity, while important, was secondary to quality. "We are not concerned with popularity," Leonard Brockington told the 1938 parliamentary committee, "We are concerned with doing our duty."

For Brockington and Plaunt, "duty" meant programs to educate as well as entertain and their ideas were shared by most of the CBC board. "Radio is the greatest university in the world," said Nellie McClung. An old Radio League veteran, Ned Corbett, now director of the Canadian Association for Adult Education, was commissioned to do a report on how the CBC could develop school broadcasting. Educational programming had been his priority since his pioneering broadcast days at the University of Alberta's Edmonton station, CKUA, in the late 1920s, and in 1938, working with provincial departments of education, he developed a plan for the CBC to produce both network and regional daily school broadcasts. School broadcasting had been around on a hit-and-miss basis on private stations for more than a decade, but with Corbett's plan more elaborate programs of talks, music, and dramatized history began. Mary Grannon, a young Fredericton school teacher, who had been reading children's stories on CFNB Fredericton for four years, brought her "Just Mary" program to the CBC in 1938 and continued for more than two decades.

Farm broadcasting also began in the CBC's early years. Radio had ended the isolation of life on the farm by bringing the world into the parlour and onto the tractor. By the mid-1930s, more than one-third of all radio sets in Canada were on farms. Orville Shugg, a young farmer in southwestern Ontario who had organized meetings for the New Canada Movement, idolized Plaunt and was inspired by his public broadcasting ideas. Shugg saw radio as a way of giving farmers market information, reports on new agricultural techniques, and news of what was happening in the farm community. He was impressed with Plaunt's activist style and he was amused when Plaunt once organized the sheep on his farm. Plaunt noticed the sheep straggling aimlessly in all directions in a field when they were supposed to be heading back to the farm. Suddenly, he took after them. He began, Shugg said, "whooping at the top of his voice and flailing his arms. The sheep looked up, startled, and then with one accord, turned and bolted down the road for home with bobbing rumps telegraphing their alarm." It was a farmyard version of how Plaunt had organized the lobby for the CBC.

Within days of the CBC's beginning, Shugg sent off a four-page proposal for farm programming to Gladstone Murray. Murray liked the idea and told Shugg he wanted him to start work with the CBC at the beginning of 1937. But months went by with no further word from Murray. "I said to hell with it! and forgot about it," Shugg remembers. Two years later out of the blue, Ernie Bushnell called Shugg to ask him to produce a fifteen-minute farm program on the CBC's Toronto station. Such a program had been started on the French network the year before, and Shugg's job was to develop farm broadcasting across the rest of the country. He started work on February 8, 1939, and had a noontime program on the air for Ontario within two weeks. By June, he had organized a daily program for the Maritimes and, by September, one for the Prairies. A year later, he had set up a program for British Columbia. To give more time for airing market and production information, Shugg lengthened the program to half an hour, and hoping to educate and inform through drama, he created an eight-minute daily soap opera about a farm family called "The Craigs" in Ontario, "The Gillans" in the Maritimes, "The Jacksons" on the Prairies, and "The Carsons" in British Columbia. The show became highly popular, a valuable training ground for Canadian actors, and a rich source of easily absorbed information for farmers.

Shugg reached back to his and Plaunt's days of organizing farmers for another program idea which became "The National Farm Radio Forum." "A sophisticated extension of the old 'New Canada Movement,'" said Shugg. The idea originated at Macdonald College in Quebec and was developed by Ned Corbett and the Canadian Association for Adult Education in consultation with farm leaders. A young McGill University graduate, Neil Morrison, who later became head of the CBC public affairs department, helped prepare the programs, which began in 1941. For a quarter of a century on Mondays at 8:30 P.M., hundreds of thousands of Canadians sat down to listen to a discussion of a contemporary social or economic issue, many listening in groups. The idea was listener participation, and there were more than 1,600 groups organized across the country, each with a secretary who sent in reports of their post-program discussions to a provincial office which, in turn, summarized the reports for "The National Farm Radio Forum" office. There was a weekly "Farm Forum" newspaper and study material was distributed to the groups before every program. The program was honoured by UNESCO and copied by many other countries. With the success of this series, and spurred by public affairs department head Morrison, in 1943 the CBC, again in co-operation with Ned Corbett's group, developed a similar but more controversial program dealing with broader issues beyond agriculture, including politics. It was called "Citizens' Forum," and it, too, had a long, successful, and occasionally pyrotechnical career.

Other new CBC programs that grew out of the sense of duty Brockington spoke of included a series called "Night Shift," celebrating working Canadians from a lighthouse keeper in Chebucto Head, Nova Scotia, to a worker in a Quebec pulp mill. There were such programs as "Our National Parks" and "I Cover the Waterfront" from Vancouver. There were talks, book reviews, and roundtable discussions. The Dominion Bureau of Statistics provided "A Fact a Day" after the nightly CBC newscast, which was read by Charles Jennings and prepared by the Canadian Press.

But it was special coverage of major events that captured the listeners' attention most sharply, including in the CBC's first year, the abdication of King Edward VIII and the coronation of King George VI, which Mackenzie King felt was handled by the CBC in a "magnificent way." The May 1937 coronation began at 5:00 A.M. EST and continued uninterrupted until 10:50 P.M. that night, with BBC coverage supplemented with CBC programs from across the country to mark the occasion. King was pleased, too, with the CBC's live coverage of his speeches and the speech from the throne, seeing in it a fulfilment of his enthusiastic forecast after the 1927 Diamond Jubilee broadcast from Parliament Hill that radio could prove to be a vital tool in developing national unity and public interest in important issues.

The prime minister's greatest program joy was the CBC's coverage of the 1939 Canadian Royal Tour by the King and Queen. His affection for the royal couple was outweighed only by his recognition of the political value of being seen and photographed with them as they travelled the country, especially in view of the federal election coming in 1940. In addition, with war clouds gathering in Europe, the prime minister felt it important to provide a demonstration of Canadian affection for the King and Queen.

The *Empress of Australia* dropped anchor at Quebec City on a sunny morning in May 1939 as a quarter-million Quebeckers watched the King and Queen begin their month-long tour out to Victoria and back to Halifax. Broadcasting the tour was the most complicated radio coverage that had ever been put together anywhere in the world, a massive feat of technical intricacy with ninety-one programs and leap-frogging production teams led by Ernie Bushnell that were always in place when the royal couple arrived.

Although he demanded massive coverage of the tour, the prime minister rejected the CBC's request for an extra $100,000 for technical and travel expenses. Initially he refused to provide any extra funds, but then he reluctantly agreed to $50,000.

The travelling teams included Bob Bowman and Frank Witters, Ted Briggs and Charles Jennings. Their gushing commentaries, stirring patriotism, and quotations from Shakespeare and Kipling all gave a reverential tone to the coverage. The commentators had pre-tour schooling on proper conduct, pronunciation, and procedures and traditions, and were advised by the BBC that "the King likes to be faced with the minimum of microphones. He always likes to talk standing." The broadcasters were concerned that the King's stammer might mean that on occasion he would not be able to finish a speech. "When he spoke," Bowman recalled, "I had to be nearby and ready to switch to a stand-by in case he broke down. He never did. . . . I used to watch the Queen while he was speaking. . . . She would be saying every word for the King and when he started to stammer, she would be trying to say it for him."

In mid-July, after an exhilarating but exhausting month of cross-country travel and an almost overdose on pomp and ceremony, their Majesties and the CBC commentators and technicians straggled into Halifax for the last stop. On a sunny early evening, amid hoots and toots and bells and whistles, the royal couple departed from Canada. The King stood on the deck of the *Empress of Britain* smoking a cigarette with the Queen beside him, waving. Perhaps the only embarrassment in the entire tour came during the farewell broadcast when the announcer described the Queen's white outfit as the ship moved away from the dock. Without indicating that he had switched to talking about the ship, he continued, ". . . and now she is turning toward us her broad beautiful white stern."

The tour had been a broadcasting triumph, the greatest up to then in radio history. Much of the programming had been carried not only on the CBC but also on the BBC and networks around the world.

The public applause for the royal tour coverage helped offset some of the brickbats hurled at the CBC on an issue which traced back a decade – religious views on the air. The Aird Commission in 1928 had been set up as a response to attacks on Roman Catholics by Jehovah's Witnesses; now, in 1937, it was Catholics versus Protestants. A program on the Protestant view on birth control broadcast by CFRB, Toronto, by Rev. Morris Zeidman, director of the Protestant Radio League, was banned by the CBC because it was considered too controversial. What made it worse for many Protestant groups was the fact that the fiery denunciations by the head of the Radio League of St. Michael's, Father Charles Lanphier, heard on the CBC, were not similarly banned. In a House of Commons debate on this issue, C. D. Howe said, "Obviously it is the duty of the broadcasting corporation to determine the character of the program and I think the first test . . . must be whether it gives offence to any part of the population."

A few months later, the CBC board banned from the air any abusive comment on any race, religion, or creed. Zeidman and Lanphier continued their radio feud, however, and the CBC finally ordered both off the air near the end of 1937. That set off another wave of protest, and thousands of letters poured into the offices of the prime minister, Howe, and the CBC, protesting against "this grave betrayal of Canadian freedom of speech" as one Toronto woman wrote Howe. Murray was accused of supporting "Godless communism," of being a "red," and denounced for allowing communists to "worm their way into public life." "Mr. Gladstone Murray, I think you should be heartily ashamed of yourself. . . ." wrote a woman from London, Ontario.

An even bigger explosion of outrage, however, came after a few CBC Radio talks by *Winnipeg Free Press* managing editor George Ferguson in which he criticized British prime minister Neville Chamberlain's appeasement policy. "Great Britain is now embarking upon an attempt to buy security for herself at the expense of the rest of Europe," Ferguson told Canadian listeners in his attack on "the Clivedon set" for seeking a deal with Hitler. Criticism of Ferguson's commentary began a war between producers and politicians, with senior CBC management caught in the middle, that has never ceased. During the next half-century and longer, the producers, and at the beginning, Plaunt and Brockington, fiercely insisted on their independence. Over the decades, however, there would be times when senior management gave in to government pressures. In Ferguson's case, the pressure came from both the Conservative Opposition and the prime minister. The Toronto *Telegram* accused Ferguson of an "anti-British bias," uttering "puerile nonsense. . . . The piffle came over the air with the authority of the Canadian Government."

One Conservative MP, C. H. Cahan, said Ferguson's radio talk was "provocative propaganda" and "common twaddle," and another, Tommy Church, said, "I think the time has come when broadcasts of this kind should be stopped . . . not only in the public interest but in the interest of the British Empire."

Mackenzie King agreed, saying criticisms of the policies of another country should be banned if they "are likely to prove embarrassing to the government and administration of the day." King said that because Ferguson was broadcasting over the publicly owned CBC, many would assume his words represented government policy. Ferguson's own paper retorted that King's comments were "a slap in the face of freedom that cannot and must not be tolerated."

Gladstone Murray was sympathetic to King's position. In a letter to CBC board member Gen. Victor Odlum he said, "The manner of advocacy as distinguished from that of exposition tended to dominate the utterances of Mr. Ferguson." But Murray was not backed up by either Brockington or Plaunt, who felt this was a test case of the CBC's freedom.

A year earlier, Brockington had told a parliamentary committee, "We believe radio speech should be allowed to be forthright, provocative and stimulating. . . . We are opposed to and shall resist, any attempt to regiment opinion and to throttle freedom of utterance." Now the prime minister seemed to be placing limits on that freedom with his statement in the House. Brockington was alarmed and dispatched a three-page letter to King saying that the prime minister's comments "have placed the Board of Governors of the Canadian Broadcasting Corporation in a position of some perplexity, uncertainty and difficulty." He reiterated the importance of independence for the CBC and quoted his earlier parliamentary testimony on the dangers of "throttling" freedom of speech. He said that to meet King's concerns about confusing broadcasts of CBC commentaries with government policy, henceforth all commentaries would carry at the beginning a statement that the commentator was speaking only for himself.

That concession resolved the dispute, as Brockington knew it would from his talks with King's assistant Edward Pickering. Pickering had helped write both Brockington's letter and King's response, which read in part, "The government is in agreement with the general principles which you have enunciated. . . . The free interchange of opinion is, as you state, one of the safeguards of democracy." King added that he had wanted to avoid any "misunderstanding or misinterpretation" of government policy that might aggravate the European political situation. "The remarks which I made in the House of Commons . . . were but an expression of anxiety I felt lest the broadcasts of certain of the news commentators selected and remunerated by the Canadian Broadcasting Corporation, should be held in Great Britain and Europe, as well as Canada, to reflect directly or indirectly, the voice of the Government of Canada. This in the circumstance appeared inevitable, seeing that it is everywhere known that the Board of Governors of the Corporation is appointed by the Government of Canada."

To C. D. Howe's outrage, Ferguson wasn't taken off the air at once, but carried on until the fall of 1938, when the weekly commentaries of both Ferguson and Halifax philosophy professor Dr. H. L. Stewart were replaced by a series of roundtable discussions and commentaries from Raymond Gram Swing in the United States and from Graham Spry who was now living in England. Spry was paid $35 a week for his commentaries.

After his election defeat in 1936 to Conservative Tommy Church, Spry couldn't find a job in Canada because of his CCF activities. He was advised by *Winnipeg Free Press* editor John Dafoe and *Toronto Star* publisher Joe Atkinson, both close friends, to look outside Canada.

"Couldn't you find me a job on your newspaper?" Spry had asked Atkinson.

"No, Graham," Atkinson had replied. "You're finished in Canada. Your only alternative is to leave the country. . . . You're labelled now. You haven't a chance of getting satisfactory employment."

A glum Spry had even appealed without success to NBC's Reginald Brophy. He had a promise of a job from Gladstone Murray as the CBC representative in the United States, but it never materialized. He was desperate when, through an old Oxford acquaintance, he found a job as an executive in a London company operated by Standard Oil of California. Calling himself Standard Oil's first socialist executive, he directed Standard Oil operations in the Middle East. Spry not only did commentaries for the CBC, but during the war he became a friend of and a personal assistant to Sir Stafford Cripps of the British War cabinet. In that role he met with, among others, Ghandi, Nehru, and Roosevelt. After the war, he became the agent-general in London for the CCF government of Saskatchewan. Spry was, in effect, a political exile, but his work as a CBC commentator pleased Plaunt enormously.

Shortly after the battle about George Ferguson's commentary, another row erupted in Parliament and in the newspapers over a series of talks the *Globe and Mail*'s publisher, George McCullagh, wanted to make. The dynamic, opinionated McCullagh wanted to buy time on a network of stations for a series of half-hour talks on his vision of a new, non-political leadership for the country. Brockington refused, saying no individual or profit-making corporation could buy any network time to broadcast opinions. McCullagh was offered a spot on a Sunday night roundtable discussion, but he declined and launched a bitter anti-CBC tirade. "This ruling is very unfair and greatly prejudices the right of free speech," he said, while his newspaper warned, "dictatorship is on our doorstep." The *Telegram* called the CBC "the servile creature of the King Government." Conservative bigwigs Arthur Meighen and George Drew agreed and condemned the CBC, and R. B. Bennett said, "Any person who can pay the price charged should have the right to buy (broadcast time)."

That was precisely what shouldn't happen, Brockington felt, and he argued before a parliamentary committee, "There should be no preference for wealth. Freedom of speech is not for sale at fifty dollars a minute on the air; if it were, then free air would soon degenerate into just a sign outside a filling station."

Brockington said he would not stop individual private stations from selling time for opinions, although he would make certain there was equal opportunity for opposing opinions. McCullagh replied that Murray supported his position and had visited his home to say so, but Brockington wouldn't budge. McCullagh eventually evaded the CBC ban by purchasing time on nineteen individual private stations and sending a transcription of his talks to each station for use at the same time.

The political fallout from the Ferguson and McCullagh cases hardened the Conservatives' antagonism toward the CBC, a feeling that strengthened over the years and eventually led the Tories to seek revenge when it came their turn to govern.

Alarmed at the political turmoil, the CBC prepared a "white paper" on political broadcasting designed to lay out the ground rules. It was prepared in consultation with the Liberal, Conservative, Social Credit, and CCF parties and drafted by Alan Plaunt and Edward Pickering, who had left the Prime Minister's Office and, at the suggestion of Plaunt, Brockington, and Murray, had joined the CBC as assistant to the general manager. The "white paper" proposed that free time be provided to political parties during federal and provincial elections, and that the amount of time be allocated on the basis of the number of elected members, the previous popular vote, with provision for new parties and other factors. Between election campaigns, parties could buy airtime, but there would be no free time. It reiterated that network time would not be sold to individuals or corporations for opinion broadcasting, although non-commercial organizations could buy time on private stations or subsidiary networks. It also committed the CBC to air programs on a wide variety of opinions on current issues. "The policy of the CBC is to prevent the air from falling under control of wealth or any other power." It said, "The air belongs to the people and the constant aim of the CBC is to have the principal points of view on questions of importance heard by the people as a whole."

McCullagh's *Globe and Mail* thought all this was outrageous and compared Brockington to Hitler. But the Plaunt-Pickering "white paper" endured and became the bible for political broadcasting. Its guidelines are still used today, more than half a century later.

Plaunt had good reason to be pleased with the policy battles won by the broadcasting creature he had fought so hard to bring into being. The "white paper" seemed to have secured political broadcasting; Brockington's exchange of letters with the prime minister seemed to have assured the CBC's independence; and the victories over C. D. Howe seemed to have enshrined the dominant role of public broadcasting. Plaunt had helped recruit some key personnel for the CBC whom, he hoped, would balance the Boys from CKNC who still ruled much of the entertainment programming.

Plaunt began casting about for new causes. "The ground work job has been done [for the CBC]," he wrote to Brockington in the fall of 1938. "In a sense, I am taking leave of a first love." Plaunt said he would like to become "an ordinary Member of the Board" instead of taking the leading role, so that he could devote more attention elsewhere.

When war threatened in Europe, Plaunt found his "elsewhere." Along with left-wing activists, the CCF, and many Liberals, including, to a large degree, Mackenzie King himself in his private thoughts, Plaunt took a neutralist stance in the European troubles.

He organized the Neutrality League with the same intensity with which he had organized the campaign for public broadcasting. Simply put, Plaunt was an Isolationist. He feared Canada might well break apart amid French-English strains if the country ever entered a war, and in that, he certainly reflected King's fears. King had endorsed Chamberlain's appeasement policy in hopes of avoiding war, but by early 1939, when that policy seemed headed for disaster, King was determined Canada would not say, "Ready, aye, ready!" and put Canada automatically at war if Britain went to war against Germany.

As part of his campaign for neutrality and because of his philosophical endorsement of many of its policies, Plaunt anonymously gave

$10,000 to the CCF. He also helped finance the *Canadian Forum*, one of the few English-speaking Canadian journals "which welcomes articles that take the isolationist position," as one of the magazine's officials told Plaunt. Plaunt spearheaded the Neutrality League's campaign by issuing pamphlets, seeking big-name supporters, and, on the advice of National Liberal Federation president and Mackenzie King confidante, Norman Lambert, he sought to broaden support beyond the CCF. He failed, however, to get the kind of across-the-board support that he had achieved for public broadcasting nearly a decade earlier.

In the draft of a pamphlet entitled "Keep Canada Out of War," Plaunt wrote: "The war hysteria which has been deliberately whipped up during the last few weeks has made clear how prone Canadians still are to be swept off their feet by moralistic and idealistic appeals which have little to do with the hard facts. . . . The proper policy for Canada is non-intervention in a European war." Plaunt denounced the "imperialist powers" and warned that Canadians would be turned into "cannon fodder." "If Canada is automatically committed to war by the declaration of a non-Canadian government, then we are still in the colonial stage and have no control over our own destinies," he said.

In promoting Canada's right to choose neutralism, Plaunt fired shots at his CBC protégé, Gladstone Murray. Plaunt had never accepted Murray's description of the CBC's programming mandate. "We are in the show business primarily," Murray had said at a parliamentary committee hearing. "We have to establish ourselves as good at the business. Secondly, there is the provision of useful information in palatable forms." Plaunt was a program missionary, seeking to expand the knowledge of the world and of the various political options, and for him, mass entertainment was secondary. That's why he had fought to bring the CBC into being in the first place and he now began to feel that Murray was sabotaging that objective.

Thus, while busily preparing Neutrality League pamphlets and positions, Plaunt also launched a bristling attack on CBC programming, especially a New Year's special on Canada and the world. "As a combination of banality, bad taste, cheap sentimentality, jingoism and incoherent production, this programme would . . . be hard to beat," he told Murray. "The parts relating to Canada and the Empire during the various

European crises and the references to the Crown, were especially objectionable. They were crude and infantile – a travesty on the real currents of thought and feelings in Canada. . . . An American listening in would get no impression other than that we were a mawkish and sentimental bunch of imperialist half wits, slavish Chamberlain worshippers with no identity or independence of our own."

Plaunt demanded the CBC allow neutralists on the air so that the CBC's total objectivity would be preserved, and he strongly supported the speeches of University of Toronto professors Frank Underhill and George Grube, who said Canada had the right to be neutral. In defending the two professors, Plaunt got into a vitriolic row with Ontario Conservative leader George Drew, calling him a "coward" who was muzzling freedom of speech. Drew responded by denouncing "parlour pinks who preach Empire disunity." Gladstone Murray, who confided in Drew, privately agreed with the Conservative provincial leader. Former Conservative prime minister Arthur Meighen joined the anti-Plaunt, anti-neutrality forces, saying that the CBC was using "some pink professor . . . to tell the people of Canada that Britain was a traitor to democracy and that the United States would soon be taking over leadership of democracy throughout the world," and he added that "a public man could not broadcast loyal words."

Plaunt, however, viewed the possibility of Canada going to war over a European crisis as "a nightmare and sheer madness." Plaunt wanted at the very minimum for Canada to make its own decision about going to war, a position King publicly insisted on. "Parliament will decide," King told Canadians. "Our effort will be voluntary." Thus, while Britain declared war on September 3, 1939, Canada waited a week before making its declaration. That week was a fateful seven days, as the Nazis overran Poland. It was a fateful week as well for Plaunt, Murray, and the CBC.

One day after Britain declared war, Plaunt called Murray's assistant Edward Pickering and complained about Murray's ruling that forbade any Canadian station from carrying news and commentaries originating in the United States. Plaunt felt the American news should be carried to balance what he considered an excessive amount of BBC news being carried by the CBC at Murray's order, and to stop Canadians from switching to American stations for their war news. Plaunt also believed that commentators advocating neutralism for Canada should be heard on the CBC at least until Parliament decided whether to go to war.

Earlier, Plaunt had been upset at Murray's prewar summer trip to London to discuss with British authorities how the BBC would operate in the event of war and was particularly distressed at reports of Murray meeting with the head of British propaganda. Plaunt was even angrier at Murray's trips to New York to confer with the British spy master William Stephenson, code-named "Intrepid," who was campaigning to get the United States to increase its support of Britain. All this, Plaunt thought, was putting the CBC into the pocket of those who wanted to stampede Canada into war. Beyond that, he feared C. D. Howe might try surreptitiously to take over the CBC, superseding the board of directors, as a wartime measure. Plaunt felt that in the event of war, the CBC board should remain in charge unless the government formally and publicly proclaimed it was taking over the CBC. Plaunt sensed that Murray was manoeuvring behind the scenes with Howe, with whom Murray had become closely allied in recent months, and that the CBC general manager preferred Howe's direction to that of the board.

Pickering communicated some of Plaunt's concerns in a memo to Murray, and the battle between Plaunt and Murray exploded. It was the nationalist neutralist versus the imperialist interventionist, aggravated by an astonishingly bitter attack by Plaunt on Murray's managerial competence. Plaunt, who had expressed confidence about the future of the CBC only a few months earlier, now suddenly feared his "baby" was in mortal danger because of Murray. Gone was Plaunt's earlier fervent admiration for Murray, and gone, too, was Murray's gratitude and respect for Plaunt. The protégé and the mentor turned on each other with a ferocity that shook the CBC to its foundations.

"He [Plaunt] saw the whole thing threatened by the vagaries of this man whom he once trusted and supported, and there was a sense of betrayal," Pickering recalls.

In Murray's opinion, Plaunt had become a left-wing, anti-British "conspirator" plotting to undermine the safety of the nation. In the week between the British and Canadian declarations of war, Murray said later, there was "a concentrated nightmare of problems. There was at once a demand from certain quarters that the BBC relays should be discontinued as a violation of our neutrality; alternatively that German bulletins in English should be carried in the name of impartiality. At the same time, there was formidable pressure to organize nationwide radio debates on whether or not Canada should enter the war. Both demands were successfully resisted." In a letter to Arthur Meighen, Murray later wrote, "As war became imminent, the left wing forces tried to stop me taking the necessary steps to prepare and warn public opinion. I was under severe pressure to advocate neutrality for Canada."

Validating Plaunt's and Brockington's fears, Murray and Howe did bypass the CBC board, dealing directly with each other for a few weeks after Canada had declared war. Pickering later said, "He [Murray] told me he expected the minister would supersede the board in the conduct of the corporation's affairs in war time. It became apparent Murray was taking directives from the minister and was bypassing the board." Murray himself later admitted to a parliamentary inquiry, "It might be argued that in practice for a few weeks after the impact of war, the management dealt directly with the government." In fact, Murray had what he himself later admitted was a "day-to-day relationship with Mr. Howe," seeing him almost every morning at 8:45 A.M. or 9:00 A.M. "It was pretty obvious that he hoped to free himself from the control of the board in wartime," Pickering says. "I could not escape the impression that the general manager would have welcomed the government taking over the direction of the CBC and thus be released from the board's control." In notes he wrote later to explain his actions to a parliamentary committee, Murray said, "Decisions had to be taken rapidly. . . . There was real anxiety of possibilities of sabotage, of 5th column activity. . . . We were venturing on uncharted seas, the predominant consideration being the security of the state." In green ink, he had added, but later crossed out, that the CBC board couldn't have handled the emergency situation at the time because "the Board would have had to be in constant session."

At the outset of war, Brockington had ordered Murray to convene a board meeting for September 6, 1939, but Howe asked Murray to postpone the meeting. Murray did and, instead, a meeting was held between Howe and the board's finance committee, including Brockington. Howe said the government wanted the board's functions to be carried on by a three-man executive committee which would be the bridge between the CBC and the government.

Angry at Howe and at Murray's manoeuvring to wrest control from the board, Brockington protested to King. Plaunt also protested to the Prime Minister's Office, saying Howe had claimed that the one reason for the need to take power away from the CBC board was that some members "were likely to be difficult" in wartime. Plaunt felt that was a direct reference to himself. Howe's relationship with Plaunt had always been tense because of their basic philosophical differences, but Plaunt had also annoyed Howe earlier for getting the CBC to reject the minister's "urgent" recommendation, endorsed by Murray, that a private radio licence be issued for London, Ontario, to an applicant Howe favoured.

Once again, Mackenzie King quietly supported Brockington and Plaunt. A few weeks after their complaints had reached King's ears, Howe began backtracking, showing "a sweet reasonableness" as Brockington told Plaunt. Howe said he now saw no reason for the executive committee arrangement, and the power of the CBC board was restored.

The CBC was left crackling with suspicions, distrust, and recriminations. The battle between Murray and Plaunt permeated the whole organization. "Alan was after Bill's [Murray's] hide," Ernie Bushnell said, adding, "The executioners were sharpening the guillotine." Bushnell privately denounced Plaunt for "treachery" and "sabotage" of the war effort. "Mr. Plaunt made no secret of the fact that he rarely listened [to radio]," Bushnell later said. "When he did, it was usually to talks or debates in which left-wing or anti-British views might be expected to bulk. He was a constant advocate of what he called 'extending the latitude of discussion,' by which he meant providing a forum in which left-wing opinion would secure the advantage in argument." Bushnell and the Boys from CKNC sided with Murray, while Pickering and those heading some of the more serious program areas, especially public affairs, supported Plaunt and Brockington. In short, it was the entertainers versus the educators.

Pickering, who had been as concerned as Plaunt about the CBC board being bypassed by Howe and Murray, assumed he had lost the general manager's confidence. Murray felt that since Pickering was Plaunt's

Birth Pains

friend and confidante (Pickering named his son after Alan Plaunt), it was dangerous to have him continue in the general manager's office. Bushnell put it more bluntly, accusing Pickering of being a spy for Plaunt and charging that Pickering "relayed inside information to his patron." Pickering denied the charges, saying he discussed CBC issues with Plaunt and Brockington only at Murray's direction. But Pickering felt he had lost Murray's confidence, and he resigned. "It was the only proper thing for me to do," he explained. Then, for his own protection, he wrote Plaunt and Brockington a memo on the events leading up to his resignation. Pickering had been with the CBC for less than a year. He went on to become a senior executive with the Robert Simpson Co. and later became a cultural mandarin in Toronto, as president of the Toronto Symphony, Massey Hall, and Roy Thomson Hall.

Soon after Pickering's departure, the battle between Plaunt and Murray escalated into an all-out war. This time, the cause was a report by Plaunt on the internal operation of the CBC which, in the words of Plaunt's diary, the board "begs me unanimously to undertake." Pickering says the board's request "was a pretty obvious sign of waning confidence in the general manager." The report came before the board in mid-October 1939, when Pickering's resignation and Howe's and Murray's manoeuvring behind the board's back still poisoned the atmosphere.

Prepared by Plaunt and the Montreal chartered accountant James C. Thompson, the report was a time bomb that, when it went off, destroyed the careers of several senior CBC officials, outraged Parliament, and scandalized the nation's media. The recriminations would last for a generation.

During the summer of 1939, Plaunt and Thompson had visited CBC stations in Vancouver, Winnipeg, Toronto, Ottawa, Montreal, Quebec City, and Halifax, talking to programmers and administrators, and came away alarmed by what they felt was the bad management of the corporation. They made general recommendations about moving CBC headquarters from Ottawa to either Toronto or Montreal, putting less money into capital expenditures and more into programming, providing more money to the French network, putting less emphasis on commercials, producing more regional programming, and paying producers and announcers more. They also wanted to see tighter financial controls and a wholesale revision of the administration of the CBC.

Plaunt was particularly caustic about CBC making what were nicknamed "cocktail party appointments." "The majority of the staff, which consists of hard working, capable, conscientious people, cannot help being discouraged to find demonstrably incompetent persons retained," Plaunt reported. It was impossible to fire anybody, Plaunt said, and he complained about the habit of turning good producers into "mediocre administrators." All this, he said, resulted in bad programs caused by "chaotic" administration which led to "a sense of discouragement and frustration throughout the organization." "If one looks for the causes of this situation," Plaunt said, "one is ultimately obliged to conclude that it lies in the inability of the General Manager to take firm action."

When Edward Pickering was asked by a parliamentary committee whether he thought the CBC was well-managed under Murray, he answered, "Oh, boy!"

"While he had superb talents for programming, Murray had no capacity for managing staff," Pickering later said. "He also had little capacity for managing finances, either the corporation's or his own."

Both in the report and in subsequent memos and conversations, Plaunt poured scorn on Gladstone Murray, whom he described as "capricious," "inefficient," "haphazard," "appalling," "unreliable," "incompetent," and "chaotic."

He wanted Murray fired.

When his report was submitted to the board in mid-October, Plaunt was in hospital for a cancer operation, and, much to his anger, the report was passed on to Murray for study. Plaunt was further distressed when Brockington decided he had had enough of fighting Murray and Howe, and resigned as chairman of the CBC board. Brockington recommended to Mackenzie King that Plaunt be made the new chairman, saying, "If I were to assess the contribution made by individuals to national radio, I would place his consistent and untiring efforts easily first." Brockington retired after the mid-October 1939 CBC board meeting, joined MacKenzie King's personal staff, and later went to London to become an adviser to the British minister of information and an occasional participant in CBC public affairs programs. After the war, he became chairman of Odeon Theatres in Canada and continued to do CBC commentaries into the late 1950s. His recommendation of Alan Plaunt as CBC chairman was not accepted, however, and instead, the vice-chairman, René Morin, a Montreal financier, took over. Morin, Plaunt feared, was too close to big business.

At a meeting in November, the finance committee stripped Murray of some of his financial responsibilities and transferred them to the assistant general manager, Dr. Augustin Frigon. That wasn't enough for Plaunt, who declared that the needed reforms could not be carried out by Murray. He demanded the board act on all of his recommendations at its January meeting. Again, however, because of a major cancer operation, Plaunt could not attend the January meeting at which the board merely confirmed the transfer of financial authority from Murray to Frigon. Plaunt did attend the next board meeting in April and outlined his report. The board agreed to set up a committee to make recommendations based on Plaunt's report, but the committee's meetings kept getting postponed or cancelled, and by the end of summer 1940, Plaunt was outraged at what he considered a conspiracy by Murray to avoid facing the issues raised in the report.

In almost indecipherable handwriting, Plaunt poured out his fury in private memos and notes. "Clear that present General Manager of CBC not a fit person to be entrusted with an essential instrument of national unity in peace or war," he wrote. "He is incapable, unscrupulous, two-faced, capricious. He is, also, a pathological drunk, more fit for a pathological ward than the executive direction of a great public utility."

Plaunt was vituperative about Murray's old drinking problem, a problem he had dismissed when he was moving heaven and earth to get Murray the job as general manager four years earlier. Now that he was trying to get Murray out of the job, he exploded with indignation about Murray's drunkenness, claiming that Murray was "always drunk, usually by 10 A.M.," that he had gone to London in the summer of 1939 to look for another job, and that "his stay in London was a continuous drunk" with "many disgraceful incidents." In another memo, Plaunt said,

"Murray's personal exhibitions throughout the length and breadth of this country, not to mention New York, and Washington, have for years been a notorious scandal."

"He [Murray] had a low tolerance for alcohol," says Edward Pickering. "The effect on Murray was not that he became drunk, but that his judgement became impaired. He became lacking in good sense, judgement, and discretion."

Ernie Bushnell said Murray "fell off the wagon" on a trip to Western Canada when friends in Calgary sent him off on the train to Winnipeg with a case of scotch. Ned Corbett said Murray was seldom drunk in Ottawa; "only when he'd go away he had those awful sprees," he added. Murray was on one of his "sprees" when he visited the CBC Winnipeg newsroom as William Metcalfe, who was then a senior editor with the CBC, described in his autobiography: "He was gently propelled into the room by John Kannawin, the regional representative. It was 10 A.M. and the General Manager seemed to be having some difficulty in getting around smartly, perhaps from some over-indulgence the night before, perhaps even from a continuation of that over-indulgence that same morning. His eyelids were closed almost tight as if he dreaded the glare of daylight and, if Kannawin hadn't aided him, he might have stumbled.

"We had been forewarned of the visit, of course, and leaped to our feet, prepared to answer any question the visitor might ask. He peered through those narrow slits, appeared to make a supreme effort and then, in a sort of quavering voice, he addressed Matt.

"'Are you happy here?' he breathed.

"'Oh yes, sir,' replied Matt beaming all over. 'Very happy.'

"'Good,' said Murray and with that he turned around and, with Kannawin's help, made it to the door and out of our lives forever."

Even the mild-mannered Graham Spry echoed Plaunt's distress at Murray. "He was a terrific mistake," Spry later said. "He was a drunkard and turned into a right winger of the most awful vintage. . . . He was just irresponsible and drunk."

Pickering feels another reason for Plaunt's antipathy toward Murray was that he no longer trusted what Murray was saying. "Bill was very glib with words," he says. "He could razzle-dazzle with words in a way that very few people could. The border between truth and falsehood, he crossed over it very freely. Alan got to the point where he just didn't believe Bill. He didn't accept anything that Bill told him as true."

The new CBC chairman, René Morin, was unhappy at "the extent and violence of Mr. Plaunt's denunciations" and suggested that Plaunt was on a vendetta, saying his comments "leave the impression that public interest is not the only motive behind this."

Plaunt wrote a note at one point reminding himself that he had to be careful not to generate sympathy for Murray through the ferocity of his attack. "Important to avoid impression I am out to 'get' Murray," he wrote. "Better appear that I am out to 'get' the Board because they failed to face up to their obligations."

He called the board "timid and vacillating," accused it of "white washing" Murray, and said the CBC was "increasingly . . . the tool of government, Mr. Howe and Big business." In another note to himself he wrote, "Convinced that on present basis, type of system I pioneered and helped create going down the drain."

Plaunt was also angry at Murray because he had tried to stamp out efforts by CBC technicians, announcers, and producers in Toronto to form a union in late 1939. Murray had issued a memo to staff saying that "such a course in wartime would involve grave considerations which His Majesty's Government in Canada could not disregard." "Thus in pompous terms, the CBC employees are warned against organizing themselves," editorialized the *Winnipeg Free Press.* The assistant program director in Toronto, taking his cue from Murray, was quoted by the would-be union organizers as warning them, "The RCMP are liable to get you for this." Plaunt was aghast at Murray's anti-union efforts, telling board member Gen. Victor Odlum, "The policy underlying the General Manager's circular of Dec. 4th on the organization of a union for CBC employees should be disavowed without any delay." It wasn't, however, and Murray was successful in preventing unionization at the CBC. It was not until 1953, when the five hundred members of the National Association of Broadcast Employees and Technicians (NABET) got a forty-hour week, that the CBC signed a formal agreement with a union.

The seriously ill Plaunt continued his assault on Murray, often from his sick bed, complaining that Murray was waging a "campaign of insinuations, innuendoes and falsehoods assiduously pushed in an effort to discredit me." While denying he was engaged in a "sinister conspiracy against Mr. Alan Plaunt," Murray's counterattack did portray Plaunt as the arch villain of a left-wing plot to take over the CBC. He never publicly named Plaunt, although he certainly did so in private. From the very beginning, he later said, "a difficulty I had to face was that the most influential of my associates wished to build a staff of left wing bias."

Murray's supporters reinforced his accusations. Ernie Bushnell, who got along famously with Murray in spite of his own hopes to be the general manager, later said, "Mr. Plaunt's idea of organization was perhaps only to be expected from one who had never done a day's work in his life, and who was guided by a curious combination of snobbery, personal prejudice and sense of inferiority." Bushnell blamed Plaunt's intense criticism of Murray on either his cancer or "frustration neurosis because of the failure of an endeavour to gain control of the CBC for his own purposes, political or otherwise."

Murray had no doubt that Plaunt's objective was left-wing political control of broadcasting in Canada. In a remarkably revealing letter he wrote to Arthur Meighen a decade later, Murray charged that Plaunt, Graham Spry, and Brooke Claxton, who was minister of defence in King's cabinet, had been plotting "a powerful conspiracy to create an absolute state monopoly of radio. . . . These people were not only left wing, but bitterly anti-British and anti-Imperialist. It emerged later that they sought my help merely to get over the first hurdle. Realizing I was right wing and Imperialist, they planned to discard me just as soon as the new monopoly was in operation. . . . Fortunately C. D. Howe turned out to be an ally and with his help, the private radio stations were saved."

In a startling admission near the end of the two-page letter, Murray wrote, "It might have been better if public radio had never been undertaken in any form."

Murray told Meighen of his battles with "the left wing forces," meaning Plaunt and Brockington, at the outbreak of war. "In the end," Murray wrote in a self-serving distortion of history, "I had to explain to C. D. Howe the existing conditions were impossible, so he suspended the

Board and Brockington resigned." In another part of the letter, he said, "Of course my numerous left wing enemies were hard at work. And ultimately they hit upon some vulnerable points." One of Murray's "vulnerable points" was that he fiddled his expense accounts, and it was this that ultimately sank him as general manager of the CBC.

Murray had long complained privately that his $13,000 salary wasn't enough, telling Gen. Victor Odlum, "I cannot go on subsidizing my own job." And it was the talk of Ottawa that Murray was living unusually well on his salary. Finally, questions were asked about his expense accounts. The auditor general, Watson Sellar, raised his eyebrows at Murray's $1,000 claim in April 1939 for "intelligence service" that was unsupported by any vouchers or explanations. Sellar was the same government financial authority who, as comptroller, had caused so much trouble over Hector Charlesworth's expense accounts at the CRBC half a dozen years earlier.

A few months later, Murray made another unsupported $1,000 claim for expenses incurred for "statistical purposes." The expenses were simply listed as "Jan. 6 Friday Toronto $75, Jan. 12 Thursday Toronto $90, Jan. 13 Friday Montreal $70, Jan. 24 Tuesday Toronto $60," and so on, and were in addition to other travel expenses and a per diem allowance he received. Murray explained to his inquiring financial staff that he had spent the money securing information about American plans hostile to public service broadcasting and related to gathering "statistical and other information relative to CBC coverage and public reaction."

At a 1942 parliamentary committee hearing, Pickering blew the whistle on Murray's expense accounts and set the ball rolling toward his dismissal. Pickering said, "I was told there was no specific budget provision and so far as could be learned, there was no Board authorization for an expenditure of this type." Pickering added in his testimony to Parliament, "Mr Murray gave me to understand that he recognized the danger of expenses of this kind, particularly when they did not have advance authorization from the Board."

One of Murray's problems was his enjoyment of the genial company he found in bar rooms and his willingness to pick up the tab. "He was a soft touch," Pickering says, remembering one night at the bar of the

Ritz Carlton Hotel in Montreal where Murray was drinking brandy and ten or fifteen friends joined him. "There must have been an alcoholic tom-tom," Pickering recalls. "The hangers-on got wind that Murray was buying drinks in the lounge. He didn't have sense enough to extricate himself. He was taken advantage of. His alertness and his astuteness abandoned him." Only after a great deal of brandy was Pickering able to get Murray out of the bar and away from his friends.

Sellar was incensed at Murray's expenses and drew them to C. D. Howe's attention. The board tried to control the damage by increasing Murray's living allowance and per diem travel expenses retroactive to April 1939. Murray then withdrew his second group of special expense claims. But in doing so, he had to revise his travel claims since he could only get the increase in travel money if he were outside of Ottawa. Unfortunately in the revision, he claimed he was travelling on several days when all evidence showed he was in Ottawa attending parliamentary hearings and other functions. As well, there was no record of any train or plane travel, and Murray explained he'd been given a free flight on a Department of Transport plane. Finally, after much juggling of dates by Pickering, the CBC treasurer, and Murray, the revision was revised, submitted, and the matter settled.

It left, however, a sour taste, and when the matter was investigated two years later by a parliamentary committee, it scandalized the government. Committee member M. J. Coldwell of the CCF castigated the CBC treasurer, saying, "I think that any treasurer of a corporation . . . [who] does not object to this procedure is derelict in his duty."

Murray again was adamant that he had done nothing wrong. "I deny this categorically," he said. "There were no irregularities, nothing not disclosed. The purpose of expenditure was always indicated." There was, he said, "nothing *sub rosa*, nothing hidden . . . nothing illegal." His explanations, however, didn't wash with the parliamentary committee or the government. Grant Dexter, the *Winnipeg Free Press* correspondent in Ottawa, wrote privately to his editor, John Dafoe, about a conversation he had had with Thomas A. Crerar, the minister of mines and resources. "Cabinet deeply shocked by revelations of financial misconduct of Gladstone Murray," Dexter said. "The accounts of the Corporation were found to be in a horrible muddle. Murray did not have one friend and Howe was the bitterest of them all." Crerar told Dexter that Murray had been ordered to refund to the government $5,697, and he "has agreed to do so."

The 1942 parliamentary committee was withering in its condemnation of Murray and of the CBC board. It attacked "the expenses of the General Manager which the Committee feels were out of all reason and much confusion was caused by the slack and unbusinesslike manner in accounting for these expenditures. Detailed vouchers were not submitted, extraordinary and unclassified expenses were included which it felt were unnecessary. . . . Mr. Murray was unable or unwilling to state to whom many of these payments were made. His explanation of their purpose is obscure. . . . Mr. Murray's denial of the existence of some of these expenditures . . . the absence of particulars or receipts justified the conclusion that at least there was gross carelessness in the way in which these expenditures had been handled and accounted for. . . . It is high time expenditures of this character and on this scale, were stopped. . . . They were never justifiable in any corporation in peace time. They are a thousand times less so in time of war when we speak of equality of sacrifice."

The parliamentary report's complete vindication of Alan Plaunt was not unexpected given the evidence and given the fact that Plaunt's old ally and Murray's adversary, Brooke Claxton, who had been elected a Liberal MP in the 1940 election, was the principal drafter of the report. In a letter to Dafoe, Claxton said, "Murray's weakness has forced him to resort to more and more devious ways to keep control in his own hands." Claxton credited Pickering for exposing Murray's expense account fiddles, saying, "I can't exaggerate the importance of your evidence in creating openings and starting the flood." He added, "I expect . . . Murray will hang on like a leech." The *Canadian Forum* demanded, "The canker of disorderly management has been eating into the otherwise sound structure of national broadcasting. It must be stopped before it is too late."

All this denunciation of Murray, however, came in 1942, more than two years after the gossip and charges about his expenses and drinking first made the rounds in Ottawa. During 1939 and 1940, the evidence was kept largely within the CBC board. Frustrated by the board's delay in acting on his report on Murray's management of the CBC, Plaunt submitted his resignation. "I feel that, as a public trustee, I should not continue to accept responsibility for the internal organization and executive direction of the Corporation when I have long ceased to have confidence in it," he wrote to Howe with a copy to Mackenzie King. With his tongue surely tucked in his cheek, Howe replied, "I had no idea that you felt so strongly."

Plaunt's resignation was announced in October 1940. Board chairman René Morin took advantage of the resignation to reject Plaunt's accusations about bad internal management. "It was resolved that the Board regretfully notes the retirement of Alan B. Plaunt and feels impelled to deplore the publicity given in the press on his retirement."

Rubbing salt into Plaunt's wounds, the board also passed a resolution which said, "all members of the board today assembled declared their full and complete confidence in the General Manager Mr. Gladstone Murray." The resolution went on to express "appreciation and gratitude" for his work. At the same meeting, however, the board began to whittle further away at Murray's authority. Primary responsibility for CBC financial, engineering, and commercial matters, and all CBC operations in Quebec were taken from Murray and given to Dr. Augustin Frigon. Four months later, the board again reduced Murray's authority, giving Frigon more responsibility for the internal management of the CBC.

Meanwhile, Watson Sellar once more zeroed in on Murray's expense accounts. In addition to his $13,000 salary, Murray had received nearly $15,000 in expenses in 1939-40 and about $14,500 in expenses in 1940-41. Sellar complained to Howe about Murray's $4,500-a-year allowance for Ottawa expenditures and his $20-a-day travelling expenses. Howe was furious, and the CBC cut Murray's Ottawa expense allowance to $3,000 and his $20 per diem travel allowance to actual expenses. Howe was angry with Murray and utterly fed up with all the troubles he'd had with CBC in general. So that Howe could devote more time to his other wartime activities, King transferred responsibility for the CBC to the minister of national war services, Gen. Leo R. LaFlèche. Murray finally was removed as general manager in November 1942. With flowery but painfully empty rhetoric, the board appointed Murray as director general of broadcasting at $12,000 a year and no living allowances, responsible for nothing at all except providing program ideas. The CBC staff was advised, "He shall have no authority to commit the Corporation to any expenditure except with the approval of the General Manager.... He is to be [an] advisor. ... He is not to look after the 'executive' field at all."

Murray's humiliation was complete when he was transferred to Toronto and succeeded by Dr. James Thomson, president of the University of Saskatchewan and a member of the CBC board. Dr. Thomson wrote to Murray, "I think it would relieve you and others from exposure to unpleasant relations if, when you require advances of cash for travelling or other duty expenses in connection with your work for the CBC you would apply directly to me. ... I would take it as a favour if in every case you gave me some exact description of what was involved in the application, including the purpose for which they are made and the duties you would expect to perform."

It was too much for Murray, and he resigned three months later to become a public relations consultant to business. The ever-loyal Bushnell maintained to the end that Murray's programming strengths far outweighed his weaknesses and that he didn't deserve "the ignominious treatment he received." Bushnell later said, "I had nothing but the greatest admiration for Gladstone Murray . . . Alan Plaunt hated the British like hell . . . and he was determined to crucify Bill Murray and he did it, and he's a son of a bitch so far as I'm concerned, God rest his soul."

Murray spent the rest of his life criss-crossing the country warning of the menace of socialism and relating the story of how he was a victim of a left-wing vendetta because of his battle to prevent a socialist takeover of the CBC and the Canadian airwaves. In his talks to Rotary Clubs, church meetings, corporate gatherings, Canadian Clubs, and Conservative conferences, he concentrated much of his free-enterprise fire on the CCF, especially party leader M. J. Coldwell and his "henchmen" who, he said, sought to turn the CBC into a proving ground for state socialism. The CCF charged that Murray had been hired as a Tory toady for $35,000 a year to undermine both the CBC and the CCF.

Murray kept up a wide correspondence after he left the CBC, including fawning letters to King, congratulating him on birthdays, anniversaries, and speeches, and offering advice and help to Conservative Party leaders such as Arthur Meighen, George Drew, and John Diefenbaker in the battle against socialism.

The *Globe and Mail* endorsed Murray's campaign, editorializing at one point in the fall of 1943, "It is of value to recall that those who, in the years between the wars, had tried to weaken our ties with the Empire and to sabotage measures of armed defense, did their best to keep us out of war and, when this failed, tried to limit our contribution . . . [Murray] reveals again the fundamental weakness of the national radio monopoly. . . . It has been the privilege . . . of a small group of Socialists to use our national radio network for the dissemination of their propaganda under the pretence of presenting 'the other side.'"

Murray's onetime supporter on the CBC board, Gen. Victor Odlum, wrote to him in 1946, "As you know, I clung to the idea that you could become a great man in Canada. You had all the necessary gifts. The only trouble was that you did not take yourself sufficiently seriously." In response, Murray wrote, "I feel the truth is, I am constitutionally incapable of any considerable administrative responsibility."

Murray died in 1970 at the age of seventy-seven, a seminal figure in Canadian radio whose broadcasting genius was betrayed by what he called his weaknesses. He had outlived his mentor-turned-tormentor, Alan Plaunt, by nearly thirty years. While Murray died declaring socialism was "the road to serfdom," Plaunt, in his dying days in 1941, was still proclaiming the CBC as a model for the future of Canada. He despaired at what he considered the CBC's virtual paralysis of independent judgement because of its obsequiousness to government, by which he primarily meant C. D. Howe, and its deference to big business, by which he meant board chairman René Morin and N. L. Nathanson, a movie distribution mogul and confidante of Howe. "We are practically back to the defects which wrecked the Radio Commission," he wrote Brooke Claxton shortly before his death. "I care not in the slightest what goddamn fools of themselves Nate, Morin and Co. make. But I do care about this enterprise a) for its own sake and b) because I believe that our Act provided a model framework for a publicly owned business which surely is of some importance to the future of democratic government in this bloody country."

Cancer finally claimed Plaunt in an Ottawa hospital in September 1941 at the age of thirty-seven, a man possessed by his visions and without whom the CBC would never have existed. If Graham Spry was the Father of Public Broadcasting for the campaign he led in 1932, Alan Plaunt was the Father of the CBC.

Leonard Brockington said on Plaunt's death, "When the history of national broadcasting is written, Alan Plaunt's name will be honoured above all others. It was he who, in spite of many obstacles, much criticism and many discouragements, did more than any other to chart the course of national control."

7

The CBC Goes to War

W hen Canada went to war, Gladstone Murray and Ernie Bushnell cried, "Ready, aye, ready!" and the CBC also went to war. More than ever before or since, during the war years the CBC became almost an arm of government.

It was a time of CBC journalistic lustre from the battlefield and, at home, of journalistic anger at an obsequious management that was too ready to accept government interference and manipulation. It was a time, too, of the CBC's self-wounding, near-suicidal affront to the Conservative Party, which prompted the Tory leadership finally and formally to turn against the CBC.

Canada's declaration of war created a minor storm for the CBC because of its almost cavalier manner of broadcasting the news. On Sunday, September 10, 1939, announcer Austin Willis interrupted a noonhour NBC show from Philadelphia called "Music for Moderns" that the CBC was carrying to read a CP bulletin he had just been handed announcing that Canada had officially declared war on Germany. Having read the bulletin, CBC promptly returned to what *The Financial Post* labelled "raucous swing band music." Willis remembers he broke into the network when "Smoke Gets in Your Eyes" was playing, read the war declaration, and then returned listeners to the playing of "Inka Dinka Doo," hardly the kind of stirring martial music associated with going to war. Charging that the CBC had failed to do a proper news report, *The Financial Post* said, "Incredible stupidity has been shown by Canada's state-owned broadcasting system. . . . No sense of sober gravity of the moment seized the CBC."

Canada's declaration of war was treated almost as a journalistic afterthought mainly because of the heavy coverage on the CBC when Britain declared war a week earlier and the coverage given the previous day to the parliamentary debate on the war. CP bulletins had been broadcast throughout the day on the German attack on Poland, as had statements by King George VI and Chamberlain from London, Daladier from Paris, and King from Ottawa.

As the war progressed, listeners heard some of the most spectacularly successful programming in CBC history from its war correspondents, a story vividly told by A. E. Powley, who was in charge of CBC war reporting, in his book *Broadcast From the Front.* The nation sat by the radio night after night through the war years, hanging onto every word from the Voice of Doom, as Lorne Greene was nicknamed for his role as the CBC national news anchor, and from Canadian radio reporters on the battlefront who became household names, such as Peter Stursberg, Marcel Ouimet, Bob Bowman, and Matthew Halton, father of CBC correspondent David Halton.

Spurred on by the patriotic fervour of Gladstone Murray and Ernie Bushnell, Bob Bowman and his engineer, Art Holmes, were aboard the *Aquitania* when she left Halifax on December 10, 1939, carrying the first contingent of Canadian troops to Britain. As Canada's first broadcast war correspondents, Bowman and Holmes were not welcomed aboard ship. "The captain didn't want to have anything to do with us," remembered Holmes. "Why, damn me eyes, sir!" the captain told Bowman, "there's a war on and they propose to send a broadcasting man on my ship? Why, damn me eyes, the answer is no!" Whereupon Bowman and Holmes were hustled off the ship, returning only after intervention from Ottawa.

Bowman's program on the troop crossing was Canada's first radio war coverage and was sent back from London by "transatlantic beam," as it was called, a few days after the convoy arrived. Holmes reported that it was the first recording ever made at sea. The young engineer had been a

Fox Movietone newsreel cameraman in 1930, then a wireless operator in the Arctic, and one of the first to join the CRBC in 1933. He became the unsung hero of Canadian war reporting, the man in the background recording the sounds of war and the words of Matthew Halton and others. Holmes' sounds of the Blitz were so vivid that almost all British war movies used his bomb and anti-aircraft gunfire sounds, as did the BBC. "You could even get the whistle of the bomb coming down, and sometimes you'd misjudge and get too close," Holmes said. He was passionate about capturing the sounds of the Blitz, going out night after night in the CBC recording van Big Betsy during the Battle of Britain, sitting for hours listening through his earphones and cutting recording discs of the German bombs falling all around him. In all of England there was nothing quite like Big Betsy with the CBC emblem on the outside and, inside, the elaborate recording facilities. Betsy was riddled with shrapnel from many a close call.

"For a moment last night," Holmes laconically reported to his bosses, "I thought the CBC were going to be minus a van as a dive bomber came straight down at it, passed over at about a hundred feet, but fortunately didn't drop anything there." It's no wonder Holmes was nicknamed "the bomb chaser."

On another occasion, Betsy took a direct hit. "A bit of a bomb came through the van, in one side and out the other," Holmes recalled. "It just left a hole in each side . . . but missed me. I was at the opposite end. But we also lost three of our offices by bombs."

Holmes' recordings of the Blitz in 1940 vividly brought the war home to Canadians as did Bowman's reports from Dieppe two years later. Reading from notes smeared with sea water and smoke, Bowman reported on the eight hours he spent sitting aboard a landing craft in Dieppe harbour watching the doomed Canadian attackers. "A.A. tracers, like red sparks, and there is a heavy red glow extending down the coast," he reported. "The sky is streaked with 'flying fools' and so is the ocean. . . . A Spitfire has just crashed off our starboard bow and into the sea like a stone. We could see the pilot trying to get out, but he couldn't. . . . The Germans on the cliffs are even throwing hand grenades on our ships below. . . . I am listening to our tank shortwave equipment and I know they are fighting like fools on shore. I can hear one of our tank captains saying, 'Come on over boys, we are killing lots of Germans.'"

Although CBC correspondents were in the thick of battle in North Africa, Italy, Normandy, and the drive into Germany, only one was killed. Eddie Baudry was hit by machine-gun fire while flying to cover the Casablanca summit conference of Roosevelt and Churchill near the end of 1942. President Roosevelt personally sent a wreath to the funeral.

Holmes was torpedoed once in the Mediterranean, just as he was eating dessert. He floated alone for four hours, worrying about sharks and German U-boats before being rescued. When his ship went down a camera he used to take pictures for the CBC went with it. Holmes requested the CBC give him an allowance to buy another one, but his request was rejected by bureaucrats who admonished him for carelessness in losing the camera and told him, "Remember there's a war on!"

Correspondents Halton, Stursberg, Ouimet, and the ever-present Holmes and his colleague Paul Johnson were among the several reporters who risked their lives to bring the Italian campaign into Canadian living rooms, particularly in seeking the sounds of battle – the booming barrages, whistling shells, chattering machine guns, tanks clanking by, and Spitfires roaring overhead. Mixed in was the talk of tank men and soldiers as they went shouting into battle. Holmes said the CBC crews were often literally in the front lines. In a note he wrote to the CBC he said, "It would be impossible to get any closer without running into enemy lines."

"The anti-chamber of hell" was the way Halton described to Canadian listeners the battle for Ortona, a little town near Rome where Canadian troops fought. "I see a picture so vivid that I clench my fists," Halton broadcast. "A convoy of ammunition trucks starting down the corkscrew road to the bridge. The Jerry gunners have every bend in the road taped, registered, and every few seconds they drop a shell here and over here and over here, but the drivers have to go. When you run the gauntlet yourself as we of the CBC often had to do four or eight times a day, it isn't too bad. There's an unholy thrill about it as well as fear. . . . It's when you are watching others do it that you grow older, especially when a vehicle is hit and goes up in a vomit of flames and smoke."

Halton went back to England to cover the D-Day preparations while

Stursberg followed the Allied progress toward Rome. Canadian radio listeners were transfixed by Stursberg's reporting on the battle for Rome. "Sheets of flame and balls of fire are leaping back and forth across the valley," he reported. "It's an amazing and terrifying sight and yet thrilling.... There are guns in front of us – they're the ones that make the sharp cracks – and guns behind us. If you listen carefully, you'll hear the whoosh of their shells going over our heads."

Stursberg reported from Rome when it was liberated on June 5, 1944, one day before the invasion of Normandy where his colleagues Matt Halton and Marcel Ouimet went ashore with the Canadian troops one hour after D-Day began. Halton and a very young Reuters correspondent from Canada named Charles Lynch brought ashore with them a basket of carrier pigeons, figuring the pigeons would be a fast way to get their stories back to England. Unfortunately, when they released the pigeons, the birds immediately flew over the German lines, seemingly headed for Berlin. Lynch rose up, shaking his fist at the rapidly disappearing pigeons and shouting, "Traitors! Damned traitors!" Halton was almost constantly in the field and on the go from that day on through France, the Netherlands, and Germany until nearly a year later when he entered Berlin with the victorious Allied forces.

Describing Canadian soldiers in Normandy two weeks after D-Day, the forty-year-old Halton waxed poetically and patriotically, "These men were new to battle. They'd never heard the screaming shrapnel before. They hadn't been machine-gunned or sniped at. They hadn't had bombs thrown in their faces. They hadn't been overrun in their slit trenches by tanks. But they have now and they know that there are no better fighting men on earth."

The cheerleader reporting by Halton and other CBC correspondents was totally unlike the much more critical reporting in later wars in Korea, Vietnam, and elsewhere. There was a boosterism to it that reflected the CBC's determination to raise morale by praising the Canadian military, vilifying the enemy, and supporting the government. "It would be regarded as ham today," veteran journalist Charles Lynch said. "We were propagandists. Let's not kid ourselves that the war coverage was objective." A good example of that was the D-Day lead story read by CBC news announcer Earl Cameron, which began, "The dagger pointed at the heart of Berlin has been driven into the side of Nazi Europe."

A news service guideline warned CBC journalists, "When the news is particularly grave, care should be taken to handle it in a way that will not unnecessarily alarm or depress listeners. . . . If more cheerful or encouraging war news is available, use it in the next item." The wording of newscasts also reflected the subjective reporting of war news. The word "announced" was used in referring to British war communiques, while for German statements, the words "claimed" or "admitted" were used.

Halton and the other CBC correspondents were the "stars" of the war, even more so than the generals, and they were called home by the government from time to time to make speeches and appearances on Victory Loan tours of the country.

Canada's most famous war correspondent, Matt Halton, was a long way from his Pincher Creek, Alberta, birthplace. The onetime teacher and *Toronto Star* correspondent added an emotional, and occasionally almost romantic, tone to his broadcasts that captured the imagination of Canadian listeners as they heard his voice sometimes softly quavering with excitement. "It's two minutes to five," he reported in a typically evocative broadcast from the front. "Two minutes to five in Normandy and the sun hasn't risen yet over us or over the Germans eight hundred yards away. It will rise on a fearful scene, because at five o'clock precisely, the Canadians are going to attack. . . . The morning is as soft and beautiful as a swan gliding down a quiet river. But just wait a minute.

"I am in a stone barn with a company of Western Canadian machine-gunners who are going into battle. . . . In front of me, not half a mile away, is the powerful German strong point. . . . We can see the Germans moving from time to time in the half light. We won't see them when the barrage begins. Little white rabbits and baby ducks are playing at my feet. They don't know that this barn will soon be shelled and machine-gunned. . . . The attack will come across right in front of us and toward us. I've never had a better observation post for a battle. And I dread what I'll see through this door."

Halton's most memorable and most emotional broadcast was his report on the liberation of Paris. He, Marcel Ouimet, Art Holmes, and

Paul Johnson entered Paris escorted by the French Underground Maquis before the main Allied forces got there. A young, beautiful, gun-toting Maquis leader named Christianne flung her arms around Halton when they first met on the outskirts of Paris, kissed him, and then burst into tears. "Forgive us," she told Halton. "We have waited so long." She and Halton leapt into a Citroën and led their colleagues into streets that were jammed with wildly cheering Parisians despite the presence of rooftop snipers. As he later broadcast, "Here the crowds were just beginning to come into the streets, mad with happiness. And my friends were shouting *Il est Canadien* – he's a Canadian. And I knew what it was to feel like a king. We were all kings that day."

In the first network broadcast out of a liberated Paris, Halton exulted, "Speaking from Paris! I am telling you about the liberation of Paris, about our entry into Paris yesterday and I don't know how to do it. Though there was still fighting in the streets, Paris went absolutely mad. Paris and ourselves were in a delirium of happiness yesterday and all last night, and today. Yesterday was the most glorious and splendid day I've ever seen." To hear a recording of Halton's report today, half a century later, still raises goosebumps.

The only day more glorious for Halton was the day the war with Germany ended nine months later. Broadcasting back to Canadians, Halton spoke of Sicily, Ortona, Normandy, Carpiquet, and "the appalling hill at Kapellen." "Remember these names, Canada," he said, "because they are written on your heart."

With much less emotion, but with what he called "a good deal of vigour," Mackenzie King also went on the air to mark the end of the war in Europe. "I am told the broadcast had the largest coverage of any the CBC has thus far given to anyone," King confided to his diary. "It included the entire Canadian network, U.S. national network and short wave to Britain, also to sailors and soldiers. It was supposed to have gone to all battlefields." Always the politician and mindful of the federal election in a few weeks time, which he would win, King added, "A broadcast of this kind is worth more than two weeks' campaigning on party matters."

Three months later on VJ-Day when the war in the Pacific ended, King was decidedly less enthusiastic about the CBC's broadcast of his victory speech. He was, in fact, mortified because the CBC broadcast a recording of his comments on Japan's surrender two days before the war was actually over. He had been told the United States would announce the end of the war on August 12, 1945, and he had gone to the CBC's Ottawa station to prepare his remarks. He waited all day at the station but the surrender announcement didn't come from Washington. He agreed to record his statement and leave. At 9:36 P.M. at his Kingsmere residence, while listening to an NBC program carried by the CBC called "The Album of Familiar Music," he heard the CBC break in with a radio flash: "President Truman has just announced that Japan has accepted the surrender terms of the Allies." Then, after a brief musical interlude, on came the prime minister's recorded statement. The flash had come into the CBC newsroom on the British United Press (BUP) news ticker: "FLASH – JAPAN SURRENDERS! REPEAT FLASH – JAPAN SURRENDERS!" The flash had also been carried by NBC. But ten seconds after King's recording began, a "KILL" came on the BUP wire warning, "DISREGARD JAPAN SURRENDER FLASH. NO CONFIRMATION." Charles Gunning, a CBC news editor at the time, recalls, "The horror of it all sank in.... The BUP flash had been a mistake, a fake, a hoax." Later, Gunning says, it was discovered that the fake story had been put on the wire by a disgruntled editor in the agency's Washington office. Rather than cut King off, his statement was allowed to finish. "It did not seem to be advisable to me to stop it," Ernie Bushnell explained.

It was, said the chief news editor, Dan McArthur, "The CBC's most historic fluff." McArthur ordered that from that moment on no flash be broadcast over the CBC until confirmation came from another news agency.

Mackenzie King moaned in his diary about the "malicious spirit" of the media which he knew would criticize him for the mistaken CBC broadcast. "I recognize," he wrote, "that the press would be certain to put the whole thing on my shoulders.... For the rest of my days, and after I'm gone, I shall not be surprised if they continue to harp on this premature announcement."

Apart from this mortifying incident, Mackenzie King had good reason to be pleased with the CBC wartime broadcasts. The war correspondents had boosted the morale of nearly 12 million Canadians. So had other programs that glorified Canada's participation in the war, such as

"Fighting Navy," "Comrades in Arms," the Airforce drama "L for Lanky," "Voices of Victory," "Soldier's Wife," "This Is Our Canada," and "Carry On Canada." There were Victory Loan broadcasts, musical salutes to the Army, Navy, and Air Force, to factory workers and farmers, and the seven-year-old Dionne quintuplets sang "There'll Always Be an England." There were programs on the history of Canadian regiments, the portrait of a day in the life of a recruit, and a series by ten leading industrialists on Canada's war munitions effort. Shakespearean plays were largely abandoned and symphony broadcasts were cut by half to make room for the war shows, comedies, and lighter musical fare such as Gilbert and Sullivan operettas and a national patriotic song contest. The CBC advised all stations in 1940, "It would not appear to be good policy . . . to use songs in Italian or German," and it said such music as "Tales from the Vienna Woods" was "not suitable."

In spite of its best efforts, however, CBC entertainment shows still couldn't match the prime-time popularity of American shows featuring Charlie McCarthy and Edgar Bergen, Jack Benny, Bing Crosby, Bob Hope, Fibber McGee and Molly, and the Lux Radio Theatre. In the afternoon, however, Claire Wallace's talk show, "They Tell Me," and "The Happy Gang" outperformed such American soap operas as "Ma Perkins," "Pepper Young's Family," and "Big Sister." Ottawa prized CBC programming and sought to manipulate it for its wartime needs and as a potent instrument of public persuasion.

A parliamentary committee in 1943 declared, "Radio . . . is the most vital morale builder at a nation's command." The CBC agreed heartily and, in essence, became a propaganda tool of government wartime policies. In a pamphlet entitled "CBC War Effort," the CBC stated that its role was "to inspire the nation as a whole and every individual to greater effort. To put everyone in the proper frame of mind to accept willingly the inevitable sacrifices involved in the war effort. . . . To invigorate every listener with new courage, mentally and physically."

The CBC told its producers it wanted "stirring dramas with propaganda themes." In 1941, it declared, "In the radio field as elsewhere, the all-absorbing task is to further the war effort. . . . There are the numerous war tasks to explain and promote. Such work takes absolute priority." A few months after the war had begun, Ernie Bushnell, as the CBC's program head, chaired a meeting of his senior staff in Toronto and told them, "We must become the vibrant, vigorous expression of a proud nation at arms in every way."

Mackenzie King's government had a particularly broad view of "every way" and not only took over much of the CBC programming itself, but interfered when it didn't like the attitude of some panelists and commentators. CBC program personnel, especially in the public affairs department, chafed at the increasing number of programs originated by the Armed Forces, government departments and agencies, and private organizations such as the Canadian Legion, which were given to the CBC for airing. Gladstone Murray had also ordered a substantial increase in BBC programming carried by the CBC, which reached 1,000 hours a year by 1942 or 7.8 per cent of all CBC airtime. Public affairs producers complained that this left practically no time for talks by Canadian speakers. What little time there was was usually filled with talks ordered on the air by Murray often after consultation with officials of the External Affairs Department or other government departments.

In reaction, the programmers protested that "the unanimous decision of the Program Board [is] that there is no merit whatsoever in [the] talks." Talks department head Donald Buchanan complained that Canadian commentators such as Bruce Hutchison couldn't get on the air and said he had been ordered to take off the national network a series of Canadian talks because of the time needed for the BBC commentaries.

It all became too much for Buchanan, an Alan Plaunt disciple, who resigned in November 1940 shortly after Plaunt himself quit. The CBC, he felt, was surrendering its programming responsibilities. "Any really effective building of national information programs soon became impossible owing to the lack of clarified direction," Buchanan told the 1942 parliamentary committee. "Various war departments of the government put on talks. The CBC management itself took advice from various quarters.... This relinquishment of responsibility, this apparent inability on the part of management to encourage the program staff to draw up a general plan for national information broadcasts ... meant to me that an impasse in the development of the CBC had been reached. So I resigned."

In an article in the Montreal *Standard* a few weeks after his resignation, Buchanan said, "The majority of the ideas used in CBC wartime broadcasts are not the creation of the CBC."

Alan Plaunt, in a note recorded in his files, put it more bluntly: "The Corporation has, since the outbreak of the war, been rapidly becoming merely the tool of the party in power. . . . Nobody except Cabinet Ministers and other government yes men are invited to speak. . . . The Corporation has lost all vestiges of independence of thought or action."

Far from being concerned about programs originating from the government, CBC management expressed pride in working so intimately with the government. In 1943, it boasted that "the war finance committee have utilized our facilities to the full . . . the Armed Services have all secured places in our programming to publicize the activities in which they are engaged. The Wartime Prices and Trade Board have regular features on our programming."

The lack of CBC-originated programs was aggravated by the absence of the head of programming for much of the early part of the war. Ernie Bushnell had been seconded to the BBC to run its North American service. But faced with Buchanan's resignation and growing internal disgruntlement, Murray recalled Bushnell in January 1941, and the CBC began to broadcast more of its own commentaries and discussion programs. This, however, brought more headaches in the form of government interference in programs. After government pressure, CBC management agreed to restrict political free time because, as René Morin told the 1942 parliamentary committee, "In time of war . . . it was not the proper time to engage in controversial broadcasts which might endanger the unity of the country." The result was a distinct advantage to the Liberal government, whose spokesmen were often on the air with "non partisan" commentaries while the Opposition was largely unheard. In 1942, for example, Liberal MPs and senators made seventy-five CBC broadcasts and Opposition members, five. King was on the air fourteen times and the leader of the Opposition, once.

The most blatant example of CBC kowtowing to government was during the 1942 conscription plebiscite. Mackenzie King wanted to be released from a pledge he had made against conscription for overseas service, and he held a plebiscite in which a yes vote would release him. In preparing for radio free-time talks on the issue, Murray drafted a plan that included the possibility of having talks by the no side, as well as the yes side, at least in Quebec where anti-conscription sentiment was strong.

A draft of his plan said, "For the French Network there will be special provision of four hours, ——— of which will be made available to the advocates of a negative answer to the plebiscite."

A share of CBC free-time broadcasting in the plebiscite debate was exactly what was demanded by La Ligue pour la défense du Canada, a Quebec nationalist group formed to fight conscription and led by, among others, Georges Pelletier, editor of *Le Devoir*, and André Laurendeau, a future editor of *Le Devoir* and future member of the Royal Commission on Bilingualism and Biculturalism. A vitriolic supporter of the anti-conscription campaign was a young Pierre Trudeau, who called the government plans "sickeningly dishonest."

In a letter dated late March 1942 to Secretary of State Norman McLarty, Gladstone Murray had written in a P.S., "In the matter of time on the national network for advocacy of a negative answer, if it seemed expedient and safe to arrange this, provision could be made." But it was neither "expedient" nor "safe" for the King government, and the CBC quickly began backtracking once it heard government voices raised in protest. The quickly revised policy allowed network talks only by speakers representing the four major political parties – all of which favoured the yes side. Pelletier and Laurendeau were told they could buy time on individual private stations, a much more expensive and much less effective way of getting out their message. They protested but to no avail. Augustin Frigon, CBC assistant general manager and, in effect, head of the French network, wrote them that the decision was taken "in accordance with instruction received from the federal government."

CBC board member Adrien Pouliot said it was a government decision and the acting secretary of state, W. P. Mulock, seemed to agree when he declared, "The use of the Canadian Broadcasting Corporation's English and French Networks, in dealing with the plebiscite, is restricted to use by the Prime Minister, Members of the Cabinet and leaders of the recognized parties in the House of Commons."

The Mackenzie King government had simply ordered the CBC to

deny the no side any radio network voice. It was as if Ottawa had forbidden the CBC to broadcast any statements by the no side in the Charlottetown accord referendum of 1992 or imposed a ban on network airtime for those favouring separatism or sovereignty association in the Quebec referendum of 1970. This intervention, however, didn't help King in Quebec. While the country as a whole voted yes on conscription for overseas service, Quebec voted no by a resounding majority.

The governing Liberals may have forced the CBC to deny airtime to the no side in the conscription plebiscite, but a few months later the CBC walked into its own trap when it said no to a Conservative Party request that outgoing leader Arthur Meighen be given CBC airtime for an address from the party's December 1942 Winnipeg leadership convention. Board members thought that granting the request would be "a new departure that might lead to innovation," and Gladstone Murray, in his last days as general manager, was instructed to tell the Conservatives that a radio speech by Meighen "would create an inadmissible precedent." The Liberal-dominated CBC board worried that if the Conservatives got airtime, similar airtime would have to be given to the CCF. In spite of the Tory's fury and their offer to purchase time on air for the address, the CBC remained adamant.

The Conservatives were outraged, charging the CBC with restricting radio "as a private preserve for those with whom it is in sympathy." They said the Conservative Party leader had "an absolute right" to airtime "on an equality with him who occupies the position of Prime Minister of Canada."

The CBC brusquely rejected the Conservative's claims, but Dr. James Thomson, who had just taken Murray's place as general manager, offered half an hour of airtime for the successor to Meighen to be chosen by the convention, provided the speech was "not of a political nature." Dr. Thomson added, "He should refrain from anything that is abusive or which would tend to cast any personal discredit on political opponents. In other words, I would suggest that the broadcast should be made in the spirit of a constructive and positive statement of policy rather than a negative attack upon the policies of other people."

That tore it for the Conservatives. The party secretary called Dr.

Thomson's offer "an empty gesture," and added, "By what right, Sir, do you venture to suggest to the Leader of the Conservative Party what are the proprieties that might be observed?"

At the Winnipeg convention in December 1942, an enraged Meighen devoted much of his speech to an attack on the CBC, calling it "an authoritarian Commission." He had spent a sleepless night before speaking tossing and turning as his anger rose at the CBC. In Winnipeg's Civic Auditorium the next day, he told delegates, "We of the Conservative Convention of this Dominion cannot be heard and we cannot pay to be heard. . . . The radio of Canada has been for years and is today, and Mr. King intends it will continue to be, the effective monopoly, tool and instrument of a partisan Government headed by himself."

Meighen accused King and his ministers of using radio for political propaganda. "Has anyone listened since the war began, or for years before, to a radio address by the Prime Minister or by any of his Ministers, which was not charged and replete with political appeal; whose purpose was not from first to last to boost the stock of the King Government? . . . Those men, month after month, week after week, day after day have gone on delivering messages to the people of Canada, the central purpose of which was to build themselves up, to popularize themselves and thus to be ready for a trial of strength when an appeal to the electors comes. And the radio commission says that is all right, it is in the national interest; that only contributes to loving harmony which must prevail in time of war. . . . That, according to Chairman [sic] Thomson, is a great patriotic purpose, but if we who think differently seek . . . to show the other point of view, he tells us that to do so is to inject political discord into a happy atmosphere, and he turns the button against millions of people whom we want to reach, and who are waiting to hear."

The Conservative Party endorsed Meighen's stance and condemned the "authoritarian" CBC for "peremptorily refusing" and "forbidding" the Conservatives from carrying "its speeches, its arguments and decisions . . . into the homes of our country." In the ensuing years, Meighen's anger at the CBC remained, and in his autobiography, *Unrevised and Unrepentant*, he called the CBC a party instrument. He wrote of "the Gestapo methods in matters of radio" and charged that the Liberals were using radio "with their eyes on the ballot morning, noon and night. . . . You might as well sit up and recognize that fascism is here." Meighen refused to appear on any CBC program for the next fifteen years.

After Manitoba Premier John Bracken was chosen as Meighen's successor, on the condition that the party henceforth be known as the Progressive Conservative Party, the CBC repeated its offer of a half-hour radio speech, and Bracken accepted. As soon as his speech was on the air, CCF leader M. J. Coldwell demanded and was reluctantly given equal time. Coldwell, too, was admonished by the CBC to "not think of yourself as a propagandist for a particular political party, but rather as a responsible political leader of a party in the Canadian House of Commons who is being invited . . . to advance his particular point of view as a general and positive contribution to the elucidation of great public questions."

Continuing on its self-mutilating path, the CBC rubbed salt into the Conservative Party's wounds a year later by refusing to let Bracken go on the air with a report on his first year as party leader. The CBC board had originally agreed to his half-hour address, but when it read his speech, it said he was being too political and cancelled the broadcast. The board, said the Conservative Party, was "so obviously steeped in politics that it would be unable to define the word 'political' without embarrassing itself." When queried about giving airtime to the prime minister and cabinet ministers but refusing the Conservative leader, Frigon said government statements were "reports to the public on governmental administration" while Bracken's proposed radio address was "political controversy."

The resulting hullabaloo eventually led the CBC to give regular free airtime for political statements to all parties between elections as well as during election campaigns. In addition to the regular free time, the recently elected Conservative premier of Ontario, George Drew, wanted the CBC to provide a provincial network once a week for a report to the people. The CBC said no, and Drew became an enemy of the CBC and its "idiotic restrictions."

Arrogantly denying Meighen's and Bracken's requests had been a fateful mistake. It seriously undermined political support for the CBC and gelled the Tory's antipathy toward the CBC. From here on the Conservatives campaigned tirelessly to split regulatory functions away from

Andrew Allan (right), premier drama producer of radio's golden age, conferring in a control room with orchestra leader Lucio Agostini. (*National Archives of Canada, PA 122555*)

Max Ferguson, aka Rawhide, CBC Radio's most controversial and iconoclastic character. (*National Archives of Canada, PA 111381*)

Lorne Greene, known as the Voice of Doom, broadcasting the war news. (*National Archives of Canada, 14467*)

Johnny Wayne and Frank Shuster in their early radio days before becoming Canada's most popular and enduring comedians. (*National Archives of Canada, PA 152119*)

Prime Minister Mackenzie King, who oversaw the birth of the CBC in 1936, making his VE-Day statement on radio. (*National Archives of Canada, C 23279*)

Radio's most popular orchestra of the 1930s and 1940s was
Mart Kenney and his Western Gentlemen.
(Sandy Stewart Photo Collection, National Archives of Canada, 12682)

The legendary "Happy Gang," who captivated Canadians from 1937 to 1959 with their
effervescent brand of music and comedy. Left to right, head "gangster" Bert Pearl,
Bob Farnon, Hugh Bartlett, Blain Mathe, George Temple, and Kay Stokes.
(*Sandy Stewart Photo Collection, National Archives of Canada, 12669*)

CBC recording engineer Art Holmes, who captured the
sounds of war more effectively than anyone else
during the Second World War.
(*National Archives of Canada, 16073*)

Matthew Halton, Canada's most famous war correspondent, broadcasting from
the Italian front near Ortona. (*National Archives of Canada, C 66626*)

Marcel Ouimet reporting from Normandy as the
Canadians attack a German stronghold. (Sandy Stewart
Photo Collection, National Archives of Canada, 6015)

CBC French network correspondent Benoit Lafleur, reporting from the Italian front
with recording engineeer J. L. Ben. (*National Archives of Canada, 14023*)

Leonard Brockington, first
chairman of the CBC, 1936-39.
(*National Archives of Canada,*
C 12857)

Dan McArthur, the colourful,
resolute founder of the CBC
News Service in 1941. He con-
sidered news to be a public trust.
(*National Archives of*
Canada, 15578)

Gladstone Murray, the talented,
heavy-drinking first general
manager of the CBC, 1936-42.
(*National Archives of*
Canada, PA 122592)

The first CBC board of governors in 1936. Left to right, N. L. Nathanson, Nellie
McClung, vice-chairman René Morin, chairman Leonard Brockington, Col. Wilfrid
Bovey, Wilfred Godfrey, Rev. Alexandre Vachon, Alan Plaunt. Gen. Victor Odlum was
absent from this meeting. (*National Archives of Canada, 12470*)

J. Frank Willis, Canada's first broadcast news "star," holding a CRBC microphone and interviewing rescuers at the
1936 mine disaster at Moose River, N.S.
(*National Archives of Canada, CBC 15284*)

Comedians Woodhouse and Hawkins were the Wayne and Shuster of early Canadian
radio. (*Sandy Stewart Photo Collection, National Archives of Canada, 6018*)

The Gang of Three who ran the CRBC. Left to right, Lt.-Col. William Arthur Steel chairman Hector Charlesworth, , and Thomas Maher.
(*National Archives of Canada, PA 122591*)

Austin Weir, progam director of CNR Radio in the 1920s, became program director of the CRBC and later joined the CBC.
(*National Archives of Canada, PA 122958*)

the CBC, lessen CBC's role, and strengthen private broadcasting's. At the Winnipeg convention, John Diefenbaker listened to and agreed with Meighen's bitter attack on the CBC. As prime minister a decade and a half later, Diefenbaker finally got the party's revenge on the CBC.

The CBC's readiness to bend to real or perceived pressures from the governing Liberals encouraged them to make more demands on the CBC; the government just couldn't keep its hands off CBC programming. The worst offender was the minister of war services, Gen. Leo R. LaFlèche, a war hero and patriot, who had taken over responsibility for the CBC from C. D. Howe. His desire to interfere was matched only by Augustin Frigon's desire to let him. Frigon had become general manager in 1942, replacing Dr. James Thomson, who had run the CBC since Gladstone Murray's demotion and had already demonstrated his deference to government in the conscription plebiscite controversy. In his new capacity he riled even program head Ernie Bushnell, as well as journalists and public affairs producers.

The first confrontation arose in late 1943 over a new discussion program series, modelled on "The National Farm Radio Forum," which grew out of the series "Of Things to Come." It would evolve into the long-running "Citizens' Forum" moderated by author Morley Callaghan and offering widely divergent and controversial points of view on current issues. Ned Corbett, director of the Canadian Association for Adult Education, developed the series in co-operation with the new head of CBC public affairs programming, Neil Morrison. The participants they chose included Liberals, Conservatives, and CCFers. The idea of CCFers getting airtime on such a program alarmed the Liberals, especially Brooke Claxton, who was now the prime minister's parliamentary assistant. Ironically, Claxton had been the principal author of the 1942 parliamentary report condemning Gladstone Murray and the CBC for not having "a wide variety of points of view" in its programming. Morrison and Callaghan went to see Claxton to tell him of their plans, including the fact that they had had discussions with the CCF. Claxton exploded in anger, saying that they could not have "those people" on the air and that he was "mad as hell."

Claxton, who had just been named chairman of the Liberal Party policy committee, feared the CCF might make inroads into the Liberals' support. His attitude was revealed in a letter he had written earlier to *Winnipeg Free Press* editor John Dafoe saying, "The CCF are ingenious and persistent in discovering means to put the radio to political use in their interest." In a memo to Mackenzie King, Claxton said the list of speakers for the program showed "a drastic loading in favour of the CCF. . . . The programs must be fundamentally changed." Morrison recalls that Claxton thought that any on-air discussion of controversial issues could play into the hands of the Opposition and threaten the government. "You can't tell me what to do!" Callaghan shouted.

The next night Bushnell went to Claxton's Chateau Laurier hotel room to discuss the same subject and again they got into a shouting match over the program, with Bushnell accusing Claxton of interfering in other CBC programming. "We went at it hammer and tong," he remembered, after Claxton demanded that Morrison and Callaghan be fired as "incompetents."

Claxton and his Liberal colleagues pressured LaFlèche to do something and he, in turn, told Frigon, "Stop those broadcasts!" Frigon tore a strip off Morrison, telling him to shape up and threatening to withdraw his exemption from Army service. "Good God," Morrison later recalled. "That guy was blackmailing me!"

The board, responding to government pressure, was moving toward cancelling the series. "They were hack political appointments, some of them," Morrison said. "There was a constant tension or frequently conflict between management and or the board, and the program staff."

"We've had terrific pressure on us to have this series stopped," Murray told Ned Corbett. CBC board member Rowe Holland was part of the pressure, telling Bushnell, "I am personally pretty well disgusted with the results we are getting with these round table discussions. I am afraid they are too obviously undermining the confidence in government. . . . When our 'way of living' is being so seriously challenged by the socialists, this is a matter which should be given our greatest consideration. The net result of most of these round tables is to disseminate criticism of government policy without any counter balancing factor."

The programmers were angered both by LaFlèche's attempt to cancel the series and by the board's giving in. "A nasty piece he was," Corbett later said of LaFlèche, and Morrison agreed, adding, "He was not one of the brightest politicians in the world." Fourteen senior program officers dispatched a two-page letter to Frigon asking him to pass on to the prime minister and LaFlèche their condemnation of the political pressure. They warned that the CBC might be viewed as "the instrument" of the Liberal Party and that political interference "will inevitably lead to the destruction of the basic principles of the organization and the demoralization of staff." The memo never got beyond Frigon who told Bushnell the series had to be postponed.

LaFlèche announced the series would be "laid aside," and the programmers didn't know what to do next. But in what was becoming a pattern, the wily Ned Corbett knew exactly what to do. A few years earlier he had been angered when the CBC threatened to stop a series of radio talks which the Liberal government thought was too left wing. Corbett leaked the story to the Toronto *Telegram,* and the CBC and the government had to bow to the embarrassing headlines. The series continued with a discussion on the value of co-operatives by Nova Scotia's Father M. M. Coady. This time, Corbett leaked the story to the *Winnipeg Free Press.* That led to screaming headlines about gross government interference, attacks on the Liberals, and an outraged phone call to the prime minister from John Dafoe. "The CBC isn't worth the paper it's written on if this is going to happen," Dafoe told King, according to Corbett. "You've got to stop this business." Corbett says King "went through the roof" in response to the press attack. LaFlèche retreated, saying, "There has not been any exercise of any political pressure or any attempt made to dominate the board politically."

After much confusion and intense political embarrassment, the series finally went ahead as scheduled. Corbett confessed to Bushnell that he had leaked the story, to which Bushnell responded, "You son of a bitch, Get out of town. But goddamn it, I'd do the same as you're doing."

Corbett said Murray also supported his action and quoted him as saying, "I wanted the public to know that this had happened. The best thing that could happen was to let it run in the papers."

But the furore didn't shake LaFlèche from his habit, and he interfered to order the cancellation of a commentary on New Brunswick mental health hospitals by reporter Kenneth Johnstone. Again, news of his intervention was leaked to the press. Frigon said that he had cancelled the talk, not the minister, and the commentary was broadcast later. "If this is a typical example of what state ownership of national broadcasting means in the shape of political control and decision, it is high time that the whole policy and set up were given a thorough overhauling," said the Montreal *Gazette*.

In spite of political embarrassment and burned fingers, LaFlèche kept on interfering. While he peppered Frigon with complaints and suggestions, his public relations staff, his secretary, and even the Liberal Party advertising agency, Cockfield-Brown, repeatedly called CBC newsrooms in Montreal and Toronto demanding stories be aired about the minister's activities, speeches, and travels. CBC chief news editor Dan McArthur recorded that LaFlèche's secretary was boasting in Ottawa that he was "running the CBC news." LaFlèche, McArthur said, "felt [he had] the right to expect certain things in the news."

The general himself forcefully sought publicity for his activities, and on one occasion, a CBC Montreal editor was ordered to LaFlèche's home to hear his demand that a speech of his be carried in full on CBC. It wasn't.

In the mid-summer of 1944, LaFlèche forbade the CBC to make any mention of the huge train station welcome in Montreal for former mayor Camillien Houde. Houde had just been released from internment for anti-war activities in urging people not to register for military service. LaFlèche said the CBC could mention the fact that Houde had returned to Montreal, but must ignore the thousands of cheering Montrealers who greeted him. The boisterous welcome was splashed across newspaper front pages and heard on private radio, but not on the CBC. "Management had given a commitment to the government over the head of the News Service to suppress the story of the demonstration," McArthur bitterly complained. He later wrote, "The basic principle of honest news reporting . . . had been swept aside by an authoritarian management at the behest, or perhaps merely at the suggestion, of the government."

LaFlèche was also behind an order to forbid the CBC from reporting demonstrations against conscription, and McArthur was admonished for allowing on the air a report of an anti-conscription parade in Montreal in which several windows in a newspaper building had been broken. The incident came before the CBC board, which endorsed the rebuke.

The official summary of the board meeting noted, "The Chairman suggested the CBC should set an example by publicly announcing that it would in future carry no news at all in CBC bulletins of anti-conscription demonstrations."

Bill Metcalfe, the CBC's senior editor in Winnipeg, recalled attending a CBC editors meeting the day after the parade. After raising his objections to the CBC's story, Frigon was asked how he would have written about the window-smashing, anti-conscription riot. "I would have written it like this," he told the editors. "'Last night a group of high-spirited young men held a protest parade through downtown Montreal. After their parade, they dispersed.'"

"Oh boy!" said Metcalfe to himself. "What are we in for? No reference to French-speaking students; no reference to police; no indication that the students were protesting conscription; and no reference to all those broken windows. If this is the kind of falsity our news service must employ, I want out."

Metcalfe's impression of Frigon was that "he seemed to have a respect for Liberal Party authority that overrode any respect he might have had for the integrity of the news."

LaFlèche was not the only cabinet minister who stuck his fingers into CBC programming. The justice minister and later prime minister, Louis St. Laurent, demanded the CBC not carry reports on prison riots. "It would be appreciated if the Editor of the CBC News could see fit to eliminate in the news, broadcasts with reference to these minor disturbances," St. Laurent wrote to Frigon. His argument was that if the CBC carried reports of prison riots, prisoners in other penitentiaries, who were not allowed to read newspapers and only allowed to listen to the CBC, might be encouraged to cause disturbances as well.

"You should be honoured to take instructions from the Minister of Justice," McArthur was told. He disagreed, calling it "a very disturbing suggestion." But despite his protests, McArthur was ordered to obey, and a story about a disturbance in Manitoba's Stony Mountain prison was withheld from the CBC News. Frigon told the minister, "I am very pleased to have had this opportunity to offer the co-operation of the CBC in a matter of such significance."

"I still take a dark view of such concessions on our part," McArthur complained to Bushnell. The *Globe and Mail*, when it learned about St. Laurent's intervention, headed a critical editorial, "GOVERNMENT COMMANDS, CBC OBEYS." The *Winnipeg Free Press* said, "Another assault on CBC independence.... The instances multiply as the years go by."

The problem for McArthur, Morrison, and their producers and editors was clearly not just government interference in programs, but CBC management's acquiesence, specifically Frigon's willingness to cater to the government's wishes. Many of Frigon's colleagues felt he had opened the gates to government invasion of CBC independence with his deference to authority. At his instructions, Frigon's secretary frequently called CBC news rooms issuing suggestions and directives to editors "in a most peremptory" fashion, according to McArthur. "Frigon's attitude," McArthur said, "was simply to bow to authority," a stance McArthur despised. He complained to his boss, Bushnell, "The Doctor has for some reason, resented what he considers the 'independence' of the news. I am also convinced that at heart he does not accept the democratic approach to news.... Each concession makes CBC News more of an 'official' news service which gives the listener only such news as those in authority consider desirable."

A major confrontation came over a news story in early 1944 on the controversy over the retirement of Gen. Andrew McNaughton, whom the government had removed from command of Canadian soldiers overseas. The CBC story quoted McNaughton as saying on his return to Canada that he was "absolutely fit." This contradicted a government statement that he had retired because of poor health. By carrying the story, CBC had embarrassed the government, Frigon felt, and he lambasted the news service for "yellow" journalism.

Dan McArthur, the creative, fiercely independent, and frequently vituperative chief news editor, was totally the opposite of the orderly, efficient, devoted public servant Augustin Frigon. They simply couldn't understand each other, and as McArthur grew increasingly furious at Frigon's interference, Frigon became deeply frustrated and resentful at what he considered McArthur's insubordination.

McArthur said Frigon had a "civil service approach to news" with an "attitude of mind completely undemocratic." Frigon consistently denied he ever bowed to government pressure and said his concern was that CBC

News should not elaborate or provide details on stories such as the anti-conscription demonstrations. In a letter to Bushnell, Frigon wrote, "No one on our staff is more determined than myself to keep our news service independent of all influence. Nevertheless, there are occasions when it becomes necessary."

McArthur became so angry, he threatened to reveal a secret dossier he had kept on Frigon's interference in the news by leaking it to John Diefenbaker, M. J. Coldwell, and Paul Martin, as well as to *Maclean's* writer Blair Fraser and others. "Blackmail maybe – but good!" he memoed Bushnell. But he backed away when Bushnell promised him he could appear before the CBC board to state his case. He did and the confrontation was papered over, although tensions between McArthur and Frigon remained.

Their clash had been inevitable from the moment the CBC News Service was established at the beginning of 1941. Each man had a profoundly different sense about the role of journalists and what CBC News should do. McArthur felt Frigon believed newsmen were "congenitally venal" and should be satisfied with low pay because they could find easy ways of augmenting their income, by which he meant through bribery. Much worse in McArthur's mind was Frigon's concept that CBC News should be the vehicle for the dissemination of government information and propaganda. When the News Service was being set up, Frigon urged "that the CBC be considered as a semi-official medium to reach the public."

Frigon, a close friend of Mackenzie King's Quebec lieutenant, Ernest Lapointe, felt strongly that the CBC should support government efforts to improve wartime morale and that this would inevitably lead to concealing or changing news stories as the government dictated. He endorsed LaFlèche's statement that "radio is a war machine, a war weapon. With it one can play upon the minds and hearts of men. It can be used to strengthen the moral fibre of a people at war or it can be used to demoralize. . . . In a war where everything we have is at stake . . . it is to be remembered that the radio is essential." The board took a similar view at the outbreak of war, saying that the CBC's role was to bring "the country's leaders in constant contact with listeners and to sustain morale."

While accepting the necessity of wartime censorship and recognizing the usefulness of some morale-building radio programs that glorified the war effort, McArthur was damned if he would allow CBC News itself to become a mouthpiece of the government. He not only fought off an interfering government, but also interfering senior officials inside the CBC, such as Frigon, who aided and abetted much of the government's intrusion. From the time he was named CBC chief news editor in late 1940, McArthur spent the rest of his life battling and, in most cases battling successfully, to maintain the independence and integrity of CBC News.

News broadcasting had not been a priority with the CBC until the outbreak of war in 1939. The new corporation had initially continued the Canadian Press-prepared newscasts of the CRBC days because they were free. To have its own news service would cost money the CBC preferred to put into new stations and general programming. By broadcasting CP-written newscasts, CBC management also thought it could avoid taking responsibility for the content of the newscasts. Still another reason was CP's insistence on being recognized as Canada's principal disseminator of news.

Ernie Bushnell, however, thought that CP was delivering an inferior product to the CBC. "What we have been getting from them is not good enough – stale news, poorly written and oft times poorly chosen," he said in a December 30, 1937, memo to Gladstone Murray. "They do not know how to write material for oral delivery; they do not know how to build a radio newscast, giving it a shape just as a musical or a dramatic production has a shape."

Bushnell was supported by E. C. Buchanan, head of CBC public relations who, a year earlier, had suggested to Murray that the CBC should take more control of its newscasts. Bushnell proposed that the CBC not only write and prepare its own newscasts, but advanced the seemingly revolutionary idea that the CBC should have its own reporters as well. Three months later, two CBC news announcers, W. J. O'Reilly and Terrence O'Dell, gave Bushnell a detailed proposal on establishing a news service. It was "absurd," O'Reilly and O'Dell said, that the CBC broadcast only one network newscast a day. Their ideas were welcomed by Bushnell, but squelched by CBC chairman Leonard Brockington, who told a parliamentary committee a few days later, "The gathering of our own news would be very expensive and one which we cannot engage in at the present time."

Bushnell's, O'Reilly's, and O'Dell's ideas were put aside but not forgotten, and in the fall of 1938, Bushnell brought them up again. "The proper presentation of news . . . is by far the most important function of a nationally operated broadcasting system such as ours," he said. His interest in news was spurred by visits to England as war neared, where he was impressed with the BBC's extensive radio news coverage, especially during the Munich crisis. Picking up much of the BBC's reports, the CBC had aired more than a hundred special broadcasts in the seventeen days of the Munich crisis. Bushnell urged establishment of a news service "at once," but his bosses still said no. Instead, a new arrangement was made with CP under which the CBC would decide the number and length of newscasts, although CP warned against changing the "integrity" of any of its stories. The CBC agreed to pay $20,000 a year to CP for technical expenses. CP, however, still determined the choice and order of news stories and did all the basic writing, with consultation from the CBC only on radio writing style. CP also often withheld stories from the CBC until they had appeared in the newspapers.

As the Second World War approached, it became increasingly apparent to both senior CBC management and to the government that the CBC should have full control over its newscasts. The chaos of war and the organizing of wartime programming preoccupied both the CBC and the government, however, and it wasn't until mid-1940 that action came. It came from Transport Minister C. D. Howe, at the time responsible for the CBC, who said, "I think I can say that within the next month there will be a new policy for news on the air which I shall announce as soon as I can and which I think will be recognized by all as an improvement . . . [but] I may be scooped by my news service." His reference to "my news service" clearly indicated Howe expected CBC News to be his and the government's, not an independent service.

By the end of the summer of 1940, the CBC had decided to set up its own news service, with newsrooms in Toronto, Montreal, Halifax, Winnipeg, and Vancouver and with Dan McArthur as chief news editor. Under the guidance of the future war correspondent and future head of the French network, Marcel Ouimet, a small French-language newsroom had been set up in Montreal for the French network a few years earlier. But now, with McArthur's appointment, the CBC was formally in the news business with a staff of twenty-five editors across Canada.

On January 1, 1941, at 8:00 A.M. EST, the CBC News Service went on air with the words, "This is the National News Bulletin brought to you by the CBC." Thus ended eight years of CP newscasts and the beginning of true broadcast news – "a running account of history in the making," McArthur called it. He soon added actuality and voice reports from war correspondents within the newscasts, and two and a half years later, a fifteen-minute program of background information called "News Roundup" was added, immediately following the "National News Bulletin." It had longer reports from war correspondents and newspapermen on the scene of important events in Canada and elsewhere.

The forty-three-year-old stubborn and mercurial Dan McArthur was born in Brooklyn and spent his childhood in England and his teenage years in a log cabin near Appin, in southwestern Ontario. His father was a noted Canadian journalist and his godfather was the Canadian poet Bliss Carmen. Carmen instilled in him a love for raffish poetry and doggerel that lasted all his life and added a certain vividness to his CBC memos, such as one entitled "Up Shit Creek Without a P & A Paddle." In the memo, he vituperatively denounced CBC bureaucratic administrators, and by implication, Dr. Augustin Frigon. He sent a copy of it to Frigon, all senior administrators, and all senior News Service personnel. In it, he called the CBC bureaucracy "that fungus growth that now covers the whole of the CBC like a green mildew." Instead of an atmosphere "that should be creative and dynamic, that needs imagination and sensitivity and flair . . . we now live in something so beautifully organized that all the guts have been squeezed out of it." Program people have had, he said, "the beJesus organized out of them."

No longer, he said, was he going to "suck up to" or "humiliate" himself "to some fatass" bureaucrat in "trying to explain in Basic English why something needs to be done about an operation of which they know nothing."

The focus of his scalding invective in this instance was a denial by Frigon's favourite department, Personnel and Administration (P & A), known to McArthur and his colleagues as the Pest and Aggravation Department. It had denied McArthur a fan to cool the central newsroom's summertime hellhole in the basement of a CBC building in Toronto. If he were given the fan, the bureaucrats explained, then other locations would want fans, too. "These buggers," he said, "want . . . uniformity and conformity, in newsrooms and in individuals, everything nicely grouped and graded from coast to coast. . . . If anything means death in a creative enterprise, it is uniformity. . . . If one of these lardasses would spend a week in a newsroom . . . he might know what in hell I was talking about. . . .

"If this creeping paralysis of P & A can't be checked, if we can't crack it up and get back the old dynamic and stimulating atmosphere and restore the vital creative juices to the CBC, then to hell with it all. Just to be one of another batch of poor old dyspeptic bastards, stewing away in a stinking mess of P & A red tape . . . then we're up Shit Creek and P & A has the paddle . . . and as far as I'm concerned I intend to jump in and swim for shore."

The fan he demanded for the newsroom was later installed, although only after McArthur resigned in protest and was then persuaded to stay on. He would remain chief news editor for thirteen stormy years. "He had a savage temper, and anybody who ever saw Dan in eruption might well wonder whether he was stable or not, especially if you were on the receiving end," said veteran journalist and McArthur's old friend, Charles Lynch. "He was an irreverent, flamboyant, profane man," Lynch added, "but he was a ferocious guardian of the CBC News department."

McArthur's eccentricity, his prodigious and colourful profanity, and his abrasive and obsessive insistence on the independence and integrity of CBC News saved the News Service from becoming an echo chamber for government propaganda. "In some quarters," McArthur remembered, "it was taken for granted that the CBC Bulletin would present only the 'official' viewpoint – would be, in other words, the mouthpiece and apologist of the party in power."

That danger was there from the start and was pointed to by much of the press. McArthur recalled a Victoria newspaper editorial in which CBC News was called "the lickspittle creature of the present government."

With much of the press suspicious of the CBC being a government voice, with government officials like C. D. Howe thinking of it as "my news service," and with some in CBC management, such as Frigon, urging it be a 'semi-official' service, there were valid grounds for McArthur's fears that CBC News would be misused and mistrusted. He had two defences: for his editors, an insistence on objectivity, which he made a holy grail; and for his bosses, an absolute rejection of any editorial interference from them or anyone else outside the newsroom. Both of these approaches he pursued with unrelenting ferocity. "The maintenance of the News Service integrity hinged on McArthur's ability to stave off challenges both from inside and outside the CBC," says broadcast historian Robert Albota.

"This service," McArthur declared, "is in the nature of a public trust. . . . Accuracy must be the first consideration. [It will] present all the significant news of the day's happenings in Canada and abroad factually without bias or distortion, without tendentious comment and in a clear and unambiguous style." That meant, he told his editors, absolute impartiality in presenting the news. In turn, that meant "rigid factuality" with no possibility of even perceived bias. "No member of CBC News Service staff will permit his personal views, whatever they may be, to exert the slightest influence on the manner in which he may handle political copy for CBC News Bulletins," McArthur warned. At one point, McArthur even issued a statement swearing political neutrality that every supervisor and senior editor in the country signed.

"I was called into the regional director's office and asked to sign a statement that I was not a member of a political group," recalls Don Macdonald, then an editor in Halifax and later one of McArthur's successors as chief news editor. "To have to do that illustrates what his concerns were and what steps he had to take to resist pressures and protect the news." McArthur himself told his bosses, "I have no political affiliation and never have had."

McArthur even ordered his editors to be careful in expressing their political opinions in private conversations. "Editors should be especially circumspect," he memoed, "in engaging in political discussions in public or with chance acquaintances, where their views might be misinterpreted and work serious harm to the reputation of the whole news service." He ordered his editors never to deviate from the facts in news agency reports and, except for war correspondents, McArthur would not hire reporters, especially in Ottawa. "This obviates any possible criticism that the CBC News Service is an official Government mouthpiece," McArthur said. It would be more than a decade before CBC News did serious reporting of its own within Canada.

McArthur had a standing rule that if anybody brought a news story to the CBC, they would be told to contact the Canadian Press. The News Service thereby lost many a scoop, but in McArthur's mind, this protected the CBC from outside influence. "We wanted to make sure no one outside the News Service no matter what his position was, would feel free to call up a news editor to say, 'Look, please handle a certain story in a certain way,'" McArthur said. He brusquely rejected suggestions from some government officials that the CBC should be given information by government departments ahead of the newspapers.

"CBC was very sensitive and very frightened of news," says Peter Stursberg, the CBC war correspondent. "They were afraid that if they had their own reporters or if they had their own reporting, the newspapers would claim that this was government propaganda... McArthur wanted the news to be purely and simply a rewrite of the agencies."

In spite of his strictures, McArthur was idolized by his staff who viewed him as a straight arrow fighting off the Goliaths both in government and in the senior levels of the CBC. He enlivened many an all-night singing and drinking session with his editors with his concertina and his sassy songs. Don Macdonald remembers McArthur visiting Halifax. "He'd have this little squeeze box with him and we'd have a few beers and Dan would play the little accordion and sing. He had a good sense of humour, but he had temper tantrums that erupted from time to time." News writer Bill Metcalfe in Winnipeg later wrote, "Whatever integrity the CBC News ever enjoyed then and now, Dan McArthur should receive the credit for it."

McArthur's strict rules didn't please everyone, however. Some Liberals complained of "a strong CCF slant" on CBC News, as did Conservative and Social Credit members, one of whom complained of "the hidden hand" of the CCF on the news. On the other hand, CCF leader M. J. Coldwell complained of "political discrimination practised deliberately" by CBC News against the CCF. He claimed, "People on this side of the House are never invited to participate in the discussion of public issues. That is reserved for members of the Government and for officials who praise them." John Diefenbaker said the CBC had "become a party vehicle" for the Liberals in its programming. George Drew called the CBC a "Government mouthpiece." One of Drew's predecessors as Conservative leader, Arthur Meighen, denounced the CBC for biased editing of one of his speeches in the early part of the war. "They had mutilated and butchered [it].... They took out everything in the nature of criticism and left a shapeless, truncated mess."

McArthur's inflexible demands for objectivity, however, sometimes shocked government authorities. Once when an official in the Prime Minister's Office called the newsroom with a statement which Mackenzie King wanted on the CBC News that night, he was told by an editor, "Tell the Prime Minister that I'm the editor and I'll decide what goes into the Bulletin."

McArthur applied his unyielding attitude on the independence of his news service to CBC management as well as to the government. Senior executives must not call the newsroom, he decreed. "If senior executives . . . felt free to call the news editors and make suggestions that certain items should be carried or should be given special emphasis for reasons that were personal or political in nature, the whole integrity of the news service would immediately be lost," he told Gladstone Murray. On this, Murray, a former journalist himself, agreed, and as long as he was general manager, Murray kept his hands off the News Service. That changed when Frigon took over and the bitter feud between Frigon and McArthur began. Frigon did not want the CBC to carry any news stories that he felt might undermine national unity or the war effort, or which might embarrass the government. His allegiance was to government not to the integrity of the news.

McArthur also despised entertainment values in the news and warned editors, writers, and announcers to avoid "anything in the nature of the exciting or the emotional." He urged them to not use sensational or scandalous stories or ones involving suicide, crime, divorce, or gambling. He wanted announcers who would neither be "histrionic" nor be dull. Their role, he felt, was to reinforce the objectivity of CBC News, and he worried about "showmanship creeping into the news . . . a sort of bang bang delivery."

He was very distressed when his principal radio news anchor from 1940 to 1943, Lorne Greene, opened one wartime newscast, which was filled with stories of Allied successes, by saying, "There's lots of news tonight and, for a change, most of it is good." Greene was reprimanded and told never to ad lib like that again. The next time he got into trouble was for a verbal stumble. Reporting on prairie crop conditions, Greene announced that "Western farmers are expecting their biggest crap in years." Stifling laughter, he corrected himself and made it worse. Greene was twenty-four when he joined CBC in October 1939 for $25 a week, a modest beginning that led to $15,000 a week three decades later as Ben Cartwright in the hit American TV show "Bonanza." But in wartime, he was known as the Voice of Doom because of his deep, sonorous voice and the fact that in the early war years most of the news was bad. In fact, Bushnell eventually replaced Greene with someone "whose tones and overtones were not quite so disturbing in periods of anxiety."

Greene's friend and fellow announcer, Austin Willis, also got into trouble after he broke into the network with a bulletin on the sinking of the British battleship *Hood* in which thousands of men had drowned. Immediately after the bulletin, Willis read a commercial saying, "Buy your son in the service a Bulova Watch. They're watertight." "They never let me forget that for the rest of the war," he says.

Gladstone Murray called Greene and his fellow CBC announcers, including Greene's successor Earl Cameron and others such as Allen McFee, Austin Willis, Lamont Tilden, and Byng Whittaker, "the living link" between the CBC and its listeners. Murray spent considerable time urging the proper pronunciation of "educated English."

"The announcer is a visitor in the home and he must be . . . careful of the feeling of his listener," said W. H. Brodie, who had been appointed coach to announcers in 1937. He warned that it was "bad manners" to hurry in delivery, shout, "show off," or "try to impress . . . with the beauty of your voice."

"The public today is hungry for news as it never was before," Murray said. This was borne out by an Elliott-Haynes audience survey which reported that 86 per cent of all English Canadian adult radio listeners tuned nightly to hear the CBC war news. "We are without question," McArthur said, "the most important medium of news dissemination in the Dominion." At C. D. Howe's insistence, the main news bulletin was moved from 11:00 P.M. to 10:00 P.M. because he felt workers were staying up too late to hear the news and consequently were not at their best at the war factories the next morning. He also said that since most people went to bed after hearing the news, an earlier broadcast would save electricity. With Canadians increasingly turning to CBC Radio, the stage was set for a postwar golden age of programming.

8

The Golden Age

When Gladstone Murray was banished both Ernie Bushnell and Augustin Frigon wanted the job of general manager, and Bushnell set out his qualifications in a letter to CBC board member Rowe Holland: "I'm not a narrow-minded nationalist . . . neither am I an ardent Imperialist . . . I have greater respect for an Englishman than I have for a Yankee . . . I have no strong political views . . . I am not a Socialist or a Communist. I hope I am a modernist and a realist . . . I believe in the old principle, 'Live and let live.'" But his pitch didn't convince the board, which was split between the two. As a compromise, a board member, Dr. James Thomson, president of the University of Saskatchewan, was persuaded to become general manager. He stayed only a year before returning to the university.

When he departed, the rivalry between Bushnell and Frigon started up again. However, this time several other candidates were also discussed, including John Grierson, head of the National Film Board (NFB). Bushnell poured scorn on his new rival, writing to Holland that Grierson was "a radical or extreme leftist. . . . He is very clever at covering his tracks." Two other candidates being mentioned for the job were Gen. Andrew McNaughton and board member Col. Wilfrid Bovey. Bushnell groaned,

"I haven't heard God's name but they will probably call on him as a last resort."

It wasn't God but Frigon who got the nod. The rivalry between Bushnell and Frigon had completely soured their relationship, and in the years to come Bushnell rarely missed a reason to complain about Frigon's management.

Their mistrust flashed into a huffy exchange over coverage of the San Francisco conference to establish the United Nations in mid-1945. Frigon had told Norman Robertson in External Affairs that commentators Willson Woodside and Elmore Philpott and the supervisor of the public affairs department, Neil Morrison, would be covering the conference for the CBC. Government officials regarded them as "politically unreliable" and protested. In mid-April, Frigon telegraphed Bushnell forbidding Morrison, Philpott, and Woodside from going to San Francisco for the CBC. Philpott had been a left-wing thorn in the government's hide for several years, and CBC board member Rowe Holland had urged that he be fired. "He seems to have the faculty . . . of arousing the active and venomous opposition of all pro-Britishers." If Philpott and Woodside went to San Francisco on their own and not on behalf of the CBC, Frigon said, they "should be very sparingly used," adding that Morrison could not go because he lacked respect for authority and "he has a faculty of causing trouble. . . . He is much more the type of propagandist than a level-headed administrator."

Morrison was outraged. "The Government, through one of its Cabinet Ministers, has taken upon itself the responsibility of dictating to the CBC who should be allowed to broadcast from San Francisco," Morrison wrote to Bushnell. "This is a clear cut case of direct political interference. . . . The General Manager is willing to accept dictation from Government officials about the duties and functions of senior staff members of the Programme Division. This undermines the whole structure and purpose of the Corporation as an independent body."

Bushnell agreed fully and fired off a stinging four-page memo to Frigon. "I realize this is plain speaking," he said, "[but] it is . . . a further attempt to retain for the Corporation the freedom it once had which, as I see it, is gradually becoming less and less." Bushnell asked what would happen if the government tried to tell Southams, the *Vancouver Sun,* or *Saturday Night* whom to send. "This is," he said, "a direct violation of the principle of free speech on the air."

"I don't understand those people in Toronto. I just don't understand them," Frigon told radio program executive Harry Boyle in exasperation. Thinking that Bushnell "had the knife out for him," as Boyle says, Frigon refused to budge, and his orders stood. His actions underlined the fact that the CBC had emerged from the war with far less independence than it had when the war began. It had moved – even leapt – under the government thumb in too many instances, had lost support among the Conservatives and Social Credit opposition parties, lost support, too, from many onetime friends, and faced a private broadcast sector that was far stronger, richer, and smarter than it had ever been before.

Much of its earlier newspaper support had waned, and even the hitherto devoutly supportive *Winnipeg Free Press* had turned on the CBC after the death of John Dafoe in 1944. The paper now recommended splitting away the CBC's regulatory powers and urged "a check upon its possible use as a political monopolist weapon by government." The *Vancouver Sun,* the Montreal *Gazette,* and numerous other papers also urged taking away regulatory functions from the CBC.

After their confrontation with the CBC over Meighen's and Bracken's speeches, the Conservatives demanded that a formal radio commission be established to set regulations for both private and public broadcasters. Their antipathy toward the CBC led the Conservatives to give up the original idea of a single system. They now viewed the CBC and the private broadcasters as competitors. "The CBC has lost the confidence of the people of Canada," said Gordon Graydon, Conservative House leader, which was an overstatement of the public's attitude but a clear reflection of the Conservative Party attitude.

The private stations fanned these flames of discontent through their aggressive lobbying arm, the Canadian Association of Broadcasters, and through the feisty industry newspaper, *The Canadian Broadcaster.* In a major advertising campaign to promote private radio, the stations asked, "Will public ownership engulf radio . . . with bureaucratic and discriminatory tendencies to limit facilities to sympathizers and stooges, and free speech become a cherished memory? Private radio is the only guarantee of impartial service to all factions."

Like a hurricane forming over the mid-Atlantic, anti-CBC sentiment was gathering strength and, ever the saviour of the Aird-Plaunt-Spry concept of public broadcasting, Mackenzie King became alarmed. In his diary he noted what he had told a cabinet meeting: "Our policy was government ownership and control and members of the party must not begin to favour private interests in competition, but hold to the policy laid down by the Aird Commission. . . . Referred to the importance of its utility in the national life of the country."

He began remedial work in 1945 by sending LaFlèche to Greece and Turkey as ambassador, strengthening the CBC board, and looking for a new chairman. He set out in his diary the qualities he wanted: "What was needed in a Chairman was one with an understanding heart and knowledge of affairs and liberal mind, broad sympathies etc., someone who could deal with prima donnas. Had high standards in matters of cultural education . . . who had vision as to [radio's] future. A belief in public ownership and control . . . someone who would be perfectly impartial as between political parties and who understood the educational value of radio."

And King had in mind just the man: B. K. Sandwell, the erudite editor of *Saturday Night*, the same job Hector Charlesworth held before he was chosen to run the CRBC by R. B. Bennett a dozen years earlier. But Sandwell turned down the job offer. A disappointed King then reached out to a candidate from a younger generation.

On the face of it, it was an astonishing choice for the old world Mackenzie King to make: a thirty-three-year-old "boy wonder" Montreal newspaperman, A. Davidson "Davie" Dunton. "He wasn't afraid of my age," remembered the pipe-puffing Dunton who, at the time, was the fluently bilingual editor of the weekly Montreal *Standard*. He had come to King's attention during the war when he headed the Wartime Information Board. There he had, among other things, played a key role in organizing news coverage of the Churchill, Roosevelt, and King conference in Quebec City.

Dunton had been a Fuller Brush salesman while he worked his way through McGill University, and after graduation he studied at

Cambridge, Grenoble, and Munich, taught English in Mexico, worked on a CPR survey party, and wrote department store advertising. In 1935, he became a *Montreal Star* reporter, and three years later at the age of twenty-five, he became editor of the Montreal *Standard.*

The CBC offer came as "a complete shock," he said, and his wife told him, "If you take the job, you'll take a beating." Even so, and even though the *Standard* offered him more money, after a week's thought he said yes. "I love newspaper work," he said later, "but I felt this was a really big job in the public interest which I could not conscientiously refuse."

A quintessential WASP, Dunton described his political philosophy as "left Liberal to right CCF." He was armed with a stronger power base than any predecessor because he was made a full-time chairman and chief executive officer at $15,000 a year, making him one of the highest paid officials in Ottawa at the time.

Dunton inherited a besieged and fractious organization, one that was quickly becoming a target in a public shooting gallery. He knew he faced a "mighty battle."

The *Telegram* described him as "a gilded fifth wheel," but the charming yet quietly driven Dunton got mostly rave reviews inside and outside the CBC, especially when one of his first actions was to defy the government and admonish his general manager, Augustin Frigon. Within days of his appointment, he revoked Frigon's order forbidding news reporting of prison disturbances, which had so infuriated Dan McArthur. In a letter to Justice Minister St. Laurent, who had requested the reporting ban, Dunton said there "could not be justification for restrictions that would prevent certain legitimate news items reaching the Canadian listening public.... Such restrictions on legitimate news would weaken the faith of the public in the impartiality and integrity of CBC news bulletins in general." He later said, "I thought it was a serious derogation of the Corporation's independence and to the integrity of the news. . . . The Minister of Justice was not very pleased."

But McArthur, his editors, and other CBC programmers felt they at last had a friend at court. To their joy, Dunton concentrated on programming, especially on the English network, which allowed Frigon happily to shift his focus to the technical side, while keeping an eye on the French network. Most program people had deeply resented Frigon's subservience to government direction, but Dunton, with typical diplomacy, said only, "Frigon had a great respect for authority and if some Minister said something he would tend to agree."

Dunton's articulate advocacy of freedom of expression, his determination to protect the independence and integrity of CBC programming, and his creative enthusiasm ushered in a golden age of CBC radio broadcasting which lasted for a decade. The CBC's war reporting had made an indelible impression on Canadian audiences. Programs such as "The National Farm Radio Forum," "Citizens' Forum," "The Happy Gang," an occasional comedy hit featuring an irascible old Irish rogue called "Mulrooney," and, late in the war, a breakthrough in drama production, Andrew Allan's "Stage" series on Sunday nights, had all been popular. For Canadian listeners, the work of Dan McArthur, Orv Shugg, Neil Morrison, and the new drama wunderkind Andrew Allan was far more interesting than the kowtowing to government of the CBC's chairman, the board, and the general manager.

Dunton's arrival heralded a sunburst of talent in drama, music, comedy, and documentaries, as well as in news and public affairs. Foster Hewitt's broadcasts of Saturday night hockey games remained Canada's most popular radio program, but Hewitt now had such rivals for stardom as Bert Pearl of "The Happy Gang"; commentator and talk show host Claire Wallace; Wayne and Shuster, who had returned to the air after a wartime of entertaining the troops; band leaders such as Mart Kenney, Horace Lapp, and Art Hallman; singers Norma Locke, Gisèle MacKenzie, Wally Koster; and in a classical vein, Lois Marshall and Maureen Forrester. There were actors such as Barry Morse, Jane Mallett, and Tommy Tweed; orchestra leaders Samuel Hersenhoren, Luigi Romanelli, and Geoffrey Waddington; and a young up-and-coming pianist named Glenn Gould. There were nationally known commentators, program hosts, and announcers such as Earl Cameron who read the "National News Bulletin," John Fisher and his patriotic talks across Canada from Trois-Pistoles to the Peace River country, Byng Whittaker with his jazz and children's shows, and a cavalcade of talents including J. Frank Willis, Morley Callaghan, J. B. "Hamish" McGeachy, Ralph Allen, and James Bannerman, all of whom enlivened discussion programs.

Dunton's golden age of radio also saw performances by the Leslie Bell Singers, the dramatization of W. O. Mitchell's play *Jake and the Kid*, and the flowering of creative geniuses such as Esse Ljungh, Lister Sinclair, Harry Boyle, and Fletcher Markle. Between 1944 and 1961, the CBC produced an estimated 6,000 plays, about 80 per cent of which were Canadian. During this time, the most extraordinary cultural series in Canadian broadcast history, the "Wednesday Night" series, started. An idea borrowed from the BBC, promoted by Dunton and run by Harry Boyle, "Wednesday Night" offered an entire evening of highbrow culture with James Bannerman as host. There were symphonies, poetry, chamber music, opera, readings, plays by Tolstoy, Ibsen, and Sean O'Casey, and, on one occasion, an entire evening devoted to one day in 1765. "Wednesday Night" programs ranged from Keynes to Kierkegaard, from Jung to Hindemith. But the highbrow programs didn't appeal to everyone. "More people seem interested in listening to the country music of 'Holiday Ranch' than *La Bohème*," Dunton said, "but we feel that people who like *La Bohème* should also have the freedom to hear opera, too."

Popular culture also flowered during radio's golden age. Don Messer, Canada's favourite fiddler, from the East, "Burns Chuckwagon" from the West, and Max Ferguson and his "Rawhide" show from Halifax were favourites. Highly popular commercial shows included "G. E. Showtime," "Ford Radio Theatre," and American shows such as "The Aldrich Family," "The Edgar Bergen Show," "Lux Radio Theatre," "Father Knows Best," and "The Roy Rogers Show."

In an editorial praising CBC programming early in the Dunton era, the *Ottawa Citizen* commented, "It has saved Canadian listeners from the worst excesses of commercial broadcasting as it is practised in the United States."

As always, Canadian talent was paid less than American. In 1946, the CBC noted that American talent costs were $22,500 per week for Jack Benny, $20,000 for Fred Allen, and $18,000 for Abbott and Costello, while Canadian talent costs ran $1,050 for the "Stage" series, $925 for "Radio Carabins" on the French network, $500 for Mart Kenney, $240 for "The Red River Barn Dance," and $60 for Don Messer.

The golden age thrived on the French network, too, with programs such as "Radio-Collège," "Le Théâtre classique français," variety shows such as "Radio Carabins," the 6:00 P.M. daily children's serial "Yvan l'intrépide," and French network versions of "Citizens' Forum" and "The National Farm Radio Forum." Téléromans and the serial drama "Un Homme et son péché" sometimes reached 80 per cent of the listening audience in Quebec.

"It didn't seem to be a golden age at the time," Lister Sinclair recollects. "We got a lot of sneers, but it was called golden because we won some awards in the United States."

About a year before Dunton arrived, the CBC had launched a second radio network, making room for both the explosion of programming talent and the heavy demand for advertising time. Austin Weir, the original program director who had been fired by the CRBC and then rehired by the CBC, was now in charge of commercial sales, and he promoted the idea of a second network. Ernie Bushnell supported him because there was, he said, "so damn much business [we] didn't know where to put it." Bushnell may have felt the abundance of commercials was a mark of success, but that sentiment was not widespread. Conservative MP R. B. Hanson said, "I am sick and tired of hearing about soap and laxatives." Social Credit MP E. G. Hansell complained of commercials on Sundays, saying, "We are permitting the commercialization of the Sabbath. . . . It is one instance of the edge of the wedge to destroy our great Christian principles and I abhor it." Distress at excessive commercials crossed all party lines, and CCF leader M. J. Coldwell called them "an insult to the intelligence of the Canadian people. I think those who sponsor those singing commercials must regard the people of Canada as a nation of morons."

The man who had invented the singing commercial, Ernie Bushnell, didn't agree, and the Dominion network was born as a young brother to the Trans-Canada network. It consisted of the key CBC station, CJBC in Toronto, and about thirty affiliated private stations across the country. Network programs, which ran only on weeknights, were heavily commercial, light in tone, and included many American shows.

Opponents of the new network were not only those distressed by commercials, but also those who were alarmed at any expansion of national public broadcasting. "Bells may shortly be tolling the death knell not just of private radio, but of the whole democratic structure of our system of competitive business," warned *The Canadian Broadcaster* in complaining about the establishment of the Dominion network.

The Dominion network thrived through the golden age of radio, but when television came on the scene, radio advertising revenue collapsed, private affiliates wanted out, and the second network died in the fall of 1962.

But in 1946 the CBC was booming and marked its tenth anniversary with a prime-time showcase of self-congratulations produced by Andrew Allen, including a statement by Dunton that "radio has come to have an intimate part in the daily lives of most of us." Elwood Glover and Allen McFee hosted the radio birthday party and played such upbeat tunes as "'s Wonderful" with singer Norma Locke and Lucio Agostini's orchestra.

Not everyone saluted Dunton's golden age, however. One of the most popular announcers in the country, Joel Aldred, was incensed at what he saw as a waste of money on highbrow programming such as "Wednesday Night," and his diatribe was quoted, ironically, in an article in Dunton's old paper, the Montreal *Standard*. "The CBC is spending an outlandish proportion of its program budget on a fifty-two-week dose of culture," Aldred wrote. "There is too much catering to the Montreal and Toronto artsy crowds. What the CBC needs in its radio fare is more corn and a lot more reality."

This public outburst, coming on the heels of accusations of professional misbehaviour on air, led the CBC to fire the thirty-year-old Aldred, "the man with the $100,000 voice," as *Maclean's* described him.

Years later a still bitter Dunton said, "He was being a skunk . . . I did not respect Joel Aldred." Besides, he added, he felt the CBC was already providing "corn" along with "artsy" programming. His approach was to serve all of the people some of the time rather than some of the people all of the time. A war-decorated RCAF squadron leader and widely heard radio voice, Aldred had many supporters and his dismissal became a *cause célèbre*. Seething with grievance against the CBC, he sought help from George Drew who called his dismissal "part of the fear complex" at the CBC. In the next federal election, Aldred campaigned for the Conservatives, saying the CBC was "a wonderful example of socialistic monopoly at work." Later, he ran and lost against Prime Minister Lester Pearson in the 1965 federal election, and he continued supporting the Conservatives and growing wealthy as one of the best commercial announcers in Canada or the United States.

No one personified the golden age of radio more than Andrew Allan, the Scottish-born son of a Presbyterian parson, who began as a CFRB dance-band announcer in the early 1930s and became broadcasting's genius of drama. Allan had wide-ranging friendships, dining with Vincent Massey and drinking with Matthew Halton in prewar London. His passion for theatre had led him to work in British radio and stage with everyone from Gracie Fields to Judith Evelyn. He was returning to Canada at the outbreak of the Second World War when his ship, the *Athenia*, was torpedoed in the North Atlantic. He and his companion, Judith Evelyn, survived but his father, who was travelling with them, drowned. On his return to Canada, Allan joined CBC Vancouver as a drama producer and came to Toronto as drama supervisor in 1943.

The heavy-smoking, heavy-drinking Allan was a bad administrator, a demanding, even frightening, and meticulous producer in the studio, and a much-loved *bon vivant* outside. "He was the kind of alcoholic who couldn't function unless he had three double scotches under his belt and then he appeared to be completely sober," recalls Lister Sinclair who worked with Allan on many "Wednesday Night" productions. The dapper perfectionist always addressed his performers in his soft Scottish burr formally as Mr. or Miss but never by their first names. "It prevented us from presuming on one another," he said. Allan also never talked to musicians directly, only through the conductor. He could be a holy terror or a Dutch Uncle – whatever it took to get the most out of his actors and writers. "There was no better studio director in the world," says Sinclair. He was the sun king of the golden age of radio.

"I had a feeling," Allan once said, "that only in radio could we have enough drama to make a theatre in Canada." And, indeed, CBC Radio was Canada's principal theatrical stage. Allan reached more creative heights in Canadian broadcasting than anyone else. Although he originally had expected to reach only a relatively small, élite audience, at one time his Sunday night "Stage" series was second only to Saturday night hockey in popularity, a situation he worried about because, as he said, "The more popular you get, the more people you reach, the more pressure groups you encounter and the more taboos and inhibitions you have." Allan spoke of "the prickly hedge" of taboos in radio and would remove words like hell or even heck to avoid giving offence, saving his creative troublemaking for bigger issues.

The taboos Allan tackled in the dramas he produced included sex and religion, and these challenges usually set off avalanches of prudish criticism. George Drew was now Conservative Opposition leader and he often spoke of the CBC's "blasphemy on the air" and "indecent broadcasts" which, he said, ridiculed religion. Canadian religious convictions were undermined, Drew said, by "this mental poison being carried over the airwaves of Canada."

John Diefenbaker complained of "pornography" on the air, the *Fredericton Daily Gleaner* thundered that CBC programs "pour smut and obscenities into the living rooms of Canadians," and the *Saint John Telegraph-Journal* talked of CBC "sex orgies."

In the late 1950s, after nearly two decades of obsessive overwork and alcoholic demons, Allan fell into a depression and a creative dry hole. "It was what the medievals called the sin of despair," he later recalled. "There was nothing worth doing." He saw the life of radio squeezed out by television and complained, "The content of TV is neither nourishing nor arresting. It's cliché."

Allan was a burned-out fifty-year-old creative casualty who eventually roused himself by writing and delivering radio essays for Harry Boyle's programs and later the morning talk show programs of Bruno Gerussi and Peter Gzowski.

Reflecting on both the golden age of radio and himself, he said near the end of his sixty-six years of life, "No age is called golden until it is long past. . . . To survive, you need a good capacity to absorb disappointments."

It was not only Andrew Allan's dramas that were assailed in the 1940s. Max Ferguson's "Rawhide" character set off volcanoes of outrage as every morning the toothy, impish Ferguson poked fun at members of Parliament, national institutions, religion, and every icon in sight. A Conservative MP from Toronto, Douglas Gooderham Ross, called "Rawhide" "that program of meaningless ravings and tripe, couched in the poorest possible illiterate English . . . an insult to the intelligence of the Canadian public." Another MP called Ferguson's "Rawhide" character "a boorish sort of nincompoop . . . loose on the airwaves doing irreparable damage to the young." Ottawa Baptist minister Rev. Stuart Ivison said Ferguson's program was a "sacrilege, blasphemy, evil public avowal of irreligion and something that Godless Soviet Russia could hardly improve on."

Dunton defended "Rawhide" publicly, and privately he sent Ferguson a telegram: "Having difficulty organizing support for campaign to make Rawhide Mayor of Ottawa. Keep your fingers crossed and six guns ready." Lorne Greene telephoned Ferguson to say, "Congratulations . . . You couldn't buy publicity like this for a million dollars. . . . You're a lucky guy to get a break like this." Ferguson's "Rawhide" character outlasted all the critics – the program stayed on the air for seventeen years.

More serious for Dunton were the attacks on the CBC for being the handmaiden of communism. One of the most vociferous assaults came following a 1956 radio drama on the life of American labour martyr Joe Hill. Social Credit leader Solon Low said it was a plot by the CBC in "partnership" with the communists to glorify "a red." The two-hour play, he said, "was communist inspired. It was communist in every way. . . . This nefarious, subversive program." Low admitted, however, that he hadn't heard the program.

The minister responsible for the CBC in the House, J. J. McCann, was also distressed about the program and apologized in the House of Commons for it. "I do not think it was a good thing," he said, "and the CBC does not think it was good. . . . We will certainly be . . . on guard to see that such a thing does not recur again." Then he added, "Apparently there are communists everywhere and they infiltrate into organizations of government as well as into places of industry."

In an oral history recording, Alphonse Ouimet underlined the cabinet's fear of communists in the CBC in relating a conversation he had with an unidentified St. Laurent cabinet minister:

"Minister: 'You are having a bunch of communists on the air!'

"Ouimet: 'We have no communists on the air. Who are you talking about?'

"Minister: 'You know goddamn well. . . . Marchand, Trudeau, Pelletier, Gagnon, Laurendeau. . . . Get rid of them all!'"

Social Credit MP Ernest Hansell agreed, saying simply, "Fire them all. . . . There should be a complete housecleaning."

The Investigator, a play about McCarthyism written by Reuben Ship, who had been blacklisted in the United States, was produced by Allan and starred John Drainie. A pirated recording of the program became a runaway best-seller in the United States, although the record gave no credit to the CBC. It was "another communist play," said an outraged Solon Low. He urged the government to "look inside the CBC to find out those who are selling the Canadian people down the river. . . . The CBC [is being] used . . . by diabolically clever subversive agencies in ideological warfare."

Dunton also came under fire for the radio commentary of Dr. Ewen Cameron, a Montreal psychiatrist. "He is propounding of a philosophy of man's dependence upon himself to a place where God is ruled out," said Social Credit MP Ernest Hansell. "And that is communism." Almost any time prominent psychiatrist Brock Chisholm spoke about psychology, birth control, or other social issues, an avalanche of scorn came down on him and the CBC. Solon Low protested the CBC's use of Chisholm and "his poisoned mind." "Atheistic propaganda," "socialism," "anti-Christian" were some of the epithets hurled at the CBC in the House of Commons, and not only by the Opposition. One of Chisholm's broadcasts about a world population explosion drew strong criticism from Prime Minister Louis St. Laurent, who had succeeded Mackenzie King at the end of 1948.

What was especially significant about these incidents was not the high-level complaints themselves but the strong defence of the CBC's independence made by Dunton. His defence of Max Ferguson reflected his support for creative daring, and so, too, did his note to writer-performer Tommy Tweed after a particularly controversial program. "Dear Tommy," he wrote. "You got me in a lot of trouble. Please do it again." On another occasion, while Andrew Allan was going through a rare period of receiving no political criticism, Dunton phoned him and said, "What's wrong? There's been no trouble for the last month. What's going on? Everything's too quiet and I hope you're not avoiding controversy." Not since the days of Leonard Brockington had the CBC had such strong leadership. In defending non-establishment, non-status-quo programs on the CBC, Dunton said, "It is not freedom when you let the tastes of a large group dominate the tastes of a smaller group. In a democracy, the majority must respect minority rights, too." Dunton elaborated on this theme when he told the Fowler Commission on Broadcasting, "One of the tests of a healthy democracy is the tolerance of unpopular minority opinions, of new expressions of art and ideas."

Dunton, of course, got no sympathy from the organ of private broadcasting, *The Canadian Broadcaster,* whose editor, Richard Lewis, described the CBC as "a power drunk tribunal" and Dunton as "this dictator."

In a *Maclean's* article, writer Pierre Berton noted the diatribe of criticism falling on Dunton and wrote about "the Niagara of vilification, imprecation, tirade and abuse which has drenched the corporate head of the CBC."

"You never know when it's going to explode," Dunton said. "When the going gets tough, I sometimes wish I were back behind a typewriter at the *Montreal Star.*"

Dunton was unable to resist witch-hunting critics in one area of the CBC, the International Service. The service had begun in 1944 to provide Canadian news to the troops overseas and then, at war's end, to promote the image of Canada abroad. Programs of news, commentaries, and entertainment were beamed mostly to countries in Western Europe and the Western Hemisphere. But the outbreak of the war in Korea and the growing fear of communism put increasing pressure on the CBC to turn the International Service into a strident instrument of Cold War propaganda aimed at Eastern Europe as the Voice of America had become. One of the central aims of the service, the government said, was "unmasking the hypocrisy" of communism and "the hypocrisy of Soviet peace propaganda."

McCarthyism in the United States and Igor Gouzenko's revelations in 1946 of espionage in Canada stimulated fears of communists and their "henchmen." In the House of Commons, Solon Low talked of the CBC's "continued pounding, pounding, pounding of indoctrination" in left-wing politics. There were demands for a purge at the CBC, especially in the International Service, similar to the one that had recently racked the National Film Board (NFB). Spurred on by some Eastern European refugee groups and the virulently anti-communist Catholic weekly newspaper, *The Canadian Ensign,* published in Montreal, Conservative leader George Drew questioned the supervision of the International Service and said there was "a great deal" in the allegations that "men with known communist associations" worked for the service. The External Affairs Department became alarmed and the RCMP began investigating. Ira Dilworth, head of the service, reported to Ernie Bushnell that "those buggahs in Ottawa" were launching a witch hunt that was destroying morale and ruining lives. Dilworth said most of the RCMP secret dossiers on suspected communists and fellow travellers were filled with hearsay evidence and guilt by association. He cited cases of employees who were called suspects because their parents or relatives were reportedly supporters of left-wing movements. Dilworth admitted some International Service employees endorsed "liberalism so far left as to verge on socialism," but he felt that that was a long way from being a communist spy or a subversive.

In the midst of the red scare, Dilworth suffered a heart attack and a search began for his successor as head of the service. One candidate in Ernie Bushnell's mind was Stuart Griffiths, the dynamic head of the International Service English-language programming. But Griffiths was being questioned by the RCMP as a possible subversive and the RCMP advised his boss, "It might be better if he didn't work there." Dilworth said External Affairs had warned him at one point that "as long as Griffiths is at the International Service there can never be the free flow of information from External Affairs . . . nor can there be complete confidence on the part of External Affairs in our Service."

Griffiths denied he was a communist and threatened to sue if he were dismissed on the grounds of security. "He was not a communist," Bushnell said later. "He was an advanced thinker, but there was nothing disloyal about him." Griffiths was not dismissed, but he did not get the job of running the International Service. The hardworking Griffiths later made enormous creative contributions to the development of CBC television programming and, later still, ran a highly successful private Ottawa television station. In another case of political persecution, author Ted Allan was fired as a CBC announcer because, he said, "some RCMP zealots went to the CBC brass and said I was a communist." Even theatre critic and program host Nathan Cohen was suspected by the RCMP of having communist affiliations.

The man finally named to replace Dilworth in 1952 as International Service head was Jean Désy, the Canadian ambassador to Italy, veteran civil servant, and the choice of External Affairs. His mandate was to clean up the "red mess" at the service, a task he vigorously pursued, firing, threatening, and demoralizing much of the staff. When he departed the CBC eighteen months later to return to diplomacy, he left a legacy of bitterness that lasted for years.

The lurid postwar accusations about communism, sex, and blasphemy on the CBC were used as weapons in the larger battle by private broadcasters and the Conservatives to weaken the public broadcaster. Echoing the position of private radio owners, the Conservative Party at its 1947 annual meeting passed a resolution declaring, "The CBC as presently administered is a menace to freedom of speech and freedom of enterprise as it occupies the untenable position of being the controller of and at the same time a competitor with private radio stations. The control of radio should be removed from political domination and vested in an independent board."

The government not only faced this demand for a fundamental shift in broadcast policy and a general concern about the future of federal government involvement in promoting the arts, but it also worried about the cost of public television that was just around the corner. The minister responsible for the CBC, J. J. McCann, told the House, "I am constantly admonishing the CBC that they are too expensive; that they are employing too many people; that I think a lot of these things ought to be cut down; that their spending program ought to be curtailed as much as possible." In these circumstances, Prime Minister St. Laurent did what all Canadian prime ministers do when faced with a difficult choice: he appointed a royal commission.

Thus the Massey Commission began a two-and-a-half-year analysis of broadcasting and the arts in Canada, hearing 1,200 witnesses, reading 462 briefs, and travelling to sixteen cities. It was a "stacked" commission, predisposed to favour federal funding of culture and, specifically, public broadcasting over private. Vincent Massey, one of the original backers of the Canadian Radio League, a friend of Alan Plaunt, and an energetic behind-the-scenes player in the development of public broadcasting, was chairman and three of the four other commissioners were leading academics. The fifth commissioner was a Montreal professional engineer, Dr. Arthur Surveyer, the lone supporter of the private sector in the commission.

There was the usual parade of witnesses – cultural organizations, educators, performers, and spokespersons for groups representing women, farmers, co-ops, unions, and churches, all favouring a strengthened CBC, and business groups, chambers of commerce, advertisers, private broadcasters, and radio manufacturers, seeking a weakened CBC. Most of the latter groups urged an end to the CBC's regulatory powers and a recognition of equality between the private broadcasters and the CBC. Supporters of public broadcasting and successive governments had always maintained broadcasting was a single system: the CBC was the dominant force and the private stations filled in around the edges with local programming while also providing extra outlets for the CBC national service. But certain private stations, notably CFRB in Toronto, had been allowed big increases in power, and now their signals reached well beyond local areas, generating more advertising revenue because of the larger audience and reinforcing the private broadcasters' argument that they were competitors of the CBC for both audience and advertising.

John Diefenbaker joined in the debate, saying that the CBC was "cop and competitor, judge and litigant, all at once." There was even some Liberal support for this idea, including the chairman of the 1947 parliamentary radio committee who said, "I personally would have no objection to a regulatory board." No evidence was ever offered to the Massey Commission of actual unfair regulatory treatment by the CBC, but the potential for unfairness was a constant theme of private broadcasters. The CAB argument, and that of its increasing number of supporters, was that the Canadian broadcasting system was now not one but two equal and competitive systems, an argument that, if accepted, would have widespread policy implications and dramatically reduce the role of the CBC from that envisioned in the original broadcast legislation of 1936 and endorsed by subsequent Parliaments. It was this issue that formed the core of concern for the Massey Commission.

When the Massey Commission Report was issued in mid-1951, its conclusion was a powerful pat on the back for the CBC and a refutation of the private broadcasters' claims. "[The CBC is] the greatest single agency for national unity, understanding and enlightenment," the commission stated. Before there was public broadcasting, the report noted, "Canada was in real danger of cultural annexation by the United States." The commission attacked much of the private broadcasters' local programming as indifferent and inadequate and commented, "The principal grievance of the private broadcasters is based, it seems to us, on a false assumption that broadcasting in Canada is an industry. Broadcasting in Canada in our view is a public service directed and controlled in the public interest by a body responsible to Parliament. . . . The statement that the Board of Governors of the Canadian Broadcasting Corporation is at once their judge and their business rival implies a view of the national system which has no foundation in law and which has never been accepted by Parliamentary Committees or by the general public."

The Massey Commission, with the exception of Dr. Arthur Surveyer, rejected the idea of splitting regulatory functions away from the CBC because to do so would "divide or destroy or merely duplicate the present system." The commission added that private broadcasters "can be useful within the national system, but they have no civil right to broadcast or any property rights in broadcasting."

Surveyer offered a minority suggestion to establish a separate regulatory authority, the details of which John Diefenbaker noted closely and remembered half a dozen years later when he became prime minister.

For the time being, however, the Massey Report kept the private broadcasters at bay, and Davie Dunton, as head of the CBC, remained the czar of Canadian broadcasting. Even so, the Tories' growing political support for private stations, the intensified lobbying and agitation by the private broadcasters themselves, and signs of a few cracks in Liberal Party support meant the struggle for public broadcasting was far from over.

The battle lines shifted, and so did the CBC's leadership. Augustin Frigon stepped down as general manager in 1951 because of ill health and was succeeded by Donald Manson, a radio pioneer whose career stretched back to 1906 when he began as a "learner" at the Marconi communication school in Liverpool. He worked with Marconi himself for three years, was inspector of radio for the Canadian government, secretary of the Aird Commission, and chief inspector of radio for Canada before joining the CBC in 1936.

But Manson was totally overshadowed by the presence of Chairman Davie Dunton and stayed as general manager for only a year. He was succeeded by a star-crossed engineering genius who was obsessed with developing television in Canada, J. Alphonse Ouimet.

9

The Magic Eye

The first face seen on television was a ventriloquist's dummy named Bill. British scientist John Baird used the dummy as a model in an October 1925 experiment. Bill's flickering image contributed to the development of the greatest instrument of mass culture ever invented, as well as the world's most potent disseminator of news.

The idea of television had been around for decades. In 1870, German inventor Paul Nipkow developed the concept of television transmission, and there had been experiments in the 1880s and 1890s in Europe and the United States. One of the first uses of the word "television" was in *The Scientific American* in 1907. "Television [is] on the way" proclaimed the *Kansas City Times* in 1910. Radio pioneer Reginald Fessenden experimented with television and then John Baird began serious work on the possibilities of the new medium in 1913. Two years later, Marconi predicted the "visible telephone" would soon arrive. The 1924 *British Radio Yearbook* spoke of "seeing electronically by wire or by wireless," and British reporters did just that when, on January 26, 1926, Baird showed them in his London laboratory televised pictures of a policeman's hat, a bouquet of roses, and a man making a face.

In March 1928, RCA predicted television would be in homes within a year. "Television may be commonplace in five years," *Canadian*

Magazine said in January 1929, in an article about "radio pictures" on a one-and-a-half-inch set. While Canadians were reading about their TV future, the chairman of the Aird Commission was sitting down in Baird's experimental London studio to become the first Canadian to appear and speak on television. John Aird's only words, however, were to complain about the hot studio lights. But it made a deep impression on him, and three years later he told a parliamentary committee, "It is coming gentlemen. . . . We should be prepared to keep the question of television before us."

It was very much before the Canadian scientists who began major experiments in Montreal in 1930 under the direction of Professor Jean Charles Bernier of L'École Polytechnique. Since 1926, Len Spencer, the chief engineer at *La Presse*'s station CKAC, had also been toying with television. From a studio atop *La Presse*'s building at 8:00 P.M. one October night in 1931, Canada's first television show was aired over a CKAC transmitter, VE9EC. Nine months later, a much more elaborate program was broadcast; Mariotte Mineau played violin, Violet Gridley sang, cartoonist Edward Picard sketched, and comedian Sydney Nesbitt told jokes. Hundreds of people crowded in front of Ogilvy's department store window to watch the black and red picture. The Montreal *Gazette* headlined its story on the event: "PRACTICAL TEST GIVEN TELEVISION. RADIO EYE ADDED TO EAR."

The equipment had been provided to CKAC by a fledgling manufacturing company called Canadian Television Ltd., run by fly-by-night stock promoters trying to sell shares at ten cents each. It had hired fresh out of McGill University an ambitious and brilliant young engineer named J. Alphonse Ouimet, who, as a child, preferred his crystal set to his bicycle. He had been fascinated by television, too, and had built his own set while at university. He was the entire technical staff of Canadian Television Ltd. and was told to build both a receiver and a transmitter from equipment he had to buy with his own money. The resulting picture quality was poor. Much later, Ouimet told Pierre Berton, "The pictures were such that if you stood close enough, you could just barely recognize your own mother on the screen." He tested his work by putting himself on camera. "It was certainly [the] first test pattern," he later said. Ouimet had a unique value for testing because he had a large gap in his front teeth which helped to measure picture definition. All his efforts for the company went down the drain however, when it went out of business, owing Ouimet several weeks' pay.

Ouimet then went on to work as an engineer for the CRBC at $2,000 a year, beginning his long climb to the CBC presidency. Meanwhile, CKAC chief engineer Len Spencer continued experimenting with TV, producing one-hour programs with amateur fiddlers, guitar players, and singers, and broadcasting twice a week by the summer of 1932. Then the experiments dropped to once a week before finally stopping altogether because of the deepening Depression.

In the United States, there were twenty-nine experimental television stations by 1932, but the world's first regular television service was started by the BBC in London on November 2, 1936, the same day the CBC was established. There were only 400 television sets in use in London at the start. A Canadian, Joan Miller from Nelson, British Columbia, who had gone to England to further her acting career, was the host of the world's first regular television program for the BBC called "World TV," which ran from 1936 to 1939. She was the first TV star.

Six months after television programming began, the BBC telecast the coronation of King George VI. The legendary CBS newsman Edward R. Murrow, based in London, had a set in his home and watched BBC TV with his colleague Eric Severeid. "That's television," Murrow said. "That's the future, my friend." A year later, on Neville Chamberlain's return from Munich, Murrow and the few hundred other Londoners who had sets watched the British prime minister wave a piece of paper signed by Hitler and declare, "Peace in our time." TV broadcasting followed within a few months in France, Germany, and Italy. In London in August 1939, Baird gave a demonstration of colour TV with a colour photograph of King George VI. One of the most popular prewar television stars in Britain was a young musician from Sault Ste Marie, Ontario, who hosted his own show called "Eric Wild's Tea Timers."

In the United States, NBC began regular television broadcasting in 1939 with programming from the New York World's Fair, where Franklin Roosevelt, who opened the fair, was the first U.S. president to appear on TV. Foster Hewitt was Canada's first TV sports announcer, covering televised boxing matches at the World's Fair. He didn't like the new medium very much.

Later in 1939, a link was established between New York and Philadelphia and the first televised coverage of a political convention came in 1940. By 1941, CBS and Dumont began television programming, as did several independent stations. Up to fifteen hours of television programming a week were offered but after the attack on Pearl Harbor programming was reduced to four hours a week carried by half a dozen stations. In Britain, television had been suspended at the outbreak of war. At noon, September 1, 1939, as German bombs fell on Warsaw, Poland, BBC TV abruptly stopped in the middle of a Mickey Mouse cartoon.

Even during the war, however, there was excited journalistic speculation about TV such as the article in *Maclean's* in 1943 which described "television's promise for the future: a front row seat in your home for theatre, movies, sports and news events." A year later, *Saturday Night* wrote that television "will one day revolutionize culture, the arts, education, communication and industry."

When the war ended, the television revolution began. Within months, there were seven stations operating in the United States, one in Britain, one in France, and one in Russia. Within a year, thirty TV stations had been licensed in the United States. NBC's Milton Berle was television's comedy king on the more than one million TV sets in the United States. In the United Kingdom, the BBC had resumed and expanded its TV broadcasting. By 1950, there were 150 stations around the world producing what the *Manchester Guardian's* U.S. correspondent Alistair Cooke called "photographed radio."

In Canada, CBC leadership didn't share the general enthusiasm for TV. CBC chairman Leonard Brockington had told a 1939 parliamentary committee that TV was too costly for Canada. "The cost of supplying daily different programs with live talent will be highly expensive. . . ." he said. "Taking into account the high cost, both of equipment and production . . . it is safe to say that it is not economically feasible in Canada at the moment." Frigon agreed, and he resented the constant pushing of television by his chief engineer, Alphonse Ouimet. "Ouimet, you and your damn TV," Ouimet remembered Frigon telling him. "Will you leave me alone? Do you seriously think people will keep sitting in front of a little screen?"

In 1936, Ouimet had proposed that the CBC establish a national TV network but his proposal was rejected. In 1944, Frigon felt TV probably wouldn't be available to the general public for another fifteen or twenty years. Two years later, he told a parliamentary committee, "It would be a mistake to encourage the introduction in Canada of television without sufficient financial support. . . . We refuse to be stampeded into premature action."

The government agreed. Eighteen applications for TV licences had been received, but Ottawa had done nothing. "It was not prudent for us to spend a lot of money as a Corporation or to encourage private companies to spend money on this until there has been some further development," Revenue Minister J. J. McCann, the minister responsible for the CBC, said in 1947.

But Davie Dunton was listening more to Ouimet than to Frigon or McCann. "I was a damn good pleader," Ouimet later said, and he was assigned to study the state of TV in the United States, Britain, and France. Dunton was concerned that American TV signals would soon invade Canada much as American radio signals had done twenty years earlier. Under Dunton's prodding, the CBC began plans for TV facilities in Montreal and Toronto. In mid-1948, the CBC board heard three private TV applications, rejecting one and deferring the others. But the board declared there were "great potentialities in television. . . . Canada should not lag behind."

The government, however, was uneasy about being pushed on TV. It rebuffed the CBC's request for extra funding for television development, and C. D. Howe, who chaired a cabinet meeting on the matter, thought the medium was too expensive and that the private sector could best develop it. "If private operators think it worthwhile to risk that much money, let them go ahead," Howe said. "For the government, it would be a dead loss. If I were living in my own town of Port Arthur, I'd kick like a steer at paying taxes to bring television to Montreal and Toronto."

Arguing in cabinet against the development of CBC-TV, Howe trotted out the old arguments he had used against Brockington and Plaunt when the CBC was getting underway in 1936. In 1948, as in 1936, CBC supporters spoke of the "very great social force" of public television and its importance to national unity. Now, as before, the persistent, persuasive arguments put forward by the head of the CBC were successful in diluting and eventually overcoming the opposition within the government, notably, Howe's opposition. Prime Minister St. Laurent agreed to set up the Massey Commission to examine the future for TV and broadcasting in general, as well as other cultural issues. Significantly, and under pressure from CBC supporters in the cabinet such as Lester Pearson and Brooke Claxton, St. Laurent also appeared to reverse Howe's private-sector approach of a few months earlier. "I do not think these frequencies," he told the House of Commons, "should be lightly turned over to private ownership and exploitation unless we come to the conclusion that there is no better way in which the Canadian public can be provided with this new form of entertainment and education."

A few weeks later, the government announced television in Canada would be developed much the same way as radio had been – as a mix of public and private broadcasting with the CBC dominating. CBC stations would be set up in Montreal and Toronto, and a program service would be developed by the CBC. Local private stations would be licensed and regulated by the CBC. "This new medium can be of great benefit to the national life of Canada if properly developed," the government stated. "It is clear that a large measure of public participation in television is necessary."

The government's action was not entirely driven by philosophical considerations. Ottawa also was spurred into a decision on television by heavy pressure from the Canadian electronics industry, which faced layoffs and wanted TV in place so it could manufacture the production and transmission equipment and the hundreds of thousands of TV sets that would be snapped up by a TV-mad population. By 1950, 30,000 sets had been sold in Canada and in the next year another 40,000 were sold, even without a Canadian TV station to watch.

At last, CBC was moving on television, ordering equipment, developing plans based on Ouimet's report, and hiring key personnel. An on-air target date for Montreal and Toronto was set for September 1951. Ouimet was named chief engineer, co-ordinator of television and, as Frigon was ill, chief adviser to the board. Ernie Bushnell was sent on a tour of British and American television facilities, looking for creative ideas, and farm broadcaster Fergus Mutrie was named director of television for Toronto and Aurèle Séguin for Montreal. Mutrie and J. Frank Willis, who had made his radio reputation in the 1936 Moose River mine disaster, reported after studying British and American TV in late 1949 that CBC-TV could take one of two routes: "On the one hand, [it] is a great new medium for entertainment and enlightenment – on the other, a great commercial enterprise." They made clear their recommendation was for the BBC's creative model, not the American commercial approach. A technological choice had to be made, too: to go with the European or the American model, and on this one, the CBC went American.

Meanwhile, the CBC stalled a flood of private station TV applicants who fumed at CBC delays, as did much of the public. So, too, did Alphonse Ouimet, who complained of how "the corporation's own lack of conviction" was encouraging the government to go slow on TV. More delay was caused, Ouimet said, "because of Maurice Duplessis's stubborn refusal to allow his old enemy, the CBC, [to put a transmitter] on Mount Royal." As Canadians had turned their dials to American radio stations in the 1920s, so, too, did the 70,000 Canadians who had TV sets and were within reach of American TV signals. Aside from delays caused by policy and politics, the on-air date for Canadian TV had to be pushed back to the fall of 1952 because of steel and equipment shortages caused by the Korean War, which delayed building the new stations. But the CBC got the blame for stalling on TV.

"Television has been held back . . . in this country by the policy of the CBC," thundered John Diefenbaker. Conservative leader George Drew also protested at the stalling of licences, and he was incensed when, in mid-1951, the Massey Report powerfully endorsed the idea that the CBC should dominate Canadian television. "The pressure on uncontrolled private television operators to become mere channels for American commercial materials will be almost irresistible," the Massey Report said.

This echoed Davie Dunton's comments of a few years earlier when he told a Canadian Association of Advertisers conference, "Television is and must be, more than just an electronic billboard. . . . It must be in the national interest . . . to have a television system that expresses Canadian ideas, that uses Canadian talent, that stimulates the thinking and imagination and creative power of Canadians, that adds to the richness of our national life. . . . It could not be in the interest of the development of Canada as a nation to have material from outside Canada swamp Canadian creative efforts on our own television."

Leading the charge in organizing "Canadian creative efforts" on TV was the old radio song-and-dance man Ernie Bushnell, who hired Stuart Griffiths from the International Service to run production and Mavor Moore, who had been acting and producing for CBC Radio since 1939, as senior producer to develop programming in Toronto. They were warned against stealing radio talent, so they brought in a new generation of creative pioneers whose exuberance and fascination with the new medium overcame their ignorance of it.

Under the thirty-three-year-old Mavor Moore's guidance, in mid-January 1952, about thirty youthful, would-be producers, directors, and technicians began their training in an old downtown Toronto building, hearing lectures from 9:00 A.M. to 1:00 P.M. and practising in a make-shift studio until 6:00 P.M. They had nine months to learn their craft. Sitting there listening to Moore's instructions were such future creative greats of television as Ross McLean, Norman Jewison, Harvey Hart, Don Hudson, Harry Rasky, and Sydney Newman. The others particularly looked up to Newman because he had worked briefly for NBC-TV in New York and had spent more than a decade producing films for the NFB. Day after day they listened to experts from New York, experimenting and learning the techniques of television. At night some of them would sit in the living room of Ross McLean's cramped, one-bedroom north Toronto apartment drinking beer and watching a Buffalo TV station. "None of us had a TV set except Ross," says Rasky. "But we thought we were going to change the world."

One of their lecturers was Gilbert Seldes, a former CBS-TV program director and author who told his students, "Television is the most powerful instrument of persuasion ever conceived." Warning of TV's impact and the producer's responsibilities, Seldes told Canada's first TV producers, "Surely it is conceivable that sometime in the future a demagogue with a great TV personality, as it is called, might be nominated and elected over a sounder statesman whose television appeal is limited. We have to wonder what television will do to our intelligence. It may stimulate us to thought, but it may also put our minds to sleep. . . . We must make sure that it serves by disturbing our complacency as often as it lets us escape from our problems."

Through the spring and summer of 1952, as the start date for Canadian TV grew closer, the neophyte TV producers were in a "state of disintegration and panic," as McLean later recalled. Dry runs began in August and a daily test run produced by Mavor Moore, called "Ex Marks the Spot," with host Rick Campbell, began during the CNE in Toronto.

In Montreal that summer, similarly apprehensive producers had experimented by televising a drama and the Montreal Royals and the Springfield Cubs in an International League baseball game. The producers became Canada's first on-air TV programmers, launching the bilingual CBFT on Saturday, September 6, 1952. CBC-TV flickered onto Montreal sets at 4:00 P.M. with an English-language children's film, *Aladdin and his Lamp.* An English cartoon followed, then a French-language film, and at 7:30 P.M., a news review of the summer of 1952, and at 8:00 P.M., a bilingual variety show. The inauguration ceremonies, which began an hour later, featured Prime Minister St. Laurent, J. J. McCann, and Davie Dunton. Midway through Canada's first TV night, Archbishop Paul-Emile Léger came to the control room to bless the television launch. While he was offering his benediction, the control room's television screens were showing a line of scantily clad chorus girls kicking their legs in the air. The evening ended with a French-language production of Cocteau's play *Oedipus Rex.*

Two days later on Monday, September 8, it was Toronto's turn, and the CBC went on the air with its identifying slide upside down. A technician had taken special care just before going on air to clean the opening slide, and when he returned it to its holder, he put it in upside down. The co-ordinating producer, Murray Chercover, who had spent five years working in television in New York and who later became president of CTV, was mortified. Chercover was also terrified. Standing right behind him at this moment of birth for television in Toronto were all his bosses: Davie Dunton, Ernie Bushnell, Fergus Mutrie, Mavor Moore, and Stuart Griffiths.

"Five different hands suddenly thumped my shoulder," Chercover remembers. Dunton cried out, "What'll we do?" Nothing could be done and the embarrassment was over in a couple of seconds. More than forty years later, Chercover still shivers at the memory. "It was painful, but we were live so we just had to keep going," he says.

Despite appearing to be "indestructibly self-confident," as his colleague Ross McLean described him, "Murray was almost at the point of nervous collapse before every show and was violently ill," McLean said of Chercover's early days in television. On a pioneering live Friday night series called "Space Command" (which featured William Shatner and James Doohan, who later became Captain Kirk and Scotty on "Star Trek"), McLean said Chercover was "reduced to quivering. . . . He would have to be walked around and calmed down by his script assistant before the show went on the air."

On opening night, however, Chercover conquered his nerves and the blunder of the upside-down slide and, with Norman Campbell producing, at 7:15 P.M., English-language television was on the air with Percy Saltzman's weather report, comments by Toronto mayor Allan Lamport, and a puppet called Uncle Chichimus that previewed the evening programs. At 7:30 P.M., Lorne Greene, anchor of "Newsmagazine," came on with a scoop – the escape from Toronto's Don Jail of the notorious Boyd Gang. "Newsmagazine" producer Harry Rasky had picked up word of the escape on his police radio and, with cameraman in tow, had climbed into his Ford to chase after the story in Canada's first TV news reportage. "BOYD FIRST STAR AS TV STARTS SMOOTHLY," the *Toronto Star* headlined in its report of how pictures of gang leader Edwin Boyd had been flashed on the screens during the day even before TV officially began. The first real star of Canadian TV was an escaped bank robber, and Davie Dunton lost no time in noting that TV had begun by using "Canadian talent." Harry Rasky recognized the impact of TV when the next day a woman greeted him on a downtown Toronto street by saying, "I want to hug you. You're the one who caught the Boyd gang."

The same trio of official welcomers as in Montreal – St. Laurent, McCann, and Dunton – formally opened CBLT at 8:00 P.M. They were followed by "Kaleidoscope," hosted by John Fisher, directed by Drew Crossan, and featuring singers Wally Koster and Terry Dale, and Geoffrey Waddington and his orchestra. Comic Don Harron did a sketch, Jan Rubes sang an excerpt from *Don Giovanni*, and a twenty-year-old still relatively unknown pianist by the name of Glenn Gould rounded out the show. Another variety program followed featuring the twenty-five voices of the Leslie Bell Singers and the Howard Cable orchestra, and at 10:00 P.M., "Newsmagazine" was repeated.

The panic of the producers in preparing for the Canadian TV debut was fully matched by that of the CBC-TV executives who were orchestrating the whole thing. Led by Ferg Mutrie and Stu Griffiths in Toronto, they battled the CBC bureaucracy for everything from studio sets, cameras, and lights to carpenters and painters. When the bureaucracy wouldn't move fast enough in approving the hiring of workers and specialists, Bushnell authorized Mutrie and Griffiths to hire them on freelance artists' contracts. When he was later admonished for cutting administrative corners, Bushnell told his Ottawa bosses, "Maybe what I did was somewhat irregular and contravened some of your bloody regulations and cut across the furrows of the bum sitters at head office. But if you don't like it, you can all go to hell or, alternatively, fire me!"

With all its jitters and frustrations, television had at last arrived in Canada, and the 146,000 Canadian black and white TV sets, which cost about $240 each, quickly became the focal point of entertainment for family and friends, just as radio had a quarter-century before. It was magic time.

Canadian TV, however, was on the air only about three hours a day and reached just 26 per cent of the 15 million population. Radio was still king of the airwaves with audiences in the millions, radios in nine out of ten Canadian homes, and stars who were leery of the new broadcast kid on the block. "At first," said Alphonse Ouimet, "most of the CBC Radio program people, announcers, and producers, and especially the supervisory echelon, were just as happy not to have anything to do with the new 'engineering toy' which they were sure would never replace the 'senior' radio service."

Popular comedians Johnny Wayne and Frank Shuster showed a typical reluctance about TV. Montreal producer Pierre Pétel recalled wooing them to go on CBFT in the fall of 1952. "They weren't interested in television," he said, "because they were big stars in radio. I courted them for days on the telephone. Then I went to Toronto, twisted their arms, broke their legs and ... they agreed to do a comedy sketch." They joked and sang in French and English a song they had written, "Mes Amis Canadiens." But even after their successful performance, they were not yet hooked on television.

Wayne and Shuster had first met when they sat behind each other in a Harbord Collegiate Grade 10 classroom in Toronto in 1931. After performing in Harbord's "Oola Boola" drama club and in productions of Gilbert and Sullivan operettas, they carried their comedy routines into the University of Toronto where an advertising agency official, Maurice Rosenfeld, saw them and said, "You guys are pretty bad, but there's a germ of something here." As "Shuster and Wayne," they did a household hints show on CFRB called "The Javex Wife Preservers" in 1941, then a comedy program "Co-eds and Cut-ups" and sketches for the Buckingham Cigarette show "Blended Rhythm" on the CBC. Later that year, they joined "The Army Show," going overseas with it in 1942. After the war, they wrote "The Johnny Home Show" for CBC and in 1946 began "The Wayne and Shuster Show." An advertising executive, Bill Byles, suggested they put Wayne's name first because it sounded better. "We were both getting the same money so it didn't matter to me," says Shuster.

Their first exposure to an American audience was in a CBS summer replacement radio show, and in 1950, they did their first TV show on "Toni Twin Time." The M.C. was Jack Lemmon, who would go on to Hollywood fame. They weren't that impressed with TV, however, although both had paid $600 for a ten-inch set that, Shuster says, "Got only one channel, Buffalo, and had more snow than Toronto in February." In 1952, they turned down an invitation from CBC-TV head of production, Mavor Moore, telling him, "Look, you guys don't know anything about television. We don't know anything either. Why don't we wait until we both know something about it."

Two years after TV arrived in Canada and after their one-shot performance in the Montreal studio, they succumbed to the lights and cameras and were on the screens together continually from 1954 to 1990 when Wayne died. "Our life has been spent with the Mother Corporation," Shuster says. Throughout their careers, even into their seventies, they were known as "the boys," who sustained their creative collaboration in part by keeping their personal lives mostly separate.

Radio stars weren't the only ones initially uneasy about television. The CBC's chief news editor, Dan McArthur, felt TV was no place for news. He agreed with Alphonse Ouimet and Ernie Bushnell who thought of TV as essentially a vehicle of entertainment: drama, music, and comedy. Journalism, they thought, would have only an occasional walk-on role. McArthur felt TV was frivolous, phoney, and not to be trusted with so important a matter as the news. Thus, there was no newscast when TV went on the air in Canada, and it was not until more than a year later that a separate television news department was formed with a staff of twelve.

That apprehension was echoed in a chorus of warnings about "TV horror-itis," just as, twenty-five years earlier, there had been warnings about "radio-itis." The so-called "boob tube" will cause "spectator-itis," it was said, and the University of Toronto worried about TV encouraging "passivity of mind," foreshadowing later concerns about "couch potatoes." Television may destroy conversation and could even make thinking "obsolete," warned CBC Radio commentator and *Globe and Mail* associate editor Hamish McGeachy. "Televidiots" may result from too much watching, warned a *Maclean's* article. "The greatest stumbling block to education we've ever had," said a Toronto school trustee. "It [TV] gives the children bad eyes, makes them unable to sleep and unable to study, and I wouldn't permit it in my house." "Television is the opium of home life," said Jack Scott in *Liberty* magazine. "TV's hypnotic eye can mesmerize your family all night."

Despite the apprehensions and warnings, a television craze swept Canada just as it had the United States. From all across the country demands poured into Ottawa insisting on the establishment of television stations just about everywhere, and the sales of TV sets zoomed. The CBC was attacked for being too slow in setting up more stations and for stalling on allowing private TV stations. The *Vancouver Sun* denounced "the CBC-loving highbrows" for frustrating free enterprise and denying TV to Canadians except those in Toronto and Montreal. John Diefenbaker demanded that the CBC authorize private TV stations and so, too, did the National Liberal Federation. Private broadcasting supporters, some of them high-ranking Liberals who had pressured the Liberal Federation, sought and got a meeting with the prime minister and several Liberal cabinet ministers to push their case. Meanwhile, the CBC was also pushing the government to set up half a dozen more CBC stations across the country.

In late November 1952, the government announced that CBC stations would be established in Halifax, Winnipeg, and Vancouver. Earlier, the government had announced a CBC-TV station in Ottawa. The CBC also wanted TV outlets in Quebec City, Windsor, and a second station in Montreal so there could be an outlet in the city for each language, and it also wanted stations in Edmonton, Regina, Saint John, and St. John's, plus a few others in southwestern Ontario. That would provide a CBC station in every province but Prince Edward Island. But the government didn't want to move that fast, worrying about the cost of such an expansion. St. Laurent was hesitant, C. D. Howe pushed for more private stations, and they both steered the cabinet into limiting CBC-TV expansion. The government said there would be hearings on private applications that proposed to serve areas without a CBC station and which would carry the CBC national service. This meant, for the time being, no private stations in Toronto, Montreal, and other cities where there would be a CBC station.

One city where the CBC was frustrated in its desire to establish a station was St. John's. Dunton thought he had cabinet approval for a station there, but he underestimated his opponents within the cabinet and the anger some CBC programs had provoked in many of the ministers, including the prime minister and Howe. The cabinet said no and instead approved a private station to be run by broadcasters Geoff Stirling and Don Jamieson, a popular radio personality and a onetime activist against Newfoundland becoming part of Canada (he campaigned for Newfoundland's economic union with the United States). Jamieson was also a spokesman for private broadcasters, later a president of their lobbying association, and more significantly, a behind-the-scenes power in the Liberal Party. He would play a key role in the life of the CBC in the years ahead as a senior Liberal cabinet minister and policy-maker and, in time, would replace Howe as the CBC's *bête noire* inside the government.

In getting his TV station, Jamieson had a powerful ally in his close friend, the key Liberal policy-maker and cabinet minister, Jack Pickersgill. It was Pickersgill who won the argument to have the cabinet reject the CBC station in favour of Jamieson's private station, the first time that had ever happened. "There were at least a dozen better ways to spend $1 million of public money for the benefit of Newfoundland," he later wrote.

The private broadcasters realized they could make a fortune in TV by importing inexpensive American programs: "It's just like having a licence to print your own money," in the immortal words of broadcasting entrepreneur Roy Thomson. The CBC, on the other hand, thought TV had the potential to be the most effective weapon ever devised against American cultural domination and *the* most valuable instrument of national unity. "No other single factor will be so influential in shaping the future life of this country as television," said CBC public affairs head Neil Morrison.

The public, emerging from the shortages and horrors of the Second World War, saw TV as a glorious new beginning, as a way of bringing into their living rooms the best of the stage, the movie screens, the radio, the sports arena, the concert halls, and the news. "REVOLUTION IN EVERYDAY LIFE," headlined the Montreal *Gazette* the day after the launch of CBC Montreal.

Revolution it was, at least for those in Toronto and Montreal through the fall and into the winter of 1953. By March, the number of TV sets in use had doubled from seven months earlier; tripled by September 1953; quadrupled by the end of that year; and hit over 700,000 by March 1954. TV programming had risen to thirty hours a week. In mid-May 1953, Toronto and Montreal were linked and the *CBC Times* cheered, "CANADA'S TWO BIGGEST CITIES CAN SEE EACH OTHER!" What they saw simultaneously the first night of linkage was the first full-length opera on Canadian TV, Mozart's *Don Giovanni*, produced in Toronto by Franz Kraemer.

As it had been on radio, Saturday night hockey was the number one show, but there were also huge audiences for the Grey Cup football final and regular programs such as the variety shows "Holiday Ranch," "The Big Revue," "The Leslie Bell Singers," a quiz show with the feisty author Morley Callaghan, a discussion program, "Fighting Words," with acerbic columnist Nathan Cohen, "The Wayne and Shuster Show," "Newsmagazine," and Ross McLean's "Tabloid," a daily current affairs program hosted by the "easy emcee" Dick MacDougal. MacDougal needed to have an easy style because the program had more than its share of unplanned moments, such as the item on carrier pigeons when one of the pigeons refused to come down from the studio's rafters. It stayed there for weeks, surviving on half-eaten sandwiches left out by the technicians, and when the lights went on, the pigeon – known as the Mad Bomber – would swoop down and occasionally drop deposits on the set, once hitting Mac-Dougal on the forehead during a live interview. In a style followed more than a decade later by "This Hour Has Seven Days," McLean irreverently opened "Tabloid"'s first program with an interview with the controversial anthropologist Dr. Margaret Mead and closed it with an interview with Samia Gamal, an Egyptian belly dancer.

To Dan McArthur's unease, "Tabloid" included a four- or five-minute newscast. The first "National Edition" of TV news began in March 1954 with anchor Larry Henderson. Initially, CBC senior management thought the anchor could just read the 10:00 P.M. radio news bulletin on TV at 11:00 P.M. with the only picture being a slide saying "The News." But TV eventually got its own newscast. Mavor Moore had wanted a news personality to anchor the CBC-TV news, much to the horror of news traditionalist Dan McArthur. The much-travelled, temperamental Larry Henderson exactly fit Moore's description, and his background of acting and reporting gave TV news flare and a high profile. He rapidly came to be the most recognized face in Canada, although TV news still had a low priority among CBC executives, some of whom accused it of offering "today's news with yesterday's pictures."

In Montreal, "Music Hall" was a smash hit and the puppets Pépinot and Capucine were adored by French-speaking children. But the all-time favourite was "La Famille Plouffe," by best-selling novelist Roger Lemelin, at 8:30 P.M. Wednesdays. Lemelin's 1948 book *Les Plouffe* had been adapted for radio in 1952 and the next year was on television. At one point 81 per cent of all TV sets in Montreal were switched to the program. It was so successful in French that the CBC produced an English-language version, but it never had the same popularity in the rest of the country as it did in Quebec. "Those plough jockeys out in western Canada just raised bloody hell," Bushnell later remembered. "Out there, nobody listened to it."

A whole new generation of stars in front and behind the cameras was developing in those beginning years of Canadian TV. Lorne Greene had switched from being a news anchor to classical drama, playing Brutus in *Julius Caesar* and the Prince of the Moors in *Othello*; William Shatner starred not only in "Space Command" but also in Shakespearean dramas on the CBC long before he became Captain Kirk. Singers Robert Goulet, Paul Anka, and Gisèle MacKenzie headed musical shows on CBC before going to New York and Hollywood. Kate Reid featured in many TV dramas both in Canada and the United States. Stars who stayed at home included such singers as the sultry Sylvia Murphy, Joyce Hahn, Terry Dale, Wally Koster, Denny Vaughan, comics Wayne and Shuster, and Canada's first TV weatherman, the chalk-tossing Percy Saltzman, who gave up his meteorology career for "show-biz" weather reporting. Behind the scenes were directors Norman Jewison and Harvey Hart, who later went to Hollywood, and others such as Ross McLean, Don Hudson, Drew Crossan, Harry Rasky, and Norman Campbell who would all leave an unmatched legacy of creativity.

Queen Elizabeth II, however, was the biggest star of all in the early years of Canadian TV when she was crowned in London in June 1953. The TV coverage of the coronation was the audience highlight of the year as well as a competitive triumph for the CBC. Those were pre-tape days, but Stu Griffiths had found a new, quick way to produce television recordings and Bushnell organized RAF and RCAF jets and helicopters in a cross-Atlantic race with the American networks to rush the coronation program onto the air.

CBC listeners heard the early morning live radio broadcast of the coronation from London with announcers Ted Briggs and Marcel Ouimet, both future CBC vice-presidents. Another CBC on-air commentator at the royal celebration was René Lévesque stationed at Trafalgar Square. There was a mad dash to be first with television pictures, especially since Ottawa, Toronto, and Montreal had just been linked by microwave.

The CBC won the race, scooping the Americans, who were furious at their failure to be first. Both NBC and ABC were forced to carry the CBC's coronation program, which was on the air at 4:15 P.M. about eight hours after the ceremony. It was the first time a TV program was seen the same day in the United Kingdom and North America. The triumph was viewed dimly by CBC bureaucrats, however, because Griffiths had broken through a forest of red tape to make it happen. "Jesus, it made everybody in Ottawa furious because he didn't go through channels," remembers Harry Boyle.

There was another confrontation with the American networks in the early days of TV which, for a while, prevented the CBC from carrying popular American shows. It was an argument about money. When the CBC carried American radio programs, it gave the originating network 15 per cent of what Canadian advertisers paid to sponsor the shows. For television, the Americans wanted 70 per cent. The CBC refused, and it was four months before a deal was struck at 50 per cent. Only then could CBC audiences see the likes of "The Aldrich Family," "The Jackie Gleason Show," or "Studio One."

The CBC also took on the advertising agencies in those early days. It was determined to have control over the content of all Canadian programs, which advertising agencies had often controlled so they could protect the image of their clients. Now, the CBC said no, although it agreed it would, if necessary, consult advertisers on program content. "They were used to paying the money and calling the piper," Davie Dunton said. "We said, 'You pay the money and we'll call the piper.'" Even so, General Motors often demanded and sometimes got script changes on the drama series "General Motors Presents" – so often, in fact, that the insider nickname for the show was "General Motors Prevents." When the CBC refused to remove a hanging scene in "Shadow of a Pale Horse," GM withdrew its commercials. When Ford protested about a play in "Ford Startime" – "Point of Departure" – the drama was killed.

Meanwhile, the battle for private television intensified as private broadcasters saw the pot of gold TV represented. They demanded fast action on their applications while opponents, such as historian Arthur Lower, warned that "private ownership means American control." M. J. Coldwell attacked the CBC board for being "weak" in dealing with private broadcasters and told Lower, "The Conservatives have for years been their [private stations'] mouthpiece in Parliament." He also said the Liberals were weakening their support for the CBC, although, speaking for the government, Transport Minister Lionel Chévrier said in the House,

"The essential reason for public development of television in this country is that we want . . . programs to be produced in Canada by Canadians, about Canada." Private broadcasters would be more inclined to import American shows, he said, and must exist "not as a competitor of the CBC . . . but as a complement to the CBC."

Responding to the private lobbyists, the CBC board, in March 1953, finally approved licences for seven private TV stations and two more were approved in June. The first one on the air was CKSO in Sudbury, Ontario, in October 1953, just over a year after CBC-TV had begun. By 1954, fourteen private stations had been approved and by 1956, there were twenty-six private stations. Between the mushrooming private TV sector and the CBC expansion to all major centres, within eight years television had reached 90 per cent of Canadians.

The one millionth TV set installed in Canada was turned on in 1954, but what the million TV screens showed was mostly American programs, except on the CBC French network where, because of linguistic necessity, nearly three-quarters of the programs were home-produced.

The CBC could buy American network programs for as low as $2,000 to $3,000, but Canadian productions such as "The Big Revue" or "CBC Television Theatre" cost over $10,000 each week to produce. The CBC-TV's first season cost $3 million, but within seven years, the cost catapulted to $65 million a year. CBC staff jumped from 1,500 when TV began to 5,500 three years later. The government advanced a total of about $8 million in loans to the CBC to finance the start of television, and TV's budget quickly zoomed past that of radio. While the CBC total annual budget had been around $10 million before TV, within a decade it was about $110 million.

The spectre of American programming swamping Canadian creativity and culture reached new heights in *Maclean's* editor Ralph Allen's 1955 satirical novel *The Chartered Libertine*. In his novel, Allen, a strong supporter of the CBC, envisioned an all-out assault on the CBC for left-wing, immoral, and blasphemous programs, which leads the government to sell the CBC to aggressive private entrepreneurs in Toronto. They, in turn, convert the CBC into an outlet primarily for American programs with the slogan, "The Best of Hollywood Is None Too Good for Canadians," and broadcast shows, such as "I Wed Wanda" and "I Admire Adele," which copied the most popular show seen in Canada, "I Love Lucy."

The large number of TV stations, long hours of programming, and growing size of staff meant that the CBC needed more money – a lot more. Some came from commercials, as more than one-half of the English network CBC-TV shows now carried advertisements, in contrast to one-fifth of radio programs. There had been special government grants and the government replaced the annual $2.50 CBC licence fee with a 15 per cent excise tax on radio and television sets and parts which would go to the CBC. But when the surge in buying TV sets slowed, the government looked for other financing methods and eventually settled on an annual grant. Not only was TV costly, but radio was too, because of the size of the country. As the Massey Commission had noted, while the BBC reached 50 million people with 975 miles of land lines, the CBC needed 15,000 miles of land lines to reach the 15 million Canadians.

Aside from the problems of financing the CBC, the government was grumpy with the CBC as the early TV years sped by for what it considered the airing of too much criticism of the governing Liberals. The Conservative and Social Credit parties, and sometimes right-wing Liberals, continued their protest about a left-wing bias in CBC news and public affairs programming, while the CCF believed that programming was slanted against them. The Canadian Congress of Labour complained to the government that "insofar as CBC Television is concerned, the balance is heavily weighted against labour."

The all-powerful "super" minister, C. D. Howe, didn't think so. In 1954, he lambasted the CBC, called Dunton "a Tory," and threatened to have everybody from Dunton on down fired over a proposed program on unemployment. In a telephone conversation with Dunton, he demanded the program be killed and accused Dunton of currying favour with the Tories by airing the documentary. When Dunton protested, an enraged Howe hung up on the CBC chairman. He then steamed into a cabinet meeting again saying everybody at the CBC should be fired if the documentary were not killed. "This was dangerous nonsense," fellow cabinet minister Jack Pickersgill later said. During a lunch break, Howe said to Pickersgill, "Perhaps I am wrong about this. The right thing for me to do is to call Dunton and tell him the cabinet is thoroughly annoyed, but will not interfere. But if he cares to postpone the broadcast, we will appreciate it." Howe made the phone call, but to his dismay, the program went ahead as planned.

Dunton faced another high-level row with Prime Minister St. Laurent, who had been one of the original backers of Spry's and Plaunt's Canadian Radio League. It was over a letter St. Laurent had written to Dunton in the summer of 1956 complaining about commentaries by University of Manitoba professor John Conway, who had criticized the "timidity" of Canadian foreign policy. Protesting "the supercilious tone used by a young man," St. Laurent said that airing the professor's views "was not a proper use of funds appropriated by Parliament." He said someone in the CBC should ensure this kind of commentary did not get on the air. Dunton diplomatically rejected the prime minister's complaint. Somehow, six months later, the exchange was leaked to the Opposition parties. St. Laurent insisted he had not improperly tried to interfere because, he said, he had written the letter as a private citizen not as prime minister. "Naive!" said the Opposition. Stanley Knowles of the CCF said, "What is at stake here is the principle of freedom of speech, the principle of the independence of the Canadian Broadcasting Corporation."

Conservatives joined in on the attack on St. Laurent. Donald Fleming called the attempt at interference "a dangerous step," and Quebec Conservative MP William M. Hamilton told the House of Commons, "If this debate does nothing else, I hope it will persuade the prime minister not to burn his little fingers by dabbling in the CBC again."

St. Laurent was also upset at a proposed broadcast discussion on a controversial book critical of Mackenzie King by H. S. Ferns and Bernard Ostry. After hearing from King's old associates, particularly Brooke Claxton, Dunton cancelled the program. "I could not conceive of Davie passing on this," Claxton wrote a friend. "It reached his desk in the ordinary course the next morning and he killed it." A few years earlier, Dunton had cancelled another program after the government had apoplexy when it heard of a proposal to discuss on "Citizens' Forum," a Defence Department scandal involving horses on the government payroll.

The CBC and the government came closest to a breaking point over the wildest parliamentary debate of this century: the spring 1956 battle over C. D. Howe's project to bring Alberta natural gas by pipeline to southern Ontario. An impatient Howe was insistent on ramming through the House the legislation enabling the project to go ahead, and more than any other event, this symbolized the Liberal government's arrogance and insensitivity at the time. CBC airwaves were filled with the vitriol of politicians on both sides of the debate and the acid comments of parliamentary press gallery members on the tactics of the government. The Liberal cabinet, especially Howe, was furious at the CBC. Dunton and Ouimet were privately vilified by Liberal cabinet members, and there were suggestions relayed to program staff by Ernie Bushnell that the CBC "lay off" the debate until the bill was passed. To programmers who protested, Bushnell said, "Well, that's the way it has to be!" Senior program officials, including Gene Hallman and Frank Peers, protested to Alphonse Ouimet, who was now general manager, and he ordered programming as usual. Having been burned before for interfering with the CBC, Prime Minister St. Laurent issued no admonition to the CBC to stop giving airtime to government opponents. Thus, uncharacteristically, the Conservatives said the CBC's coverage of the pipeline debate was very fair.

There is no doubt that the coverage on the CBC and elsewhere in the media given to the raucous House of Commons debate vividly underlined the government's bull-in-a-china-shop style and had a profound effect on Canadians for which Howe and the Liberals would pay dearly. Because the CBC was the only national broadcasting outlet and because some influential Liberals still thought of it as "our creature," the CBC was the focus of the Liberals' fury. After the election a year hence, the Liberals vowed, they would move in with tighter controls on the CBC.

Even Health Minister Paul Martin, a longtime CBC supporter, demonstrated his frustration with the CBC, calling it "that holiest of corporations" and denying Conservative charges of interference. "All I can say is that any such alleged intervention has proven to be wholly ineffective," he said.

Less than a year after the pipeline debate, while the Liberals' anger was still simmering, the Conservatives jumped all over the CBC for being unfair to them. Leslie Frost, the Ontario premier, led the charge in a fiery exchange of letters with CBC chairman Dunton. Frost charged that the CBC was developing "into a propaganda machine for the party in office in Ottawa . . . the Liberal Party. . . . It seems to me that everything is being loaded against the Opposition parties." He cited coverage of External Affairs Minister Lester Pearson's Suez crisis activities at the United Nations (for which Pearson would later be awarded the Nobel Peace Prize) and coverage of speeches by other cabinet ministers such as Paul Martin, Jack Pickersgill, and Jimmy Gardiner. Frost felt the coverage was "heavily weighted in favour of federal Liberals." Federal Conservatives provided a background chorus of support for Frost's charges, and Dunton quickly made a delicate refutation proposing that representatives of the CBC and the Premier's Office together examine the CBC newscasts item by item.

Frost replied by reiterating his accusations of bias and rejecting Dunton's proposal. The premier also released some of his correspondence with Dunton to the *Globe and Mail*, whereupon Dunton released all of it to all the media. Both sides retired muttering to themselves, letting the accusations and refutations stand.

The private broadcasters escaped almost all the political attacks the CBC suffered by the simple expedient of carrying little or no critical commentary or serious news programming, although MPs were given free broadcast time. Nor did the private broadcasters offer much, if any, serious or controversial dramas or satires. They were growing fat, rich, and popular from airing American dramas, soap operas, sitcoms, a few Canadian variety shows, and tame journalism. Titillate, not stimulate, was their approach. It was a creed of greed. There was just too much money to be made in the "vast wasteland" of television as Newton Minow, John Kennedy's chairman of the U.S. Federal Communications Commission, later described the medium.

Some of this had been foreseen by the Massey Commission, which had recommended there be a special study of Canadian television by 1955. The present government agreed that, given the turmoil in TV with two million sets now in use and thirty-eight stations on the air, an examination of broadcasting was in order and in 1955 announced the establishment of the Fowler Commission. Brooke Claxton, who had proposed Vincent Massey to head the last royal commission, was also instrumental in getting Robert Fowler, president of the Canadian Pulp and Paper Association, to head this one. Unlike the Massey Commission however, this one was not loaded with public broadcasting supporters from academia. The other members were an ambassador and a banker, and together they travelled to twelve cities and received 276 briefs. Once again, debate was focused on the merits of public versus private broadcasting. The president of the Canadian Association of Broadcasters, Halifax broadcaster Finlay MacDonald, charged in a Halifax speech that the noted historian and leader of a pro-CBC organization, Professor Arthur Lower of Queen's University, was "one of the best known socialists in Canada." MacDonald said he did not mean to "infer that [Lower's] organization is communist dominated." The Halifax *Chronicle-Herald* accused him of using "one of the oldest of propaganda devices," and Dalhousie University philosophy professor George Grant charged MacDonald with "demagoguery." "Having listened to the radio station of which Mr. Mac-Donald is the manager, I can well understand why he objects to the intellectual," Grant said.

A short time later, after he had left the CAB presidency, MacDonald took a much softer approach, telling the Fowler Commission that he disagreed with the idea of splitting regulatory control away from the CBC. Furthermore, he told Fowler, the private stations were "not . . . equal elements . . . but links in the national system" of the CBC.

The CAB and most private broadcasters, however, took a very different view, thinking that those who supported the CBC were, as Newfoundland broadcaster Don Jamieson suggested, "misguided eggheads or bribed stooges . . . who advocate state control." They declared American television programs were no threat to Canadian culture and they also said the CBC should get out of selling commercials and pay the private stations for carrying ad-free CBC programs. In addition, they wanted a private network. There were also suggestions the CBC should stop all broadcasting and only produce programs, something like the NFB, which could be aired by private broadcasters.

But the most intense debate swirled around the old charge that the CBC was both "cop and competitor." Try as they could, however, the Fowler commissioners could not get from the private broadcasters any substantial evidence of unfair treatment by the CBC. Indeed, if anything, evidence indicated the CBC had regulated the private stations with an extremely light hand. It was noted that in 1952 the CBC had proposed that radio stations be required to have a minimum percentage of time devoted to Canadian programs. After vigorous protests from the private stations, the CBC had backed down, and in fact, gave the stations more time for commercials. The CBC's timidity enraged Professor Lower. "I am beginning to despair of the CBC authorities," he wrote to Graham Spry. "They seem to have no reply at all to the aggressiveness of the private broadcasters. Between you and me, I think we probably need a change of personnel there."

Maclean's editorialized about Robert Fowler's efforts to get evidence of CBC unfairness. "Time after time," it said, "he demanded and failed to get examples of the tyranny and persecution by the CBC that elicited such heart-rending screams from the private stations. Some of the examples submitted were palpably false.... Others were nearly twenty years old.... Fowler didn't hesitate to give this sophistry the drubbing it deserved." *Maclean's* spoke of "the loose, ill-tempered, hyperbole of the private stations ... telling their story ineptly and at times misleadingly."

After a year of hearings and travels, the Fowler Commission presented a 518-page report that somehow pleased everyone, if not by much. The commissioners criticized the quality of private station programs, but opened the door for more private TV, saying it was now time for the establishment of second TV stations per area. They praised CBC programming but, recognizing the financial problems of the CBC, urged a more vigorous pursuit of advertising revenue. That recommendation had a lasting impact on CBC-TV schedules as CBC programmers were encouraged to put more emphasis on programs that would "sell" to advertisers. The former CBC commercial manager and longtime public broadcasting activist, Austin Weir, lamented the change of program direction implicit in the Fowler recommendation. "The saleability of programs now became a prime consideration," Weir later wrote. "And the thinking of program staff consciously or unconsciously, but inevitably, was directed very largely to the production of saleable programs." That direction was pushed even harder two years later when a parliamentary committee picked up the theme and said, "Increased efforts should be made to ensure the emergence of vigorous commercial policies." Those policies led to the programming of popular Hollywood shows that made the CBC more akin to private broadcasting and more competitive with private stations. "Commercial pressures are natural, persistent and inexorable and those who have never been in the business have no idea how insidious and compelling they can be in the face of tightening budgets," Weir said.

The implications of this march into a more commercial ethos, which would haunt the CBC unto the eve of the twenty-first century, was at first largely overshadowed by Fowler's more controversial recommendation of a new structure for Canadian broadcasting. The commission criticized the CBC for being too soft in its regulation of private stations, but it also recognized the level of concern, if not the validity, of the private broadcasters' complaint about the CBC being both "cop and competitor." It recommended the establishment of a board of broadcast governors to oversee all broadcasting and to which both the CBC and private stations would report. The CBC board would be eliminated and the CBC would become an operating arm of the new overall board. This was only half a loaf for the private broadcasters who had wanted a fully independent regulatory board unrelated to the CBC, but they and their supporters reasoned half a loaf was better than none. For its part, the CBC now seemed content to be rid of its tiring and frustrating regulatory role. The commissioners expected the single overall board to be much tougher on private stations than the CBC had been. "Some stations may lose their licences because of a shabby performance," the commission warned.

The report was well-received and ready for implementation as soon as the June 1957 election was out of the way and, as everybody believed, the Liberals were returned to office.

But John Diefenbaker was not mollified by the commission's report and complained of "hog wild spending" by the CBC, calling it a "mass propaganda agency" and its policies "an unjustifiable challenge to freedom of speech." Diefenbaker's words carried more weight now because he had succeeded George Drew as the leader of the Progressive Conservative Party. He had been chosen at the end of 1956 when Drew, exhausted from the pipeline debate, retired from active politics.

CBC television's live coverage of Diefenbaker's victory at the Tory leadership convention changed forever the very nature of Canadian politics. TV had brought politics into the living rooms of the nation, and the television set had become the country's political stage. Canadians were fascinated by the flamboyant Prairie political evangelist who seemed such a refreshing change from the staid, atrophied Liberals. And while he had said some nasty things about the CBC and had become a powerful supporter of private broadcasters, Diefenbaker nevertheless had good relations with much of the press and many CBC reporters and producers. They began to smell a coming seachange in Canadian politics.

When it came to the election itself, television provided the *coup de grâce* to the Liberals. On TV, Prime Minister St. Laurent was the epitome of grey. He didn't like TV, felt and looked uncomfortable in front of the camera, and spoke haltingly and stiffly. He was a relic of the past compared to the vibrant, fresh image of John George Diefenbaker, and it could all be seen on CBC television, which provided the only national TV news coverage.

Charles Lynch, the CBC's UN correspondent, who was assigned to cover the election, marvelled at what he called "the magic of Diefenbaker" on television. Travelling the country with his TV cameras and his producer, Morley Safer, who later went on to "60 Minutes" fame, Lynch knew he had a good story. He didn't know how good until election night, June 10, 1957. To the astonishment of the nation and of CBC anchors Lynch and Blair Fraser, Diefenbaker won. And to his astonishment, C. D. Howe was beaten in his Port Arthur, Ontario, riding by a local school teacher, CCFer Doug Fisher, largely, Howe said, because of television. Fisher was good on TV and knew how to use it; Howe was awful and didn't know how to use it. The CBC's Liberal *bête noire* for more than two decades was gone from public life.

Amid the election night excitement, Lynch pulled out a foot-and-a-half-long cigar while on air. "I lit the damn thing and away it went," he said. "I said this is to mark a great story, an event in the history of the country." But the ever politically sensitive CBC officials were alarmed at what they feared might be perceived as a pro-Conservative gesture. "They made me kill the cigar and the next day there was a tremendous inquisition about this cigar, whether it compromised the network," Lynch laughed. The CBC had much more to worry about than Lynch's cigar, however.

A foretaste of the future came when the new prime minister said he would strip regulatory powers from the CBC and set up a whole new system – a system that would profoundly change public broadcasting and lessen the dominance of the CBC. In effect, the private broadcasters were being told they would get what they always wanted; the single system of the past two decades would end and the CBC would no longer be, as Diefenbaker so often said, "acting as both judge and jury." It was the beginning of a diminished role for the CBC and the unravelling of Graham Spry's and Alan Plaunt's dream. Diefenbaker, however, refuted rumours of the CBC being sold to private broadcasters for $50 million. "No offer has been received or will be considered," he said. But he also made it clear that more private TV stations would soon be authorized, including some in cities where the CBC stations were located.

He sought to soften the blows to the CBC by naming as revenue minister, through whom the CBC reported to Parliament, Nova Scotia MP George Nowlan. Nowlan had been supportive of the CBC on several occasions and knew broadcasting from his role as president of a small Annapolis Valley broadcasting company. It was, however, little consolation for what was to come. Nine months after his minority government upset win, Diefenbaker won a second general election by a landslide and now he began to focus on changing the CBC.

10

Canadian Stars Arising

While the CBC as an organization began to tremble in antici-
pation of John Diefenbaker's changes, CBC stars were beginning to shine
on the nation's television screens. Canadians still preferred American
shows, watching in the millions as Ed Sullivan, Milton Berle, Dinah
Shore, Perry Como, Sid Caesar, and Jackie Gleason sang, joked, and
talked, but Canadian performers were starting to challenge them. The
biggest star of all was Canada's best-known voice for the past quarter-
century, Foster Hewitt with his Saturday night hockey, although he was
never as comfortable on TV as he had been on radio. The telecast of
hockey games usually began after the first period so that fans in the arena
would see more than fans at home. NHL president Clarence Campbell
felt TV was a "menace" to hockey and worried about ticket sale losses.
The CFL met that worry by blacking out local games.

Listening to Hewitt from Toronto and Danny Gallivan from Montreal
and Gallivan's French-language counterpart, René LeCavalier, was a
bond for two and a half million English-speaking Canadians and for two
million French-speaking Canadians even before a full national TV
hook-up existed. Sydney Newman, pioneer TV producer, who later
became head of BBC drama and boss of the NFB, was the first hockey
television producer. He knew little or nothing about the game, but said he

used his cameras during a game as if he were a ballet choreographer. New-man applied the same choreography in producing the first televised Grey Cup game in 1952 and the first boxing match seen on Canadian TV.

Although they didn't reach the same audience heights as the Stanley Cup and Grey Cup games, variety programs were having their heyday on the CBC. Never again would there be so many, so popular. Wayne and Shuster successfully transferred their talents from radio to television as did "Our Pet," Juliette, and the Maritime fiddling favourite, Don Messer. In fact, "Don Messer's Jubilee," with Charlie Chamberlain and Marg Osburne and their corny country music and jokes, at one point even out-drew hockey and Ed Sullivan to the mystification of sophisticated big city critics who couldn't understand the attraction of homespun programs like Messer's, "Country Hoedown," "Holiday Ranch," or "Red River Jam-boree." Messer, according to ratings surveys, at his height reached 25 per cent of all TV homes in big cities, 50 per cent of all farm homes and, in the Maritimes, according to the Elliott-Haynes survey, at one point captured 96 per cent of all TV homes.

In comedy, Wayne and Shuster not only captivated Canadian audiences on the CBC but also were a hit in the United States through "The Ed Sullivan Show," where over the years, they appeared more times than any other comics – live on fifty-eight occasions, plus nine repeats. Although strongly wooed, they refused to move to the United States, however. "Johnny and I really hated the gypsy life of show business," Shuster says. "Our roots were in Canada and we wanted to stay here." Success came from their rare brand of literate slapstick such as their legendary 1958 "Rinse the Blood Off My Toga," a satiric skit on Shakespeare's *Julius Caesar* done in the style of a 1930s tough-guy private eye novel. They occasionally were taken aback, however, by Canadian viewers who contrasted their Ed Sullivan shows with their CBC shows. "How come you guys are so much funnier on Sullivan than the CBC?" they were asked. In fact, the material was the same on both.

"The Big Revue" had begun regular variety programming on CBC in 1952, with Don Hudson and Norman Campbell producing, Norman Jewison floor directing, and starring such performers as Phyllis Marshall, Shirley Harmer, Alan and Blanche Lund, and comics Frank Peppiat and John Aylesworth. It was quickly followed by a kaleidoscope of song and dance shows such as "Cross Canada Hit Parade," "Showtime," "Pick the Stars," "The Denny Vaughan Show," "The Jack Kane Show," "The Jackie Rae Show," and many others. The CBC looked to its variety shows for mass audiences and high commercial revenue to help finance its more serious cultural and journalistic programming, which generally drew smaller audiences.

Of all the Canadian stars who challenged the American show-biz big names there was none brighter than Juliette, who, her onetime writer Alex Barris said, was "flirty . . . but nice . . . a coquette but not a seductress." She was "Our Pet" who said, "Goodnight Mom" after every show to her Ukrainian mother in Winnipeg. Singing was her life. She had begun in amateur shows at age six singing "Buddy Can You Spare a Dime," going professional at age thirteen in Vancouver with the Dal Richards band and at fifteen she had starred on CBC Radio. She became known as the Belle of the Chuckwagon on the "Burns Chuckwagon" radio show in 1951. Her first TV appearance in 1954 was with Cliff McKay on "Holiday Ranch." By 1958, she was a full-blown star on radio, TV, and at the occasional nightclub. Tough, demanding, but with generosity and innocence encased in a show-biz veneer, Juliette became a Canadian icon, making the most lasting impression of any of the early Canadian singers who took TV by storm. Her Saturday night post-hockey show lasted from 1954 to 1966. Although she had offers from Perry Como and Arthur Godfrey, she, like Wayne and Shuster, said no to all proposals to work in the United States. When her post-hockey show was cancelled, it came as a blow. "I had no idea I was going to be dumped," she says. "But I should have had an idea when I saw my producer in the Celebrity Club nibbling on the ear of my replacement."

Rivalling Juliette in popularity was "Front Page Challenge" which began as a summer replacement quiz show in 1957 with a joke-cracking Alex Barris, glamorous Toby Robins, and the all-time curmudgeon, Gordon Sinclair, along with handsome Paramount Newsreel announcer Win Barron as host. Barron, however, wasn't comfortable on TV, quit after a few months, and was replaced by Fred Davis. Pierre Berton soon joined the panel and Betty Kennedy came along four years later when Toby Robins left over a salary dispute. When it began, the panelists got $60 per program. The show became the longest running Canadian network TV program in history, although its popularity with the audience was not always reflected by the critics, most of whom panned the first show and have poked fun at it ever since.

But not every performer enjoyed TV as much as Juliette or the "Front Page Challenge" personalities. Dr. Leslie Bell, whose choir was one of the first to experience TV death by ratings, said TV was a rat race. "I left it," he wrote in *Maclean's*, "because I saw how rapidly it burns up talents . . . TV performers for the most part, fall into two groups – those who have been dropped and those who are going to be dropped."

There was other criticism, too. Performers complained of there being no "star system" in the CBC to develop TV headliners, although most of the country thought they were stars. Variety show host Alex Barris said, "The CBC's determination to deflate show business egos is clear. . . . The CBC has always been uneasy about proclaiming anyone as a 'star.'" Juliette agrees, saying, "The corporation I don't think ever really wanted anyone to have the kind of power a real star has because then they couldn't control them." In truth, at the CBC it was the producers not the performers who were treated like stars, with rare exceptions such as Wayne and Shuster and Juliette.

There were complaints, too, about CBC-TV being too American. "Many of our shows are pallid imitations of American shows," said Johnny Wayne. "Stop trying to copy what the Americans do best," said leading producer Mavor Moore.

But there were differences. Canadian drama had less violence and action and more substance and controversy than American TV drama. There was, for instance, "Flight into Danger" by a thirty-six-year-old advertising executive and future best-selling writer named Arthur Hailey and productions by Bernie Slade, whose future lay in Hollywood. Others whose creative work got national attention by being showcased on CBC-TV included W. O. Mitchell, Joseph Schull, Len Peterson, Tommy Tweed, Lister Sinclair, and George Salverson.

Pushed by the effervescent enthusiasm of drama producer and supervisor Sydney Newman, drama series such as "General Motors Theatre," "Folio," "First Performance," and "On Camera" heavily featured Canadian-written plays, giving Canadian writers the greatest opportunities and biggest audiences they had ever had.

Opera, ballet, and Shakespearean drama were sprinkled through the CBC's television schedule. They were expensive productions, superbly done, but they drew only modest-sized audiences and criticism from some politicians for "forcing" culture down Canadian throats. New Brunswick Liberal MP Henry Murphy complained about "long-haired nut boys cavorting around in tight, long underwear."

There was not much of this kind of criticism of CBC French network TV, however, which featured even more high cultural programming than the English network. But, as on English television, the biggest audiences to CBC French television were for hockey, football, music shows such as "Music Hall" and "Au P'tit Café," "Café des Artistes," and of course, "La Famille Plouffe."

From Montreal to the Gaspé, television opened a new world to Quebeckers, lifting the veil on hitherto taboo subjects and slashing into two centuries of church and state paternalism, submissive conservativism, and old-fashioned values that were vividly upheld by the regime of Premier Maurice Duplessis. But since the CBC was a federal institution, Duplessis, to his distress, could not control its programs. The extent of the social and political impact of TV in Quebec was something never experienced in English-speaking Canada. The greatest TV challenge to Quebec's established authority were the new ideas and stimulating insights provided by the most controversial program on the French network, the weekly half-hour show "Point de Mire," featuring René Lévesque. Writing on a blackboard, pointing to a map, and interviewing guests, the chain-smoking news correspondent and onetime war reporter achieved a popularity with the audience never reached before or since by any broadcast journalist on Canadian television. He seemed hopelessly unorganized, untidy, and world-weary, but his engaging and sometimes shy smile and style, combined with his razor-sharp insights, gave him an uncanny ability to touch the public as he explained wars, revolutions, and political upheavals. He had covered the Korean War for the French network and later began co-hosting the CBC Radio program "Carrefour" with Judith Jasmin, focusing on major political issues. In 1955, he and Jasmin began a TV version of "Carrefour," along with Solange Chaput-Rolland and Jean Ducharme. But it was "Point de Mire" that made him by far the most popular journalistic "star" in Quebec. The charisma that gave him stardom would later make him one of the century's most important Quebec political leaders.

The only program on the CBC English TV that came close to Lévesque's "Point de Mire" was Ross McLean's "Close-Up." McLean had produced a CBC youth radio show called "Young Ideas" with, he said, "half-pint pundits" and then was entranced by the new medium of television. He brought together for "Close-Up" a constellation of present and future journalistic TV stars including J. Frank Willis, Pierre Berton, Charles Templeton, Jack Webster, and June Callwood. There were soon-to-be star directors such as Allan King and Daryl Duke, as well as a couple of neophyte producers named Patrick Watson and Doug Leiterman of whom much more would be heard within a few years. Others who later worked with McLean included future English network vice-president Peter Herrndorf, future press secretary to Prime Minister Trudeau Patrick Gossage, future vice-president of news and current affairs Tim Kotcheff, and writer Barbara Amiel. McLean's celebrity-loving, controversy-seeking "Close-Up" did interviews with everyone from President Tito to Red Skelton, from Lucky Luciano to Ann Landers. What he sought, McLean said, was "information masquerading as entertainment." His program explored the social issues of divorce, homosexuality, unwed mothers, crime, and it tackled political exposés and separatism in Quebec, featuring the comments of University of Montreal professor Pierre Trudeau.

McLean, the wicked-tongued *enfant terrible* of CBC-TV, admitted he had his troubles with his bosses. "A number of people found me prickly and very hard to love," he said. CBC management found him hard to trust, as well, especially after "The Shady Lady" program, an exposé of Canada's divorce laws that included a woman who said she was a professional co-respondent who faked evidence to get divorces. The trouble was, she wasn't, and red-faced CBC officials endured public humiliation at the hoax. "A very stupid thing to do," recalled Keith Morrow, head of the CBC in Toronto at the time. "Ross McLean didn't level with me about it." It was, said Morrow, one of several similar incidents that upset management.

McLean's undisguised contempt for most senior officials at the CBC did not help. "I have been saddened by years of simple [management] incompetence, profound ineptitude, or just runaway timidity and obtuseness," he later said. Eventually and inevitably, the CBC could take no more of his programming controversies and lacerating contempt, and after what he called a "Queegian court martial scene," he and the CBC parted company.

While "Close-Up" and "Point de Mire" captured the most attention, old reliables such as "The National News" and "Newsmagazine" increasingly set the national agenda with a less flamboyant approach to the news, thanks to the legacy of Dan McArthur. As TV began to overwhelm radio, McArthur, who despised what he saw as the frivolous "show-biz" tarnishing of the news by TV, quit his job as chief news editor and went to CBC headquarters in Ottawa to spend the rest of his career in a backwater advisory role.

"Newsmagazine" was the creative spark which began to change CBC News from the relatively staid coverage of Dan McArthur's day to a much more aggressive coverage by CBC reporters, especially in Ottawa and outside the country. Just as the nation had been transfixed two decades earlier by J. Frank Willis' radio reporting from the Moose River mine disaster, Canadians were captured by televised reports of the 1958 Spring Hill mine disaster and Queen Elizabeth opening Parliament in Ottawa in 1957. Dramatic pictures from the British-French Suez invasion and the Hungarian Revolution in the fall of 1956 drew huge audiences, as did the Kennedy-Nixon debate in 1960. Never before had such vivid, breaking news actually been seen by so many Canadians. And never before had Canadian politicians been under such intensive journalistic scrutiny or had issues been examined more critically by so many people. In January 1958, four million Canadians watched the Liberal leadership convention choose Lester Pearson as the new party head; five and a half million watched the Stanley Cup play-offs that year; and almost eight million watched John Diefenbaker defeat Pearson in the March 1958 federal election. An audience height for the era was reached a few years later when twelve million Canadians tuned into CBC-TV to see a recording of Princess Margaret marrying Anthony Armstrong-Jones.

Altogether, there was an astonishing array of radio and TV programming on the CBC that went far beyond the wildest dreams of Graham

Spry, Alan Plaunt, Leonard Brockington, and even Gladstone Murray. There was news, public affairs, music, comedy, and drama; children's programs such as "Small Fry Frolics"; farm programming, arts, and religion. Even the veteran radio program "Citizens' Forum" was now on prime-time television, as was its French-language counterpart "Les Idées en marche," with the likes of Pierre Trudeau, Jeanne Sauvé, and André Laurendeau, who had fought the CBC over its conscription referendum ban of the no side. The Quebec government of Maurice Duplessis demanded the CBC take off the air "hot-headed leftists" such as Laurendeau, and Quebec Conservative MP Louis-Joseph Pigeon warned the CBC, "Let us throw out those people with warped ideas, leftist ideas, who grab half the television programs, such as, for example . . . Pierre Elliott Trudeau, Gérard Pelletier and Jean-Louis Gagnon, who should be permanently kept away from the national network. . . . Let these gentlemen be replaced by people imbued with democratic and Christian ideals."

Until mid-1958 there was, in fact, a patchwork rather than a true national network, but on July 1 that year, less than six years after the birth of television in Canada, the nation finally was linked by TV, Atlantic to Pacific. It was an engineering triumph, the most complex TV system in the world at the time, stretching about 4,000 miles. It also was Alphonse Ouimet's finest hour, since most of the credit for this electronic highway was his. It was, he said, "The story of a nation that can see itself at once in a sort of giant full-length mirror."

To mark the East-West link, a TV celebration was hosted by René Lévesque and Joyce Davidson entitled "Memo to Champlain" because the date of the link-up coincided with the 350th anniversary of Quebec's founding. The three million TV screens in Canada showed in a split-screen picture four Canadian cities: Vancouver, Winnipeg, Toronto, and Halifax. Canadian stars, officials, and personalities saluted a nation that from Sydney, Nova Scotia, to Victoria, British Columbia, at last could simultaneously see and share a hockey game, a parliamentary opening, or some other major live event. A year later, the final link was made to St. John's, Newfoundland.

Also in 1958, the CBC took over radio broadcasting in the North from ten scattered military and community stations. A decade later, the CBC introduced television to the North, shipping tapes from Toronto and telecasting for four hours a day, and by 1973, the Anik satellite was feeding a full TV northern service all the way from the Yukon to Baffin Island. At first, programs were only in English or French, but in time, CBC was broadcasting in eight northern languages as well, from Dogrib to Gwich'in. Cree sportscaster Sidney Ottereyes became the Foster Hewitt of the North, broadcasting NHL hockey games and even echoing Hewitt's famous "He shoots! He scores!" in Cree: "Shoochabadawmaw! Beechabadun!" One problem when hockey broadcasts in Cree began was that there was no Cree word for "puck," so Ottereyes referred to it as "the round thing."

As well as Ottereyes, the CBC made northern stars of singers Susan Aglukark, Daniel T'Len, and Charlie Panagoniak and gave a shared experience and a self-awareness among Northerners that, because of their isolation, they had never before had. Opening up new worlds sometimes could be confusing, however. Once, at the end of a program of classical music from the Frobisher Bay radio station, the Inuit announcer advised, "That's enough of the white man's foolish music for this week." TV in particular worried local leaders, as it transformed life in the North even more than it had in the South, bringing with it all the attendant worries of creating couch potatoes. But like their counterparts in the South, they couldn't stop the onrushing television age.

Planning the CBC Northern Service and the coast-to-coast TV linkage had been one of the last undertakings of the Dunton era. They were a swan song for the man who had been the most effective chief executive officer the CBC ever had or would have. Three days after the national system was inaugurated, Davie Dunton announced his resignation. He had been chairman of the CBC for nearly thirteen years, generating more loyalty from his staff, more respect from politicians, and more admiration from the broadcast industry than any leader of the CBC before or since. His success came from his boyish charm, his zest, his cultural enthusiasms, his integrity, and his pragmatism. He was able to ward off his enemies' blows with a velvet glove on an iron fist – a very different manner from the steamrolling style of his most successful predecessor, Leonard Brockington.

"A brilliant CBC head," said the *Ottawa Journal* on Dunton's departure. "His brains, temperament and civilized outlook made it a great broadcasting institution."

With the engineering and managerial detail work led by Alphonse Ouimet and the programming guided by Ernie Bushnell, Dunton had reversed the CBC's wartime subservience to government, had overseen the golden age of radio, and had launched television in Canada. Under him, the CBC had exploded from less than 1,000 employees when he began to more than 6,300 when he left, and the budget had gone through the roof, all because of the gargantuan human and financial appetite of television. Dunton had come closer than anybody else to managing the Herculean task of translating Plaunt's and Spry's dream into a radio and television reality. But by mid-1958, with John Diefenbaker poised to weaken the CBC and strengthen the private broadcasters, Dunton saw the future and didn't want to be part of it. Although at forty-five he was still a relatively young man, Dunton retired to the gentler environment of the presidency of Ottawa's Carleton University and took up the role of moderator and commentator on numerous CBC public affairs programs.

Others, however, still wanted to fight Diefenbaker's vision of a less dominant CBC, and out of London, England, where he was representing the Saskatchewan government, the old public broadcasting warhorse Graham Spry galloped onto the Ottawa scene. "The dangers to the CBC are not those of extinction but emasculation," he wrote to the CCF leader and his old friend, Tommy Douglas. He wrote in a similar vein to Professor Arthur Lower. Lower, worried about the lessening government support for the CBC and the growing power of private broadcasters, had in 1951 brought back to life Spry's and Plaunt's old lobbying organization and renamed it the Canadian Radio and Television League. It had faded away after a few years, however, but now Spry, alarmed at Diefenbaker's plans for the CBC, again revived and renamed his lobby group. In June 1958, he announced the formation of the Canadian Broadcasting League. Supporters included some of the same old gang of a quarter-century before, including Ned Corbett of the Canadian Association for Adult Education. Spry told Douglas he was alarmed that Conservative policies might force the CBC into "dependence . . . upon American broadcasting and advertising agencies. To me this result would be disastrous to the national life of Canada. Frankly, there is no length to which I would not go, no personal sacrifice I would not make, to forestall such a consequence."

He charged into Ottawa, bouncing from office to office in his quest, meeting, cajoling, pleading with senior civil servants, members of the prime minister's staff, including Rod Finlayson, his old friend and collaborator from the campaign to persuade R. B. Bennett to favour public broadcasting, and even private broadcasters such as Finlay MacDonald of Halifax, a friend of the minister now responsible for the CBC, fellow Nova Scotian George Nowlan. Spry described MacDonald as "a rather James Stewart type . . . a most liberal, open-minded, sophisticated character."

While many of the longtime advocates of public broadcasting joined in Spry's efforts, his new organization lacked the critical newspaper, business, and multi-party support it once had. In addition, he faced a far more powerful private broadcasting industry and a fiercer political determination to cut the CBC down to size. Spry wrote to Tommy Douglas that private stations may have made "a deal" to favour the Conservatives in news coverage in exchange for getting the kind of new broadcast legislation they wanted.

The attitude of many of the now governing Conservatives was reflected in the comments of New Brunswick Conservative MP J. C. Van Horne who thundered, "If this government ever inherited a mess, it was when we took over the CBC. The whole top echelon of the CBC seems to be blinded by the wrong kind of liberalism. The CBC is the source of more complaints than any other branch of government. I suggest that the government sell the CBC." Quebec MP Louis-Joseph Pigeon demanded, "Let the CBC do away with smutty stories and with daring costumes. . . . A clean-up job is necessary."

Diefenbaker used these outbursts to validate his own attacks on the CBC. Although the private broadcasters brought in a flood of American programming, Diefenbaker concentrated his venom on the CBC. The CBC, he said was "dumping" American programs into Canadian prime-time television. "The CBC had become so indoctrinated with the Liberal viewpoint," he said later, "that it indiscriminately embraced North

American continentalism and could not differentiate, its academic and intellectual pretence to the contrary, between American national opinion and true internationalism."

The new prime minister, who had the backing of his huge majority government, was determined to change fundamentally the idea of a single Canadian broadcast system in which the public broadcaster was dominant and private broadcasters secondary and supplementary. In short, he wanted to "get at" what he felt was a Liberal-dominated CBC which his then executive assistant, Gowan Guest, says Diefenbaker believed was trying to undermine his administration in general and himself in particular.

First, however, he had to face his fellow Westerner Graham Spry, who arranged for the Canadian Broadcasting League to meet the prime minister two days after Dunton resigned. Knowing Diefenbaker's personal hero and role model was Sir John A. Macdonald, Spry named Macdonald's biographer, history professor Donald Creighton, head of the more than two-dozen leaders of labour, farm, church, and educational groups who crowded into Diefenbaker's office at noon. Creighton opened the meeting by evoking the memory of Canada's first prime minister, saying, "Sir John A. Macdonald's national policy provided the framework for an integrated trans-continental economy. A national broadcasting system can do for us, in the realm of the mind and the spirit, precisely what these old and tested national policies have done for the political and economic spheres. A steady flow of live programs along the east-west lifeline will express Canadian ideas and ideals, employ Canadian talent and help unite our people from sea to sea and from the river unto the ends of the earth."

It was Spry, however, who did most of the talking. Although the group claimed to represent ten million Canadians, Spry began with a shy grin, saying, "We do not pretend to be a high-powered group. Sir, we are merely disinterested amateurs profoundly concerned with broadcasting as an instrument of national unity. . . . Our vision is that of Sir John A. Macdonald and not of the disc jockey."

What Spry, Creighton, and their public broadcasting supporters wanted was implementation of the Fowler Commission's recommendation for a single system with a national regulatory board to which the

CBC and private broadcasters would be accountable. They also wanted more funding for public broadcasting and a reinforcement of its dominant role in Canadian broadcasting. The ideas were not dissimilar to suggestions floated by CRBC chairman Hector Charlesworth in 1934. They had been abandoned then but now had come back to life.

Much the same advice had reached Diefenbaker's ears two months earlier from a surprising source: Finlay MacDonald in Halifax, who had been asked by Nowlan to head a study on broadcasting. MacDonald strongly supported the main recommendations of the Fowler Report and a continuation of the single system approach with one overall board. He felt Nowlan agreed with him, but cabinet ministers Donald Fleming and George Hees, who worried about "lefties" in the CBC, strongly disagreed, as did Diefenbaker himself.

As Spry and Creighton outlined their views, the prime minister listened, said he was impressed with the broad public support represented by the delegation, but did not reveal that, in fact, he had already made up his mind to give the private broadcasters most of what they had been seeking for the past two decades.

Within a month after the meeting, the new broadcast bill was introduced by the government. It proposed profound changes to the Canadian broadcasting system, and rejected the aims espoused by Plaunt, Spry, R. B. Bennett, and Mackenzie King. No longer would the CBC and public broadcasting dominate a single system in which the role of private broadcasters was to carry CBC national programming, provide supplementary local coverage, and follow the rules of broadcasting as laid down by the CBC.

The Fowler Commission had advocated a system with one overall board that would regulate all broadcasting and supervise the CBC, but Diefenbaker established two boards; one regulatory board under which the private stations and the CBC would, in effect, have equal status, and a second board to run the CBC. That meant all Liberal-appointed members of the existing CBC board would be dismissed, and Diefenbaker would choose a new board that would reflect the pro-private attitude of his government, as would most of the members of the new regulatory agency, the Board of Broadcast Governors (BBG). Diefenbaker had rejected the substance of the Fowler Commission recommendations, but he had taken Fowler's proposed name for the regulatory board.

Not only did the legislation give new status to private stations and diminish the CBC, it opened the door to more private TV stations and a private TV network. The CBC was also financially restricted to annual parliamentary appropriations instead of gaining the security of long-term funding recommended by the Fowler Commission. Having to get money every year from Parliament gave the government a tighter rein on CBC operations and made a nightmare of long-range programming plans. Much of the push for all this came from Finance Minister Donald Fleming.

The Liberals and the CCF, dramatically reduced in the House of Commons by the Diefenbaker landslide, put up only weak opposition in the debate. Liberal leader Lester Pearson spoke philosophically, warning that the new law weakened the public role and strengthened the private sector. "What was . . . a privilege for private broadcasters had gradually become a vested interest and eventually has been invoked as a right," he said. But Don Jamieson's increasing influence among the Liberals, Jack Pickersgill's waning enthusiasm for the CBC, the pallid opposition of the CCF and the Liberals, and the huge Conservative majority ensured a quick approval of the House for a diminished CBC. Graham Spry, although feeling his lobbying had prevented even more damage to the CBC, remained gloomy. "I am convinced that those in the government hostile to the CBC gained powerful opportunities to interfere with and even drastically weaken the CBC," he wrote to a colleague.

The CBC was heading into the most tumultuous era in its history.

I I

The Father of Canadian TV,
A Flawed Genius

The man who piloted the CBC through the political tumult and creative rebellion of the Diefenbaker and Pearson years was a technological genius, a committed nationalist and public broadcaster, a centralizing manager, and a man who was singularly incapable of understanding either the creative or the political process. J. Alphonse Ouimet had been named general manager in 1953, and now at age fifty he was the new CBC president.

The orderly, straight-arrow Ouimet was an innocent abroad in a world of chaos. He was repeatedly booby-trapped by the private agendas of Machiavellian politicians, by the jealousies, turf wars, personal peccadillos, and frequent incompetence of his senior bureaucrats, and by the raging passions of his crusading, rebellious producers. Ouimet didn't drink, was prissy and proper about women and swearing; he was a loner who shied away from camaraderie and whose competitive aggressiveness was largely hidden behind a smiling, shy countenance, except while playing Ping-Pong in his basement recreation room. "Ouimet wanted so desperately to be liked, but he didn't know how to go about it," says Harry Boyle, Network Radio program director in Ouimet's era.

Admired but not loved by close colleagues, Ouimet was a meticulous workaholic with a furious determination and a thin skin when criticized.

"He could not take criticism any time," said Ernie Bushnell, who remembered Ouimet once admonishing him, "Promise me you will never criticize me before my colleagues."

Ouimet also knew little about the creative community of English-speaking Canada. "He had a tremendous inferiority complex about the English side," says Bill Armstrong, his executive assistant and director of press and information in Ouimet's early presidential years.

Ouimet's painfully honest, tightfisted, and straightlaced nature was in extraordinary contrast to the profane, boozy, womanizing predilections of many of his senior executives. His character was a product of his strict, Quebec upbringing during which he had to come in first in his school class every month before his parents would give him his ten-cents allowance.

He was properly recognized as the Father of Canadian TV, but for all his hard work, his technological brilliance, and his managerial savvy, Ouimet never could comprehend what made creative people tick. "Why can't they be more orderly, more obedient? Why don't they see it? Why don't they understand?" he would ask his associates. Ouimet didn't understand their high emotions, and he would tell colleagues, "Passions must be controlled." Bill Armstrong says, "He had the logical mind of an engineer scientist."

Ouimet was appalled at what he felt was the ignorance of many political leaders about the purpose of the CBC and public broadcasting. Why don't the politicians think more of the country and the CBC's unifying role in it, he wondered, instead of being obsessed with petty ambitions and quarrels? It was a problem not only among Conservatives but Liberals, too. He recalled attending a Montreal dinner with the then Liberal trade minister Robert Winters, who told him, "Al, when are you going to earn your way? Why have we got to pay a lot of money for the CBC when the private stations pay their way? Why can't you do the same thing?" Ouimet was astonished that Winters wasn't aware of the basic difference between public and private broadcasting. He felt the same incomprehension when John Diefenbaker, shortly before becoming prime minister, said, "I find it difficult to understand why the CBC, having available to it the best outlets in Canada, is continually in the red. . . . Private stations make money . . . [the CBC] should make profit."

Behind his disarming chuckle, Ouimet was a cool agnostic, affronted by anything that seemed illogical to his rigid mind-set. As an engineer, he deeply resented "the scientific illiteracy of the humanists," and he felt creative people lacked the discipline necessary for leadership. Alphonse Ouimet was a hardware man in a software business, and his failure to understand the creative mind, combined with his political naiveté and his warring associates, resulted in organizational bedlam. It was a fatal flaw that would eventually destroy his CBC presidency.

After Dunton's resignation, the job of finding a new head of the CBC had been given to George Nowlan, who was under intense pressure from newly elected Conservative ministers, including the prime minister, to find someone who would clamp down on CBC spending and provocative programming, who was ideally a Conservative or at least certainly not a Liberal, and who preferably was not part of the existing CBC management. "The praetorian guard of bureaucracy, the CBC since World War II, had become a government within a government, answerable only to itself," said Conservative insider Tommy Van Dusen in a comment reflecting the attitude of the new Conservative government.

Nowlan did not entirely share the paranoia of many of his colleagues, including the prime minister, but he did look for a fresh face, even though Dunton had recommended Ouimet. Among others, he consulted commission chairman Robert Fowler who, although admiring Ouimet's engineering brilliance, felt he could not provide the necessary creative leadership. Nowlan searched, but could find no one who had the ideal qualities and who wanted the job. "I was not the man the Conservatives had been looking for, but they were not able to find the candidate of their choice," Ouimet later said.

Both Nowlan and Diefenbaker were anxious not to affront Quebec, where the Conservatives had made a political breakthrough in the recent election, winning an astonishing fifty seats. Ouimet was one of a handful of Quebeckers who had risen to the top of the public service, and at least he seemed to be politically indefinable. They hoped he would be a quiescent cultural *apparatchik*. So, after four months of fruitless searching following Dunton's resignation, in a last-minute decision, Nowlan presented his recommendation to the cabinet: Ouimet as president and

Bushnell as vice-president. The prime minister and his colleagues reluctantly agreed, and Nowlan called the two CBC men to his office to tell them. As they entered, Nowlan stood beaming and said, "Congratulations, Mr. President!" Ouimet, who had thought Nowlan wanted to talk about CBC policies, was startled and, uncharacteristically but ever pragmatic, said the first thing that popped into his head: "What's the salary?" It was $20,000.

The two new CBC leaders were as diametrically opposed in their characters as any two humans could possibly be. In contrast to Ouimet's austere, cold logic, his engineering orderliness, his fascination with hierarchical management charts, and his teetotalling purity (he drank endless amounts of Coca-Cola), Bushnell was the fun-loving, hard-drinking, profane antithesis of a bureaucrat. At one point, CBC board members pushed Ouimet to mingle socially more with Ottawa's high and mighty. He went to a few cocktail parties, forcing himself to sip a drink and trying to be convivial, but he hated it and quickly gave it up. Partying, however, was not a problem for Bushnell, who later admitted he was drunk much of the time in his first six months as CBC vice-president. Bushnell hated what he felt was the oppressive and tense atmosphere of the CBC's Ottawa bureaucracy and longed to put his feet up, share a bottle or two of scotch, and exchange stories with his programming cronies.

He admired Ouimet's intelligence and integrity but theirs was a wary relationship, not the least because Bushnell had played a more senior role than Ouimet for most of their careers at the CBC and had resented being passed over in favour of Ouimet for the post of general manager. His hero remained Gladstone Murray, and he would later say, "There wasn't a soul at the top after Gladstone Murray who knew broadcasting from a bale of hay!" Presumably, that included Alphonse Ouimet.

Bushnell said he was utterly loyal to the CBC: "I believe in the damn thing." But Ouimet came to think that Bushnell had few deep convictions about public broadcasting and that "his positive contribution to its development was outbalanced by the serious negative aspects of his role with the CBC." More to the point, Ouimet added, "Bushnell definitely did not like engineers, particularly French-speaking ones from Montreal." Harry Boyle, Bushnell's close colleague, confirmed that, saying, "'Bush' was bigoted as hell. He was anti-French and anti-Catholic.... He was riding a tiger all the time. He was a private enterpriser. His normal instincts were to side with all the people we were fighting."

In one of his extensive private memos on his CBC years that he later circulated among his former colleagues, Ouimet wrote of Bushnell as a participant in "Dan McArthur's revolt against Dr. Frigon in the late '40s." Ouimet remembered Bushnell "with tears running down his cheeks" apologizing for an attack on Frigon, and crying again at an executive meeting when he did not become general manager.

"The fact that he wanted to be head of CBC did not increase his love for either Frigon or myself." Ouimet said "When he was senior vice-president and I was president, he was constantly critical of my actions and decisions." Beyond this, Ouimet said, "Bushnell's ethics were as unpol-ished as his manners [but] there was also his roguish appeal."

If Bushnell was a burden for Ouimet, so, too, was John Diefenbaker, who carried intensifying suspicions that the CBC was plotting against him. Ouimet privately attacked Diefenbaker's "anti-CBC bias and his Francophobia." "The problem was the temperament of Diefenbaker," Ouimet later said. "He always thought somebody was knifing him."

Diefenbaker had been enraged at Ouimet in 1956 when the Conserva-tive leader had gone to the CBC Montreal studios for a broadcast and had been given only a tiny office in which to wait until airtime. He felt this was a slight and never forgave Ouimet or the CBC. Two years later, as prime minister, he was back in a Montreal studio for a TV broadcast and was unhappy about the studio background for his talk. He wanted something dignified behind him, and after a rush call to the Royal Canadian Hussars, the producer got a cloth coat of arms for the background. Although the picture looked fine, Diefenbaker was livid after the broadcast, shouting, "Damn it, this is a horse blanket!" He also said the technicians were snick-ering at him and that the cameraman concentrated the camera on his hands, which were shaking.

A short time later, Diefenbaker came to the CBC Ottawa studios for a TV speech, the text of which had been delivered to the station late and hurriedly reprinted on the teleprompter. In the rush, the teleprompter's letter "s" broke and so there were none in the prime minister's script. When he arrived, Diefenbaker was beside himself in rage at the "s"-less script, saying he couldn't go on if the "s"s were not there. As the time to go on air neared, and it appeared that the teleprompter couldn't be repaired, a studio assistant quickly used a felt pen to put in the hundreds of missing "s"s. Then, two minutes to air, the teleprompter broke down entirely and Diefenbaker went berserk. Trembling in the control room and watching the prime ministerial fury was Alphonse Ouimet. Finally, seconds before airtime, the teleprompter was repaired, the camera's red light went on, and Diefenbaker delivered his speech.

Afterwards, Ouimet dashed out of the control room to apologize to a still fuming prime minister. "He just let go," Ouimet said. "He gave it to me for ten minutes in front of sixty people."

Waving his arms and shaking his jowls, Diefenbaker threatened to fire the technicians responsible for the teleprompter problems, and he thundered, "St. Laurent would never stand for this. I've had the horse blanket incident in Montreal. It's a French Canadian plot!" With that, he stomped off, leaving a pale and shaken Ouimet.

"So he was never my great supporter," Ouimet said. "[It was] a bad time, a hazardous time." "When the Conservatives came in after twenty-two years in opposition," he said later, "they were determined that they would have it their way, and when we were not complying, they thought we were just a bunch of Liberal activists." Diefenbaker, in fact, was so angry with Ouimet that he froze his salary for nearly five years. Only when Mike Pearson and the Liberals came to power in 1963, did Ouimet get a pay raise.

The other new burden that Ouimet had to deal with was the BBG which, under Diefenbaker's new broadcast law, took over the responsibility for broadcast regulations. The new legislation, Ouimet said, was designed to "cut the CBC down to size." But, in truth, Ouimet didn't feel as strongly as his predecessors had about the removal of regulatory responsibilities from the CBC, believing it would leave the CBC freer to concentrate on programs.

In Ouimet's view, the CBC and the BBG would have "a platonic enmity," and he found the new BBG chairman, University of Alberta president Dr. Andrew Stewart, less troublesome than he had feared. Aside from Stewart, however, the BBG members were mostly prominent

Conservative Party activists, former party officials, and supporters, including Diefenbaker's dentist in Prince Albert, Saskatchewan. The prime minister had initially wanted Allister Grosart, national director of the Progressive Conservative Party, to be the head of the BBG, but Grosart declined.

Diefenbaker's choices for the new CBC board were far less blatantly political than for the BBG. The CBC board members were, however, under specific orders from the new government to slash what it considered to be the CBC's programming extravagance. To that end, Nowlan wanted Montreal businessman R. L. Dunsmore to be named chairman. Ouimet resisted, saying he wanted to be both CBC president and chairman. Although annoyed at Ouimet's insistence, Nowlan reluctantly acquiesced, and Dunsmore became chairman of the board's finance committee with a specific responsibility to ride herd on CBC spending.

For all his apprehension about Diefenbaker's hostility toward the CBC, the first of a series of numbing crises to assail Ouimet came from quite a different and unexpected source. It had a profound political impact that reverberates in Quebec and Canada to this day. It was the beginning of Quebec's Quiet Revolution, expanding on the Asbestos strike of a decade earlier. It brought about the politicization of René Lévesque and also tore apart the CBC French network, where the scars are still evident.

It began in November 1958 when a TV children's program producer, Pierre Leboeuf, angrily refused a program assignment and was warned by management that his refusal would be remembered when his next contract was negotiated. Leboeuf retorted, "My next contract will be a collective one!" At the time twenty-two producers' contracts had run out, leaving them with no job security. That confrontation whirled into the worst strike in CBC history.

The strike grew from a combustible combination of intellectual ferment, political activism, and creative frustration. Ouimet blamed it on "socialistic and nationalistic forces" and said it was caused in part by an atmosphere created by "the Laurendeaus, the Pelletiers and the Trudeaus. . . .the left wing of the Jesuits. . . .their counterparts in Radio-Canada – its writers, its artists, some of its producers and some of its program executives."

Added to that brew was the rampant frustration of producers result-ing from the explosive growth of television in its first five years, the con-fusing lines of authority, and especially in Montreal, management's determination to chip away at their authority. What particularly stirred the producers' ire was what they felt was the arbitrary arrogance of their boss, André Ouimet, the director of television in Quebec who also hap-pened to be Alphonse Ouimet's younger brother. "A martinet," said one colleague. "Remote and formidable," said producers who blamed him for slow contract renewal negotiations with producers. Even his own senior colleagues were leery of Ouimet. "It was something very personal with André Ouimet. . . . He was so arbitrary, it was deplorable," says then pub-lic affairs supervisor Marc Thibault.

Altogether, the CBC French network was a powderkeg ready for a lit fuse. But in Ottawa, the new and out-of-touch CBC senior management and board had no idea of the ferment and was astonished, confused, and angry when the strike exploded. "We had been in office for only six weeks when the roof fell in, taking us completely by surprise," Ouimet said.

As soon as he stomped out of his boss's office, Pierre Leboeuf began organizing producers with the help of the Confédération des travailleurs catholiques du Canada (CTCC) led by Jean Marchand. The CTCC had its own reasons to support the producers, including a desire to make a breakthrough in organizing professional employees and to gain public attention for its efforts.

The first general meeting of producers was held on Friday, December 5, 1958, in the Windsor Hotel, hosted by the CTCC, one of whose officials urged producers to organize and affiliate with the CTCC. The sixty or so producers on hand agreed to form an association and chose Leboeuf as president and fellow producer Guy Parent as secretary. André Ouimet read of the session in the next day's papers and called a meeting of pro-ducers for the evening of December 11.

At that meeting, Ouimet categorically rejected any recognition of a producers association for bargaining purposes, but he and the producers did agree to study the status and responsibilities of producers. They set a deadline of March 12, 1959, to reach an agreement. CBC management thought it was a good meeting, but the producers did not, and they began criticizing their representatives for a poor presentation of their case. On

December 18, another general meeting of producers was held at which they formally established a producers association and sought to be affiliated with Marchand's CTCC. Leboeuf and Parent were replaced by a new executive, with producer Fernand Quirion as president. Quirion met the next day with André Ouimet who reiterated the CBC's refusal to recognize the Montreal Producers Association for bargaining purposes. Four days later, at another general meeting, Quirion reported the CBC's refusal and the angered producers voted to strike "at a time it [the Association executive] will judge appropriate."

André Ouimet was warned of the strike threat the next day, Christmas Eve, and he was quoted by producers as calling them "fools," "children," and "incompetents," whose strike threat was "crazy." Both sides, however, agreed to meet at 10:00 A.M., Monday, December 29.

The CBC head office in Ottawa, meanwhile, was unaware of the ticking time bomb in Montreal. Alphonse Ouimet had gone to Miami for a holiday because he was "dead tired." André Ouimet assured Ernie Bushnell that the Montreal problem was nothing serious. But on December 28, Bushnell was telephoned by André Ouimet's boss, Gérard Lamarche, CBC director for Quebec who, "in tears," according to Bushnell, warned him that the situation in Montreal was getting out of hand. Bushnell decided to send the comptroller of operations, Jimmy Gilmore, to Montreal for the planned meeting with the producers.

At 10:00 A.M. on December 29, André Ouimet met the producers and said *non!* to their demands for union recognition. The producers then met Lamarche and Gilmore and got the same answer. At noon, they lunched with local leaders of the unions representing CBC writers, performers, editors, reporters, announcers, stage-hands, office workers, and technicians, and they all agreed not to cross the producers' picket lines if there was a strike. The producers were egged on by CTCC officials, who told them that, because of public reaction to a strike, the CBC would cave in within a day or two. After lunch, the producers met again with CBC executives, who once more rejected their demands. The producers left the meeting frustrated, angry, but excited at the prospect of a brief but dramatic strike.

At 4:40 P.M., Quirion announced in the first-floor lobby of the CBC building that the strike was on, and the walkout began in an almost care-free mood. "An air of festivity resembling that of school children going on a picnic," Alphonse Ouimet described it. Most CBC officials believed that after a few hours of exuberance the producers would come to their senses and call off the strike. "This will be a small strike," André Ouimet told his colleagues. "Don't worry. They will come back." Some of his senior staff were not so sure. Marc Thibault warned him, "You will have the strike and it will be a general strike." Ouimet brushed off the warning.

The producers set up picket lines, waved placards they had previously prepared, and called for a mass meeting that night. The seventy-four producers who went on strike (eleven refused) and their 1,200 supporters jammed into a nearby Canadian Legion Hall to hear a fiery Jean Marchand who enthused the strikers and their supporters. Pledges of help were made by officials of all unions at the CBC except the American Federation of Musicians.

On New Years' Eve, two days after the strike began, Bushnell called an unaware Alphonse Ouimet, who was sitting in the Miami sun, to advise him of the walkout. "You don't have to come back, Al," he said, "but you should know the producers have walked out."

An angry Ouimet rejected Bushnell's advice to stay in Miami and immediately packed his bags and flew back to Ottawa that afternoon. By 7:00 P.M., he was getting off the train in Montreal. "I knew how vital a quick settlement would be and, frankly, thought I could achieve it without any great difficulty," he later said. Besides, he thought "most of our producers were still young, sensitive and romantic."

To his astonishment, he was met at the railway station by a delegation of striking producers and their supporters. Together they drove over to the CBC building where, in the bitter cold and behind mufflers, raised collars, and pulled down toques, the shivering strikers marched back and forth in front of the entrance. "Spontaneously and, I suppose now, with rather childish naiveté," Ouimet said, "I started to shake hands with those closest to me. I told them I thought it was silly for them to risk catching pneumonia and invited them to do their picketing inside the lobby."

Alarmed at the president's fraternization with the strikers, his management colleagues grabbed Ouimet and shoved him inside to be briefed by his officials. The next day, New Year's Day, he met Quirion, but "I just did not get anywhere with him." The reason, Ouimet thought, was because "the producers had . . . completely lost control of the strike to the union," and it was now a major confrontation between Marchand's CTCC and the CBC on the broad principle of union representation for what the CBC considered to be management personnel. As Ouimet recounted later, Marchand told him to "capitulate or else," and when the CBC president said there was no way the union could win the strike, Marchand told him, "Yes, Mr. Ouimet, you can win the strike, but before we are through with you, your institution will never be the same again."

Ouimet also got nowhere with Gérard Pelletier, who was Marchand's adviser, an influential journalist, a close friend of Pierre Trudeau, and the backroom *éminence grise* of the whole strike. Ironically, Pelletier had encouraged Ouimet to accept the CBC presidency a few weeks earlier, telling him, "You are far more intelligent than Frigon. . . . You are more open and have more imagination." This time, Pelletier wasn't at all supportive, telling him the strike would go on until the CBC gave in.

After more fruitless meetings with the producers, Ouimet returned to Ottawa to brief George Nowlan. Articulating the attitude of the Diefenbaker government, Nowlan told him, "This is your chance to get rid of the whole bunch of leftists and radicals you have been harbouring in your French Network. Be tough and don't you give in!" That afternoon Ouimet met with Labour Department senior officials who, contrary to Nowlan's advice, urged compromise.

In between hectic meetings and conflicting advice, Ouimet was conferring with the CBC's executive committee, whose disparate composition did not offer any consolation to the increasingly agitated and besieged Ouimet. There was a power battle between himself and Nowlan's favourite, R. L. Dunsmore, which, he said, "took a lot of my energy and undoubtedly his also, to avoid our clashing temperaments from impairing the group effort." Raymond Dupuis was an ultra-conservative aristocrat whose family department store had just lost a strike and who offered little hope for the CBC. Veteran broadcaster Kate Aitken was a bright, lively, and elderly lady who, Ouimet said, "was really out of her element." The other committee member was Ernie Bushnell who, when not well into liquid stimulation, was so sharp-tongued that,

Ouimet remembered, "he had Mrs. Aitken in tears and asking for his removal."

For all their conflicts and idiosyncracies, however, Ouimet steered his executive committee into strong endorsement of the CBC's refusal to recognize the Montreal Producers Association as a bargaining unit. They had powerful support from both Nowlan and the minister of labour, Michael Starr, both of whom considered the strike illegal and refused to have the government intervene. The committee announced that the producers and the 1,200 employees who had refused to cross the picket lines had broken their contracts and, thus, no work, no pay. "Intimidation," said *Le Devoir* of a CBC back-to-work order.

As the strike wore on, an increasing number of employees did go back to work, and the producers began to realize this would be a long and costly strike with an uncertain outcome. But there were cracks, as well, in the CBC's support. Even in the Diefenbaker cabinet there was dissension as Solicitor General Léon Balcer supported the producers. So, too, did the Quebec intellectual community and most of the media. Even Cardinal Léger came out in support of the producers, saying, "Everyone has the right of association. The CBC strike is nothing else than that. That right . . . must be asserted."

Support for the producers was evident, too, among the five million Quebec viewers, who grew increasingly impatient with the diet of old movies, stale reruns, and skimpy newscasts caused by the strike. Gone were the broadcasts of Montreal Canadiens games and everybody's hero "Rocket" Richard; gone were the immensely popular variety shows, dramas, and soap operas; and worst of all, gone was the most beloved of all programs in Quebec, "La Famille Plouffe."

The Plouffes were on the picket lines as cast members trudged back and forth in the sub-zero weather. They were joined by what was perhaps the most eclectic picket line ever seen in Canadian labour history. Best-selling authors, star performers, university professors, leading journalists, and even some politicians marched with the producers. One puzzled policeman muttered to reporters, "This is no strike. They all have university degrees." Hobbling on a leg injured in a skiing accident, Pierre Trudeau couldn't march, but still came several times to the CBC building by taxi to demonstrate his support of the strikers.

Actresses Denise Pelletier and Giselle Schmidt made vast quantities of soup and paté at home and brought them to the picket lines for hungry strikers. "A strange sight, indeed," said Ouimet, "to see the top men of the Quebec theatre, performers, writers and intellectuals marching arm in arm with the riff-raff of professional picketing. . . . A strange but also highly moving spectacle which, with the help of the artistic and intellectual community soon won the sympathy of the Montreal population."

Alphonse Ouimet and the CBC were simply no match for the strikers and their supporters in the contest for public support. While harassed CBC officials dashed from meeting to meeting trying to fashion counterproposals that would meet some producer concerns yet still not recognize the producers' bargaining unit, the producers themselves captured the sympathies of the media and Quebec's cultural and academic community. They held mass meetings, benefit concerts, and variety shows, and politicians, especially prominent Liberals such as Maurice Lamontagne and Lionel Chévrier, began to show their support.

Other support for the strikers came from restaurants which gave the picketers free meals, grocery stores which provided free food, and doctors and druggists who offered free services. Workers inside the CBC contributed $3,000 to the strikers, a tag day was held, art works donated and auctioned off, and appeals made at public meetings. Altogether, $125,000 was raised.

Public endorsement of the producers' strike came from some of Quebec's cultural folk heroes, including Gratien Gélinas, Roger Lemelin, André Laurendeau, and Monique Leyrac. But it was René Lévesque who came to symbolize the strike. His charisma leapt off the screen and onto the street and he was the star of a variety show which put on more than fifty performances in Montreal and other Quebec cities, raising $70,000 for the strikers. Thin, stooped, balding, and burning with resentment, Lévesque was the hit of the show when he came on at the end, rasping out in his scratchy, cracked voice the latest news of the strike. "You may not realize it," André Laurendeau told Lévesque after watching him one night, "but you're about to launch a political career which might really take you places."

"That's where Lévesque learned he could really get the crowds moving," Ouimet later remembered. He called Lévesque "a brilliant but chronically discontented man." The tumultuous public applause and his effectiveness in rallying support for the strike radicalized Lévesque and sent him on his way from TV into the centre of Quebec and Canadian politics.

The CBC was losing the battle for public support – in fact, it almost abdicated it – and it was getting nowhere in the flurry of proposals and counterproposals that sought to resolve the increasingly bitter strike. In mid-January, negotiations broke down, and Ouimet called a meeting of his board's executive committee in Montreal for Saturday, January 17. "I wanted the corporation to stand firm on the question of principle," he said. "But I also wanted to be sure that if we maintained our position now, we would not give in later on when the pressures became even greater."

At the meeting Ouimet suggested the CBC tell the striking producers there would be no more negotiations and that they would all be fired. He also wanted to put similar pressure on those who had refused to cross the picket lines. This would demonstrate, he thought, that the CBC wasn't bluffing in its tough stand and would, he hoped, break the strike or at least bring back to work all but the most militant strikers.

At the end of the day, the executive committee meeting adjourned for the night, and an exhausted Alphonse Ouimet returned to his hotel room for a troubled sleep.

At 10:00 A.M. on Sunday, after having breakfast with his wife at the hotel and an hour before the resumption of the executive committee meeting, Ouimet was struck by a serious heart attack. A shaken Ernie Bushnell broke the news as the committee members gathered. He assumed the duties of the president and chaired the meeting.

In the next few days, with Ouimet in hospital fighting for his life, Bushnell rejected a producers' proposal for compulsory arbitration and letters of dismissal were sent out to striking producers. Those who had remained out in support of the producers were warned that they, too, would be fired if they did not go back to work immediately. The threat was reinforced by Ron Fraser, the CBC's public relations director, who warned at a news conference in Montreal that the CBC was "prepared to start from scratch if necessary to rebuild the French Network."

All this set off a storm of union protest in Montreal and across the country and, ominously, even among middle and senior managers in the CBC French network. That same day, Jean Marchand met with Prime Minister Diefenbaker, Labour Minister Michael Starr, and George Nowlan, and their earlier support for a tough CBC stand began to waiver. Bob Bryce, secretary of the Privy Council, suggested federal intervention, and the next day, Saturday, January 24, the deputy minister of labour called Bushnell to suggest mediation.

The day after the dismissal letters went out, twenty-five CBC managers in Montreal held a protest meeting and said they would refuse to train new producers hired to replace the strikers. That same day, Marc Thibault and Roger Rolland, the regional program director in Quebec and a friend of Pierre Trudeau, rushed to Ottawa to present the French supervisors' protests to Bushnell. Sunday afternoon, Bushnell faced more pressure from another protesting delegation, this one headed by Neil Leroy, representing the Council of Broadcast Unions, a grouping of the various recognized CBC unions. They, too, urged delay and mediation.

Faced with overwhelming pressure and taking solace from Johnny Walker, Bushnell caved in and announced a reversal of the ultimatum to the producers and their sympathizers. He would "defer action for the time being," he said.

In his Montreal hospital bed, Ouimet was unaware that his basic strike strategy had been changed by Bushnell. Later he would groan, "It was now unfortunately clear to all concerned that the corporation could be made to back down under sufficiently well-concerted pressure."

Some senior CBC negotiators, such as legal counsel Hugh Laidlaw and personnel official Guy Coderre, talked of Bushnell's "surrender" and, as quoted later by Ouimet, placed "great emphasis on Bushnell's concessions which had demoralized the CBC negotiating team."

Two days after Bushnell's policy switch, 1,500 strikers took a special train from Montreal and, waving placards, marching, and shouting, they poured onto Parliament Hill to protest against the CBC. Led by well-known stars, writers, and journalists, they presented a petition with 22,000 signatures to Labour Minister Michael Starr. The convivial strikers thought that they had the CBC on the run.

Over the next few days, pressures on Bushnell intensified with demands for a further easing of the CBC position, and he increasingly retreated to the bottle. Associates described him at times as "drunk out of his skull." Admitting to "a sharp tongue," Bushnell later said, "too much of the grape certainly did not lessen its abrasiveness." Because of his diabetes, Bushnell said he could drink heavily one night without apparent effect, but another night take only a few drinks and "I assumed all the characteristics of a drunk." Ouimet later reported a conversation with Bushnell in which "he also confirmed that he had been drinking heavily during the strike." When Ouimet noted he was "alleged to have conceded some important points to the union while he was intoxicated," Bushnell responded, "This is quite possible."

Another factor inflaming the strike was the accusation that the CBC's intransigence was an "English plot" against the French. René Lévesque drew cheers with his repeated charges of discrimination and said he had "a tired and unworthy feeling that if such a strike had happened on English CBC, it would . . . have lasted no more than half an hour."

Lévesque charged the English press of Montreal with "slanted and biased reporting" on the strike. "A shameful travesty of the facts," he said. There were accusations that English-speaking Canadians throughout the country were deliberately kept in the dark by the English media about the issues of the strike. In *Le Devoir*, André Laurendeau spoke of Quebec being "abandoned" by the indifference of English-speaking Canadians. "The whole bloody French network became virtually non-existent, and nobody English cared," Lévesque said later.

There was an English-French clash within the labour movement, too, as CBC locals in Montreal, affiliated with unions whose headquarters were in Toronto, were incensed with what they felt was little support from Toronto. The producers also resented the fact that the annual salaries of their Toronto counterparts averaged $2,000 to $3,000 more than theirs. Toronto producers and performers mostly stayed away from the strike, fuelling an everlasting resentment that led to the establishment of totally separate union groups in many cases in Montreal.

With Ouimet still in hospital, the control of CBC policy was in the hands of unilingual anglophones such as Bushnell, Jimmy Gilmore, Ron Fraser, and CBC lawyer Hugh Laidlaw. The strikers complained that even the CBC's principal negotiator, Marcel Carter, had an English-sounding last name. "So the old rivalries and prejudices between . . . English and French had raised their ugly head early in the game and the whole affair had rapidly taken strong nationalistic overtones," Ouimet later noted. At a party marking the twenty-fifth anniversary of the strike, Lévesque said, "The strike was a watershed in the development of nationalism."

Impatient and embarrassed at CBC management's inability to resolve the strike and faced with growing political agitation from Quebec Conservatives, Diefenbaker, Nowlan, and Starr increased their pressure on Bushnell. Forgetting about his earlier support for a tough stand by CBC management, Nowlan grumbled at its intransigence and said the strike should have been settled long ago. "It was," said Nowlan, "the most unfortunate and unnecessary episode in labour relations in Canadian history."

Five weeks after the strike began, Diefenbaker, Nowlan, and Starr decided to intervene. The first clear sign of this came out of the blue when Montreal Conservative MP Egan Chambers asked to meet the strikers, many of whom lived in his riding. He suggested he act as a middleman between them and the CBC. They met on February 1 and developed a proposal. The next morning Chambers called Bushnell to say he had "a simplified proposal." Bushnell said he was busy with a meeting of the board and referred him to Ron Fraser, with whom Chambers had a four-hour session. Meanwhile, Nowlan called Bushnell to say he "might want to have a chat with board members." Bushnell thought Nowlan was being pushed by Starr to force the CBC to give the producers what they wanted. Nowlan also began talking privately with Ouimet's rival on the board, R. L. Dunsmore, whom Nowlan had wanted to be CBC chairman.

While these behind-the-scenes moves were taking place, out on the picket line in front of the CBC Montreal building a three-hour riot broke out when policemen on horses charged into the shouting, placard-waving, singing picket lines. The police had received a tip that the strikers were going to break into the CBC building, and 200 police officers, including 10 on horseback, rushed the crowd of 1,000 picketers, swinging clubs and arresting 29, including René Lévesque and Jean Marchand, who told reporters, "I was just beginning to sing 'O Canada' when the police came with horses and arrested me."

For the government, the riot dramatically underlined the urgency of settling the strike, and Nowlan's "chat" with the board of directors took place at the Chateau Laurier a few hours later. Out of this discussion came a "suggested formula for [a] CBC producers' settlement" which was almost exactly the same, including much of the same wording, as Egan Chambers "simplified proposal."

The board's new proposal repudiated Ouimet's and Bushnell's previous stand against recognizing the producers association as a bargaining unit. Detailed negotiations began at once, and over the next few days a deal was worked out with Chambers presiding over the talks, shuttling between the two sides, and bringing in Bushnell from time to time to make critical concessions to the producers.

Settlement was finally reached sixty-eight days after the walkout began. What Ouimet called "the most serious crisis CBC has had to face" was over and the producers had won. The CBC conceded they could organize an association to bargain with the corporation, and the only concession the CBC got was that the producers would not affiliate with any other union or federation of unions. Even so, union officials were exuberant at the triumph and the breakthrough in collective bargaining for people whom the CBC had considered as management. Years later, as a minister in Trudeau's cabinet, Gérard Pelletier, the *éminence grise* of the strike, leaned across a dinner table and told the CBC president, "Mr. Ouimet, the Montreal strike at the CBC was one of the most important landmarks in the development of the union movement in Canada." Ouimet nearly choked, recalling his humiliation as he lay in his hospital bed still recovering from his heart attack and what he considered a CBC "catastrophe." "It was a disaster . . . awful," he said. "[The CBC] never found its spirit for at least ten years."

The strike left French TV audiences resentful and the staff hostile. "The price the CBC had to pay for the political accommodation of its inexperienced board," Ouimet said, was "an immediate loss of institutional prestige" and a "substantial and dangerous erosion of the supervisory authority it must maintain over its producers." He later said, "The Corporation's capitulation contributed greatly" to problems of separatist influence in programs and "even the temerity of the Toronto Seven Days rebels in 1966."

But Ouimet saved most of his anger for the government and its "improper, unnecessary and . . . unwise" interference in the CBC-producer negotiations. "I denounce this type of political meddling as extremely hazardous in terms of public interest and inconsistent with the autonomy given to the Corporation under the law," he said. "The government intervention . . . was deliberately hidden from the public, apparently for reasons of political expediency. I wish I knew just what leverage 'socialist' Jean Marchand used to scare Diefenbaker, Starr, and Nowlan into their one-sided intervention."

Years later, looking back at who his adversaries in the ordeal had been, Ouimet lamented, "Marchand, Pelletier, Trudeau, Lévesque! No wonder I had a heart attack!"

René Lévesque, the most popular journalist ever on the CBC French network, was a war correspondent in Korea, a far-ranging political reporter, and host of the hugely successful "Point de Mire." (*National Archives of Canada, 14954*)

Norman DePoe, one of the CBC's most memorable journalists. His encyclopedic knowledge of Canadian political history and articulate, charismatic delivery have not been matched since. (*National Archives of Canada, 14581*)

"Our Pet," Juliette, TV's most glamorous and popular regular performer. Her show, which ran after "Hockey Night in Canada" from 1954 to 1966, became a Canadian institution. (*National Archives of Canada, 16072*)

Robert Goulet, an early Canadian TV star who went on to success on the American stage and screen, starred in the CBC's "Show Time" with singer Shirley Harmer. (*National Archives of Canada, 16074*)

CBC strikers march on Parliament Hill during one of the most damaging crises in CBC history, the 1959 Montreal producers' strike. It left scars on the CBC for a generation. (*National Archives of Canada, CBC 914*)

George Nowlan (left), the minister responsible for the CBC under John Diefenbaker, consults with radio pioneer and CRBC and CBC executive Ernie Bushnell. (*National Archives of Canada, 160079*)

"Front Page Challenge," the grandfather of English-language TV programs. Here, in the early 1960s, is the most memorable Challenge team: left to right, Gordon Sinclair, Betty Kennedy, Fred Davis, and Pierre Berton.
(*National Archives of Canada, 7692*)

Ross McLean, pioneer TV producer, and an eclectic, creative genius who inspired a generation of journalistic producers with his provocative style and defiance of authority.
(*National Archives of Canada, 16075*)

Wilf Fielding, then a cameraman and later a producer, behind an early TV camera.
(*Courtesy of the CBC*)

"La Famille Plouffe," the most popular series in Quebec in the early years of TV. Left to right, standing, Pierre Valcourt, Jean-Louis Roux, Denise Pelletier, and Emile Genest; seated, Amanda Alarie and Paul Guèvremont. (*National Archives of Canada, 6949*)

The Leslie Bell Singers, featured on CBC Toronto's opening night, were stars of early TV. (Sandy Stewart Photo Collection, National Archives of Canada, 12674)

Canadian TV's first chorus girl, Lorraine Thomson, was hired by the CBC in 1952. A trained ballet dancer, she went on to host and produce CBC Radio and TV programs. (*National Archives of Canada, 16083*)

Canadian TV's first star weatherman, the chalk-tossing Percy Saltzman. He was on the first CBC-TV Toronto program in 1952 and continued on TV at the CBC and, later, CTV until 1974. (*National Archives of Canada, 13675*)

TV began in Canada on September 6, 1952, in Montreal, with Davidson Dunton (at the microphone) opening the new era of broadcasting. (*National Archives of Canada, 12456*)

The control room during TV's opening night in Toronto, September 8, 1952. Director Drew Crossan is seated at the microphone and senior TV producer Mavor Moore is on the telephone. (*National Archives of Canada, 6615*)

Davidson Dunton, arguably the best leader the CBC has ever had. As chairman, 1945-58, he oversaw the golden age of radio and the launch of television.
(*National Archives of Canada, 16080*)

Alphonse Ouimet, CBC president, 1958-68, posing with Canada's first commercial TV set, which he designed in 1932
(*National Archives of Canada, CBC 28059*)

12

Ernie Bushnell's Woes

In the wake of the strike, Ernie Bushnell had the delicate job of, in effect, firing the president's brother, André, who had become a symbol of CBC authoritarianism. "All the hatred was directed at André," Bill Armstrong recalls. The producers had demanded his head, and in the spring of 1959, Bushnell "reluctantly" removed André as director of television in Montreal and gave him a makeshift staff job as director of planning. André resigned a few months later to go into private broadcasting.

About a month after the strike ended, Alphonse Ouimet had recovered well enough to be back at his office for a few hours a day. But he was under strict orders "not to expose myself to any kind of stress which, in effect, meant doing nothing." The stress was all on Bushnell, who reeled under the disorder left in the wake of the Montreal strike, the frustration of dealing with an increasingly anti-CBC John Diefenbaker, and coping with various program crises. Then, suddenly, Ouimet was again flat on his back, this time with a gall-bladder attack and subsequent surgery that took him fully out of action until mid-summer. As his troubles mounted, Bushnell increasingly found solace in George Nowlan's company and, fuelled by scotch, the two frequently escaped from their burdens in a camaraderie rare, if not unique, between a cabinet minister and the boss of a Crown corporation. They became close friends which, in the end, led to Bushnell's worst crisis and his resignation.

While Ouimet was away from the office again, Bushnell was hit with a few program embarrassments that turned into crises offending just about everyone. On the French network, a drama to mark the beatification of Mère Marie-Marguerite d'Youville, founder of the Grey Nuns in 1755, turned out to be a bawdy romp featuring a young Marguerite in a startlingly low-cut nightgown and her lover bouncing in and out of bed. The play, called "The Prettiest Girl in Town," scandalized Quebec, infuriated the Catholic Church, outraged politicians, and mortified CBC officials. It was made all the worse because parish priests throughout Quebec had told their congregations not to miss what they thought would be a reverential salute to Mère d'Youville, who was to be beatified in Rome on the day of the broadcast. Even though it was largely historically correct, the soap opera was hardly what the parish priests were expecting. "I think the people responsible for it should be fired," Nowlan told Bushnell. The CBC suspended the producer and the supervisor quit. Bushnell told a parliamentary committee, "We have offered our abject apologies."

Bushnell had to offer more apologies at about the same time when English network talk show personality Joyce Davidson told Dave Garroway's NBC audience on the eve of a Canadian tour by Queen Elizabeth, "I, like most Canadians, am rather indifferent to the Queen's visit." "An insult," cried Toronto mayor Nathan Phillips, and hundreds of calls of protest flooded the Prime Minister's Office. United Empire Loyalists protested about "this woman," whom they considered to be outrageously insolent. MPs demanded action, and for the royalty-loving Diefenbaker it was yet more proof of the subversiveness of the CBC. Bushnell apologized once more and suspended Davidson.

Almost simultaneously, Bushnell was besieged by two other program controversies that brought more political pressures. In one, a Toronto producer wanted to interview Nazi military hero Otto Skorzeny, but when the government found out about it, he was refused a visa to enter Canada. The determined producer then sought to interview Skorzeny in New York. Nowlan made the government's objection vividly clear to Bushnell, who cancelled the interview.

In the other case, the prime minister of France had protested CBC French network plans to interview some Algerian political leaders who were highly critical of French policy. Nowlan warned Bushnell, who ordered the interview cancelled. However, the producers then interviewed other Algerians who also complained about French policy, and an exasperated Nowlan told Bushnell, "This is an example of loose management and defiance of management in the organization."

About the same time, apprehensive about his controversial personality, the CBC French network offered to renew René Lévesque and his "Point de Mire" program, but only if Lévesque would stop his highly opinionated commentaries on CKAC and sign an exclusive contract with the CBC. The offer, made by Marc Thibault as head of public affairs, was rejected. "I have no interest now," Lévesque said, and he began to move into politics.

Meanwhile Bushnell was blindsided by CBC News on the night of the Ontario election in mid-June which re-elected Conservative Premier Leslie Frost. Frost had earlier clashed with Davie Dunton over charges of a pro-Liberal bias at the CBC. This time Frost's anger exploded when the CBC, because of technical problems, was unable to televise from the premier's home in Lindsay, Ontario, coverage of his victory statement while live coverage was given to his defeated Liberal rival, John Wintermeyer, in his home town of Kitchener, Ontario. Frost fumed about abolishing the CBC.

The stress continued for the CBC and Bushnell, including audience anger at the June cancellation of the CBC's most popular daytime radio program, "The Happy Gang," after twenty-two years on the air – Canada's then longest running radio show. "The Gang" was replaced by a young, up-and-coming country singer named Tommy Hunter, known as the Singing Guitarist, who was born when "The Happy Gang" began on the network in 1937. The six-foot-four Hunter, who favoured cowboy boots, Stetsons, and a "Hi folks!" approach, went on to have an even longer broadcasting career than "The Happy Gang" as a weekly star on CBC Radio and -TV until the 1990s. His first show featured The Rhythm Pals and a guest appearance by "Our Pet," Juliette.

But CBC Radio was ignored and increasingly bitter about the corporation's obsession with television. Radio audiences were shrinking, and many of the big shows and stars, overcoming their initial hesitancy, had now emigrated to televisionland. As much as the postwar era had been the golden age of radio, this was now, as broadcaster and author Sandy Stewart has labelled it, the dark days of radio. Even on television, there was change when Canada's first TV news anchor, Larry Henderson, quit in a salary dispute, to be replaced by the comforting, granite-faced Earl Cameron as the voice of "The National News." And increasingly, what Cameron was reporting was public distress at John Diefenbaker's government.

Two or three times a week Bushnell, as acting president, and George Nowlan would meet to share a glass or more of scotch while pouring out their miseries to each other: Bushnell on the CBC and Nowlan on his troubles with John Diefenbaker, who was distinctly unhappy to hear any pause in the roar of adulation, let alone the kind of criticism he was hearing on the CBC. Diefenbaker and many Conservative MPs were convinced the CBC was conspiring to undermine their public support, and the Tories repeatedly pointed accusingly to a four-minute morning radio program called "Preview Commentary." It was heard after the 8:00 A.M. news and carried commentaries by Ottawa press gallery reporters, who were paid $25 for each one. While it sought a balance of political opinion, Diefenbaker thought the program was blatantly targeted against him. At a cabinet meeting that spring, Diefenbaker said he wanted an investigation into how the CBC chose its commentators, and the cabinet agreed saying that, according to the minutes, "far too many of them were being unjustifiably and unnecessarily critical of the government."

Diefenbaker talked of "cleaning up the CBC." He called CBC officials and producers "Pearsonalities" in his accusations that the CBC was an unfriendly Liberal establishment that made him a victim of its hostility to his government. Increasingly he became less concerned with the CBC as a public broadcaster and more obsessed with how it portrayed his prime ministership. His old friend Toronto MP David Walker later spoke of "how disgustingly one-sided the CBC commentators have become."

Diefenbaker's rancour poured onto the shoulders of George Nowlan, whose gentle smile and genial style softened his intimidating six-foot-five frame and made him seem like the lion in *The Wizard of Oz*. Time after time Nowlan sat with Bushnell in the subdued lighting of his cabinet office wearily warning Bushnell of the prime minister's anger at the CBC and that of most of the cabinet. Nowlan frequently warned there would be "a political blow up" unless the CBC changed its ways. Nowlan was, in his own way, a strong defender of the CBC against the emotional excesses of Diefenbaker and much of the cabinet. For instance, he rejected Finance Minister Donald Fleming's demand that the CBC Symphony Orchestra be disbanded because it was, according to Fleming, a waste of money. At another point Nowlan chastised his cabinet colleagues for the intensity of their anti-CBC animus, saying that if they kept up their attacks and demands on the CBC, they might have "to get themselves a new boy." Nowlan, in fact, was up to his ears in frustration over the CBC and told Bushnell he was "sick and tired of these criticisms coming in from all over the country, from members of Parliament, from my colleagues and from the public in general." He was also fed up with frequent calls from Diefenbaker complaining about programs which Diefenbaker felt were tainted with liberalism and out to get him. Shortly after, Nowlan told a parliamentary committee, "There is nothing I would rather do, frankly, than to be rid of reporting for the CBC."

Even so, Bushnell regarded him as the best minister the CBC ever had to deal with, and there was general agreement at the CBC about that. Bill Armstrong says, "Nowlan was wonderful, one of the best ministers ever. He gave the best speeches, although he was sometimes totally plastered beyond words."

As acting president, Bushnell not only idolized the minister but was also close to Nowlan's secretary, Ruby Meabry, who at times acted as Nowlan's alter ego. She would often relay suggestions to Bushnell when the minister was busy.

When Bush and Nowlan did confer, Bushnell would often seek

Nowlan's advice on how to deal with the CBC's problems, saying ruefully at times, "I'm coming to you as man to man for some advice.... What the hell would you do?"

"Ernie, that's your problem.... You're running the CBC ... pull up your socks," Bushnell remembered being Nowlan's usual response.

But by the middle of June 1959, the political pressures on Nowlan had become ferocious, and he warned Bushnell, "The whirlwind has developed into a tornado and all hell has broken loose." What had broken it loose was the controversial program "Preview Commentary," on which some of the commentaries, Bushnell felt, were "almost an outright fabrication and a deliberate attempt to do a first-class hatchet job on the prime minister." He even suspected some press gallery commentators may have been in the pay of the Liberals. R. L. Dunsmore, the influential and highly connected Conservative and powerful CBC board member, was also growing angry at the program. Diefenbaker told aides that "Preview Commentary" was deliberately trying to get him.

Bushnell was told in no uncertain terms that he, Ouimet, and even Nowlan himself might be fired by Diefenbaker unless something was done about the program. Exactly how Bushnell received this warning is still unclear. Ouimet said it may have come when Nowlan "bared his soul to Bushnell on some convivial occasion." Nowlan himself admitted, "Once I told him ... I thought the thing [the CBC] was very loosely run, that the CBC reminded me of a cabbage patch with a great lot of heads, each one trying to get bigger than the other – and you know what happens when they get too big. They burst." The warning of possible executive manslaughter may also have been relayed by Ruby Meabry, who talked to Bushnell regularly. But however it came, the warning was effective. Bushnell cancelled "Preview Commentary." He told Charles Jennings, then the controller of programs, heads would roll if "Preview Commentary" were not cancelled. The warning phrase probably originated with Diefenbaker, who often said privately that "heads will roll" if something he wanted were not done.

The CBC's public affairs supervisor, Frank Peers, was astonished on Monday, June 15 when he was advised of "Preview Commentary"'s cancellation and replacement by news agency summaries of daily parliamentary events, effective June 22. "Such a peremptory command from the

chief executive to kill a series without consulting the programmers concerned was unprecedented," the impeccably and steely independent
Peers later wrote. Peers, who was visiting Ottawa at the time, immediately
tried to see Bushnell to protest, but was told the acting president was "too
busy" and that in any event, the cancellation "was final." He went back to
Toronto, but returned to Ottawa on Wednesday evening with two public
affairs department colleagues. They met Bud Walker, the English network head, who said it was "an unfortunate decision" made necessary by
external political pressure. As Peers recounted the conversation, "He said
that Mr. Bushnell had been given two alternatives: either to take the program off the air or the corporate structure of the CBC would be
endangered."

The next day, the programmers were told Bushnell was sick and
couldn't see them so they returned to Toronto, talking about resigning in
protest at the cancellation. Friday and Saturday saw frantic meetings
among the programmers in Toronto and among the executives in
Ottawa, most of whom were unhappy with Bushnell's action. The programmers drew up a protest petition, made more threats of mass resignations, and got support from most of the Toronto CBC senior executives,
including the director and the program director of radio, the program
director of television, and the chief news editor. Finally, they met Bushnell in Toronto on Sunday night, June 21, and he ingenuously explained
the program wasn't being cancelled; it was just that a new program experiment was being tried out for parliamentary reportage. In response to
tough questioning by Network Radio program director Gene Hallman,
Bushnell said it was sometimes better for the CBC to lose a skirmish in
order to win a battle. He was asked what would happen if the CBC board
of directors reversed his decision, and Bushnell said, "I suppose I'd be
sent to Siberia." He pleaded for understanding, but left the programmers
discouraged and dissatisfied.

By pure chance, the CBC board of directors was arriving in Toronto
for a meeting the next day, and Hallman and two senior network colleagues left the session with Bushnell to meet with University of
Manitoba historian and board member W. L. Morton, who opposed the
cancellation of "Preview Commentary." Peers had met Morton earlier in
the day.

On Monday, the board refused to meet the protesters and endorsed Bushnell's cancellation of the program. In organizing their strategy, Hallman told Peers, "You fight outside and I'll fight inside," and at 1:00 A.M., Peers and his senior colleagues announced their resignations. Hallman, meanwhile, sought a meeting with the board the next day. That Monday night, Bud Walker called Ouimet, who was abed in his Ottawa home recovering from his gall-bladder surgery. It was the first time Ouimet had heard of the crisis, and he was appalled. He thought the program was "an acute irritant" to politicians but he felt "its excesses were not sufficiently serious to warrant its removal from the air." He decided to call Bushnell the next morning.

Bushnell didn't return Ouimet's call until late on Tuesday, June 23. It was the most damaging and publicly examined phone call in CBC history. Meanwhile, newspapers across the country had front-paged the previous night's resignations, which were then joined by those of thirty-two other producers. More said they would join in Halifax, Winnipeg, and Vancouver, all of which threatened to destroy the entire public affairs department.

The *Toronto Star*'s headline read, "CBC SURRENDERS." Bushnell denied he was surrendering to government pressure and said that he would not resign. More tension was added when Liberal leader Lester Pearson demanded the House of Commons adjourn for an emergency debate on the CBC crisis and charges were heard in the House of "clandestine political influence" behind Bushnell's decision to cancel the program.

Ironically, of all days, this Tuesday was also the day members of the parliamentary broadcasting committee had come to Toronto to tour the CBC facilities. In all the offices, studios, and corridors, the staff was racked by the tensions of the day.

So, too, was Ernie Bushnell who, after an exhausting, emotional day, retreated to his favourite watering hole, the Celebrity Club, located in an old Victorian mansion just across Jarvis Street from his CBC Toronto office. With a drink in hand and two colleagues in tow – Bud Walker and Charles Jennings – at 5:30 P.M. Bushnell finally got around to returning Ouimet's phone call of that morning. "The Celebrity Club was hardly the place for sober reflection," Ouimet later remarked. "Bushnell sounded very emotional as he usually was in such circumstances."

Bushnell indeed was angry that Ouimet did not support his action to cancel "Preview Commentary." "Why don't you trust me and leave this in my hands, Al?" Ouimet remembered him saying. "It is this megalomaniac Diefenbaker . . . I am not doing this for myself but for the Corporation – for all of us, the minister, you, me. Otherwise we will all lose our jobs."

"It would be disastrous," Ouimet said, if he gave in to political interference, and he urged Bushnell to tell the board "everything."

"Heads will roll. Nowlan's, yours and mine," Ouimet heard Bushnell say excitedly as he argued about the implications if "Preview Commentary" were not taken off the air. He asked Ouimet "to support me and to pay scant heed to the rebellious, self-established monarchs of the Talks and Public Affairs Department."

Bushnell had asked Walker and Jennings to be with him when he called Ouimet, and after the emotional and inconclusive conversation, the three went back to the club's bar. The next day, Wednesday, the controversy was fuelled by a flood of telegrams and phone calls protesting the program cancellation and by former CBC chairman Davie Dunton, who issued a statement saying, "If the Board of Directors of CBC do not put 'Preview Commentary' back on the air they are selling out the principles of national broadcasting in Canada."

While Dunton was talking to the Canadian Press, the CBC board was, in fact, reconsidering its endorsment of Bushnell's action. Nowlan had met with several CBC directors that day while he was passing through Toronto enroute to a meeting in Niagara Falls. Meanwhile in Ottawa, the parliamentary broadcasting committee met and issued an immediate call to Peers and his fellow protesters to come to Ottawa to testify on their accusations of political interference.

Amid Ouimet's doubts, the parliamentary agitation, and the hailstorm of headlines and accusations, the CBC board unanimously agreed to reverse its earlier approval of Bushnell's actions and ordered the program back on the air. Bushnell felt betrayed and accused the board of "throwing me to the wolves." He accused board member W. L. Morton of plotting against him by spending "two days closeted with several of the ring leaders of the mass resignees" and hearing only their side of the story. He was further angered the next day when the *Toronto Star* editorially attacked him for giving "a tangle of contradiction and slithering evasion." His humiliation deepened when the board issued instructions that management should refuse to accept the resignations of Peers and his colleagues and said it hoped they "will find it possible to resume their duties."

The board took another slap at Bushnell and indirectly at Ouimet, by deciding that it would take the CBC chairmanship away from the president or acting president and name one of the directors to the post. R. L. Dunsmore was elected chairman. This was a long-delayed triumph for Nowlan, who the previous November had told Ouimet that's what he wanted. Ouimet had refused at the time, but this time, still away recovering from his surgery, he could not prevent the board from taking action on its own.

Bushnell's agony wasn't over yet. He was called to appear before the parliamentary committee along with Frank Peers, Bud Walker, Charles Jennings, several others from the CBC, and Nowlan himself. From his sick bed at home, Ouimet urged Bushnell to tell the truth about political pressures, but Bushnell said he would deny receiving any political direction to kill the program. He made it clear he would protect Nowlan at any cost. "He was a very loyal associate of the minister, George Nowlan, who may have thought his job was in jeopardy," said Gene Hallman. Nowlan himself said, "Mr. Bushnell and I have been very close. We have talked freely and met two or three times a week in discussing the affairs of the Corporation."

Bushnell told the parliamentary committee, "Never at any time has an order or a directive been given to me, or to my President, Mr. Ouimet, by the Honourable Mr. George Nowlan or by any Member of Parliament, or by anyone else who could be said to wield political influence." Bushnell's own colleagues, however, testified he had talked to them of political pressures, if not a specific directive. Bud Walker, the head of the English network, and Charles Jennings, controller of programs, Bushnell's closest colleagues, created a sensation when they gave detailed testimony of conversations with Bushnell and the Celebrity Club phone call to Ouimet, revealing the "heads will roll" comment. Bushnell was especially incensed with Walker who, shortly after the phone call to Ouimet, had gone back to his hotel room and made notes of the conversation. Walker told colleagues he was going to quote from the notes in his testimony. Capt. W. E. S. Briggs, a friend of Nowlan, a former special events commentator, and now the head of the CBC in the Maritimes, called Walker the night before his parliamentary appearance urging him not to talk about political pressures on Bushnell. To do so, he said would have "dire consequences." Walker, who may well have had his eye on Bushnell's job, refused, saying, "I'm going to tell the truth." Briggs considered both Walker and Gene Hallman disloyal because of their roles in the affair.

After the testimony of Walker and others, newspaper headlines across the country screamed of high-level political interference at the CBC. Bushnell was outraged at what he considered treason by Walker, who had been a close colleague since their days together at CKNC in Toronto three decades earlier. "I've never forgiven him," he said years later. "I've never seen the son of a bitch since and I don't intend to. I don't think Bud was a very loyal person. To hell with him!"

Bushnell's attitude is echoed by CBC Radio pioneer Harry Boyle, who held a number of senior programming roles during the late 1940s, 1950s, and early 1960s. "Walker destroyed a lot of people," Boyle says. "He was a no-account guy." Boyle says Walker began his rise in the CBC when he was named to run the Dominion Radio network. Austin Weir, head of the CBC commercial department at the time, was instrumental in launching the Dominion network and was, says Boyle, "A foxy old bugger, looking for a dummy . . . he could manipulate and he accepted Walker. Walker covered his tracks all the time. He was an engaging guy, personable, but he didn't have a clue about programming."

When Nowlan testified, he denied pressuring Bushnell to cancel "Preview Commentary," although he admitted telling Bushnell that with all the program problems of the CBC, including the Montreal strike, "You had better tighten up this organization or something will happen to somebody around here."

After hearing all the testimony, the Conservative-dominated parliamentary committee said it could find no evidence to support the charge of "clandestine political influence." It was an inconclusive and unpersuasive end to the latest torment for Bushnell, who was still the CBC's acting president. In a private letter to *Financial Post* editor Ron McEachern, Bushnell was scathing about the CBC public affairs department. "The Talks and Public Affairs Department of ours has tried to be a law unto itself and even so much as the lifting of an eyebrow to criticize anything they have done immediately brings forth loud cries of protest and insinuations of political interference from Ottawa."

Alphonse Ouimet did not share Bushnell's assessment and felt Peers and his colleagues "had good and sufficient reason to suspect undue political influence." "I must tip my hat to Frank Peers and his colleagues for the manner in which they conducted themselves during this trying business," he said. A year after the crisis, Ouimet brought Peers to Ottawa to be director of information programming, a job more advisory than operational, and his colleague in the "Preview Commentary" confrontation, Bernard Trotter, was named head of public affairs. Peers later retired to academia at the University of Toronto.

Ouimet's tip of his hat to Peers and his colleagues was not the president's usual attitude toward program people. "I have always found the role played by some of the Corporation's intellectuals, who think of themselves as the sole guardians of CBC's institutional morality, highly presumptuous and equally detestable," he wrote in a memo to himself. "Generally speaking, I have not seen any evidence over the years that the high priests of CBC's intelligentsia have much to teach to their less pretentious colleagues in the field of ethical behaviour. If anything, it is generally the other way around."

In his postcrisis misery, Bushnell licked his wounds from not only the "Preview Commentary" fiasco but also the Montreal strike, plus assorted other controversies of his acting presidency. Bushnell's woes were a manifestation of Yeats' poetic cry that, "Things fall apart; the centre cannot hold. Mere anarchy is loosed upon the world." He was comforted, however, by his old mentor Gladstone Murray, who had been extinguished by a similar parliamentary inquiry. "Cheer up," Murray wrote. "In my twenty years of radio I went through at least a dozen similar ordeals."

In reply, Bushnell was both jocular and tormented about his future. "Please get me a gasoline concession in the Township of Durham, at least ten miles off the highway," he said. "It must have a good trout stream adjacent.... Whether I can ride out this storm remains to be seen."

"Of course you can and will ride out this storm," Murray responded.

As was his habit, Bushnell retreated to liquid comfort, often alternating between being tipsy and being falling-down drunk. He desperately needed a rest. "The last six months have been probably the most hectic in the history of the Corporation," Nowlan said. "Mr. Bushnell has worked tirelessly ... on many occasions seventeen or eighteen hours a day ... Mr. Bushnell is completely and totally exhausted."

The CBC board gave him two months leave and named a management committee to run the CBC until he or Ouimet returned to work. Bushnell fled to his cottage on the Gatineau River just outside Ottawa, feeling abused and used as a political scapegoat. He wanted time to assess his future and his health, and what he called "a calamitous six months trying to run the CBC as its chief executive officer." His continued affection for alcohol led to arguments with his wife, and that summer he caused embarrassment by staggering and falling at an Ottawa diplomatic cocktail party. Even he realized he had to stop drinking, especially in view of his diabetes. "I just came to my senses," he later said. "I finally realized that I was making a fool of myself." He gave up drinking in a typical Bushnell manner: he bought a bottle of rye, drank it all by himself, and said, "That's the last." He fell off the wagon once a few months after that, but then remained sober for the rest of his life.

Ouimet came back to work as CBC president early in August and Bushnell returned in September. The first thing on Ouimet's plate was his plan to reorganize the CBC. Sifting through the organizational debris of the past six months, he decided a major bureaucratic restructuring was needed. Besides, the parliamentary broadcasting committee had demanded a shake-up. "The administrative structure of the Corporation is weak and in need of thorough review," the MPs had said in denouncing the CBC for divided authority and lack of clarity in direction.

Ouimet's answer to charges of managerial chaos was to name a bevy of vice-presidents and general managers, trot out complicated organizational charts, reshuffle responsibilities, and focus authority on Ottawa, all of which dismayed and peeved Bushnell, who felt it was an elaborate demotion for him. Ouimet even barred him from attending the board of directors meeting that approved the reorganization plans, fearing Bushnell would speak out against them. Bush began thinking of quitting, which probably was what Ouimet wanted in the first place, and he began, too, to get offers from private broadcasting, where he had come from more than twenty-five years earlier. He would get much more money than the $16,000 a year CBC was paying him, the bureaucratic headaches and heartaches would be far less, and there would be no politics and no Al Ouimet. In late November 1959, he walked into George Nowlan's office and told the minister he was quitting. "Ernie, you don't have to quit," Nowlan told him. "Tell those bastards who are hounding you over there to go to hell."

"Sorry, Mr. Minister," Bushnell replied, "my usefulness has ended. I have little or no responsibility. There are people working for me who in my judgement have been disloyal and others in whom I have no confidence and for whom I have no respect. I couldn't possibly continue to work in such a climate. I'm through as of December 31."

With Nowlan's praise in his ears, the fifty-nine year-old Bushnell went back to the CBC to tell Ouimet he was resigning. He did not get any praise from Ouimet who, to his dying day, blamed Bushnell for much of the CBC's troubles over the years.

One major difference between the two men who had played such a critical role in development of broadcasting in Canada was their attitude toward politicians. Years later Bushnell told Ouimet, who always maintained a protective, stiff-necked distance from politicians, that he lacked "political savvy." Bushnell said this had angered Nowlan, his colleagues, and especially Nowlan's secretary, Ruby Meabry. "You have no idea," Bushnell told Ouimet, "the scunner that Ruby had taken against you." Thinking back to that conversation, Ouimet wrote, "He also philosophized on the need of Crown Corporation executives to play ball with politicians. . . . We had to keep political imperatives in mind. All our predecessors had done it, Murray, Brockington, Frigon, Dunton." They also talked about Bushnell's heavy drinking, and Bushnell told him proudly that he hadn't had a drink in fifteen years. "Too bad you didn't stop fifteen years before," was Ouimet's sour response.

Ouimet's scarred relations with Bushnell are reflected in conversations he recorded between himself and Bud Walker, whose distaste for Bushnell was palpable. Walker told Ouimet he didn't think Bushnell had any convictions about the CBC, did more damage than help during his years there, plotted against Frigon, and forever criticized Ouimet. Walker admitted, though, that Bushnell "was always jolly, never missed a party, drank and cursed a lot . . . and had a knack of surrounding himself with good men."

When Bushnell marched out of Ouimet's office for the last time at the end of 1959, he left behind a giant footprint of creative leadership and chaotic management. He had been a seminal figure in Canadian broadcasting since the late 1920s, vitriolically arguing against public broadcasting in the early 1930s, joining "the enemy" soon after the CRBC began, and championing programming over bureaucracy for more than a quarter of a century. For a generation, Canadians had listened to the magic of radio and the miracle of television programming as shaped by Ernie Bushnell. But the old song-and-dance man's heart was always in entertainment shows and, with few deep philosophical roots, he was for the most part at best tolerant and at worst contemptuous of the more serious side of programming. As he had been from the beginning, he remained sceptical of the idea of a public service mandate to educate, enrich, and help unify the nation through broadcasting. But he brought a sense of fun to his job, a concept the unemotional Al Ouimet, with his dedicated sense of duty, had difficulty understanding.

Far from quitting with his tail between his legs, however, the lovable, infuriating old rascal rejoined the world of private broadcasting by establishing a TV station in Ottawa that, to his private satisfaction, competitively kicked the hell out of the local CBC station. Bushnell was proud of his contribution to Canadian broadcasting, but always feared that his epitaph would be that in the 1920s as a broadcast advertising pioneer, he had invented the singing commercial in a promotional campaign for the Toronto Wet Wash Company.

13

The Troubles Continue

George Nowlan didn't look very far to find Ernie Bushnell's successor; he chose his old friend, the CBC's Maritimes director Capt. W. E. S. "Ted" Briggs. An intimidating, spit-and-polish old Navy man, Briggs had been one of the stars of early CBC Radio, anchoring special events such as royal tours and royal weddings. He was a decorated Second World War hero and had run a tight ship on North Atlantic convoy duty. Nowlan wanted him to do the same at the CBC.

Ouimet was furious and astonished at the appointment. He had not been consulted at all by Nowlan and did not believe Briggs had the right qualities for the job. Also furious was corporate affairs vice-president Ron Fraser, who had fully expected to get the job. Many of his CBC colleagues also resented Briggs' constant use of nautical terms, issued in a booming, British-accented voice, a left-over from his days at an English boarding school during the First World War.

Built like a combination of a British bulldog and a Japanese sumo wrestler, Briggs liked his nickname of "the old man" but hated the whispered moniker "Uncle Bulgy." His hearty bluffness and pleasure at "splitting the main brace" appealed to Nowlan who, above all, prized Briggs' loyalty. The new CBC executive vice-president, however, could not speak a word of French, nor did he have any reputation for intellectual depth or executive leadership. He knew little about television or the creative world, and producers such as Ross McLean referred to him as "Captain Queeg" and said he once "tried desperately to explain television to Captain Briggs."

Nowlan and Briggs developed a hearty friendship, if not as intimate as Nowlan's and Bushnell's it was at least as productive for the minister in getting his views into the CBC management without having to deal with Ouimet. Once when Ouimet made one of his rare visits to see Nowlan, seeking support for increased funding, he sat sipping Coca-Cola while the minister and Briggs downed glass after glass of scotch.

Nowlan's unease with Ouimet and Diefenbaker's contempt of the CBC president gave Briggs an important role as the principal channel for government communication with the CBC. Over the next few years, that channel was filled with multiplying denunciations of CBC programs.

Altogether, the CBC was now producing more than 100,000 radio and TV programs a year, and as television became a four- or five-hour-a-day habit, people began eating in front of their TV sets and depending on the magic box of wires and tubes for most of their information on what was happening and why. That caught the attention of politicians, who began to appreciate the power of television to shape public attitudes. Political careers were being made and lost on television, and society itself was being mirrored on the living room screen with more impact than radio had ever achieved even in its heyday.

Television was king, and everybody wanted to be on the air from the youngest MP to cabinet ministers and the prime minister. Their executive assistants lobbied for interviews and coverage of speeches and activities, giving an unheard of power to the producers and editors who decided whom and what would get on the air. Upwards of 1.5 million Canadians watched the CBC-TV "National News" every night at 11:00 P.M. (11:30 P.M. in Newfoundland), and they began hearing a steady beat of Opposition complaints about Diefenbaker and seeing the signs of a coming anti-Diefenbaker revolt within the Conservative Party itself. His notoriously thin skin was repeatedly pierced, and pain for the man Peter Newman called "the Renegade in Power" came particularly from programs such as Patrick Watson's "Inquiry," with host Davie Dunton, a weekly look at Ottawa politics, and Ross McLean's "Close-Up."

Television relayed the volcanic changes of the early 1960s: the sleepy Eisenhower-St. Laurent era was out and the Kennedy zest was in, Fred Waring and Guy Lombardo were fading and The Beatles and Elvis were breaking loose, Norman Vincent Peale was giving way to Jack Kerouac, and traditional values were under siege from a confident, questioning new generation.

In drama, music, current affairs, and news, CBC-TV echoed and stimulated these generational changes, mystifying and frightening the old élites and politicians. Producers approvingly quoted BBC head Hugh Green as saying, "The heresies of today are often the dogma of tomorrow."

The Mère d'Youville program and Joyce Davidson's comment on the Queen were examples of the new attitude, as were the obscenities in a program called "The Zoo Story," a drama written by Edward Albee for which Ouimet had to apologize, and especially the series "Quest" with its upsetting avant-garde approach. A 1962 "Quest" program, "Crawling Arnold" by cartoonist Jules Feiffer, was a stinging satire on sex, psychiatry, and the atom bomb which brought cries of rage. Medicine Hat Conservative MP E. W. Brunsden, to the nodding agreement of many fellow MPs, quoted constituents telling him it was "depraved, disgusting, absolutely immoral garbage . . . and a rank violation of the sanctity of the Canadian home and family." "As a good Baptist," Nowlan responded, tongue in cheek, "I am in church Sunday nights so I have not had occasion to watch the program in question."

Other drama series such as "Festival" and "Folio" drew similar cries of righteous outrage about profanity, immorality, and anti-establishment attitude. One play on "Folio" was bitterly attacked because brutal soldiers shown battling terrorists in an occupied country had English accents. The complaint was that anyone with an English accent could not possibly be brutal. Not only drama was under fire. Alberta Conservative MP Jack Horner unleashed a bitter assault on the CBC for having an American commentator anchor a program on the Calgary Stampede.

Social Credit leader Robert Thompson said the CBC was undermining family life by showing unmarried couples in the same bed. Alberta Premier Ernest Manning denounced CBC programs as "pornographic, trash, filth" and the governments of Manitoba and Prince

Edward Island complained that the CBC was portraying their provinces in a bad light.

BBG chairman Dr. Andrew Stewart did not share these apprehensions about controversial programming. He strongly defended the CBC, saying, "It would be a sad state of affairs if, in any sector of broadcasting . . . the only permissible material was in defence of the establishment or the established ways of doing things or even was in support of the mores of the majority."

Among some critics, the old refrain was heard of the CBC being "riddled with communists" and "subversives," and charges were again made that "reds dominate the CBC." Alberta Social Credit legislator William Tomyn declared the CBC was airing "nefarious and subversive propaganda" and went on to accuse it of "brainwashing" and promoting "the Kremlin neutralist disarmament line . . . designed to stir up anti-American feelings in Canada." He declared the CBC was airing "nauseating . . . subversive skulduggery."

Newfoundland Liberal MP Chesley Carter was no less strident in attacking the CBC. "I am a little frightened at the amount of brainwashed and subversive propaganda which goes out over the CBC day after day at the taxpayers' expense," he said. "I'm appalled at the extent to which the CBC provides a national platform for subversives . . . a barrage of ideas and points of view which have their origin in the Kremlin." He cited, as an example, a CBC interview with noted scientist Dr. Linus Pauling, who opposed nuclear testing. "There is," Carter said, "a liaison between communist headquarters and the CBC." That led to the *Ottawa Citizen* headline, "MP BARES CBC-KREMLIN 'LINK'."

A "Close-Up" interview with singer Paul Robeson on folk songs was ordered delayed several times because he was controversial. The program was seen a year after the original air date and still drew criticism as left-wing propaganda. Diefenbaker himself talked about the CBC French network having "left wing communist infiltration" and there were demands to remove René Lévesque from any appearances on the air. At the same time, the CBC was being attacked for creative timidity by some, such as the *Winnipeg Free Press*, which editorialized that since Diefenbaker had been prime minister the CBC had demonstrated "all the independence and courage of a rabbit confronted by a tiger."

CCF broadcast critic Doug Fisher said CBC public affairs program- ming was "scared . . . gutless." "The programming situation has gone to the dogs," he said. "There is a gutlessness in the organization. . . . We are getting more and more vacuity and a poorer and poorer job in public affairs. . . . They are scared stiff." Critics pointed, as an example, to a CBC comedy sketch in which Diefenbaker had been referred to as prime min- ister "for the time being" and which management had ordered killed. Faced with criticism from all sides, a seemingly friendless but bemused Alphonse Ouimet sighed to a Toronto Canadian Club luncheon audience that no other organization has been so "damned, slurred, supported, inquired into, ignored, blamed, upheld, detested, liked, criticized or praised, as the CBC."

Criticism poured out of the parliamentary broadcasting committee which Graham Spry labelled "a witch hunt." He said the CBC was being "noisily drawn and quartered" by Conservative politicians. He was angered, too, at CBC management, saying the CBC might either "be slaughtered by its enemies . . . or commit suicide because of its own mis- takes and mistaken leadership." In a letter to Spry from Walter Gordon, Spry's friend and an influential Liberal, there was more foreboding about the CBC. "I do not think there is much doubt that the Tories are out to wreck the CBC," Gordon wrote. "They are helped by the fact that it seems to have been incredibly badly managed since Davie Dunton left and Ouimet's illness."

But Diefenbaker and his cabinet were listening increasingly to the CBC's critics, and the prime minister's disgust with much of CBC pro- gramming grew along with his wrath at Ouimet. His anger encouraged hostile Conservative MPs to lash out at the CBC through the 1961 parlia- mentary broadcasting committee. Significantly, this parliamentary com- mittee was the first not to uphold the importance of public broadcasting in specific terms. It proposed to weaken CBC network controls, sug- gested action to remove Ouimet and Briggs from the board of directors, and attacked CBC management for everything from mishandling of cap- ital investments to weak program script control.

The Conservatives' and the committee's heartburn was aggravated by the testimony of Maxwell Henderson, who had been the CBC's chief financial officer prior to his recent appointment as the government's auditor general. Ouimet thought Henderson had not been a "team player" when he had been with the CBC, and he had reduced his authority in the management shuffle of 1959. Ouimet felt he had been forced to hire Henderson shortly after Diefenbaker's 1957 election by his then boss Davie Dunton. Dunton, in turn, had been under pressure from Donald Fleming's Finance Department to give the CBC financial job to Henderson. In his testimony to the parliamentary committee, Henderson was highly critical of the way Ouimet was running the CBC, and his firsthand experience at the CBC lent credence to Conservative accusations of bad management. "Vicious defamation," was the way Ouimet characterized the criticism.

The CCF's Doug Fisher said some Tory MPs "want to destroy the CBC." The *Montreal Star* called the parliamentary report "biased," and the *Globe and Mail* suggested Conservative "spite" may have led to "needling of a distasteful sort." "The management changes recommended in the report are of dubious origin," the *Globe* said. Even Toronto radio station CFRB, an adversary of the CBC for a generation, editorialized on air, "Notwithstanding its shortcomings, the CBC does a good and necessary job for Canada," and it urged listeners to protest the threats to the CBC to their MPs.

Faced with this heavily negative reaction, the Diefenbaker government shelved the parliamentary committee's recommendations, although it did ask for an inquiry into CBC operations by the Glassco Commission, which was then carrying out a broad review of government departments and agencies. When it made its report in 1963, the Glassco Commission tone was highly reproachful of the CBC, saying, "The Corporation is in need of extensive reorganization to secure efficiency and economy in the operations."

"Hatchet job" Ouimet labelled the criticism and "entirely wrong." He called for a royal commission, which led to the establishment of the Fowler Committee a few years later.

Already under attack from the government, Ouimet also faced Diefenbaker's growing support for the private broadcasters. That support would change the nature of Canada's broadcast system as dramatically as the removal of the CBC's regulatory powers and licensing of more private TV stations had earlier.

The private stations gave Diefenbaker no offence because they were offering no controversial dramas and their thin journalistic coverage angered no one. Their objective was simply to make money, which they were doing in astonishing amounts. "The sweetest music is the sound of the thirty-second commercial at thirty dollars a time," said early private broadcaster Roy Thomson. The industry was third in profitability among 140 leading Canadian industries, the Bank of Commerce had reported. The best way to sustain that was with inoffensive programming, dominated by American imports interspersed with a handful of pallid Canadian imitations of American talk and game shows.

Eugene Forsey, a friend of Graham Spry and one of the few non-Conservative members of the BBC, wrote Spry decrying what he called "the miserable" private broadcasters. "They are for the most part a collection of bandits . . . a terrible crew," he said.

The highly principled, gentle but determined chairman of the BBG, Dr. Andrew Stewart, was insistent that private stations produce more Canadian programming, even if that did cut into their profits. At first, he thought the CBC should produce programs that would be aired on those private stations not affiliated with the CBC, but Ouimet rejected the idea because he thought it might weaken the CBC network. Then the BBG hit on the idea of a regulated amount of Canadian content, something the old CBC board had tried but failed to enforce earlier. Inevitably, the BBG's proposal was received by howls of protest from the private broadcasters who feared what Roy Thomson called their "licence to print your own money" was being threatened. It might lead to "mediocre" programming, said CAB president Malcolm Neill. "Quality broadcasting . . . cannot be achieved by percentage requirements," he said, although "quality broadcasting" had not been much in evidence without Canadian content rules. Canadian advertisers also made it clear they did not want any Canadian content requirements. Although they modified their original proposals, Stewart and the BBG finally ruled that all TV stations must have 45 per cent Canadian content by April 1961 and 55 per cent by the following year. That was no problem for the CBC which already had more than 60 per cent Canadian content on the English network and 85 per cent on the French.

The percentage was achieved by most grumbling private stations through low-cost game shows, bare-bones newscasts, and amateur talent shows. Some filled endless hours with low-paid performers playing an organ or a piano. Hamilton broadcasting mogul Ken Soble later noted, "Why spend $3,000 or $4,000 when you can get the same credit for hiring a piano player."

More contentious for the BBG and more worrisome for the CBC was the government's determination to increase greatly the number of private TV stations. The Diefenbaker government had made clear it was going to expand private broadcasting and shrink public broadcasting, and one way of doing that was to open the airwaves to the eagerly waiting entrepreneurs who saw television as a cash cow. "One of the quickest roads to a fortune in Canada," Graham Spry commented.

The high-rollers of Canadian broadcasting, publishing, and industry in general scrambled for a place in the TV sun. Roy Thomson wanted in and so did Jack Kent Cooke, Don Jamieson, Finlay MacDonald, the Siftons, oil tycoon Frank McMahon, department store owner John David Eaton, Henry Borden, a nephew of the former prime minister, and countless publishers and broadcasters. Many an old CBC face was seen in the race for a TV licence, including Ernie Bushnell's and Stuart Griffiths'.

The biggest controversy in the licence-granting scramble was in Toronto where *Telegram* publisher John Bassett, with John David Eaton's money, won with CFTO. Eaton was a financial angel for the Conservative Party and Bassett was a powerful Tory insider whose newspaper support was important to the Diefenbaker government. Thus, the Conservatives owed a debt of gratitude to Eaton and Bassett. Even before he was granted the licence, Bassett, supremely confident that he'd get it, had bought a site and drawn up the blueprints for the studios. That inevitably led to accusations that "the fix was in." That suspicion was inflamed after Bassett bragged to friends that he had the licence "in the bag." Mavor Moore, no longer with the CBC and now another contender for the Toronto licence, remembered Bassett telling him, "Mavor, don't worry. I have been promised the licence by John Diefenbaker and George Hees." Hees later admitted to a reporter that as a Diefenbaker cabinet minister, "I was very helpful to him [Bassett] in getting his television licence." The *Telegram*'s

Ottawa bureau chief and friend of Diefenbaker, Peter Dempson, later said he had been a go-between on the matter between Bassett and several cabinet ministers, and he said that in a private conversation the prime minister had implied he had had a role in securing the licence for Bassett.

Eugene Forsey chided Bassett and his friends who "had let their tongues wag," but he defended giving the licence to Bassett on the grounds that Bassett had made the best presentation. The Toronto publisher had also surrounded himself with big-name broadcasters, including the controversial former CBC announcer Joel Aldred, who was made president of the new station, future cable king Ted Rogers, and hockey's Foster Hewitt, who was named vice-president. Together, they promised a creative nirvana that would rival the CBC, including ballet, opera, Shakespeare, symphonies, dramas, and big-time variety shows. Little of it materialized, however, after they got their licence.

With five new second stations, private TV was now in every major city of the country, and the next step in the private broadcasting march toward the dominant role in Canadian radio and TV was obvious: a private network. "We have been in a sense promoting this," one BBG official admitted. After Ouimet had rejected the idea of the CBC providing programs to the new private stations, the idea of a private network began to take shape. Ouimet himself said he wouldn't mind the competition. Newfoundland Conservative MP J. A. McGrath said, "We now have second television stations in major cities and there is the possibility of a second network which takes the exclusive national service away from the CBC; in other words, there are other people who are now capable of providing a national service . . . with no cost to the taxpayer."

In July 1960, an informal program exchange arrangement was set up by the private stations, and October 1, 1961, the Canadian Television Network (CTV) went on the air, linking stations in eight cities: Vancouver, Calgary, Edmonton, Winnipeg, Toronto, Ottawa, Montreal, and Halifax. Only Toronto, Montreal, and Ottawa were linked by microwave; programs were carried on a delayed basis in the other cities. CTV founder Spence Caldwell, who had worked with the CBC Dominion Radio network when it was set up in 1944, made it clear that CTV programming would be significantly different from that of the CBC. "Ours is going to be commercial TV, an advertisers' network." he said. He hired CBC veteran producers such as Ross McLean and Michael Hind-Smith, yet the eight and a half hours a week of programming he offered consisted largely of game shows, American westerns, and detective shows, a barn-dance program, and sports. CTV went to fourteen hours a week in 1962, and a newscast and a public affairs program were added. Caldwell, meanwhile, continually pressed the BBG for a lower Canadian content rule for CTV.

Alphonse Ouimet commented that "the CBC is an instrument of national purpose – the CTV of commercial purpose." CTV's arrival, however, had a disquieting effect on the CBC. The new competition encouraged the CBC to chase audiences more vigorously, which led to more mass-appeal programming, and Diefenbaker's financial squeezing led the CBC to seek more advertising revenue. This was hailed by the CBC's private affiliates and by advertising agencies but lamented by public broadcasting supporters. Eugene Forsey warned his BBG colleagues, "The CBC is under constant attack, constant pressures to go more commercial, which means almost certainly less and less Canadian."

The Father of public broadcasting, Graham Spry, was the most worried and disillusioned of all the CBC supporters because he saw the dream he and Alan Plaunt had shared more than thirty years before being shattered. "The CBC has been outflanked, surrounded and hemmed in to a subordinate place in the structure of Canadian broadcasting," he wrote in the *Queen's Quarterly* in an article entitled "The Decline and Fall of Canadian Broadcasting." The Canadian system, he said, had now become "essentially a merchandising system on the American commercial model, . . . The CBC has been maligned, misrepresented, savaged, nagged and subjected to meanness and indignation by hostile and sometimes greedy competitors and ill-informed politicians." Spry's pessimism worsened as time went on, and a few years later he said, "I profoundly regret that the CBC prime time is now primarily devoted to selling American goods, financed by American advertisers, and very largely with American programs."

Meanwhile, John Diefenbaker was increasingly paranoid and resentful about the way he was being portrayed on the CBC. "Something will have to be done about the CBC," said Tory strategist Allister Grosart, who charged that the CBC had become a Liberal propaganda agency. In March 1961, the cabinet, with Diefenbaker and Nowlan absent, decided action against the CBC had become necessary. The cabinet minutes recorded the government's bitterness at CBC programming which, it said, was "part of a campaign to discredit the government." The cabinet declared, "Consideration should be given to the establishment of a Cabinet Committee to assist Mr. Nowlan in investigating the programming of the CBC." Cooler heads later prevailed and the committee was never created.

But Diefenbaker's agony intensified as he sank lower in the public opinion polls, and many of his erstwhile Conservative Party friends, including John Bassett, turned against him. In 1962, he got into an unwinnable squabble with the Sir Lancelot of politics, John Kennedy. He felt surrounded by mutinous colleagues and blamed the media, especially the CBC, for his impending political doom. Seeking support, he had promised to "clean up" the CBC French network in an effort to woo Réal Caouette and his Quebec Social Crediters, who wanted Diefenbaker "to remove the socialists and like-minded persons from the CBC."

But nothing helped, and Diefenbaker's doom came in the spring election of 1963 which threw him out and brought in Lester Pearson and the Liberals. For Alphonse Ouimet, it seemed like a deliverance.

Pearson had been a longtime supporter of the Canadian Radio League and a friend of Graham Spry and Alan Plaunt. In his memoirs, Pearson stated his view "that broadcasting should be treated as education and that there should be the greatest possible public control; that the emphasis should be on the public system and private broadcasting should be very much a subsidiary."

Pearson's election made life easier for Ouimet because not only was Diefenbaker no longer there to torment him, but one of the first things Pearson did was to double Ouimet's salary from $20,000, where it had been frozen by Diefenbaker for five years, to $40,000. Ouimet also got rid of his boardroom nemesis, R. L. Dunsmore. The government decided the heavily Conservative board had acted illegally when it named Dunsmore as chairman after the "Preview Commentary" crisis, and Ouimet was restored as both chairman and president. Dunsmore resigned a short time later.

There was, however, a discordant note to the music in the ears of CBC supporters. It lay in the influence of Newfoundland private broadcaster Don Jamieson, CAB president and a powerful backroom operator in Liberal politics. Another worry was Jamieson's friend Jack Pickersgill, the political wizard behind Pearson and the man Pearson picked as secretary of state, responsible for the CBC.

Pickersgill had prevented the establishment of a CBC-TV station in St. John's in preference to a station run by Jamieson, and he had protested the granting of a CBC-TV licence for Edmonton, saying it was "an unnecessary waste of the taxpayers' money." He thought CBC stations in Vancouver, Winnipeg, Toronto, Ottawa, Montreal, and Halifax were enough "to provide national network coverage and . . . all the rest of the field should be left to private initiative." So it was no surprise that he was uneasy with the CBC's desire to establish new stations in St. John's, Saskatoon, Sudbury, New Brunswick, and Prince Edward Island.

Graham Spry wrote from London to Eugene Forsey expressing misgivings regarding Pickersgill's appointment and worrying about the relationship between Pickersgill and Jamieson. Forsey agreed, responding that he was "most uneasy about Pickersgill, especially in combination with Jamieson; both are as clever as paint, and neither to be trusted farther than you can kick him."

Pickersgill's attitude reflected the new world of broadcasting in Canada. There were now more than 250 radio stations in Canada and 70 TV stations. No longer was it one system run by the CBC in which affiliated private stations carried CBC programs and only serviced local communities. No longer did anyone seriously talk of the CBC taking over the private stations as had been envisioned in the 1930s. Private broadcasting was big business, had big influence, and was now the senior partner in the business of Canadian broadcasting. Pickersgill and Jamieson were determined to keep it that way.

Balancing Pearson's strong pro-CBC instincts with what he perceived as the new broadcasting reality, Pickersgill tiptoed into action. Within weeks of his appointment, he named a troika of wise men to help establish a new broadcasting policy: CBC president Alphonse Ouimet, BBG chairman Andrew Stewart, and CAB president Don Jamieson. Now even the Liberals viewed the private sector as an equal partner in broadcasting, something Mackenzie King and R. B. Bennett had never done.

When the troika met, Jamieson brought to the table a dramatically different attitude toward the principles and purposes of public broadcasting from that held by Ouimet and Stewart. The CBC, he felt, had "a woefully ill-defined sense of purpose," and he believed it was a "potential threat to our free society." As he later wrote in an attack on the idea of a CBC monopoly, "Hitler was using just such a monopoly to prostitute radio to the basest needs of his regime." With his slap-on-the-back heartiness and booming, sonorous voice, Jamieson inveighed against "well-meaning moralists," "crusaders," "missionaries" and the "well-intentioned" who got involved in broadcasting. He discouraged the idea of more Canadian programming on the grounds that Canadian talent was generally inferior and inexperienced, and anyway, he was sure Canadian audiences wanted American programs. "Public preferences for U.S. programs of virtually every type is obvious and growing," he said. "There is a surprisingly small amount of truly professional, thoroughly competent and well-disciplined talent available to Canadian TV today." And he added, "There are few better places than a state-controlled broadcasting system within which mediocre talent can rationalize its failures so conveniently while calling on the state for help."

Jamieson was especially critical of CBC journalism and what he felt was runaway freedom for producers. It was dangerous for the CBC to report the news, he said, because it could not be trusted on political stories. He also thought satire was "tasteless and pointless," and he would later exclaim in his book *The Troubled Air* that "CBC uses its own personnel and public monies to survey and report on the likely outcome of national elections."

CCF broadcasting critic Doug Fisher said Jamieson could "be as brutally frank as any old robber baron and as piously high-minded as an Archbishop." He used both talents effectively in trying to shape Canadian broadcast policy and cut down the CBC.

The troika was able to agree on some broad generalities, but fundamental differences remained unsolved. Ouimet called the year-long troika discussions "an exercise in futility." Distressed at the continuing disarray of radio and TV policy, Prime Minister Pearson retreated to the timeworn approach of Canadian governments by appointing in 1965 yet another major investigation into broadcasting. This time, he brought back Robert Fowler to head an advisory committee with a more modest agenda than the royal commission on broadcasting Fowler had led in the last days of the previous Liberal government. Fowler totally disagreed with Jamieson's broadcasting ideas and would seek to outflank him and Pickersgill.

Other members of the Fowler Committee were Marc Lalonde, a Liberal lawyer, friend of Pierre Trudeau, and strong public broadcast advocate, and veteran deputy minister Ernie Steele. Their report was a blockbuster; a scathing indictment of almost everything Jamieson, the private broadcasters, and the Conservatives held dear in broadcast policy. Even the CBC did not elude censure for carrying too much American "escapist programming," for too centralized management, and for failing to be a better bridge between English- and French-speaking Canadians. One surprising and troubling recommendation that seemed out of harmony with the rest of the report was a recommendation that CBC-TV should capture at least 25 per cent of Canada's TV advertising, and 30 per cent would be "so much the better," it said. That was tempting advice for the financially hard-pressed government, but Ouimet said it would have a disastrous effect on CBC programming.

While private broadcasters also worried about too much commercial revenue going to the CBC, it was the ferocity of the attack on their own programming that set the station owners' teeth on edge. As for private radio, Fowler said, "In many cases radio has become a mere machine for playing recordings of popular music with frequent interruptions to carry as much advertising as can be sold." For TV, while saying there were a few good information programs on private stations, the report concluded, "for the rest, the systematic mediocrity of programming is deplorable."

In his criticism, Fowler was echoing the words of U.S. Federal Communications Commission chairman Newton Minow, who had lacerated American TV four years earlier, calling it "a procession of game shows, violence, audience participation shows, formula comedies about totally unbelievable families, blood and thunder, mayhem, violence, sadism, murder, western bad men, western good men, private eyes, gangsters, more violence and cartoons. And endlessly, commercials – many screaming, cajoling and offending. And most of all, boredom."

Canadian private TV, said Fowler, was much the same, and he condemned private broadcasters for scarce and scrawny Canadian programming. No amount of private broadcasting rhetoric could hide the reality that Fowler noted: Canadian private radio stations were each paying an average of $22.29 per day for Canadian talent, while private TV stations were averaging $110 each a day. "Deplorably low," Fowler said, although he added that French-language private stations were doing much better than their English-language counterparts.

Beyond that, the report concluded that the addition of private stations had simply increased the viewing of American programs. In Toronto, for example, the viewing of American programs had risen to 75 per cent in prime time by 1963, a fact that would be repeated down through the years whenever new channels, new networks, and new cable systems were established.

The root philosophy of the Fowler Committee was etched in a paragraph on what broadcasting should be all about. It was an exact reflection of what Spry, Plaunt, Brockington, Dunton, and all the other public broadcasting missionaries had sought and what private broadcasters deplored: "A broadcasting system must not minister solely to the comfort of the people. It must not always play safe. Its guiding rule cannot be to give the people what they want, for at best this can be only what the broadcasters think the people want; they may not know and the people themselves may not know. One of the essential tasks of a broadcasting system is to stir up the minds and emotions of the people and occasionally to make large numbers of them acutely uncomfortable. . . . In a vital broadcasting system, there must be room for the thinker, the disturber and the creator of new forms and ideas. He must be free to experiment – to fail as well as to succeed."

The Fowler Committee was a throwback to the pre-Diefenbaker days in its powerful advocacy of the CBC as the paramount force in the Canadian broadcasting system. Indeed, Fowler proposed a return to his one-board system recommendation of 1957 for a Canadian broadcasting authority directly supervising the CBC as well as setting rules and regulations for the private and public sectors. The committee also proposed decentralizing the CBC's authority by putting network managers in Toronto and Montreal instead of Ottawa where Ouimet wanted them.

At once the private stations lashed back with accusations of "fascism," "communism," and "dictatorship." CAB said the ideas were "repugnant to our sense of democratic freedom." Philosophical soul mates of the CAB within the Liberal Party waged guerilla warfare to delay or modify any legislative action based on the report. The new broadcasting act would not come for three years, and when it did it would be much watered down from the Fowler Committee proposals.

While he was pleased with some of the Fowler recommendations, Ouimet rejected any return to a one-board system that would produce a czar of all broadcasting. He also was furious about Fowler's criticism of CBC management, especially the opening sentence of the report, "The only thing that really matters in broadcasting is program content; all the rest is housekeeping." "Simplistic," Ouimet replied as he argued that management, engineering, and programming were all equally important. Producers, however, cheered Fowler's words, and his "housekeeping" comment became an oft-repeated, venerable truism to use in arguments with management.

Fowler's support for avant-garde programming contrasted sharply with a new wave of puritanical attacks on CBC programming. The Supreme Council of the Knights of Columbus said the CBC was "allowing fellow travelling leftists, agnostics, terrorists and other troublemakers on certain programs, class struggles and contempt for religious, civil and legal authorities." Quebec cabinet minister Bona Arsenault warned, "There has been left wing communistic infiltration of the French network of the Canadian Broadcasting Corporation."

In English-speaking Canada, women's and church groups circulated a "Declaration by Canadian Women" with 70,000 signatures condemning the CBC for spreading "propaganda for perversion, pornography, free love, blasphemy, dope, violence and crime."

A network drama called "The Open Grave" had used an allegorical Easter story to tell a contemporary tale of the last days of a Canadian peace advocate who was tried and executed. That brought John

Diefenbaker to rhetorical heights. Even though he hadn't seen it, he condemned the program as "a flagrant, scandalous and sacrilegious insult to a majority of Canadians."

Diefenbaker also demanded an investigation into the drama series "Festival," and Alberta Conservative MP Clifford Smallwood demanded removal of the "Quest" series of dramas. When a commentator on the CBC-TV program "Viewpoint" said the Queen would not be welcome in Canada on her forthcoming visit, Manitoba Conservative MP Nicholas Mandzick called for laws "to prevent the . . . expression of . . . disloyal utterances through the medium of the publicly owned CBC."

But the biggest program fuss was over a new style *cinéma-vérité* documentary on a day in the life of Prime Minister Pearson. "Mr. Pearson" became a major problem for Ouimet and the prime minister, and was a precursor to the "This Hour Has Seven Days" immolation that was waiting in the wings.

Producer Dick Ballentine, with the encouragement of Ross McLean who had returned to CBC after a brief fling with CTV, had put together a graphic, candid camera portrait of the prime minister. It showed Pearson at the United Nations, at home eating breakfast, watching the World Series on his office TV set, and dealing with a myriad of crises from a dock strike to a filibuster in the House of Commons. A few "God"s and "damn"s were captured, as well as some private joking and gossip. Portable cameras caught an informal, highly human prime minister, but did so in sometimes out-of-focus, occasionally jerky, and often jump-cut sequences. On top of that, McLean had violated a fundamental CBC rule by agreeing beforehand that the Prime Minister's Office would have editing rights. A number of cuts were made after several screenings by the Prime Minister's Office, including by Pearson himself. There was still some niggling about more cuts when the CBC said the film would be shown as is, with or without the prime minister's final approval. That distressed Pearson's advisers, some of whom demanded more cuts.

CBC officials in Toronto and Ottawa, most of whom had screened the film several times, wanted one last viewing before giving their final go-ahead. Suddenly, they decided the film was technically inferior, a conclusion with which Ouimet vociferously agreed, and its air date was cancelled. "Pearson thought that was crazy . . . the worst of all worlds from our standpoint," says Dick O'Hagan, who was then the prime minister's press aide. The Opposition was handed a political issue and the story, complete with overtones of prime ministerial interference, inevitably leaked to the media. A major storm broke in the House of Commons.

"The CBC has allowed itself to become the government's catspaw," Diefenbaker charged, and the House reverberated with accusations of censorship and political pressure.

"There was no interference whatsoever," Pearson said. But to still the parliamentary and media furore, he called the CBC president to plead that the film be broadcast. Ouimet recounted the conversation as follows:

"Pearson: It's Lester Pearson speaking.

"Ouimet: How do you do, sir?

"Pearson: You probably know what happened in the House this morning.

"Ouimet: Yes, I do.

"Pearson: Then you know the leader of the Opposition, Mr. John Diefenbaker, has asked me to use my good offices to try to get you to release this film.

"Ouimet: I know you were asked and that you would do your best. Are you calling me as the prime minister of Canada, sir?

"Pearson: Oh no!

"Ouimet: Are you calling me as head of the Liberal Party?

"Pearson: Oh no!

"Ouimet: Then you must be calling me in a personal capacity.

"Pearson: Yes.

"Ouimet: We will consider your views in that light. Thank you very much."

Ouimet did consider and then said no to Pearson. The program was not shown until 1969, after Ouimet had resigned from the CBC, Pearson was gone as prime minister, and new program leaders had taken over in Toronto.

The parliamentary furore over "Mr. Pearson," the headlines, the agitated producers, and the defensive management were all a prelude to the final chapter in Alphonse Ouimet's star-crossed role as president of the CBC.

Ouimet was a centralist who wanted operational program control in

Ottawa. This contrasted sharply with Fowler's recommended decentralization and transference of program control to Toronto for the English network and Montreal for the French. At the heart of their argument was a question that had bedevilled CBC since its beginning: Who had control?

When Augustin Frigon was general manager he, in Ouimet's words, "tended to be ignored and resented in Toronto . . . so Bushnell operated pretty well on his own." It had been much the same under Gladstone Murray. Ouimet had been determined to change that, and when he became general manager he moved most of his senior officials to Ottawa from Toronto and Montreal over their strong objections. In Montreal, programmers and executives feared Ouimet's centralization would undermine creative freedom and Quebec's bid to break out of English domination. Quebec intellectuals and journalists were alarmed, and Ouimet had lunch with writers André Laurendeau and Pierre Laporte "to try to reassure them regarding the future of French Canada, which they considered was endangered by such a centralizing move."

In Toronto, the ever-present smouldering resentment against Ottawa and the CBC head office's remoteness from the creative heart of CBC English programming intensified among both program executives and producers when they heard Ouimet's plan. One of the Toronto senior executives at the time, Keith Morrow, later noted, "Anyone who lives in Ottawa in the milieu of head office gets farther and farther away from programming and casts themselves in the role of second guessers. . . . The longer the umbilical cord, the less confidence."

Sensing the resistance to his centralizing plans, Ouimet pulled back. As he later said, "It did not take very long before practical difficulties of communication and the refusal of leadership by Toronto Supervisors forced us to move both [Bud] Walker and [Jean-Marie] Beaudet to Toronto. We were convinced that as Head Office trained people . . . they would not have any great difficulties in ensuring that Toronto operations would be in conformity with Corporate plans and philosophy. It did not take more than two months, however, before our two new emissaries from Ottawa to Toronto began to behave exactly as if they had been part of the Toronto team all their lives."

When Ouimet pulled his corporate reorganizing plan out of his presidential hat in August 1959, it was another, more rigid centralization scheme to provide, he said, "much stronger control and leadership for Ottawa." But the move angered producers in Toronto who had lost none of their anti-Ottawa, anti-head office animus. They also feared that program decisions taken in Ottawa would be far more susceptible to political interference.

The Fowler Committee had heard powerful denunciations of senior Ottawa management from the producers, and in its report it noted, "CBC Television has been marred by a smouldering dissatisfaction among producers. . . . Occasionally this slow fire bursts in a blaze of resentment. . . . The blaze subsides but the dissatisfaction of the producers smoulders on."

This malaise among the producers was, however, dismissed by Ouimet, who resented the producers talking to Fowler and denied their accusations. Ideally, he wanted a single, fluently bilingual person to be in charge of both the English and French networks, but neither Bushnell nor his successor, Briggs, could speak French, and so he opted to have a chief operating officer for each network: the onetime announcer Bud Walker for the English and the veteran journalist and war correspondent Marcel Ouimet for the French. Marcel Ouimet was no relation to Alphonse, which was evident from his totally different personality. Both Walker and Marcel Ouimet were essentially radio men of the prewar generation.

"The system worked well, at first," Alphonse Ouimet said later. "But the particular hazards of the '60s, that is, the general contestation and crisis of authority, the permissive society, weak parliaments and odd ministers, separatism, the impact of the BBG, second station competition, and the advent of the second network, so complicated the operations of the Corporation that leadership from Ottawa became more and more difficult."

What also complicated the system was one of the oddest, most eclectic collections of management talent seen this side of *Dr. Strangelove*; a disparate group of defiant barons, war lords, courtiers, and discontented, frustrated executives, most of whom Ouimet did not really know or understand.

At the top was Captain Briggs, the executive vice-president Ouimet never wanted and never liked. "I might as well say," he later commented, "that I did not agree with the style of my executive vice-president, but there was nothing I could do about it. He had been appointed in spite of my protests." Sitting in his sixth floor office, decorated like a ship's cabin with naval portraits and paraphernalia, "the old man," who was in his late fifties, fired off bolts of authoritarianism, occasionally went down to the basement cafeteria to mix with "all hands," and was feared by executives and ridiculed by producers. Ross McLean called Briggs "an idiot" and Patrick Watson said he was "poison." While he was never vindictive, he was brutally open with his criticisms and unswervingly loyal to Ouimet despite their strained relationship. He gained only modest sympathy for his increasingly painful and crippling arthritis. Briggs had, however, the no-nonsense qualities the Diefenbaker government had wanted when it appointed him.

The man running the English network, Bud Walker, was scared to death of Briggs. As Walker told Ouimet, "Life was not easy under Briggs' authority." Briggs considered Walker disloyal for giving his revealing "Preview Commentary" testimony to the parliamentary committee that had sunk Ernie Bushnell. Briggs was especially unhappy because he had expressly asked Walker not to testify, but at the time Briggs was only Walker's colleague, not his boss. Walker was a handsome, free-drinking, affable dandy with the reputation of being a lady-killer. "When Walker came to town, the secretaries would scurry," says one senior secretary from that time. Producers considered him intellectually shallow with little knowledge of television production. One of Walker's colleagues, Harry Boyle, says part of Walker's corporate success was his friendship with Ouimet. "Ouimet was very lonely and Walker really sucked up to him."

Walker was, indeed, one of the few of his executives that Ouimet admired. They had travelled to Europe together to study TV in preparation for its introduction in Canada, got on well together, and Ouimet appreciated that Walker was an organization man who would take orders. "I do not think he would consider himself as an intellectual," said Ouimet, adding that his advice always "seemed well thought out, completely sound, practical and lucid." And it usually was what Ouimet wanted to hear.

"No one is perfect," Ouimet said in a comment that summed up his attitude toward Walker. "But I am convinced that ... Walker did as good a job as anyone else available at the time."

It was not a feeling shared by the producers, most of Walker's colleagues, and by most politicians he dealt with. Walker had a reciprocating low opinion of most of his colleagues. In a remarkably frank conversation with Ouimet which, in retirement, Ouimet detailed for former associates, he and Walker tore apart just about every one of their senior colleagues, characterizing them as ineffective and incompetent, or drunk, disorderly, and disloyal.

As a senior executive, Gene Hallman, who had been a key supporter of the public affairs department during the "Preview Commentary" crisis and who was a brilliant program developer, got little respect from Walker. Ouimet noted that "Walker still holds Hallman responsible for many of the Corporation's problems with its Toronto dissenters. He also talked about his indecision, his ineffectiveness as an executive, his politicking, his disloyalty to his colleagues, his reported encouragement to rebels, etc." Years later, long after Walker came under public attack for his own deficiencies and was removed from his job, Hallman went on to a distinguished career as head of the English Radio and TV networks in an expanded version of the job Walker had held. But he, too, eventually fell victim to a later CBC president.

In his conversation with Ouimet, Walker also attacked his own deputy in Toronto, Keith Morrow, who at one point Ouimet had seriously considered as a possible overall boss of the English networks instead of Walker. But Walker complained that Morrow's thinking had become erratic and distracted. To others, however, it appeared that Walker's distress with Morrow stemmed from the fact that Morrow's sympathies lay more with the creative programmers in Toronto than with the bureaucrats in Ottawa.

Walker's key program director in Toronto, who worked under Morrow, was Doug Nixon, whose mercurial creativity and lifestyle affronted Ouimet. "Doug Nixon ... had started out very well," Ouimet said, "but had ended up being very much involved in illicit relations complicated by a drinking problem." "A rather regular drunk," said Ross McLean. "He was untidy in that aspect of his life." Nixon was a programming wizard, whose ideas, enthusiasms, and support for producers and contemporary programming continually plunged him into bureaucratic hot water. He ran into trouble, as well, with some Toronto public affairs producers because of his emphasis on entertainment shows, especially American. He loved the glamour of Hollywood, and his partying during his annual trips to buy American network shows in Hollywood became legendary.

Nixon was not alone in his difficulties. Women and booze became such problems that, as a senior secretary recalls, at one point a directive was issued for Toronto executives to get rid of their mistresses.

At first Ouimet credited chief news editor Bill Hogg with carrying out his job "with distinction," but then complained that when Hogg took on overall responsibilities for both news and public affairs, his health deteriorated, his wife got sick, and he lacked strength. "Walker and I consider that his appointment had been a mistake," Ouimet noted.

The most vitriolic Walker-Ouimet assessment of their senior staff was reserved for the head of the public affairs department, Reeves Haggan, who had succeeded Frank Peers and Bernard Trotter. Haggan, they moaned, refused to follow instructions and couldn't manage difficult producers. They felt he was a traitor to management because of his strong sympathies for producers and the intellectual and creative community, and his endorsation of controversial, even provocative, programming. Ouimet said Haggan encouraged "open revolt" among producers and actively plotted against senior Ottawa management.

There were also strains within the Ottawa management. Aside from problems with Briggs and Hallman, Ouimet and Walker faced the barely hidden hostility of the vice-president of the French network, Marcel Ouimet, and the vice-president of regional broadcasting, Charles Jennings. Both were fun-loving men, whose roots lay in programming and who escaped what they felt was the oppressive head office atmosphere to long lunches together, featuring double martinis in huge goblets, where they were joined occasionally by Walker. During these lunches they would pour out their bitterness and frustration. "When he'd be drunk, Charles would be very wise," Ouimet's aide Bill Armstrong remembers. "He'd go home after lunch. Marcel would go back to the office and start on the scotch."

Marcel Ouimet sublimated his frustrations by concentrating on what he feared was a growing separatist sympathy in the French network.

Jennings became increasingly involved in the Ottawa social scene, propelled by his ebullient personality and his wife's money. He was highly
visible among Ottawa politicians and senior mandarins and became the
most effective lobbyist CBC ever had in Ottawa, with the exception of
Alan Plaunt in the mid-1930s.

Ron Fraser and Jimmy Gilmore, the other vice-presidents, were basi-
cally non-drinking "goody goodies" who tut-tutted about Jennings' and
Marcel Ouimet's alcoholic antics and loyally came running when Al
Ouimet called.

The mistrust among CBC senior management, the mine field that lay
between programmers and bureaucrats, and the antipathy between
Ottawa and Toronto lent an appropriate cacophony to the anti-
establishment turmoil among many producers. It set the stage for a
mortal confrontation of a new generation of TV producers versus an old
generation of radio bureaucrats – a confrontation that would explode
into nationwide headlines, destroy a CBC management, wipe out the
CBC's most successful creative team, and endanger a government. Nothing was ever quite the same again after the crisis of "This Hour Has Seven
Days."

14

The Glory and the Hell
of "Seven Days"

What would become the most talked about program in Canadian broadcast history had its genesis on a big rock on the shore of Go Home Lake in Muskoka, a two hour drive north of Toronto. Patrick Watson and Douglas Leiterman, two mutually admiring, brilliant new generation producers both had cottages on the lake. One summer afternoon in 1962, they sat in the sun swapping ideas on how to make informational programs "more compelling." They had talked about this many times before as they worked together on documentaries and programs such as Ross McLean's "Close-Up," but this time, their ideas began to crystallize. "Patrick and I . . . talked about how exciting it would be if somebody could produce a television program which would be so compelling that nobody could not watch it whenever it was on," Leiterman recalled years later, "which would occupy prime time on Sunday night . . . which could be so daring that it would not fear to attack any subject, which would become a kind of television ombudsman and which would somehow fulfil that tremendous potential all of us had seen in television and which to that time had never really been fulfilled in current affairs. . . . Entertaining and exciting, fast moving, well-paced [with] a lot of variety."

As the lake water lapped their rock, Watson and Leiterman grew excited at the prospect of a public affairs show with, as Watson later said, "the same kind of power as the Western and the cops and robbers shows. . . . Nobody had ever done a television public affairs program whose first intention, and first priority, was to get the biggest damned audience possible."

The bad boy of Canadian television, producer Ross McLean, had, in fact, sought big audiences with his pioneering, provocative style of public affairs programming, but Watson and Leiterman wanted to go much farther than McLean had dared. Still, they wanted his help in developing the style of their dream program. Because McLean was still on the outs with CBC management, Watson and Leiterman didn't put him on the payroll when "Seven Days" began, but instead paid his wife, comedian Jean Templeton. "Ross was an irrepressible busybody who never did anything but listen and watch everybody's programs," says Watson. "He was a superb teacher who didn't open his mouth unless he had a phrase ready. He was very complicated, tyrannical, and incredibly insensitive to other people's feelings. . . . He was a very insecure man. I both liked and was afraid of and disliked Ross, but he was for me, a guide, a teacher and an uncle."

Another major influence in shaping their thinking was the BBC satirical current affairs blockbuster, "That Was The Week That Was," which had achieved phenomenal popularity in Britain. *New York Herald Tribune* critic John Crosby called it, "The best TV show in the world." TW3, as it was nicknamed, combined biting wit, music, sketches, and interviews to reach the biggest audience ever achieved for a British current affairs series. But it soon became too hot for the BBC to handle and was killed after two years – a bad omen for what Watson and Leiterman were planning.

Marshall McLuhan and his "global village" concept was another unseen hand in the birth of the Watson's and Leiterman's baby. "Television is essentially a sensation instrument," Watson, a McLuhanite, once said in a *Globe and Mail* article, "a device for communicating, or inducing, sense impressions. It works on the senses. Marshall McLuhan says it's tactile." Television is "cool," McLuhan said.

Watson and Leiterman believed McLuhan's dictum that the medium is the message and agreed with his ponderous profundity that "the implosion of electric technology is transmogrifying literate, fragmented man into a complex and depth-structured human being with a deep emotional awareness of his complete interdependence with all of humanity."

Watson and Leiterman knew a picture was worth much more than a thousand words and together they rode this belief in the theatre of journalism into broadcasting history. They fit together perfectly. "It was a kind of love affair, Doug and I," Watson muses nearly three decades later. "We were on the phone all the time and Doug came to accept my notion that television was theatre."

Leiterman was thirty-seven, a loner, a non-smoking, non-drinking Christian Scientist who had studied economics, government, and Soviet affairs at Harvard on a Nieman Fellowship. He was a onetime police reporter and political correspondent for Southams who passionately believed in making society better. He became a prize-winning documentary maker for the CBC, producing vivid portraits of political leaders and incisive examinations of such things as poverty in Brazil, segregation in the American South, and the "wasteland" of television. He was the more pragmatic one of the two dreamers.

The thirty-five-year-old Watson was congenial and relaxed and had studied philosophy and linguistics. His first on-air role was as a thirteen-year-old playing "Jake," the villain in the CBC Radio series "The Kootenay Kid," and then he was on teenage radio shows for CFRB in Toronto. At age twenty-five, he was a freelance host on the CBC-TV program "Junior Magazine" and, he says, "I just became absolutely intoxicated with television." Watson gave up working on his PhD, took a CBC-TV training course, and was hired for various production jobs, including directing "The National" with anchor Larry Henderson and producing the "Mr. Fix It" do-it-yourself TV show. He was drawn to Ross McLean's iconoclastic production genius, and after working with McLean on "Close-Up" he went to Ottawa in 1960 to produce "Inquiry," an earnest weekly public affairs discussion program on Parliament and government activities. Former CBC chairman Davie Dunton was his first program host. Watson lusted after a more dynamic program, however, one that would break through broadcasting traditions. He wanted a leading edge public affairs show that would use McLuhan's ideas, show business techniques, controversial topics, and even some of the magic tricks Watson had learned as a child and still practised.

In January 1963, Watson and Leiterman presented to their bosses their ideas for a new show. "We propose," they said, "a new kind of journalism which will bring the whole range of human experience to Canadians with the impact of live-picture television; which will bring public affairs to ordinary citizens whose normal viewing is Ed Sullivan and 'Bonanza'; and which will, if successful, become mandatory Sunday night viewing for a large segment of the nation." Over the next year, they refined their ideas and wrote more "pretentious and purple prose," as Watson describes it, and were given a go-ahead for the fall of 1964.

In their determination to use entertainment to capture large audiences, Watson and Leiterman were echoing the comment of the *Spectator* of 1711 which said, "Whosoever would influence the public must first learn to entertain it." They were reformers who wanted to change society; to encourage Canadians to throw off the shackles of old values and traditions and embrace the new, liberating, permissive, questioning and questing mores of the new generation. "We were McLuhanites," said "Seven Days" reporter Larry Zolf. "And we really believed . . . you could actually get a revolution in the streets and change society through the boob tube; that people would sit in their living rooms and get so outraged at whatever indignities were being shown them on the air that they would end the Vietnam War, bring peace and security and happiness."

"We believed in change," Leiterman later told Judy LaMarsh, who was the minister responsible for the CBC during the "Seven Days" years. "We thought this society needed many things it wasn't getting. That a lot of people were being hurt by this society. That the machinery to bring their grievances to public or government attention was not available. That politicians needed a kind of special examination that they were rarely getting in television and radio."

Leiterman's mother had wanted him to go into politics, but he was more interested in using television as an instrument of political activism. "The basic thing," he said, "was that we were not afraid of controversy. In fact, we felt this was vital and essential [to] stir up all pressure groups. . . .

331

stir up for sure the politicians and the government, and particularly the CBC brass who over the years have had an unenviable reputation for having their heads buried in the sand . . . so they won't hear the controversy and won't see it, won't smell it and won't be disturbed by it."

"Doug was trained as a journalist and was more rigid in the principles and practices of journalism than I was," says Watson. "But he was very much interested in putting journalism into a theatrical framework. I never considered myself and still don't consider myself to be a journalist. I always thought of myself as a theatrical producer putting journalism into a theatrical frame. I thought of it as non-fiction theatre." He and Leiterman would spend hours experimenting with ideas to dramatize their programs: staging techniques, camera angles, lighting, getting people to smoke in the studio to produce a hazy atmosphere, and using, as Watson describes it, "a shotgun microphone with its penile thrust right in the shot aiming right at the guy being interviewed." He and Leiterman dismissed "the old myths of objectivity and studious neutrality" for journalism, "myths" that Alphonse Ouimet and Dan McArthur considered immutable values.

The two producers were lucky in their immediate bosses, all of whom were dedicated, ex-program people and all of whom were at odds with their superiors in Ottawa. The head of public affairs was Reeves Haggan, a former program organizer, lawyer, and business executive, and a managerial loose cannon who encouraged the adventurousness of his producers. The Belfast-born forty-one-year-old Haggan was a convivial colleague, a friend of many politicians and those he called "persons of consequence," and a man who loved having power and influence. He approved the Watson-Leiterman proposal, as did his bosses, Keith Morrow and Doug Nixon, both of whom liked the idea of what Nixon called "a popular, shit-disturbing show with a serious purpose."

The Watson-Leiterman dragon-slaying approach, however, deeply offended Alphonse Ouimet's sense of journalistic responsibility. Ouimet also despised the flashy program style espoused by Watson and Leiterman. "This is exactly the creed which motivates Madison Avenue and commercial broadcasting entertainment generally," he said later. "It is a socially reprehensible approach for them and even more condemnable for public service broadcasting such as the CBC to apply it to the coverage of current affairs."

It was clear, therefore, right from the very beginning that Watson and Leiterman were on a collision course with senior management. It became even clearer that the CBC had a tiger by the tail when a press preview of "This Hour Has Seven Days" was held in late September 1964, eight days before the launch of the program. It featured snippets of program items to come, including a wicked satirical sketch on John Diefenbaker in full oratorical flight with quivering jowls, waving hands, and wagging head, all moving in time to music; and interviews with the mother of Kennedy assassin Lee Harvey Oswald, with American Nazi leader George Lincoln Rockwell, and with Justice Minister Guy Favreau on an Ottawa crisis. There was a sampling of a report on The Beatles performing in Toronto, a lampoon on the Cold War, and glimpses of the issue of homosexuality.

"A TV SHOCKER," headlined the *Ottawa Journal*. "STORM BREWING OVER TV SHOW," said the *Ottawa Citizen*. "CBC TO OFFER SHOCKER SERIES MOCKING CANADA'S LEADERS," the Vancouver *Province* headlined.

"I can see no good coming out of it," warned Social Credit MP Bert Leboe, a comment that captured the apprehensions of the Opposition, the government, and CBC management. When the program officially began on October 4, 1964, its mocking, popularizing style, so unlike most broadcast journalism, stunned viewers. As well as stories on Kennedy's assassination and on the long-missing, corrupt seaman's union leader Hal Banks, there was a salute to Harpo Marx and one to The Beatles, an interview with the mother of a murdered U.S. civil rights worker, a report on a plane crash, and a Second City satirical skit. It was all mixed together with upbeat music, fast cuts, and brisk scripting.

"Phenomenal . . . energy, vitality, intelligence," said the *Vancouver Sun*. "A show that can hardly be ignored," said the *Calgary Herald*. With Watson and Leiterman producing, hosts for the show were Canada's distinguished radio actor John Drainie, who brought to his role Canadian rectitude and impeccable professionalism, and McGill University history professor Laurier LaPierre, who brought neither. What LaPierre did bring, however, was emotion, excitement, and a highly evident, passionate commitment to right wrongs.

Drainie and LaPierre had been chosen as hosts after many auditions and turn-downs. Among those considered were a young Peter Gzowski; an even younger Peter Jennings; critic Robert Fulford; the future Margaret Trudeau's father, James Sinclair, a onetime federal Liberal cabinet minister; Bernie Braden, a Canadian star on the BBC; and Pierre Trudeau. Trudeau was tempted by the allure of what he called "a great soap box" but decided he was more of a writer than a performer, although he said he would be willing to be an occasional freelance interviewer for the program.

With its irreverence and impudence, the first program set the pattern of controversy that would engulf "Seven Days" for the two years of its life. The government complained about the unfair editing of Justice Minister Favreau's interview; Diefenbaker loyalists raged about the unfair portrayal of The Chief; there were cries of "pornography"; and CBC head office killed a spoof on the Queen's visit to Canada.

The royalty-loving Captain Briggs, on hand when the Queen arrived in Quebec to begin her visit that fall, was appalled at hearing that the CBC planned to cover demonstrations that might occur against Her Majesty. He forbade any such live coverage and banned "Seven Days" reporter Larry Zolf's man-in-the-street interviews on the Queen, most of which had been negative. Also banned was a "Seven Days" satirical skit portraying the Queen delivering her annual Christmas message dressed as a mop-holding cockney in curlers.

The rumpled and rotund Reeves Haggan called Briggs' ban "a drop of poison." The "Seven Days" team did, however, slip through one impudent reference to the Queen in the program in a skit on birth control pills in which pills for royalty were coloured pink with Her Majesty's picture on them.

For the rest of the 1964-65 season "Seven Days" rocked the country, the government, and CBC Ottawa with scandals, sensations, sex, political intrigue, injustice, and a new style of interviewing called the "Hot Seat." The interviewers would provocatively grill politicians in a Perry Mason style in the interests of "illuminating theatre." The interviewers, usually host Laurier LaPierre and reporter Warner Troyer, but sometimes others such as Pierre Trudeau, would prepare extensively to entrap the unwary victim. He or she would be lit, positioned, and shot in an unflattering way that sometimes produced beads of sweat, furtive glances, and verbal stumbles. At times the questions were savagely hurled by the "Seven Days" inquisitors. Some interviewees became flustered, badgered into imprudent or revealing remarks, so much so that Lester Pearson eventually banned all cabinet ministers from being interviewed on the program. "He had a great respect for serious journalism . . . and was deeply committed to the principle of public broadcasting," Pearson's former press aide Dick O'Hagan says. "But I think his nature rebelled against what he saw as a combination of presentational gimmicks." Pearson had been hounded by the "Red Hunters" of the McCarthy era, accused of abetting a communist spy when he was stationed in Washington and so had a special abhorrence of public bullying.

But the "Seven Days" antics made rivetting viewing and audience numbers skyrocketed. "This hour has oomph!" said *Ottawa Citizen* TV critic Frank Penn.

There was an uproar in the House of Commons when John Diefenbaker, who was a constantly inviting target for "Seven Days" barbs, demanded a parliamentary committee investigation of the CBC president. The former speaker, Conservative MP Marcel Lambert, denounced the program and the CBC for concentrating on "anything which is wrong, or a deviation or detracts from common decent morality." "Filth!" said other MPs, and Parliament reverberated with charges against "Seven Days" of glorifying, as one MP said, "perversion, pornography, free love, blasphemy, dope, violence, crime and Nazism."

"I'm all for sensationalism, but only if it is responsible sensationalism," Leiterman told a *Toronto Star* interviewer. Part of the sensationalism was the ombudsman role "Seven Days" undertook in its efforts to right wrongs such as its investigation into accusations against an Ontario United Church minister, Rev. Russell Horsburgh. He had been jailed for encouraging teenage sexual activity, but was later exonerated, in part because of the publicity given to the case by the program.

"Seven Days" also helped to free an Ontario farmer, Fred Fawcett, who had been improperly locked away in a hospital for the criminally insane. "Seven Days" producers got an interview with him in the hospital by posing as family friends and smuggling cameras into the hospital in a picnic basket. That upset Ouimet who felt that "CBC should do nothing illegal . . . even to achieve great goals." C B C head office demanded the item not be aired, but it was anyway. Bud Walker was uneasy with this self-appointed ombudsman role, feeling it was "a precarious business to always champion the underdog."

Not only were politicians, the government, much of established authority, and C B C senior executives shocked by the program, but public affairs producers in other programs were jealous of all the attention and money pouring into the Watson-Leiterman hour. "Seven Days" was spending about $32,000 a show, far more than any other public affairs program. There were also accusations of reckless journalism by C B C News reporters and editors whose union, the Canadian Wire Service Guild, charged "Seven Days" personnel with stealing news files and film. Calling the "Seven Days" staff "unscrupulous and diabolical," the union issued a six-page statement saying, "Our reputation for honesty, objectivity and balanced news coverage is being destroyed by charlatans with little or no experience. . . . The Guild demands that these wanderers of the night, these semi-professional merchants of the strong arm method of film procurement, these pilferers of pictures and slap-happy exponents of the sly lie, be forbidden access to the . . . offices occupied by the News Department."

Less colourfully, the *Globe and Mail* columnist George Bain denounced Watson and Leiterman for having "cut-rate courage to expose ersatz menaces." The *Globe*'s T V critic, Dennis Braithwaite, was more caustic. "'Seven Days,'" he said, was "a sort of intellectual 'Beverley Hillbillies'" filled with "pretension," "juvenile frivolity," and "vulgarity."

But Watson and Leiterman were having the time of their lives. "The intelligentsia call us cheap journalists, but Watson and I are as responsible a pair of birds as you could find," Leiterman declared. They had said their program would be "vital, compelling, probing, provocative and vigorous" and it was all that and more. The year before, the public affairs program "Horizon" in the same 10:00 P.M. Sunday slot had reached an audience of 650,000. Within its first month, "Seven Days" reached 1.6 million; more than 2 million by the end of the season; and would reach more than 3 million the following year, rivalling even N H L hockey, Don Messer, and Juliette in audience enjoyment. Clearly, Watson and Leiterman had achieved their goal of winning truck drivers and stenographers to their audience as well as the traditional public affairs program watchers.

No applause for the program could be heard, however, on the sixth floor of the CBC's head office in Ottawa. Bud Walker didn't know what had hit him. In a meeting before the program had gone on the air, he had assured Ouimet and his senior colleagues that there would be no trouble with the program. The minutes state, "Mr. Walker said he was satisfied this was going to be a responsible series." Now, he was being pummelled, caught between the quarterdeck furies of his boss, Captain Briggs, the confrontational defiance of Watson and Leiterman, and what he felt was the obstinacy of his Toronto managerial colleagues. "It was a constant battle between Toronto and Ottawa," says Keith Morrow.

Briggs kept demanding to know what was coming up on the program five or six days ahead of airtime, but in a current affairs show like "Seven Days," changes were made up to the last minute and no one knew for sure what would be in the show until shortly before it actually went on the air.

The minutes of meetings of the board, the president, and the program council all reflect the upper echelon's obsession with the program. "The program needs a man who is by temperament and interests not always seeking the sensational or picayune," state the minutes of one presidential meeting. Another said the program was "not up to the usual standards," and still another discussed "the apparent philosophical gap which exists between the Network program and supervisory staff and senior management at Head office. . . . [and] the 'avant garde' thinking at the program production and other levels which is in conflict with . . . traditional values held by senior management."

Ouimet decided a Toronto management shake-up was needed to make "Seven Days" more responsive to those "traditional values." Its boss in Toronto, Walker's deputy Keith Morrow, was considered to be too sympathetic to the programmers and antipathetic to head office, and so he was banished to the obscure role of special assistant in management studies at CBC Ottawa. Morrow's number-two man, Doug Nixon, saw his powers severely curtailed. Both had paid the price of their support for "Seven Days." Three new players were brought in to impose stronger controls on Watson and Leiterman. Bob McGall replaced Morrow as Walker's Toronto deputy; Marce Munro came in from Vancouver to run television; and chief news editor Bill Hogg, a strict journalistic tradition-alist, was named overall head of news and public affairs, specifically to ride herd on public affairs boss Reeves Haggan and his "Seven Days" pro-ducers. Bill Hogg memoed Haggan, "Renewed efforts must be made to improve communications up and down the 'Seven Days' line." Haggan was denied a pay raise because of, as Hogg told him, "Management's dis-pleasure [that] ... supervisory performance has not been up to expecta-tions."

Ouimet and Walker even spent five hours "really knocking it out," in Watson's words, with the two producers in a Westbury Hotel room in Toronto discussing program philosophy and ethics. While he accepted that there was a place for controversial journalism, Ouimet wanted it to be safe and responsible so that it, as the minutes of one president's meet-ing noted, "could bring credit to the Corporation without running too many risks and creating too much difficulty." Ouimet wanted tame, "common sense" controversy, quite different from the much more ram-bunctious, even outrageous controversy that Watson and Leiterman were producing.

That courting of controversy was evident in the first show of the new 1965-66 season. A satirical skit on Pope Paul II's visit to New York had him considering umpiring a baseball game and trying to get tickets to *Hello Dolly*. Ouimet, himself an agnostic, felt the skit was in bad taste and that it was dumb to offend a large portion of the population. Walker thought the skit was "quite stupid" and "highly offensive and improper."

"Only a public apology from the CBC could erase our memory of this insulting event," cried Toronto Liberal MP Ralph Cowan. The CBC obliged when Ron Fraser, vice-president and assistant to the president, issued a statement saying the CBC was "guilty of an error of program judgement.... This needlessly gave serious offence to the feelings of many of our viewers ... and we regret this mistake." Watson was furious because he and Leiterman had not been consulted on the apology. This, he said, "created a fair amount of bad blood between us and the president."

One major change in the new season was the appearance of Watson as co-host of the program with Laurier LaPierre. CBC's policy was that a producer could not be a host on his own program, and Watson had stayed off the air while he was co-producer with Leiterman during the first year of "Seven Days." But before the new season had begun, John Drainie had to leave because of cancer, from which he died the next year. Head office was pleased with Watson as co-host largely because it thought he was the leading activist of the program and that, with him no longer co-producer, the program would be more manageable. They were dead wrong, and it was years later that Ouimet said he had finally realized "Leiterman was the brain and strong man of 'Seven Days,' its unquestioned leader."

In the second season, Leiterman led his producers into ever-deeper hot water and ever-bigger audiences who were swept up by the most defiant, controversial program in the history of Canadian broadcasting. In one program, a confrontation was staged between Ku Klux Klan leaders and an associate of Martin Luther King. Wearing their pointed hats and white gowns, the two Southern racists flatly refused interviewer Robert Hoyt's on-air request that they shake hands with the black civil rights leader. It made dramatic television but CBC head office said it was "gimmicky."

"Sleazy, sensational and trivial," said the Ottawa sixth floor to the "Seven Days" racy portraits of movie sex goddess Ursula Andress and San Francisco topless go-go dancer Carol Doda. The focus was on Andress's nude *Playboy* pictures and on Doda's silicone-enhanced breasts, from which "Seven Days" said it drew social significance.

All the breasts, sex, scandals, confrontations, revelations, and pugnacious interviews were more than Briggs and Walker could stand. Briggs was especially irate about the show's references to homosexuality which, he felt, was not an issue in Canada. He claimed, by way of illustration, that there were no homosexuals at all in Saskatchewan. Briggs confronted Walker, demanding the program be neutered or killed. Walker himself was fed up with defiance from the program staff, lack of control by his managerial team in Toronto, and the thunderbolts from Briggs. What had begun as creative indigestion for him was now a bleeding ulcer. He wanted to kill the show, and he memoed Briggs in mid-November 1965, echoing Briggs' own feelings that the program was "arrogant," "yellow journalism," and "sensationalism."

"Can we go on any longer with this program?" he asked. "Can the Corporation's reputation for integrity, fairness and responsibility . . .

stand much more of this program? I think not. I feel we must seriously consider terminating this series within the next few weeks."

Walker's dyspepsia was aggravated by "Seven Days" host Laurier LaPierre who, in a talk to University of Manitoba students that fall, urged the firing of the CBC brass. "They will have to go," he said. "It's a miracle the show goes on at all. . . . They are always trying to censor 'This Hour'. . . . They are putting the screws on us. The end result would be to take us off the air."

Briggs and Walker went wild. LaPierre's later apology was "utter drivel" Walker said, and he began hardening his determination to move against the program. He examined Watson's, LaPierre's, and Leiterman's contracts, noting that LaPierre was paid $150 per program, Watson about $18,000 a year, and Leiterman just under $19,000.

Alphonse Ouimet, while distressed with the program, was also aware of its enormous popularity and shrank from the public and political fall-out that might descend on him if "This Hour Has Seven Days" were cancelled in mid-season. Besides, he was not as offended as Briggs and Walker about the program's anti-establishment style. In a speech that fall in Nigeria at a Commonwealth Broadcasting Conference, Ouimet had said, "We must never fear to show our present day society as it is, even if the picture may sometimes be disturbing or unpleasant. We must never fear to make room for new ideas, artistic innovations, new ways of thinking, notwithstanding the protests of certain elements in our audience."

Later, he commented, "I happened to feel that many of society's cherished conventions and traditions should have been buried long ago." What upset him, however, was "Seven Days"' defiance of CBC Ottawa's authority. He rejected Walker's proposal to kill the series outright and then directed him to put an ultimatum to Watson and Leiterman warning them that if they did not follow Ottawa orders, others would be found to produce the program. Ouimet described it as "a sanitary operation" and told Briggs and Walker to act immediately. Walker flew to Toronto and presented his ultimatum, which included an end to the "hot seat" interviews, an end to "irresponsibility," and an end to talking freely to the press about the program. Faced with "a list of our sins" and threats of cancellation, Leiterman reluctantly agreed to tone it down. "I personally felt it was a dishonourable acceptance," Leiterman later said. "We decided, however, that we really had no alternative. . . . We thought the best thing to do was to accept what was demanded of us and do the best we could." But Leiterman's accommodating comments belied his determination. He was prepared to take one step back while planning two steps forward. When Ouimet realized this, he called Leiterman "devious" and an "evil genius."

Walker left his Toronto boardroom meeting with the "Seven Days" personnel in good spirits, feeling he had done what nobody else in management could do: get "Seven Days" to toe the line. His euphoria didn't last long. Even with the compromises Leiterman had agreed to, the program continued to stir controversy, and Walker told Bill Hogg, "Please plan on wrapping up the series permanently at the end of the season – mid-May." Walker complained to Hogg about the program's "conscious non-conformism with shooting down the establishment, with journalistic crusading." He also told Hogg that Watson's contract as host would not be renewed, although he left the door slightly ajar for "some kind of association later on," and Leiterman, he said, would be reassigned to producing documentaries.

Watson and Leiterman knew none of this and had been encouraged in their battle with management by the release of the Fowler Committee report in the fall of 1965, which had been highly critical of CBC management and supportive of both producers and controversial programming. Ouimet was furious at what he believed was Fowler's encouragement of rebellious programmers. "It was undoubtedly the most compelling encouragement to stand against Management they could possibly have received," Ouimet later noted, "an exhortation to continue the good fight. . . . The whole Fowler Report was so obviously another hatchet job on Management that the 'Seven Days' people can hardly be blamed for believing that the continuous erosion of Corporate authority . . . would have left the Corporation pretty well at their mercy. . . . Had [they] not been convinced by the Fowler Report that Management was already down, they would not have taken the risk of a revolt."

The corporate "housekeepers," however, were resolved to get rid of what Ouimet was now calling this "splitting headache" and "problem child," "Seven Days."

Ouimet was confident he would be able to contain any outcry from an

end-of-season cancellation of the program because of the strong government backing he felt he had. He had just been reappointed by Lester Pearson to another seven-year term as CBC president, and that fall had also
seen the Liberals re-elected, although still with a minority government.
One result of the election was a cabinet shuffle which saw the rambunctious Judy LaMarsh named as secretary of state, the minister responsible
for the CBC. She was everything Ouimet wasn't: emotional, disorga-
nized, hard-drinking, heavy-smoking, party-loving, and a political mav-
erick. She also knew and admired the creative brilliance of Watson and
Leiterman. "My view of the program is quite enthusiastic," LaMarsh told
reporters. Although Ouimet didn't realize it as 1965 ended, she and he
were heading for a fatal collision in mutual hostility, even hatred.

Through the winter of 1966, however, Ouimet's most visible adversary was "Seven Days." The program continued to generate headlines,
protests, bureaucratic frustrations, huge audiences, and even foreign
critical acclaim. Writing about the program in the *New York Times* at the
end of January, TV critic Jack Gould said, "There is no doubt that Canadians are journalistically adventurous in a way that does them proud."

Larry Zolf was particularly "adventurous" when he sought an interview with former associate defence minister Pierre Sévigny, a key player
in the Gerda Munsinger sex and spies scandal of the Diefenbaker era.
When, with cameras rolling, Zolf knocked on the front door of Sévigny's
Montreal home, the one-legged, much wounded, much decorated Second World War hero raised his cane and whacked the intrepid "Seven
Days" reporter over the shoulders and chased him to his car. Sévigny then
called Judy LaMarsh demanding she stop "Seven Days" from showing
any of the film taken. She discussed it with Lester Pearson who told her to
do "nothing," and nothing was done. The "Seven Days" producers, however much they thought the film was great theatre, decided it would be
legally prudent to not show it.

The Vietnam War was another area for "adventurous" programming.
Interviews with anti-war advocates such as Bertrand Russell and skits
lampooning the Americans outraged head office and many Conservative
politicians. Walker was especially upset about the satirical skits, saying in
a memo that he wanted to stop them because "it is quite improper to
satirize war." Peter Campbell, number-two man in the public affairs

department, a former Canadian diplomat in Southeast Asia, and a classical scholar, begged to differ. "War," he wrote back, "has been long established in the tradition of Western civilization as a subject for satirical treatment. . . . The great comic dramatist Aristophanes wrote a trilogy lampooning war." Walker, who didn't have a clue and didn't care who Aristophanes was, continued to complain.

An interview with White House aide McGeorge Bundy raised an international ruckus when Bundy protested that unfair editing made him look more hawk-like on Vietnam than he was. Only eight minutes of the forty-three-minute interview were shown, and the White House issued the full transcript to defend its anger and distributed it in Canada as well as in Washington. Saying the CBC was "untrustworthy," the state department retaliated by imposing a ban on CBC News in Washington, cutting CBC off from official sources of information for several months.

The most vivid anti-war statement made by the "Seven Days" producers was "Mills of the Gods," an hour-long documentary by Beryl Fox, who later married Leiterman. It was one of the series of documentaries that filled every fourth "Seven Days" program, and it was unforgettable. The screen came alive with images of American soldiers and Vietnamese, devastated villages, foreboding jungles, and the victims of war. The documentary was shown on the BBC, on the educational network in the United States, and had theatrical release. *New York Times* critic Jack Gould said it was, "not the shrill cry of the pacifist. It was a chilling poem of resignation to the inevitability of man's inhumanity to man." Novelist Hugh MacLellan called it "the most beautiful, disturbing and moving work of art I have ever seen on television." Even Walker told Fox, "The film was tremendous." Later, however, he criticised the film as being part of "Seven Days"' "misleading" and "snide poker" at the United States.

In the spring of 1966, the most dramatic, most publicized single moment in "Seven Days"' history was Laurier LaPierre's tear. He later claimed he was fired for crying on air when head office used his tear as proof positive of his uncontrollable bias. The tear came when LaPierre was on air, watching an interview with the mother of a fourteen-year-old boy, Stephen Truscott, who had been sentenced to hang for the rape and murder of a twelve-year-old girl, although his sentence had later been reduced to life in prison. Questions had been raised about his conviction, and after the highly emotional interview with Mrs. Truscott ended, LaPierre rubbed a tear away from his eye. In a hoarse voice, he connected the sentence of hanging to an upcoming debate in the House of Commons on capital punishment. There was no doubt where LaPierre stood on the issue. "I still have goose pimples when I think about it," LaPierre says. Three years later, Truscott was released on parole after ten years in prison. Ouimet suspected there was more show business than real emotion in LaPierre's tear and he said it demonstrated LaPierre's "unprofessional" behaviour. "I always suspected there had been no tear to wipe off but that, as the good actor he is, he had made the quick tear-wiping gesture to heighten further the highly emotional charge of the particular broadcast," Ouimet said. He later regretted voicing his criticism of the tear. "I might as well come out against motherhood and the monarchy," he said. "My blunder cost me unending headlines right across the country and overnight I became a cruel and cold-blooded technological tyrant who refused its staff the right to cry."

As instructed by Walker, Bill Hogg had told Reeves Haggan in December that "Seven Days" would not be renewed for the following season. But Haggan had not told Watson and Leiterman. He said he was not "a drain pipe" for senior management and, besides, he thought Ottawa probably would change its mind. He was right, for in January, Hogg advised him that "Seven Days" would be renewed, but not with Watson and LaPierre as hosts. Again, Haggan didn't relay this information to "Seven Days" because he thought it would destroy the morale of the program staff, and he also thought CBC Ottawa might well change its mind yet again.

Meanwhile, a new program proposal had come forward for a show called "Quarterly Report," a series of public affairs programs produced jointly by the CBC French and English networks and planned to start in the fall. Patrick Watson had been suggested as executive producer for the English team, but Ouimet wasn't sure it was a good idea. "We were delighted with this new opportunity to put his talents to good use, but we obviously didn't want to repeat the experience of 'Seven Days,'" Ouimet said. He asked Walker to go to Toronto to talk to Watson about it.

Walker felt he could solve two problems with one move: get Watson off "Seven Days" and break up the Watson-Leiterman team; and then get the obviously talented Watson to run what would be a "safe" centennial-year CBC showpiece.

Walker and Watson had diametrically opposed agendas for their meeting, and the CBC vice-president was walking into a trap that would, within weeks, spin him into a name-calling, ruinous public donnybrook. He wanted what he affably told Watson was "a man-to-man chat" and assurance that Watson would behave if he were to produce "Quarterly Report." He assumed, incorrectly, that Watson knew that his and LaPierre's "Seven Days" contracts were not being renewed. Watson, for his part, was prepared for a showdown over "Seven Days" and, if necessary, to trap Walker into self-incriminating statements that could be used if open hostilities broke out. Walker was walking into a powderkeg carrying a lit match.

They met in the early afternoon of Tuesday, April 6, 1966, in an office in "The Kremlin," the nickname for the building housing CBC Toronto executives at the time. "You seem to be an angry young man, a man with a chip on his shoulder," Walker said as he outlined why Watson and LaPierre's contracts weren't being renewed and talked of Watson's possible involvement in "Quarterly Report." Watson was less interested in the latter subject than he was the former. "I'm arbitrarily severing the relations between you and 'Seven Days,'" Walker said first to Watson's surprise and then to his quiet delight when he realized it was a clear violation of the producers' agreement with the CBC for a vice-president to shortcircuit the executive producer and directly fire a program employee.

Watson knew he'd "got him," and as Walker talked on, Watson, with what he called "controlled fury," said little and scribbled Walker's words in a pad on his knee. Walker didn't seem to notice the note-taking. "Anti-President, anti-management, perhaps . . . anti-CBC. . . . We believe you to be not one of us. . . . We are afraid you are not with us and I don't want anyone in the CBC who is not with us. . . . I do not know whether you believe in Canada or not." Walker mentioned LaPierre was being removed because "he's clearly not with us either and we cannot afford the luxury of a person whose feelings are worn on his sleeve." Watson's notes also quote Walker as saying that " 'Seven Days' brought out the bad side of Patrick Watson."

As Watson wrote down Walker's incendiary comments, his fury turned to increasing confidence and "a sweet sense of calm." He knew he had enough on Walker to "destroy him." "I quite frankly manipulated that conversation for all it was worth," Watson says. To Walker, however, Watson seemed almost contrite and agreeable, and they smiled and shook hands at the end of the conversation. Walker was sure Watson had learned his lesson and would be a well-behaved executive producer of "Quarterly Report," doing what he was told. A contented Walker immediately flew back to Ottawa, went straight to Ouimet's office, and told him, "Al, we should see those fellows more often. I had the most gratifying talk with Pat. He's the nicest guy." He burbled on about how "sometimes we misjudge these people," that Watson was such "a great guy" who "now understands our problems and . . . will go along with our plans."

Back in Toronto, Watson was confident he had the goods on Walker. Years later he told Ouimet, "I fooled him. When he said I wouldn't be the host any more and that LaPierre wouldn't be host, I knew we had the handle we'd been looking for." Ouimet later wrote that Leiterman told him, "Look, Walker is a two-faced liar. Watson knew he couldn't trust him and he decided to fool him and Walker was so dumb he was completely taken." Ouimet ruefully agreed, saying "Watson had completely fooled Walker."

While Walker left the president's office daydreaming about Watson being co-operative, the "Seven Days" host was meeting colleagues, including Haggan, regaling them with his notes on the conversation. They agreed that Watson's and LaPierre's removal was simply a backdoor way of killing the program. That night Watson called Leiterman who was holidaying in Florida, and they agreed to hold off any specific action until Leiterman returned on April 13. "We did not have a revolt plan all mapped out, but . . . I quickly recognized the great possibilities of the cause Walker had just placed in my hands," Leiterman told Ouimet years later.

The "Seven Days" rebels, as they became to be known, laid their plans, and when he came back from Florida in mid-April, Leiterman protested the dismissals to Walker. At the same time, Haggan dispatched a memo to Walker also protesting the decision and the process. "Only chaos can result . . . from attempts by Head Office to undertake detailed direction of particular programs and their personnel," he said. "This breaks the established line of responsibility." The day after sending the memo, Haggan saw Ouimet and Walker and told them that he was not prepared to accept the Watson-LaPierre dismissals. "Haggan . . . [is] already one of the rebels," Ouimet thought.

The crisis burst into public with screaming headlines in the *Globe and Mail* about the dismissals. One of the decisions taken by the "rebels" when they met on Leiterman's return at mid-week had been to leak the story to *Globe and Mail* reporter George Bain. The following wild weekend, Watson, LaPierre, and Leiterman held press conferences and told reporters of the management interference in the program. A nationwide Save "Seven Days" committee was established, headed by the politically well-connected York University professor Bill Kilbourn. The committee set up a command post in a motel across Jarvis Street from the CBC, and local committees were established in numerous other cities. Motivated by what they thought was a bureaucratic squashing of freedom of speech and unjust creative interference, senators, MPs, and academics publicly supported the "Seven Days" rebels, as did luminaries such as René Lévesque, Pierre Berton, Marshall McLuhan, Gilles Vigneault, and Leonard Cohen.

The rebels phoned hundreds of community activists, church leaders, professors, journalists, politicians, and even some CBC board members, especially E. B. Osler of Winnipeg, who was known to be sympathetic to the program. Staff members made personal donations to pay for some of the activity, but much of it was charged to CBC accounts.

Illustrative of the country's obsession with "Seven Days," most newspapers bannered or gave front-page attention to the dismissals on the weekend the story broke, while relegating to a secondary position a statement by UN Secretary General U Thant that the world was on "the edge of nuclear disaster."

CBC offices were picketed by "Seven Days" supporters carrying signs saying, "We want Patrick. We love Laurier. This Hour Has Courage. Hands off!" An avalanche of telephone calls, telegrams, letters, and petitions to "Save Seven Days" began pouring into CBC head office, Parliament, and the Prime Minister's Office. Bell Telephone later reported that 7,000 calls had reached CBC switchboards during that first weekend. Ouimet was bombarded with viewers denouncing the "Seven Days" dismissals. "This family protests your arrogance, dishonesty and gross mismanagement of public broadcasting. Stop. Resign." said a telegram from Dr. Peter Brawley. The North Battleford and District Labour Council sent in a petition attacking Ouimet, and the members of the Mine, Mill Ladies Auxiliary No. 117 wrote Ouimet, "We are concerned about the future of Patrick Watson and Laurier LaPierre."

A few of his correspondents gave Ouimet some comfort. Mrs. Aileen Sivell of Edmonton wrote, "Those gentlemen offend and insult . . . with a dirty sneer and a dirtier leer." He also felt reassured by a letter from Mac-Millan Bloedel chairman J. V. Clyne, who warned that unless Ouimet asserted management rights "against the dictatorial attitude of producers, then . . . it is the beginning of the end of the CBC."

There was, too, a ghost from the past; CBC radio pioneer Bob Bowman wrote a sympathizing letter to Walker. Since Bowman was out of work, it was also a pleading letter, "I have applied for minor jobs in Vancouver and Halifax, but have been rejected, even though I am one of the most experienced broadcasters in Canada. . . . But I can't get anywhere. . . . What price loyalty?" Walker didn't get him a job, and within a few months, Walker himself would be out of a job.

One key source of support Watson and Leiterman sought and got was Judy LaMarsh, the secretary of state and the minister responsible for the CBC, who had respect for them and no love for the CBC president. Bill Neville, who was Judy LaMarsh's executive assistant, says, "Ouimet expected Judy to defend him, but he was very selective in what he would tell her, and that was the cause of some tension between them."

By chance, on the day when the "Seven Days" revolt first hit the news, Ouimet had a meeting with LaMarsh on the Broadcasting Act. She warned him, "There might well be a hot public debate over this whole mess." Describing the conversation in her autobiography, LaMarsh said, "He poo-poohed my alarm and indicated that . . . if left alone, he would soon have the revolt under control." What Ouimet sensed as an organizational tremor, was, in fact, an earthquake and, as his then aide Bill Armstrong says, "He couldn't grasp the danger of the wheels flying apart."

The Young Liberal Conference, which was being held that weekend in Ottawa, requested that LaMarsh appear to explain the "Seven Days" firings. In a question-and-answer session with delegates, LaMarsh fanned the flames of the "Seven Days" revolt by saying it represented "only the tip of the iceberg" at the CBC.

Privately, the minister thought Ouimet, while a brilliant engineer, was a rotten CBC president, and, as she later said, "the wrong man in the wrong place." She talked of his "stultifying presence" and his being "always wary, always nervous." During the "Seven Days" crisis, her distaste for Ouimet strengthened as did her thoughts about getting rid of him as president, even though Lester Pearson had reappointed him to another seven-year term only six months earlier.

So Ouimet now not only faced a revolution from "Seven Days," public humiliation over his inability to control his producers, and a broad attack by supporters of the program, he also faced a minister who wanted him out of the president's chair. Privately, he fumed at LaMarsh, calling her "totally irresponsible, indiscreet and destructive . . . a menace."

Ouimet's self-imposed isolation from the political world and his wariness of the intellectual, academic, media, and cultural communities was in sharp contrast to the well-connected "Seven Days" producers.

"The speed with which 'Seven Days' launched its attack was nothing short of phenomenal and it still stands as a tribute to the extraordinary organizational talents of its leaders," Ouimet later commented. "It stands also as a tragic warning of what can happen when the raw power of television falls into the hands of people who know how to use it. . . . The 'Seven Days' coup had been carried out smoothly, efficiently and mercilessly."

During the height of the "Seven Days" storm an electronic "bug" was discovered in the program's office by a staff assistant who happened to be a technological whiz. "He found it in the wall," says Peter Campbell, then Haggan's deputy, "and the suspicion was that CBC Ottawa had put it there. He took it out."

On Monday, April 18, Ouimet met a delegation led by Haggan who warned of widespread angst in the public affairs department. Earlier, Walker had dismissed Haggan's warnings and said the CBC was like "a plant turning out tin cans. . . . You've got to expect a few bent cans." Haggan later said, "I have never had a useful, helpful or positive program suggestion from management." He also rejected Walker's and Ouimet's accusations of disloyalty. "Loyalty to management is not a matter of any interest to me whatsoever," he later said, "I think employees have confidence in management or they do not. . . . A demand for loyalty is usually an admission that confidence does not exist."

Ouimet also met a delegation from the Toronto Producers Association who protested that "due process" had not been followed in the dismissals of "Seven Days" hosts Watson and LaPierre. That same night, Ouimet held a press conference in which he attacked his rebellious staff.

The next day, Opposition leader John Diefenbaker told Parliament there was a "crisis of uncertainty and chaos in the affairs of the Canadian Broadcasting Corporation," and he demanded an emergency debate in the House of Commons. "I do not think," he said, "there has ever been a matter which in so short a time has brought about so much antagonism in all parts of Canada." Diefenbaker's demand was rejected, but the prime minister became so alarmed at the political storm that he arranged for the parliamentary broadcasting committee to launch its own investigation.

Amid all this, the CBC board began meeting in Halifax on Wednesday, April 20. It was angered that the parliamentary committee had entered the dispute and was calling witnesses. While Walker, Haggan, and Leiterman were being questioned in Halifax by the board, in Ottawa, LaMarsh and Watson were being questioned by the parliamentary committee. At its meeting, the CBC board took three actions: it attacked the parliamentary committee for interfering in the internal affairs of the CBC and making settlement of the dispute "more difficult"; it supported Walker's dismissal of Watson and LaPierre; and it said "there had been a serious breakdown in formal communication between management and the producers of "Seven Days." It "directed that steps be taken . . . to ensure effective communication."

Nobody was happy with these judgements. Walker was upset that the board had not given him stronger support and feared he might be made a management scapegoat in the affair. Watson, Leiterman, and Haggan denounced the board's affirmation of the hosts' dismissal, and Leiterman said he would quit producing the program if Watson and LaPierre were not reinstated. Several MPs on the parliamentary committee thought the board's admonition to the committee was arrogant, and John Diefenbaker said the CBC board was in contempt of Parliament.

More frenzied activity, accusations, and acrimony flared across the country that weekend, especially in Ottawa and Toronto, while the "Seven Days" program itself carried on on Sunday at 10:00 P.M. with its usual irreverence and defiance.

On Monday, April 25, while Watson continued to testify before the parliamentary committee in Ottawa, Ouimet and Walker flew to Toronto to meet in an emergency session with the agitated public affairs supervisors. Walker apologized for violating line authority by talking directly to Watson, and Ouimet appealed for support, which he did not get. A few hours later, Ouimet and Walker met with recalcitrant Toronto producers in a meeting that flowed from a boardroom to the Toronto airport cafeteria and continued on the plane to and in Ottawa that evening. It was to no avail. "It's a mess," said Toronto Producers Association president Tom Koch, and the following day, Ouimet issued a statement on his inconclusive talks with producers.

The next day, from Ottawa on a nationwide closed-circuit radio hook-up, Ouimet appealed to CBC staff to support management. He detailed the "sins" of "Seven Days," specifically attacking LaPierre for crying in the Truscott interview. In Toronto, led by Peter Campbell, the department staff walked out of the studio where they were listening to Ouimet. Campbell said he was protesting Ouimet's misuse of CBC facilities to attack his own staff. Watson and LaPierre demanded, but did not get, equal time for a similar CBC internal hook-up, and LaPierre denounced Ouimet for defending the dismissals by "the sneer, the innuendo, the half truth and the lie." A few days later, LaPierre told a Vancouver news conference, "The CBC top brass must go. CBC President Alphonse Ouimet and other top officials have shown a bankruptcy of leadership." At another point, LaPierre told a reporter, "I do not feel I owe loyalty to [the] CBC. I owe loyalty to a concept of broadcasting." "I was on an immense ego trip," LaPierre later confessed. "I had the feeling really that the world was centred around me and if I wasn't there, the world would stop turning."

When Watson finished testifying to the parliamentary committee, Leiterman began, and at the same time the Toronto Producers Association formally threatened to go on strike. Meanwhile, the prime minister had stepped into the crisis, conferring with Ouimet and meeting directly with the association in two days of attempted conciliation. Pearson finally backed away, persuading *Vancouver Sun* publisher Stuart Keate to launch "in the national interest" a special investigation for the Prime Minister's Office.

Fighting a cold and fed up with what, to him, was a time-wasting storm in a teacup, Pearson sought to convince both Ouimet and the producers to accept Keate's mediating effort. After endless phone calls and using all his Nobel Prize-winning diplomatic skills, Pearson finally got a reluctant consent both from Ouimet and from the producers, who agreed to suspend their strike threat. Pearson couldn't believe so much time and effort was being spent and so much political and public turmoil was erupting over what to him was "a mere communications issue." He had many other major foreign and domestic issues to deal with and felt the whole affair was just nuts. "Why do I have this? Why am I dealing with this?" he asked aides. He remained committed to the CBC as an institution, but he felt "Seven Days" had become an intolerable thorn in his side.

In the meantime, Ouimet named CBC administrative vice-president Guy Coderre to conduct an internal CBC inquiry into the crisis, adding yet another investigation to those already underway by the CBC board, the parliamentary committee, the prime minister, and Stuart Keate.

On Sunday, May 11, "This Hour Has Seven Days" opened for its second to last program of the season with an announcer saying, "Ladies and gentlemen, thanks to the good offices of the prime minister of Canada, this hour HAS seven days." The luminous, twenty-two-year-old, guitar-strumming Dinah Christie, who opened each program singing its highlights in mocking lyrics, said to Watson and LaPierre, "With you fellows losing your jobs, I feel so left out. I wonder what a girl has to do to get noticed in Ottawa?"

"Don't ask!" said LaPierre.

During the first two weeks of May, headlines and newscasts continued to wail with the clamour of rhetoric on management rights versus producer freedom. Alphonse Ouimet expected support from Judy LaMarsh and was astonished at her hostility towards him and her admiration for Watson and Leiterman. She was a soft touch for the imprecations of the "Seven Days" rebels and, as she later said, "I had a regular

parade of people in to see me [demanding] ... some relief from the stultifying presence of Ouimet and his phalanx of Kremlin dwellers."

In an extraordinary breach of ministerial ethics, LaMarsh secretly
conferred, if not conspired, with the "rebels," talking frequently on the
telephone with Watson and Leiterman and their associates, and on one
occasion had a clandestine rendezvous with Leiterman in a Mack Sennett
setting. She came to Toronto and drove to a downtown street corner
where Leiterman was waiting. He ducked into her car and, as they talked
and drove toward Hamilton on the Queen Elizabeth Highway, LaMarsh
glimpsed in her rear-view mirror a pale blue auto tailing them. She had
visions of being kidnapped, but it turned out to be a car that would take
Leiterman back to Toronto after their secret conversation ended. "It's
hilarious to look back on," she later said. "But at the time everybody was
scurrying around [saying] mustn't let people know that the Minister who
doesn't run the CBC is having a conversation with an employee. I think
that's the nuttiest thing I've heard of." When he later heard the story,
Ouimet was startled, saying, "This cloak and dagger story shows what
damage an indiscreet or immature minister can do to the CBC."

Damage was also being done to the CBC at the parliamentary committee which, altogether, met thirty-two times in two months' of hearings, listening to half a million words of testimony. To Ouimet's chagrin,
his old nemesis from the Montreal producers strike, Gérard Pelletier, now
an MP, was chairman of the committee and, Ouimet thought, clearly
sided with the "rebels." They got to tell their story first in the jammed
committee hearing room, grabbing the headlines, the initiative, and the
sympathy of the committee members.

"Whatever the reason," Ouimet said, "his anti-management anteced-
ents or inexperience, Pelletier had certainly placed the Corporation at
great disadvantage. ... [He] handed the 'Seven Days' rebels on a silver
platter a fifteen-day monopoly of the highest and most effective soap box
in the land." Later, the CBC president blamed a "'Seven Days' lobbyist,"
the suave and powerful Ottawa insider, CBC Ottawa public affairs supervisor Bernard Ostry, for persuading Pelletier to put on the "rebels" first.

With the consummate skill of polished communicators and with
boyish smiles and earnestness, Watson and Leiterman wove their tale of

management interference and incompetence, with strong supporting testimony from Reeves Haggan and his French network counterpart, Marc Thibault, both of whom said the management malaise went far beyond "Seven Days."

At one point in the Toronto-Ottawa confrontation over "Seven Days," Ouimet and Haggan had exchanged advice on how to handle the problem. "Make some mistakes, Reeves," Ouimet had urged. "That'll make it easier for Bud [Walker]. Don't always defeat him." Haggan, in turn, told the precise, orderly CBC president, as Ouimet remembered it, "that I shouldn't look for rationality in the anatomy of a revolt." Both good pieces of advice were ignored as the "Seven Days" warfare erupted.

Walker, nervous and defiantly defensive, stumbled through his testimony to the committee, denouncing Watson and Leiterman and saying, "What we do not want and what we will not have are constant challenges to basic ethics, standards, policies and all the old fashioned things like respect for personal privacy, good taste and integrity and so on."

Walker denied he had said Watson was disloyal to the CBC, in spite of evidence to the contrary. Bill Hogg had planned to testify on Walker's assertions, but he collapsed from nervous exhaustion before being called. Although uncomfortable about doing so, he made it clear that, had he testified, he would have demolished Walker's credibility. Although a loyal and longtime CBC employee, Hogg told an associate, "I would have had to tell the truth and that man [Walker] was lying." While Ouimet didn't know exactly what Hogg had planned to say, he noted, "Hogg seemed to have become somewhat erratic and confused as to his responsibilities."

Walker was under particular attack from David Lewis of the New Democratic Party (NDP) who privately referred to him as "that bastard Walker," and who publicly accused him of being "irresponsible." "Why did you go out of your way to create one of the nastiest situations which the Corporation has been involved in over many years?" he asked Walker.

"I did not!" Walker spluttered. Calling "Seven Days" the "root evil," Walker put much of the blame for what he called "the mutiny" on the middle management of the CBC in Toronto for failing to see that Ottawa's orders were carried out.

Even Ouimet, who steadfastly defended Walker, admitted that "his goose is cooked" and later said, "Watson, with all the ease of the charismatic television persuader, had Walker looking like a fool and most committee members eating out of his hand."

Ouimet was contemptuous of Watson's and Leiterman's testimony, calling them "two prima donnas," and of Haggan, whom he considered a traitor to the CBC. Ouimet was also incensed at what he believed was a plot by committee chairman Pelletier to undermine the CBC president with the testimony of Marc Thibault, who complained of CBC Ottawa's "interventionist supervision" that caused tension among the French network producers. By that, Thibault specifically meant Marcel Ouimet, who daily fired off lengthy memos to Montreal protesting against what he saw as a separatist bias in programs. He prepared lists of separatist sympathizers who had been on the air, and he sought constantly to undermine Thibault's authority.

Thibault and Pelletier had been friends since 1955, and together with a colleague of Thibault, on the day of Thibault's testimony they drove together in Pelletier's car from Montreal to Ottawa, arriving forty-five minutes late for the day's hearing. To a suspicious Ouimet, that was proof of collusion. Thibault and Pelletier had had little time to talk on the trip, however, because Thibault slept in the back seat most of the way, having been up all night writing his testimony.

Thibault particularly roused Ouimet's ire with his comment, "I don't believe that the CBC has the task of promoting national unity. The CBC is a public service with the task of providing a national broadcasting service to reveal the problems that exist in the whole of the country." The CBC, Thibault said, "powerfully contributes to the shaping and influencing of public opinion, to instigate and promote far-reaching social and political changes in our milieu."

Philosophically, Thibault shared much of Watson's and Leiterman's program objectives but few of Ouimet's. "By his very presence in the stand Thibault succeeded in bolstering Miss LaMarsh's mistaken claim that 'Seven Days' was only the 'tip of the iceberg,'" Ouimet said. He dismissed Thibault's forty-page statement as "imprudent," a "harangue," and "hyperbolic," adding that "Thibault's credibility [was] already half shot because of the suspicion of separatist sympathies in his department."

One of Alphonse Ouimet's nightmares was the possibility of French network producers joining the "Seven Days" rebellion. In spite of the strains between them and CBC head office, they never did, however, partly in memory of the lack of support from Toronto producers seven years earlier at the time of the Montreal producers strike.

When he got his chance to testify, Ouimet let loose his denunciation of Thibault, Watson, Leiterman, Haggan, and "This Hour Has Seven Days." With barely suppressed rage, he said, "I reject the assumption that production people, through management's default, have become the sole keepers of the conscience of the Corporation and so, guardians of its ideals." He talked of "sexy, sleazy or badly done" items on "Seven Days," and he attacked the program for "inexcusably" using "deceit, misrepresentation, invasion of privacy and possibly the simulation of actual events."

"'Seven Days,'" he said, was "a little empire within the CBC [which] consistently resisted the observance of CBC policy." Ouimet was especially angered by being "defied and attacked . . . torn to shreds" by the "Seven Days" press statements. "It is almost unheard of for employees, while still employed, to challenge publicly the management and policies of their organization," he said. "Resignation usually precedes such action. I know of no precedent for the challenge to corporate authority which we are now witnessing." He also rejected Leiterman's claim that the producer should have "co-equal authority" with management on program matters and that producers should not be overruled by management on such matters.

On a philosophical note, Ouimet said, "CBC was not brought into being to instigate or stimulate social changes. It was intended to use the communication techniques for broadcasting to help the Canadian people make their own choices of what their future should be."

Two days after Ouimet's statement to the parliamentary committee, the last "Seven Days" of the season, the fiftieth program to date, aired a defiantly provocative show with satirical skits, investigative reports on aircraft sabotage and Canadian economic nationalism, and an interview with the program's guru, Marshall McLuhan. A skit by the Second City Co. ridiculed an anti-communist Christian crusade, urging, "Kill a Commie for Christ." As the show ended, LaPierre said, "See you in seven weeks. Well, maybe. *Au revoir.*"

15

Judy LaMarsh,
"A Runaway Horse"

The second season may have been over for "This Hour Has Seven Days," but it was still open season on the program, its producers, and their bosses, not only in the parliamentary hearing, but in Stuart Keate's inquiry. For a few weeks, assisted by Judy LaMarsh's aide Bill Neville, Keate interviewed thirty people, including all the principals. Prime Minister Pearson hoped Keate's effort would cool things down. "It was simply designed to smother the thing for a while," Neville says.

In late May 1966, Keate issued his report, which on the surface criticized both sides in the "Seven Days" dispute, but the subtext of which tilted toward Watson and Leiterman. He deplored the CBC board's refusal to reopen the question of Watson's and LaPierre's dismissals. "The board's intransigent stand was an affront to an instinctive Canadian sense of fair play," Keate said.

He poked fun at the CBC's near-retirement "radio age" senior bureaucrats, quoting American comedian Fred Allen's attack on NBC vice-presidents who are, Allen said, "men who come to their offices at 9:00 A.M., find a molehill on their desks and have until 5:00 P.M. to build it into a mountain."

Keate applauded "Seven Days" for its irreverent tone and investigative reports, but was critical of some of its interviewing techniques which, he said, "too often ... descended to the level of a brutal, almost savage, inquisition." He hailed Leiterman as a gifted journalistic "generalissimo" who was also "stubborn, prickly and relentless." Keate didn't mind LaPierre's tear, but felt his attacks on CBC management in speeches and press statements suggested he had a death wish. Keate also noted the comment by Dick Nielsen of the Toronto Producers Association who had told him, "We not only agree with management's right to manage, but to mismanage. What we are concerned with is due process and cogent reasons."

The *Vancouver Sun* publisher picked up this theme in his recommendations, urging the CBC board to re-examine the question of "due process and cogent reasons" for the dismissals. He also urged the producers to remove their strike threat and hoped the parliamentary committee would conclude its "Seven Days" hearings and concentrate on the whole question of a new broadcasting act.

Within a day, the board issued a statement promising that the CBC would hereafter abide by its agreement with producers not to make any change in program performers "without full consultation with the Executive Producer and Producer concerned." But the dismissal of Watson and LaPierre as "Seven Days" hosts was non-negotiable, the board said. Producers rejected the statement, complaining of the board's "intransigence" and saying they no longer trusted CBC management and would not remove their strike threat.

Ouimet, who repeatedly said he wanted a cleansed "Seven Days" to return in the fall, began to have doubts that this could be achieved with Leiterman as executive producer. He called Leiterman to Ottawa for a star-chamber grilling, not unlike "Seven Days" own "hot-seat" interviews. For an hour Ouimet, Briggs, and Walker hurled questions and accusations at a defiant Leiterman, and then he and Ouimet talked privately for another hour. It led Ouimet to the conclusion that Leiterman had to go because of the fundamental differences in their approach to broadcasting: the old traditionalist versus the young rebel.

By late June, when the national hysteria over the "Seven Days" crisis was cooling down, the parliamentary committee issued its report, which was highly critical of CBC management. "The Committee was faced," it stated, "with evidence of deep divisions within the CBC among top management, middle management (Supervisors) and production people....

Dissension ... seemed deeply rooted in the very structures of the CBC....
The problem went far beyond the individuals involved."

Basically, the report echoed the criticism of the Fowler and Glassco
reports, saying that lack of clarity in lines of authority had led CBC management into "extreme nervousness or jumpiness ... and extreme touchi-
ness or irritability on the part of the creative personnel." The MPs said the
malaise at the CBC was, indeed, widespread and recommended more
opportunities for "younger, more dynamic" staff members to reach the
CBC top echelon. They urged a formal collective agreement between the
CBC and Toronto producers, similar to the one that had been won in
Montreal after the producers strike there. With a swipe at Captain Briggs,
the parliamentarians said it was wrong to try to run the CBC in a military
style and attacked CBC head office's "remote control of programming."
They recommended the two senior vice-presidents be moved to Toronto
and Montreal to be responsible for the English and French networks.
Keate had recommended a new vice-president be appointed to be
responsible for all news and public affairs programming. The MPs agreed
that CBC staff must not promote their personal views on programs, but
heartily endorsed controversial and adventurous public affairs programming with "strong" and "lively" hosts.

After the parliamentary committee report came out, the CBC board
held another tense, emotional meeting in Ottawa. The board agreed to
appoint vice-presidents for Toronto and Montreal as recommended by
the committee, reaffirmed an internal grievance procedure and the right
of producers to be consulted before any on-air personnel changes, and, at
Ouimet's particular insistence, criticized Reeves Haggan's supervision of
"Seven Days." The most heated arguments were over the central players
in the crisis. Leiterman and Walker. Ouimet wanted Leiterman out, but
he and Briggs were outvoted, and the board agreed Leiterman could produce "Seven Days" the next fall, provided he signed a specific pledge to
"accept CBC policies, procedures and direction." It now would be up to
Leiterman.

There was even more emotion over Bud Walker. Board member E. B.
Osler, more sympathetic to "Seven Days" than most of his colleagues,
moved a resolution to remove Walker, pushing him into another job or
early retirement. The *Toronto Star* headlined, "OUIMET ON CBC CARPET

FOR NOT FIRING WALKER." LaMarsh had also been pressuring Ouimet to fire Walker, but he rejected her "constant complaints" and in the boardroom won the day for the man he relied on most at CBC. Osler's resolution to get rid of Walker was voted down.

In a fatal pre-emptive strike, Walker immediately flew to Toronto and announced that, in conformity with the board's decision to have a vice-president in charge of the network in Toronto, he was moving to Toronto as of October 1 to carry out these functions. He had always felt the job should have been located in Toronto, not Ottawa, as Ouimet had previously insisted, so such a move fitted him perfectly. The words had no sooner flown out of Walker's mouth when an "anguished phone call" came in to Judy LaMarsh from a friend of hers at the CBC. Walker had been singled out by the Toronto production staff as the villain of the "Seven Days" crisis, and what was widely regarded as his ham-handed, stumble-tongued manner of dealing with the crisis had swung support to "Seven Days" even from those who previously had been leery of the program. "Here was the man they hated most," LaMarsh later recounted, "sent down to lord it over them ... I called Ouimet myself and asked him what in hell he was trying to pull off, whether he was himself deliberately fomenting another palace revolution."

Ouimet, who seemed unaware of Walker's statement or his trip to Toronto, contacted members of the CBC board, and the next day, the CBC announced that Walker would not be moving to Toronto to take on the new vice-presidency. It was a humiliating denouement to Walker's three-decade CBC career. A few months later, he was removed from his job and dispatched to Jamaica to head a project advising Caribbean governments on broadcasting. Ouimet later said, "It is not a healthy thing for any executive, even a good one, to have a revolt in his department. So Walker had to pay for having been revolted against."

Public affairs executive Peter Campbell has a simpler explanation for Walker's downfall: "He was dumb, basically. Thickheaded and dumb and tried to cover it by being a bit of a martinet ... I don't think he really understood programming at all."

On the same day of Walker's failed coup, Leiterman was directed to sign the loyalty oath the board had demanded. He told reporters the "obedience oath" was "childish and redundant." At the same time, his boss Reeves Haggan memoed Ouimet that the demanded oath was "insulting and degrading."

The protests were rejected, and Leiterman was told to sign the oath by 4:00 P.M., Thursday, July 7, 1966, or else. The "or else" meant dismissal, and the threat was given to him via Haggan, but it originated with Marce Munro, who literally minutes before had been appointed to succeed the ailing and increasingly disillusioned Bill Hogg as head of news and public affairs. While frantic phone calls went back and forth, the deadline came and went. At 10:00 P.M., Leiterman announced on CBC Radio news that he would accept the CBC offer, but he made no specific mention of agreeing to the oath. Munro listened to the statement in the office of Bob McGall, Walker's deputy in Toronto, and they decided it was now time to fire Leiterman. They immediately issued a news release announcing his dismissal, knowing that it would be carried by the CBC-TV news at 11:00 P.M.

"You're fired!" an exhausted Haggan said as he phoned Leiterman. "And I have resigned." At 1:00 A.M., Haggan issued his own news release saying, "I am resigning tonight because of the sordid manoeuvres the corporation has been going through to rid itself of Douglas Leiterman. . . . He has been pushed too far by an intransigent and insensitive senior management."

The next day, Watson also resigned, as did several key producers in the program. For Watson, it had been a giddy, ego-swelling roller-coaster ride as he and Leiterman had imagined their efforts leading to the expulsion of senior CBC management and the replacement of Ouimet, possibly by Watson himself. He felt he had an ally for his ambitions to be president in Judy LaMarsh, who found Ouimet arrogant and secretive. "In my opinion," she wrote later, "he [Ouimet] was tragically miscast by temperament to be the President of the Corporation."

But the bloodletting was over. With Watson and LaPierre gone, Leiterman gone, the key producers gone, the program was also gone. "7 DAYS CAPUT," headlined the *Toronto Star*.

Ouimet and Walker had repeatedly said they wanted "This Hour Has Seven Days" back in the fall. "We want a bigger and better 'Seven Days,'" Ouimet had told the parliamentary committee. At another point, he said, "It was our hope that with the 'sleazy' items removed and more honest techniques of news gathering employed, it could return in stronger form next season." But while he paid lip service to the idea of the program returning, his lips weren't moving very much. What he really wanted back was a tame version of "Seven Days" with a defanged production staff. "It would seem that programs which depend too much on provocation, sensationalism and shock carry within themselves the seeds of their own destruction," he later mused.

To the end of his life, Alphonse Ouimet bitterly denounced Watson, "the extrovert," and Leiterman, "the introvert," noting that "Leiterman . . . called the shots but Watson seemed to make all the noise . . . Leiterman appeared quiet and restrained while Watson was impulsive, emotional and rebellious." "Their thirst for power and freedom had given them delusions of grandeur," Ouimet later wrote. "They were both cocky and ambitious young men who became dazzled by the magnified image television gave them of their own brilliance . . . inflating their already massive egos to the point where they did not really give a hoot about management directives." But Ouimet grudgingly admitted that Watson and Leiterman had put together "a superbly organized and executed attempt to supplant or force out a management which they considered hostile to their concept of television journalism."

With almost paranoid resentment, Ouimet also never forgave others he considered his adversaries in the "Seven Days" battle. He denounced as uncooperative, incompetent, or disloyal almost every one of his senior- and middle-level managers, with the notable exception of Bud Walker. He attacked, with much justification, the slash-and-burn style of the irrepressible and uncontrollable Judy LaMarsh, the minister through whom he reported to Parliament. "Miss LaMarsh must have had a very strange concept of her responsibilities," he said.

Ouimet also denounced Lester Pearson for the "silly" action of being a "self-appointed conciliator" during the dispute. He said Pearson had helped "to fan [the crisis] with the hot winds of politics and to allow the media's insatiable appetite for conflict to do the rest." He felt Pearson not only worsened matters with his own actions, but did so, too, in launching Stuart Keate's investigation and allowing the parliamentary committee hearings.

Ouimet reserved particular scorn for the committee, denouncing both the committee and its chairman Gérard Pelletier. Pelletier had, he said, an "anti-management prejudice" which led to the committee's vindication of "Seven Days." He decried the committee for sticking "both feet in an internal CBC matter which was none of its business." The effect of the hearings, he said, was "to encourage the rebels to prolong... their mutiny.... To lead power hungry young men, already on an ego trip, to believe their goal was within reach.... To have irremediably biased public opinion ... [and] to have done all this without contributing one iota to the solution of the conflict."

The parliamentary committee, he said, "transformed a case of straight mutiny into the most notorious, if not the most serious, crisis the CBC ever had." Thus, Ouimet said, the government, the prime minister, Judy LaMarsh, Stuart Keate, Gérard Pelletier, the parliamentary committee, and Parliament itself "compounded the problem immeasurably," and he added them to his list of adversaries in CBC management and production.

For their part, Watson and Leiterman relished all the publicity, argued forcibly for their new brand of journalism, and denounced Ouimet for what they felt was his wimpy sense of journalistic tradition. "It was Mr. Ouimet who felt we were a gang of troublemakers, that we were an evil compact of people trying to overthrow the country," Leiterman told a reporter a year later. "They called it irresponsibility. But from where I sit, there was only one real issue: their lack of guts."

Before Leiterman left the CBC, the new news and public affairs head, Marce Munro, demanded that he repay the CBC for long-distance phone calls and telegrams the "Seven Days" group had charged to the CBC during their anti-management campaign. "They amassed a tremendous amount of popular support on our money," Munro snapped in an archival audio interview, and he deducted about $4,000 from money the CBC owed to Leiterman to pay the charges. "He didn't resent it very much," Munro said. "He thought it was fair enough."

Leiterman left Canada for New York to work for CBS, which borrowed some of his program ideas in developing "60 Minutes," a subdued version of what had been Canada's most-watched journalistic program. After two years, however, Leiterman quit in frustration over CBS program restraints and he came back to Toronto, forming his own production company and later operating a cable firm and a major international production financing company.

Some years after the program ended, Watson admitted the "Seven Days" team was "unmanageable," "cocky," and had tried to create "an empire in a kind of counter-power centre within the CBC and that was intolerable to any management." In an interview with Judy LaMarsh on her CBC radio program almost a decade after she had left politics, Watson said the program had been produced with a "kind of recklessness and . . . kind of total commitment. It's like a destructive love affair. You know that the farther you plunge into this thing the more you're going to ruin your life. But by God, it's worth it!"

"What could we do with such romantic immaturity?" was Ouimet's tart comment on hearing Watson's words.

On the same radio interview program, LaMarsh and Watson reminisced about an extraordinary sideshow in the whole "Seven Days" crisis: her effort to fire Ouimet and Watson's campaign to succeed him as president.

What LaMarsh did not know was that just before the "Seven Days" public explosion Ouimet had privately told Pearson that he wanted to be relieved of the CBC presidency. Pearson had asked him to stay on until the new broadcasting legislation had been passed, which he thought would occur within several months – in fact it took nearly two years. Unaware of this, LaMarsh actively examined several possible candidates to replace Ouimet, including CBC-TV production pioneers Mavor Moore and Stuart Griffiths – and Patrick Watson. In her typical bull-in-a-china-shop style, she once brought Moore and Ouimet together in her office while she was courting Moore to replace Ouimet. As recounted by onetime CBC broadcast executive and writer Erich Koch, LaMarsh heartily escorted Moore into her office, saying, "I've got a friend of yours in here." Whereupon Moore saw a subdued and uncomfortable Ouimet slouched deep in an armchair. LaMarsh handed Moore a scotch, put her foot on her desk, and loudly said, "All right Mavor, what are we going to do about all those queers at the CBC?"

She was just as indiscreet with Watson, who was a more than willing presidential aspirant. Encouraged by colleagues and by his own ambitions, Watson took LaMarsh to dinner in Ottawa one evening during the

"Seven Days" crisis and said he wanted to be president of the CBC. Watson later recounted the story on LaMarsh's radio program: "You asked me whether I chased boys and got drunk a lot and was otherwise clean or dirty because that was the first consideration. You couldn't even talk about [the job] if I had any blackmail chinks in my armour." Hearing of no such chinks, LaMarsh told Watson, "If you're serious about it, here's what you've got to do. You've got to do some lobbying with key ministers."

Watson prepared his recommendations on how to run the CBC and lobbied with several ministers for their support, including Paul Martin, Paul Hellyer, and Maurice Sauvé. He later said he was "pretty stupid . . . naive anyway," and told another interviewer, the CBC's Michael Enright, "I suggested myself as a possible president. . . . Sure I went down and lobbied on behalf of me . . . I thought it [the CBC] was in such a miserable state at the moment that it really couldn't be done worse and that it maybe ought to be done for a while by somebody who understood programming and cared about programming and program makers."

At one point, LaMarsh had her aide Bill Neville arrange for Watson to meet the prime minister as part of his lobbying effort. Pearson was preoccupied with other matters, however, and, said Watson, "he could hardly listen to what I had to say." Pearson, in fact, had listened and, although he admired Watson, he did not like what he had heard. He later told friends privately that Watson had lectured him saying, "If I become president, I'll be travelling all the time and nobody will tell me what to do." Watson seemed too aggressive, Pearson thought, and one of the prime minister's colleagues later commented, "Pat burned himself with Pearson. . . . Pearson got very annoyed." The prime minister admired Watson for being bright, young, and articulate, but felt he was not sufficiently weighty or knowledgeable about managing a huge corporation.

Watson was equally unpersuasive with the ministers he met and his bid for the CBC presidency was stillborn. LaMarsh blamed the "Seven Days" crisis for destroying Watson's chances. "The person who is the assassin can never be put in the position of the assassinated," she told Watson. "And I really grieved at the fact that your public connection with the whole dissolution of this was going to destroy you as a person who might hold that office."

"Well you shouldn't have," Watson told her, "because it would have been a terrible thing for me and the CBC if I had ever become president." A quarter of a century later, after a distinguished career as a documentary maker and Canada's most eloquent TV interviewer, Watson became chairman of the CBC board.

Shortly after the "Seven Days" débâcle, Watson did contract work at Montreal's Expo '67 and for the NFB, and in 1969, he and his "Seven Days" co-host, Laurier LaPierre, were teamed up by Stuart Griffiths, at the time running CJOH-TV in Ottawa, to add program excitement to the station. Their irreverent style produced more excitement than Griffiths bargained for, and the two left the station after one season. LaPierre ran and lost federally for the NDP, went back to university teaching and writing, and worked for some years in television in Vancouver. After CJOH, Watson went to New York to work for public television for a few years before returning to Canada and, eventually, to the CBC's airwaves.

After his resignation, the head of public affairs programming, Reeves Haggan, went to work as assistant secretary to the cabinet in the Prime Minister's Office, then became an assistant deputy minister, and later a senior adviser to the government on constitutional issues.

The fall of 1966 brought colour to CBC-TV and a new program to replace "This Hour Has Seven Days" called "Sunday." Run by another young, iconoclastic producer, Daryl Duke, "Sunday" plunged the CBC into almost as much public hot water as its predecessor. It was lacerated in Parliament and in the pulpit for undermining Christian values, public morality, and the establishment. "Utter garbage," said British Columbia Conservative and former cabinet minister Davie Fulton. Quebec Conservative Sen. Josie Quart said one program that showed an unmarried couple in bed together was "a diabolical scheme to tear down the sanctity of marriage." "The program has a flavour of perversion," said another Quebec Tory, Sen. Louis Philippe.

This time, however, the producer was not as rebellious, and CBC management was more forceful than in the "Seven Days" era. "'Sunday' needs more time to find its bearings and to show whether it can measure up to management requirements and public expectations," Ouimet told a parliamentary committee, adding that if it did not measure up, it would be cancelled. The public affairs department eventually decided the program was not working out, and it was cancelled at the end of its first season. "It had been a mistake," Ouimet said.

The fate of "Warrendale," a spellbinding documentary by famed film-maker Allan King on the treatment of emotionally troubled children, was another casualty of a nervous management. The CBC refused to air it because it was too controversial, too emotional, and included too much foul language. The film was aired to rave reviews in the United States and Britain. "Extraordinary," said the *New York Times*. "A very nearly perfect documentary," said *Newsweek*. "No," said the CBC as the post-"Seven Days" chill settled in on TV programs.

As Ouimet and his colleagues were clamping down on adventurous CBC programming, Judy LaMarsh began her organizational housekeeping. She wanted to fire not only Ouimet but also BBG chairman, Dr. Andrew Stewart. Earlier, the government had refused to reappoint Carlyle Allison as BBG vice-chairman because of his Conservative Party connections, and now LaMarsh searched for a Quebecker to become vice-chairman. She first tried to get the head of the NFB, Guy Roberge, who turned her down, and then she sought Roberge's young, ambitious, and highly regarded deputy, Pierre Juneau, who was head of NFB French production. Although reluctant, the tough-minded Juneau agreed, and LaMarsh planned to recommend him for chairman of the new regulatory agency, replacing Dr. Stewart when the new broadcasting act was passed.

LaMarsh also was determined to get rid of Diefenbaker's appointee Captain Briggs, whose term as CBC executive vice-president was up in early 1967. She gave him six-months' notice and was infuriated when the CBC board gave Briggs an augmented pension and a year's salary as a retirement bonus. "I blew up," she said, but there was nothing she could do to stop it.

It was, however, the hunt for a new CBC president that preoccupied her. "I was really seeking a new broom to clean up the situation and restore the Corporation to a lively and informative family with scope for creative people, and firm, sympathetic direction from above," she later wrote in her autobiography.

What outraged LaMarsh about Ouimet was not only his handling of the "Seven Days" crisis, and his crisp and imperious style, but also what

she claimed was his bad management. She had become a magnet for mal-
contents from the CBC, and a stream of complaining CBCers marched in
and out of her office with tales, she said, of "waste, extravagance, and
sheer stupidity, sometimes downright cupidity."

She heard stories of thefts of large quantities of film and other sup-
plies from CBC Montreal, scandalous waste of facilities and needless
extra staff, exorbitant expense-account-living by CBC executives, and
excessively high prices paid for Hollywood productions. Don Jamieson
fed her some of this gossip which she accepted as true (and a small part of
it was), saying the CBC was "notorious" for paying Hollywood more than
the private stations and getting "dogs" that no one else wanted. A senior
news editor, who had just quit CBC in an internal news department
squabble, came to regale LaMarsh with stories of extravagant and wasted
office space in New York, waste in foreign news assignments, high-living
and overstaffing of major events. "This threw new light on the way
Ouimet worked," she said. "Up until then I had thought him merely ill-
suited by temperament.... Report upon report piled up of waste and lack
of any kind of coherent organization."

The Fowler Report, the Glassco Report, the Keate Report, and the
parliamentary committee report had all attacked CBC management, and
Ouimet had dismissed them all as "hatchet jobs," the products of anecdo-
tal evidence, sour grapes, and ignorance. LaMarsh suggested to Ouimet
that he hire Fred Friendly, Edward R. Murrow's onetime producer and
former head of CBS News, to study CBC's management, and when that
was rejected by Ouimet, she suggested someone from the Australian
Broadcasting Commission or the BBC. All suggestions were rebuffed,
but Ouimet had earlier set up a special internal task force – The President's Study Group – which, LaMarsh claimed, was aimed at producing a
whitewash. Certainly Ouimet did not expect a critical report on CBC
management from the study group and was angered when he heard it was
straying off the reservation. Spearheaded by his own executive assistant, a
managerial whiz kid named Michael Harrison, the study group recommended major organizational changes. Ouimet was outraged at what he
considered a runaway internal study aimed at destroying his presidency,
and he never forgave Harrison, especially since he had given him specific
instructions on what the study group should deal with. "I was trying to

avoid the possibility that a committee of inquiry might use the report of the P.S.G. to clobber the Corporation," Ouimet said later.

All of this left LaMarsh brimming over with distrust and disgust with Ouimet's management, and in the fall of 1967 in a television interview with Pierre Berton, she blurted the fateful words, "I think there is some rotten management in many places in the CBC." She also said there were too many separatists in the CBC French network. Her comments validated NDP leader Tommy Douglas's description of her verbal clumsiness when he said, "The only time she doesn't have her foot in her mouth is when she's changing feet."

The *Globe and Mail* editorialized that her statements were "a kick in the teeth to every single CBC employee with a management function. . . . Whatever their weaknesses, they do not deserve to be subject to this kind of sweeping, non-specific insult."

Her words whipped up a storm in the House of Commons, mortified the prime minister, made Alphonse Ouimet's blood boil, and infuriated the CBC board of directors. Ouimet immediately wrote and had hand-delivered to LaMarsh what his aide Bill Armstrong describes as "a scathing denunciation of her interference. . . . He felt it was absolutely unforgivable . . . a really terrible thing to do. . . . When she used those words, that was the end." In his letter, Ouimet said, "Such accusations are capable of destroying public confidence in a national institution. . . . If your charges are correct . . . the Corporation will take appropriate action. If they are not justified, then the reputation of the Corporation and its people must be cleared at the earliest possible moment."

"Arrogant," responded LaMarsh, who was infuriated not only by Ouimet's letter but by the threat of mass resignation by the CBC board members. The board issued a statement declaring, "The Directors reject categorically Miss LaMarsh's sweeping allegations concerning 'rotten management' and related unsubstantiated statements as being utterly without practical value and gratuitously offensive. . . . In the face of a provocation that may have deserved the response of a mass resignation, the Directors have decided to carry on."

LaMarsh called the board "dead wood" and "a rubber stamp" for Ouimet. She said the board statement was a demand for her resignation, something the beleaguered prime minister likely would have dearly welcomed. LaMarsh defended her accusations of "rotten management" but refused to substantiate them. In fact, she said, she had learned the situation at the CBC was even worse than she had originally thought.

Pearson was furious with LaMarsh – "a runaway horse" he called her privately – and he demonstrated his anger by inviting to his office Ouimet and Jimmy Gilmore, who had special responsibilities for the CBC programming on Canada's centennial year. Pearson personally thanked them and their "dedicated" employees for the 1,500 hours of CBC Radio and -TV coverage of the centennial events of 1967, including Montreal's Expo '67 extravaganza. The prime minister also met with the CBC board to sympathize with their agitation over his minister's statements, and he privately encouraged his cabinet to speak out in support of Ouimet.

"I know of no Canadian . . . who is more passionately and sincerely devoted to a simple love of Canada and the cause of national unity than this very honourable man," said parliamentary secretary John Munro of Ouimet. "He has been a committed devotee to the concept of public broadcasting. . . . We owe him a debt of gratitude which cannot be repaid in words."

In what LaMarsh called "a great growl," the House of Commons debate raged for three days over her attacks on CBC management. The debate broadened into attacks on CBC programming in general from Conservatives and Social Crediters and even from a few friends of the CBC.

Yukon Conservative MP Erik Nielsen complained of CBC management allowing programs such as "Seven Days" and "Sunday" to air "an unending parade of drug addicts, black power advocates, prostitutes, purveyors of filthy literature, Nazis and pseudo Nazis. All the scrapings and leavings of society sooner or later turned up on the CBC. No one in the CBC apparently was able to exercise any control over what went on." Ontario Conservative M. T. McCutcheon asked, "How can we control and, yes, cut down on the woeful extravagance of this juggernaut?"

It was an eccentric debate, for much of the Opposition supported the minister while most of her own party publicly rejected her complaints about CBC management. "I faced utter hell," she later complained. "My colleagues writhed in their seats in embarrassment."

The raucous and inconclusive parliamentary and media circus over the "rotten management" accusation provided a noisy background to the passage of a new broadcasting act. Lester Pearson had named himself chairman of the cabinet committee on broadcasting, which was shaping the new broadcasting legislation, and his style irritated Judy LaMarsh. She complained of his frequent absences from meetings as well as what she considered his interference in her responsibilities. At one point she got so furious with the prime minister that when he began chairing a meeting of the cabinet committee, she hurled her briefcase across the table at him, startling Pearson and astonishing her cabinet colleagues. Later, she also threw a file across a cabinet table at Justice Minister Pierre Trudeau at the climax of an argument with him over a judicial appointment.

Amid these occasional fireworks, the cabinet concentrated on its white paper on Broadcasting, which LaMarsh tabled in the House of Commons on July 4, 1966, while the CBC was going through its final self-immolation over "Seven Days." The white paper rejected the Fowler Committee's recommendation for a return to the old one-board, single system and endorsed many of the ideas of the Liberal backroom power and private broadcasting leader, Don Jamieson, and his friend and political mentor, Jack Pickersgill. Pickersgill was highly influential in the cabinet and knew how to lobby effectively to get across his points. "I have a predilection for the free play of economic forces," he had once said about his attitude toward broadcasting. "But ... there would be no distinctively Canadian content to radio broadcasting if it were left to undiluted commercial enterprise." So he sought some, but not too much, public broadcasting.

To Ouimet's consternation, the Liberal government said the CBC should seek to retain a 25 per cent share of television advertising in Canada. Ouimet feared this would make CBC programming more susceptible to commercial considerations in both the scheduling and the type of programs. "The ideal commercial policy for the CBC," he said, "is to be out of commercials. . . . We are too commercial. We don't know what we are."

The white paper did, however, endorse the commitment that the

CBC should keep its traditional mandate within the Canadian broadcast system and urged minimum standards of Canadian content. Based on these recommendations, the government's new broadcasting act evolved amid fears of people like Graham Spry, who felt that the CBC would continue "to get weaker and weaker and have more and more problems."

The evolution of the white paper into a bill provoked further efforts to weaken the CBC by some cabinet members, notably Forestry Minister Maurice Sauvé whose wife, Jeanne Sauvé, was a CBC employee. Later she became minister of communications and ultimately governor general of Canada. In cabinet, Maurice Sauvé argued for the CBC to be split into two organizations: one for program-making only; the other to handle broadcasting facilities. His ideas were not accepted.

The act, which went through five formal drafts, generated much debate, and the CBC successfully sought to be less under the thumb of the new regulatory agency, retaining most, if not all, of its existing powers – still far less, however, than it had had between 1936 and 1958. LaMarsh said it was "a tilt" back to the public sector compared with the Diefenbaker government's 1958 legislation. The new act did declare that "radio frequencies are public property" and stated that in any conflict between the objectives of the national broadcasting system and private broadcasters, that paramount consideration would be given to the national interest. This was a slight weakening of the suggested language in the Fowler Report and in the original white paper. Pearson personally would have preferred a stronger, less commercial CBC, but the bill was as good as he could get through his ministers and MPs with his minority government. In the end, Ouimet was not especially unhappy about it, although many of his suggestions had been rejected. Don Jamieson, who, with Jack Pickersgill, had helped to shape it, said it was "the best piece of broadcasting legislation we have had." His comment alarmed Graham Spry.

One new and significant element in the bill was the requirement that the new cable industry would come under the jurisdiction of the regulatory agency. That had immense implications for the future cable explosion across Canada.

One of the most contentious issues in the act which reverberated down through the years was the requirement that the CBC "contribute to the development of national unity." CBC French network producers protested this was tantamount to censorship, but LaMarsh, worried about reports of rampant separatism among the producers, rejected their plea to remove the clause. Opposition MPs and some high-profile Liberals condemned the idea of committing the CBC to "contribute" to national unity. The NDP sought to delete the clause altogether because, as British Columbia MP Robert Prittie said, the words could lead to a "witch hunt against the people employed in broadcasting." Prince Edward Island Conservative MP David MacDonald was also worried. "When we begin to move into areas such as . . . national unity, we are, in effect, moving away from the concept of public broadcasting toward the idea of state broadcasting whereby the broadcasting system of the country becomes an extension of the state," he said.

In the debate, an effort was made to change the word "contribute" to "promote," but it was turned down because "promote" was felt to have a whiff of propaganda about it. The idea of the CBC promoting national unity had actually been part of Graham Spry's and Alan Plaunt's initial concept of a public broadcasting system. It had also been in the Aird Report and part of Premier Bennett's rationale for establishing public broadcasting back in 1932. Moreover, the Massey Commission had called the CBC "the greatest single agency for national unity," and the Fowler Committee had specifically said that encouraging national unity was part of the CBC's mandate.

Conservative spokesman Gordon Fairweather, however, said the phrase "contribute to the development of national unity" was too nebulous, and Liberal MP John Reid echoed that concern when he told the House that the word "contribute . . . is a pious word you cannot define and you cannot define how you are going to achieve it." LaMarsh fudged by responding, "It is not for the government to define," presumably meaning the CBC would define it. Within two years, however, politicians from the prime minister on down did indeed define it and claimed that under the law the CBC had an obligation to "promote" national unity, not just "contribute" to it. Those claims, in turn, led to a vicious and dangerous attack on the CBC for encouraging separatism. The argument went on for more than twenty years before the phrase was removed in 1991 by the Conservative government of Brian Mulroney in a new broadcasting act.

On the heels of the CBC's programming success during the Centennial Year, 1967, and with the prime minister praising him in one ear and Judy LaMarsh berating him in the other, Ouimet decided it was now definitely time to go. He had already stayed much longer than he had anticipated after telling the prime minister in mid-winter 1966 that he wanted out. He asked Pearson to set a specific date, and they agreed Ouimet could leave by the end of 1967.

Ouimet had presided over the most convulsive years in CBC history, betrayed, he felt, by colleagues on the inside and mauled by adversaries on the outside. His voluminous and meticulous private notes about his CBC presidency, which he later shared with some old colleagues, reflect a driven, almost desperate search for self-justification. In them, Ouimet pays grudging praise to very few of his associates and shows contempt for most of them. His conclusions after hundreds of pages of analysis and evaluation were that he had done almost everything right and the few failures of his presidency were caused by others.

It was his technological brilliance and determination that built the world's biggest and most complex television system, and it was under his direction that CBC programming ballooned to more than 200,000 individual radio and TV programs a year. The CBC produced more French-language programs than the national system in France, and the CBC was much bigger than NBC, CBS, or ABC. "For Alphonse, it was his whole life," says Bill Armstrong. But for all his genius, his tenacity, and his rigid integrity, he could never fathom the creative side of the business. "He had no comprehension of programming," says Harry Boyle.

"He was a person of principle and integrity but he was puzzled by the impact of television programming on a changing society," says Peter Campbell. "He never really understood television as an instrument of change." Nor did he understand, says Patrick Watson, "the insecurity of people working in our trade and their need for him to be a supporter, a fan, a father figure. And his political ignorance was appalling." Ouimet's inability to deal with politicians and program makers was his fatal flaw.

He expected of them the same cold, hard logic he used, and by his yard-stick, they failed to measure up.

From 1969 to 1980, he was chairman of Telesat Canada. He also worked with UNESCO, served on innumerable committees and task forces, and wrote about the dangers of communication technology erod-ing Canadian sovereignty. He died in 1988.

As he retired from the CBC, Lester Pearson saluted him for thirty-three years of "untiring, unselfish and experienced service." LaMarsh finally had what she wanted: Ouimet was out. But Pearson, fed up with LaMarsh and doubting her judgement, had taken the selection of Ouimet's successor totally out of her hands.

"What Pearson wanted," she said, "was a lid for the whole mess – someone who would keep the Corporation quiet, out of the public press and the Government's hair."

Pearson ignored LaMarsh and personally interviewed possible candi-dates – men who had public prestige and who would, indeed, keep the lid on the CBC. He talked to NFB head Sydney Newman, but was turned off him, he told colleagues, when Newman told him the first thing he would do as CBC president would be to buy a plane to get around the country. That affronted Pearson's Methodist frugality, and he went on to other possibilities. He tried Claude Bissell, president of the University of Toronto, who said no, and he also got a no from the Canadian ambassa-dor to France and future governor general, Jules Léger.

Pearson tried others in business, academia, and journalism, but none wanted the large headaches and relatively modest salary that went with the job. Ouimet had recommended his vice-president Jimmy Gilmore, who became acting president after Ouimet retired and who badly wanted the job. But Pearson said no.

At one point, LaMarsh even suggested she'd like to be president of the CBC, "but," she added in an interview, "I don't think it's in the cards." It certainly wasn't as far as Pearson was concerned. He was appalled at the very idea. "My faith in him was shattered beyond repair," LaMarsh later remarked. "Whenever he looked at me he saw only trouble." Pearson told LaMarsh he was having a hard time finding a CBC president because of all the trouble she had caused. His search was endless, she said, because "Pearson . . . dithered and dallied."

16

A Good and
Grey Presidency

W hat Prime Minister Lester Pearson wanted in the president of
the CBC was someone who would provide peace, order, and good government. He had "had it" with the CBC. Besides, he was resigning as
prime minister shortly and didn't want his final months stained by any
more CBC crises.

Judy LaMarsh had insisted that she choose the new CBC president,
but their bitter arguments on the choice finally ended when she told Pearson, "All right, you choose your own man!" That's what he was going to
do anyway because, he said, "The post of top man at the CBC was, to my
mind, the most difficult appointment my government had to make."
Pearson agonized for months over his choice, talking to more than a
dozen potential candidates. "Mike had been peddling this thing around
for God knows how long," says George Davidson, then head of the Treasury Board and the man Pearson finally approached with a two-headed
proposition. He invited Davidson and Jules Léger to his office and put to
them the idea that Davidson would in charge of all programming for the
CBC and Jules Léger would be in charge of administration and management. After expressing their hesitancy to Pearson, Davidson and Léger
left his office and, over lunch, decided their answer was no. "This was a

complete misfit for both of us," Davidson says, and they formally rejected Pearson's proposal.

A few months later, the prime minister again called in Davidson and this time told Davidson he had to accept the job as the CBC president. "No, I'm not going to do it," responded Davidson. "I've had enough trouble with the Treasury Board. Why should I go from one frying pan into another fire?"

"George," Pearson replied, "you've got to take this. I've been looking around for somebody and have been turned down by God knows how many people. . . . I've had enough of this. This is a job I want you to do. This is not either, or. This time, I can't take no for an answer."

"Well, you're the boss," sighed Davidson. Later he explained, "If the prime minister of this country says 'I want you to take on this as a public duty,' I feel I have no alternative. . . . I guess I'm an old firehorse. I have to respond. And somebody has to do the job."

The job was a mess. Internally, the CBC was demoralized, confused, and threatened in the wake of the "Seven Days" fiasco. Externally, the CBC was a besieged island in a typhoon of "rotten management" charges from Judy LaMarsh and others. All of this was being played out in full public view, on the front benches of Parliament and on the front pages of the papers. Underlining the malaise was Ouimet's protracted departure, which Davidson later bemoaned, saying, "Poor Alphonse. He died by inches." Davidson feels Ouimet's biggest failure was that "he couldn't communicate with artistic people."

Davidson knew he was headed into a maelstrom and told reporters that his favourite program was "Run For Your Life." He said he was an "average viewer," watching everything from wrestling to "Front Page Challenge." As he took on the job, the onetime classical scholar, who wrote his PhD thesis on the techniques of Greek plays entirely in Latin, sent a telegram to Prime Minister Pearson saying, "*Caesar, Morituri te salutamus!*" – "Caesar, we who are about to die, salute you!" – a salutation given by Roman gladiators when they entered the arena to do battle until death. Pearson's reply was, "You're not going to '*morituri.*' You're not talking to 'Caesar,' either. But we do '*salutamus*' you."

Pearson breathed a sigh of relief that the CBC was now in good, grey,

and mature hands. If, under Davidson, there would be no burst of program creativity, that was fine with him. Judy LaMarsh told colleagues,
"We needed a CBC leader, but we got a lid."

Davidson's appointment, however, was hailed by the Father and
grand old man of public broadcasting in Canada, Graham Spry, who,
travelling in Europe at the time, said, "Davidson is a very good man . . . I
don't envy him his job – it is the most merciless task in Canada except
being P.M." Davidson disagreed, and today laughingly says, "Oh, no, no.
Much worse!"

One story illustrative of Davidson's ability to handle a "merciless
task" involves his dealings with the sometimes cantankerous style of one
of his political bosses, Paul Martin, who was minister of health and welfare when Davidson was deputy minister. Once Martin called in a rage
about some long-forgotten issue, and as his tirade continued, Davidson,
in a typical use of humour with a bite to dissolve Martin's anger, broke in
with, "Who is in the room with you, Paul, you're trying to impress?"

As president, Davidson's first task was to find an executive vice-
president, and he was heavily pressured to choose Pierre Juneau, the
vice-chairman of the BBG and soon-to-be chairman of the new regulatory agency, the Canadian Radio-television and Telecommunications
Commission (CRTC). Three heavyweight Quebec Liberals, Gérard Pelletier, Maurice Sauvé, and Jean Marchand, took Davidson to lunch to
press for Juneau. "It was a friendly lunch in which they proceeded to tell
me that it would be excellent if I were to select Pierre Juneau. I said I had a
great respect for Pierre Juneau – which was stretching a point a bit, but I
said it anyway – but our chemistries were not compatible. I can't see it."

Pelletier, Sauvé, and Marchand kept pressing for Juneau and a slightly
exasperated Davidson said, "Look, I'm perfectly willing to step aside and
let them take Pierre Juneau as president. I just can't agree with this."

"Who, then?" said the three Quebec Liberals.

"Laurent Picard. I was much impressed with him."

"Fine," they replied.

Shortly afterwards, Pearson asked Picard to be the CBC executive
vice-president, and at a meeting, Pierre Trudeau, Marchand, and Sauvé
urged Picard to accept.

Davidson had met Picard about a year before when Picard came to

Ottawa to discuss the offer of a senior Treasury Board post. Picard had turned down the job, as he had turned down other offers to be assistant or deputy minister in Ottawa. Davidson had been impressed with both Picard's mind and his style, however, and believed he and Picard would be compatible. Picard felt the same way. "We were on the same wavelength," he says.

Davidson's rejection of Juneau would come back to haunt him, however, whenever, as CBC president, Davidson had to appear before the CRTC and its chairman, Pierre Juneau. "Juneau found I had turned him down and that coloured our relationship," Davidson says. "I just felt that every time I appeared before the CRTC, in the back of Pierre Juneau's mind was, 'This guy didn't have enough confidence to accept me as his deputy.'"

Fifty-eight-year-old George Davidson, the mandarin's mandarin, and forty-year-old Laurent Picard, a modern labour-management expert, were the ideal couple to deliver Prime Minster Pearson's desire for tranquility at the CBC. Both knew a lot about managing and bureaucratic finessing, but neither knew anything about broadcasting, although Picard had helped to develop a training program for CBC French network managers and a few years earlier had been asked by Alphonse Ouimet to take a senior management job at the CBC which he had turned down. Their lack of experience in broadcasting outraged Judy LaMarsh. "She thought it was crazy that I should be put in there," Davidson says. "She thought it was a ridiculous appointment and she was very miffed at Mike Pearson."

The Nova Scotia-born and British Columbia-raised Davidson and the Quebec-born and -raised Picard both went to Harvard but were as educationally apart as they had been geographically. Picard had a business degree while Davidson's degree was in classical languages. "My study of Greek has been a great help in understanding bureaucratic documents ever since," Davidson quipped in reflecting on his thirty-four years in provincial and federal bureaucracies. He'd been brought up by an aunt, a school teacher, following the death of his mother just after he was born. His father was confined to a wheelchair. He enrolled at the University of British Columbia at age fifteen, and at thirty-five, Davidson became Canada's youngest deputy minister at the Department of Health and Welfare, where he spearheaded the introduction of the Canadian family allowance program and universal old-age security. He then spent three years as deputy minister of citizenship and immigration, following which he directed plans for government reorganization, based on the Glassco Commission's recommendations. He went on to become secretary of the Treasury Board, where Judy LaMarsh nicknamed him "Mr. Misery" for his tough controls on government spending. Davidson got a taste of his own medicine when, in his first years as CBC president, the government froze CBC's budget. Although he and LaMarsh got on well together, Davidson says, "She was a negative, ornery person" who was forever stabbing Pearson in the back. "She was yapping at him all the time and undercutting his position quite considerably," he says.

LaMarsh was not the only challenge Davidson faced. Ninety minutes after he and Picard were appointed, they were under attack in the House of Commons. "It is regrettable that neither has had experience in broadcasting," said the NDP's broadcasting critic, Robert Prittie. The Conservatives also voiced concern that neither Davidson nor Picard had any broadcasting background. "I make no bones about that very real gap in my armoury of knowledge about broadcasting," Davidson responded. "I'll have to learn fast."

Neither man had any creative credentials, either, which in time led the Globe and Mail to editorialize, "The great sin that the CBC continues to commit . . . is not to let the creative person into the upper councils. This is a basic error." Davidson, however, dismisses the idea that a CBC president needs to be creative. "It may help," he says, "but his creativity may get in the way of other people's creativity. His strength needs to be that of allowing creativity to flourish. He has to be able to understand creativity when he sees it and to encourage it."

Thus, Davidson's first priorities at the CBC were administrative not creative. The CBC, he says, "was in disarray. Nobody was really able to exercise effective control and command the respect of the organization as a whole because Alphonse, by this time, God bless him, had outlived his usefulness. . . . It was leaderless, and Judy LaMarsh was heckling on the side." Davidson also wanted to ensure that the managerial "goat" of the "Seven Days" crisis, Bud Walker, was organizationally isolated, so he maintained Walker's assignment in Jamaica and later kept him out of the line of fire by making him head of the CBC overseas broadcasts. "Bud Walker's presence was a constant reminder that . . . Bud had dirt on his hands in the minds of a good many people and that affected the atmosphere," Davidson says. The atmosphere was also affected, he says, by "a bitter animosity shown toward the CBC in the last two years of Alphonse." One small but typical change of style from Ouimet to Davidson was Davidson's rejection of Ouimet's advice to get an unlisted telephone number so he wouldn't be bothered with crank phone calls.

"My first job was to settle the place down," Davidson says. He also wanted to get away from the "high degree of centralization . . . very much of an authoritarian approach." Picking up the recommendation of the parliamentary committee report on "Seven Days," Davidson appointed a senior vice-president in both Toronto and Montreal, transferring program decision-making power out of Ottawa. His choices were instructive for he reached below the surface of the managerial old guard and selected two men whose roots were in programming and who had opposed much of Alphonse Ouimet's and Captain Briggs' autocratic management style. The two were: Raymond David to head the French network in Montreal, a former producer and program manager with whom Ouimet had felt ill at ease because "he does not react the same way as we do," and Gene Hallman, a public affairs programmer and vice-president in charge of program policy who had sided with the "Preview Commentary" producers in their battle with CBC Ottawa and whom Ouimet had felt was not "a team player."

"Our purpose," Davidson said in announcing the appointments, "was to place those in charge right at the scene of network operations." It was a clear signal that Davidson was serious about decentralization, and the fires of discontent in Toronto and Montreal began to cool. "The centralization, the phalanx of vice-presidents in a protective circle around the president's office, whatever its reasons or merits or advantages, resulted in a lack of communication." Davidson said. "There have been examples, too numerous perhaps . . . of trying to impose a position by direction from above."

But decentralization also had its problems. Bill Armstrong, director of corporate relations at the time, recalls, "He handed all the power away. Nothing wrong with doing it, we all agreed on that. But he should have put a few policies in place first because what happened was it just started to divide."

The decentralization, in time, led the French and English divisions into different program approaches and different administrative actions, some of which were in conflict with each other such as, as Armstrong says, "totally different, incompatible computer systems. That cost millions of dollars because they can't talk to each other." The decentralization reinforced the image of the two solitudes as there was little inclination to share program projects between Toronto and Montreal.

But at the time, the transfer of authority out of Ottawa was hailed as enlightened management, although, later, under Pierre Juneau and Gérard Veilleux, much of the substance of power was brought back to Ottawa. That, Davidson says, is wrong. "It's a mistake to recentralize," he says. "How do you get the people on your side? You don't do it by centralizing everything in Ottawa. You have to put some content and substance and quality into the regional part of the operation. I think that is where we're taking a backward step now. Sometimes I wonder if the CBC has lost track of the importance of the decentralizing factor." Referring to the inclination for centralization among past and future CBC presidents Ouimet, Juneau, and Veilleux, Davidson adds, "This is a racist remark, but the French logical mind is much more likely to be centralist inclined."

LaMarsh, squeezed out of the decision to choose Davidson as CBC president, was determined to get her choice as head of the new regulatory agency, the CRTC. She wanted to get rid of Diefenbaker's appointee, Dr. Andrew Stewart, and put in Pierre Juneau. With the help of Trudeau, Marchand, and Pelletier, she finally convinced Pearson, but the prime minister kept procrastinating on dismissing Stewart, and in the end, she had to swing the axe herself. "It was yet another of the instances when Pearson left the dirty work to someone else," she said. Stewart finally resigned in mid-March 1968, and Juneau was chairman of the BBG for two weeks before becoming chairman of the CRTC when it was established on April 1 under the new broadcast legislation.

The government appointed as vice-chairman of the CRTC another man who had already had enormous influence on Canadian broadcasting and the CBC, the former producer and program manager, Harry

Boyle. From the start, Juneau, Boyle, and a highly talented group of full-time CRTC members took an activist, interventionist approach, which contrasted sharply with its tranquil predecessor, the BBG. Inevitably, it would clash with the CBC.

One early example of Juneau's and Boyle's more assertive style was the CRTC's investigation of a CBC documentary exposé on the dangers of air pollution. Prepared by farm department producer Larry Gosnell and hosted by news anchor Stanley Burke, "Air of Death" was broadcast in October 1967 and caused a sensation. "One of the most terrifying documentaries I have ever seen . . . It's a shocker!" said *Globe and Mail* columnist Bruce West. It was the first major network anti-pollution program, regarded so highly by the CBC that it pre-empted the Sunday prime-time "Ed Sullivan Show." It stirred up protests that, in time, led to public pressure forcing governments to introduce anti-pollution legislation. Immediately after the broadcast, the companies accused in the film of polluting raised such a ruckus that the Ontario government appointed a commission to investigate the claims of the documentary. In a highly controversial conclusion, it said the documentary was irresponsible. Then the CRTC entered the controversy in the winter of 1969. With Harry Boyle chairing the meetings, the CRTC probed not only the accuracy of the program claims, but explored the whole purpose of controversial documentaries, the techniques used, and the issue of rebuttal. The idea of point-of-view documentaries was assailed by some, including J. Angus Maclean, former Diefenbaker cabinet minister and future premier of Prince Edward Island. He told the House of Commons, "It is almost as if an employee of the Royal Canadian Mint were given an opportunity to mint his own money on the side." *Hamilton Spectator* editor William Gould retorted that the CRTC investigation of the CBC's "Air of Death" was "a monstrous invasion of freedom of the press. . . . The absolute independence of CBC newsgathering . . . is at the root of our entire experiment with [the CBC]."

A parade of witnesses testified for and against "Air of Death" in particular and controversial documentaries in general. They included not only CBC staff, but Graham Spry, private broadcasters, and the guiding light of "This Hour Has Seven Days," Doug Leiterman. The CBC was uneasy about this CRTC intrusion into programming, and Gene Hallman,

Davidson's new man in charge of the English Radio and TV networks, made a powerful case for producing controversial programs. Sounding like Alan Plaunt of thirty years before, Hallman said, "One of the tests of a healthy democracy is the tolerance of unpopular minority opinion . . . . The CBC has a responsibility to see that seriously held minority views . . . find a place in its programs along with the more conventional, despite the discomfort and criticism this may provoke among some sections of our audience." Davidson agreed, and in a speech in Ottawa to the Women's Canadian Club, he said the CBC cannot "turn a blind eye and show Canadians only those insipid, sentimental, satisfying myths of what we would like our lives to be. . . . Nor can you expect the CBC to turn the lights out, to put the cap on its film camera, to turn its back on the events of our own turbulent society." Altogether the hearings listened to the most intensive philosophical discussion on the issue of controversial programming in the history of Canadian broadcasting.

When the CRTC made its report, there was some criticism of the extent of the research in the program, much praise for it generally, and a ringing endorsement of the program philosophy articulated by Hallman. It was an endorsement that was particularly relevant to the CBC but only marginally relevant to the private stations, which were still concentrating on the more profitable entertainment programs that diverted and relaxed viewers, not the politically troublesome programs that stimulated and challenged their audiences.

But the private stations were very much involved in another CRTC action on Canadian content. At Juneau's insistence, the CRTC established stricter Canadian content rules for broadcasting, which, George Davidson said, were "consistent with . . . our goals." They certainly weren't the goals of private broadcasting, however, and most of the private stations howled that they would go broke. They had a powerful political friend in former CAB head Don Jamieson, who was now in the Liberal cabinet and who was bitterly opposed to Canadian content rules. He thought Canadians wanted to see American performers, not Canadian, and besides, he believed there was insufficient Canadian talent to meet the quotas. His ideas found support among some Liberal members of the parliamentary committee on broadcasting, who gave Juneau what

Bob Homme, the star of "The Friendly Giant," the long-running children's program which started in the late 1960s. (*National Archives of Canada, CBC 10020*)

Since 1964, Ernie Coombs, as "Mr. Dressup," has been entertaining millions of Canadian children on CBC-TV. His friends Casey and Finnegan retired in 1992, but he kept going. (*Courtesy of the CBC*)

Mavor Moore, the CBC's first senior TV producer, later performed in many CBC dramas. Here he portrays the colourful Calgary editor Bob Edwards in a 1964 edition of "Telescope." (*Courtesy of the CBC*)

Gordon Pinsent starred in the highly popular "Quentin Durgens, M.P." in the late 1960s. (*Courtesy of the CBC*)

Al Waxman and Fiona Reid in the 1970s hit "King of Kensington." (*National Archives of Canada, CBC 27078*)

Laurent Picard, CBC president 1972-75, testifying before the CRTC, flanked by his executive vice-president, Lister Sinclair. (*National Archives of Canada, 16076*)

CRTC chairman Pierre Juneau (right) and vice-chairman Harry Boyle in 1974. Juneau went on to become CBC president and Boyle the chairman of the CRTC. (*National Archives of Canada, 16077*)

George Davidson, CBC president 1968-72, autographing picket signs outside CBC's head office during a technicians' strike. (*National Archives of Canada, 16078*)

Graham Spry continued his battle for public broadcasting until his death in 1983. (*National Archives of Canada, 16071*)

A quarter-century of hosts of "The National," 1953-78. Left to right, Larry Henderson, Earl Cameron, Stanley Burke, Lloyd Robertson, Peter Kent.
(*Norman Chamberlin, courtesy of the CBC*)

"The National" anchors 1978-92, Peter Mansbridge and Knowlton Nash. (*Courtesy of the CBC*)

Alison Smith, anchor of "The National" when it switched to CBC Newsworld in 1992. (*Courtesy of the CBC*)

"As It Happens" with Barbara Frum and Harry Brown was a key part of the CBC "radio revolution" of the early 1970s. (*Sandy Stewart Photo Collection, National Archives of Canada, 6419*)

Peter Gzowski hosted CBC Radio's short-lived "Radio Free Friday" in 1968, his first taste of radio stardom. (*National Archives of Canada, 14334*)

A new radio show featuring Tommy Hunter replaced "The Happy Gang" when it went off the air in 1959. Then he shifted to TV and starred in his own country music show for twenty-six years. (*Courtesy of the CBC*)

Anne Murray, a CBC superstar. When she signed on with the CBC she met Gene Hallman, the English network vice-president, in her bare feet. (*Courtesy of the CBC*)

"This Hour Has Seven Days," 1964-66, was the most popular and most controversial TV journalistic series ever aired by the CBC. On the set are, left to right, host Laurier LaPierre, executive producer Douglas Leiterman, and host Patrick Watson. (*National Archives of Canada, 6951*)

The homespun humour and toe-tapping fiddling of "Don Messer's Jubilee" made it one of the most beloved TV shows ever seen. It made national stars of Messer (centre), Marg Osburne, and Charlie Chamberlain. (*National Archives of Canada, 13982*)

he calls a "very, very tough time" when the CRTC appeared before the committee to discuss the content proposals.

The CAB and its supporters felt that encouraging more Canadian programming through quotas was a dictatorial limitation on freedom of speech. The *Calgary Herald* took the same line and denounced the CRTC for "abrogating the freedom of Canadian citizens." It warned, "These people [the CRTC] seem to have little comprehension of the meaning of freedom." Jim Allard, the CAB's executive vice-president, complained that the quotas would be outrageously expensive, adding, "I do not think you can stimulate Canadian production by regulation." Juneau recalls Allard telling him in his rich, ex-announcer tones that "there is no talent in Canada and when there is talent, they prefer to go to California where they will have a much bigger salary, a new house, and a pool." The president of CAB, W. D. McGregor, told Juneau, "What do you want to turn out – quality meat or sausages?" CTV president Murray Chercover claimed the quotas would cost CTV $6,765,000 and mean a total loss to CTV stations of up to $15.5 million.

What Juneau wanted was 60 per cent Canadian programming in prime-time TV and 30 per cent of all music on radio to be Canadian. "Dictatorial," "isolationist," "fascistic," "Hitler," "muzzled," "communist," were some of the private broadcasters epithets hurled at Juneau's Canadian content proposals. *Broadcaster*, the magazine voice of private radio and TV, sputtered that the quotas were a "rampage . . . aimed at the total subjugation of the Canadian broadcast media."

Juneau fired back at what he calls the "horrendous opposition," saying the complainers were "the prophets of doom, the messengers of mediocrity . . . Canadian broadcasting," he said, "should be Canadian." His NFB background meant he was well aware of what had happened to the Canadian film industry. He thought that for years Hollywood had bled Canada, taking all the profits from Canadian movie houses and returning nothing to help develop a Canadian film industry. "They're not going to do the same thing to Canadian television," he said. "We're just getting whispers of our own material onto the pictures. We're just trying to breathe, for God's sake, in an atmosphere completely dominated by U.S. material."

The private broadcaster continued to rage at these ideas, however, especially at the CRTC hearings. "They filibustered the CRTC," Juneau says, with such intense and long-winded rhetoric that three key CAB members disowned the anti-Canadian quotas campaign. John Bassett of CFTO, Toronto, and Stuart Griffiths of CJOH, Ottawa, announced their resignations from the CAB, and Télémetropole in Montreal formally disassociated itself from the vitriolic campaign against Canadian quotas.

In the end, Juneau won, and the quotas were set at 30 per cent for Canadian music on radio and 60 per cent for TV prime time by October 1972. However, a number of concessions were made to the private broadcasters, including permission to average the percentage over the year instead of in each calendar quarter. The quotas were a bonanza for Canadian songwriters, producers, performers, and entrepreneurs, as Canadians began to discover their own music on the radio. Within a short time, thirty Canadian single records and ten albums hit the international charts, three singles sold more than a million, and three Canadian records went gold in the United States. While Canadian programming did increase on television, it was not in the qualitative way the music quotas had enriched radio. TV was much more expensive and many private stations sought ways to obey the letter but not the spirit of the quotas.

One unusual result of the Canadian content battle was the development of a personal friendship between the buccaneering entrepreneur and Tory stalwart, John Bassett, and the disciplined, intellectual public servant, Pierre Juneau. They became close friends and tennis competitors – Bassett was the better player – and Juneau regarded Bassett as a strong supporter of Canadian content. "I like interesting people, and I found John an interesting person," says Juneau.

While the CRTC under Juneau and Boyle was heating up, the CBC under Davidson and Picard was cooling down. The government's three-year budget freeze dampened spirits, and the dramatic management reorganization failed to generate much excitement. Nor did most of the programming. Radio wallowed in its doldrums and television quivered in its apprehensions. The ghost of "Seven Days" hovered over management and programming, dulling the creative edge. Nobody wanted to go through such a trauma again. Ross McLean was back producing the second replacement for "Seven Days," this one called "The Way It Is," and

Patrick Watson had resurfaced with the new program. But even such a potentially combustible combination of talents produced only flickers of controversy and spawned few headlines. Most of the headlines through the winter and spring of 1968 focused on Vietnam, Lyndon Johnson, the murder of Martin Luther King, the last campaign of Bobby Kennedy, and the Liberal leadership campaign to replace the retiring Lester Pearson. When Pierre Trudeau was chosen Judy LaMarsh quit, and Alphonse Ouimet's longtime adversary Gérard Pelletier was named secretary of state and the minister responsible for the CBC. Pelletier brought a more liberal attitude toward broadcasting, and he dismissed as irrelevant the residue of bile among the CBC's traditional enemies, who continued to rant in the House of Commons. Alberta MP and former Social Credit party leader Robert Thompson attacked the CBC for "a straight, deliberate mockery of Christianity. . . . Wake up Canada. There are men in the CBC who would betray Canada."

Another MP, Ontario Conservative Percy Noble, told the House of Commons, "It is time to halt the headless horsemen of the CBC. . . . The CBC, or a section of it, has been a Trojan horse in our midst, attacking, destroying and spreading filth and disease in the nation." Saskatchewan Conservative Frederick Bigg screeched, "I say there is a plot, a well thought out and clever plot . . . to bastardize the Canadian airwaves."

All these jibes were sloughed off by Davidson, whose first serious trouble was not over programming about sex, drugs, violence, or anti-Americanism but about a parade. In keeping with head office's desire to have pageantry in the foreground and protest invisible, CBC management had ordered that coverage of the annual St. Jean Baptiste Day parade in Montreal should focus on the floats and avoid reference to any protests. "Ignore any demonstrations and concentrate on the parade only," a producer had advised his broadcasters. When rioting erupted and bottles were thrown at Prime Minister Trudeau in the reviewing stand, CBC announcers reporting live on the parade had to turn away. "Here I was," said French network announcer Henri Bergeron, "seeing police cars and ambulances racing by, hearing the smashing of bottles and the shouts of the demonstrators, seeing the parade jammed and stopped by disturbances ahead, and having to report how pretty the girls in the float looked." French network reporters covering the parade for programs later in the evening leapt into action, however, in spite of the "lay off" orders. One reporter, Claude-Jean Devirieux, was suspended for allegedly exaggerating the violence. In protest, the French newsroom went on strike, refusing even to cover the federal election four days later. French network management got a lesson in how serious Davidson was about decentralization when Montreal officials called him for advice on what to do. "You make the decision," Davidson snapped. "You take the responsibility for living with the decision. We're not going to take you guys off the hook. . . . It's up to you."

As much as Davidson liked to decentralize decision-making, he hated surprises, and insisted on being kept aware of any significant program changes. A few years later when the Saturday late-night edition of a current affairs program called "Week End" was cancelled without his knowledge, he made a blistering telephone call to his Toronto managers. "What the hell are you guys doing down there?" he roared. "You never told me a thing about the 'Week End' cancellation for God's sake. Do you think I'm some office boy? You guys don't tell me anything!"

He was even more distressed when he was publicly booby-trapped by CBC Toronto's abrupt cancellation in 1969 of the onetime smash hit but now fading show "Don Messer's Jubilee," a shamelessly hokey country music program. The cancellation was part of English TV network entertainment program director Doug Nixon's attempt to get a younger image for CBC variety programming. "I am," he told a colleague, "bloody well going to kill the geriatric fiddlers." What he hadn't counted on, nor had Davidson, was the firestorm of protest from St. John's to Victoria that in public outrage rivalled that of the "Seven Days" débâcle. Unlike the "Seven Days" campaign, however, this was utterly spontaneous. It deluged Davidson, as well as the Prime Minister's Office, with tens of thousands of telegrams, telephone calls, letters, and petitions from individuals, service clubs, women's groups, churches, boards of trade, and community groups, all demanding a return of Don Messer and his Islanders with the friendly, familiar faces of Messer, Charlie Chamberlain, and Marg Osburne. Although it was now twenty-second in popularity, the program had been in the top ten Canadian TV shows for each of the previous ten years and for twenty-seven years before that had captivated CBC Radio audiences with its homespun humour and toe-tapping fiddling. What especially upset Messer was that nobody from CBC Toronto had talked to him or offered an explanation for the cancellation. All he got was a telegram from Nixon notifying him of his program's termination. "No one had the guts to tell me. . . . They couldn't care less," he said. "Tarnation poop!" he added, hurling the harshest epithet in his vocabulary.

The shy and gentle Messer from Tweedside, New Brunswick, had begun fiddling when he was seven (and was paid thirty-five cents per barn dance), and in 1934 formed his first musical group called The New Brunswick Lumberjacks, with Charlie Chamberlain. Messer made his first radio appearance on a Saint John station shortly afterwards and went on to become one of the CBC's greatest stars, although the most it ever paid him was $25,000 a year. His small-town manners and morals never left him, and the killing of his cornball country show by the slick, big-city Toronto broadcast hotshots stirred deep emotions in the country, especially in rural Canada. There were protest marches to Parliament Hill, pickets at the CBC's Ottawa and Toronto offices, and 300 square dancers whooped it up in front of the CBC's head office with plunking fiddlers and square dance callers. "We are here to serenade people in protest against the arrogance of the CBC," one square dance caller said. "The intellectuals in Toronto are trying to destroy the last bit of Canadian folklore," said Don Gilchrist, a teacher of traditional Canadian dance.

The protesters denounced the CBC's destruction of what, for them, was a way of life. The cancellation of "Don Messer's Jubilee" was a philosophical Rubicon the CBC crossed. It was throwing away a hitherto loyal constituency in favour of the glitzy allure of rock and roll and all that the new Woodstock generation stood for. For many Canadians, killing the Don Messer show was more significant and tragic than the end of "Seven Days." The new prime minister, Pierre Trudeau, who didn't have a clue who in the world Don Messer was, was baffled by the protest.

Pencil scrawls, blotted letters, and scribbled notes poured in not only to Trudeau and Davidson but to ministers, MPs, and newspapers. "Please, please tell them to continue our show," said a letter to Trudeau signed "an old lady" from the Ottawa Valley. "We will so miss Marg and Charlie," she added. "It is all we have left worth watching," said Mrs. Kathleen Sanderson from Lennoxville, Quebec. "I am an old man, 74, and live alone," said another letter. "I am protesting that you are taking the Don Messer show off the air." "Why can't we have some say in what we want to see?" asked Mrs. Ruth Saunders of Wainfleet, Ontario. "It is a clean, wholesome show. You are not embarrassed to watch it with your family."

The Prime Minister's Office replied to the thousands of letters that flooded in, "On behalf of the Prime Minister I would like to thank you for your recent letter concerning the Don Messer show. We were very pleased to receive your views. . . ."

"HELP SAVE THE MESSER SHOW," headlined the Halifax *Chronicle-Herald* and even a *Toronto Star* editorial was headed, "BRING MESSER BACK."

In the House of Commons, NDP leader Tommy Douglas pleaded that Messer be kept on the air, and John Diefenbaker said it was contemptuous that the CBC aired programs on the Black Panthers while killing the Messer show, of which, he said, he was "fond."

In spite of the national outpouring of affection for Messer's show, Doug Nixon refused to budge, saying, "Godamnit, they won't stop me! That stuff has had its day!" Backed by Davidson, the decision stood, another example of Davidson's devotion to decentralized decision-making. At the same time, it marked the beginning of the end for the impetuous and at times imprudent Nixon, who quit a short time later when his fiery enthusiasm collided with what he felt was some new CBC bureaucratic indignity. He was succeeded by Thom Benson, an iconoclastic enthusiast with a strong streak of Canadian nationalism.

As for Don Messer, he and his Islanders took off by bus on what he called his "35th Farewell Tour of Canada," later did a syndicated TV show from Hamilton, and he died at age sixty-three in March 1973. He was, along with Bert Pearl, Juliette, and Anne Murray, one of the all-time stars of CBC musical programs. In 1992, the CBC revived the Messer show in a repeat series that drew nostalgic reviews and large audiences.

The colourful Gordon Sinclair was another problem for George Davidson. The old curmudgeon and radio pioneer frequently upset some viewers with his bold and, some thought, insensitive questions on "Front Page Challenge," particularly about religion and money. But he was immensely popular, too, with his gaudy attire and Rolls Royce. He was called everything from "the Puck of the Airwaves" to "this cantankerous old man ... a rude bully." A Nova Scotia MP called Sinclair "that bombastic, overstuffed, conceited nothing," and demanded that he be fired. Complaints poured in to Davidson when Sinclair broke a TV taboo by asking champion swimmer Elaine Tanner if she swam when she was having her menstrual period. She said she did. Twenty-five hundred letters poured into Davidson, all but twenty-one attacking Sinclair. Several MPs professed to be scandalized by Sinclair's question and demanded he be fired. Davidson refused, although he apologized to Tanner. The storm of protest was so great that Sinclair offered to resign, but Davidson would have none of it. Sinclair carried on with the grandfather of all TV programs, "Front Page Challenge," until he died in 1984.

George Davidson had far more serious problems on his hands than Gordon Sinclair in the accusations of separatism in the CBC. As an activist professor, supporter of causes, and founder of *Cité Libre*, Pierre Trudeau had been called a communist, a fascist, a revolutionary, and an all-round disturber of the peace. Quebec Premier Maurice Duplessis had raged against Trudeau's CBC Radio and -TV commentaries, as Réal Caouette and his Créditistes had later. They had demanded the CBC remove Trudeau from the air. Now, however, Trudeau was prime minister and it was his turn to rage at the CBC. His target was separatists whom he earlier had said "swarm at the CBC" and whom, he now said, poisoned CBC French network programming with separatist propaganda. In October 1969, he told CBC French network interviewers that he might put the network into trusteeship if separatist propaganda continued. "It is possible. Yes, it is possible," he said. A few days later at a fifty-dollar-a-plate Liberal Party banquet in Montreal, Trudeau let loose his first major prime ministerial torpedo at separatism in the CBC. Saying he was "fed up with the non-objectivity of Radio-Canada," and warning of a "sickness of the spirit" at the CBC French network, Trudeau said that if the separatist influence were not wiped out at the CBC, "we will put a lid on the place ... we will close up the shop. Let them not think we won't do it. If need be, we can produce programs, and if not, we will show people Chinese or Japanese vases instead of the nonsense they dish out. That would be of some cultural benefit." It was vintage Trudeau being mischievously absurd to underline a fundamental complaint.

In a final thrust at the CBC, he told the 3,000 cheering Liberals, "It is not their role to use public funds to destroy the country." He specifically condemned a French network reporter's question to American banker David Rockefeller about what impact on American investment in Quebec there would be if Quebec became a separate country. Rockefeller said it wouldn't affect investment; Trudeau said the question showed a separatist bias.

The next day, Davidson defended the journalist, saying the question to Rockefeller was a legitimate one and "just good journalism." Phoned by a reporter for a comment on Trudeau's threats, Davidson said, "Mr. Trudeau is a taxpayer and he's got the same right to express his opinion about the CBC as any other taxpayer. And we'll pay the same amount of attention to his comments as to any comment we get."

When he saw Davidson's words, Trudeau telephoned the CBC president, "congratulating me," Davidson says. He had a good relationship with Trudeau in part because the prime minister enjoyed Davidson's sometimes whimsical sense of humour. They had met at a cocktail party before Trudeau became prime minister and during their conversation Davidson had explained how he would have responded to General DeGaulle's "*Vive le Québec libre!*" statement. "I'd go to Paris," he told Trudeau and several others, "hire a car with the top down, and ride down the main street shouting, '*Vive St-Pierre and Miquelon libre!*'" Some time later, Trudeau was riding in an open convertible at noon through a busy downtown Ottawa street and spotted Davidson on the sidewalk. He rose from the seat, stretched out his arms, and shouted at a laughing Davidson and astonished passersby, "*Vive la Martinique libre!*"

In contrast to Davidson, Pierre Juneau took a far more worried view of Trudeau's threat to close down the French network. He arranged for a meeting with Trudeau the day after Trudeau's speech, arriving at the prime minister's office shortly before 9:00 A.M. Trudeau ushered him into his office, and for ten minutes Juneau politely but firmly berated his old colleague while Trudeau shuffled papers from his briefcase with his head down, saying nothing. Finally Trudeau looked up and said, "Well, you may be right. But if you think I'm going to say so, you're wrong."

A short time later, the minister responsible for the CBC, Gérard Pelletier, came to Trudeau's office also to protest the extremity of his

Montreal remarks. "Pierre, never do that again," he admonished. Years later, Trudeau would say privately that he regretted having lost his temper in public and that Pelletier and Juneau were right to come to the defence of the CBC.

A day after talking with Davidson and seeing Juneau and Pelletier, Trudeau eased away slightly from his rhetoric, telling reporters, "I would hope it would give management additional support and strength in making sure their directions are followed."

What Trudeau's "close-up-the-shop" threat did, however, was to stir up a frenzy of separatist accusations against the CBC, making them seem legitimate now that they had a prime ministerial blessing. Some Liberal cabinet ministers, mostly from Quebec, blamed the CBC for spreading separatism and not just reporting on it. The dividing line between spreading and reporting became blurred, and many Quebec Liberals felt the mere reporting of René Lévesque's activities was, in fact, showing a bias in favour of the Parti Québécois (PQ).

There were, indeed, separatists among the French network journalists, just as there were in Quebec universities and newspapers, but the CBC was singled out for particular attack because it had the greatest influence. The key question was not whether there were separatists in the CBC, but whether they were propagandizing the separatist movement.

John Diefenbaker joined the attacking chorus and charged the CBC was "pandering to separatists" and "welcoming revolutionaries." Talking to reporters, he broadened his assault on the CBC beyond separatism, saying the CBC "calculated to incite student riots . . . glorify violence, worship revolution and condemn law and order. . . . These broadcasters preach the gospel that wrong is right, that decency is dirty, that observing the law of the land is lunacy."

Réal Caouette accused the CBC of "loading the French network with separatist propaganda." Judy LaMarsh said the CBC French network was "not only infested by separatists, but even by subversives who were turning [it] into a propaganda machine to advocate a separate state in Quebec. . . . Control over Radio-Canada had been completely lost."

Quebec Liberal MP André Ouellet asked Gérard Pelletier, LaMarsh's successor as secretary of state, if he would "at last agree that a clean up is required . . . so that the CBC will no longer be used as a medium for separatist propaganda." Ontario Liberal Harold Stafford said that covering the news about separatism helped to "spread the disease."

George Davidson spent three harrowing hours before the parliamentary broadcasting committee defending the CBC against Quebec Liberals howling about separatism in the CBC. He admitted there were separatists in the CBC but denied they were "propagandizing" on the air. He said separatism was not illegal, and in a speech to a Conservative policy conference, he said the "most important political fact of life in Quebec today is the emergence of separatism as a political force. . . . It is the obligation of the media to reflect political and social facts of life in Canada even if they are unpalatable and unpleasant." More than two decades later, Davidson reiterated his position, "It's inconceivable that we would create a situation in which the fact of separatism's existence in the Canadian body politic should be suppressed."

It was not an attitude that commended itself to the Quebec Liberals, especially to Liberal MP Jean Chrétien, with whom Davidson "had quite a tangle" over Chrétien's accusations about separatism in the CBC.

Early in 1970, CBC French network journalists were ordered to stop any freelance work for pro-separatist publications, and one reporter who refused was fired. But Davidson denied he or the government would launch any "witch hunt," saying separatists could continue to work for the CBC so long as they "keep their opinions to themselves and retain their integrity on air." In a CFRB radio interview he warned against "condemning men for what they are rather than for what they do."

What now seems clear is that the intensity of the accusations hurled at the CBC by the Quebec Liberals was rooted in fears of the growing popularity and political strength of René Lévesque and his Parti Québécois. The fears were well-founded: the PQ won 30 per cent of the vote in the 1973 provincial election, making the party the official Opposition, and won power in 1976.

The attack on the CBC for fostering separatism turned out to be just a dress rehearsal for the relentless assault that besieged the CBC later and continued for the next decade.

The immediate challenge for Davidson came during the October Crisis of 1970 when the Front de libération du Québec (FLQ) kidnapped

British trade commissioner James Cross and murdered Quebec's deputy premier, Pierre Laporte. What the PQ sought to do through political evolution, the FLQ sought through violent revolution, and their terrorist bombs killed and maimed dozens of people and spurred fears of destruction, murder, and insurrection.

As the single most important source of information for the public, the CBC was in the middle of the crisis. That role was very much on his mind when Pelletier called the CBC president after Cross and Laporte were kidnapped to urge that the CBC avoid "inflammation" of the crisis in its coverage and commentaries. That day, cabinet ministers, stunned by the information on the FLQ provided by the RCMP, had talked of the possibility of imposing censorship and bringing in the War Measures Act. They envisioned hundreds of bomb-throwing, murdering terrorists rampaging through Quebec threatening revolution and were further agitated by Quebec Premier Robert Bourassa's anxious plea that troops be sent into Quebec for protection against the FLQ.

"There were so many foolish rumours about what was going on," says Marc Thibault, then CBC French network news and current affairs head. He had been warned that an apartment building in his neighbourhood was filled with FLQ dynamite. The warning was passed on to him by Laurent Picard, who had been given the information by Ottawa "officials." Picard told Thibault, "If you can, try to take your family out of this region." Thibault did, sending his family to the country for several days.

As it turned out, the FLQ was a tiny, rag-tag collection of self-styled revolutionaries who, through the RCMP's exaggeration, held the nation on the edge. But when Pelletier called George Davidson, they both believed the RCMP's erroneous information. "There could be bloodshed on the streets of Montreal before many hours have passed," Pelletier said. "The government is very much concerned that there be as little as possible of unnecessary inflammation in reporting the events in Quebec."

Knowlton Nash, who had left his job as Washington correspondent to become the director of news and current affairs for the CBC English network, was in Davidson's office when Pelletier called. After the conversation, Davidson outlined what Pelletier had said: that the country was in danger and that there was a very real possibility of insurrection. Davidson had acknowledged Pelletier's concerns, but he had made no promises. In talking with Nash, however, he made it clear that CBC journalists should avoid "speculative stories" and "inflammatory commentary." Guidance to that effect was sent out to CBC English network journalists, leading to the cancellation or delay of a couple of local discussion programs, but no news stories were killed. There were immediate accusations of censorship, nevertheless, and when Davidson arrived home late that same night, his phone was "ringing off the hook." He told the Canadian Press, "The policy of the CBC is to broadcast all the facts there are, but not gossip and rumours." "There had been instances of inaccuracies in CBC coverage as well as other reporting," CP reported him as saying, "and all sorts of wild rumours and speculation. When you're playing with men's lives, it's necessary to be somewhat more serious." Then, caught off balance by questions about censorship, he added, "I think it's time to cool it."

That phrase captured the headlines, brought more charges of censorship, outraged CBC journalists, and infuriated his executive vice-president, Laurent Picard, whom Davidson had not consulted before making his comment. "Laurent was pretty rough with me," he says.

As soon as he saw what Davidson had said to the Canadian Press, Picard called to give the president an unusual tongue-lashing, warning, "I have the resignations of half of the French network managers." Later, Davidson told a colleague, "I have never been blasted in my life like that."

The next day, Trudeau invoked the War Measures Act, and the day after that Laporte was found murdered. CBC News coverage so far had been, for the most part, a comprehensive, balanced, and fair account of the crisis, all the more reason why CBC News people resented Davidson's "cool it" admonition. French network journalists also protested that management wanted to play down the military intervention and the mass arrests made under War Measures Act. Clearly, the police zeal in making arrests outstripped its wisdom, but the country strongly endorsed the comments Trudeau made in a CBC News interview about "weak-kneed, bleeding hearts" who criticized tough action against the "outlaw bandits" of the FLQ.

One painful stumble by the CBC was an erroneous report carried by both English and French networks that the kidnapped James Cross had been killed. That editorial error was matched by a management misjudgement when the English network, in response to French network pleas, cancelled a documentary on Lenin because it was feared the program would encourage FLQ terrorists. "A document for revolution," Conservative MP Lloyd Crouse had said. In truth, it was a plodding documentary that was more in danger of boring than inciting the public. Davidson was again the focus of media attack for being "craven," "timid," and mindless," but, in fact, the decision had been made without his participation at all. In an ironic twist, as a substitute for the film on Lenin, the CBC put on a documentary about avalanches which included instructions on how to produce a home-made bomb which could be used to control avalanches.

One of the FLQ's demands had been for a CBC broadcast of its manifesto. Picard remembers Davidson telling him, "We have to act before the government is forced to act, because if the government is forced to act it will have to do that openly, and it will be embarrassing to the government. So we are going to put it on the air without talking to Ottawa, for humanitarian purposes." There was a flurry of phone calls with Mitchell Sharp, Marc Lalonde, and Trudeau. Sharp, who as external affairs minister was responsible for the safety of British trade commissioner Cross, recalls approving the CBC broadcast and getting hell later from Trudeau for doing so. "What is this you've done . . . given away to blackmail!" Trudeau told Sharp. Picard, who was the CBC's principal link to Trudeau, had several tense telephone conversations with him, but came away from it all with a high regard for Trudeau's commitment not to interfere in the internal operation of the CBC. He recalls Trudeau telling him at one point, "Laurent, you run the CBC. I'm keeping the right to call you a stupid ass in the House of Commons. But you do what you want. . . . You run the place. . . . If you think you're right, do what you think."

After one other occasion when Trudeau criticized the CBC in the House of Commons, he apologized to Picard, saying, "I may have gone a bit too far." Picard agreed and told Trudeau, "Pierre, I'm going to say you're wrong."

"That's your right. Fine," said Trudeau.

Throughout the October Crisis most Canadians got their news from television. With the arrival of TV, radio listening had collapsed, and CBC Radio got few headlines, minimum attention from politicians, except for its morning news and commentary, and only passing glances from most senior CBC management. Private radio had followed the American model of programming popular music interspersed with snippets of news and, on some stations, highly personalized and opinionated phone-in shows. Families no longer sat around listening to the big radio in the living room, they had switched to watching television. The advent of the transistor had made radio mobile, and now people wanted faster-paced programs, as they were listening only for short periods in their cars, or while shaving or putting on makeup in the morning.

The CBC Radio turn-off began first in English-speaking Canada, but quickly spread to Quebec. Its radio programs had not changed with the times and audiences were plummeting – only an estimated 325,000 Canadians were now listening to CBC programs for any extended period. Laurent Picard knew it was change or die for CBC Radio. He launched a revival campaign designed to make radio programming more relevant and more popular. "We have to redefine the medium," Picard said. For the English network, two keen intellectuals who later became CBC vice-presidents, Peter Meggs and Doug Ward, were assigned the task of drawing up a blueprint, which they called "CBC Radio in the Seventies." A similar undertaking was launched for the French Radio network. In April 1971, after two years of study, they presented their reports which argued vigorously for a resuscitation of CBC Radio. Sen. Keith Davey in the 1970 report of his commission of inquiry into mass media had said CBC Radio was "a national medium in a country unable to support a national press." Meggs and Ward and their French colleagues wanted to prove the validity of that comment and recommended a much expanded program range and the establishment of a CBC Radio One on AM and Radio Two on FM. CBC Radio One would concentrate on news, commentary, information, providing light entertainment and more live and local programming. CBC Radio Two would be more leisurely paced, focusing on music, drama, and the arts.

The revival of CBC Radio was a key project for Picard, who said he feared that unless there were changes, the CBC might become third in a two-station market. He believed that the implementation of the two radio reports would put CBC back on track, bringing in new listeners, encouraging the private affiliates, setting a new creative standard, and giving more emphasis to local programming. The spirits of radio producers soared at the prospect of a rejuvenated CBC Radio, but came down to earth a year or so later when the CRTC refused to approve the plans for Radio One and Two because, it said, they would make the CBC too commercial in its style. The plans, however, had sparked new enthusiasm among programmers, and what became known as the CBC "radio revolution" began to transform the schedules. The CBC also started an FM stereo network. CBC-FM stations had been established in 1946 in Montreal and Toronto, but after an experimental FM network in 1960-62 was scrapped, FM had returned to purely local service. In 1964, FM became network again, and in 1975, a nationwide FM stereo service was begun.

Davidson's new program leadership in Toronto had encouraged local Winnipeg radio producers to develop a 6:00 A.M. to 8:30 A.M. program on AM of news, weather, sports, traffic reports, and analysis of local issues. It was a success, and the idea became part of the "radio revolution," spreading across the nation to other local CBC stations. A similar approach was developed at noon with local programs that had an agricultural or consumer orientation. For the late afternoon, preceding the 6:00 P.M. network news, producers developed local, light information programming. That meant a total of seven hours a day of CBC local programming of news, current affairs, sports, and weather.

"Aux Vingt Heures," "Présent," and "L'écoute" emerged on the French network. And on the English network the previous, rigid fifteen- and thirty-minute programs gave way to longer formats. Under radio director Jack Craine, experimentation with new program styles had begun a few years earlier with the introduction of a two-hour evening program known as "Radio Free Friday," hosted by Peter Gzowski, who had been managing editor of *Maclean's*. It was short-lived, but another, more lasting show called "As It Happens" was developed simultaneously. A little more formal and structured than "Radio Free Friday," "As It Happens" became one of the most popular radio programs in Canadian broadcast history. It also was a national launching pad for one of the country's greatest journalists, Barbara Frum. She, however, was not the host when the program began in November 1968. Veteran CBC announcer Harry Brown and host Phillip Forsythe anchored the two-hour Monday night program, featuring, as the CBC announced, "interviews and telephone conversations with people who are where it's happening: an up-close blend of music and current affairs." Under the direction of executive producer Val Clery, the first program aired a Beatles recording and cancelled an interview with a man who was too drunk to come to the phone. "At least it is different and therefore refreshing," said *Toronto Star* columnist Patrick Scott. By 1971, "As It Happens" was a smash hit. It absorbed "Radio Free Friday," going to five nights a week for ninety minutes. The thirty-four-year-old Barbara Frum joined the program with, as co-host, the controversial artist William Ronald. A year later, after Ronald had left, she and Harry Brown anchored the program, the audience for which had increased by 30 per cent.

After graduating from the University of Toronto where she majored in history, Barbara Frum had written book reviews and hosted a local CBC Toronto TV current affairs program before joining "As It Happens." Frum said that her politely persistent and sometimes insistent style was designed "to find out from these people, 'What's going on in your brain? What's cooking in your gut?'" As she said a few years after making the program and herself a national institution, "I like to have my preconceptions shattered, to find that something is the opposite of what I imagined. I like the complexity of issues and the way they contradict each other."

While Frum began her climb towards stardom so, too, did Peter Gzowski with the national radio show "This Country in the Morning." Gzowski, who must have been born rumpled, hosted it for three years before being lured in 1976 by the siren song of television for what turned out to be a disastrous late-night show called "Ninety Minutes Live." He licked his wounds for a few years and then returned to radio to host the network 9:00 A.M. to 12:00 noon program "Morningside" and captivate listeners from coast to coast. Frum and Gzowski were both backed by enthusiastic, youthful, jeans-clad producers and researchers, working in a creative free-fire zone, whose offices gave new meaning to the word "cluttered." With Peter in the morning, Barbara at night, local early morning and late afternoon information programming, and other new programs such as "The Royal Canadian Air Farce," which debuted a few years later, the "radio revolution" put CBC Radio back on track. The distinguished editor of *Channels* magazine in the United States, Les Brown, said CBC Radio was "arguably the best radio service in the world."

By the winter and early spring of 1972, Davidson could look back with some comfort at his four years as CBC president. He had brought about a successful organizational decentralization, the "radio revolution," and the beginnings of creative rebirth in some TV programming, especially on the information side. This period was also the heyday of children's television programming. New favourites with children were Bob Homme as the Friendly Giant with Jerome the giraffe and Rusty the rooster, and Ernie Coombs as Mr. Dressup with his pals Casey and Finnegan. Chez Hélène, which featured French story-telling, was also very popular. Later, the CBC began broadcasting the American show "Sesame Street" with its own inserts on Canadian history and the French language.

For the most part, however, CBC-TV had retreated from much of its earlier creative daring and had flopped with its confusing $2-million drama spectacular "Jalna." But it was developing a series of impressive and popular historical documentaries, including vivid biographies of Pearson, Diefenbaker, and other Canadian political, cultural, and economic heroes. The most spectacular success was "The National Dream," which transformed Pierre Berton's books on the CPR and the opening of the Canadian West into perhaps the most evocative, effective, and popular visual history lesson the country ever had.

The only cloud over his presidency that Davidson could discern was a nasty strike of technicians which had strangled much programming in the late winter and spring of 1972, including Stanley Cup play-off games. Although he left the hard bargaining to his associates, Davidson occasionally injected himself into the strike, driving his labour relations specialists to distraction. They didn't like seeing the president chatting amiably with picketers in front of CBC's studios and buildings and cheerfully autographing picket signs. Davidson always did more listening than talking, but his labour experts feared he might weaken the CBC's negotiating position. Even more distressing to them was the fact that the woman with whom Davidson was living at the time was a union member who was picketing in front of the CBC's head office building. "She had to go on the picket line, so she found the most obscure place she could find," Davidson remembers. "One night in our apartment, about half a dozen CBC picketers came up, knocked on the door and said, 'Can we come in and have a drink?' That means something."

What it meant to Davidson was that, even while he was refusing the union's demands, he could still communicate with the strikers and maintain good personal relations with them. He ranks the ability to communicate well the number-one prerequisite for a CBC president and says, "If I can contrast myself with Alphonse Ouimet or Laurent [Picard], I think it was in my ability to communicate through interpersonal relations. . . . There weren't very many people who said, 'Davidson, that son of a bitch!'"

In spite of the strike and the occasional political firefight, Davidson was having the time of his life. "The job is more fun than anything I've found in years," he told a reporter in early 1972. He had not only brought a measure of tranquility to the CBC but had reduced staff by 500 to about 9,000, taken over private stations in Charlottetown and Regina, added 40 new TV and 62 new radio transmitters, and increased Canadian content in prime time from 52 per cent to 68 per cent. He still felt the CBC was too commercial, although he was proud that cigarette advertising had been banned during his presidency. Altogether, commercials provided the CBC with about $40 million in a budget of about $225 million, and while he wanted to reduce reliance on commercials, he didn't want to eliminate them entirely. Advertising, he told a parliamentary committee, "helps keep us in touch with the real world." But he worries today about commercialization. "Public broadcasting in Canada is a bastard," he says. "It's one-half commercial and in many ways getting more than half commercial. That's partly a factor of the government squeeze on revenues. But there is not a clear cut choice between private and public broadcasting."

Despite of his love for the job, the sixty-three-year-old Davidson couldn't refuse the even more alluring prospect of a top job at the United Nations when he got an offer from the UN Secretary General Kurt Waldheim. An old friend from the days when he had been the Austrian ambassador to Canada, Waldheim asked Davidson to be his second-in-command as an undersecretary general in charge of budget, finance, and administration. It was an offer Davidson couldn't decline even though he still had three years to go on his seven-year CBC appointment. "Hate like hell to leave . . . but I can't resist a challenge, a new adventure," he said. He had served on various Canadian delegations to the UN and had been president of the UN Economic and Social Council in 1958. His distress at leaving the CBC was real. Bill Armstrong remembers, "He came to my house and burst into tears the night he decided to go to the UN."

"ANOTHER CBC FAILURE," read the *Globe and Mail* headline over an editorial which said, "Mr. Davidson leaves the CBC as troubled as he found it; his administration has been completely ineffective." That excessively harsh verdict was not shared by the government, for Davidson had done exactly what he had set out to do and what the prime minister wanted him to do: he had brought peace, order, and good government to the CBC. The last thing the government had wanted was charismatic, creative inspiration in the head of the CBC, preferring that Davidson keep his public image of a bureaucratic, grey man.

Today, in reviewing his public service career with characteristic irony, Davidson muses, "I set up the machinery for family allowances. They've been wiped out now. I created with Paul Martin and the parliamentary committee . . . the introduction of universal old-age security. That's wiped out now. I tried to decentralize the CBC and strengthen the regional component. That's being wiped out. So," he laughs ruefully, "what the hell have I lived for?

"My greatest satisfaction was that I left the CBC as a more harmoniously working organization than it was when I came," he says. This was true, and if the CBC was less vibrant and daring in its TV programs, at least its reputation with the government had been restored and the organizational wheels rolled more smoothly. It was now the turn of the modern management than to take over.

17

The Risk-taking President

Just about the last thing Laurent Picard wanted was to become president of the CBC. He had taken on the executive vice-presidency as a project not a career, and he wanted to get back to Montreal, where he could make more money, as quickly as possible.

When he took the job with the CBC back in 1968, he had been paid even less than he had expected. Three days before he was to start, Judy LaMarsh called to tell him the planned salaries for him and George Davidson were too high and she was arbitrarily cutting them by $5,000 each. Picard would earn $40,000 and Davidson $45,000. "Laurent, what can you do?" Davidson said in telling Picard it was too late for either of them to back out. "You've said yes and I've said yes." It was a particular blow for Picard who was paying for a house in Montreal where his family still lived, renting an apartment in Ottawa, and commuting each week-end between the two. He kept telling Bill Armstrong that he needed more income so he could finance his five sons' university educations at Harvard. Armstrong remembers, "He used to say, 'Do you know what that costs, Bill? I have to make money. I have to make money.'"

Picard even sold off some of his personal investments in order to finance himself while he was president of the CBC since his salary was about one-half what he had been earning before he joined. "I lived on my shares for seven years," he says. It's no wonder Picard was miffed not only at Judy LaMarsh's action but also when the Conservatives, angry at the CBC over a claimed administrative failure, sought in the House of Commons to reduce his salary to a dollar a year. They failed.

Picard was the obvious successor to Davidson, although a few other men were gossiped about: Sydney Newman, head of the NFB and early CBC-TV producer; André Fortin, assistant undersecretary of state; and Raymond David, head of the CBC French Service. But Picard's was the only name seriously considered, and because he still had things he wanted to achieve at the CBC, he agreed, and his appointment was quickly announced.

Under Davidson, Picard had been virtually the invisible man, working quietly in the background to streamline the organizational machinery and to develop planning processes. Upon becoming president, he said he wanted to change the CBC from an organization that was "large and heavy to light and flexible."

The sturdy and bespectacled new president was uncomfortable with the limelight and criticism that goes with the job of the head of the CBC. "The life of the president is too public for me," he told an interviewer. "Love is never having to say you're sorry. And sometimes I think the job of president is always having to say you're sorry." He was realistic about all the troubles that get hurled at the CBC president, saying, "The role of the leader is to have the privilege of being the first one to be shot at if there's a war."

Although he had a physics degree from Laval University, he had been a professor of business management at Laval, a research associate at the Harvard Business School, and associate director of the business school at L'École des hautes études commerciales in Montreal. In addition, he had headed a controversial inquiry into labour conditions on the Montreal waterfront, consulted widely for major companies on labour-management relations, and served on numerous government commissions.

His approach was often imaginative. He once taught a business course using as a textbook Mao Tse Tung's The Revolutionary War so that budding businessmen could learn, as Picard said, "all there is to know about timing and about preparing your resources." He also referred occasionally to Mao's approach in discussions with his CBC colleagues because he believed Mao's book was "a masterpiece of strategy."

The CBC's predilection for extemporaneous management drove Picard to distraction. His special assistant, David Lint, said that MBA did not mean Master of Business Administration in the CBC at the time, it meant "Management By Anecdote." The comment reflected the worst management problem Picard faced – lack of planning. Executives were experienced "crisis managers" and effective in dealing with day-to-day issues, but, he felt, were so consumed with short-term demands that they had little or no time for long-term planning.

Picard had been Davidson's enthusiastic co-author of the decentralization of the CBC, which he felt was fifteen years late in coming. All Picard's planning and creative management had one objective: "How do we make ourselves so clearly identifiable that we are different from anyone else?" he asked. To do that, Picard said, he wanted to develop a system "in which more risks are taken" and in which the quality of programs was paramount.

The young but greying Picard was preoccupied with the management of creative people. "It's a new problem: how to deal with creative people in industry," he said as he began his CBC presidency. His way of dealing with them was to push as much authority as possible down from senior officers to the program creators. Much of the cause of both the Montreal strike and the "Seven Days" crisis, he thought, could be traced to the tensions aroused by Alphonse Ouimet's penchant for centralization. One proposal, for instance, had been to have only one newsroom, to be located in Ottawa, that would cover the entire country. The object of the proposal was to have more central management control over news programming. "The desire for management control over an organization like [the CBC] just didn't make any sense. . . . You cannot do it," he says. "It's not a car factory with an assembly line. The man who creates the product is the man in the studio. It's not the administrator. The people who are creative should be running the show and you're there [as management] to support them. Because of that you need decentralization. It's the only way to manage it.

"We need to bring much more feedback from the producers into the administration flow. We need much more input from producers and

creative people. The conventional system of a pyramid doesn't apply to a creative organization."

As an example of the new management style he wanted, on one occasion Picard agreed to go on the "Ombudsman" TV program to answer a cameraman's complaint that he had been unfairly treated by the CBC in being denied some work benefits and overtime pay. Picard, as usual, had done his homework, and before an audience of 1.5 million Canadians, told program host Robert Cooper that the CBC had indeed been unfair and promised to rectify the injustice immediately.

Picard pushed both the decentralization of power and the decentralization of money. This meant that the heads of the networks could not come running to head office for special funding for unexpected events such as an election or royal visit since all the money would have been disbursed to them and there would be no head office "slush fund" to "corrupt the system." His approach meant the president and executive vice-president would have less power, but that was essential, he felt, in a creative organization.

He startled both the CBC management and its creative community by plucking out of the ranks of producers and naming as his executive vice-president, the longtime writer, performer, and producer for both radio and television, Lister Sinclair. Sinclair and an up-and-coming young programming executive named Peter Herrndorf and a half-dozen others had been chosen by Picard as a "kitchen cabinet" advisory group, and listening to Sinclair's ideas in meetings, Picard thought that he'd met a genius. "He was absolutely enchanted by this brilliant, articulate man, and Laurent thought, 'This man represents the finest example of English Canada,'" Herrndorf recalls.

While producers thought it was wonderful to have one of their own in top management, much of management itself was baffled, and Picard's predecessor, George Davidson, was upset. He doubted the wisdom of any producer as number-two man in the CBC's senior management. "That was pathetic. That was a mistake," Davidson says, shaking his head at the memory of Sinclair's appointment.

"We chose him," Picard said at the time, "because of his tremendous quality, his knowledge of the media, his capacity to learn anything, his incredible inquisitive mind." The media and the creative community agreed, hailing the news that at long last creators could enter the top ranks of CBC management. The Bombay-born, fifty-one-year-old Lister Sinclair also thought that producers belonged in management, and visions of becoming president played through his mind, knowing as he did that Picard would leave the job within a few years. Sporting a small white beard and horn-rimmed glasses, Sinclair had neither the management image nor management experience, but his creative credentials were impeccable. He had begun writing for radio and stage while at university in 1944 and gained prominence acting and writing for Andrew Allen's "Stage" series during the golden age of radio. He had spent eight years in radio and twenty in television, establishing a high profile as a writer, actor, panelist, commentator, lecturer, and producer in arts and sciences. Sinclair even produced a radio program on sports writers. He was a polymath if there ever was one. Fluently bilingual and articulate, Sinclair bowled over Picard, who had never heard of him before joining the CBC. "Zapped him with his intelligence," Bill Armstrong remembers. In fact, Picard knew next to nothing about English Canadian radio and had spent little time watching any television. He knew "Seven Days" more as a labour-management conflict than as a program. He was, said his special assistant, David Lint, the typical French Canadian with next to no experience in English-speaking Canada.

"Lister's judgements are based on thirty years as a broadcaster, and with a man like him, it's much easier to develop new ideas and bring in new writers," Picard told an interviewer shortly after Sinclair's appointment. In a prophetic comment at the time of the appointment, *Toronto Star* columnist Jack Miller wrote, "Poor Lister. I wonder if he knows what he's getting into."

The problem was that he didn't, and the romance between Picard and Sinclair was on the rocks almost as soon as it began. "It was a little like a man falling in love with a dancer onstage, marrying her, and then resenting the fact that she's never home," says Herrndorf. "Lister is one of the great intellectual forces in the country, but was far less interested in the details, the tactics, the strategies, the managing of a big organization."

Picard soon felt Sinclair had taken the post as a consecration, not as a job, and became agitated at Sinclair's extensive travelling. "He was never there. His secretary never knew where he was," Picard remembers. When he was at head office, Picard still had problems with Sinclair. "He couldn't make a decision. He was jumping on one side and then jumping on the other. Facing your mistake every morning for two years is not great fun."

Meanwhile, Sinclair rued facing his frustration every morning "Picard was a very different personality from the way he appeared," Sinclair says. "He was really not rational at all. Rather, as a personality, he was an intuitive person, very, very emotional and very egotistical. He really wanted to be in charge of everything. We had different concepts of the job. He was disappointed in me because he felt I would not be an appropriate successor."

Picard's subordinates tried to keep Sinclair away from Picard as much as possible. "It was so tense," recalls Bill Armstrong, "I can't remember if he [Picard] was speaking to him or not, but he would avoid Lister." Denis Harvey, at the time a senior executive in Toronto, adds, "Lister would go for days and days and never see Picard. He'd ask for meetings and Laurent would keep putting him off and putting him off."

Sinclair had plenty of program ideas, especially in the arts and sciences, but he did not have the ear of the French and English network leaders, let alone the attention of the president. "I met him on a plane once and he wanted to do a special program on Nobel Prize winners," Harvey recollects. "I said 'Yes, Lister,' but nothing was done. We never dealt with Lister. Basically for us, he was non-existent." Sinclair resented that the network heads went around him and dealt directly with Picard. "He [Picard] should have said, 'Don't talk to me, talk to Lister,'" Sinclair says. "He never did that."

At first Sinclair had plunged into his new role, trampling on some administrative toes, audaciously lecturing private-affiliated stations, and using his executive muscles on his former bosses to change schedules. He felt he was under pressure from Picard to "do something," but often when he sought to, Picard criticized him, "How dare you get the English network all riled up? Now what have you done?" Sinclair remembers Picard saying when he pushed through some TV program schedule changes. "He certainly lost patience with me," Sinclair smiles. Sinclair occasionally put his foot in his mouth as when he publicly questioned the propriety of a popular local Gaelic radio program in Cape Breton. Since Gaelic was not one of Canada's official languages, he feared the program might lead to other language groups, such as the Ukrainians, demanding airtime. Gaelic music was all right, said the Gaelic-speaking Sinclair, but not Gaelic conversation. Picard was distraught at the controversy and, says Sinclair, "He blamed me for all the bad publicity."

Sinclair's future seemed in doubt after Picard made an offhand comment at a CRTC hearing. "It's a funny thing I've noticed since I came to CBC. These men are brilliant when they are producers. They become stupid when they come into management – within half a day." It was interpreted as a slap at Sinclair with whom he was by then totally disillusioned, but in fact, Picard had meant his comment as a criticism of those who automatically complain about executives even when they come from the creative ranks. As Sinclair himself says, "The hosannas from the producers at the start lasted about a week. I underestimated the degree to which the producers would become very hostile."

After an uncomfortable two years in the job as executive vice-president, Sinclair shifted over to a lesser vice-presidential job which gave him more of an advisory than decision-making role, and, in time, he returned to production in Toronto, working in radio and becoming the smoothly erudite host of the evening radio program "Ideas." His time as executive vice-president, he says, was "very bruising."

Picard not only had problems with Sinclair. In the first year of his CBC presidency he was in a mood for change, and he unceremoniously removed as head of the English network the cultivated, white-haired veteran of many an internal CBC battle, Gene Hallman. Picard felt Hallman had made major contributions in encouraging Canadian production, but had become insufficiently decisive and "extremely Hamlety." Picard appreciated Hallman's instincts, but he wanted a more muscular executive to run the English network. "Hallman liked best the philosophical and policy aspects and program initiatives," says Herrndorf, who at the time was Hallman's executive assistant. "What he didn't like so much was resolving turf warfare and reconciling really impossible disputes. He just didn't like the down and dirty bureaucratic stuff. And also Picard wanted his own person. He wanted a much more aggressive, cutting-edge kind of style." Although offered other lesser CBC jobs, Hallman chose to go back to university as a middle-aged law student and begin a new career as a lawyer.

He was replaced by Don MacPherson, who joined the CBC in 1952 as an accountant, became a control room director, moved over to CTV where he became head of news, and returned to the CBC to run Toronto operations. For MacPherson's deputy, Picard chose Denis Harvey, the TV chief news editor, who had been hired the previous year from the Montreal *Gazette*, where he was the managing editor. Picard barely knew the two men, and the appointments came totally out of the blue for both. Picard originally wanted Harvey as the vice-president of the English service, with MacPherson as his number two. "He liked Harvey's management style . . . rolled up shirt-sleeves and very strong in getting in there and giving orders," says Sinclair. But Picard was talked into reversing their roles by Sinclair and David Lint, on the grounds that Harvey had only a year's experience in broadcasting compared to MacPherson's twenty-one years. "You're taking too much of a risk," Picard's colleagues told him, and he reluctantly said, "Well, maybe I am going too fast." So MacPherson got the senior job, although in the end, Picard felt his original idea would have been better.

He told MacPherson and Harvey, "Look, I don't want to know what you're doing all the time, but I don't want surprises. If anything is a problem, you tell me before it happens." Picard seldom came to Toronto, spending much more time in Montreal with the French network. "I think he was uncomfortable in English Canada," Harvey says, "and he said to us, in effect, 'It's your baby.'"

Picard not only wanted new management, but also a new corporate face for the CBC. He had designers develop a logo, which became known as "the exploding pizza," that would identify the CBC on the air, on billboards, buildings, advertisements, and letterhead. Even a new name was proposed for the CBC – Radio-Television Canada – which would read the same in English or French, but Picard rejected the idea. Others thought the ideal name, which would be valid both in French and English, would be Air Canada, but that was pre-empted by the national airline.

At the same time as these executive changes in the English networks, the CBC got into a showdown with the CRTC in the 1974 licence renewal hearings, which were held in an Ottawa motel basement meeting room. Sen. Keith Davey, in his report on the media, had said "sniping at the CBC has become a national pastime" and proof of that was at hand. More than

300 different groups, mostly critical of the CBC, flooded the CRTC with their statements. Pierre Juneau called the assaults "a peculiar sport."

The hearing pitted two strong-willed French Canadians against each other: Laurent Picard, president of the CBC and Pierre Juneau, chairman of the CRTC. Juneau, who endorsed the principles of the CBC and public broadcasting, nevertheless had for some time been dissatisfied with CBC programming, especially on the English network. "Either we have a country, or we don't!" he had snapped at a private dinner just before the hearings as he urged more Canadian programming.

It was ironic to see these two francophones arguing in public, and mostly in English, over the future of English Canada's most important cultural instrument, the CBC. Picard and Juneau had known each other for years. "I knew Laurent very, very well," Juneau says. "We were close." They had worked together on the board of an experimental children's school and moved in much the same social circles. "I was very pleased when he [Picard] became vice-president and then president of the CBC," Juneau says, "and we got along very well. He is an intelligent man, but Laurent is an extremely emotional person and he got very upset. He got very irritated about some of the questions and some of the things that were said, so he was boiling up."

"It was never for me a personal matter," says Picard. "I don't dislike Pierre. We don't agree on a lot of things – there is a lack of chemistry between the two of us – but I can work with people I hate provided we stick to the job. It was always a principle."

What especially irritated Picard were the CRTC's questions and comments about too many American shows and too many commercials on the CBC. He was insistent that "the CBC was not under the CRTC and this was critical." The CBC, he believed, was responsible only to Parliament and to the public, and he thought the CRTC was improperly intruding into the business of the CBC.

Exacerbating the wounds inflicted by the CRTC was a stinging denunciation of CBC programming by a group of querulous English Canadian writers and producers headed by Robert Fulford and Patrick Watson, called the Committee on Television. "Our aim," said writer and committee member Morris Wolfe, "is to move the elephant one-quarter of an inch."

In a lengthy submission, the committee said CBC current affairs programming "had never been worse," drama had reached "a new level of inconsequence," and they felt "betrayed by the mélange of triviality, inconsequence and bureaucratic paralysis which has now become the hallmark of public broadcasting." A few months earlier, Fulford had written in *Maclean's* that years before, when the CBC showed Canadian programs, viewers had "yawned and they switched their dials." So, he wrote, the CBC had begun airing more American shows to give the people what they seemed to want.

In a direct slap at Picard, Fulford, Watson, and their colleagues said, "The true if unwitting enemies of public broadcasting are now at the helm." Watson earlier had sought to have Lister Sinclair as a member of the Committee on Television, but Sinclair had brusquely rejected the idea. "It can't be done," he told Watson. "We naively thought that he would see this as a way of helping the corporation," says Watson. "But he was furious with us and threw us out." Watson and his colleagues also saw Picard, but also got nowhere with him. "He was courteous but he was impervious to our ideas. His preoccupation was financial," Watson recalls.

Picard felt he was being eaten alive by missionaries and told writer Val Clery, "Every president of the CBC has been labelled a failure. Is the CBC so close to Canadians that we have the feeling that it cannot and should not succeed?"

At the CRTC hearing, Picard responded to the flotilla of critics and to Juneau with what one critic called "a bravura performance." Sometimes almost shouting, sometimes almost whispering, and waving a cigar in one hand, with the other he stabbed a pointer at charts and diagrams. Picard sat, stood, or walked, while he poured out a torrent of facts, figures, and philosophy. His counterattack illustrated the difference between he and Juneau. One emotional, the other ice cool. Picard noted that Canadian content had risen during his time at the CBC from just under 52 per cent in 1969 to nearly 70 per cent in 1974. Successful new programs had been broadcast, including the hit series "The National Dream," the consumer program "Marketplace," "Ombudsman" with storefront lawyer Robert Cooper, "The Beachcombers" with Bruno Gerussi, and Al Waxman's "King of Kensington." There had also been a revival in the area of drama with the hiring of John Hirsch to produce with Sunday night dramas and "For the Record," an experimental series of journalistic dramas. Picard noted, too, one of the most thrilling moments in the history of broadcasting when in late September 1972, the CBC aired Paul Henderson's last-minute winning goal in the Canada-Soviet Union hockey championship series. It was one of the country's most unifying moments of the century, with Canadians from St. John's to Victoria, from Windsor to Yellowknife, letting loose a national scream of elation as they heard and saw the goal on the CBC.

When the white-haired Father of public broadcasting, Graham Spry, testified that the CBC's licence should be renewed with no conditions, Picard rushed up to him to shake his hand.

Picard also urged the hearing to clarify the CBC's role in national unity, insisting that the Broadcasting Act's admonition that the CBC "contribute" to national unity did not mean it should be a propaganda agency for unity. "The national broadcasting service," he said, "must be a clear mirror in which the Canadian people can see themselves in all their diversity. . . . Those who would deny . . . unity are themselves part of the diversity and to exclude them would be to falsify the reflection of the Canadian people to themselves."

In its report, the CRTC supported Picard's approach on national unity, but at the same time it said the CBC must be "consciously partial to the success of Canada as a united country." This issue would come back to challenge the CBC within a few years in a particularly nasty political confrontation over the CBC's role in national unity.

The most contentious matter in the showdown between Picard and Juneau, however, was advertising on the CBC. In its report, the CRTC demanded that the CBC eliminate commercials on radio and during children's TV programs, which Picard had already decided to do, and to reduce them on TV by one minute per hour each year for five years – an eventual cut of about 50 per cent – and then to review whether there should be more reduction. "Commercial activity deflects the CBC from its purposes and influences its philosophy of programming and scheduling," the CRTC said. The "commercialization of the schedule," the CRTC believed, led to the "exaggerated predominance of American entertainment programs on the English-language service during prime-time hours."

Outraged by Juneau's report, Picard told Sinclair, "How dare he think he has the right to say that!" "If we abandon American programs now," Picard told a reporter, "we lose our audience and there is no way Parliament will fund a minority network. . . . Sure, I'd like to reduce the commercials, but where's the money to come from? . . . Just give us time."

Ridiculing the CRTC's recommendation to his colleagues, Picard recited the fable of the centipede and the wise old owl who advises him to cut off his legs to relieve his pain. "How then would I get around?" the centipede asks. "Don't ask me," the wise old owl replies. "My job is policy, not operations."

Furthermore, Picard said, Canadian audiences were not seriously irritated by commercials. "I see much more important things to do than to get out of commercial revenue," he said. If the government were prepared to provide money for the CBC to get out of commercials altogether, he felt it would be better spent on improving programs.

The argument over commercials was an old one for Juneau who, four years earlier, had tackled George Davidson at a similar hearing, saying the CBC was "caught between two fires" and was making an "uneasy compromise" between commercial revenue and public service. The CBC, he said, should stop chasing advertising dollars. Davidson had admitted it amounted to a dual personality for the CBC, but said that every time he went to the Treasury Board, he was pressured to earn more advertising revenue. "They asked why it wasn't even higher," he told Juneau.

Over the intervening years, the CRTC chairman had hardened his attitude on commercials and the CBC. "There is a contradiction," he said, "between the CBC's public service preoccupations, which are the reasons for its existence, and its marketing preoccupations. . . . A corporation that is financed by public funds and gets marginal revenues from advertising should not be influenced forcefully by the marginal part of the revenues."

"The CRTC is telling us how to manage," Picard told Montreal *Gazette* columnist Ian MacDonald. "This I find difficult to agree with.

The management of the CBC cannot be held responsible for decision-making if decisions are taken out of its hands."

Although apparently locked in verbal combat, Picard and Juneau were talking past each other. Picard was obsessed with meeting present challenges while Juneau was looking to the future. Ideologically, the two were, in truth, not far apart, but their timing and styles were profoundly different. Picard, the pragmatist, felt the CBC could not cope with a loss of about one-third of its total budget which, he said, the commercial reduction would mean, while Juneau, the idealist, felt commercial reduction was necessary to save the CBC's soul.

As they squared off, Picard said, "I'm not going to let the CBC be pushed around," and he later added, "I am not a loser. The CBC cannot afford to lose any more. It will kill the CBC if we go back to where anyone can kick us whenever they want to." To which Juneau said, "The Commission has lost fights before. . . . But let me make it clear that we cannot afford to and do not intend to, lose too many fights."

In the end Picard won, and the CBC kept its commercials. The CRTC's conditions, by law, could not be imposed on the CBC, and any disagreement had to be referred to the minister of communications for a final decision. The minister, Gérard Pelletier, a friend of both Juneau and Picard, didn't want to intervene, and he knew the government would not increase its grant to the CBC to make up for any loss of commercial revenue. In the face of Juneau's demands for reductions and Picard's adamant refusal, a cabinet committee was set up to review the issue, but its meetings kept being postponed and it never met. By default, the CBC won and kept its commercials. "We just said we wouldn't do it," Picard says. While simply ignoring the CRTCs demand for cutbacks in advertising, the CBC voluntarily gave up commercials on radio, which were valued at $2 million, and commercials on children's TV programming, valued at $1.5 million.

The confrontation illustrated just how far power had shifted away from the CBC. Before Diefenbaker's 1958 law, such a showdown could never have happened because there had been a single broadcast system run by the CBC. The confrontation demonstrated the power the regulatory agency could have under a strong, assertive leader such as Juneau.

While he couldn't force his recommendations on the CBC, he scared the dickens out of its executives.

At the same time the CBC was winning this battle, Picard won another fight when he wrestled $50 million from the government to extend CBC Radio and -TV into remote regions of the country. Every community in the country with more than a 500 population would now be served by the CBC within five years, bringing the CBC to 99 per cent of Canadians.

Perhaps Picard's most important triumph, however, was that he finally persuaded the cabinet to provide a funding formula guaranteeing both long-term financing and an annual increase in funding over and above increases for inflation. In May 1975, the cabinet approved a six-year financing formula that provided an allowance for inflation and a 5 per cent budget increase every year. It was something every previous leader of the CBC had sought but failed to get. Ominously, however, the cabinet said special circumstances might arise which could mean a temporary suspension of the formula. In the end, the government never did officially approve the formula. Lurking in the background and arguing against the whole idea was Auditor General Maxwell Henderson, Alphonse Ouimet's old adversary and a man who had been critical of CBC financial affairs ever since his brief but unhappy period as a CBC financial officer.

In another case, and in spite of Henderson's objections, Picard persuaded the government to allow the CBC to keep half of any money it might save from one year. Previously, any surplus had gone straight back into government coffers.

Having won these concessions from the government and won the battle with the CRTC over commercials, Picard decided now was the time to leave. "I felt sad that I had to go," he says. "It had been challenging, funny, exhilarating and exciting." But personal financial needs forced him to go. At one point, Transport Minister Jean Marchand had offered him the post of chairman of the CNR, but he had turned it down. Possible successors who were mentioned included Claude Bissell, University of Toronto president; Douglas Fullerton, former chairman of the National Capital Commission; Allan Gottlieb, deputy minister of manpower; Peter Newman, editor of *Maclean's*; Mavor Moore, who had been among presidential possibilities for a decade; and Bernard Ostry, secretary general of National Museums of Canada and a former CBC public affairs department executive.

But none of them got the job. It went, instead, to a man who seemed to be the quintessential cautious bureaucrat with the dull grey background of being a deputy minister, a Treasury Board head, an adviser to the prime minister, and a senior Saskatchewan civil servant. Albert Wesley Johnson was a Harvard graduate and a Prairie preacher's son, an insider's insider whose career had been totally in the provincial and federal civil service. He was utterly unknown to Canada's cultural community and without a moment's experience in broadcasting.

18

Canadianize! Canadianize!

$\mathbf{W}$hat the CBC needed was a young, tough-minded, idealistic cultural crusader who could articulate a deep feeling for the country and effectively manage the unwieldy CBC. What it seemed to be getting in Al Johnson was a worthy, prudent, middle-aged financial expert who might be seen anonymously walking the corridors of power, trailing behind a cabinet minister and occasionally whispering into his ear. But looks were deceiving. Beneath Johnson's bureaucratic fifty-year-old year old breast beat the heart of a culturally sensitive nationalist, far more intrigued with policy substance than constraints and processes, and a man whose deep enthusiasms bubbled out in conversations with his colleagues. Pierre Juneau remembers going to a meeting with Johnson to discuss the NFB's budget when Johnson was secretary of the Treasury Board. Juneau recalls Johnson's sense of excitement at what the Film Board was doing. "My what an exciting job you have!" Johnson enthused.

"Al got involved in the substance. He got very worked up about concepts," says Juneau. "He was a public thinker, a public policy man."

The roots of Johnson's enthusiasm for public policy go back to his childhood in Saskatchewan. His father, a close friend of reformer J. S. Woodsworth, was first a Methodist and then a United Church itinerant preacher who travelled to the small towns of Saskatchewan such as

Insinger, where Johnson was born, Riceton, where he went to public school, and Wilcox, where he went to high school.

Johnson's social conscience was formed during the Depression when, as a teenager, he helped his father hand out food and clothing to destitute farmers. His sense of Canada and the world came from listening to the CBC on a crystal set or an Atwater Kent radio. He grew up listening to "Citizens' Forum," "The National Farm Radio Forum," Foster Hewitt, "The Happy Gang," and dramas such as W. O. Mitchell's *Jake and the Kid*. "It was the CBC that introduced me to Canada," he says. "The CBC was Canada. Without it, for me, Canada would only have been Saskatchewan. It was our Canadian theatre and newsmagazine and music hall. We loved it. And we needed it."

Johnson went to college at age fifteen, and after graduating from the University of Saskatchewan, he went to the University of Toronto and then to Harvard. He joined Tommy Douglas's CCF government in Saskatchewan as a budget analyst, and at age twenty-nine, clearly a "comer," he became a deputy minister. "My father wanted me to go into the church," he once said. "I wanted to go into politics. I ended up a career civil servant."

When the Liberals of Ross Thatcher took power in Saskatchewan, Johnson left, snatched up by Ottawa Liberals in 1964 as assistant deputy minister of finance where, as in Saskatchewan, social reform was his lode star. His idealism, enthusiasm, and love of his country made Johnson one of Ottawa's noted mandarins. He became deputy minister of Welfare in 1973.

After nearly three decades as a civil servant, Al Johnson was a golden boy to government insiders, but he was an unknown to the country at large. Laurent Picard, however, knew exactly who Al Johnson was and wanted him as his successor. "He was the obvious choice at the beginning," Picard says. Unlike any CBC president before or since, Picard had the power to make his wish happen. "Laurent Picard . . . had been given a hunting licence by the prime minister to find a successor," says Johnson. Picard had approached Johnson a few years earlier to be his executive vice-president. Johnson, who was in the midst of helping to revise the social security system, declined and the job had gone to Lister Sinclair. Now, in 1975, Picard took a different approach. When they met, Picard pulled a sheet of paper from his pocket and said, "Here's a list of names and I want your advice."

The list of about eight names had been boiled down from an initial fifty that Picard had considered as a possible CBC president, and he had gone across the country taking soundings on the "possibles." He never explicitly offered the job to anyone except Johnson. What he really wanted was Johnson to look at the list and say that he could do a better job than any of them. As he read the list Johnson felt Picard was "managing me. He was really very clever." Johnson sensed that indeed this might be the job of a lifetime. He knew its reputation as a killer job but the very challenge of it tantalized him.

"Yes, I would be interested. I would like to do that now," Johnson said. "I've done what I want to do in the public service."

When the announcement was made that Al Johnson was to be the new leader of the CBC the headlines, in effect, said, "Al Who?" The scepticism of the outsiders was matched by the doubts of the CBC insiders who didn't know Johnson either and were largely dismissive of his civil service credentials. What they saw when Johnson took the elevator to his sixth floor office in his early days as president was a stocky, bespectacled, soberly suited man of medium height with wavy grey hair and a smile that crinkled his square face. Occasionally he whipped out an inhaler for his asthma.

"The big question," he told an interviewer, "is whether I can be [an] energizing force. Whether I can make the things that must happen, happen. . . . What I have to do is provide the kind of leadership that will help creativity." Nearly twenty years later, recalling his early months as president, he says, "I had to decide what are the one or two things I want to accomplish."

Gladstone Murray had got the CBC going. Davie Dunton had brought in the golden age of radio. Alphonse Ouimet had brought television to Canadians. George Davidson had brought order to the CBC out of the post-"Seven Days" chaos. Laurent Picard had streamlined and decentralized CBC management. Al Johnson wanted to bring to the CBC effectiveness not merely efficiency, and he was basically indifferent to technology, administration, and management systems. For him, they were only instruments to be used to achieve the one accomplishment he wanted passionately: Canadianization of the airwaves. He was frustrated by the early sessions he had with his senior staff. "The briefings I was getting tended to be more of a management kind," he says. "That took me aback. I had to push these people away from me."

Rejecting "these people" led some of them to criticize Johnson as a poor manager. The new CBC president, however, reached out to programmers in a way that none had tried since Davie Dunton three decades earlier. He established personal relationships with network program directors, producers, columnists such as Joan Irwin of the *Montreal Star*, and an ever-widening circle of creative people who kept pushing him on the need for more Canadian and more creative programming.

As these people "bugged me and pushed me and pulled me," and as his own predilection propelled him, Johnson took a significantly non-bureaucratic approach to running the CBC. Picking up Laurent Picard's theme, Johnson says, "Giving some kind of direction to a creative organization is profoundly different from managing anything else because the whole idea is that you must have cells of creativity. They have to be free. They have to be free of administration and bureaucracy. It's almost a benign anarchy."

When he articulated these ideas to some politicians, they'd say, "No goddamn wonder the CBC has trouble." Some CBC head office bureaucrats privately disagreed with Johnson's approach, too, but his style won him high marks from a creative staff that had expected so little from a seemingly dull civil servant.

What he desperately wanted to do was increase the quality and the quantity of Canadian programming. "He wasn't very interested in the day-to-day management of the CBC," says Peter Herrndorf, who served as Johnson's vice-president of planning after he left the TV current affairs area in Toronto. "He was much more interested in ideas and concepts. He was also the most passionate nationalist . . . hellbent to turn the CBC into an instrument of Canadian cultural nationalism. This is a man who is very liberal intellectually and quite conservative emotionally. He loved the swirl of ideas, but he had to have a fair degree of emotional comfort as well."

Denis Harvey was in the middle of many a creative debate with Johnson and recalls, "We'd stay to twelve or one o'clock in the morning debating and discussing. He loved that kind of thing. He always felt journalists in Canada had too much power and that they didn't understand things. We had some terrible, angry debates, but one thing about Al is that the next day it was all forgotten. He was terrific that way."

He would suggest program ideas but seldom insist on them. "I don't like using brute force," he says. "Once you use brute force with creative people you have changed the relationship and you can no longer have the kind of easy and informal and almost creative exchanges about the direction you want to go." Head office's use of brute force in the "Seven Days" crisis, Johnson believes, happened because there was no agreed-upon journalistic code of ethics and no continuing personal relations with the programmers. When all that is missing, he says, "then you have a disaster on your hands." None of this stopped him from vigorously arguing with programmers about his pet peeves such as advocacy programs, what he felt was occasionally excessive criticism of government, dramatized documentary sequences, and ombudsman-type programs.

Radio programming came in for Johnson's particular attention. The preferences of his wife, Ruth, a CBC Radio devotee, were memorized by Bill Armstrong, who had become head of English Radio. "She lived and died with CBC Radio, and we used to hear a lot through Al about what she liked and disliked," says Harvey. In 1976, when Bill Armstrong made dramatic program changes, especially in the arts and music programming, the Johnson household was upset with some of the alterations. "Ruth was very, very interested, and she also had a very good friend called Adrian Lang [Transport Minister Otto Lang's wife at the time] who was very, very interested, too, and they would chat daily about any changes," Armstrong remembers. He heard the president's reports of those chats, spiced with Johnson's own, sometimes biting, criticisms.

Armstrong heard complaints from inside the CBC about these radio changes as well, including one from a producer of a series cancelled to make way for Mark Starowicz's "Sunday Morning." The producer threatened to get her uncle, a cabinet minister, to protest the change by asking the Treasury Board to reduce the CBC's budget. "Altogether, the complaints brought terrible pressures. It was just awful. But the ratings went up," says Armstrong, adding, "Johnson was quite cross with me for about a year." Johnson, however, came to appreciate Armstrong's talents, promoting him to be number-two man for all English services under Herrndorf and later recommending him as executive vice-president of the CBC.

Given the lead time of a year or two needed to develop TV programs, most productions in Johnson's first few years were inherited from the Picard era and included some significant successes such as Al Waxman's "King of Kensington," "Marketplace," "Ombudsman," and major documentaries on the fifth anniversary of the October Crisis in Montreal, on crime in Canada, and portraits of Trudeau and Lévesque.

There were a few creative disasters as well, including a current affairs program still unsuccessfully chasing the ghost of "Seven Days." "Up Canada" was intended to be cheeky but turned out to be, as one critic wrote, "the worst tragedy since Shakespeare wrote *Hamlet.*" In the fall of 1976, with much fanfare and at considerable cost, the CBC launched "Ninety Minutes Live," a late-night variety and current affairs program hosted by Peter Gzowski and designed to woo Canadians away from Johnny Carson. It didn't. Critics nicknamed it "Ninety Minutes Dead" and pronounced the program "lacklustre," "an inexcusable affront . . . a monument to CBC incompetence." It was a 1970s version of the same fate that, in the 1990s, would befall another late-night show, "Friday Night! with Ralph Benmergui." Most of the blame for the "Ninety Minutes" flop unfairly fell on the drooping shoulders of Gzowski, who was described by one columnist as "a fumbling amateur." His shambling, meandering style seemed out of sync with the slick, fast-paced aura that the producers of the show sought to project. Hurt and harassed, Gzowski fled before the program died, and his TV career went with it. Later he returned to his natural home in radio, where his air of innocent exuberance and endless curiosity made him a national cultural hero for his morning network program, "Morningside." What did not work on television for Gzowski clearly worked on radio, and he became one of Canada's all-time favourite radio personalities.

The fall of 1976 also brought another TV program problem to Johnson's door when Lloyd Robertson, anchor of "The National" for the past half-dozen years and the CBC's most visible face, was suddenly wooed away by CTV. It was bad enough to lose his smooth, familiar, and friendly presence, but losing him to the opposition's newscast was especially worrisome for the CBC. Correspondent Peter Kent took his place and, in fact, the audience loss the CBC had feared never occurred.

One program triumph of Johnson's first few years was the coverage of the 1976 Summer Olympics in Montreal. For more than two weeks, the nation was united as seldom before in watching on CBC-TV the best athletes in the world race, jump, swim, hurl, and otherwise compete.

For Al Johnson, however, the pivotal event of his entire presidency had nothing to do with programs. It was the November 15, 1976, election victory of René Lévesque and his Parti Québécois. No event so shaped his CBC presidency as did the political, philosophical, and creative fall-out from that election.

"My presidency," he says, "was characterized by the omni-present problem of the Parti Québécois having been elected, of the impending referendum, and by the obsession of members of Parliament from Quebec and the élites of Quebec with the notion that CBC, Radio-Canada, had contributed to separatism and was responsible for the election of the Parti Québécois. They believed that." For them, proof came on election night from the Montreal TV studio, where an invited audience, accompanied by some French network personnel, burst into cheers at news of Lévesque's victory. Industry Minister Jean Chrétien complained that the cheers drowned out the words of anchor Bernard Derome, although, in fact, the noise was relatively muted.

Within two months of the PQ victory over the Liberals in Quebec, an all-out Liberal assault began on the CBC. The first salvos were fired by a longtime friend of Johnson, Jean Marchand, who had played a key role before in the life of the CBC as the "generalissimo" of the 1959 producers strike in Montreal. Since then he had gone into politics, been a Trudeau cabinet minister, and in January 1977, he was making his first speech as a new member of the Senate. "If this country is ever destroyed, it will be in large measure because of one Crown corporation – Radio-Canada," he told the Senate.

Immediately after making the speech, Marchand telephoned Johnson to say, "Al, I want to tell you that I have created difficulty for you. It was a political imperative in my judgement. I know Quebec, and I know I had to say this." Johnson thanked his old friend for calling and then watched the roof cave in as one cabinet minister after another and then the prime minister himself poured vitriol on the CBC for promoting separatism and tearing the country apart. The logic of their argument was that there were separatists in the French network, which meant programs were biased in favour of the PQ, and in any event, the mere reporting of PQ statements and activities in recent years had helped to spread separatist ideas.

Jean Chrétien accused the CBC of forgetting that its objective was to promote national unity. "I am frustrated every night by it," he said, citing as one example of separatist bias the fact that French network had stopped using "O Canada" when it signed off each night. The CBC said it had been omitted because of technical problems, and it was promptly put back on. There were complaints, too, that the French network referred to Trudeau as "the federal" prime minister.

Trudeau came to feel he would never be fairly reported on the French network and, echoing his anti-French network comments of eight years earlier, he told the House of Commons, "When the taxpayer picks up half a billion dollars a year to have a public broadcasting system, he is justified in ascertaining that the public system does not set out to destroy the country." He warned of Radio-Canada "propagandizing" separatism and said, "The overwhelming majority of employees in Radio-Canada are of separatist leaning." Fingers were pointed at René Lévesque, who had been a high-profile CBC commentator, and at Lise Payette, who had been the popular TV host of a CBC French network late-night talk show and was a close associate of Lévesque in the PQ.

Finance Minister Donald Macdonald joined the assault, as did the government Senate leader Ray Perrault, Labour Minister John Munro, Monique Bégin, Mitchell Sharp, and other prominent Liberals such as Simma Holt, a British Columbia MP who said, "The CBC has divided Canada.... If we don't clean it up, our country is going to pieces." Quebec Liberal Maurice Dupras demanded that all CBC employees take loyalty oaths and Urban Affairs Minister André Ouellet said, "Every night there's bias and every night it's in favour of the separatists." He demanded that Johnson "fire the bloody guys who are working separatists," and he said he had a list of separatists working in the CBC to "destroy the country."

As part of his proof of separatist leanings at the French network, Jean Marchand cited Radio-Canada's treatment of René Lévesque in reporting a late-night car accident in which Lévesque had hit and killed a sixty-two-year-old derelict lying on the street. The CBC, Marchand said, had called the victim "a wino" and had not mentioned that he was a war veteran "who fought for his country."

Opposition leader Joe Clark sprang to the defence of the CBC, saying the accusations were "a deliberate attempt by the Liberal Party and by its senior ministers to try to create the impression in English Canada that separatism was created by the CBC." His charge may have been right in part for the Quebec Liberals were seeking to blame anyone but themselves for their election loss to the PQ. But also the federal Liberals hoped their firestorm would intimidate the CBC and Al Johnson to limit coverage of PQ activities and to openly propagandize federalism. Trudeau told a news conference, "If you work for the CBC, you must produce national unity."

Johnson, apprehensive but not cowed, knew he was striding through a political minefield. Meeting privately with Quebec MPs, he agreed there were separatists in the CBC, but said, "The CBC has never given political blood tests and we're not about to start now." Responding to demands that he fire employees who were separatists, he asked the MPs, "Have you expelled the members of your family who are separatists?"

As George Davidson had reasoned eight years earlier, Johnson argued that the test was whether separatist employees were slanting the news. "And by that test, I believe firmly that the news coverage was fair," he says.

Pierre Trudeau and his Quebec Liberal caucus did not agree and would long remember what they considered Johnson's refusal to act. What they didn't know about was Johnson's subtle internal struggle with the French network and to a lesser extent with the English network. He was sparring with the powerful head of French network news and current affairs, Marc Thibault, who had loomed significantly in the Montreal producers strike of 1959 and during the parliamentary hearings into "Seven Days" in 1966. He was a friend of former communications minister Gérard Pelletier, knew Trudeau, and by 1977, was the *éminence grise* of the French network.

Thibault, his boss, Raymond David, who was in charge of the French network, and his colleague Jean-Marie Dugas, the head of French TV, were known as "The Jesuits" who ran the French TV network with a missionary zeal. They had led the fight for programs that were harbingers of the Quiet Revolution. As Quebec writer and TV host Guy Fournier has written, "It is thanks to television that our society began to exist. . . . Television is not the consequence of the 'Quiet Revolution,' it preceded it and brought it about." "The Jesuits" were among the leaders within the CBC who helped shape the social impact of television in Quebec. Inside the CBC they fought against the domineering centralization of the Ouimet era. "The Jesuits" were much more philosophically driven than most of their English network colleagues. Now they were in charge and were the targets of much Ottawa invective about coddling separatists and were even accused of being separatists themselves.

Thibault had joined the CBC in 1950 as a producer, popularizing educational programs for radio, and became the program director of network radio before taking over public affairs programming. He was a proud, passionate Quebecker who understood the feelings of his separatist colleagues in the CBC, but at the same time, he was eloquently and sometimes hot-temperedly insistent on journalistic balance and fairness. He knew there were active separatists in the French network newsroom, and he tried to weaken their influence. "Oh yes, sure, we had serious problems with a few of them," he says. "During the October Crisis two of them were fired. . . . Those two were very activist in the newsroom on political matters. . . . Many wanted to break the limitations within the French network and they engaged in outside initiatives we didn't approve."

Thibault's English network counterpart, Knowlton Nash, didn't have to face the accusations of separatist bias in programming but, like Thibault, he was determined that the CBC journalistic programming would not become a propaganda machine either for any type of separatism or any particular brand of federalism. The CBC's job, they argued forcefully with Johnson, was to maintain its journalistic credibility by reflecting the reality of the country, including the reality of separatism. Their fear was that the federal government wanted CBC journalistic programming transformed from being a public watchdog to being a government lapdog, as other Canadian governments in other years had also sought. Only during the years of the Second World War had CBC management succumbed to such government pressure.

428

Johnson listened and accepted Thibault's and Nash's arguments on the overriding importance of journalistic integrity, but he had other ideas of how to make the CBC more reflective of the nation as a whole. He demanded and got much more French network news coverage of Canada outside Quebec which hitherto had been sharply limited on the grounds that more than 90 per cent of the French network audience was in Quebec. He also demanded and got more English network coverage of Quebec, and he had the two networks launch a joint prime-time series called "Quarterly Report" on the major issues facing Canada, including French-English questions. It was an idea that had been considered more than a decade earlier but had been lost in the throes of the "Seven Days" crisis. When it aired on the English network, Barbara Frum was a co-host. Johnson also wanted joint network drama and variety shows so the country could see more of Quebec and Quebec more of the country.

There was some resentment and resistance in the French network where these changes were viewed by many as bowing to pressures from the prime minister. Thibault, pushed from the top by Johnson and from the bottom by much of his staff, walked a political tightrope and argued with Johnson for less than the CBC president wanted and with his colleagues for acceptance of "Quarterly Report" and other such programming, which was more than most of them wanted.

The French network senior officers were all, or mostly all, federalists but many of them had sons and daughters who were separatists, and what played out between Ottawa and Montreal also played out between father and son and father and daughter. Some French network officials were accused by senior Quebec Liberals of being separatists. The accusations were whispered in private among themselves and into the ears of CBC head office officials. Specifically, Marc Thibault and Raymond David were accused of being separatists. "I was told that very often," says Laurent Picard. "Trudeau was convinced I was a separatist," says Thibault. "I have the feeling they were not comfortable with all of us. They felt that we were encouraging [separatists]. They tried very hard to prove that we were doing a very dirty job."

Thibault believes Marcel Ouimet, the onetime head of the French network and later vice-president of CBC program policy, privately encouraged the cabinet in its belief that Thibault, David, and others in the

French network were unwilling or unable to control the separatists. Thibault said he thinks he was first labelled a separatist because of his parliamentary testimony during the "Seven Days" crisis, in which he had said the role of the CBC was not to promote national unity but rather to reflect the reality of the nation and the constitutional options facing Canada. "We had no responsibility to promote any options, but we had to reflect all the positions," Thibault says.

Despite Johnson's efforts, the political hammering of the CBC continued with much of the argument based on the cabinet's interpretation of the Broadcast Act, which said the CBC must "contribute to the development of national unity." Everyone from the prime minister down kept saying the CBC must "promote" national unity. To Johnson and most of his senior executives, "promote" meant propagandizing, and "contribute" meant reflecting what was going on in Canada. The latter had been Parliament's understanding when the Broadcast Act had been passed nearly a decade earlier, but there had been no René Lévesque and no Parti Québécois in power then. Johnson told reporters he would resign rather than submit to political pressure and interference in CBC programming.

In a way, this was Johnson's finest hour as CBC president. His emotions were pushing him to share much of Trudeau's national vision of Canada yet his intellectual side resisted the political pressures on the CBC to become a federalist propaganda agency. "He felt very strongly and very emotionally that we were a national instrument, and it was our job to rally the forces," says Peter Herrndorf. "As the debate went on he became more of the view that it was really the CBC's job not to proselytize for a particular view but to provide information so Canadians could make their own choice. Al's intellectual instinct about how a democracy had to work prevailed, much to the chagrin of people in political office."

That chagrin was easily seen in the cabinet, which felt Johnson was too defensive and not in control of French network programming, a feeling shared by even a few CBC board members at the time. There was a sense among some of the more politically active Liberal appointees to the board that Johnson was far too easy on separatists in the French network. They were sceptical of his arguments about journalistic freedom in the face of the threat that they, as well as Trudeau and most of the cabinet, believed the nation confronted. "The separatists were running the French network and he was much too tolerant of them," one then board member says.

"Trudeau came to feel that the French Service of the CBC management was really not in charge. I was startled by Trudeau's intensity of feeling," says Dick O'Hagan, then the prime minister's media adviser. "I was told that in the caucus a lot of voices would say, 'They're either separatists or fellow travellers.'" Liberal Quebec MPs and much of the cabinet began to believe that everything produced by the French network was calculated to serve the cause of separatism.

In the late winter of 1977, Trudeau further inflamed the debate by telling the House of Commons of "a loud, continuing and even agonized cry" in Quebec about the CBC destroying the unity of the country. He then set up a committee of inquiry into the CBC headed by Harry Boyle, who had succeeded to the CRTC chairmanship on the departure of Pierre Juneau in 1975.

It had been a long climb for Boyle, who as a teenager had been a truck driver, a house painter, and a hobo who'd been thrown off a westbound freight train by railway security men in 1932 near the Ontario-Manitoba border. By the time he was nineteen, the red-faced cherub had started writing for weekly newspapers and shortly after began his broadcast career. He became a radio announcer in Wingham, Ontario, at a salary of three dollars a week, then ran the CBC farm department and became CBC Radio's director of programming, achieving cultural heights with the golden-age program "Wednesday Night" while simultaneously battling CBC bureaucracy. At one point, Alphonse Ouimet had asked Boyle to resign. "Screw you, Al! You have to fire me," was Boyle's response. Ouimet shrank from that, although he kept Boyle in the corporate doghouse.

Although Boyle still bore a few personal grudges against the CBC and felt strongly that it was not portraying the regions as well as it should, he was, nevertheless, a devoted public broadcaster. Now, as one of Ottawa's top mandarins, he knew how angry the cabinet was at the CBC. Simma Holt said in public what others only muttered in private: "Take the CBC off the public purse. Sell it!" she told the House of Commons. Recalling the ferocity of the anti-CBC feeling in the Trudeau cabinet at the time, Boyle says, "The CBC was vulnerable because the Quebec caucus was absolutely fired up. You have no idea of the vehemence of it. But, [John] Turner, [Donald] Macdonald and six or eight of them were more violently opposed to the CBC than [to] the French network. Macdonald was advocating, and Turner was advocating, selling the CBC. And they weren't fooling. Macdonald said, 'Let's sell it and get rid of it. We've had enough.'" Mac Donald today doesn't remember the statement, but Boyle says it was accurate. "This I got leaked back from cabinet. I don't think the CBC was ever as vulnerable as it was at that point. Trudeau was pissed off with it. He was sick and tired of it." If the CBC were not to be sold, one cabinet minister proposed its budget be reduced to one dollar, in effect, abolishing the CBC.

Boyle remembers being told by a close friend of Trudeau, "Pierre was just on the verge. He had been fed up with the whole thing. God knows what he could have done." On the question of selling the CBC, Boyle says, "The whole thing, in retrospect, strikes you as being stupid. Nobody would think of selling the CBC. But then, they've sold a lot of other things since then."

Boyle says the CBC didn't realize how much danger it was in, and so he had the CRTC examine CBC programming, searching for a way to appease Trudeau but at the same time endorse the role of the CBC and public broadcasting. When they finished, he produced a sweeping set of charges, attacking the CBC for failing to reflect the country as a whole adequately and emphasizing the importance of the role of public broadcasting. In a headline-grabbing accusation, the CRTC said that all the broadcast news media in both English- and French-speaking Canada "are biased to the point of subversiveness," a statement insisted upon by CRTC member Northrop Frye. Frye had been warned that the phrase might be misconstrued but had refused to abandon it.

The CRTC said the broadcast media were biased because they didn't provide enough information, because the news they aired was primarily what happened in Toronto, Ottawa, and Montreal, and because the networks assume Quebeckers don't care about what happens in English-speaking Canada and vice versa. "These assumptions are intolerable," the CRTC said. "They also are extremely stupid." Boyle had long felt it was critical for the CBC to gain more support in small-town and rural Canada, and he argued forcefully in private for more CBC transmitters to reach these areas.

Boyle's report generally dismissed accusations of separatist influence on CBC French network programming, saying only 13 per cent of Quebeckers thought there was a separatist bias while 12 per cent thought there was a federalist bias. Much of the CRTC's criticism of the CBC was an echo of its attack on the CBC in Picard's and Juneau's confrontation three years earlier. "The CBC, the English network particularly," Boyle said, "seems to have fallen between its mandate of being an instrument of Canadian public interest and a more or less deliberate self-imprisonment in the North American mould of entertainment and commercial sponsorship."

Boyle had succeeded in diverting the assault on the CBC French network for its separatist bias by berating the English network for its failure to reflect the country. At the CBC, that set tempers flaring, especially Al Johnson's and the English network journalists', who resented what they felt was a grossly unfair criticism, particularly the accusation of "subversiveness." "Gratuitous and insulting," Johnson said, and he attacked the "unsubstantiated and unqualified assertion that the CBC has failed to contribute to the development of national unity." In retrospect, however, Johnson feels that while the charge was flamboyant, "It was an excessive statement that was easy to handle." Boyle says his report "didn't waver" in support of the CBC and only denounced some of the execution of its responsibility. Thus, Boyle believes, his report may have saved the CBC from some dramatic and damaging action by the Trudeau government.

The Conservatives and the NDP demanded that Trudeau apologize to the CBC for his accusations of separatism which, they said, Boyle had disproved. Trudeau, however, said Boyle's report had supported his charges. "Mr. Boyle says there is subversion and there is bias," Trudeau responded, adding that the findings "bear out some of the suspicions." At a news conference he called the CBC Canada's "sorcerer's apprentice . . . out of control of Parliament in many senses . . . [and] a world in itself."

But whether because of Boyle's report or because of simple exhaustion, the intensity of the Trudeau and Quebec Liberal attack on the CBC faded, especially after René Lévesque's Quebec referendum defeat in 1980.

With the board of directors and management carefully monitoring the coverage, there was no substantial complaint from either side about the way the CBC handled the referendum campaign, except on the night of the vote itself. Jean Chrétien, as justice minister, had been the key federal player in the campaign in Quebec, but on referendum night he wasn't interviewed at length by CBC-TV and was fit to be tied. The CBC had interviewed Trudeau and Quebec Liberal leader Claude Ryan and had decided that was enough for the anti-separatist side. Chrétien fumed that the separatists were keeping him off the air, and he complained to the cabinet about a CBC conspiracy against him.

Although the issue never again aroused the flaming intensity that it had between 1960 and 1980, the political resentment against Johnson for not being tougher on the separatists in the CBC sharply intensified. The irony was that Johnson was also accused by much of Quebec's creative community of bowing too much to federalist pressures.

Johnson and the CBC got into more trouble with the Trudeau government a few months later when the English network news service broke wide open to public view the RCMP's barn burnings, office break-ins, unlawful mail openings, telephone-tappings, and a whole series of botched illegalities in Quebec all designed to combat "subversives." Led by investigative reporter Brian Stewart and researcher Joe McAnthony, night after night CBC News uncovered more RCMP Security Service misdeeds, mortifying the government and leading to further attacks on the CBC. Solicitor General Francis Fox said the CBC was wasting public money by "irresponsible" reporting, and he suggested that funds should be taken away from the CBC and given to the RCMP. Fox later apologized, and even Trudeau admitted that the RCMP's actions had been "technically illegal." The scandal tarnished the RCMP and also aggravated the cabinet's distress with the CBC and Al Johnson. The government felt especially aggrieved since arguments about the RCMP's misdeeds echoed in the House of Commons, which was now under the watchful eye of television, and thus seen and heard by millions of Canadians.

The fall of 1977 had seen a breakthrough for television when cameras were allowed to record the House of Commons debates and Question Period. TV cameras had first been allowed inside the House a quarter of a century earlier to record the visit of U.S. president Dwight Eisenhower. Since then, the CBC had televised special ceremonies of Parliament and had carried out experiments in provincial legislatures, but it wasn't until October 17, 1977, that the first televised regular session of the House of Commons was seen, pre-empting the soap opera "The Edge of Night." The government was not altogether enthusiastic about TV in the House because it was the embarrassing questions and clash of Question Period that were usually seen on the nightly news. Inevitably the footage showed the Opposition on the attack and the government on the defensive. It did, however, also show Canadians for the first time on a regular basis their government and their Parliament in action. With the same sense of magic that they had when they first heard radio and saw television, Canadians were fascinated by the early broadcasts from the House of Commons. They, for the first time, could actually see the prime minister and his cabinet ministers being peppered with questions and defending their actions. It was the fulfilment of Prime Minister MacKenzie King's dream half a century earlier. He had been astonished at the effect of his 1927 nation-wide broadcast from Parliament Hill marking Canada's Diamond Jubilee and impressed with how broadcasting could be used to spread political and national awareness throughout the entire country, a possibility now dramatically enhanced by television.

TV in the House of Commons made MPs abandon the tradition of thumping their desks in approval of some comments. The politicians thought it looked bad on TV so they switched to hand clapping instead. Television, in addition, led to increased heckling. MPs also wanted the viewing public to think they were always present in the House and so rushed to fill seats around the prime minister or whoever had the floor so the public would not see empty chairs. The MPs learned, too, to be more fastidious after NDP leader Ed Broadbent was seen scratching his crotch live on the first day of television, and Federal-Provincial Relations Minister Marc Lalonde was seen picking at his teeth.

During his years as CBC president, Al Johnson shared MacKenzie King's dreams of the nation-building possibilities of broadcasting, and he was captivated by the idea of "Canadianizing" the airwaves. That would be, he decided, his monument. It would also reinforce the "Canadianization" Pierre Juneau had sought during his years at the CRTC and would be Johnson's answer to accusations from Quebec Liberals that the CBC was betraying Canada.

He was encouraged to draw up his manifesto by a speech by Secretary of State John Roberts who, in late May 1977, had said TV had failed Canada because it was too Americanized. "As a business, television is a success story," he said. "But as a positive force for the development of a national consciousness and pride, it has been a failure. . . . I am determined [to stop] . . . more foreign cultural penetration." Johnson determined to go beyond Roberts' rhetoric and make specific proposals, in effect, asking the government to put its money where Roberts' mouth was.

Using as his ghost writer a similarly committed Knowlton Nash, director of the English TV news and current affairs, Johnson began to develop a major policy statement. It was considered unusual by both the media and the Ottawa civil service because of its passion, its personal nature, its willingness to admit errors, its blunt accusations of government failures to deliver on government rhetoric, and its boldness in offering a blueprint for broadcasting of the future. Out came all of Johnson's bursting pride and personal commitment to Canada, all his emotional ties to his Prairie roots, all his exuberance at the nation-building possibilities of public broadcasting, and all his private love of the arts. Called "Touchstone," the document possessed Johnson, frustrating some colleagues who felt his near-obsession with the statement distracted him from more practical, day-to-day management issues, and some who disagreed with his emotional rhetoric and his criticism of some past CBC actions. Undeterred by or unaware of the criticism, Johnson was boyishly enthusiastic about what he called "my credo," which would be the first full-scale articulation by a president of specific guiding principles for CBC programming. In his sweeping *cri du cœur*, Johnson was impelled by one of his favourite quotations: "Dream no little dreams. They have no

436

magic with which to stir men's souls." Stirring souls was exactly what Johnson wanted to do. "If you don't have a grand dream for the CBC and public broadcasting, you can be sure you're never going to achieve one," he says.

In distinctly unbureaucratic language, Johnson declared in "Touchstone," "The hottest place in hell is reserved for responsible authorities who, in times of crisis, remain cautious and circumspect. I have no intention of going down to that place, and there is absolutely no way I'm going to be circumspect in the cultural struggle of our nation. You develop a culture with passion, not passivity. In this plan for Canadian culture and public broadcasting in Canada and its reinforcement of our nationhood, I am going to be as fighting, aggressive, bold, loud and honestly nationalistic as I am capable of being.... We are in a fight for soul, for our cultural heritage and for our nationhood."

He began by saying the statement "is a confession in that I believe we in the CBC have failed to play our proper leadership role in the national battle for Canadianism.... It is an accusation in that I believe successive governments and their agencies have failed to provide the policies and funding necessary to safeguard Canadians and our culture through broadcasting, especially in English Canada. And we in the CBC have failed to be sufficiently forceful in dramatizing the need for appropriate policies and funding."

The personal style, the accusations, the confessions of failure, and the warnings of "cultural invasion" and "electronic rape" of Johnson's eighty-page "Touchstone" statement captured headlines across the country. Most of it was laudatory, if sceptical, about the possibilities of Canadianizing the TV airwaves to reach a target for Canadian programs of 50 per cent of all viewing. Ironically, that was the same target Charles Bowman had urged in the late 1920s for radio listening. Surveys showed Canadian TV programs were watched by about 20 per cent of the total viewing audience at the time, which also was the same percentage of Canadians who were listening to Canadian radio programs back in 1927. "AL STICKS HIS NECK OUT," headlined the Vancouver *Province* over a column by Charles Lynch, who said, "Brave Johnson's heart is on his sleeve and I greatly fear it's going to end up broken."

"A COURAGEOUS STATEMENT," said the Montreal *Gazette* headline.

Montreal Star columnist Joan Irwin wrote, "No chief executive of the CBC has ever made so passionate a commitment to the principles of public broadcasting."

"MR. JOHNSON'S DREAM," said the Halifax *Chronicle-Herald*, and the Antigonish *Casket* headed its story, "A. W. JOHNSON'S IMPOSSIBLE DREAM." The scepticism was rooted in a feeling that Canadians would rather watch American programs than those made in Canada. Syndicated columnist Basil Deakin wrote, "Frankly, I don't believe they would really care for all that emphasis on home-made, home-grown productivity. It would go against Canadian social inclinations and history."

Johnson not only aimed his "Touchstone" manifesto at the politicians but also at the CBC staff. He criss-crossed the country, selling his public broadcasting ideas in big and small meetings, lunches, dinners, and bull sessions with CBC producers, technicians, office workers, and bureaucrats. He particularly targeted the senior program managers, some of whom were dubious about "Canadianizing" and whose vision of the CBC was more market oriented. He had to be a missionary among the hired guns who worried about losing audiences with too much Canadian programming. In response to their doubts, Johnson said, "It matters because they [the audience] are soaking up American values and attitudes and history and mythology, and they are soaking up the values of American commercial television. . . . Of course there are North American values we share with our American neighbours, but there are Canadian values, too, and Canadian traditions and history and institutions and you sure don't get them on American television."

"Touchstone" had scores of specific recommendations, most of them focusing on "Canadianizing" CBC prime-time television to 80 per cent by the early 1980s, with special emphasis on the English network. A second CBC-TV channel was proposed. It would be commercial free, culturally rich, somewhat like BBC-2, and repeat many of the main channel's programs. There was a promise to move "The National" from late night to prime time; commitments were given for more Canadian dramas and documentaries and a reduction of American programs; and more co-operative projects between the English and French networks were promised, as was more coverage of all of Canada by the French network and of Quebec by the English network. Many of the fundamental changes in CBC-TV programming over the next decade and a half had their roots in "Touchstone," including putting "The National" and "The Journal" at 10:00 P.M. and a predominantly "Canadianized" prime-time CBC-TV schedule.

Johnson's focus on Canadianizing CBC-TV did not distract him from the problems of commercial revenue and its impact on CBC programming. "Too often public broadcasting needs are overridden by commercial considerations," Johnson said. ".... public service needs always must come first for the CBC."

The CBC's commercial department and some senior English network officials were dismayed by that statement, but, in any event, the CBC remained in the grip of the commercial culture because of government budget cuts that made commercial revenue even more important.

Johnson, to this day, remains distressed by the ethos of commercialization, which he feels has "polluted" public broadcasting. "CBC would have been better off never having started getting into commercials," he says. He feels CBC programs are forced into a form of split personality by the CBC being mandated to reflect Canada, but at the same time being ordered to earn ever-higher commercial revenue, which is attracted by mass-appeal programming. "We at the CBC were always trapped with the tensions between commercials and public service," he says. CRTC chairman Harry Boyle felt the same way about those tensions, and later wrote in *Maclean's*, "The Corporation is neither fish nor fowl, and that makes it vulnerable."

Some politicians and senior bureaucrats were uneasy over Johnson's "Touchstone" manifesto because they felt he was appealing over their heads to the public and beginning to establish a constituency of his own for support of Canadian programming. If it took hold, they feared, it might limit the political manoeuvrability of the government in setting broadcast policy. "I knew I had to put my dream, my sense of direction, before the CBC people and the audience," Johnson says.

Describing the need for a campaign for public broadcasting, Johnson says, "Somebody and some people in the CBC have to be constant crusaders, including the president and leading programmers. We in the CBC have never been good at mobilizing our own audience, which politicians never want you to do. They can get cross with you. But in the final analysis, they will listen to public opinion. They might hate you for having organized public opinion, but they have to listen to it."

"Touchstone," in effect, was a counterattack to the separatist charges made against the CBC, and Johnson used it as the CBC's statement to Boyle's CRTC inquiry. "I accelerated the timing of it," he says, "because of the pressures we were under in the Quebec situation. We were on the defensive. I can't say enough about how that obsessed and oppressed the CBC, at least was oppressive on the president, to cope with the situation effectively. We had to get off the defensive."

Johnson had more success in articulating his "Canadianizing" ideas than implementing them. The government was becoming tight-fisted and less supportive of the CBC president, at least partly because it was losing faith in his ability or desire to clean house in the French network. "He didn't deliver to Trudeau and his colleagues what Trudeau expected of him," says Marc Thibault. Retribution came financially as the government initiated its economic restraint program and reneged on earlier promises of increased and long-term funding. "The Quebec crisis blew up, and that blew up our funding formula, too," Johnson says.

Just over a month after Johnson issued his "Touchstone," Trudeau chopped $71 million out of the CBC's 1979-80 spending plans of $574 million. So much for Johnson's plans and Secretary of State John Roberts' brave words. "The cut in the CBC's budget, I'm sad to say," Johnson said, "seems to represent a willingness on the part of the government – conscious or otherwise – to accept what amounts to a continuing drift towards cultural colonialism in Canadian broadcasting."

The government's harsh budget cuts made Johnson look inward, juggling finances to try to achieve as much "Canadianization" as he could, especially on the English TV network. Staff was reduced, old equipment and studios patched up, and program plans downsized. On the nation's twelve million TV screens, "The Beachcombers" and "King of Kensington" continued as smash hits playing to bigger audiences than most of the best American imports, and a showcase of Canadian talent such as Gordon Pinsent, Wayne and Shuster, Oscar Peterson, Anne Murray, René Simard, Bruce Cockburn, Hagood Hardy, and Tommy Hunter was offered. A performance of *Giselle* with Karen Kain and Frank Augustyn complemented the popular music, as did a concert with Glenn Gould and the Winnipeg Mennonite Choir. Portraits of Emily Carr, Lucy Maud Montgomery, Sir Wilfred Grenfell of Labrador, Nellie McClung, and Northrop Frye were seen. In current affairs, "Marketplace" was drawing 1.7 million viewers, "the 5th estate" 1.5 million, and "Ombudsman" 1.4 million, while "The National" at 11:00 P.M. was watched nightly by an average of 1.3 million and reached a total of 3.6 million different Canadians every week. "The Nature of Things," Roy Bonisteel's "Man Alive," and "Quarterly Report" were both audience and critical successes. It was a breathtaking array of programming, achieving 74 per cent Canadian content on CBC English TV, far beyond anything that Graham Spry and Alan Plaunt dreamt about when they began campaigning for public broadcasting nearly fifty years earlier. Nor would they have dreamed that Canadians would be spending an average of twenty-two hours a week watching television – roughly half of all their leisure time. In journalism alone, the CBC was providing 75,000 hours a year of programming on radio and television, including 500 different radio and television newscasts a day.

The hurrahs for these achievements were not universal, however. Some performers and producers felt Johnson was not doing enough. That was evident at a black-tie dinner in Toronto, where Johnson was in the audience when Patrick Watson accepted a 1977 ACTRA Award as the best TV public affairs broadcaster for hosting "The Last Nazi" about Albert Speer, aired by Global. In his acceptance speech Watson said, "At the CBC, milk rises to the top." It was a joke Watson had heard that afternoon from Marshall McLuhan, and he almost immediately regretted repeating it. "I thought I was being very clever," he says. "I was a smart alec and cocky. It was very thoughtless." That night, however, it set off a series of attacks on the CBC for creative timidity by other award winners, so much so, that M.C. Pierre Berton responded that without the CBC, there would be no awards, adding, "We're all part of the CBC."

Watson seemed to be still fighting his "Seven Days" battle. He had become embittered while negotiating his host contract for Ross McLean's "The Way It Is," when he had been told by CBC-TV boss Marce Munro, "Don't kid yourself Patrick, the CBC is never going to give you a contract as a producer again."

There also was distress in the English network executive suite. Denis Harvey was growing restive, feeling he was carrying more than his full share of the management load as number-two man of the network. His relations became increasingly strained with his boss, vice-president Don MacPherson, because of what he felt was MacPherson's irresolute management style. "I had to do every tough thing," he recalls. "I got fed up." Their arguments erupted more frequently and publicly, unnerving their subordinates. "I don't like it when Daddy and Mommy are fighting," cracked Jack Craine, the English TV network program director. Finally Harvey quit and when he did, Peter Herrndorf took his place, and shortly after was elevated to the English network vice-presidency, replacing Mac-Pherson. Herrndorf became the driving force behind implementing Johnson's "Touchstone" promise to expand "The National" and put it into prime time. Herrndorf, a dynamo of cultural activism, had been head of TV current affairs on the English network, briefly a CBC vice-president of planning, and was now the head of the English Radio and TV networks. Aged thirty-eight, he had a law degree, a journalistic background, a Harvard Business School education, a fascination with power brokering, and an intense commitment to public broadcasting. The bald eagle wunderkind angered many in his relentless, hyperactive determination to get what he wanted. He put in fifteen- to eighteen-hour work days and expected his senior associates to do the same, which sometimes led to resentment among his subordinates. Herrndorf's style was to trample on bureaucratic toes, bully his bosses, and inspire his producers.

In the summer of 1979, he had established a task force which recommended moving "The National" from 11:00 P.M., where it had been for nearly three decades, to 10:00 P.M. to be followed by a current affairs interview and documentary program, which would come to be known as "The Journal."

The announcement stirred doubt about putting news in the heart of prime time. Most commentators and observers felt it was suicidal because, they said, Canadians wanted to watch American shoot-'em-ups and soap operas in prime time. "The safest bet to make is that it simply won't happen . . ." editorialized the *Globe and Mail*. "It will face a loss of audience and a loss of revenue. The network can't afford either."

While most of the news people were enthusiastic at achieving their old dream of a prime-time slot, they were in the minority. Advertisers were unhappy at the idea, private broadcasters thought it was just dumb, the CBC commercial department forecast a loss of $6 million a year in advertising revenue, CBC plant officials initially were not consulted and, when they eventually were, they warned of havoc caused by the demand for new technical facilities, the CBC private affiliates were aghast, demanding and getting a CBC guarantee that they would not lose advertising revenue, and the non-journalistic CBC programmers protested at the priority given to news and current affairs. Even most of his senior executives opposed Herrndorf's project. "Nobody believed we could compete at ten o'clock with news and current affairs every week night," Herrndorf says. "They thought it would be a fiasco."

Unpersuaded and undismayed by the naysayers, a bull-headed Herrndorf stomped ahead. "I really thought that with 'The National' as the engine and with a very strong 'Journal' behind it, we finally would be a national stage for events of the day every night, and that for the audience it would be irresistible," Herrndorf says. "I had little doubt that it would work." He felt the risk was minimal because he knew current CBC ratings at 10:00 P.M. were weak. "We were just dying," Herrndorf says.

His biggest challenge was the financial improbability of the CBC being able to afford "The National" and "The Journal" at 10:00 P.M. as well as more drama and CBC-2, more ambitious than originally conceived and which would cost anywhere from $9 million to $16 million a year to operate and up to $82 million for capital costs. Clearly, increased government funding would be required to pay for all this. Johnson's heart lay in more drama and CBC-2, rather than in news and current affairs at 10:00 P.M. "I would have preferred to put a good Canadian drama on the air every night, but I knew I couldn't afford it," Johnson says. Executive vice-president Pierre Desroches was also dismayed at the costs. At a reception in Ottawa he pulled aside one of the news project's key planners, Bruce McKay, and told him, "What the hell are we going to do? We can't afford to do both of these things." Herrndorf doubted that the CBC would get CRTC approval for its CBC-2 proposal, although Johnson still had some hopes.

With single-minded tenacity, Herrndorf argued with Johnson who, Herrndorf says, "was sceptical because it wasn't really where he wanted to go. But he was terrific, and he and I came to an understanding. He would let the game go on. He could have killed it at half a dozen points. As time went by he became less sceptical." For about a year, Herrndorf conducted his selling job, massaging the CBC bureaucracy, senior officers, and the board of directors, and talking of the program as "an engine of reform." He found growing support among board members, particularly in Dan Hayes of Calgary and John Young, who had gone to law school in Halifax with Herrndorf. Initially, the board had favoured a 7:00 P.M. to 8:00 P.M. airtime for the program, although it quickly adopted the 10:00 P.M. start. There was less enthusiasm on the board for Herrndorf's creative estimates of the cost. "The budget got bigger and bigger, and there were some estimates that didn't turn out to be entirely accurate," laughs Johnson in recalling Herrndorf's budgetary juggling. "He can't add!" exclaimed a later CBC president, Pierre Juneau, in exasperation over Herrndorf's budget control. At one point, Herrndorf's program planners found they had forgotten to request a necessary $7 million in capital spending for the new program. He flew to Ottawa to face a clearly angry president and head office executive to seek additional money.

"You have to explain this to the board tomorrow," Johnson told him.

"I can't," said Herrndorf. "I'm getting married in Toronto at nine-thirty tomorrow morning."

"Well, you just have got to make this presentation!"

Reluctantly, Herrndorf called his bride-to-be, CBC program executive Eva Czigler, to postpone the wedding for a few hours. The next morning he faced an exasperated board of directors. "They just trashed me," Herrndorf remembers. "Around noon, after trashing me some more just for the fun of it, they approved it." He immediately flew back to Toronto and, in Judge Rosie Abella's chambers at 4:45 P.M. on June 6, 1980, the wedding ceremony was held.

The problem of financing both the 10:00 P.M. program and a CBC-2 disappeared a few months later when the CRTC rejected Johnson's CBC-2 idea on the grounds that the CBC should concentrate on improving its existing channel. The CRTC did leave the door slightly ajar in expressing some philosophical support of the kind of programming a second channel could generate. Encouraging Johnson's "Canadianization" objectives, the CRTC also said, "The transformation of the

Canadian system into an appendage of an American programming system is both unacceptable and unnecessary." The CRTC's statement seemed to be directed as much or more at the Trudeau government as at the CBC.

With board approval of the 10:00 P.M. "National" and "Journal" – the biggest gamble up to then in Canadian TV programming – television history was made. In announcing the new programs, Johnson said, "We've got to try some bold moves." The key producers who would make those bold moves a success or failure were Tony Burman, executive producer of "The National," and Mark Starowicz, executive producer of "The Journal." They would spend a year and a half getting ready. Both were hyperkinetic Montreal print and broadcast journalists in their early thirties who had catapulted up through the CBC ranks. Starowicz had been a fiery-eyed student radical in Montreal who had become executive producer of "As It Happens" and then launched "Sunday Morning." But all his CBC experience had been in radio, not television, and thus his appointment added to the gamble being taken. Like Starowicz himself, many of his key program staff came from radio, including the principal host, Barbara Frum. She and Mary Lou Finlay on "The Journal" and Knowlton Nash on "The National" (who had moved from the executive suite to the anchor chair) became the public faces of Johnson's most visible example of "Canadianization" and, contrary to the doomsayers, the 10:00 P.M. to 11:00 P.M. hour (10:30 P.M. to 11:30 P.M. in Newfoundland) was a hit from its first night on Monday, January 11, 1982. Burman, aided by the creative zest of director Fred Parker, had turned the venerable, slightly stodgy "National" into a fast-paced, production-rich newscast. Meanwhile with "The Journal" Starowicz had introduced a new kid on the journalistic block that became "must" viewing for much of the nation. "Our goal," said Burman, "is . . . to make the hour an essential hour in the lives of Canadians . . . a service they can get nowhere else." Overnight, audiences for "The National" doubled and all the doubting Thomases were converted. The popularity of "The National" and "The Journal" was a joyous surprise to Herrndorf and the board since they had low-balled their audience expectations.

There had not been so much focus on journalism since the heyday of Patrick Watson and Doug Leiterman. The ghost of "Seven Days" finally had been put to rest sixteen years after the program's demise. Starowicz had toyed with the idea of having Watson do documentary work on "The Journal," but the plan fell apart after loud exchanges among Watson and Starowicz and his staff. Watson didn't hesitate to offer criticism of the program, especially since half a dozen years earlier Watson and Ottawa producer Cam Graham had proposed a similar Monday-to-Friday prime-time current affairs program. The idea had been rejected by senior management at the time as being too costly. "Mark didn't like what I had to say about his program," Watson says. "When the program went off the air that first summer for a two-month holiday, I said, 'Give it to me. I'll keep it on the air with a skeleton staff.'" To reporters he complained of the "glibness" of "The Journal" and said it was too "mechanical." "It's so con-trolled," he said, "that it leads me to think it's being careful not to offend." His criticism was taken badly by Starowicz and the program staff, and the clash ended Watson's involvement in "The Journal." He went to New York to host the short-lived CBS Arts Cable Network.

The success of "The National" and "The Journal" seemed even more impressive when the French network launched its prime-time journalis-tic twin a year later. While a major success, "Téléjournal" and "Le Point" never made quite as big an impact as did the English network program, in part because it wasn't given as many resources or as much money.

The success of "The National" and "The Journal" did not, however, burnish Johnson's image in the government's eyes, and while he wanted to be renewed for another term as CBC president, Trudeau and his col-leagues had other ideas. "It was clear for anybody who knew what was going on in Ottawa," says Johnson's successor, Pierre Juneau, "maybe wrongly, unfairly, but it was clear that Al's mandate would not be renewed. . . . He went through a very difficult period during which it was very difficult to run the CBC."

Trudeau and most Liberal MPs thought that Johnson was a "bleeding heart manager" and that the CBC was "out of control," especially in the French network. Trudeau had argued that there were times when the commitment to free speech had to be abridged and he, his Quebec cau-cus, and many other Liberal MPs felt Johnson had not accepted this in the crisis over separatism. "Don't these people realize what's happening?"

they would say in discussing Johnson and the CBC. "They're naive fools. In such a crisis, you're either for us or against us."

Johnson didn't see it that simply, and so he paid the price of his convictions and his defence of the CBC against the charges of Trudeau and the Quebec Liberals. "He badly wanted a second term and was very upset when he didn't get it," says Denis Harvey. "Johnson was the last of the builders, the last president to have the concept of an expanding CBC," says John Young, a CBC board member from 1976 to 1986. "After him, it was all contraction."

After the end of his seven-year presidency, Johnson taught at Queen's University and then at the University of Toronto, headed the Canadian Broadcasting League, and became a consultant for numerous provincial and federal government agencies. When 1982 began, he buoyantly told employees to have pride in CBC achievements in producing "some of the best radio and television programs in the world" in spite of disappointments in not having the finances to do more. Seven months later, he was gone, many of his dreams unrealized. Nevertheless, he had spurred the CBC into an irreversible "Canadianization" of its TV schedule. Aside from that legacy he also left his heart at the CBC. "The best job I ever had," he says. "The best seven years of my life."

19

Pierre Juneau,
The Defiant Lone Ranger

Not since Gladstone Murray ran the CBC had anybody brought to the presidency the credentials carried by Pierre Juneau. The fifty-nine-year-old Lone Ranger of broadcasting rode into the CBC in 1982 armed with an unmatched background of commitment to creativity and communications leadership. He had been a senior executive at the NFB, chairman of the CRTC, an adviser to Prime Minister Trudeau, and a deputy minister. The hooded-eyed cultural nationalist was a hero to Canadian music because of his CRTC order of 30 per cent Canadian content in radio music – the Juno Awards are named after him. He was also a hero to broadcast nationalists for his advocacy of more Canadian TV programming; a hero to public broadcasting purists for his assaults on commercials; and a hero to those discontented with the CBC's past performance who saw in him glimpses of their own vision of the CBC's mandate for service. As much as Picard was primarily concerned with process and Johnson with substance, Juneau was preoccupied by policy.

Juneau's detached elegance, his tenacity, and his coiled combativeness led to descriptions of him as being "disciplined," "austere," "incorruptible," "a perfectionist," "demanding," and "autocratic." Trudeau wanted someone to go into the CBC and shake the trees and regarded Juneau as the ideal tough manager. Juneau also knew how to weave through the

448

Ottawa bureaucracy with his implacable logic and his impeccable personal connections to the prime minister. In short, Pierre Juneau looked like he had just about everything the CBC could possibly want in a president. There was, however, one seemingly inconsequential speck on his curriculum vitae that would, in time, blacken his universe and destroy his dreams.

The speck was a political misadventure that his friend Pierre Trudeau had talked him into. In late June 1975, Trudeau had called Juneau and surprised him by saying, "Pelletier's leaving . . . I'd like to talk to you about this. . . . Would you accept the job of minister of communications? I have to have an answer for the beginning of July."

Trudeau and Juneau were longtime colleagues and friends, having first met in their Left Bank student days in Paris in the late 1940s, sharing interests and ideas. Juneau, from an old Montreal family, had been trained, like Trudeau, by the Jesuits – Trudeau at a rich boy's residential school and Juneau at a bare-bones day school in downtown Montreal. Juneau had been an activist organizer for an influential student Christian movement called Jeunesse étudiante catholique, where he worked closely with Gérard Pelletier in pursuing religious freedom and social progress. When Juneau and Trudeau returned to Montreal from their European studies, they joined Pelletier in founding *Cité Libre* as an activist intellectual voice of reform in Quebec. René Lévesque also joined them as a contributor.

Juneau had been interested in seeing how film could be used for popular education and social advancement and was delighted when the NFB offered him a job. "The Film Board was very attractive because it combined social activism and film," he says. There, he was essentially a bureaucrat, never a creator, although he often appeared on CBC programs as a commentator or host, usually discussing films. After working for the board in Montreal and Ottawa, he was sent to London to represent the NFB for two years. He came back to be secretary of the board and then head of French production. It was when he was in that job that Judy LaMarsh, after consulting the new Liberal political star from Quebec, Pierre Trudeau, asked Juneau to be the vice-chairman of the BBG, which launched him on his career as the regulatory czar of Canadian broadcasting.

449

While generally hailed as a crusader for Canadian programming, Juneau was criticized by some because during his CRTC years he had licensed more private stations, the Global Network, and cable services, all of which had the effect of boosting the viewing of American programs. Critics such as Robert Fulford and Morris Wolfe denounced Juneau as the architect of increased American viewing. "He established a pattern of CRTC decision-making that has succeeded over the years in undermining the central role of the CBC in the Canadian broadcasting system," Wolfe later wrote. Commenting on his appointment as CBC president, Fulford wrote, "If Pierre Juneau today looks around the CBC and sees a once great corporation that has been pushed into a desperate corner, he must know that he bears some part of the responsibility." Their views were in the minority, however; most observers regarded Juneau as a strong cultural nationalist.

When Trudeau called him, Juneau had had seventeen years with the NFB, two years as the BBG's vice-chairman, seven years as chairman of the CRTC, and he was looking for new ways to implement his nationalistic vision for Canadian broadcasting.

Juneau had never thought of going into politics, but as he considered Trudeau's invitation, he began to feel that many of the objectives he couldn't achieve as a senior bureaucrat could be reached as a minister. He recalled meeting with Al Johnson when Johnson was Treasury Board secretary to try to find "any trick that we could use, any means that we could use, to force more money into production by some kind of levy."

"You don't have the power to do that," Johnson had told him. But now, he realized that, as a minister, he could have that kind of power. "I had been convinced," he said, "that regulations and quotas were indispensable, but that the main problem was production. If we could not increase the capacity to produce programs and particularly fiction, then quotas were a bit artificial and I felt that could only be done at the political level.... So I accepted."

He was sworn in as minister of communications replacing Pelletier and then had to face a by-election in Pelletier's old, working-class riding of Hochelaga in the east end of Montreal, a riding that had been solidly Liberal since 1921. It was a cinch, he was told. There was no way he could lose. But as a wide-eyed political innocent, he could and he did. "I discovered that so-called political machines are sometimes pretty run down, and mine was," he laughs now. There were also charges that the Liberals had parachuted an anointed candidate into the riding. In addition, as a colleague said, "He had all the right instincts and sympathies, but he just couldn't talk to those working-class people." The final blow to Juneau's short-lived political career was the announcement on the eve of the by-election of Trudeau's wage and price controls. "The impact of that was devastating," Juneau says, and he was handily beaten by an unknown Conservative, a mailman, who later became a Liberal.

Juneau resigned as communications minister and Trudeau hired him as an adviser. He then served as chairman of the National Capital Commission for a few years. In 1978, he became undersecretary of state and then deputy minister of communications. When Joe Clark won the 1979 election, Clark asked him to stay on as deputy minister, which Juneau believed indicated that the Conservatives regarded him as a public servant and would not hold against him his fleeting moment of political fame as a Liberal cabinet minister. As a deputy minister and CRTC chairman, he had concentrated on broadcast policy and had never envied the operational role of the CBC president. He considered the CBC presidency a nightmare job of harrowing complexity and Byzantine bureaucracy.

"No, no, no." he kept saying to friends who suggested he would be offered the job of CBC president, and when Communications Minister Francis Fox told him, "People were talking around the table today that you are going to the CBC," Juneau replied, "Francis, I am not going to the CBC." He didn't want the job for two reasons: first, he found it exciting and rewarding to be developing cultural policy as a deputy minister, and second, he was scared to death of the job. "I was a bit terrified," he says. "You know the rumours that the CBC is filled with intrigues."

At lunch one day a group of friends attacked his attitude. "You're crazy! You're absolutely crazy!" they told him. "You're interested in culture. Policy is all very well, but the CBC is it. That's the cultural scene in the country." Juneau began to have second thoughts. Although he worried about what he had heard of backstabbing at the CBC, he reasoned that most people there were "nice" and he decided, "I'll make use of the positive people and I'll manage the others. I let it be known that I'd changed my mind."

In fact, nobody had formally asked him to be CBC president, although he was aware that Trudeau had decided he would not renew Al Johnson's term. The prime minister wanted a Quebecker and thought of Quebec Liberal leader Claude Ryan or de Montigny Marchand, deputy minister of external affairs. But it was his old friend Pierre Juneau he chose. Besides, he may well have felt he owed something to Juneau after talking him into his political misadventure in Hochelaga. Certainly he also felt Juneau would take control of the CBC in a much tougher way than Al Johnson had.

One of the first things Juneau confronted as CBC president was the decentralization implemented by Davidson and Picard and continued by Johnson. It ran against Juneau's grain. He believed the president and his board were under so many pressures that they had to have strong control to "run the place." "Juneau felt he had a mandate to get this thing under control, and he was horrified at the lack of controls in the CBC," says Bill Armstrong who became Juneau's closest associate. "If you're spending a billion dollars, people expect some kind of controls." Shortly after he was named president, John Bassett gave him a dinner party at which Bassett jokingly noted that if any of Juneau's new CBC colleagues thought he wouldn't be a strong-minded boss, they had better think again.

Juneau wanted more financial control and he felt too much authority was held by the English and French network vice-presidents. His centralizing predilections were a partial throwback to Alphonse Ouimet's management style, and they inevitably meant pulling some power from Toronto and Montreal and putting it in Ottawa. It was the classic dilemma of running the CBC: centralization for better presidential control versus decentralization for more programming freedom. Juneau decided not only to wrest some financial controls from Toronto and Montreal, but he also wanted more involvement in senior network appointments. "I don't want to read in the papers about the new head of a department," he said. To get the control he wanted, he split up the English and French network vice-presidents' jobs, which angered the network heads and left them dramatically reduced in power. The move initiated a reversal of the decentralizations achieved by Davidson and Picard.

"Pierre initiated his reorganization without any consultation or any involvement of mine or of any of the other senior people," says Peter Herrndorf, then vice-president of the CBC English Radio and TV services. Juneau also had sharp stylistic differences with Herrndorf. "He was small and shy and Peter was big and confident," says Trina McQueen, a senior English network executive at the time. Juneau's changes were too much for Herrndorf, who saw his job chopped into three pieces. His responsibilities for the regions were taken away and put into the hands of a new vice-president located in Ottawa, and his responsibilities for radio were given to another new vice-president. "Peter was left with what we thought was the biggest single, most important job, which was English television," says Bill Armstrong, who had particularly wanted radio to have a separate vice-president.

Herrndorf also had a problem with Juneau's appointment of Armstrong as CBC executive vice-president and Herrndorf's immediate superior. Armstrong had been Herrndorf's deputy a short time before, and he and Herrndorf had long had an uneasy relationship. Their values and styles differed, with Herrndorf more the assertive buccaneer with a specific program agenda and a much more pluralistic style, and Armstrong the prudent traditionalist and highly competent professional manager. Herrndorf's first love was journalism and Armstrong's was the arts; Herrndorf came out of programming and Armstrong came out of management. Their differing backgrounds made a professional, if not personal, clash almost inevitable. With Al Johnson's strong endorsement, Armstrong had been appointed as head of English radio by Don Mac-Pherson and Harvey, and when they departed, the newly-appointed Herrndorf inherited Armstrong as his deputy. Herrndorf thought Armstrong had done "a superb job in radio," and there was never open warfare. But Armstrong resented the manner in which he felt Herrndorf used him to lobby with the board in the campaign to win approval of the 10:00 P.M. to 11:00 P.M. "National" and "Journal" programming and was acutely uncomfortable with Herrndorf's budgetary juggling in projecting the costs of the new programming. He also was annoyed when Herrndorf went off on a holiday in France, leaving Armstrong to deal with financial problems of how to fund "The Journal." "His style was certainly not mine," says Armstrong. "There wasn't any personal antagonism. We were quite friendly. But I was fed up with the lack of attention to the managerial side." Armstrong left the CBC to run the new concert venue in Toronto, Roy Thomson Hall. His chairman at Thomson Hall was Ed Pickering, who had played such a key role in the establishment of the CBC in 1936.

When Juneau was named CBC president and was looking for a number-two man, Al Johnson told him, "Bill Armstrong's your man," recommending the fluently bilingual veteran CBC executive as the executive vice-president. Armstrong, however, was happy with his new adventure at Thomson Hall and turned down the first invitation to return to the CBC. Juneau flew to Toronto and successfully wooed Armstrong at lunch. He was aware of strains between Armstrong and Herrndorf. "Bill had been Herrndorf's assistant in Toronto and the relations between them were not the best in the world," Juneau says.

It was, however, Juneau's removal of much of his authority that irked Herrndorf the most. He described Juneau's management changes as "a fairly conscious, aggressive effort to cut my wings," which he had been told about only at a breakfast meeting four days before they were announced. "Peter thought it was a terrible mistake," Armstrong says. "I'm sure at that moment he set the wheels in motion to get out." Right after the breakfast Herrndorf began preparing a lengthy memo on why he thought the changes wouldn't work and on what he felt was Juneau's effort to control rather than to liberate his senior subordinates. Creativity, Herrndorf felt, could only come from liberation. His protests were rejected, however. The changes, he says, produced "absolute chaos inside the CBC."

"I'm not getting much sense of support from Ottawa," Herrndorf finally told Armstrong six months later, "and unless there is some kind of sign of support, I'm simply going to pack my bags and go."

"Peter said very frankly if we did not change our position that he would leave," Juneau says. "We did not change our position, so he left."

The breaking point came in early October 1983 at a three-day "think in" about the CBC's future that Herrndorf was holding for about sixty-five television producers and executives at a resort on the shores of Lake Couchiching, north of Toronto. Trying to be both an inspirational as well as a managerial leader, Herrndorf sought to motivate his colleagues with a positive creative vision. Juneau, who was in agony from a hiatus hernia, spent only part of a day with the group. He took a decidedly less hopeful view of the CBC's financial future than Herrndorf offered. "We do not expect new funds," Juneau said, and he also did nothing to dispel the CBC producers' fears that an increasing amount of program production would be taken from their hands and given to independent producers. Juneau's grim demeanour reflected his physical pain, and on his way back to the Toronto airport he had to stop the car several times to throw up. At Couchiching he left behind a disgruntled band of senior producers and executives and a dispirited Herrndorf. "He came in and rained on our parade," one producer said. For Herrndorf, it was the final straw.

The prospect of leaving the CBC was heartbreaking for Herrndorf. His aggressive insistence (pushiness to others) had been responsible for some of the CBC's most successful creative achievements, including the new "National" and "Journal," "the 5th estate," and a range of prize-winning documentaries. His name often figured in speculation about future CBC presidents, and he spoke frequently across the country about broadcasting. Juneau had appreciated these creative achievements, but the clash of styles between Herrndorf in Toronto and Juneau and Armstrong in Ottawa and their tightened financial grip made Herrndorf's departure inevitable. Herrndorf handed Armstrong his letter of resignation and tearfully left CBC, saying, "I've loved the job." Within days, he became publisher of the magazine *Toronto Life*, which had approached him earlier, and later he took over TVOntario, the provincial public broadcaster. Herrndorf and Juneau have met frequently since at broadcasting functions and still share many of the same public system ideals, but they have never again talked to each other about their bureaucratic confrontation.

To replace Herrndorf, Juneau selected Denis Harvey, the man Laurent Picard had originally wanted for that role nearly a decade earlier but had been talked out of. Harvey had left the CBC in 1978 to be editor in chief of the *Toronto Star*, but later quit and had been brought back to the CBC by Herrndorf to head the sports area. Now, he took Herrndorf's place and, with his combative style, rapidly became one of the few vice-presidents who dared talk back to Juneau, although he generally accepted Juneau's centralizing moves. "I decided, 'Look, he's done that, there's no point in fighting that because it's a *fait accompli*,'" Harvey says.

"Denny is a bit like me," Juneau says. "He's not afraid of saying no to people. He's much blunter than I am but we got along marvellously. The people who may have trouble working with me are the people who are impressed with the fact that I argue strongly and they may withdraw too early."

They had only two major battles in their six-year working relationship, but both fights were explosive and, for a while, both refused to talk to each other. The worst happened at a late-night budget meeting in the Toronto boardroom, when Juneau became irritated at Harvey's continuing criticism of the French network's advertising revenue. Exasperated by Juneau's tart comments, Harvey noisily picked up his papers, glared at Juneau, snarled, "I'm not taking this!" and stormed out of the room. Harvey realized at once that he'd gone too far and, as he sat alone in his office, thought he would be fired. An associate came in urging him to apologize, but Harvey said, "I'm fucking not going to do it!" He even took Juneau's briefcase out of his office and left it outside his closed door. Juneau flew back to Ottawa without speaking to him, but the next day Armstrong persuaded the president to call Harvey. "Denny, you were wrong, but so was I," Juneau told him. "Can we forget about this?"

"Absolutely!" said Harvey.

It was a reverse situation in their other big battle and Juneau wouldn't speak to Harvey for days. Finally, they found themselves alone in the same elevator at the CBC head office, and after several tense moments of silence, Harvey said, "Pierre, look, I'm very sorry. You know I feel very strongly about these issues and I sometimes lose my temper. I'm sorry. I was wrong."

Juneau smiled, said, "Can I drive you to the airport?", and their fight was forgiven and forgotten.

The new CBC president shook up the French network as well as the English. Shortly after he took office, Juneau had sent Pierre Desroches to Montreal to run Radio-Canada, replacing Raymond David, who had resigned. Now, Juneau clipped not only Herrndorf's wings, but

Desroches's as well, and in much the same abrupt way. Although he stayed on, Desroches hated Juneau's centralizaling moves and told friends that he now had only "as much power as a janitor." Juneau increasingly felt Desroches was being stubbornly unco-operative, and their relations, like those between Juneau and Herrndorf, deteriorated steeply. After four frustrating years, Desroches left, took on a diplomatic assignment in Paris, and in 1988, became head of Telefilm Canada, where he remained as executive director until June 1994.

Juneau's first major program decision got him into politically scalding water and brought to the surface the Conservatives' conviction that Juneau was too close to Trudeau. Trudeau wanted to give the country a lecture on Canada's economic problems and asked the CBC for fifteen minutes of prime-time television on three consecutive nights in October 1982. The CBC president's office had been called directly, whereas the usual practice was for such requests to be discussed initially at a lower level. Thus, Juneau was personally involved in the decision from the start. It was, in fact, an unprecedented demand since it was not a national emergency, and the prime minister had no major announcements to make. In recent years, the CBC had carefully weighed each of the prime minister's requests for airtime, granting most, but rejecting some. Now to ask for three nights in a row seemed excessive. If Juneau said no, however, the prime minister could legally command the airtime, but governments find it less awkward politically to have the CBC grant the airtime.

In the end, Juneau felt he had to give Trudeau the airtime. To achieve balance, he gave airtime to the other parties for a response. Trina McQueen says, "Juneau had the belief that when the prime minister wanted airtime, it was not for the public broadcaster to decide whether or not what the prime minister had to say was important." It was a damaging judgement, long-remembered by the Conservatives and denounced in most newspaper editorials across the country as a surrender to the government. "MANIPULATING THE CBC," was the heading of a *Winnipeg Free Press* editorial which noted, "The [Liberal] party's campaign is now to be abetted by the public-owned CBC. The President of the CBC is Pierre Juneau, a former member of the Liberal Cabinet and a former unsuccessful political candidate for the Liberal party." Juneau knew his brief political past might come back to haunt him some day. Even Douglas Fisher, a politician-turned-journalist, had described him in the *Toronto Sun* as "a worn Grit carthorse."

Joe Clark said Juneau was "honour bound" to resign for failing to stand up to the prime minister's demand. "You have the obligation to exercise discretion," Clark said to Juneau. Ed Broadbent said the decision raised questions about the CBC's integrity and Juneau's political independence. In reply, Juneau admitted Trudeau's request may have been "unusual and indeed unprecedented," but he felt the criticism of his decision was "unfounded and unfair" and said he would not resign. Adding insult to injury in the ruckus, Trudeau's three talks pre-empted normal, popular programming and cost the CBC $100,000 in lost advertising revenue.

A year later, the man who had fought consistently against political intrusion into the CBC and had seen more battles over the CBC than anyone else, the Father of public broadcasting in Canada, Graham Spry, died quietly in his sleep in Ottawa at the age of eighty-three, after spending the evening discussing the future of public broadcasting with a friend. Flags on CBC buildings were flown at half-mast for the man who had promoted public broadcasting since the 1920s. Twelve years earlier he had been honoured by friends with a birthday party hosted by former prime minister and friend of half a century, Lester Pearson. The daughter of his old comrade-in-arms, Alan Plaunt, was there, as were Alphonse Ouimet, George Davidson, Al Johnson, Pierre Juneau, Patrick Watson, and 250 others who came to salute the man who had been there at the creation of national public broadcasting. Now, in 1983, this gentle Hercules of public broadcasting was gone, leaving his followers to wrestle with the problems that threatened his creation.

One of those problems came a few months later in the form of recommendations from yet another government commission investigating the CBC, the Cultural Policy Review Committee, co-chaired by Louis Applebaum, a prominent Toronto composer, and Trudeau's old friend, writer and later senator, Jacques Hébert. The CBC, they said, was the broadcasting heart of Canada, but they also said the CBC was radically wrong in the way it was doing its job. Focusing on television, Applebaum and Hébert said the CBC's contribution to Canadian culture had been "meagre," too commercial, and was losing popularity. They suggested that the CBC give up program production except for news and instead purchase programming from independent producers. They proposed that the CBC sell off most of its facilities, fire much of the staff, stop selling commercials, kill local programming, and discontinue its affiliation with private stations. In this way, they said, the CBC could become "better, more vital, more effective, more cherished." The CBC welcomed Applebaum's and Hébert's rhetorical support and condemned most of their specific proposals, calling them "unsupported and unsupportable conclusions and recommendations." "Weak . . . cavalier. . . . The Applebaum recommendations represent a huge gamble for Canada – it gambles millions of dollars and thousands of people on a totally unproven hypothesis, or a form of wishful thinking."

As a deputy minister of communications, Juneau had played a key role in establishing the Applebaum-Hébert study, but now in his new role, he attacked its conclusions. Because of his private lobbying and the Applebaum-Hébert report's excessively dramatic proposals, most of their recommendations were sidestepped by the government and the CBC. The government, however, did announce a broadcast strategy for Canada, filled with eloquence on the importance of public broadcasting, the need for a stronger CBC, and a series of recommendations to move towards "Canadianizing" the CBC, such as 80 per cent Canadian content in television. It also suggested 50 per cent of programming, other than journalism and sports, should be purchased from independent producers. The latter recommendation was an impressive triumph for two hard-lobbying former CBC current affairs producers who had gone independent, Pat Ferns and Dick Nielsen. For all the silver-tongued rhetoric of its proposals, however, the government provided no extra money to the CBC to meet the new "Canadianizing" targets.

One source of indirect funding came from the establishment of the Canadian Broadcast Program Development Fund. Over the ensuing years, it annually poured tens of millions of dollars into productions for the CBC and private broadcasters (both of which provided matching funds) in dramas, children's programs, variety shows, and documentaries. In its first eighteen months, the fund stimulated $156 million in productions. It was a remarkable success story, backing award-winning programs from "Anne of Green Gables" to "Codco" and "E.N.G." In ten years, the fund invested a total of $650 million. This backdoor way of channeling extra funds into broadcasting was considered more politically palatable than giving more money directly to the CBC, and it had the added advantage of encouraging private broadcasters to air more Canadian programs. The long-term consequences of the government's new approach was a burgeoning of private production companies, a sharp drop in the number of CBC in-house variety and drama productions, and the resultant elimination of almost all CBC staff producers in drama and variety.

Juneau clearly was highly effective working in the corridors of the Trudeau government among old Montreal friends and colleagues. His world, however, was suddenly turned upside down in 1984 when, in rapid succession, Pierre Trudeau left, John Turner came and left almost before he arrived, and a new breed of politician, a new party, and a new attitude toward the CBC arrived in Ottawa in the form of the new prime minister, Brian Mulroney.

A pragmatic politician, Mulroney had little philosophical identification with the mandate of the CBC, and like most prime ministers, his view of the CBC was based on how it covered his activities. "He viewed the CBC through the microcosm of how it dealt with him," says Paul Curley, onetime national director of the Conservative Party and campaign manager. Time after time in caucus meetings and conversations with friends, including some on the CBC board, he would say, "Jeez, did you see what those bastards did to me on 'The National' last night?" At one point he threatened to sue the CBC and reporter Mike Duffy over a report Duffy had done. At another time, he bitterly complained to news anchor Knowlton Nash about a report on a Montreal meeting where he had spoken to more than 3,000 supporters. "Unfair . . . wrong," he said in complaining that the CBC had underestimated the crowd size. "I've been short-changed by you guys," he said. "I'm bloody mad about it."

Except during the brief interlude of Joe Clark's government, Juneau had never worked at a senior level in Ottawa with Conservatives in government, and he had difficulty adjusting to the two kinds of Conservatives now competing for power. There were the so-called red Tories or Camp Tories who shared the more sophisticated, culturally sensitive views of the Tory guru Dalton Camp and whom Pierre Juneau understood, and then there were the raw-boned Tories from small towns and rural areas and the hustling entrepreneurs who felt culture and the CBC were for sissies. These, Juneau never understood. The mouths of many such Conservatives watered at the prospect of recapturing the $1 billion or so that went each year to the CBC. Some ridiculed the "long-haired" music of Beethoven and Brahms carried by the CBC, dismissed "foreign writers" like Shakespeare and Molière, denounced "degenerate" modern dramas, condemned investigative reports on "the 5th estate" that alleged government misdeeds, seethed at some of Barbara Frum's hard-edged interviews on "The Journal," and accused reporters on "The National" of offering anti-government opinions instead of facts.

What resulted was Mulroney rhetoric in favour of public broadcasting and the CBC some of the time in recognition of one section of his party, and Mulroney action torpedoing the CBC most of the time in a bow to the other. He sympathized with his International Trade Minister John Crosbie who, when angered at the cultural community as a whole, denounced the "CBC-type snivellers and encyclopedia pedlars."

Although he constantly felt wounded by its news coverage of him, Mulroney did not have the degree of visceral hate for the CBC as an institution that many of his supporters had. "I don't think Mulroney had any personal philosophy about the corporation," says Bill Neville, CBC board member and political ally of the prime minister. "In the whole area of cultural policy, he just didn't have a view. So, therefore, in terms of caucus management and trade-offs, it became an easy area for him to trade off."

After their election triumph, the hot-eyed, revenge-bent Mulroney Conservatives came whooping into power looking for the blood of every suspected Trudeau-ite in Ottawa, not unlike the Tory assault on "Pearsonalities" when Diefenbaker came to power twenty-seven years earlier. This time, Pierre Juneau was at the top of the hit list. "Juneau had by his own decisions established himself as a partisan, [he had been] a minister and tried to become an MP," says Neville. "You live by the sword and die by the sword. He stepped over the line and left himself vulnerable and made it difficult for him to wrap himself in the flag of independence." Few were more determined to get rid of Juneau than Marcel Masse, Mulroney's newly appointed minister of communications. While he publicly spoke glowingly of the CBC, privately he had very different things to say about Pierre Juneau. Masse and most of the Tory caucus felt Juneau and the CBC were "anti-Tory, anti-Conservative... trying to do us in," as one senior Tory insider puts it. "They [the CBC] thought we were a bunch of right-wing nuts."

"They hate the CBC," said Cathy Chilco, president of the Canadian Television Producers and Directors Association, after meeting with Conservative MPs.

Masse was determined that if Juneau didn't quit, he would "embarrass the shit out of him," says one party insider and colleague of Masse. "He kept him waiting for meetings ... wouldn't take phone calls."

"I've always thought that Masse handled it abysmally in the sense that here was a guy [Juneau] with certain pride and ego, and you don't stick it in his nose the way Marcel did," says Bill Neville.

They didn't know each other personally, but Masse and Juneau knew of each other professionally and were like chalk and cheese philosophically. While Juneau and his *Cité Libre* friends and colleagues like Pelletier and Trudeau had abhorred the old-style Duplessis politics of the Union Nationale, Masse had been a Union Nationale cabinet minister in the post-Duplessis era. "None of us really knew Masse," Juneau says. "He was a Union Nationale member. There was no question that our whole group were strongly opposed to the whole Duplessis crowd." Juneau had little in common with his new minister, and Masse had little respect for Juneau – and he also had a long and vengeful political memory.

Juneau had first met his new minister half a dozen years earlier when Juneau was undersecretary of state and Masse came to Ottawa seeking a grant for a Quebec festival. Juneau found him "charming" and Masse got his grant. But charming was not the characterization that leapt to Masse's mind when he thought of Juneau. Masse not only bitterly opposed many of Juneau's friends and ideals, but his flamboyant, good-time-Charlie lifestyle contrasted sharply with Juneau's austere, undemonstrative manner. According to some of his associates, Masse also deeply resented being snubbed by Juneau and his friends by never being invited to visit their summer retreat around a lake in the Laurentians, even though he had a cottage nearby. One colleague remembers Masse angrily saying, "The bastards would never ask me over. They thought they were better than me."

In fact, it had never occurred to Juneau to invite Masse to what was, in effect, a compound of friends' cottages, including Pelletier's. Trudeau had bought a lot in the thirteen-acre compound but never built and later sold the land. Today, ironically, Masse lives in the same Montreal apartment building as Juneau. "We meet in the elevator sometimes," Juneau smiles. "He's always very courteous and even sometimes charming."

The CBC president not only had a queasy relationship with Masse, but he faced antipathy, too, from Mulroney, most of the Quebec Conservative MPs, many of whom had been Union Nationale supporters, and many Tories from the West and small-town Ontario who felt the CBC was a money-wasting, do-good organization that tried to force culture down Canadian throats and misrepresented their part of the country. Worse, it was run by a Quebecker who aroused all their anti-Trudeau rancour. They were determined to get rid of Pierre Juneau one way or another. "It was a different attitude toward the whole public service," Juneau says. "And I was not the only one. I was more of a target, I guess, than others. Maybe I should have tried more to deal with Mulroney himself, which I didn't because I'm independent. I may be too independent."

Within a few months of coming into office, Mulroney made massive budget cuts in government spending, with a particularly savage chop to the CBC, proportionately far heavier than to other areas of government spending. Seventy-five million dollars were slashed and, on top of that, the CBC was told it would not get its usual extra funding for inflation costs, its capital budget would be cut back by $10 million, and it would have to find an extra $20 million to cover the cost of layoffs. Altogether that meant a budget haemorrhage to the tune of about $120 million. That, in turn, meant hundreds of jobs would be cut and scores of dramas, documentaries, and arts programs would be killed. It was a long way from Juneau's optimistic comments at the start of 1984, when in a speech to fellow broadcasters, he had spoken of plans for a second CBC-TV channel, more dramas, more variety shows, and more children's programs, amounting to an extra 150 hours a year of Canadian programming on English television and 80 hours more on French TV. All that was now lost. The budget cuts forced the CBC to put greater effort into earning commercial revenue, and commercials were introduced into numerous hitherto commercial-free information programs and entertainment shows were encouraged to have more mass appeal, American style.

"A catastrophe" was Juneau's characterization of the cuts. Little did he realize that it was only the beginning of the Mulroney government's slash-and-burn budget attack on the CBC.

The message was clear: the CBC was going to be cut down to size. The government sought to soften the blow to cultural nationalists and the CBC with reassuring rhetoric. Just after he made the budget cuts Mulroney declared, "Cultural sovereignty is as vital to our national life as political sovereignty," and Masse a short time later said, "This Progressive Conservative government intends to ensure that public broadcasting not only survives, but prospers in the coming years." He called for a "new look" at the CBC and publicly praised the CBC, noting in a speech, "For fifty years now a strong, vibrant CBC has been central to the health of the Canadian broadcasting system, indeed to the Canadian community as a whole. That was true in the 1930s. . . . It is especially true today now that the cascade of technological change has gained such momentum. All these events have presented the Corporation a series of great challenges. It has met these challenges triumphantly."

The words were nice, but the reality lay in the government's budgetary devastation, and Juneau would later complain that the government seemed to "say one thing and do another." But, although they set off alarm bells among public broadcast supporters, when the cuts to the CBC were announced in the House of Commons, Conservative MPs erupted in prolonged, loud cheering. The Tories' election triumph showed that they had abundant public support.

Reluctantly, the CBC acquiesced. "We felt there was no way we would win with public opinion at that stage," Juneau says. "So we said, 'Well, fine, it's tough, but we'll do our best.' We wouldn't really protest against the cuts."

After telling this to Masse at a meeting, Juneau asked, "Could we meet privately?" The minister took him into his office and Juneau raised the question of his resignation, noting that twenty reporters were waiting outside. He told Masse, "They will ask me whether I'm resigning and I intend to tell them that I'm not resigning."

Masse nodded and Juneau added, "But they will also ask me whether you asked me to resign, and I intend to tell them that you have not asked me to resign." Again, Masse nodded and said, "That's fine."

The issue of Juneau's resignation never came up again between the two of them. But Masse's colleagues vividly recall him saying repeatedly in private, "It's time for him [Juneau] to go. If he doesn't do it voluntarily, we'll do it for him."

"It was clear Masse viewed Juneau as a competitor and as a threat. . . . He and Juneau had widely different views," says John Young, then a C B C board member. "Juneau was part of the Quebec intellectual élite and Masse and Mulroney were not."

"There was no misunderstanding on anybody's part that they wanted him out of there," says Paul Curley. "The question was how do you do it? A lot of them assumed that he would automatically go." But Juneau says, "[Masse] never, never asked me to resign. Flora did. Flora was a friend and Masse was not."

Flora MacDonald succeeded Masse as minister of communications in 1986 but for the two years before that, Mulroney, Masse, and others waged a relentless undercover campaign to force Juneau out. They looked enviously at the American system where all senior officials automatically leave their jobs when the government changes. Conservatives had now taken over in Ottawa and felt that the president of the C B C, the most important cultural leader in the nation, should reflect Conservative values. "The problem with Juneau as president of the C B C," Paul Curley says, "is that he was seen by Tories as the enemy, not because he was, but the perception was that. Here was a Liberal who had done everything that the Tories were against in all those years of Trudeau. Here is a guy who was one of the main architects [of Liberal cultural policy] and now he's running one of the main institutions. We just got elected. Why can't we put someone in there who at least has some understanding of our philosophy?"

"Oh, there were offers and little quiet dinners and they tried to wave carrots," says Bill Armstrong. Although nothing specific was ever offered to Juneau himself, hints were dropped in friendly ears about other jobs such as ambassadorships. Conservative impatience grew at Juneau's refusal to take the hint and go, and there were warnings of retribution against the CBC if he didn't. At one point, Juneau faltered in his certainty about refusing to go and sought advice from Bill Armstrong and Denis Harvey, wondering if he might be wrong in staying. But they strongly supported him. "Don't go.... Don't give in to the fuckers!" Denis Harvey told him. Although less passionately put, Juneau was getting the same advice from two close friends, Rand Ide, former head of Ontario's provincial educational network, and former Ontario premier Bill Davis.

With his resolve reinforced by the views of Harvey, Armstrong, Ide, and Davis, Juneau told his colleagues, "I won't be the first president of the CBC to be pushed out by political reasons. It would be an intolerable precedent for the CBC and its future heads."

Juneau's old bureaucratic adversary, Peter Herrndorf, strongly supported his position. "Removing him in those kind of circumstances," he says, "would have destroyed public broadcasting in Canada. You can't get rid of a CBC president for what are essentially political reasons in the middle of his term because it turns the CBC into a kind of state broadcasting." Herrndorf personally told Masse, "From your point of view, it isn't worth it because it'll haunt you politically forever.... It will alter forever the nature of the organization and you simply can't do it."

One who disagrees with Juneau's position is his successor as CBC president, Gérard Veilleux. "I would have gone," Veilleux says. "If you don't, you personalize the institution ... the cult of personality, and then it's too easy for governments to hit the individual."

Another form of pressure on Juneau came from the new, Mulroney-appointed members of the CBC board of directors. One, Robert Kozminski, a Winnipeg entrepreneur, made that clear while dining with a Liberal-appointed CBC board member whose term was not yet up, Paul Fraser of Vancouver. Kozminski mistakenly thought Fraser was one of the new Mulroney-appointed board members and told him, "I'm here, we're all here, to get rid of Juneau."

"I think you'd better stop," Fraser responded. "I happen to be a strong supporter of Juneau." Kozminski and other anti-Juneau board members had several informal sessions to discuss the CBC presidency, and as time went on the chasm between the board and the president grew, especially as more Conservative members were appointed. "He fought us all the time," says Kozminski. "Many times in public statements he did not reflect the board's view. We were angry that sometimes he was not following the board's views. He was also completely uninterested in day-to-day management. There was a fundamental mistrust. Yes, the CBC suffered because he didn't go. . . . It would have been better for the CBC if he had gone."

The new board appointees felt Juneau kept information away from them, but anonymous "brown envelopes" were sent to board members, apparently from disgruntled staff. Kozminski received three carrying the message: "This isn't what was said, but this is the real story." Bill Neville also received secret messages, including late-night phone calls from senior CBC staffers, saying, "You heard this today, but let me tell you what the truth is."

"[Juneau] knew the ones who didn't like him . . . they were all the Mulroney appointments," says Denis Harvey. "They were led by about four of them and . . . Juneau had a very difficult time with them."

Most of the Tory caucus thought the CBC board, despite its new Conservative members, didn't do enough to bring the CBC to heel. The board was, one caucus member comments, "a rubber stamp for the leadership of the CBC."

"They were appointed because they were to bring a Conservative policy view to the CBC," Paul Curley says. "But once they were there they became spokesmen for the institution." The board members "were used" by the CBC, Curley says, to try to alleviate its problems with the Conservative government.

Denis Harvey holds a different view and thinks that the new board members acted differently from the old ones. "The Liberals lost their political allegiance almost on the day they walked into their first board meeting," he says. "This group was totally different. They never lost their Tory feelings, and they got very tough on the journalistic end of things. They were constantly looking to find fault with our journalism."

Regardless of the pressures, Juneau wouldn't give in to the campaign to get him to go. He says, "It was wrong because it sacrificed the most important principle of the CBC, independence. . . . The independence of the CBC starts with the independence of the president."

"I've never seen under such attacks and meanness, such fortitude as that man's," says Armstrong. One example of meanness, Armstrong says, was that in Juneau's seven years as CBC president he got not a single increase in pay. "It never bothered me," Juneau says of the salary freeze. "The principle is wrong, but I said I'm not going to make the staff suffer [in their pay levels] by the fact that the government is not increasing my salary." At the end of his terms, Juneau was earning about $124,000, his deputy, Bill Armstrong, was earning about $30,000 more, and the salaries of the network vice-presidents in Toronto and Montreal were also more than Juneau's.

For reasons of political delicacy and not wanting to appear heavy-handed with Juneau, there was never a formal demand for his resignation or a decision to fire him. Masse even told a reporter, "Oh, I can live with Pierre. . . . In fact, I defend him and the CBC in caucus because there are some who want him out."

The prime minister was always courteous with Juneau. "Whenever we met, he was always extremely charming," Juneau says. But behind the scenes, the charm was not much in evidence.

When Masse left the culture portfolio, Mulroney insisted that his successor, Flora MacDonald, again probe Juneau about resigning. She was a red Tory with sophisticated tastes and a politician Juneau considered a friend. They met over dinner, and she raised the question, asking if he were asked to resign, would he? "Flora, no, I don't think so," he told her. "I won't because I feel it would be wrong for me. It might be much easier if I did something else, but I feel that it would be a very, very bad precedent for governments in the future. They don't like the president of the CBC. They make some pressure. They offer something, and then he leaves. . . . I'm a prisoner of that job."

When Flora got a no, others were asked to try. If Juneau wouldn't succumb to political pressure, perhaps, the Prime Minister's Office thought, he might listen to one of his civil service colleagues, and a senior mandarin was delegated to take him to dinner to try to get him to quit. "They're going to get you one way or the other, so wouldn't it be better if you went?" the mandarin asked Juneau.

"He was doing his job, so I'm not blaming him. He was very courteous," Juneau recalls with a rueful smile. The CBC president's response was the same as he gave to Flora Macdonald. Juneau gave the same answer, too, to a onetime CBC producer, broadcasting entrepreneur, and influential Conservative, Roy Faibish.

"If you are as concerned about the future of the CBC as you say you are, you should go," Faibish told him over lunch in his office.

"I won't be pushed, Roy," Juneau replied testily. "I am not going to be pushed out."

The persistent Faibish had a second conversation with Juneau, but all he got was another defiant *no!*

The Conservatives then began putting out the word that if Juneau went, he not only could have "an interesting job" somewhere else, but the CBC itself would be treated better by the government. In effect, it was a bribe. The CBC had been developing a plan to get a Canadian channel on American cable systems – a plan later known as Northstar – which needed Ottawa's approval. "Word would come back that we could have had Northstar," says Bill Armstrong. "Everything was lined up. Ready to go. And the word was, the day after Juneau goes, it will be approved. That's pretty rough stuff."

It was, however, effective stuff for some public broadcasting supporters, who began to feel that the CBC was suffering unnecessarily because of Juneau's stubbornness. Officials of the lobby group the Friends of Public Broadcasting concluded that it would be better for the CBC if Juneau did go. They worried that his staying exacerbated the anti-CBC feeling among leading Conservatives who would take revenge against the CBC by more budget cuts and policy actions. Leaders of the group included the writer Peter Newman, who had been considered as a CBC president possibility, editor John MacFarlane, and Friends of Public Broadcasting executive Ian Morrison. MacFarlane and Morrison were designated by their steering committee to sound Juneau out on the subject of quitting. They met for dinner at Ottawa's Westin Hotel.

As they sat down, Juneau ordered a double martini to ease the pressures of an exhausting day, and MacFarlane and Morrison knew they were in for "a tough dinner." "We think you should consider the option of resigning," Morrison said to the shocked Juneau. "You mean resign and leave the CBC to that bunch!" exclaimed Juneau in bitterness, and Morrison saw a tear form in Juneau's eye. He felt deeply wounded that such a suggestion was coming from those he had felt were friendly toward him. They talked for two or three hours over martinis, a couple of bottles of wine, and their meal, but Juneau remained deeply hurt. "I strongly disagreed for the same reasons I mentioned to Flora," Juneau says, "and I don't think it's one of the best moments in the Friends' history." Morrison now says, "In retrospect, he was right and we were wrong." Juneau was especially distressed with the role of his old friend Peter Newman. "He kept saying that he had tried to reach me and had not succeeded, and that's not true," Juneau says coldly. It did not escape his attention that Newman at the time was in close touch with Mulroney.

"The suggestion of the Friends shocked him more than anything, really shocked him," says Armstrong. "He didn't believe it. Newman had been very friendly." A well-known communications lawyer and friend of Patrick Watson, Michael Levine, also discussed some of the Friends' concerns in a phone call with Denis Harvey. But he didn't get very far. "Michael, you've got to stop it," Harvey told him. "He will not quit. . . . If you people come out with a statement, I'm telling you he's going to dig in deeper."

Juneau believed it was completely illusory to think the CBC would be better treated by the government if he had quit. "That was terribly naive," he says.

Juneau sustained his independence, but he became isolated. "There was no relationship at all between cabinet members and Juneau," says Kozminski. "There was just no communication with the shareholder, other than formal occasions." "I sat on the board under him for two and a half years," Bill Neville says, "and came to believe he was a disaster as a president and certainly in his relationship with the board. It was not only that he didn't level with us. You also never got anything approaching independent input."

There was also no intimacy between Juneau and Felix Holtmann, the chairman of the House of Commons communications and culture committee. Holtmann, a rural Manitoban with little interest in culture, demanded that CBC Radio carry advertising and that the CBC have more mass-appeal shows and less highbrow cultural programming. "The need for a publicly owned broadcasting company as a nation-builder is past," Holtmann said. He advocated more cuts to the CBC budget, more efficiency, and more commercials on TV as well as on radio, all of which, he said, would "breathe new life into a stagnating agency."

Juneau understood the intensity of the Conservative antipathy toward him but was reluctant to acknowledge it, "even to himself," Armstrong says. "Not ever did he let on to anyone just how awful it was." "It was preoccupying," Juneau admits. "I don't mind a good fight. But it was more the damage it was doing to the CBC. The guerilla warfare went on in various ways and that absorbed a lot of energy. But I was sure I wouldn't lose."

As Al Johnson had in his "Touchstone" paper, Pierre Juneau articulated his vision for the CBC in a major statement called "Let's Do It!" Working with Knowlton Nash, who had performed the same ghostwriting role for Al Johnson, Juneau and his colleagues sketched an ambitious blueprint for "Canadianizing" broadcasting. He proposed the removal of American mass-appeal shows from the CBC, 90 per cent prime-time Canadian content by 1987 including ten hours a week of prime-time drama, the establishment of a series of specialty channels, including CBC-2 with a regional programming emphasis, a children's TV channel, a channel of Canadian programming beamed to American cable systems, an all-news channel, and several joint venture broadcasting plans with both private and public organizations. The multi-channel proposals were designed to put more Canadian programs on the air so that half the TV broadcasts seen in Canada would be Canadian productions. It would cost money that he knew was not forthcoming, but at least it laid down an agenda to challenge the government.

"Let's Do It!" was submitted to a task force Mulroney named to make yet another major study of Canadian broadcasting and especially the CBC. This one was headed by Gerald Caplan, a prominent NDP insider, and Florian Sauvageau, a Quebec educator and journalist. Travelling the country and listening to submissions, as so many royal commissions, committees, and task forces had before them, they essentially came to the same conclusions: the need for more money for the CBC to "Canadianize" television; the necessity for private broadcasting to do much more Canadian programming; and the critical role broadcasting, especially the CBC, plays in encouraging a sense of nationhood. The task force called CBC news and current affairs "the great Canadian success story," but noted a paucity of Canadian drama, saying that only 2 per cent of the drama seen on English-language television was Canadian-produced.

They criticized the CBC's reliance on commercials and worried that too many American shows were being carried by the CBC. The report called for "a substantially expanded public sector in broadcasting with the CBC as its major component." Caplan and Sauvageau recognized their recommendations would cost a lot of money – $270 million a year more if fully implemented – but said, "Paying for the new system is the easy part of the problem. The more difficult question is whether we have the will, whether we care enough about the role Canadian broadcasting plays, to do so."

It was a good question because their approach did not mesh with the thinking of most of Mulroney's cabinet. Bits and pieces were picked up by the government in its new broadcast legislation, but the main thrust was put on the back shelf with all the other task force and royal commission recommendations over the past half-century. The task force had been appointed essentially to try to soften the cultural community's growing distaste for the Mulroney government and to give Masse some time to develop his own ideas. By the time it reported, Mulroney and Masse had hoped Juneau would be gone and a new Conservative-appointed CBC leader would be in place.

One Caplan-Sauvageau recommendation that was picked up was to split Juneau's job in two so that, in future, there would be both a president and a chairman of the CBC, something the Diefenbaker government had wanted and now the Mulroney government would get. Although it would not affect him personally since his term would be up before it came into effect, Juneau opposed the split because he felt it might lead to an adversarial relationship between management and the board. Besides, he just didn't like the idea of diluting the power of the office of the president. Juneau's opposition got him into more hot water with his board, which favoured splitting the president's job and told the government it disagreed with its president's position.

Juneau was a lingering reminder of Trudeau for the Mulroney government, and on one issue he was a disappointment to the public broadcasting purists, as well. They had expected him to chop commercials from CBC-TV, something he had been ardently advocating for more than a decade. As CRTC chairman, he had sought a 50 per cent reduction in commercials and had warned, "Our broadcasting system has become involved to a large extent in the entire North American merchandising mechanism. . . . We do not want broadcasting to be only an extension of the market plaza. . . . Over the years, we have maintained a concern as a nation about the marketing managers of North America becoming the gate keepers of broadcasting." On another occasion as CRTC chairman, he said he was "convinced that the disentanglement of the CBC from the commercial context is an urgent priority," and he warned that the CBC was "especially threatened if the criteria of the marketplace are permitted to predominate." So how could he turn his back on all he had urged other CBC presidents to do? How could he fail to act on his own words?

He could and he did on the grounds that in his previous life at CRTC he had been dealing with policy objectives and now he was dealing with operational reality. As president of the CBC, he knew the government would not replace lost advertising revenue with a higher grant to the CBC. When the Applebaum-Hébert report urged getting rid of commercials, Juneau said, "I don't see why we should throw all the ad revenue away. I don't know if Parliament would be willing to make up the difference." A few years later in his "Let's Do It!" statement, he noted commercials brought $220 million a year to the CBC and said, "It is impractical to think Parliament would be willing to increase the CBC subsidy sufficiently to allow the CBC to abandon commercial activity on television." In fact, the CBC had become more aggressive in its commercial policy, accepting advertising for a wider range of products than ever before and putting commercials in programs that previously had been commercial-free. "The CBC is," Sauvageau and Caplan said in their report, "an institution with very mixed values."

Juneau scored a few victories along the way in spite of the government's campaign against him. The most significant was the CRTC's decision to grant the CBC a licence to operate an all-news channel, "Newsworld." In his appearance before the CRTC, Juneau joked about Mulroney's assault on him, saying, as he began his testimony, "My name is Pierre Juneau and I am still with the CBC. This, Mr. Chairman, is not an expression of arrogance, but maybe one of surprise."

The idea of an all-news channel had been percolating within the CBC for years, and in this case, the board strongly supported Juneau's plans. The CBC board developed what Juneau describes as "a combat strategy" to achieve them. There was, however, powerful opposition from an Edmonton broadcasting entrepreneur, Dr. Charles Allard, who put in his own application for an all-news channel. The CRTC was more impressed with the CBC's presentation and granted the licence to the public broadcaster, especially since the CBC would locate major "Newsworld" production centres in Halifax and Calgary. Fuming, Allard enlisted his influential Conservative supporters, including cabinet minister Don Mazankowski and the chairman of the parliamentary communications committee, Jim Edwards, to help overturn the CRTC's decision. Edwards resigned as committee chairman to fight the CBC application, and he worked with Allard in an appeal to the cabinet. Because of the anti-Juneau feeling within the cabinet, the ministers were sympathetic to Allard. "They really took it very seriously, and we had a feeling that they might go along with Dr. Allard and reject the CRTC decision," Juneau says.

Juneau began a vigorous counterattack. Flora MacDonald was key in pleading the CBC case, and as a CBC board member, Bill Neville was especially effective in developing plans to counter Allard's move and in using all his close connections within the government and cabinet. Neville, who had worked with Judy LaMarsh more than two decades earlier during the "Seven Days" crisis, had switched loyalties to the Conservatives and had become one of the most influential backroom operatives in the Conservative government. His advice and actions proved invaluable in persuading a reluctant cabinet to agree to the CRTC decision to give the all-news channel to the CBC. It went on the air on the very last day of Juneau's term, July 31, 1989.

Another victory for Juneau was the decision to construct a new CBC building in downtown Toronto to house the CBC office and production facilities that were scattered all over the city in twenty-six buildings. For about thirty years, various announcements had been made about consolidating the CBC Toronto facilities. Finally, pushed by private-sector enthusiasm for the profits and the jobs that would be generated by the construction of the new building, the Conservative government okayed the plans. Even Juneau's *bête noire*, Marcel Masse, seemed enthusiastic. "Masse was funny, you know," Juneau recalls. "During our first year, our relations were very cool and then suddenly, everything changed. There was an announcement in Toronto [about the CBC building] and Masse spoke, and he was very, very positive about me."

What Canadian audiences saw at the end of the Juneau years was a lot more Canadian production on the air, in spite of the budget cuts. By squeezing money out of the bureaucracy and other program areas, Juneau's network colleagues had spent more on drama and journalism. Twenty years earlier, when George Davidson and Laurent Picard had taken over the CBC, Canadian content had been at about 52 per cent. They raised it to 68 per cent; Al Johnson pushed it up to 74 per cent; and Juneau had moved it up to just over 80 per cent. The English TV schedule was anchored in "The Journal" and "The National," and dramas had been seen such as "Riel," "Anne of Green Gables," "Empire," "Chatauqua Girl," "Charlie Grant," "John and the Missus," "Love and Larceny," and series including "The Beachcombers" and the children's show "Fraggle Rock." There was a revival of performance programs, too, with presentations by the Montreal Symphony, local theatres from Halifax to Vancouver, and ballet companies, all intended by the CBC to reflect more fully the culture of the country.

Battered and bruised by the *sub rosa* campaign to force him out,

Juneau, with quiet defiance, stuck out his seven-year term, increasingly isolated from the Mulroney government and much of the senior Ottawa mandarinate. "Juneau hung in there until the last moment knowing he wouldn't be renewed and in the last eighteen months of his presidency, nothing got done," says his successor Gérard Veilleux. "And it did damage to the institution."

Rarely did Juneau respond publicly to his critics, although in a Winnipeg speech he lashed out at criticism of CBC spending and management, saying, "Some of the clichés I hear on this subject are becoming quite insulting, irrelevant, and sometimes downright dishonest," and he added ominously, looking at the CBC budget cuts, "The survival of the CBC as a whole may be in jeopardy. . . . We are eating our own seed potatoes."

The battle with Mulroney and the Conservatives had dominated his presidency, and his greatest accomplishment may well have been simply surviving. As a going-away present as his term neared its end in mid-1989, the Mulroney government provided a budget cut of $140 million over four years. The cut, said Juneau, was "a catastrophe. . . . It will make the CBC unrecognizable in five years." It was a burden Juneau's successor would have to deal with.

20

Patrick Watson
and Gérard Veilleux,
The Icon and the Enigma

A twenty-year-old dream danced through Patrick Watson's mind when his old "Seven Days" comrade Roy Faibish mused, "How about being president of the CBC?"

Faibish had good reason to raise the question because he knew his longtime friend Prime Minister Brian Mulroney was desperately anxious to get rid of Pierre Juneau as CBC president and needed a successor who would be credible and politically popular. Who better than Patrick Watson, the cultural icon of Canadian broadcasting? The way it was put to Watson was that if Juneau left before his time were up, would he be interested? You bet, was the answer.

Actually, Faibish's and Watson's conversations with Mulroney had begun even before Mulroney became prime minister. Faibish brought the two men together after a Sunday morning speech Mulroney gave during the 1984 election campaign. They hit it off well, and both men were taken with the idea of Watson running the CBC.

Faibish knew how to move around the corridors of Ottawa, having been Ottawa editor of "Seven Days," a senior executive of CJOH-TV in Ottawa, and a commissioner of the CRTC. He first met Watson in 1955 at university, and a few years later Watson hired him to work on "Inquiry" out of Ottawa. In the late spring of 1964, he and Watson had spent two months in China working together on a documentary called "The 700 Million," and it had been Faibish's contacts that got them into China. Faibish had known Mulroney since 1956 and in 1962 had given the future prime minister a job when Faibish was executive assistant to Alvin Hamilton, minister of agriculture in John Diefenbaker's government. Later, he also became a friend of Pierre Trudeau, advising him to run for the Liberal leadership. Faibish was certainly no Liberal, but he and Trudeau enjoyed conversations about music and poetry, and he felt Trudeau would make an exciting leader. Faibish also was a friend of powerhouse civil servant Michael Pitfield. He worked on Mulroney's first attempt to win the Conservative Party leadership in 1976, and after Mulroney became prime minister, he took Faibish to a dinner with British prime minister Margaret Thatcher. After his CRTC years, Faibish had moved to London to represent cable entrepreneur Ted Rogers in the United Kingdom and Europe.

"He sold Mulroney on Patrick . . . no question," says Bill Neville. "It was the only time in my life that I asked a favour," Faibish says. "But I thought Patrick could regain the CBC's lost constituency . . . its lost support."

He took Watson to dinner with Mulroney to talk about Watson as CBC president. The prime minister was intrigued by the possibility of pulling off the double coup of getting rid of Juneau and replacing him with Canada's renowned, renaissance broadcaster. Watson, Faibish, and Mulroney discussed how the CBC should be run, and Watson had three or four phone conversations with the prime minister over the ensuing months. He then had more detailed policy discussions with the prime minister's chief of staff, Derek Burney, particularly on how to tighten up CBC spending. Watson was critical of what he felt was Juneau's confrontational approach with the government on budgets, for his autocratic management style – "destructive centralism" Watson called it – and for "a confusion of reporting lines" in the CBC. He also believed that Juneau improperly kept information from CBC board members. Wise to the ways of power politics, Faibish warned Watson not to overestimate Mulroney's enthusiasm for Watson as head of the CBC. "He loves you now," Faibish said. "He may love you tomorrow. But a time will come, as with all prime ministers, when he will become paranoid and say, 'You let me down.'"

As to his discussions with the Prime Minister's Office, Watson says, "There never seemed to be any kind of rush about it," which was because Juneau was stubbornly resisting the pressure on him to resign. Although intrigued with the idea of being CBC president, Watson says he was in no hurry, especially since he was in the middle of putting together his ten-part, $8-million TV documentary series "Struggle for Democracy." The series would take him around the world and would be seen on the CBC French and English networks as well as on networks in the United States and the United Kingdom. On the eve of the series première in January 1989, Watson was asked by *Maclean's* what he would do if he were chosen as CBC president. "My prime interest would be programming," he said. "My secondary interest would be to rehabilitate the position of the CBC as a national treasure because I think that it's largely lost its constituency, those who were once willing to go to the barricades." Asked what his weakness was, Watson answered. "Impetuosity . . . an ill-considered tendency to jump into things."

But he wasn't quite ready to jump immediately into the CBC presidency in spite of his ambitions. "Wait a minute, guys!" Watson told Derek Burney and his colleagues when they began getting more specific about the CBC presidency. "I'm up to my ears in the 'Democracy' series . . . and besides, I don't think Mr. Juneau will want to go. . . . I'm not looking for a job, but if it becomes vacant, I've certainly got lots of ideas I'd be happy to talk to you about."

The on-and-off discussions with Watson continued through 1986, 1987, 1988, and into 1989, and Watson not only discussed his ideas with the prime minister and his aides, but also with a key CBC executive, Denis Harvey, the vice-president of English TV. Trina McQueen, director of TV news and current affairs, also met Watson with Harvey at one point. A number of others in the cultural community were aware of the government's talks with Watson, including officials of the renamed Friends of Canadian Broadcasting who were pushing Juneau to resign.

Watson's friend and agent Michael Levine, who had been among those actively encouraging Juneau to resign, told Harvey in a telephone conversation that Watson was going to be the next president of the CBC.

Harvey expressed reservations. "The next thing I knew, I got a call from Patrick," says Harvey who remembers him saying, "Denny, could we have lunch? I understand you would be unhappy with me as president."

Harvey recalls that, at their first lunch, Watson said the prime minister had told him he would be the next CBC president, "Patrick had no doubt he was going to be president," Harvey says. He remembers him saying, "My big thing will be English Television and that's what I'll be spending most of my time on. I'm going to bring in a new director of programming from PBS in New York."

"Patrick, you're crazy! You can't bring in an American as head of English television programming," Harvey said. "First, you don't appoint my people. You have veto rights on my choices, but I have veto rights on your choices. We don't agree on it, no one gets appointed. If you're going to run English Television then you won't have a vice-president. You're not going to sit behind my chair and run English Television."

They argued through three lunches during the course of a year on their president-vice-president relations. "He finally backed off and agreed that we would have mutual veto rights," Harvey says.

"Denny was a very, very good adviser," Watson recalls. "He was very careful and very thoughtful."

Meanwhile, Pierre Juneau remained president of the CBC, and Harvey was urging him not to resign. As time went on, it became apparent Juneau would frustrate Mulroney, keep Watson waiting, and remain as president of the CBC until his term expired at the end of July 1989. At the same time, Mulroney began to cool on the idea of Watson as president. "He got a lot of advice, from me included, that that wasn't a good idea," Bill Neville says. "There was no evidence to make one believe that Patrick could manage the place." Besides, Mulroney now had in hand the recommendations of the Caplan-Sauvageau Task Force on Broadcasting Policy which had recommended, among other things, that the CBC presidency be split in two: a chairman and a president. Task Force co-chairman Gerald Caplan had told his friend Peter Herrndorf he had "traded off" this recommendation for something else he'd wanted in the report. Herrndorf had exploded, "You're crazy! You're absolutely crazy!" Herrndorf thought a split could lead to conflict between an activist chairman

"The Journal" with Barbara Frum (left) and Mary Lou Finlay on the program's opening night, January 11, 1982. (*Courtesy of the CBC*)

Mark Starowicz, executive producer of "The Journal." (*Fred Phipps, courtesy of the CBC*)

"Canadianize!" was Al Johnson's battle cry during his CBC presidency, 1975-82. (*National Archives of Canada, 14487*)

Peter Herrndorf, one of the most creative executives in CBC history, climbed the corporate ladder quickly until he ran into president Pierre Juneau. (*Courtesy of the CBC*)

Bruno Gerussi, a star of the Shakespearean stage, of radio talk shows, and most prominent of all, of "The Beachcombers," is seen here off the B.C. coast with Robert Clothier as the "Beachcomber" character Relic. (*National Archives of Canada, 16084*)

"North of 60," the 1990s TV hit set in Lynx River, N.W.T. Left to right, Tracey Cook, Tom Jackson, Tina Keeper, and John Oliver. (*Courtesy of the CBC*)

Trina McQueen, the most prominent woman in the CBC heirarchy until her career was derailed by president Gérard Veilleux in 1992. (*Courtesy of the CBC*)

Denis Harvey, the hard-as-nails head of CBC English TV, whose confrontation with Gérard Veilleux shook the corporation. (*National Archives of Canada, 16082*)

Patrick Watson, one of Canada's great TV journalistic performers, became a much troubled and frustrated chairman of the CBC. Named to the position in 1989, he resigned in the spring of 1994. (*Courtesy of the CBC*)

Gérard Veilleux, whose presidency, 1989-93, was plagued by government budget cuts and internal turmoil at the CBC. (*Courtesy of the CBC*)

"The Royal Canadian Air Farce" brought their radio success to television in the 1993-94 season. Left to right, Don Ferguson, Roger Abbott, Luba Goy, and John Morgan. (*Rodney Daw, courtesy of the CBC*)

"Street Legal" was the most successful serial drama in CBC history, lasting eight years before its end in 1994. Left to right, back row, Anthony Sherwood, Julie Khaner, Ron Lea. Front row, Maria Del Mar, Albert Schultz, Eric Peterson, Cynthia Dale, David C. Johnson. (*Courtesy of the CBC*)

Anchors Peter Mansbridge and Pamela Wallin launched "CBC Prime Time News"
in 1992 to widespread catcalls, especially over its 9:00 P.M. start time
(9:30 in Newfoundland). It went to 10:00 P.M. in the 1994-95 season.
(*Courtesy of the CBC*)

"Friday Night! with Ralph Benmergui" collapsed in 1994 after two seasons. It was
murdered by knives wielded by critics both inside and outside the CBC.
(*Courtesy of the CBC*)

"The Kids in the Hall" was a huge comedy hit on TV in the early 1990s. Left to right,
Kevin McDonald, Scott Thompson, Mark McKinney, Dave Foley,
and Bruce McCulloch. (*Courtesy of the CBC*)

Tony Manera, named
CBC president in 1994,
faces a broadcasting
revolution that will
propel the CBC into
oblivion or renaissance.
(*Courtesy of the CBC*)

and a president. He told Caplan he had a terrible feeling that the recommendation would be the only thing in the task force report that would be accepted by the Mulroney government. As it turned out, this was close to what happened when the government drew up the new broadcast legislation.

In the meantime, the prime minister's phone line to Watson had gone dead. "It went quiet for a long time," Watson recalls, "and then there'd be a little flurry and then a quiet, then all these rumours about all the other people who were being looked at."

"Patrick was left hanging for months, and he was really upset that he didn't know whether he was going to run the CBC or not," says Harvey. "Patrick hung out there in no man's land," adds Neville.

Watson began to look forward to taking a year off to "recharge batteries" after a gruelling year finishing the "Democracy" series. When he heard nothing further from Mulroney, he says, "I assumed by early 1989 that it was gone and they wouldn't be interested in me, and I wouldn't be interested in them. The prospect of jumping into the chairman's job was not very attractive." Indeed, as Neville says, "He had a hard time figuring out what the role of chairman was." Neville himself had been advocating someone like former Conservative premiers Peter Lougheed or Bill Davis as CBC chairman. But Faibish kept pushing for Watson.

Finally, when Derek Burney called from the Prime Minister's Office to say, "What about the Chair?" Watson replied, "I'll think about it." While he thought, the phone again went quiet and Watson began to plan his time off.

Meanwhile, the search for a CBC president other than Watson focused on the number-one mandarin in Ottawa, the clerk of the Privy Council, Paul Tellier. He, however, said no, and the spotlight shifted to Gérard Veilleux, the secretary of the Treasury Board, who had earlier served as number-two man in the Privy Council. Mulroney much admired the young, strongly federalist, bilingual, and bicultural Veilleux, who had worked both with Pierre Trudeau and Mulroney on constitutional issues before rejoining the Treasury Board. As board secretary he had been an efficient, tough planner of Mulroney's budget cuts and government downsizing. "Here was a guy whose role has been to help us reduce the cost of running the government," says Paul Curley. "He's done it very well. He put the plan together. It was thought, 'Gee, maybe he can do that to the CBC.' . . . Probably all of a sudden a light flashed on and Mulroney said, 'Gee, that's where I should put him!'"

Gérard Veilleux had come a long way from his dirt-poor beginnings in Asbestos, Quebec, where his mother transformed their living room into a millinery and yard goods shop and rented rooms to lodgers to make a living. When he was five, his father had died in a mining accident and his mother was left to raise five children, of whom he was the youngest. "It was poverty, real poverty . . . those were not good years," Veilleux remembers. Since his family couldn't afford a TV set, on Sundays he would visit a next-door neighbour to watch "Pépinot et Capucine," a French network children's show, and sometimes he also would watch "The Ed Sullivan Show," although he couldn't understand English. As he grew older, he knew he didn't want to be a miner and wanted out of Asbestos's grinding poverty. His ticket to the outside world was a $600-a-year Johns-Manville scholarship to study commerce at Laval University. "I was very lucky," he later told an interviewer. "I had an economics professor at Laval named Marcel Bélanger. He made me his protégé. . . . He made me feel that economics could be something really fascinating."

At Laval, Veilleux was a few years behind another power-to-be in Canada, a law student named Brian Mulroney, whom Veilleux had heard make speeches in the university cafeteria when Mulroney was involved in student politics. After graduating from Laval, Veilleux, still speaking hardly any English, got a job in the Manitoba Finance Department and gradually learned English, in part by listening to CBC Radio, keeping the radio on in his room all night, even when he was sleeping. In 1970, he spent an unhappy year with the Quebec government where he found too much separatist politics among senior civil servants for his liking. "I didn't like politicians disguised as civil servants," he later told a reporter. He was lured to the federal government in 1971 by Al Johnson, who was then secretary of the Treasury Board. He worked closely with both Prime Minister Trudeau and later Mulroney in federal-provincial relations before going back to the Treasury Board as secretary in 1986. It was a behind-the-scenes, nose-to-the-grindstone rise from Asbestos, Quebec, to the sixth floor CBC presidential office, dramatically different from the spotlit public role that took Patrick Watson to that same sixth floor.

But Veilleux had a problem when Paul Tellier told him, "You know the prime minister is considering this appointment as CBC president, and I should tell you that you're on a very short list." The problem was, he didn't want the job. Veilleux had been thinking of leaving the public service altogether after a quarter-century of working for the government and besides, he says, "I didn't feel I had any background that would prepare me for the job. . . . In the area of broadcasting I knew very little . . . I said, 'Why don't you find someone who has better qualifications for broadcasting?'" But, as Denis Harvey says, "Governments have always been afraid to give the job to anyone but one of theirs. They've all thought the place is out of control. They've all thought a real good administrator could go in there and clean it up." Finally, Veilleux sighed and agreed to become the CBC president for, as he says, in the public service "when your boss says that's where you go, you go."

Veilleux was dismayed at the relatively low salary paid to the CBC president and drove a hard bargain. He was shocked that his CBC predecessor Pierre Juneau, had had his salary frozen at about $124,000, calling it "atrocious" because it damaged Juneau's pension. "I intend to fix that, although I may have to wait until the government changes," Bill Armstrong remembers him saying. It was, however, not fixed. At the time, Armstrong was the executive vice-president and serving as president for three months between Juneau and Veilleux. Veilleux negotiated a salary of about $220,000. When he saw the figure, Armstrong exclaimed, "My goodness, that's quite a change." In his previous job as Treasury Board secretary, Veilleux had known all the salaries of the Crown corporation heads and was thus able to negotiate his own pay level more effectively. But, like Juneau's, Veilleux's pay was also frozen by the government for his term as president.

There was also a problem in the lack of clarity about the president's role under the proposed new broadcasting act. The president would be appointed by the board, yet would not be a board member, and the act's language on the roles of president and chairman was confused. To strengthen the presidency, the government changed the legislation so that the president was a board member, was appointed by the government, and was clearly the CEO. The chairman's position was described as a part-time job. Then, Mulroney's attention returned to Patrick Watson and the chairmanship. "He saw that was the place for Patrick," says Faibish.

The phone call Watson had first sought twenty-three years earlier finally came to his room at the Mayflower Hotel on Central Park West in New York City, where he was preparing to host a PBS broadcast from the Lincoln Center for the Performing Arts. Stanley Hart, who had replaced Derek Burney as the prime minister's chief of staff, was on the phone. He said the prime minister wanted Watson as CBC chairman and told Watson that Gérard Veilleux would be president. "When he told me," Watson says, "that the president was a man named Veilleux whom I'd never heard of and who was secretary of the Treasury Board, I thought, 'Oh, no! Not again! What's going on?'" Watson, however, agreed to fly to Ottawa, hung up the phone, and walked over in a black mood to Lincoln Center to do his broadcast, fearing the continuation of a civil service mindset at the CBC.

His foreboding grew as he took off from LaGuardia Airport the next morning when, out of the plane window, he glimpsed the carcass of a DC-9 that, the previous night, had crashed into the river off the airport. "That's symbolic," he thought, and his dark mood continued when the person supposed to meet him at the Ottawa airport wasn't there, nor was there any welcoming emissary of the prime minister at the hotel where a reservation had been made under a false name for his secret meeting. He was still brooding when he met Hart, Tellier, and Veilleux, but soon his apprehension began to lift. When Hart and Tellier left after half an hour, the CBC's future president and future chairman got down to the one-on-one business of evaluating each other. They left the hotel suite for Veilleux's home, where they ordered in pizza and talked some more. Watson was impressed with Veilleux's energy, his eagerness to learn about broadcasting, his managerial sharpness, and his political shrewdness.

"Coming out," Watson says, "I was very exhilarated, thinking, okay, we can do some work together." Watson then caught the last plane to Toronto. Veilleux called him the next day to underline a point they had discussed about their working relationship. Veilleux knew Watson had campaigned for the president's job, and he told him on the phone, "You know Patrick, I understand you wanted to be president, but you understand that you're not and that I am." "Yes," said Watson.

When the appointments were announced, Watson exulted to the *Toronto Star*, "It's going to be a zipper, a high speed trip . . . I'll bet you they [morale-wounded CBC staffers] have already started to heal because of the signal given to the troops by these two appointments." And he later told the *Star*, "The prime minister had a stroke of genius when he put [Gérard] and me together." They were dramatically dissimilar. As much as Watson was an icon, Veilleux was an enigma.

Veilleux was forty-six, a bureaucrat who had worked unseen in the back corridors of Ottawa, a managerial and financial wizard who knew nothing whatever about broadcasting. Watson was about to be sixty, a white-haired, battle-scarred, much-honoured broadcaster who knew nothing about managing. While Watson loved centre stage, as a public personality Veilleux was a fish out of water. But as CBC president he could no longer be an anonymous, grey civil servant. Reporters asked questions, even personal questions, all the time, cameras and microphones poked into what hitherto had been his privacy, and service clubs and universities wanted him to address meetings.

"I've found all the attention difficult," he said in his first days as president. "Suddenly people are prying into my life. They want to know who I am, where I live, what I do." Also, he had always been persuasive in closed-door meetings with ministers and mandarins, but dealing with the sometimes rambunctious, uninhibited CBC employees and inquisitive reporters was very different. He tried to shy away from the spotlight. "I didn't cope well," Veilleux says. "It was very intrusive and a source of tremendous stress for me right to the end. I never really got used to it . . . I am a very private person, and I found it one of the most difficult dimensions of the job."

For Watson, of course, all this was old hat, and he revelled in his high office. The differences between Watson and Veilleux shaped their professional relationship: Watson would be the diplomat and Veilleux would run the place as the chief executive officer. Veilleux wanted to make it perfectly clear to everybody that he was the CEO, and on a visit to London

shortly after taking on the presidency, he briskly told a senior BBC official, "I wouldn't have taken the job unless it was absolutely clear that I was
the CEO." On almost all of his letters, memos, and statements, he called
himself "President and CEO."

Veilleux's entrenchment as undisputed boss of the CBC was reinforced by the extraordinarily long time it took for the new broadcasting
act to become law. He was named president under the old law, but Watson's appointment couldn't be formalized until the new law, with its provision for a chairman, was proclaimed. That would take more than a year
and a half, and in the meantime Watson languished in a kind of corporate
purgatory as "chairman-designate." He was hired as a special consultant
to Veilleux under a contract negotiated by his agent, Michael Levine, a
tough-talking, razor-sharp lawyer whose show-business approach
startled the government bureaucrats hiring such a senior official. Watson
couldn't chair meetings of the board and couldn't vote, and he grew
increasingly frustrated with the longevity of his neutered role and even
considered quitting. Finally, he was formally named chairman in June of
1991. "By that time, Veilleux had completely taken control of everything,"
says Bill Armstrong.

The most controversial aspect of the new broadcasting act, however,
was not the chairmanship, but the removal of its role in fostering national
unity from the CBC's legal mandate. It had bedevilled the CBC for years,
especially during the Trudeau era. Mulroney's Broadcasting Act had
failed to get through Parliament before the 1988 election and had been
reintroduced in 1989, running into a buzzsaw of Liberal opposition to the
removal of the national unity role. The old act stated that the CBC must
"contribute to the development of national unity." The Caplan-
Sauvageau task force had urged the provision be rescinded. Mulroney
and Marcel Masse, who had retaken his old portfolio as communications
minister, agreed, warning against the CBC becoming a propaganda
agency. They said the provision was "an intolerable interference" in CBC
programming and "a constraint on freedom of expression." Veilleux
agreed, saying, "National unity is a political objective.... The CBC is not
a political institution nor should it be."

The Liberal communications critic, Montreal MP Sheila Finestone,
rejected these arguments and told the House of Commons, "What better

role is there for broadcasting and the CBC than to unify Canadians at this critical point in our history?" Her arguments failed, however, and the twenty-two-year-old mandate to "contribute to national unity" was replaced by the requirement that the CBC "contribute to shared national consciousness and identity."

CBC programmers felt comfortable with the new wording and with the new law's explicit declaration of the independence of CBC journalism from any government interference. For the first time, its traditional independence, occasionally violated by past governments, was written into a law designed to "protect and enhance the freedom of expression." It was a long way from C. D. Howe's attitude that the CBC News would be "my news service." It would, however, be sorely tested in a few years' time when the issue of free expression erupted in a crisis over the documentary series "The Valour and the Horror."

Provisions in the new law also tightened the government's financial controls on the CBC and that, in turn, affected its ability to manage. Much of the act detailed how the CBC would be audited in the future and also reduced the president's term of office from seven to five years.

What was much worse for the CBC, however, was Mulroney's financial crackdown on the corporation. It had begun as soon as the Conservatives took office in the fall of 1984 when their budget slashing was spurred by an anti-Juneau, anti-CBC zeal. CBC spending cuts since Mulroney's election victory had totalled about half a billion dollars and there were more to come. A subtext of the cuts had been the hint that the CBC might fare better financially if Juneau resigned and Mulroney was able to appoint his own man to the CBC helm. Juneau had dismissed the idea that the Tories would stop there as "naive." Patrick Watson didn't think it was. He believed that he and Veilleux had been given assurances of support by Mulroney and Masse, although they had given no explicit promises about no more budget cuts. "We want you to go in there and strengthen the institution and turn it into the first-class broadcasting organization that it's meant to be," Watson remembers Mulroney and Masse telling him.

"I've had an unequivocal statement of support from the politicians involved that they are completely behind the revitalization of the CBC," Watson told a reporter just after his appointment. Veilleux agreed.

"Listen," he said, "the prime minister told me he wanted a first-class public network and I'm taking his word on that."

"His word," however, would turn out not to be something you could take to the bank. Within days of settling into his office on the sixth floor of CBC headquarters, almost the first thing to hit Veilleux's desk was a report on the implications of the government cutbacks announced the previous spring of $140 million by 1994.

In January 1990, Veilleux announced a $35-million chop in spending in the next year to help meet Mulroney's target. Much of the cutback came out of what Veilleux deemed to be the fat CBC bureaucracy, and more than 300 employees were laid off. By spring 1990, Veilleux's finance people were telling him he might have to make another $15 million in cuts, but the new CBC president felt that while this was tough, it was reachable, especially since he wanted to streamline the CBC anyway.

His ideas didn't encourage the 35,000-member Friends of Canadian Broadcasting who were campaigning passionately against government budget cuts to the CBC – "the priceless asset," they called it – and who warned of the possibility of losing programs such as "The Journal," "Morningside," and "As It Happens." "It's simply not true," an angry Veilleux wrote to Friends spokesperson Ian Morrison, denying that those programs might be cancelled. He accused Morrison of using sensationalism which "does the cause of public broadcasting great harm." In response, Morrison said he feared future budget cuts by the government might well endanger CBC programs, especially those in the regions – a forecast that came painfully true in six months' time.

As Veilleux dug into the many-layered CBC with its 11,000 employees, billion-dollar budget, regions, networks, divisions, turf wars, and fiercely independent creative programmers, he was surprised at the complexity and what to him seemed almost the anarchy of the corporation. Most of all, he was shocked by what he felt was a reluctance to make tough decisions. "There would be a great to-do to try to avoid making a decision, so they would sweep it under the carpet and bob and weave, and that was not my style," he says. It was never like this in the civil service. You issued an order and something got done. The absence of such simplicity and obedience baffled Veilleux, who grew increasingly discomforted by the managerial looseness, arguments, and resistance he felt he was encountering among many of his senior executives, especially in Toronto. It seemed to him at times, as he told one visitor, "like the goddamn Vietnam War." Some of his executives, in turn, began to feel he equated debate over some of his proposals with disobedience and even betrayal. "At first he would have us at meetings and listen to us," says Denis Harvey, then the vice-president in charge of English Television. "But it soon became very apparent that he wanted yes-men around him and that he didn't really want a debate on anything."

It was true that Veilleux put a high premium on loyalty and positive response, and when a decision was made, he wanted it carried out quickly with no more discussion. In a major document issued in the fall of 1990 entitled "Missions, Values, Goals and Objectives," he warned the staff, "No more 'splendid isolation,' no more 'whining and complaining,' no more 'surprises.'" What he wanted, he said, was to do "constructive damage to the status quo." To help achieve that he urged more "team effort and a greater spirit of unity, vigour, and trust.... We intend to take a team approach to management: an approach based on internal unity and mutual trust. All components will recognize that they are working toward common goals; counterproductive tensions and divisions will not be tolerated."

Within a few months, however, "tensions and divisions" exploded all over the CBC as a combination of government-ordered budget cuts, excessively optimistic targets for advertising revenue, and unexpected costs combined to maim the CBC and dramatically undermine Veilleux's presidency. Revenue from commercials in the booming late 1980s had helped to offset the government's initial budget cuts. But the economy had since turned sour.

In the fall of 1990, Veilleux came back from a two-week trip to Cyprus to be told that he had a $100-million problem not just a $50-million one. "What happened?" he asked Tony Manera, his senior vice-president. "The commercial revenue just nose-dived," Manera told him. He explained the projections for next year's commercial revenue had been calculated during the earlier boom times. At the same time, the government budget cuts for the year ahead were higher than the CBC had anticipated.

"I just about died," Veilleux says. He despised management surprises, and this was, as one of his colleagues described it, "an unexpected shit sandwich." Over the next few months, his executives were obsessed with finding ways to chop back their spending by at least $100 million and find almost that much again to pay the costs of getting rid of more than a thousand employees. "Everybody was trying to protect their ass and cut the other's guy's budget," one senior executive says. From his perspective as the director of CBC-TV in British Columbia, Wayne Skene has written, "From the beginning, there was confusion, disorder, bickering, infighting, power posturing, errors, misjudgements and the odd bit of character assassination thrown in for good measure." It was a nightmare, but Veilleux felt that as a good public servant, he would do "the job I am given to do." Most of his senior managers told him, "Go to the government and tell them that you are drawing the line in the sand and that this is war." That kind of talk made him nervous. It was a winless fight, he felt. "Look," he told them, "we may go to war, but I'm not sure we're going to have all the ammunition. . . . That's fine to go to war, but if nobody cares about what you're doing, then you're alone at the barricades. I'm not going to risk the lives of ten thousand people who are still working for the CBC." Besides, he felt that since the entire Canadian business sector was undergoing a massive readjustment and the size of government was being reduced, the CBC could not be exempted.

Patrick Watson picked up the same theme, explaining to the *Globe and Mail*, "If we had gone to war the way Juneau did, we would have won a series of stiff arms and would have corrupted the relationship with the senior public servants. . . . The CBC fucked up. It has drifted in the field of English and French television by making them more commercial which allowed people to say that it was not distinctive." While saying the CBC was "far too commercial," Watson maintained that the commercials now were necessary until the government provided additional funding.

But the commercial boom had faltered and dramatic measures seemed to be the only answer to the budget crisis. Denis Harvey was a key member of a committee established to come up with proposals. "We were not to come up with recommendations," he says. "Options yes, but, we were not to make a recommendation." They presented their ideas to Veilleux, then heard no more for a few days until rumours began circulating about different ideas, even the possibility of closing the local Toronto TV station. Harvey wasn't the only one who felt left out of the decision-making process. "I thought perhaps with the wealth of experience I'd had that I might have been consulted at least a bit," says Bill Armstrong. The most painful moment of Armstrong's career would be when he had to fly to Windsor to tell the staff that their TV station was closing, without his having had any input whatever into the decision.

If Armstrong was remorseful at feeling left out of the decision-making, Harvey was outraged. He had heard that final decisions on what cuts were to be made would take place in Ottawa on a late November weekend, and he called Veilleux's executive vice-president, Michael McEwen, a CBC veteran who came out of the CBC Calgary radio station. "Michael, what's going on? Are you people meeting on Sunday?" "Well, yes," said McEwen. "We're meeting to make the final decisions." Harvey blew his top. "You stupid buggers are going to make the biggest mistake you ever made in your life if you don't have the four vice-presidents of the media there to at least guide you in your decision-making!" McEwen called back an hour later after talking with Veilleux to say, "All right, get on a plane and come down here."

At the Sunday meeting, Veilleux seemed to Harvey to be impatient, cold, and angry at having so many present. There were about a dozen around the sixth floor boardroom table. Veilleux had a plan of what cuts had to be made and where, and he didn't relish the prospect of more arguments. But he told his colleagues, "Make the case for one or the other and we'll think about it."

"He just wanted to go through them, bam, bam, bam," says Harvey.

"Okay, we'll start with the West Coast," Veilleux began in a fast, tension-laced voice. "Sure it was tense," says McEwen. "All the choices were awful. There were a lot of undercurrents because we were moving from theory to painful reality." Veilleux wanted symmetry in the cuts such as having only one CBC-TV station per province. The first problem came over Alberta where it was proposed that the Edmonton station be shut down and Calgary be kept open.

"Just a moment," said Harvey. "I really think that's a problem. . . . You've got to have a common thread that you're staying in the provincial capitals." Harvey argued that the Calgary local CBC station should be closed instead of Edmonton. Veilleux quickly said, "Are we agreed? All right, Edmonton stays there."

The discussions got sharper when they got to Ontario, where Veilleux thought of closing the CBC Ottawa station. A number of those around the table disagreed sharply, including McEwen and Harvey. "You can't do that," Harvey snapped. "You just cannot close Ottawa. This is the capital of the country!" After more wrangling, Harvey remembers Veilleux saying, "Well, all right, but if you want Ottawa open, you're going to have to close Toronto." "You can't close Toronto for God's sake!" Harvey fumed. "There are three million people there!"

At the end of the meeting Harvey was still not clear whether Veilleux was going to close the CBC Toronto station and so he appealed to John Shewbridge, the vice-president of planning. "John, you've got to persuade him he just cannot close Toronto." In the end, Veilleux kept open both the Ottawa and Toronto TV stations, but Harvey was told to find money in his own TV division budget to pay for part of the cost of keeping Toronto open.

Veilleux downplays the tension of the Sunday meeting and Harvey's worries. "He may have felt distressed because the decision was not what he was recommending," Veilleux says. Harvey originally had urged ending local programming altogether, and he had some support for that in the CBC board, especially from Bill Neville. "Denny was pushing very hard for that," Veilleux says. "But I couldn't buy it because I think that would have been the end of the CBC." "I pushed it but in the end we sawed off," says Neville, and as a result, the regions were hit with a bit less than half of the total budget cuts.

The cuts were announced on December 5, 1990: $108 million; 1,100 jobs; closing or sharply reducing the operations of TV stations in Calgary, Windsor, Saskatoon, Sydney, Cornerbrook, Goose Bay, Matane, Rimouski, Sept-Îsles, and the CBC French-language station in Toronto. Local programming at the stations kept alive would be slashed, killing all local and regional programming except news. "Newsworld," however, would continue its network operations from Calgary. Radio would be chopped by $20 million, much of it coming from closing the International Service, and the parliamentary TV channel would be eliminated. In these last two cases, the government found other ways to keep those services going. Two months after the CBC budgetary bloodbath, the government provided $50 million to help cover the termination costs of making the cut.

In his announcement of the "downsizing" and "restructuring," Veilleux said, "We take these steps with the greatest reluctance and regret.... These changes will have a profound and permanent impact on the CBC.... The CBC of the future will be smaller than the CBC of the past."

The cuts, which had been decided upon in such great secrecy, jolted the CBC, and the process of announcing them was brutal. "Mangled ... mangled," is how Trina McQueen describes it. The anchor of the Calgary TV station was handed the story while on air and he read the news of the station's closing.

Programs were instantly off the air; there was not even time for them to say goodbye to their audiences. Veilleux says Harvey had urged the quick killing. "How do we do this?" Veilleux had asked, and he recalls Harvey responding, "Look, there's only one way. The moment the decision is announced, you just pull the plug." But Veilleux had made the decision, and he now says, "If I had to revisit what was done, I would have let people do one last show. It would have been better to let them say good-bye."

McQueen says there was no plan to deal with, and much confusion about, those who were being fired. "It was Veilleux's mistrust," she says. "He felt there was nobody he could bring into the circle except the board and two or three other people." Tony Manera, a key player in the budget-cutting, defends the secrecy, saying, "The more people involved, the more likely there would have been leaks. A number of options looked at and later discarded would have generated an awful lot of bad feelings. Whenever you're in a period of crisis and tough decisions have to be made, invariably the decision-making process becomes centralized and shifts up."

The cuts were dramatic and draconian and their repercussions were devastating, hurling Veilleux and the CBC into a whirlwind of public denunciation, political attack, vicious backstabbing, and traumatized morale. The CBC would never be the same again. Nor would its president.

The storm concentrated on the slender frame of forty-eight-year-old Gérard Veilleux, who was astonished, appalled, and then angered by the vilification that drenched him. He was particularly incensed that CBC News broke the story of the cuts the night before they were to be announced, getting its information from various sources, including verification from a CBC board member. "He felt 'The National' had been wrong, probably maliciously wrong, in breaking the story," says McQueen. He thought it badly damaged his strategy for announcing the cuts and that "they" were out to get him. He complained that CBC News had given far too much coverage to the story and, McQueen adds, "that we had portrayed the CBC and the government in an entirely negative way." CBC board members shared Veilleux's distress. "It was an abuse of creative privileges of news and current affairs," says Bob Kozminski. "It was self-serving and hypocritical and the CBC was hurt politically and with the public." Wayne Skene later recalled Veilleux telling him "I have a feeling the goddamn journalists think the airwaves belong to them. They don't think they are working for the public."

Veilleux was particularly distraught because the breaking of the news of the cuts by "The National" brought him into his first major confrontation with a media scrum in a very public setting, something he had been utterly unprepared for. His wall of secrecy about the cuts had broken on the night of the Gemini Awards in Toronto where, in black-tie formality, he and the whole broadcast industry celebrated TV program achievements of the year.

"I was sitting by him and it was an electric moment," says Ivan Fecan who, at the time, was in charge of entertainment programming on the CBC English TV network. "The press by then had heard of the cuts and a horde was waiting to scrum him. He had an entire plan laid out, how to tell people and how to help people cope. All of a sudden, it went to an instant death situation. That's where his anger was . . . people weren't going to find out the way he had planned." That particularly hurt him because, as he had told the *Toronto Star* the previous April, "The people here are . . . not in a factory. They are in a creative business, therefore . . . you have to treat them with a great deal of sensitivity." Now the cutback story was crashing all around him in headlines and there was no time for sensitivity. "It was just brutal, brutal," Veilleux remembers with a grimace. "We had no chance to get plans in place to do it properly. It conveyed a feeling of total insensitivity just because of a leak. You can't fault the journalists. What I was concerned about was who leaked it and why."

The slaughter of stations, programs, and people plunged CBC morale to its lowest ever, and demands ricocheted across the country for Veilleux's resignation. His picture was spread across a huge "Wanted" sign that went up in St. John's. Five thousand people protested the cuts in a mass rally in Windsor, and another five thousand protested in Rimouski. Gerald Caplan wrote of "insensitive, merciless management," and in a raucous parliamentary communications and cultural committee meeting, Liberal MP John Harvard, a former CBC journalist, bristled, "Damn it, Mr. Veilleux, we can't have someone with a deputy minister's mentality running the Corporation!" Conservative MP Geoff Scott, also a former broadcaster, called Veilleux's closing of the Windsor station "insensitive and insane." Veilleux lost his temper, and in a finger-pointing rage, he snapped, "Just a goddamn minute!" as he blamed the politicians for betraying their responsibilities. "I lost my cool" he says. "The ultimate decision for the survival of the institution depends on political will and that's their job. Obviously they were not providing it, and I said, 'You're all failing in your job and you should all resign!'"

"CBC-bashing is a kind of Canadian national sport," he said later in a speech to the Canadian Club in Toronto. "But lately, I've been getting the uneasy feeling that it's turning into a blood sport. CBC is in very real and serious danger of dying."

He not only lashed out at politicians, but also at many CBC managers whom he felt were defying and undermining him by not being team players. He warned them against talking to the media. "You people in CBC don't understand the meaning of public service," one senior executive remembers him telling a meeting of vice-presidents. "He was quite upset about it," Bill Armstrong recalls. "He would say, 'I don't tell you things because I don't trust you.' He was paranoid about leaks and so his reaction was, 'Don't tell anybody anything. Just spring it on them.'"

Veilleux was indeed obsessed with leaks, but what, to him, was a leak, to many of his managers was simply a conversation with their associates to refine their responses to his proposals. Clearly, Veilleux wanted to limit awareness of many of his embryonic ideas. "I work as a team," he says.

"And if you can't trust the team members, I don't know who you can trust. How can you consult people if they forego their right to be consulted by going out and leaking?"

He was outraged to read in the papers confidential information on his plans or excerpts of private correspondence with ministers, and he blamed the leaks both on some of his staff members and on media-friendly politicians.

It hadn't seemed that way in the beginning. Denis Harvey remembers that in the first few months after Veilleux's arrival, the new president was anxious to consult, eager to learn about broadcasting, and seemed very articulate and persuasive. "He was brilliant," Harvey says. "I never saw anyone so mesmerize any group so well. He once talked to a group for two hours without a note. He was moving, powerful, dedicated. You could hear a pin drop." But as months went by and tensions mounted, Harvey saw Veilleux increasingly retreat into secrecy and isolation, especially after the firestorm following the pre-Christmas 1990 budget cuts. "He wanted to make all decisions himself," Harvey recalls. "He didn't want to consult with anyone. He didn't want to listen to anyone's opinions or have to explain why he was doing something."

Veilleux had never before experienced a rebellious staff, managers who argued so forcefully with him, especially after he thought decisions had been made, and certainly he had never been so publicly second-guessed and publicly denounced. He was particularly upset at "getting shat upon even in our own programs," as Patrick Watson says. "He just never came to terms with it." His quick temper intimidated some of his senior executives and infuriated others. He felt maligned by the media, misunderstood by many politicians, and undermined by some of his staff. He withdrew more into himself and thought, "maybe I should just pack it in." But his combative nature, his conviction that what he was doing was the only possible course of action, even if painful, and his determination to transform the CBC into a lean, mean team overwhelmed his agonies. "People here think they own the goddamn jobs!" he exclaimed to an interviewer. The CBC president's job was much tougher than he had ever thought, and he was beginning to realize it would take drastic surgery and attitude changes within the CBC to make the changes he wanted.

He sought the help of his chairman-designate, and Patrick Watson went off speech-making across the country, saying the budget cuts, while momentarily painful, would mean a better, more focused CBC that would concentrate on its priorities. The cuts "were not the end of the world," Watson said, telling the CBC staff, "We just have to tighten our belts and pull together." He also assured CBC staff that "there are no more cuts on the way." It wasn't too comforting for staffers who remembered Watson assuring them two years earlier, "I don't think we'll see any more cutbacks."

After reading Watson's explanation of the budget cuts, Liberal MP Sheila Finestone snapped, "He didn't stand up when he was needed and then had the gall to say the CBC will be better than before."

The hossanahs that had greeted Watson's arrival at the top of the CBC fell silent, and Watson suddenly found himself reviled by producers as "one of them, not us." The creative community's unachievably high expectations of Watson's CBC chairmanship had come face-to-face with reality. Especially in the hard-hit regions he came across as "a network guy," insufficiently sensitive to the importance of regional CBC programming.

Veilleux, too, faced the producers' ire, and at a staff meeting in Vancouver was told by producer Cathy Chilco, "The corporation has had its roots sliced. . . . It is a disaster. There is no future any more. . . . Your position is just not acceptable."

As the CBC was stumbling through this anguish and organizational chaos, it was called before the CRTC to review the impact of the cuts and sketch the future.

"We have been gradually losing the CBC. . . . It has been put on a steep, slippery slope downwards," former CBC president Pierre Juneau told the CRTC as he attacked the government for chopping the CBC budget. He wouldn't, he said, want to be in Gérard Veilleux's shoes.

The CRTC also heard complaints from the mayors of Sept-Îles, Calgary, and Windsor about the killing of CBC stations in their cities. Windsor Mayor John Milson snapped, "Just give us our damn station back!" He was especially angry because the station closing meant Windsor viewers would switch to Detroit stations.

A parade of CBC witnesses, including Watson, Veilleux, and a bevy of vice-presidents, sought to put as positive a face as they could on the budget cuts. On the eve of the hearings, Watson announced "an electrifying new direction for the CBC," and he talked of a renaissance. Supported by their colleagues, Veilleux and Watson outlined the "new direction," which would boost Canadian prime-time programming to over 90 per cent. The new direction would focus on a program called "Newsmagazine" which would reflect the regions and be, the rhetoric seemed to suggest, God's gift to Canadians, practically single-handedly saving the nation from disintegration. Between them, Trina McQueen, Denis Harvey, Watson, and Veilleux bamboozled the CRTC into paying less attention to the impact of the budget cuts and focusing on the CBC's "new direction."

Veilleux celebrated the role of the CBC and painted a luminous future if only the government and the politicians would seize the opportunity to properly fund the CBC. Harvey thought Veilleux's final statement to the CRTC hearing was inspiring and afterwards effusively congratulated him. Veilleux threw his arm around Harvey and told him, "I want you with me forever." The president also embraced McQueen over her statement to the CRTC, telling her, "I saw something in you today I've never seen before and it was tremendous." Veilleux glowed with pride over his rhetorical triumph and took congratulations from everyone.

That night there was a small, celebratory party in the boardroom at head office. Everyone was flushed with a sense of success. The mood didn't last long, however, because Veilleux was furious when, at 10:00 P.M., "The National" did not carry a story on his CRTC statement. Since Harvey had gone back to Toronto, McEwen was the target of Veilleux's fury. "How could they spend ten minutes on the budget-cuts leak and they can't spend a couple of minutes on this!" the CBC president yelled at McEwen. Although the French network had carried a story on its TV news, in Toronto, editors, faced with a particularly heavy night of news, had dropped the idea of carrying a report on Veilleux's statement. He was seething. Here he was fighting for the CBC, he fumed, taking incredible abuse while battling to save the life of the organization, and his own news people didn't think his words were worth a report. His own news people were the ones, in fact, who had ruined his strategy on the budget cuts in the first place by leaking the story ahead of time and who had reported all the criticism of him. The CBC Producers Association had even called for his resignation. The failure or refusal to do a report on his statement was, he felt, symptomatic of a major problem in the CBC, and it was more than he could take.

The next morning, McEwen phoned Harvey in Toronto. "The president is absolutely livid," he warned. "You're going to hear from him. He is so angry he can't stop talking about it. He's been at it all morning long." Veilleux, however, did not call Harvey, and a few days later, McEwen called again. "It is still going on," he said. "He can't talk of anything else. Journalism is out of control because it didn't carry his statement." While Veilleux never did talk to Harvey about it, months later he was still angry. Sitting beside news anchor Peter Mansbridge at a dinner in Banff, he asked, "Why didn't you run that?"

"He took it very personally," says Watson. "He saw himself as a champion going into the lists and carrying the flag. He was and remains very hurt that what he did as president was seen by our newsroom as a story not meriting any special attention. He found that very, very tough." McQueen says, "Veilleux's temper was at its worst when it was something that concerned his own accomplishments . . . that drove him crazier than anything else." Veilleux wasn't the only one angry after the CRTC hearing. Sensitive about the criticism he'd been getting over the budget cuts and feeling the prime minister had reneged on promises of support, Watson had earlier publicly crossed swords with Mulroney. The prime minister had sought to downplay the government's role in the budget cuts by implying that they were choices made by the CBC, not the government. He quoted Watson as saying that, "It is difficult to complain of the generosity of the people of the country in that they give us $1.4 billion a year." Veilleux was concerned that the prime minister was using Watson's comment against the CBC and told him, "Patrick, you fix it!" Watson walked out of the CRTC hearing room and met the media.

"Unfair" and "out of context" Watson told reporters, adding, "The prime minister was well aware of the CBC's precarious financial situation. Here he is playing games with the people of Canada in a way that expresses a lofty kind of contempt for all those people who've lost jobs and all those communities that had service taken away from them." Michael McEwen was astonished and rushed over to Veilleux. "Did you tell him to meet the media?" he asked. "I told him to fix it!" Veilleux said. "Well, he is!" said McEwen.

In response and in pique, Mulroney raged about "that goddamn Watson" and, in a fury, promptly named to the CBC board of directors for a three-year term University of Toronto professor of political economy John Crispo, one of the country's most outspoken critics of the CBC. Watson first heard of the appointment to his board when he read about in the newspapers and exploded. "It's totally unacceptable," he shouted to friends. But he was eventually, if reluctantly, persuaded that nothing could be done about the prime minister's appointment. Nine days before his appointment, Crispo had testified to the CRTC that the CBC was a "lousy, left wing, liberal, NDP pinko network." He denounced "red Tories" and "pink Liberals" who were heard on Peter Gzowski's "Morningside," said "The Journal" was "lousy," and that the CBC was so anti-American and pro-Iraq during the Gulf War that it should be called "Radio Iraq." "I don't know why we didn't ship it to Baghdad," he said.

"I hold the CBC in contempt . . . for what I perceive to be deliberate, continued and repeated intellectual dishonesty in virtually all of its news and public affairs programming," Crispo had told the CRTC. "It has lost anything resembling journalistic integrity." He urged more budget cuts to the CBC unless "you clean up your act in terms of balance or lack of balance." "The board of directors of the Canadian Broadcasting Corporation will benefit greatly as a result of Professor Crispo's contribution," said Communications Minister Marcel Masse.

Crispo, an occasional government adviser, private consultant, and ardent advocate of free trade, especially lambasted the CBC for, he claimed, undermining public support for the Free Trade agreement with the United States. Later, as a member of the CBC board of directors, he demanded that a special check be kept on CBC coverage of free trade issues, which was agreed to and done.

CBC news and current affairs, he had told Reader's Digest, was "atrocious" and "one-sided. . . . The bias was so pervasive that it was a disgrace." He also charged that the CBC French network was undermining the country and that "the CBC almost alone killed Meech Lake, then reversed themselves in the last three sickening weeks and were so pro-Meech it was equally appalling."

"I understand you have some concerns about the CBC," Mulroney had said when he called Crispo. "He asked me if I'd like to do something about it by sitting on the board," Crispo recalled. Crispo said he certainly would, although he worried that by making the appointment Mulroney might be trying to limit Crispo's criticism of government economic policies. It was greeted as a scorched-earth appointment. "The appointment is malicious and irresponsible," said Southam columnist Christopher Young. The Opposition in the House of Commons demanded the appointment be rescinded. Crispo himself was astonished at the vitriol, although, coming from the Don Cherry school of communications, he cheerfully admitted, "I'm a walking mouth!"

He said he had never advocated the abolition of the CBC, only that it provide balanced news and current affairs. The engaging and noisily articulate Crispo seemed to love the theatre of debate as much or more than the substance. His public pyrotechnical comments about the CBC subsided, however, after he was warned that as a board member he could speak out in the privacy of the boardroom, but not in public, and he reluctantly agreed. Nevertheless, he and a few other board members occasionally telephoned producers and editors to complain directly about programming, but they were cautioned by Watson and Veilleux that it was an improper interference with management.

"He's a cowboy," says Watson, and "from time to time John has just had to be sat upon, generally by the board as a whole." At board meetings, a table-thumping Crispo spearheaded demands for more of his brand of journalistic accountability and fairness. But Veilleux felt Crispo lost most of the effectiveness of his arguments with his excesses, "and at times his facts are wrong, very often."

Watson was chairing a board that was the most aggressive the CBC had ever had especially regarding journalism and programs like "The Journal" and "The National." Previous boards had not been so intrusive in programming but, as McQueen says, some did "fiddly little things. I remember a board discussion [on] whether or not to cancel 'Bugs Bunny.' After that, Bugs was toast."

Veilleux had no hesitancy in intruding and making his own criticisms of CBC journalism. "I am entitled to be concerned about my news or current affairs product," he said. "I am at arm's length from the government, but journalists are not at another arm's length from me. One arm's length is enough." An old friend of Veilleux's, Liberal leader Jean Chrétien, was once a beneficiary of this approach. At a meeting in Montreal, Veilleux told French network programmers, "Why is it that Chrétien never appears? He's the only spokesperson for the federalists in Quebec and somehow he's never on the airwaves. So is this balance?" Almost at the same time, Watson called another Montreal programmer with the same question. French network officials agreed Chrétien should be seen more, and a prime-time interview was done a few days later.

CBC journalists are apprehensive about head office meddling in journalistic judgements and feel, in the tradition of CBC News founder Dan McArthur, that the CBC newsrooms must be free from not only political intrusion, but senior management interference as well. "Veilleux is very interventionist and very much a centralizer," says Marc Thibault. "I don't think he understood the importance of the independence of journalism ... He didn't understand that at all," says Peter Campbell, former head of CBC public affairs and at the time an adviser to Denis Harvey. "The difference between Veilleux and Juneau," Harvey says, "is that Juneau understood the importance of journalistic integrity and independence ... I didn't have to explain it to him."

Veilleux finds criticism of his attitude perplexing and has recounted to aides a conversation he once had with his friend André Desmarais, whose father-in-law was Jean Chrétien and whose newspaper broke a story about charges against Chrétien's son. "Weren't you ever tempted to go in there and say, Jesus, guys, cool it! That's my father-in-law?" Veilleux asked him. "Are you kidding!" exclaimed Desmarais. "Me go into the newsroom and tell them how to run that story? Are you kidding?" "I found that story helpful because it's the rule of journalism in the private sector, too," Veilleux says.

During the "Seven Days" revolt, Patrick Watson had demanded far more independence than was being exercised by programmers in the 1990s, but now he had transformed himself from a rebel to an elder statesman. He remembers numerous quiet conversations with Veilleux on the importance of at least a degree of journalistic independence. But, says Watson, "he found it very difficult to understand and be sympathetic to the values and traditions of an organization that is so decentralized with so much distributed autonomy. I was trying to persuade him that there was value in certain elements of the Corporation being close to being uncontrollable, particularly in the area of journalism. While journalism had to respond to the principles of accountability and standards, it had to be seen to be radically independent." Veilleux says, "I never recall those discussions."

While Veilleux at an intellectual level might have seen merit in journalistic independence, emotionally he rejected the notion of his journalists being "radically independent." In fact, he went absolutely ballistic over a clash involving the chief of the CBC English TV network Ottawa bureau, Elly Alboim.

In November 1987, Alboim, a widely respected, well-informed Ottawa journalist, made a speech at a University of Calgary conference on the Meech Lake accord in which he questioned the motives of Prime Minister Mulroney. After ruminating for nearly four years on the speech, Queen's University professor and former CRTC chairman John Meisel wrote an article on the media's role in the Meech debate, citing Alboim's comments as evidence that CBC coverage was, in the early stages of the debate, deliberately tilted against the accord. Meisel's charge reinforced John Crispo's accusations and struck a nerve with Gérard Veilleux, who had spent years as a senior civil servant dealing with federal-provincial relations. Meisel's allegations created a front-page storm in the media and enraged Veilleux. "He was unbelievably upset about it," Denis Harvey recalls.

Veilleux was furious about what to him was a clear violation of CBC policy and also about not being told of the matter before he read it in the newspapers. He couldn't understand why Alboim was being defended by the journalists and their managers and by Harvey. He told Harvey he felt Alboim had made a "serious and grave" error that was "clearly wrong and reprehensible." Alboim recognized his comments had gone too far, and he worried about all the publicity because his children were being asked at school about their father. "It would not have been investigated unless I raised it," Veilleux now says. He walked into Harvey's Toronto office and snapped, "What are you going to do?"

Veilleux says Harvey "tended to dismiss the whole question as unimportant since it was three years old." In a memo to the president, Harvey sternly denied saying it was "unimportant," adding, "I told you and Michael McEwen that Alboim had done a very stupid thing. I also argued that there were extenuating circumstances and that his record had been impressive and unblemished until this point." "He never specifically said to fire Alboim," Harvey says, "but there was no question that's what he wanted us to do."

But Trina McQueen, chief news editor Tony Burman, and Harvey were adamant that while Alboim should be reprimanded and perhaps suspended for a week, he should not be dismissed. One compromise proposed by head office was for Alboim to be reprimanded, suspended for a period of time, and then resign quietly three or four months later. Again Harvey and McQueen refused to accept the proposal. Meanwhile, the newsroom, aware of the controversy, warned Harvey that there would be mass resignations if Alboim were fired.

When Harvey handed Veilleux a file on the case, the president, in a clenched-teeth response, said, "I'm not reading that! I'll take it home for the weekend. And I'll see you in Ottawa on Monday."

All Monday morning, Veilleux conferred with Harvey and other executives about CBC affairs, but not a word was said about Alboim. When they broke for lunch, Harvey approached Michael McEwen and said, "Michael, I thought we were going to discuss Alboim." "Well," McEwen replied, "it's been taken out of your hands. He's ordered me to conduct an investigation, and he's issuing a statement tomorrow, and here it is." As he scanned it, Harvey saw it was a total condemnation of Alboim. "You can't put this out!" Harvey said. "Can you at least leave it with me and let me rewrite it?"

That was agreed to, and Harvey phoned McQueen to discuss the planned statement. Her initial response was "Oh, my God! This is awful!" As soon as she hung up, McQueen called Tony Burman to get his guidance, and he, in turn, talked to Alboim. It was a chaotic night of writing, rewriting, and phone calling. CBC chief political correspondent David Halton heard about the planned press release, and at about 8:00 P.M. called Veilleux to try to soften the president's attitude. Halton had known Veilleux for years, felt they were friends, or at least acquaintances, and he explained the chill the newsroom felt about Alboim's punishment. While

Halton saw it as a relatively innocent and friendly phone call, Veilleux saw it as a challenge to his authority. As soon as he got off the line with Halton a seething Veilleux called Harvey.

"I've had a call from our Ottawa news bureau about this statement being put out in the morning," Harvey recalls Veilleux saying. "And only three people knew about it. . . . Me, you, and Michael. Michael and I have been together all day, so you obviously have told the news department about it."

"I felt he had betrayed a conversation we had," Veilleux now says. "I said, 'How can I deal with my senior manager if that conversation finds itself in the parliamentary bureau in Ottawa? How can I deal with you, Denny?'"

Veilleux also was outraged at a suggestion from Alboim that Alboim might write a letter to the president asking for a review of the affair. This, Alboim thought, would minimize the appearance that Veilleux was under pressure from the board to take action and would thus also "avoid a war with our newsroom." Harvey thought it was worth considering, but the president rejected it bitterly. "I cannot emphasize enough how much I resent Alboim's assumptions," Veilleux told Harvey. "He led me to believe a story was going to be on 'The National,'" Harvey says, and he explained to Veilleux that he had earlier talked to McQueen and would talk to her again.

"You will talk to me at nine o'clock in the morning," the president said, abruptly ending the conversation. Alarmed at the intensity of Veilleux's emotions and worried that "The National" might be carrying a story, Harvey called McQueen. "What are you trying to do, fuck me completely?" Harvey demanded. "Do you want me to get fired? What is this?" "What are you talking about?" a startled McQueen replied. "I've never ordered you to do a thing on 'The National,'" Harvey said. "But I'm ordering you now to take that item off 'The National.'"

Harvey told her, she recalls, that, "Veilleux said the news department was on a deliberate campaign to intimidate him, and 'Was it that awful woman once again? Couldn't he [Harvey] control his people?'"

McQueen was puzzled, called the newsroom, and found no item had been planned on Alboim, and Harvey relayed the information to Veilleux. The president, however, remained indignant, and a few days later he dispatched a five-page letter to Harvey smouldering with censure and suggesting Harvey and McQueen may have deliberately leaked information on both the Alboim incident and the budget cuts of the previous December. "Discussions between senior management should never be coloured by suspicion that they may be leaked," Veilleux wrote. "Obviously that is not the case any more. Indeed, suspicion is heightened now."

"It was unbelievable," says Harvey. "I thought he was going to fire me. So I wrote a reply and just destroyed his fucking letter. . . . But I knew I was dead as soon as I wrote it. He can't stand that kind of insubordination." In his seven-page response, Harvey denounced Veilleux's suggestions of being undermined by leaks by himself or McQueen. "I . . . reject your insinuation. . . . My record with the Corporation does not warrant such an accusation," he said.

A long silence followed, and Harvey never did hear back from Veilleux on the letter. In the end, Harvey and McQueen were asked by an exasperated head office what they would accept. Finally, Alboim was given a letter of reprimand and suspended for one day. Two years later, he resigned from the CBC.

One week after the Alboim crisis had been settled on May 14, 1991, Harvey knew for certain that he was finished. McEwen told Harvey that his relations with Veilleux were now "beyond rescue." "In effect, he said I was on my way out," Harvey remembers. McEwen had earlier hinted about the possibility of Harvey retiring, but now it was clear Harvey had to go. "The sense Denny was bringing to the table was not what I was trying to develop in the corporation," says Veilleux. "I felt he was out of place."

In the end, it was Michael McEwen who swung the axe on Harvey. "Denny was bypassing him and undermining him and abusing his friendship," says Veilleux. The end came after loud arguments between Harvey and McEwen in front of half a dozen associates over an administrative issue. Meeting right after in Harvey's office, McEwen told him, "Your comments were not appropriate." "Neither were yours," replied Harvey. McEwen, who felt he had been a "good friend" of Harvey, believed their professional relationship "had rapidly become untenable," and he told Harvey he was "on his way out." McEwen then flew back to Ottawa to tell Veilleux.

"I did something that I don't know whether you will support me or whether I overstepped," McEwen said. "What?" asked Veilleux. "I told Denny he was fired," McEwen admitted. "You what? Why did you do that?" Veilleux asked. McEwen explained that he felt Harvey was challenging his authority, and Veilleux agreed that Harvey had to go.

In August 1991, Harvey was out as vice-president in charge of English TV, replaced in a surprising move by the unlikely duo of Trina McQueen, now elevated to the news and current affairs vice-presidency with responsibilities for other areas, and Ivan Fecan, who was made vice-president of entertainment programming and other departments. When Veilleux had approached McQueen about becoming vice-president, a promotion was the last thing McQueen thought was coming. They were attending a meeting in Banff when the CBC president asked her to go for a walk by the Bow River. "Denny had kept telling me that I'd be fired, too," she says. "I was nervous as a cat, and at one point as we walked he [Veilleux] picked up a stick and I flinched." She remembers him telling her, "You know that Denny is not as much a team player as I thought he would be, I think it's time for him to go and I want him to go with honour and dignity."

He told her he was considering her to succeed Harvey in a joint leadership with Fecan. "He wanted to be assured that I was tough enough to do it," she says. She said she was and said, if offered, she would accept the job. Back in Toronto, McQueen and Fecan discussed their possible vice-presidential roles and then, as she recorded in her diary, "A fax arrives offering me a job as Vice President of News and Current Affairs . . . Denis Harvey tells me the President still doesn't like me and Michael McEwen says that's all gone away. So many questions. Is there a deal with Ivan that I don't know about? What is my budget? My real role? Can I survive let alone prosper with this President?"

McQueen had steadily risen through the ranks from her first CBC job in 1967 as a summer relief reporter to be a producer, executive producer, network program executive to the pinnacle of CBC journalism.

Fecan's roots were in radio, where he was the first producer for the science program "Quirks and Quarks" and worked for Mark Starowicz on "Sunday Morning." He had been news director of Toronto's independent CITY-TV station, came back to the CBC to run its local Toronto station, then became head of the network variety department, and later went off to be NBC creative development vice-president in Hollywood. There, he was involved with programs such as "Saturday Night Live," and David Letterman's and Johnny Carson's talk shows before being wooed back to Canada in 1987 by Denis Harvey as CBC director of TV programming. In that job, he moved the drama series "Degrassi Junior High" into prime time, energized "Street Legal," launched the hugely successful "Road to Avonlea" and "Codco," and got three million viewers and an American network sale for the docudrama on Colin Thatcher, "Love and Hate." Except for Fecan's relatively brief detours to CITY and Hollywood, both he and McQueen were old CBC hands. But each harboured apprehensions about the other.

21

A Repositioned CBC

With new TV management in Toronto, Gérard Veilleux turned his attention to the need to shake up the CBC in a more fundamental way. He had to face not only the continuing budget cuts but a coming revolution in the marketplace of TV specialty channels. What could he do to prevent the CBC from being marginalized and to gain the support of his political masters and mandarin colleagues? He brought in consultants and talked with close associates about the need for dramatic change at the CBC. Patrick Watson sent Veilleux a detailed memo on the changes he thought were needed.

At the mid-November 1991 board meeting in Edmonton, board members and Veilleux tongue-lashed each other over what to do. Watson later told a meeting of producers, "The board of directors felt a sense of urgency . . . that outraced the sense of urgency felt by management. The board [was saying] we must give . . . a quick and visible demonstration that the Corporation is in motion."

"We had to take control of our fate before the axe fell," says Bob Kozminski. The board felt shaking up the CBC was necessary to generate the public support which might inhibit the government's budget-slashing. "We didn't have a constituency of support which might discourage the government from doing it," Bill Neville says. "We needed to mobilize a broader constituency."

While the board was pushing Veilleux to do something, they blasted him for something he had done: he had hired an old colleague, Robert Pattillo, as CBC communications vice-president, a job Veilleux had abolished as being superfluous earlier in the year. "It got very heated," Neville remembers, "[but] Veilleux had already cut the deal." Watson says, "He blew his cool. He just let them have it in terms of the burden he had borne and how they were making unrealistic demands on him."

As he boarded his Canadian Airlines flight back to Ottawa from the Edmonton board meeting, Veilleux was in a foul mood but he knew something had to be done. "We can't manage in a defensive stance all the time and in a crisis atmosphere," he thought. "We'll destroy the place." As he settled into his business-class seat he pulled a legal-size notepad out of his briefcase and began scribbling furiously while his 707 soared over the snowcovered Prairie wheat fields below. Toying with his tortoise shell glasses, putting them off and on his slim face, he wrote in English and drew diagrams for four hours enroute to Ottawa via Toronto.

He was a troubled man, as all presidents of the CBC are, nervously assessing the political, financial, technological, and competitive pressures that threatened him and the CBC with oblivion. He was exasperated by the frequent indifference and antagonism of the government in Ottawa. And now, his own board was in a bullying mood.

"Why should the CBC get more money?" the Ottawa mandarins had asked. "Why, when Newfoundland fishermen are being wiped out? Why, when companies are going broke and unemployment is going up? Why, when we can't finance the health care programs; when we're cutting back on old-age pensions, on education, on transfer payments to the provinces? Where do you think the CBC fits in against those priorities? Nowhere near them! So, why should we help you? You better help yourself."

It was a challenge that both frightened Veilleux and goaded his fiercely competitive nature. Adding to the pressure were more minor annoyances, such as the recent Conservative Party policy conference's resolution to privatize the CBC. Although the suggestion had been rejected by the government, it still stung.

In the two years since he became president, he had become possessed by the challenge confronting him. A decade earlier, CBC's English network share of viewers in prime time had been about 30 per cent; five years ago, 22 per cent; and now was around 15 per cent, and likely to sink further. Meanwhile, CTV, with its heavy menu of Hollywood programs, hovered around 23 per cent. The CBC French network did better with a prime-time share of about 30 per cent. The focus groups that Veilleux had ordered on what Canadians think of the CBC revealed that most people said they could hardly tell the difference between the CBC and the commercial stations. That startled and alarmed Veilleux. "People didn't recognize what we were doing," he says.

On top of the lack of money and the identity crises, the CBC faced the terrifying prospect of "death stars" powering down 100, 200, or 500 video channels, threatening to change the nature of broadcasting profoundly; in fact, to transform *broad*casting into *narrow*casting with a multiplicity of specialized channels. So many channels would end traditional office gatherings around the water cooler to share impressions about the previous night's big TV program, such as "The Journal" or "Street Legal," which could only diminish the national sense of shared experiences. The CBC would lose its audience share as viewers zipped and zapped their way across the channels, unless CBC offered something distinctive.

The future lay in specialization, Veilleux believed. Just as the magazine industry had repositioned itself from a few huge, general interest magazines – *Life, Look, Saturday Evening Post, Colliers* – to a multitude of specialized magazines exploiting niche markets in sports, business, money, or fashion, so, too, broadcasting needed to reshape itself. But he doubted the government would allow the CBC to expand into more specialized channels beyond "Newsworld" and maybe another channel to carry CBC programs to foreign cable companies.

As he thought of this, a revolutionary idea began to hatch in his mind. Repositioning was the answer! "The first thing we have to do is to reposition ourselves in the minds of Canadians," Veilleux thought. It was like any marketing problem, he felt. If your market share is shrinking, change the product – or at least the packaging and branding – and reposition the company, and if your shareholders and directors are dyspeptic, show them some muscular action within the company and bring in "agents of change." He felt that even his vice-presidents didn't really grasp the immensity and the immediacy of the dangers confronting the CBC. Time was short, desperately short, he thought, and abruptly turning around this creative *Queen Mary* demanded a faster response from his colleagues than he felt some of them could manage. He was angry at the sluggishness, if not defiance, that he felt some of his present senior managers showed toward his innovations. Too many, he felt, had "a sense of ownership" in the past. He was not trying to win any popularity contests; his job was to get results. He would simply have to change the way the corporation was run to make it more quickly responsive to the president's wishes, even if that meant being ruthless. "I wanted CBC to demonstrate that it could change its image out there," he says.

Now, as his plane whistled through the Canadian skies, he began to draw "highways" through the 1990s: seven "highways" of action, including, at centre stage, repositioning the television schedule and new approaches to corporate identity, production efficiency, industrial relations, and management effectiveness. "My whole mind was focused on doing something," he recalls. By the time he landed, he had finished his "highways to the future."

When he got to the office the next day, he called in his vice-president of planning, the BBC-trained John Shewbridge, and said, "Here's what we have to do. . . . You're going to help me see how we organize this." He talked to Ivan Fecan and then to Robert Pattillo, asking them, "Is it do-able?" "Shit, sure I think it's do-able," said Pattillo, who leapt at the idea. Veilleux tore his scribbled notes from his pad and made a copy for Pattillo. "It was very clear we were talking about a massive reorganization," Pattillo says. "He had this all figured out in stages with arrows shooting everywhere. Veilleux had us all spellbound."

Trina McQueen was brought into the discussion and then the number crunchers were asked, "Can we afford it?" Veilleux set loose a whirlwind of task forces, executive conferences, and board meetings to hammer out the details of repositioning. Reflecting on those hectic days, Pattillo says, "Working for Gérard Veilleux is like working on something that moves twice as fast as a rocket sled."

Pattillo would quickly get a reputation as "the evil genius" manipulating support for Veilleux's ideas, trampling through CBC traditions, offending programmers, and ardently advocating a dramatic change in the English TV schedule. A onetime bank teller, he had worked with Nova Scotia Premier Gerry Regan and with the Trudeau government, giving a public relations shine to government programs and, later, he became a vice-president of public and corporate affairs for the Bank of Nova Scotia. Along the way, Pattillo had been host of a CBC morning radio news and current affairs program in Fredericton. His real skill, however, was in burnishing corporate and government program images, and it was in this capacity that he had been hired as a consultant to the CBC's president. They had known each other when Veilleux was in the Finance Department and Pattillo was working with Finance Minister Allan McEachen, and earlier when Pattillo was in the Prime Minister's Office. In helping to examine CBC's problems, Pattillo had provided Veilleux with a "communications audit." "Pattillo was an agent of change," says Veilleux, "and Fecan was, too."

"It was a question of image and marketability of CBC and the relevance of it," Pattillo says. One of his and Veilleux's concerns was the lack of shared values among the various CBC divisions, programs, radio and TV. "We also had a marketing problem," he says. "Nobody knew who we were. We had absolutely no distinction on the street. My largest frustration of all was [feeling] that 'I've got to brand this thing. . . . We've got to have a street address.'"

Pattillo's job was to deal with the cosmetics, but he also became an eager missionary for Veilleux's repositioning ideas, which were presented to the board of directors in late January 1992. Two weeks later, in a rhetorical swamp of bureaucratic mumbo-jumbo, Veilleux made the first announcement about his plan for CBC salvation. Repositioning, he said, "will result in a better articulation of roles and of program rationale. It is a vehicle for change drawing the strengths of the Corporation together in a single image of shared purpose, principles and values. . . . [It] will launch a continuous process of improvement." Nothing was spelled out, although what Veilleux wanted was revolutionary corporate change, new "strategic alliances" with other broadcasters, much more co-operation between French and English Television and between CBC Radio and -TV networks, a cable service to the United States, a new look in television scheduling, more accountability for CBC journalists, more efficiency, a new public image for the CBC, and a more distinctive, Canadianized CBC. None of this was referred to in the February announcement, however, and was not fully developed until the following summer.

Most of the CBC staff greeted the vague repositioning statement with apprehension, incredulity, questions, and incomprehension. Something big was about to happen, but it wasn't clear exactly what. Clarity came with startling impact three months later. In a Richter-scale jolt designed to change Canadian viewer habits, Veilleux "niched" the English TV network evening schedule into four distinctive sections: regional information from 5:30 P.M. to 7:00 P.M.; popular family shows from 7:00 P.M. to 9:00 P.M.; "The National" and "The Journal" from 9:00 P.M. to 10:00 P.M.; and adult programming after 10:00 P.M. "What we really wanted to do was to create a multichannel environment on the main channel," Pattillo says. Changes were made to French TV, too, but relatively minor compared to the sweeping transformation of English TV. "The changes represent," Veilleux said in his announcement, "one of the most significant departures from traditional program scheduling in forty years of CBC . . . television broadcasting."

There was immediate concern that television watchers, strongly addicted creatures of viewing habits, might resist Veilleux's changes. He knew that was possible and that he was taking a massive gamble. He believed, however, that only such dramatic change could transport the CBC into the "new age of technological abundance" with its specialized satellite-delivered specialty channels. Besides, he felt only such bedazzling change could demonstrate to the Mulroney government that the CBC was now a very different, efficient, aggressive, contemporary organization on the leading edge of broadcasting. The changes in the television schedules, he said, were only the beginning of a total reshaping of the CBC. Supporting Veilleux's changes, Ivan Fecan told reporters, "We saw the future coming and we decided it would be better to deal with it on our terms instead of waiting for it to deal with us."

But Veilleux was playing with destiny for, if his plans didn't work, they could sink the CBC into irrelevance and oblivion. The zeal and rhetoric of his predecessors Pierre Juneau and Al Johnson had not secured government support of the CBC, Veilleux felt. What was needed now and what Ottawa would respect, he believed, was a vivid demonstration of entrepreneurial management. Gérard Veilleux, the ice-cold professional with a red-hot temper, was now rolling the dice on the CBC's future and on the long-ago dream of two young men, Graham Spry and Alan Plaunt.

Veilleux's biggest gamble was moving the news to 9:00 P.M. and using that switch as the catalyst of change. The idea of news at 9:00 P.M. had been debated for years and had been a winner for the BBC. But with the success of "The National" and "The Journal" at 10:00 P.M., interest in the earlier time slot had waned. Still, McQueen and others worried about the fall off of audience that happened about halfway through the 10:00 P.M. to 11:00 P.M. hour.

The real impetus for the shift to 9:00 P.M., however, came not from concern for the news but out of a concern to make, and to be seen making, a major change in the nighttime English TV schedule. It emerged out of discussions between Veilleux and Fecan. "Ivan says I gave the idea of nine o'clock. . . . This ('The National' and 'The Journal') was the flagship we had to use," says the CBC president. Veilleux recalled that the focus groups he had commissioned had said that the one distinctive and popular part of CBC English TV was "The National" and "The Journal" at 10:00 P.M. He suggested the two programs would be the ideal bridge between the family and adult programming segments that he and Fecan envisioned. One other implication was that in dramatically revising the schedule, local news at 11:00 P.M. would disappear from CBC, leaving the late-night news field wide open to CTV. As they discussed a new programming approach, Veilleux says, "Ivan and I sat there and we called Pattillo to see how he saw this from a marketing and communications standpoint, and his eyes lit up."

Veilleux also questioned the division of the hour between "The National" and "The Journal." "Robert, why does the news end at twenty-two minutes past the hour?" Veilleux asked Pattillo. He thought the time allotted for news should be more flexible and said the current rigid time division reminded him of Alice having to go through the looking glass in Lewis Carroll's story. Pattillo agreed, saying, "From a marketing point of view, 'The National' and 'The Journal' just don't make sense."

McQueen liked the idea of a 9:00 P.M. "National" and "Journal," although she wanted a year or two to prepare for the change. "This nine o'clock idea of yours, I like," McQueen told Pattillo, "But I'm worried about the timing. We're moving too quickly."

Some board members who strongly supported the concept echoed McQueen's apprehensions about the timing. In a corridor conversation after a summer board meeting, Bill Neville told Fecan, "Jesus, Ivan, if you try to get this thing on in the fall it has got to be launched properly. Otherwise, what may be a good idea is going to suffer because the programs are not going to be adequate."

Fecan assured him the programs would be fine. But a year and a half after the launch of "CBC Prime Time News" at 9:00 P.M. and the other TV schedule changes, Neville said, "They dug themselves a hole that they've taken a long time to get out of. The great mistake was trying to do it too quickly."

Veilleux, however, wanted immediate change. He felt it was necessary to demonstrate that the CBC was taking a dynamic new direction. Pattillo played an important role in making the dramatic schedule change happen, largely because he had such close access to Veilleux. "Pattillo seized on it and started selling it to the president as a radical difference," McQueen says. Veilleux knew he had a devoted colleague in Pattillo, whose total, unswerving loyalty was in sharp contrast to the lukewarm support he sensed from some of his senior managers. He could trust Pattillo, who supported his ideas, especially on repositioning.

Even so, Veilleux was worried that the change might be too dramatic. "I'm worried this might be my free trade issue.... Like everything Mulroney does is seen through the filter of free trade," McQueen remembers him saying.

"I have to tell you, I was scared," Veilleux says. He had thought of applying the same changes to the French network, but when they considered the proposed TV schedule, Montreal executives said no. They figured they would lose at least 15 per cent of their audience and would suffer a significant loss of advertising revenue if "Téléjournal" and "Le Point" were moved to 9:00 P.M.

Worried about his "free trade issue," Veilleux hesitated. At one meeting he told his senior managers, "I think we should pack up all this." He now says it was a ploy. "I wanted to test to see how convinced they were," he says. Their response warmed his cold feet, and he then took the same apparent hesitancy to the board of directors. "I'm not so sure," he told them. "I'm not so sure. This is one hell of a big gamble. We could all break our necks on this one." The directors, however, remained enthusiastic, and Veilleux heaved a sigh of relief. "I wanted to make sure everybody was onside," he says.

Some of his executives, like Pattillo and Fecan, were excited about the idea. Others were more cautious, and still others were privately apprehensive. "I kept arguing that we should move slowly on it," McQueen says. "That's why he saw me as resistant to it and Ivan as the true embracer and innovator. I was resistant to it simply because I believed that we did not have the programs to back up the schedule. We had a good schedule idea, but we had done no program development to implement that schedule. Why not wait a year and see if we could develop a number of programs? But it was sort of put together catch as catch can. He [Veilleux] saw this as opposition to his desires, and he saw that he would have a continuing struggle with me about it, and he was right. I was really strongly opposed to moving so quickly."

While McQueen was having her problems with Veilleux, Fecan got along swimmingly with him, partly because of his enthusiasm for the changes Veilleux wanted, and partly because he was used to having tough, hands-on bosses such as Moses Znaimer at CITY and Brandon Tartikoff at NBC. Fecan also always made sure Veilleux was fully aware of program plans. "He hated surprises. He got very resentful if he got surprises," Fecan says.

When he announced the schedule changes, Veilleux sat back apprehensively waiting for a reaction. It came quickly and was, he says, "massively positive." "There is this big, unwieldy, heavy CBC that can never make a decision, heavy in bureaucracy," he says. "Here they are taking the lead, changing. It was like we had shaken the image, which is, frankly, what I was trying to do. And then it got back to the government." What especially pleased Veilleux was that the new communications minister, Perrin Beatty, said he was impressed with the changes.

Not everybody was impressed, however. Negative reaction came from Gerald Caplan, co-chairman of the government's 1985-86 task force on broadcasting. "Its intention was to demonstrate ... some changes for the sake of changes," he said. "I think it's a way to make sure I watch as little

CBC television as possible, and it's working brilliantly." Ian Morrison, head of the Friends of Canadian Broadcasting, dismissed repositioning as "a packaging exercise to try to establish a marketing position."

For Veilleux, his announcement on May 13, 1992, of the CBC's New Jerusalem was marred by what he deemed was another demonstration of a lack of managerial discipline, if not deliberate sabotage. Veilleux had warned his senior managers to tell no one about the schedule changes until he announced them. "We were not allowed to tell anybody," McQueen remembers. "It was a top down thing." The news department, however, again made Veilleux's life miserable. To avoid having his staff first read about the changes in the newspapers and to soften the blow of cancellation of the much vaunted program "Newsmagazine" to make way for the new scheduling, Tony Burman issued a memo to his staff a few hours before the president's statement outlining the new schedule. It was another leak and presumptuous, Veilleux felt. It would never have been tolerated in the Treasury Board or the Finance Department. "He could have found out from only one or two sources," Veilleux says. "Again, it undermined the relationship of trust that has to exist at all times between senior managers. I said, 'How can you operate a corporation when your senior managers leak decisions to which they were a party?'"

Burman's memo not only went out to his staff but also to radio newsrooms and regional executives as well. The regional executives were shocked by the wide-ranging changes, especially the killing of their late-night local newscasts. After reading Burman's memo, several of them phoned Ottawa to find out what was going on. Veilleux purpled with rage. He grabbed the phone and hauled McQueen, Burman's boss, out of a meeting. She heard him shouting, "Why is it always your department? Why is it always your department that messes up my strategy? You've ruined the whole strategy . . . the whole thing we set out to do!"

Palpitating with a sense of betrayal, Veilleux hung up and put in a call to Burman directly. Pattillo was with Veilleux at the time and says, "My secretary placed the call but didn't tell Burman that it was the president calling, just saying, 'Can you take a telephone call?' Burman said, 'No, I'm busy.' She came back and told the president, 'Sorry, he says he's too busy.'

Veilleux's rage quadrupled. He put in another call and finally got Burman, who was in the same meeting as McQueen. She walked him to the phone warning, "He's really mad." Burman, whose memo had been explanatory and supportive of the changes in spite of his private misgivings and who had rarely spoken to the CBC president, was taken aback to hear him say, "I'd like to kick your fucking balls!"

As soon as he slammed down the phone, Veilleux realized he'd gone too far and wanted to apologize to Burman. "I was very angry . . . [but] it was uncalled for," says Veilleux. "I very much wanted him to know there was no damage in our relationship."

"He was upset about the conversation," Pattillo recalls. "He never liked beating up on people. He went back to his office, calmed himself down . . . and asked me to arrange a meeting with Burman." (When they did meet, Veilleux was impressed by Burman, and more so later, when Burman took over the 9:00 P.M. to 10:00 P.M. hour as executive producer.) After a shaken Burman had ended his phone conversation with Veilleux, McQueen says, "Then I made a stupid mistake. I could see that Tony was really upset. I couldn't help it, and I phoned Gérard and told him that I didn't think he should have talked to Tony that way." What upset her, she says, was the fact that Veilleux "was capable of extraordinary explosions. . . . The complete lack of control, the vulgarity, and crudeness of the language . . . there were times when he went beyond a certain point where you knew he was out of control."

The incident sealed McQueen's fate. "That was the final thing," she says. "Somebody told me he told the board, 'Whenever it's a choice between the president and her department, she chooses her department' . . . I knew my time was up."

"And he was right about me," McQueen says. "I did see my job in a way to be a job that defended the department against the CBC. Journalism in the CBC was an irritation. It does make the board of directors and politicians uncomfortable. There are a lot of pressures in that. And the department deserves a certain amount of defence and protection. Our job is to bite the hand that feeds us. You have to defy and oppose and explain. I don't think he felt comfortable with me in that role. One of the things about being a CBC vice-president of news and current affairs, there was no buffer. There was nobody there to defend me." Pattillo says, "I think Trina pissed him off from time to time and I knew he pissed her off, but he certainly respected her."

Veilleux had other bones to pick with McQueen. He was angry when veteran journalist Wendy Mesley anchored "The National" on occasion because she, at the time, was Peter Mansbridge's wife. Veilleux had heard complaints about it from friends, and he didn't realize that the executive producer, not Mansbridge, selected the anchors. "But he somehow believed that Peter had chosen his wife and asked how that could be justified," McQueen recalls. He complained, too, that the news service was proceeding with the assignment of correspondent Joe Schlesinger to a Berlin bureau without first discussing the posting with him.

McQueen believes one reason why Veilleux got upset with her at times was her strong defence of "The Journal" when it came under attack, as it often did, in board meetings. "That was a program that had very deep critics [on the board]," she says. "'The National' was never seen to be as contrary as 'The Journal.' I think they didn't want a current affairs presence. They wanted straight news. There was always a nervousness about 'The Journal.'"

Denis Harvey is more explicit about "The Journal" and the board, saying, "There was tremendous pressure from the board. The board did not want 'The Journal' and had not wanted it the last couple of years." The directors wanted, in effect, to cancel the program, he says, and they thought some kind of merging with "The National" would lessen the more aggressive aspects of "The Journal" and save money, too. Crispo was especially insistent on this.

McQueen was widely honoured by her CBC colleagues; she was "the good soldier," a reporter who had come up through the ranks and who, in spite of her strong personal feelings, always spoke supportively with her colleagues about Veilleux and his repositioning ideas. She was admired by the board, too, for her spirit and her intelligence. But, given her clashes with the president, it was inevitable that she would be sidelined. "There is no question it was ruthless," says Patrick Watson. "It was backed up by the board, but I think the board kind of flinched to realize just how ruthless it was because Trina was popular with the board and with the troops."

Veilleux was sure he had to have new executive blood to implement his changes. He believed too many of his senior managers such as McQueen were rooted to their own agendas and not his. As he was taking such a huge calculated risk with repositioning, he wanted his associates to be enthusiastic about it. "I was concerned about transmitting from conceptual to operational," he says. "It's all nice to have this conceptual design but if we don't operationalize it, we're not going to get very far. We had to deploy our internal resources in a way that would assist in the implementation of this. I thought we had resources there that needed to be redeployed for their own growth and development, and my own sense of having a better system of personnel planning. When people have been attached to one place, they develop a sense of ownership and it's more difficult." One way or another, he was determined to teach the elephant how to tap dance.

In a pep talk to network programmers in Toronto, Veilleux warned, "There are too many people who will dump on one part of the Corporation to promote their own part. That is deadly and it is corrosive."

Displaying a streak of frigid ruthlessness, he was determined to get rid of those senior managers not 100 per cent behind the new direction of the CBC and thereby send out a message to the rest of the staff. He wanted "agents of change" who would produce a new dynamic because, he says, "I wanted to take the place somewhere."

Denis Harvey had been removed a year earlier for his lack of total support, and now Veilleux moved again. For Trina McQueen, the change came in Ottawa at 9:30 A.M. in late June 1992, when she was summoned to the president's office. "I knew I was going to be fired," she says.

"This will be a positive conversation," he told her. "I want you to be the vice-president of regional broadcasting." "What about my old job?" McQueen asked. "Well, I've hired Tim Kotcheff to be head of news and current affairs," he replied. Some of McQueen's colleges complained she had been done in partly by Fecan "pouring poison" into Veilleux's ear. Veilleux offered no criticism of McQueen, and he said the new challenge in regional broadcasting would be interesting for her. He had to know her answer immediately since a news release had been prepared and was going out in an hour. McQueen said she wasn't going to quit, said she would do her best, and left the office. When she took up her new duties, Veilleux came to her office and told her that she was one of three or four people he would recommend as his successor as president. He never mentioned it again.

The next to go was Donna Logan, who had annoyed Veilleux over her persistent pushing of a project known as Creative Renewal. She was out as vice-president of English Radio and moved to be an adviser to the president on media accountability. Through task forces, workshops, and conferences, Logan had pushed a plan to make FM a mainstream service as the key element in revitalizing CBC Radio. Radio program director Gloria Bishop was also shoved out of her job. Some radio traditionalists were distressed at the changes proposed by Logan and Bishop, and Veilleux, who prized the CBC Radio service, was loath to go along with the changes, at least at this time, when he had so many other changes going on. When Logan and Bishop continued to push them both privately and publicly, they, too, seemed to him to be following their own agendas, not his. In time, though, Veilleux came to admire greatly Logan's work as a vice-president in charge of journalistic accountability.

In addition to sidelining McQueen, Logan, and Bishop, Veilleux shifted Michael McEwen from being executive vice-president to senior vice-president of both French and English Radio services. Some of the changes, such as abolition of McEwen's old job and the setting up of his new role as head of English and French Radio, came from a desire to restructure the CBC organization rather than dissatisfaction with loyalty. There also was a dramatic change of executives in Montreal where the head of the French networks, Guy Gougeon, suddenly banished many of his senior officers. Veilleux was outraged because he hadn't been consulted.

Veilleux's English network changes were all aimed at the fast implementation of the new schedule. "In the coming months," Veilleux said, "Canadians will . . . see for the first time what repositioning means in terms of what they see on CBC television. . . . This will be the first visible milepost on a long voyage that is ahead for the CBC . . . This is a voyage of change. . . . Change is about breaking from the herd and pioneering new approaches, new programming, new ways of scheduling."

When Tim Kotcheff, the vice-president of news at CTV, was first approached about the possibility of moving back to the CBC, it was a bolt from the blue. He had been executive producer of CBC news specials in 1976 when he was wooed by CTV at the same time as Lloyd Robertson left CBC to co-anchor the CTV News with Harvey Kirck. Kotcheff became CTV News vice-president in 1987. The first CBC overture to him came in March 1992. Robert Pattillo knew Veilleux was looking for new senior management faces, and he had suggested Tim Kotcheff, an acquaintance, who he thought might be interested. In May the offer was made to Kotcheff, and at a secret dinner meeting at the Four Seasons Hotel in downtown Toronto, he met Veilleux for a few hours to discuss the job, his past experience, Veilleux's expectations, and his views of the future.

"I was nervous and so was Gérard," Kotcheff says, because both were petrified of any possible leaks. "I'd never met him before, and I was quite impressed with him. Very aggressive and far thinking. Very zesty. His style was to get things moving. He was trying to change and found the people around him less adaptable to change and obviously, like any other business, when you want to change, you start with changing two or three key people."

By late June, Kotcheff had been hired to replace McQueen. When he sat down at what had been McQueen's desk, he found she had left him a bottle of scotch, a jar of anti-nausea pills, and a book about Australia. "This is a wonderful job," she said in a note to Kotcheff. "But it does have its bad days. Here's an emergency kit for bad days. You can read about life in Australia, take your anti-nausea pills and drink your little bottle of scotch."

There was, however, one important difference to the job in that Kotcheff would report to Ivan Fecan instead of being his equal partner as McQueen had been in running English network television. Fecan would be the head of CBC English TV programming, although Kotcheff would deal directly with Veilleux on some issues.

Veilleux gave Kotcheff no specific program directives, except to say, "You're the expert on this. It's not my job to do programming, but I think you have to produce the nine to ten program more efficiently." Kotcheff's only mandate from the CBC president was for change and efficiency. The first change he made was to kill "The Journal" and blend the prime-time journalism hour, a move that reflected the desires of Veilleux, Pattillo, and the board. In the fall Canadians would see not only a new time for the news, but a totally new program as well.

Shockwaves rolled through the CBC at the news for it meant a death blow to what had been the CBC's greatest journalistic success story. "The National" and "The Journal" had been innovative only ten years earlier, but Kotcheff believed they were beginning to show signs of age and falling audiences, and besides, sensitive to Veilleux's concerns about money, he felt they cost too much.

So he officiated at the shotgun marriage of two often warring areas of CBC programming. For "The Journal" current affairs traditionalists, it represented a final surrender to the news department since Tony Burman would be in charge of the new hour-long program. Some "Journal" producers called Burman's news staffers "the occupying forces" when they took over the "Journal" offices and studio. On top of that, the whiz kid of CBC current affairs, Mark Starowicz, was out of a job. The man who was the driving force behind the success of "The Journal" toyed with an offer to take Kotcheff's old job running CTV News. Eventually, however, he was persuaded to stay with the CBC and take over the documentary unit of current affairs.

"I was trying to establish a new vision for news and save some money, too," Kotcheff says. He was shocked at how CBC news and current affairs had grown since he'd left CBC in 1972, and he found the CBC's "culture" totally different from CTV's. He felt that, with two different staffs, two different studios, and different hosts, "The National" and "The Journal" were wasting money. "It was very inefficient," he says. "I saw two studios to do one hour. I was knocked out by it. My instinct was, this is ridiculous." Kotcheff's reaction echoed that of the board, which believed, as one director says, "We had to recharacterize the hour. The cost was too high, there was duplication and empire-building. Senior management had been unable to come to grips with it." Another board member, Bill Neville, says, "It was very inefficient. We couldn't afford to do this indefinitely. 'The Journal' was, in a budgetary sense, not ready to adjust to reality."

At the same time, Kotcheff wanted to rejuvenate "Newsworld" which he considered "a little slow, a little sleepy." To do that, he moved the popular "National" over to "Newsworld" at 10:00 P.M., significantly increasing the channel's prime-time audience. He thought this would offset any audience drop which might occur with the new 9:00 P.M. news program on the main channel.

There still was, however, grave apprehension in the news department about the rush to air with the new program in the fall of 1992. It was pointed out that while "The National" and "The Journal" had had a year and a half to prepare their staffs, facilities, studios, and concepts, the new program would have only three months. But sensing the head office's desire for fast change, and with his own predilection for a new face for CBC journalism, Kotcheff rejected all pleas for delay and ordered full steam ahead.

In an eerie way, what made it possible to make the change was "Journal" host Barbara Frum's death from leukaemia four months earlier. She was both the star and the steadfast symbol of the quality of the program's journalism. The public saw on "The Journal" for a decade, and heard on "As It Happens" for an earlier decade, a no-nonsense, persistent, knowledgeable interviewer, who asked the questions they wanted answers to. Her friends and colleagues knew her as a sensitive, compassionate woman who cared deeply about her profession and her friends. She was, above all, courageous in her journalism and in her personal life. For eighteen years, she had quietly battled leukaemia, discussing it rarely and only then with intimates. "It's too bad," she told her friend, writer and broadcaster June Callwood, "I would have been a great old lady."

When she died at age fifty-four in March 1992, for most Canadians Barbara Frum *was* the CBC. "When she died yesterday," the Montreal *Gazette* editorialized, "people across English Canada felt as if a piece of their own lives had ended with hers."

"It won't be the same any more," said the *Ottawa Sun*, and for the CBC, as well as for the nation, it was certainly true.

"I don't think they would have been able to kill 'The Journal' if Barbara had been there," says Trina McQueen. "When I went with Veilleux to Barbara's funeral, person after person came up to speak about her, and I thought that maybe Gérard would understand what CBC journalism meant to so many distinguished people. I could tell it was having an effect on him. I later thought that what he got out of it was that 'The Journal' was such a powerful program that he couldn't hope to control it or mould it. [He] saw it as something outside him – that there was a CBC out there that he wasn't truly in charge of."

Kotcheff agrees that Barbara Frum's death was a key factor in the end of "The Journal." "It was a wonderful program when it started," he says, "but when Barbara died, it was diminished. It lost something. It lost Barbara."

Now, Kotcheff focused on the future, and he and his colleagues hurtled hellbent toward a fall launch of the new program, "CBC Prime Time News," hosted by Peter Mansbridge and Pamela Wallin, brought over from CTV's "Canada A.M." Fecan, meanwhile, concentrated on developing the entertainment side of the new schedule.

While Fecan and Kotcheff were lashing themselves through fifteen-hour workdays to be ready for the launch of the new CBC-TV schedule, they and Veilleux were sideswiped by the documentary series "The Valour and the Horror." Produced by the McKenna brothers, Brian and Terence, and supervised by McQueen and her current affairs executives, the three-part, $3.5-million CBC-NFB co-production combined drama and documentary in a controversial examination of Canadian participation in Second World War campaigns in Normandy and Hong Kong and the bombing of Germany. In a revisionist approach, the McKennas showed the Canadian wartime leadership as far less than the heroes portrayed by much traditional military history. Two and a half years in preparation, the series aired in January 1992 and was hailed by critics. "CBC DOES ITSELF PROUD WITH A STUNNING SERIES EXPOSING OBSCENITY OF WAR," headlined the *Toronto Star* review.

The McKennas saw the production as a salute to the bravery of young Canadians in the face of sometimes rotten leadership and needless sacrifices. A good many Second World War veterans, especially the airmen of Bomber Command, had a decidedly different viewpoint, and charged that they had been maligned in the series by being portrayed as insensitive, unintelligent, and little more than mass murderers for their bombing raids of Germany. They were deeply offended by the portrayal not only of themselves, but also of Bomber Command head Sir Arthur Harris, who was depicted as a ruthless brute, callously unconcerned about the civilian deaths caused by his raids on Germany.

The McKennas were defended by McQueen, whose department had had script control and who believed the production was a valid interpretation of the research. "My argument was that the CBC had time and time again portrayed the Nazi regime for what it was," she says. "I did not see it as extraordinarily controversial, and after it was on the air there was almost no controversy from the general public." McQueen grants that there likely were some relatively minor factual errors in the documentary, but she remains a strong defender of "The Valour and the Horror."

In the weeks after the series aired, a barrage of denunciation erupted from veterans groups led by Cliff Chadderton, chairman of the National Council of Veterans Associations and chief executive officer of the War Amps, and by Sen. Jack Marshall, chairman of the Senate Subcommittee on Veterans Affairs. It wasn't the first time Senator Marshall had attacked what he considered a slur on the portrayal of Canadian wartime exploits. A decade earlier, he had condemned an NFB documentary which took a sceptical view of the heroics of First World War flying ace Billy Bishop, and he had persuaded the Film Board to relabel the production a docudrama. Now, he had bigger fish to fry on a bigger stage, and he called a special hearing of his Senate subcommittee.

The uproar startled Gérard Veilleux, whose original reaction had been to support the program. That support began to soften, however, as criticism mounted and the CBC board became increasingly apprehensive about the rising furore. Board member John Crispo later said the series "represented one of the most flagrant forms of revisionist history I [am] ever likely to view." Crispo felt that, by airing the series, the CBC was helping to diminish rather than celebrate national achievement. When he read Crispo's comments in December, Watson immediately issued a statement saying that Crispo's criticisms "do not represent the view of the Board of Directors of the CBC nor of management."

But while it rejected the tone and extremity of Crispo's words, the CBC board agreed with much of what he said, and Veilleux's own position was inevitably affected by the board's hardening attitude. "He responded by defending the program until it became a huge problem for the board," says Trina McQueen. Watson, whose rebellious role in the "Seven Days" crisis had made him a hero to millions of Canadians, this time found himself trapped between his past and his present; between his instinct and his loyalty. He chose his present and his loyalty. He remembers talking privately with Veilleux about the need for a large degree of producer freedom. Other board members such as Bob Kozminski remember him in some "very emotional arguments" over producer independence and the importance of taking risks. "And if you take risks, you have to accept consequences," Kozminski recalls Watson saying. "He was intolerably pulled in two directions," Kozminski adds. "Patrick's problem is that he never quite figured out who he's there for," says Bill Neville. "He seems to vacillate at times from one role to another and that's a prescription to leave all your constituencies unhappy."

No matter what he might have said privately, in public Watson sided totally with Veilleux and the board. Even when CBC executives were present at the board meetings, he restrained his comments to the point that most of the executives were astonished at what they saw as his lack of participation. "He was present at every meeting of the board and many management meetings that dealt with the issue," says Ivan Fecan. "I don't think I ever witnessed him speaking about what his point of view was at a board meeting or at a management meeting." Another person who sat in on the meetings says, "The impression I got was that he agreed the McKennas were guilty, but he wanted to commute their sentence. He really didn't defend them. He just was never there and never spoke up." Veilleux was surprised at Watson's largely silent role at board meetings on this issue. "He never said anything," Veilleux says, "and I must say I deplore it very much because I was hoping he would use his considerable experience."

Watson's friends spoke up, however, and one close colleague even helped the McKennas prepare their defence against the CBC board and management. The McKennas felt Watson was a moderating force in the board discussions, had frequent phone conversations with him, and met him a few times in Montreal during the following summer. The McKennas' producer, Arnie Gelbart, says of Watson, "He understood our position. He was sensitive to our concerns about the process. He certainly was supportive of us in the trench warfare." Gelbart also tried to see Veilleux, but the CBC president declined.

Some of Watson's friends were incensed at Veilleux, one intimate friend even called the CBC president "an ice-cold little fascist." They urged Watson to resign, fearing he would lose all his credibility if he did not. They felt he should speak out against the "kangaroo court" treatment the McKennas were getting. At one point Watson seriously thought of resigning, but decided against it, arguing that if he did, the situation would be worse for the producers. "I was dealing with a number of people who would cheerfully have murdered the McKennas," he later said. Nevertheless, publicly he continued to support Veilleux's and the board's growing unhappiness with the program.

Watson says he put a high premium on keeping any policy disagreements with Veilleux hidden from view. They were two very different people from two very different backgrounds, and Watson says their conversations ranged from harmonious discussion to shouting matches. "We worked very hard at swallowing our personal distress from time to time," he says. "We both recognized that we either come before the board with a united front or we split up, and we both felt that an open split would be very, very destructive." Veilleux says he doesn't remember those conversations.

Watson's public support of criticism of the program led critics within and without the CBC to refer back to his "Struggle for Democracy" series and speak of a new Watson series called "Struggle for Hypocrisy." But Gelbart rejects that cynicism. "Patrick was the last rampart keeping the barbarians from the gate," he says. "He and Trina McQueen, too, were very supportive."

In May, Veilleux, seeking to lessen the heat in the controversy, requested a review of the whole issue by the CBC ombudsman, Bill Morgan, a former head of English network news and current affairs. Michael McEwen had argued against this but his advice had been rejected. In June, Senator Marshall held a Senate subcommittee hearing, calling selected witnesses who uniformly attacked "The Valour and the Horror" as inaccurate and unfair. Through the summer, Morgan consulted historians, producers, and executives, and read scripts, letters, and memos. The McKennas complained that Morgan had faxed them "a mountain of very aggressive questions." By late summer, the McKennas feared Morgan was going to be critical, and by September 1, 1992, he had a draft report which was a harsh denunciation of the series. "We were absolutely floored by it," says Gelbart. McQueen was also angry because she felt the historians chosen to be consulted by the ombudsman had not been thoroughly checked out for bias. As well, she had wanted her department's and the McKennas' responses to the report to be part of it before it was made public. "None of the those conditions were applied," she says. McQueen also remembers being upset when she was told that John Crispo had phoned Morgan several times while the report was being written. Morgan denies receiving any such calls.

When she first saw the draft of the report, she told Veilleux it was "full of holes and could easily be attacked." When the McKennas saw it, they demanded more time to respond before it was finalized. Over the next few weeks, the McKennas and McQueen continued to complain, and the producers sought legal advice. As a consequence, the report's censure was toned down. But it remained a damning indictment supporting the veterans' claims about inaccuracy and unfairness.

Veilleux had hoped the ombudsman's report would end the controversy, but when he saw it "he felt terribly torn," Watson says. "I think he had hoped that the ombudsman's report would be no problem. When the first hints [of its tone] came back, he began to worry. He felt whatever the ombudsman said would be determinate, crucial, and that he would have to support it." Seeking to lessen the pressures on the CBC, Pattillo visited Senator Marshall in Ottawa and suggested that as the CBC was handling the issue internally Marshall's Senate committee might ease up on its lacerating views of the CBC and the program. It was an ill-fated and, in the end, bruising exercise for Pattillo. News of his request was splashed over the front pages, and the CBC found itself in the middle of a squabble between Senator Marshall and Cliff Chadderton of the veterans' organizations, which focused even more attention on the judgements of the ombudsman.

In an extraordinary demonstration of bad timing, the CBC issued the ombudsman's report on the eve of Remembrance Day, November 11. "Are you out of your mind? Are you completely out of your mind?" Pattillo recalls telling board members. But he says the prevailing view was that since it would be released on the eve of a holiday, the press might not give the story much prominence. Besides, the board was worried about a news leak if it delayed putting out the report.

Earlier, when it had been proposed to release the report at the beginning of October, Watson had persuaded Veilleux and the board to delay publishing it, and its tone was moderated. By November, however, he couldn't stop the steamrolling board and president.

"The Valour and the Horror," the ombudsman's report said in its dozen pages, was "flawed and fails to measure up to CBC's demanding policies and standards." The series "stacked the deck" in some cases, used selective editing of witnesses, questionable dramatic sequences, and contained inaccuracies, all, the report said, designed to prove the McKennas' thesis which condemned Canadian military leadership. The ombudsman said the McKennas also erred by presenting their series as if they were "letting the audience hear the 'full' or 'real' story for the first time."

The McKennas lived up to their reputations as "street fighters" and immediately fired back a twelve-page salvo denouncing the ombudsman's report. Uninhibited by any self-doubt, they rejected accusations in the report of major errors. They charged the historians consulted by the ombudsman were either misquoted or biased themselves, and said the CBC journalistic standards had been followed. They warned of the report's chilling effect on controversial programming, saying, it was "an ice age that they're trying to impose . . . They've run amok." Morgan issued a stinging response defending his report and detailing more criticism. Watson said CBC journalistic independence had not been compromised but on "As It Happens" he admitted, "It has been a dreadful process. There's been so much anger . . . [an] atmosphere of nastiness." But even so, he said, "We have the strongest, most responsible journalistic organization in the country, if not the world."

Although Watson kept a line of communication open to the McKennas and Gelbart, Veilleux would have little to do with them. He says that at one point they even sought to blame McQueen for the problems. "I know damn well and I have it in writing that the McKennas were prepared to hang 'Irina. I protected Trina and a few others around her," he says. On the contrary, Gelbart says, they much admired and appreciated McQueen's support.

Tim Kotcheff found himself squarely in the middle of a battle that he knew little about. "It was an awful situation," he says. "Internally a lot of people felt the president was not supporting the creative side. We were getting beaten about by everybody. I've never seen such a deluge of organized mail. It became a battle of organized groups, the creative people and writers on one side, the veterans and critics of the CBC on the other, and in the middle you had the CBC management."

Ivan Fecan, who was miffed because McQueen had not shown him an advance screening of the series, was again miffed because he had not been provided with the early drafts of the ombudsman's report. He knew, however, that given his background, Veilleux would side with the ombudsman and against the series. "He saw the higher calling being to public accountability and not to the craft of journalism or to the mantra of protecting one's own," says Fecan. "When choosing between moral ideas, I think he saw the public accountability mandate as being the most important. He was surprised when the house [CBC staff] didn't agree with that." Fecan's basic criticism of the series was the "blunder in how it was platformed. It was platformed as an objective piece of work. It was never platformed as an essay or a point-of-view piece. There has to be room for all kinds of different points of view, but when you're doing something controversial you have to work twice as hard to make sure your facts are correct and you have to platform it correctly."

The question of "platforming" is a 1990s echo of a 1930s issue. When MacKenzie King objected loudly to a 1938 CBC commentary because he felt listeners might think the anti-appeasement views expressed were those of the government, CBC chairman Leonard Brockington settled it by "platforming" future commentaries as the views of individual commentators. McQueen says she would have so labelled "The Valour and the Horror" if she had realised how controversial it was going to be. Her successor, Tim Kotcheff, takes the approach that the series should not have implied that "this was the ultimate truth." But, he adds, "There were no clean hands in this thing."

Like Fecan and Kotcheff, Watson concentrates his criticism on the appearance of the series being "the ultimate truth," but he also attacks the McKennas for being "fearfully inept" in their dramatic sequences. That, he says, "was the major, single source of the problem in the goddamn thing. . . . They don't know how to do it."

If Veilleux had simply accepted the ombudsman's report and passed it on to Kotcheff and his current affairs department executives to deal with, he might have avoided much of the abuse that subsequently cascaded over him. But with the board pushing him, he felt he had to make a public comment. He sincerely regretted, he said, "any distress the programs may have caused members of the audience." What sent a shiver through the creative community was his added comment that, "The Corporation will learn from this and as part of our emphasis on media accountability, our scrutiny of programming of this kind will be improved substantially." To programmers, that meant Big Brother would be watching, and cries of "censorship!" could be heard from across the country.

It was the start of "the month from hell" for Gérard Veilleux. The president of the Writers Guild of Canada, Jack Gray, demanded Veilleux's resignation for "spineless toadying to authority and popular prejudice." In a column entitled, "COWARDLY BROADCASTING CORPORATION," Montreal *Gazette* editor Norman Webster called Veilleux's statement "a craven disavowal," and he denounced the ombudsman's report as "one of the most pitiful, inadequate, lightweight, pettifogging, truly embarrassing reports since the Vatican condemned Galileo." The *Gazette* lead editorial said the CBC board "should be ashamed of itself" and urged Watson's resignation.

The Alliance of Canadian Television Radio Artists, the Association of Television Producers and Directors, the Canadian Association of Journalists, the Canadian Independent Film Caucus, and the Quebec Federation of Journalists all denounced Veilleux and the ombudsman's report. "The CBC's journalistic reputation lies in pieces today, slit wide and deboned like a fresh caught trout," said the *Globe and Mail*. It attacked "the servile timidity of the CBC" and ridiculed "the craven efforts of the Corporation's senior executives to appease the program's enemies in

Parliament. This is the stuff of resignation." "A snivelling apology," said Pierre Berton in the *Toronto Star*. "The CBC has crawled on its belly."

Veilleux was beside himself with rage, with pain, and with confusion; never before had he experienced such public vilification. It was even worse than the budget cuts of December 1990. The protective anonymity of his public service career had been brutally stripped away by the uproar. At one point he looked out his office window and in a whispery voice told a colleague, "Jeez, this is tough. Really tough." He simply had never dreamed there would be this kind of spotlit cruelty when he took the job as CBC president. At best, he thought, it was a very vivid learning experience. At worst, it was intolerable.

"He was just about ruined by it," Patrick Watson says. "He lost a lot of sleep. He felt it was slipping through his fingers and he didn't know quite how to handle it. He feels that sometimes opposition from people who are supposed to be in your camp is some kind of betrayal. He felt personally betrayed." Remembering the impact of the criticism, Robert Pattillo says, "The CBC is such an unforgiving place."

The McKennas, on the other hand, were hailed as heroes by the creative community. When they walked into the CBC cafeteria in Montreal they were greeted with a standing ovation. The McKennas also found comfort in the CRTC which said, "While many, including veterans, historians and the Ombudsman, have cited material which seems to indicate that parts of the films may have been incorrect, the filmmakers too appear to have reasonable grounds for the assertions made."

The McKennas won three Gemini Awards when "The Valour and the Horror" was declared the best documentary of the year. "It's the revenge of the arts community," said Sen. Jack Marshall. "A disgrace and a travesty," said John Crispo. In an article in the *Toronto Star*, Crispo denounced critics of Veilleux and of the ombudsman's report both inside the CBC and outside, saying they were "ill-informed and inaccurate at best and dishonest, malicious and vicious at worst." He condemned the "wide array of lies, slanders and smears" against Veilleux and the board, complaining, too, that in response to the critics, CBC management had been "meek, mild, and muted." He also denounced CBC Radio and -TV for their coverage of the controversy, as well as CBC employees for having "parroted their evident bias" and for their "lack of knowledge."

Crispo's protests were echoed by Senator Marshall's veterans sub-committee, which demanded the NFB stop distributing copies of "The Valour and the Horror," that the CBC produce another program "which redresses the imbalances and corrects the inaccuracies," and that drama sequences be avoided in future documentaries. The advice was noted but disregarded. A year later, an Ontario judge threw out on technical grounds a libel action launched by Air Force veterans, adding, "I do not believe the film is disparaging of Canadian air crews [but] reflects how courageous they were." In 1994, official RCAF historians took much the same attitude towards Allied terror bombing of Germany as did the McKennas, thus validating the McKenna's position.

"The Valour and the Horror" scarred the CBC and Veilleux's plans for journalistic accountability. To many suspicious journalists, "account-ability" now sounded like censorship, making it that much more difficult to sell Veilleux's ideas of journalistic responsibility. "It was like throwing a hand grenade into a tent," says Pattillo.

By the end of 1992, the CBC was staggering not only from the *contretemps* of "The Valour and the Horror," but also from a shaky launch of the 9:00 P.M. to 10:00 P.M. "CBC Prime Time News." "CBC LAUNCHES A PRIME TIME TURKEY," was the headline in the *Calgary Herald* over a review typical of the media's response. The problem, as Trina McQueen had warned, was the insufficient time spent on sharpening the program's concept and refining its production. Opponents of the hectic pace of change quoted the Duke of Albany in *Lear*: "Striving to better, oft we mar what's well."

Also insufficiently recognized in the planning was the qualitative difference in the audience at 9:00 P.M. "The National" and "The Journal" at 10:00 P.M. had been watched especially by so-called "communicators" – teachers, executives, politicians, journalists, and social activists of all kinds. They were committed viewers of public affairs programming and were in sharp contrast to the "grazers" with shallow commitments to journalistic programming who dominated the 9:00 P.M. audiences. It was true the audiences had slipped for "The National" and "The Journal" in the past year or two, but they dropped sharply for the new "CBC Prime

Time News." Once the program's weaknesses were seen on air, however, quick action was taken to reshape it which, in turn, led to the angry departure of the program's executive producer Ron Crocker. In a farewell memo to his staff, Crocker said he had been "crudely" forced out. "A soldier is fragged," he told CBCers. "Some permanent scarring of soul tissue. A legacy of seething rage."

All this creative turmoil aggravated the ravages of the Mulroney budget cuts. "It's inevitable we're going to be a smaller corporation," said Tony Manera, the CBC's senior vice-president. "That's a given. The issue is not whether we become smaller, it's whether we can manage it without it becoming a bloodbath."

By spring 1993, the chance of there being a "bloodbath" became much more likely. Finance Minister Don Mazankowski announced more cuts to the CBC beyond those the corporation was already facing in the next two years. He wanted another $100 million in the two subsequent years. "It was a very cheap shot on the part of a departing government which said that, before they slam the door, they would give another kick at you and then escape," says Veilleux. "That's cheap and that's gutless."

Veilleux was also distressed at the inaction of Watson and the board on the cuts. "I wanted the board and the chairman to go to work on this, but nothing happened. I was left alone again," Veilleux says. "Again I said to the chairman, 'Mobilize! Mobilize the board! Just go! Play hardball!'" But his plea was met with further inaction, perhaps in part because half-a-dozen board members were busy working on Kim Campbell's political campaign. "I said to Patrick, 'You've got to confront them. It's your board.' But he didn't do that. It's not his style."

Initially, relations between Veilleux and Watson had been relatively smooth and mutually supportive, but close associates say that shortly after Watson was finally confirmed as chairman in June 1991 their mutual appreciation began to deteriorate. "Coolish" is the way one colleague describes their relationship in 1992 and 1993. "Patrick's instincts were right, but his credentials lay in creativity not management and strategic thinking," the colleague says.

In commenting on the Conservative government's spring 1993 budget cuts, the Montreal *Gazette* said, "Finance Minister Don Mazankowski may go down in history as the man who delivered a fatal blow to the

CBC." Inevitably, the cuts would mean more firings, less money for programs, and a further draining of the CBC's creative juices. It was a dramatic fulfillment of the revengeful dreams of those right-wing Conservatives who had poured into Ottawa in 1984 determined to put what they felt was an anti-Tory CBC in its place. If they hadn't yet destroyed the CBC, they were well on the way, and all under the mantle of fiscal responsibility. Thirty-five years earlier, John Diefenbaker had cut the CBC down to size through legislation. Brian Mulroney did it even more effectively through budget cuts. He did it, however, less on his own initiative and more by acquiescing to the Don Mazankowskis, Jim Edwards, and Michael Wilsons of the party, who powerfully influenced the government's expenditure review committee and were propelled by the anti-CBC sentiments of most Alberta Conservative MPs. "It's not that Mulroney initiated the cut proposals, but he never overruled them and never discouraged them, and it was part of his broader lack of interest in the whole area," says Bill Neville.

"There is no longer any reason why we need a state broadcaster," cabinet minister Garth Turner had said earlier, apparently unaware that the CBC was an arms-length Crown corporation, not a state broadcaster. Monique Landry, who in a Kim Campbell cabinet shuffle in the summer of 1993 had become the minister responsible for the CBC, talked publicly about selling off some of the CBC to private interests. "We're just starting to look at this," she said. Veilleux brusquely rejected the idea.

"Any government that wants to kill an institution like the CBC," former CBC president Al Johnson once said, "would never just close it down because that would be politically impossible. No, it would starve it to death slowly over a period of years."

Johnson's nightmare seemed to be coming true and, just after the Mazankowski budget cuts, Gérard Veilleux, the very proper public servant, stepped out of character to deliver a combative, gloomy private warning to the communications minister. "This budget has serious implications for the Corporation's finances," he wrote. "If left unchanged, its full impact would impair our ability to deliver CBC-mandated radio and television services." The new budget cuts would leave the CBC about $300 million short by 1996-97, nearly a third of its current federal funding. Five months earlier, Veilleux had had to dip

Into the surplus in the CBC pension fund to help finance corporation spending. Although he accepted that the CBC had to share in general government restraint, he told the minister, "the CBC is not being dealt with fairly." He also noted that not only was the CBC being cut, but so, too, were Telefilm and the NFB, which were key players in the production of Canadian TV programming. In return, he received platitudes, but no signals of hope from the government.

Veilleux had finally run out of his ability and his patience to deal with the government's budgets cuts. Since 1984, those cuts and the non-provision of funds for inflation had totalled more than a billion dollars. Some of that had been offset by Veilleux's impressive financial skills and backroom persuasiveness, which had secured special, extra allocations he used to reduce the net amount of the accumulated cuts to about $635 million. Among other things, the cuts had led to a reduction in CBC staff from more than 12,000 in 1984 to 9,370 ten years later. Now, Mazankowski was chopping another $100 million, and Veilleux's only consolation was the promise of a communications department committee study of the CBC's financial problems.

It was too much, and after thirty years of public service, Gérard Veilleux wanted out. He was exhausted, eaten up by frustration, anguished by the government's unfairness to the CBC and, he felt, misunderstood by much of the CBC staff. He wanted a less frenetic life, more time for his family, and a better paid private-sector job. He envied both the professional and personal lifestyle of private sector CEOs such as Mickey Cohen, his friend and onetime Finance Department mentor and now Molson Co. boss. He also viewed dimly the prospect of the lame-duck status he felt he would have in his last year as CBC president. As well, there was the possibility that someone new might have a fresh chance at dissuading the government from its budget-slashing vengeance. Within nine months of leaving the CBC Veilleux found a less stressful and more rewarding role as president of Power Communications Inc., a subsidiary of Power Corp. of Canada.

"The guy had just burned himself out," says Bill Neville. "He was spiritually exhausted," says Patrick Watson, whose own twinkly eyes had dulled under the intensity of all the budget cuts, conflicts, and turmoil. "He couldn't take it any more," Watson adds. "I think he had to draw himself up to the task every morning. I've seen him on a Friday afternoon just pale, shaken, totally emptied of all resources, trying to hold on."

In late July 1993, Veilleux wrote Prime Minister Kim Campbell that he was quitting as CBC president in November, a year early in his five-year appointment. It was a time for a career change, he said in his sparse, two-paragraph letter. Watson immediately sought advice from CBC lawyers on whether he could assume the presidency on an acting basis, but he was told no because, by law, such a role can only be filled by a CBC management officer.

To the very end, Veilleux had kept his close-to-the-vest style, not telling his closest colleagues of his plans. He called a meeting of his senior associates ostensibly to discuss other matters, but really to tell them of his resignation. The meeting was scheduled for half an hour before the formal announcement was to be made. An hour or so prior to the meeting, he had confided to a few associates. "I thought it was a joke," Ivan Fecan says, but it was no joke. "You bastard!" Fecan laughingly thought, remembering how Veilleux had sweet-talked him out of leaving the CBC for a million-dollar job offered by an American specialty channel not too long before. "It's been a hell of a learning experience for him," Fecan says, "but painful and hard on his family. It was just time."

It was time, too, for Fecan. Within a few weeks of Veilleux's departure, Fecan also left the CBC to become a vice-president for Baton Broadcasting, where, with his popularizing predilections, he would find the challenge of the marketplace more comfortable than the policy mandate demands of the CBC. Shortly after he left, the axe fell on two Fecan-nurtured series: the beleaguered "Friday Night! with Ralph Benmergui" and "Street Legal," the CBC's highly popular serial drama that successfully mixed soap opera and Canadian topicality. The program had run for eight years and 124 episodes, and the CBC decided to end it while it was still on a high. Shortly after he left, another Fecan-era program announced it would depart in 1995. "The Kids in the Hall," one of the country's most successful comedy shows, would be leaving TV for Hollywood. Fecan had been especially pleased that "The Kids" had been picked up by Home Box Office (HBO) and later by CBS. Now they were going into moviemaking with Paramount Pictures.

Within a few weeks of Veilleux's departure, another of his "agents of change" quit when Guy Gougeon, vice-president in charge of CBC French TV also resigned. He had been with the CBC thirty-six years. Gougeon, too, went into private broadcasting, joining the Montreal communications firm COGECO Radio-Television, Inc. as vice-president and general manager.

While sharing many of Veilleux's frustrations, neither Fecan nor Gougeon had had to face the sharp attacks Veilleux had endured. Tim Kotcheff saw the pain etched in Veilleux's face and says, "My God, to be exposed to that kind of constant criticism, internally and externally, that was a big load to carry. I don't know how he did it." He did it through his own tight focus and discipline, and he told a private gathering of colleagues that he had learned through pain. The emotional nourishment this very private man drew from his wife, Celine, and his teenage daughter, Elaine, also helped him to cope. At a farewell reception in Toronto, Veilleux came close to tears when presented with a composite portrait of his CBC years that prominently featured his wife and daughter.

A few weeks before Veilleux announced his resignation, Trina McQueen, whom he sometimes referred to as "that woman," resigned from the CBC to run the proposed specialty service "Discovery Channel Canada." She says Veilleux was an incredible communicator and devoted public servant. "He's a committed Canadian nationalist and a committed believer that the CBC is an important part of the expression of Canada."

For all that, however, McQueen quit because she felt uncomfortable with Veilleux, as well as being "bone-numbingly weary" at the prospect of more budget cuts. When she was leaving she did not want to say anything that might be construed as criticism of Veilleux and suggested to him through Pattillo that she might express concerns about the government budget cuts to the CBC. The message she remembers getting back was, "No, don't say that, but perhaps you could say something nice about the president." She couldn't, nor could she cope with Veilleux's tough style. "I resented his temper tantrums," she says. "I resented his inability to trust people. I resented his secrecy and his favouritism, and I probably resented what was, in effect, a very shy man."

Veilleux was, indeed, a sharp-elbowed taskmaster. "I'm not paid to be a figurehead," he once said. He was a prisoner of a manner learned during his civil service past and so, as one of his close colleagues says, "He's brilliant, but he could use more interpersonal sensitivity."

"You could argue with him," another says, "But after he'd decided, you'd better support him." When frustrated, he occasionally used or simulated anger to get what he wanted. "Nobody was better at the strategic temper tantrum than Gérard," says Bill Neville. "At times, he was genuinely angry, but he also knew that it was a great way to browbeat people into getting your way."

"Gérard knew exactly where he wanted to go, and you were either on the train or off the train," says Pattillo. "He doesn't hope for things, he believes in things, and I think he believed that history will look back at this time as being the turning point for the CBC."

Veilleux believes his "repositioning" strategy is his greatest legacy for the CBC, but many of his actions began to unravel almost as soon as he was out the door. The CBC reopened its closed Windsor, Ontario, station for local newscasts, and the local Calgary station was also back with news programming. The 11:00 P.M. local news was also reinstituted for the 1994-95 season for all other CBC stations, reversing a key element of Veilleux's actions in the December 1990 budget-slashing.

Most significant of all, however, the high-profile crown jewel of Veilleux's "repositioning" – the 9:00 P.M. "CBC Prime Time News" – was moved back to 10:00 P.M. for the 1994-95 season, a painful confession of the audience failure of the scheduling scheme that had been so noisily trumpeted. The audience for the prime-time news and current affairs program had fallen by 17 per cent from "The National" and "The Journal" of two years earlier. "'CBC Prime Time News' at 9:00 P.M. has been unable to secure a place in the minds of a consistent audience," said Jim Byrd, Ivan Fecan's replacement as English TV vice-president. The move back to 10:00 P.M. was a CBC *mea culpa* and response to public preference. Even Robert Pattillo, the repositioning enthusiast, had switched positions after Veilleux's resignation and urged a return to a 10:00 P.M. start for the news. The seemingly conscious unravelling of the Veilleux era continued apace when another of his "agents of change," Tim

Kotcheff, was dismissed as vice-president of TV news and current affairs. He was a victim of the Byzantine politics at the CBC and paid the price for his hard-nosed implementation of Gérard Veilleux's objectives. The top-level house-cleaning even shook "Prime Time News" in the midst of all its program changes as anchors, producers, and editors nervously watched and occasionally agitated in discordant response to the corporate ferment. They wondered what other changes there might be. One of them was the noisy departure from "Prime Time News" of anchor Pamela Wallin.

As the months went by after Veilleux's departure, the once muffled ire of some of his CBC executives grew loud. Even some of those referred to quietly as "collaborators" seemed to be seeking redemption by privately calling their onetime leader "that son of a bitch." Still, Veilleux believes his repositioning in the schedule and elsewhere for the CBC was a worthwhile risk. He also proudly notes Canadian content under his presidency rose from 82 per cent to more than 88 per cent in prime time, and that there is more cross-cultural programming than ever before. Since 1992, 130 hours of French network dramas such as "Scoop" had been translated for the English network, while French-language viewers saw dubbed versions of programs such as "Road to Avonlea," "North of 60," and "The Boys of St. Vincent."

A year before his resignation he looked out his sixth floor office window and mused about his eventual departure, saying, "My objective is to leave the place in better shape than when I took it." He feels it is better because of repositioning, tighter management, and greater efficiency. Those were what mattered to him.

But the relatively quick departure of Veilleux's "agents of change" after he resigned, and the rescinding of many of his more visible repositioning actions, cut the heart out of his legacy. His footprints were those of a stranger. He came in to the CBC as an enigma and left the same way. He never became a part of the CBC the way, for example, Al Johnson had. Throughout his four-year presidency, Gérard Veilleux was an outsider.

In an odd way, so too was Patrick Watson, who resigned in June 1994, four months before his term as chairman was up. He had ached to be head of the CBC ever since his "Seven Days" rebellion, yet when he became chairman three decades later, the job turned to ashes in his mouth. "One of the toughest periods of my life," he said on quitting. Burdened by impossibly high expectations, he acidly noted, "Some of my colleagues expected me to reverse the law of gravity, and when I proved incapable of that, there were sometimes very bitter expressions of disappointment." Like Veilleux, he professed pride in what had been accomplished during his tenure, not in creative programming, but in the bureaucracy: a stronger board of directors and more journalistic accountability. But Gérard Veilleux had made sure Watson had little authority, and what he had he often seemed uncertain how to use, all of which led to his increasing frustration. As a legendary figure in Canadian broadcasting, his rightful acclaim rests on his many creative triumphs rather than on his executive skills.

"It's going to be a zipper," Watson had said when he and Veilleux were named to lead the CBC. In truth, for both there were many more moments of cheerless angst than of zip.

22

Oblivion or Renaissance?

For almost a decade, Pierre Juneau and Gérard Veilleux had faced a government that, inch by inch, whipped the CBC away from its public service mandate. It was not done by declared government policy, but rather through the backdoor of dramatic and disproportionate budget cuts. The Diefenbaker government shrank the CBC by boosting the role of private broadcasters, and the Mulroney government did it by financially penalizing the CBC, reducing public funding in real terms every year it was in office.

As Ottawa's support diminished, the CBC went out into the marketplace, becoming increasingly dependent on revenue from commercials – more than $300 million in 1993 – and, inevitably, that affected programming. More commercials meant more American-like, mass-appeal programs, which took the CBC further into the private broadcasting ethos than it had ever been before.

The dilemma of the corporation's pragmatic need for commercial revenue and its philosophical commitment to public broadcasting has plagued it from the very beginning. In the 1930s, Graham Spry and Alan Plaunt tiptoed into commercialism, and so too did Hector Charlesworth and the CRBC. Later, Austin Weir warned about the insidious impact of commercialism on a public broadcasting system, and so has every leader of the CBC since then. At the same time, every CBC leader has also increased commercial revenue as a proportion of the total budget because the cost of fulfilling its parliamentary mandate outran government subsidies.

"Overmandated and underfunded" was the apt description given to the CBC by Carleton University professor Bruce Doern. From the earliest days, the Treasury Board, the occasional parliamentary committee, and even the Fowler Committee told the CBC that if it needed more money, it would have to get it from the marketplace not the public purse.

The danger for public broadcasting was that the more commercial the CBC was seen to be, the more it was perceived as being not much different from private stations, and thus, why spend a billion dollars of public money every year for the same thing. It was a question that alarmed Juneau and Veilleux, trapped as they seemed to be between Charybdis and Scylla, and it led them into accelerated but underfunded "Canadianization" of the TV schedules. Under Veilleux, Canadian content reached 88 per cent in the 7:00 P.M. to 11:00 P.M. prime time for the English and French networks in the 1992-93 season. Veilleux went one step further in reaching for distinctiveness by intensively branding the CBC "a public service" and risking audience alienation by dramatically repackaging the television schedule. Indeed, for whatever reason – the rising number of TV signals, rescheduling, or quality of programs – the CBC's share of the TV audience in Canada, like that of other broadcasters, has dramatically shrunk over the years in the increasingly fragmented market. It now is less than 13 per cent, or about 15 per cent for English TV when "Newsworld" is included. "You're going down the tubes here in ratings. You're going into oblivion," warned CRTC chairman Keith Spicer in early 1994.

The election of Jean Chrétien's Liberal government was no answer to the CBC's prayers, given Chrétien's long-time distaste for the intellectuals of the French network and his past accusations about separatism among its programmers. But at least philosophically, Chrétien recognized that the CBC was one of Canada's defining institutions and by far the single most important cultural instrument reflecting and shaping Canada's identity.

While the CBC no longer confronted the deep-rooted cultural negativity and political suspicions that had infused the Conservative government, it still faced a reduced budget, a technological revolution, and a market challenge. It also faced, as it always had, the morose predictions of internal and external naysayers who viewed the future of the CBC through the lenses of their own disillusionment. What was needed to run the place was a smooth-talking, culturally sensitive visionary who was also one tough son of a bitch.

Into this witch's brew of financial and technological perplexity and cultural challenge strode a totally unexpected and extraordinary choice to run Canada's most important cultural instrument. He was fifty-three-year-old Tony Manera, an Italian immigrant from outside the milieu of Canadian élites and government mandarins. Manera was eleven years old when his parents emigrated to Montreal from their native Sicily. He learned English and French, moved to California to get his engineering degrees, became a teacher, and headed several community colleges before coming to the CBC as vice-president of human resources in 1985.

In February 1993, he had announced he was retiring at the end of the year, but when Veilleux resigned, he agreed to stay on as acting president until a successor to Veilleux was found. The last thing on his mind, and the last thing on everybody else's mind, was that he might be chosen for the permanent position. He wasn't the only one surprised at his appointment; so was much of Canada's cultural community and his eighty-two-year-old mother, who still finds English difficult and was also confused over his new job. He had told her he was going to be president of the CBC, but when she saw a *Maclean's* article headline, "THE CBC'S NEW CAPTAIN," she asked him, "It says you're a captain. You told me you were going to be president. What happened?"

The only time a CBC president has real leverage with the government is when he's being wooed to take the job, and so Manera sought to get some visible financial relief for the CBC. "I asked for a lot," he says. After several meetings, a deal was reached with Heritage Minister Michel Dupuy. The deal was that the $100 million in cuts ordered by Mazankowski would be spread over five years, not two as Mazankowski had planned, with no cuts in the first two years. There would also be long-term, five-year financing for the CBC, something CBC presidents had been seeking for years; the

CBC would be allowed to borrow up to $25 million, and, most important of all, there would be no other budget cuts for five years.

Manera felt good about what he considered to be these iron-clad promises from the minister and the Liberal government. He was less successful with his own board of directors, however, in his first major appointment. In an uncharactersitic display of management muscularity, chairman Patrick Watson led the board to reject the new president's choice to replace Ivan Fecan as boss of English TV. Manera had sought to name to the job the seasoned and sophisticated head-office veteran vice-president John Shewbridge. Watson, however, insisted on someone more popular "with the troops" and with more "ground level" experience. Manera was forced to accede and named to Fecan's old job his second choice, Newfoundlander Jim Byrd, a much admired TV executive who had won plaudits from programmers for his work in both the regions and the network.

This confrontation with his board may have been an omen of dark days ahead for Manera, although in his first months he plunged into the job with great zest. Soon, however, his enthusiasm was tested as ominous budget-cutting rumblings began rolling out of Finance Minister Paul Martin's office. Confident of the government's financial promise that he had secured, Manera couldn't believe the government would reneg. But reneg it did in the 1995 budget. It was a mortal blow to Manera's sense of integrity. He couldn't accept the broken promise and had no stomach to enforce the huge cuts: $350 million by 1997, he calculated, which could mean 3,000–4,000 employees fired, reducing CBC staff from 12,000 in 1984 to 5,000–6,000 in 1997. This, he said, would "cut the heart and soul" out of the CBC and, in an action seldom seen in contemporary Ottawa, Manera resigned on principle.

To everybody's astonishment, including his own, the long-time "boy wonder" Conservative, Perrin Beatty, was named to succeed Manera. "Do you want to serve your country?" the prime minister had asked him, and he couldn't say no. Besides, the challenge was irresistible. Ironically, Beatty would now have to implement the massive budget cuts of both the Liberals and his own Conservative government, in which he had sat, among other cabinet posts, as the communications minister with responsibility for the CBC. Chickens had come home to roost with a vengeance and Beatty, along with the new chair of the board, Guylaine Saucier, a Quebec businesswoman, now confronted the most traumatic re-organization of public broadcasting that Canada had ever faced. Unlike Manera, Beatty came with no promises from the government other than what he believed was an iron-clad commitment to public broadcasting by the prime minister. But the key question was, in what form? With the government essentially setting cultural policy by the balance sheet, Beatty's job was fundamentally to recast public broadcasting to meet a financial policy. The budget cuts were of such daunting dimension that it became no longer possible to "water the soup" with across-the-board percentage reductions. Surgery was necessary, and that meant Beatty faced agonizing and bloody decisions if the CBC was to exist at all.

While making these decisions Beatty and the government were inundated by a deluge of advice. some came from politicians, especially M.P. John Godfrey's parliamentary committee on Canadian Heritage, and some from a special advisory committee appointed by Ottawa in the wake of Paul Martin's budget cuts to examine the future of the CBC, the National Film Board, and Telefilm Canada. The latter committee included two old CBC bureaucratic adversaries but philosophical soul mates: former president Pierre Juneau and former vice-president for English broadcasting, Peter Herrndorf. Hovering over Beatty and his colleagues as they rooted through the advice was a merciless short time-frame for their decisions on the shape of public broadcasting in Canada. To meet the government's budget targets for 1996 and 1997, they had only months in which to revise sixty years of CBC's purpose.

The billion-dollar-a-year public subsidy for the CBC works out to about a dime a day for each Canadian, and the crucial question the CBC now faces is, can a worthwhile service be provided for less than seven cents a day? And is there the political will to make it work at all? Everything depends on how the CBC mandate is defined in a future of 100, 200, or 500 channels of television and the interactive convergence of the television and the computer screens on the much heralded "information highway."

In whatever way the CBC reinvents itself, more important than any-thing else is the absolute necessity for it to recognize the old Fowler Com-mittee dictum that in the end, the only thing that really matters is pro-gram content. The CBC could be the best managed, most efficient, soundly financed organization in the country, but unless its programs are exciting, enriching, and distinctive, it won't be worth a saucer of warm spit. The one lesson clearly etched over six decades of CBC history is that programs are primary; everything else is supportive and secondary. While every CBC president and chairman has rhetorically supported that belief, few have committed their heart and soul to it. Davie Dunton did, and two decades later, Al Johnson did. They knew that, in the end, the producer in the studio or the performer on the air has far more to do with the success of the CBC than any chairman or president. As a university is the sum of its scholars, the CBC is the sum of its producers and perform-ers. The bureaucrat's job is to provide the tools; the programmer's job is to captivate the public.

With programs placed first, then the decentralization of the CBC inevitably follows. George Davidson and Laurent Picard were right in taking power out of Ottawa and putting it where programs are made in the network centres of Toronto, Montreal, and the regional studios from St. John's to Vancouver. The CBC is more like a university than a business and its creative health is nurtured by a dispersion of power.

Decentralization is, of course, messy, noisy, and often a pain in the presidential ass, but the creative liberation that decentralization brings is, in the end, far more valuable than the neatness, efficiency, and control of consolidated presidential power.

As there are ever-present strains between CBC bureaucrats and creators, there are, too, inexorable tensions between the CBC and the government of the day. At some point, inevitably, the interests of the government and the CBC diverge, for the two cannot be blood brothers. No prime minis-ter from Bennett to Chrétien has ever been satisfied with the way the national public broadcaster has been run. They all, eventually, want tougher management and programming more responsive to government priorities. Even a government that heartily endorses the principles of public broadcasting – such as Mackenzie King's – will find itself, in time, seeking to have the CBC reflect the government's self-image. All the rhetoric about CBC independence melts when a government confronts what it considers to be a major crisis, as did Trudeau's administration over the separatism issue. It melts even when the government faces smaller issues such as when Louis St. Laurent tried to stop the CBC from reporting prison riots. To satisfy a government always, the CBC would have to defy its own mandate since its loyalty lies first with the public. Defence of that independence from government demands a great deal of courage in a CBC leader, such as was demonstrated by Leonard Brockington, Davie Dunton, and, at his own high personal cost, Al Johnson. The crucial test for any CBC president is how to preserve CBC independence without destroying the respect, if not the affection, of the government.

While it is not the CBC's role to espouse any particular form of constitutional arrangement, there is no question the CBC is the chosen instrument of Parliament to be the key cultural adhesive and to make Canadians more aware of each other and proud of their nation. That was the reason national public broadcasting began in the first place. It was the theme of the crusading *Ottawa Citizen* editor, Charles Bowman, in the 1920s, the central argument of Graham Spry and Alan Plaunt, and it was the rationale that persuaded R. B. Bennett and Mackenzie King to support public broadcasting. But, as in so many things, on the question of national unity, every CBC president walks a tightrope to avoid the dangers of the CBC appearing to be propagandistic to some or traitorous to others.

Al Johnson promoted the "Canadianization" of the CBC-TV schedule partly as a non-political answer to the demands of the government for a more supportive role on national unity. His legacy has been enriched and expanded by his successors and may well be the salvation of the CBC when hundreds of channels start to rain down on the country. Even before that downpour begins, Canadians are spending about 80 per cent of their viewing time watching American programs, ironically the same percentage of time Canadians spent listening to American radio programs in the late 1920s. Without the CBC, it would probably be close to 100 per cent. This is part of the painful reality that Canada's culture is the most foreign dominated of any nation in the Western world.

And the one quality that the CBC can provide better than anyone else and that will make it stand out amid the multitude of specialty American programs that will flood the country in the near future is Canadian programming. In spite of the occasional pratfall, that has been especially true in the area of journalism, where CBC's comprehensiveness and thoughtprovoking programming has been unmatched. It also has got the CBC into more political trouble than anything else. But this is not necessarily a bad thing.

Private broadcasters are now doing better than they ever have in providing quality Canadian programming, but inevitably their output is limited by the reality that their bottom line is in profit. As a taxpayer-supported body, for the most part, the CBC's bottom line is public service, and its effectiveness in providing that depends on the programmers and the leadership they are given.

CBC's history provides a map to one of the country's most formidable challenges. Never before in all of the CBC's triumphs and betrayals has any new leader confronted a more daunting mission or had more need of a good map in the search for quality, distinction, and impact than Manera does today.

"In recent years," *Maclean's* has written, "the CBC has been publicly called bullheaded, autocratic, dictatorial, spineless, weak, pathetic, extravagant, cheap, high handed, bumbling, nonsensical, dishonest, power crazy, idiotic and absurd. It has been called a milch cow, a centaur and a dog." *Maclean's* said that in 1951 at the height of the so-called golden age of radio. In different words the comment had been made before that and has been repeated many times since, for no other Canadian organization has endured the intensity of scrutiny the CBC is constantly under. Whether it's over "Mr. Sage" in 1935, over "Preview Commentary" in 1959, over "This Hour Has Seven Days" in 1966, over "Air of Death" in 1968, or over "The Valour and the Horror" in 1992, inquisitions will always occur whenever the public broadcasting system offers challenges to conventional wisdom. And so they should as the CBC is a creature of taxpayers' money. But as the Fowler Committee once said, "A broadcasting system . . . must not always play safe. Its guiding rule cannot be to give the people what they want. . . . One of the essential tasks of a broadcasting system is to stir up the minds and emotions of the people and occasionally to make large numbers of them acutely uncomfortable. . . . There must be room for the thinker, the disturber and the creator of new forms and ideas."

That, indeed, is the CBC's role.

Sources

A multitude of sources is available for research on the CBC, and this book has drawn heavily on the vast amount of material in the Federal Archives of the National Archives of Canada for documentary information and for oral history tapes at the Visual and Sound Archives section of the National Archives. The CBC itself, especially the CBC Reference Library in Toronto, was another central source of information for both documents and oral history tapes. The University of British Columbia and the Metro Toronto Reference Library were thorough and helpful sources of both published and non-published material. *Hansard* was invaluable in providing a record of parliamentary debates on public broadcasting, as were scores of official government, CRBC, BBG, CRTC, and CBC reports and a myriad of magazines, newspapers, and books. A good deal of material also has been drawn from the author's private records of letters, documents, papers, and notes. A key source for the book has been personal interviews by the author with many of the players in CBC history. Many such interviewees preferred to remain anonymous and others are listed below.

Primary Sources

Personal Interviews by Author

Armstrong, Bill (Toronto); Boyle, Harry (Toronto); Campbell, Norman (Toronto); Campbell, Peter (Toronto); Chercover, Murray (Toronto); Curley, Paul (Toronto); Davey, Sen. Keith (Toronto); Davidson, George (Vancouver); Faibish, Roy (London, England); Fecan, Ivan (Toronto); Gelbart, Arnie (Montreal); Guest, Gowan (Vancouver); Harvey, Denis (Toronto); Herrndorf, Peter (Toronto); Holmes, Art (Toronto); Johnson, Al (Ottawa); Juliette (Vancouver); Juneau, Pierre (Montreal); Kotcheff, Tim (Toronto); Kozminski, Robert (Winnipeg); Lynch, Charles (Ottawa); Macdonald, Donald (St. Mary's, Ontario); Manera, Tony (Ottawa); McEwen, Michael (Ottawa); McKay, Bruce (Toronto); McQueen, Trina (Toronto); Morrison, Ian (Toronto); Neville, Bill (Ottawa); O'Hagan, Dick (Toronto); Pattillo, Robert (Toronto); Picard, Laurent (Montreal); Pickering, Edward (Toronto); Rasky, Harry (Toronto); Sinclair, Lister (Toronto); Shuster, Frank (Toronto); Stursberg, Peter (Vancouver); Thibault, Marc (Montreal); Veilleux, Gérard (Ottawa); Watson, Patrick (Toronto); Willis, Austin (Wetaskiwin, Alberta); Young, John (Halifax)

Oral History Tapes

Allard, T. J. (National Archives of Canada, Ottawa); Bowman, Bob (National Archives of Canada, Ottawa); Bowman, Charles (University of British Columbia, Special Collections, Vancouver); Boyle, Harry (National Archives of Canada, Ottawa); Briggs, Capt. W. E. S. (National Archives of Canada, Ottawa); Bushnell, Ernie (CBC Reference Library, Toronto; National Archives of Canada, Ottawa); Carlyle, Jack (National Archives of Canada, Ottawa); Coderre, Guy (National Archives of Canada, Ottawa); Corbett, E. A. (University of British Columbia, Special Collections, Vancouver); Crossan, Drew (National Archives of Canada, Ottawa); Cunningham, Bill (Ibid.); Dunton, Davidson (Ibid.); Ferguson, Max (Ibid.); Fraser, Ron (Ibid.); Hallman, Eugene (Ibid.); Halton, David (Ibid.); Hewitt, Foster (Ibid.); Holmes, Art (Ibid.); Keate, Stuart (Ibid.); LaMarsh, Judy (Ibid.); Lint, David (Ibid.); Lyons, Margaret (Ibid.); Lynch, Charles (Ibid.); McArthur, Dan (CBC Reference Library, Toronto; National

Archives, Ottawa); McLean, Ross (CBC Reference Library, Toronto); Morrison, Hugh (National Archives of Canada, Ottawa); Morrison, Neil (Ibid.); Morrow, Keith (Ibid.); Morrow, Marianne (Ibid.); Munro, Marce (Ibid.); Mutrie, Fergus (Ibid.); Ouimet, Alphonse (Ibid.); Shugg, Orville (Ibid.); Spry, Graham (National Archives of Canada, Ottawa; CBC Reference Library, Toronto); Steel, Lt.-Col. William Arthur (National Archives of Canada, Ottawa; CBC Reference Library, Toronto); Watson, Patrick (National Archives of Canada, Ottawa); Willis, J. Frank (National Archives of Canada, Ottawa)

Private Papers

Bowman, Charles (National Archives of Canada, Ottawa); Bennett, R. B. (Ibid.); Brockington, Leonard (Ibid.); Bushnell, Ernie (Ibid.); Charlesworth, Hector (Ibid.); Dafoe, John (Ibid.); Diefenbaker, John (Ibid.); Dunton, Davidson (Ibid.); Eggleston, Wilfrid (Ibid.); Jennings, Charles (Ibid.); King, W. L. M. (Ibid.); Manson, Donald (Ibid.); Murray, Gladstone (Ibid.); Odlum, Gen. Victor (Ibid.); Plaunt, Alan (University of British Columbia, Special Collections, Vancouver); Shugg, Orville (National Archives of Canada, Ottawa); Spry, Graham (Ibid.); Weir, E. Austin (Ibid.)

Reports

Major Government Commissions and Task Forces

Royal Commission on Radio Broadcasting, Sir John Aird, 1929.
Survey of National Radio in Canada, Gladstone Murray, 1933.
Royal Commission on National Development in the Arts, Letters and Sciences, Vincent Massey, 1951.
Royal Commission on Broadcasting, Robert Fowler, 1957.
Advisory Committee on Broadcasting, Robert Fowler. 1965.
White Paper on Broadcasting, 1966.
Special Senate Committee on Mass Media, Sen. Keith Davey, 1970.
Royal Commission on Government Organization, Grant Glassco, 1963.

Consultative Committee on Implications of Telecommunications for Canadian Sovereignty, J. V. Clyne, 1979.

Federal Cultural Policy Review Committee, Louis Applebaum and Jacques Hébert, 1982.

Task Force on Broadcasting Policy, Gerald Caplan and Florian Sauvageau, 1986.

House of Commons

Parliamentary Committee Reports, 1932-1993

Hansard, 1925-1994

Major CBC Documents

Touchstone for the CBC, 1977

The CBC: A Perspective, 1978

The Strategy of the CBC, 1983

Let's Do It! 1985

Annual Reports, 1937-1993

Miscellaneous Documents

CRBC Annual Reports, 1933-1936

CRBC Minutes, 1933-1936

"Building for the Future: Towards a Distinctive CBC," Francis Fox, 1983.

Albota, Robert. "Dan McArthur's Concept of Objectivity and his Struggle to Defend the Integrity of the CBC News Service 1940-45." Carleton University, Ottawa, MA Thesis, 1988.

McKay, Bruce. "The CBC and the Public." Stanford University, Stanford, California, PhD Thesis, May 1976.

O'Brien, Rev. John. "A History of the Canadian Radio League 1930-36," University of Southern California, PhD Thesis, 1964.

Secondary Sources

Magazines and Newspapers

Broadcaster

Canadian Broadcaster

Canadian Forum, from 1931

Canadian Geographical Journal, 1962

Canadian Historical Review, 1965

Canadian Journal of Communications, 1982

Canadian Journal of Economics and Political Science, 1946

Canadian Magazine, 1929

Canadian Unionist, 1935

CBC Program Schedule 1939-1946

CBC Times 1948-1969

CBC Closed Circuit

Chatelaine, from 1934

Content

Chronicle-Herald, Halifax

Financial Post, from 1932

Gazette, Montreal

Globe, Toronto

Globe and Mail, Toronto

Illustrated Canadian Magazine, 1920, 1937

La Presse, Montreal

Liberty

London Daily Mail, 1920

Marketing

Montreal Star

New York Times, 1900

Ottawa Citizen, from 1920

Ottawa Journal

Performing Arts

Queen's Quarterly

Saturday Night

Star Weekly

Telegram, Toronto, from 1925

Time

Toronto Star, from 1922

Vancouver Sun

Winnipeg Free Press

Books

Allan, Andrew. *A Self-Portrait*. Toronto: Macmillan of Canada, 1974.

Allen, Ralph. *The Chartered Libertine*. Toronto: Macmillan of Canada, 1954.

Allard, T. J. *Straight Up*. Ottawa: Canadian Communications Foundation, 1979.

Audley, Paul. *Canada's Cultural Industries: Broadcasting, Publishing, Records and Film*. Toronto: James Lorimer & Co., 1983.

Barris, Alex. *Front Page Challenge*. Toronto: CBC Merchandising, 1981.

———— *The Pierce Arrow Showroom Is Leaking: An Insider's View of the CBC*. Toronto: Ryerson Press, 1969.

Beyond The Printed Word: Newsreel and Broadcasting Reporting in Canada. Ottawa: National Archives of Canada, 1988.

Bird, Roger. *Documents of Canadian Broadcasting*. Ottawa: Carleton University Press, 1988.

Black, A. J. *Chronology of Network Broadcasting in Canada 1901-1961*. Ottawa: CBC, 1961.

Bothwell, Robert and Kilbourn, William. *C. D. Howe*. Toronto: McClelland & Stewart, 1979.

Boyle, Harry. *Mostly in Clover*. Toronto: Holt, Rinehart and Winston, 1973.

Briggs, Asa. *The BBC: The First Fifty Years*. Oxford, England: Oxford University Press, 1984.

British Radio Yearbook. London, 1924.

Charlesworth, Hector. *I'm Telling You: Being the Further Candid Chronicles of Hector Charlesworth*. Toronto: Macmillan of Canada, 1937.

Conrad, Margaret. *George Nowlan: Maritime Conservative in National Politics*. Toronto: University of Toronto Press, 1986.

Diefenbaker, John. *One Canada*. Vols. 1-3. Toronto: Macmillan of Canada, 1976.

Downing, John. *Tune in Yesterday*. Englewood Cliffs, New Jersey: Prentice-Hall Inc., 1976.

558

Ellis, David. *Evolution of the Canadian Broadcasting System 1928-1968.* Ottawa: Department of Communications, 1979.

—— *Networking.* Toronto: Friends of Canadian Broadcasting, 1991.

English, John. *Arthur Meighen.* Don Mills, Ontario: Fitzhenry and Whiteside, 1977.

Faris, Ron. *The Passionate Educators.* Toronto: Peter Martin Associates Ltd., 1975.

Ferguson, Max. *And Now Here's Max.* Toronto: McGraw-Hill Co. of Canada, 1967.

—— *The Unmuzzled Max.* Toronto: McGraw-Hill Co. of Canada, 1976.

Frum, Barbara. *As It Happens.* Toronto: McClelland & Stewart, 1976.

Forsey, Eugene. *A Life at the Fringe.* Toronto: Oxford University Press, 1990.

Gossage, Patrick. *Close to the Charisma.* Toronto: McClelland & Stewart, 1986.

Graham, Roger. *Arthur Meighen.* Ottawa: (S.N.), 1965.

Granatstein, J. L. *Canada's War: The Politics of the Mackenzie King Government 1939-1945.* Toronto: Oxford University Press, 1975.

Gratton, Michel. *"So What Are the Boys Saying?"* Toronto: McGraw-Hill Ryerson, 1987.

Gwyn, Richard. *Smallwood: The Unlikely Revolutionary.* Toronto: McClelland & Stewart, 1968.

Hallman, Eugene. *Broadcasting In Canada.* Toronto: General Publishing, 1977.

Hardin, Herschel. *Closed Circuits: The Sellout of Canadian Television.* Vancouver: Douglas & McIntyre, 1984.

Harkness, Ross. *J. E. Atkinson of the Star.* Toronto: University of Toronto Press, 1963.

Hewitt, Foster. *His Own Story.* Toronto: Ryerson Press, 1967.

Hindley, H. *Broadcasting In Canada.* Toronto: General Publishing, 1977.

Jamieson, Don. *The Troubled Air.* Fredericton, New Brunswick: Brunswick Press, 1966.

Kesterson, Wilfrid. *Canadian Annual Review.* 1964.

Koch, Eric. *Inside Seven Days.* Scarborough, Ontario: Prentice-Hall/Newcastle, 1986.

Lambert, R. S. *School Broadcasting in Canada.* Toronto: University of Toronto Press, 1983.

—— *Mass Media in Canada.* Toronto: University of Toronto Press, 1983.

LaMarsh, Judy. *Memoirs of a Bird in a Gilded Cage.* Toronto: McClelland & Stewart, 1969.

Lewis, David. *The Good Fight: Political Memoirs.* Toronto: Macmillan of Canada, 1981.

Lightly, Lawrence. *American Broadcasting.* New York: Hastings House, 1975.

Meighen, Arthur. *Unrevised and Unrepentant: Debating Speeches and Others.* Toronto: Clarke, Irwin & Co., 1949.

Metcalfe, William. The View from Thirty: A Veteran Newsman Files his Last Dispatch. Winnipeg: W. H. Metcalfe, 1984.

MacDonald, L. Ian. *The Making of the Prime Minister.* Toronto: McClelland & Stewart, 1964.

McIntyre, Ian. *The Expense of Glory: A Life of John Reith.* London: HarperCollins, 1993.

McNeil, Bill. *John Fisher: The Canadians.* Markham, Ontario: Fitzhenry & Whiteside Ltd., 1983.

———— *Signing On: The Birth of Radio in Canada.* Toronto: Doubleday Canada Ltd., 1982.

Nash, Knowlton. *History on the Run.* Toronto: McClelland & Stewart, 1984.

———— *Prime Time at Ten.* Toronto: McClelland & Stewart, 1987.

Nolan, Michael. *Foundations: Alan Plaunt and the Early Days of CBC Radio.* Toronto: CBC Enterprises, 1986.

Newman, Peter. *Renegade in Power.* Toronto: McClelland & Stewart, 1963.

Pearson, Lester B. *Mike: The Memoirs of the Right Honourable Lester B. Pearson.* Vols. 1-3. Toronto: University of Toronto Press, 1972-75.

Peers, Frank W. *The Politics of Canadian Broadcasting 1920-51.* Toronto: University of Toronto Press, 1969.

———— *The Public Eye: Television and the Politics of Canadian Broadcasting, 1952-1968.* Toronto: University of Toronto Press, 1979.

Pickersgill, J. W. *My Years With Louis St. Laurent.* Toronto: University of Toronto Press, 1975.

Potvin, Rose. *Passion and Conviction: The Letters of Graham Spry.* Regina: Canadian Plains Research Centre, 1992.

Powley, A. E. *Broadcast From the Front.* Toronto: Hakkert, 1975.

Rutherford, Paul. *Prime Time Canada.* Toronto: University of Toronto Press, 1990.

———— *When Television Was Young.* Toronto: University of Toronto Press, 1990.

Raboy, Marc. *Missed Opportunities: The Story of Canada's Broadcast Policy.* Montreal: McGill-Queen's University Press, 1990.

Ruby, Ormond. *Radio's First Voice: The Story of Reginald Fessenden.* Toronto: Macmillan of Canada, 1970.

Santerre, Roger. *History of Telecommunications 1820-1987.* Ottawa: CBC Enterprises, 1987.

Shea, Albert A. *Broadcasting the Canadian Way.* Montreal: Harvest House, 1963.

Siegal, Arthur. *Politics and the Media in Canada.* Toronto: McGraw-Hill Ryerson Ltd., 1983.

Siggins, Maggie. *Bassett.* Toronto: James Lorimer & Co., 1979.

Skene, Wayne. *Fade to Black, A Requiem for the CBC.* Vancouver: Douglas & McIntyre, 1993.

Stewart, Sandy. *A Pictorial History of Radio In Canada.* Toronto: Gage Publishing Ltd., 1975.

———— *From Coast to Coast.* Toronto: CBC Enterprises, 1985.

———— *Here's Looking at Us.* Toronto: CBC Enterprises, 1986.

Stursberg, Peter. *Mr. Broadcasting.* Toronto: Peter Martin Associates Ltd., 1971.

Stroup, Herbert Hewitt. *The Jehovah's Witnesses.* New York: Columbia University Press, 1945.

Troyer, Warner. *The Sound and the Fury.* Rexdale, Ontario: John Wiley and Sons, Canada., 1980.

Trueman, Peter. *Smoke and Mirrors.* Toronto: McClelland & Stewart, 1980.

Topping, Malachi. *American Broadcasting.* New York: Hastings House, 1975.

UNESCO. *Canada Farm Radio Forum*: Paris, 1954.

Van Dusen, Tommy. *The Chief.* New York, McGraw-Hill, 1968.

Vipond, Mary. *The First Decade of Canadian Broadcasting 1922-1932.* Montreal: McGill-Queen's University Press, 1992.

Weir, E. Austin. *The Struggle for National Broadcasting in Canada.* Toronto: McClelland & Stewart, 1965.

Wilbur, J. R. H. *The Bennett New Deal: Fraud or Portent?* Toronto: Copp, Clark, 1968.

Wolfe, Morris. *Jolts: The TV Wasteland and the Canadian Oasis.* Toronto: James Lorimer & Co., 1985.

———— *Signing On: The Birth of Radio in Canada.* Toronto: Doubleday Canada Ltd., 1982.

Young, Scott. *The Boys of Saturday Night.* Toronto: Macmillan of Canada, 1990.

———— *Hello Canada: The Life and Times of Foster Hewitt.* Toronto: Seal Books, 1986.

————— *Gordon Sinclair: A Life and Then Some.* Toronto: Macmillan of Canada, 1987.

Zimmerman, Arthur Eric. *In the Shadow of the Shield.* Kingston, Ontario: A. E. Zimmerman, 1991.

Index